Donald E. Newcomer
385 old Garden Lane.
York, Pa 17403

845-3033

CIVIL WAR BOOKS

A Priced Checklist

With Advice

By

TOM BROADFOOT

Compilers:
Janet Hewett
Julia Nichols
Jocelyn Pinson

———

Third Edition

1990
BROADFOOT PUBLISHING COMPANY
Wilmington, North Carolina

"Fine Books Since 1971"
BROADFOOT PUBLISHING COMPANY
1908 Buena Vista Drive
Wilmington, North Carolina 28405

THIS VOLUME IS PRINTED ON ACID-FREE PAPER

1st Edition 1978
Reprinted 1979
Second Edition October 1983
Third Edition October 1990

ISBN 0-916107-85-X

Additional copies are available from:
BROADFOOT PUBLISHING COMPANY
1908 Buena Vista Drive
Wilmington, North Carolina 28405
(800) 537-5243

This volume is dedicated to my father,
Winston Broadfoot,
who urged me to become a bookdealer
rather than get a job.

CONTENTS

Acknowledgement With List Of Civil War Dealers i

What's In This Guide ii

How To Use This Guide ii

Prices iv

Book Condition iv

The Civil War Market v

Factors Affecting Civil War Book Prices vi

Reference Works vi

Book Trade Abbreviations And Terms viii

Where To Buy Civil War Books ix

Where To Sell Civil War Books ix

Civil War Books As An Investment..ix

Advice to Wives And "Significant Others"...ix

Care Of Books x

Appraisals—Insurance—Estates—Gifts x

General Books 1

Introduction To Confederate Imprints..509

Confederate Imprints 511

Appendix

The Atlas To Accompany The Official Records. Explanation
And Binding Instructions 555

Confederate Military History. Explanation and Checklist For
Extended Edition 556

Great Commanders Series Checklist...557

Official Records Of The Union And Confederate Armies Checklist 558

Periodicals. A Brief Note On What May Be Valuable. 560

Thanks Be To All

The following notables have been most kind and gracious in providing advice and allowing me to use their Civil War listings and catalogs in compiling this guide. Most of them are engaged full time in the Civil War written market and would welcome your business. I commend them to you. They offer a wide selection of Civil War books.

Symbols:

N = New Books
O = Out-Of-Print and Rare Books
C = Catalog
S = Open Shop (However, we suggest a call before visiting. Hours vary.)
BA = By Appointment

Abraham Lincoln Bookshop
Dan Weinberg
River North Gallery District
357 W. Chicago Avenue
Chicago, IL 60610
(312) 944-3085
N-O-C-S

Bohemian Brigade Bookshop
Ed Archer
7347 Middlebrook Pike
Knoxville, TN 37909
(615) 694-8227
N-O-C-S

Breedlove Enterprises
Linda Breedlove
1527 E. Amherst Road
Massillon, OH 44648
(800) 426-4659
N-C-S

Broadfoot Publishing Company
1908 Buena Vista Drive
Wilmington, NC 28405
(800) 537-5243
N-O-C

Broadfoot Publishing Company
—Store Location—
6624 Robertson Pond Road
Wendell, NC 27591
(800) 444-6963
S

Burke's Bookstore, Inc.
Harriette Beeson
1719 Poplar Avenue
Memphis, TN 38104
(901) 527-7484
O-N-C-S

Butternut & Blue
Jim McLean
3411 Northwind Road
Baltimore, MD 21234
(301) 529-2224
N-O-C-BA

Cather & Brown Books
Pat Cather
P.O. Box 313
Birmingham, AL 35201
(301) 529-7284
O-C-S

"The Conflict"
Pauline Peterson
213 Steinwehr Avenue
Gettysburg, PA 17325
(717) 334-8003
N-C-S

David Doremus, Books
100 Hillside Avenue
Arlington, MA 02174
(617) 646-0892
O-C-BA

Goodspeed's Bookshop, Inc.
Bailey Bishop
7 Beacon Street
Boston, MA 02108
O-C-S

Gary Hendershott
P.O. Box 22520
Little Rock, AR 72221
(501) 224-7555
O-C

Michael A. Hogle
P.O. Box 82
Okemos, MI 48864
(517) 349-2497
O-BA

The Jenkins Company, Rare Books
Mike Parrish
Box 2085
Austin, TX 78768
(512) 444-6616
N-O-C-BA

Bob Lurate
P.O. Box 1428
Lexington, VA 24450
(703) 463-2615
O-BA

Bill Mason Books
Bill Mason
104 N. 7th Street
Morehead City, NC 28557
(919) 247-6161
N-O-C-S

McGowan Books
Doug Sanders
P.O. Box 222
Chapel Hill, NC 27514
(919) 968-1121
O-C-BA

Morningside Bookshop
Bob Younger
P.O. Box 1087
Dayton, OH 45401
(513) 461-6736
N-O-C-S

Mount Sterling Rebel
Terry Murphy
P.O. Box 481
Mount Sterling, KY 40353
O-C-BA

Owens Civil War Books
Michael & Linda Owens
P.O. Box 13622
Richmond, VA 23225
(804) 272-8888
N-O-C-S

Olde Soldier Books
Dave Zullo
18779-B North Frederick Road
Gaithersburg, MD 20879
(301) 963-2929
N-O-C-S

L & T Respess Books
Lin & Tucker Respess
P.O. Box 236
Bristol, RI 02809
O-C-S

WHAT'S IN THIS GUIDE

In this volume we have listed every Civil War Book for which we can reliably estimate a price. "Reliably" means we have offered the volume ourselves, or have certain knowledge that it was offered on the market.

It's impossible to keep track of all the new Civil War books being published — not our aim anyhow. However, you should find almost every Civil War title ten years or older within these pages and 998 of 1,000 titles worth $25 and over. If your book isn't listed, accept the fact with neither agony nor ecstasy. Your volume may be valuable, or more likely, was not offered for sale in the last twenty years and thus, not listed. Between the last edition of this guide in 1983 and this edition (1990), we have added almost 3,000 entries.

HOW TO USE THIS GUIDE

First, determine the category of the volume you wish to evaluate. You've got two choices:

GENERAL BOOKS

This category contains all Civil War volumes except Confederate Imprints.

CONFEDERATE IMPRINTS

Material printed in the Confederate States during the War is considered to be of Confederate Imprint. For a more detailed explanation of Confederate Imprints see the introduction to the Confederate Imprints section.

Second, find your particular title within the category.

GENERAL BOOKS

- Look under the author's last name.
- If no author is given, look under the name of the editor or compiler.
- If neither author nor editor is given, look under the title.

CONFEDERATE IMPRINTS

In this volume, Confederate Imprints are listed in numerical sequence in accordance with the standard guide in the field, *CONFEDERATE IMPRINTS: A Bibliography* by Parrish and Willingham. See the introduction to the Confederate Imprints section for instructions on how to identify and locate Confederate Imprints.

A SAMPLE LISTING WITH EXPLANATION
OF ABBREVIATIONS & SYMBOLS

BROWN, Jim Worth	Last Name, First Name, Middle Name
The Civil War	Title
1863	Date of publication
(1863)	Date of publication-Not stated in book
(Circa 1900)	Educated guess as to date of publication
New York	Place of publication
(New York)	Place of publication-Not stated in book
$100	Price
Ltd.	Limited edition
Wraps	Paperback
DJ	Dust jacket

PRICES

The prices in this volume are our estimate of the full retail value for copies in good condition in the market of late 1990. This "estimate" is based on 20 years in the Civil War book business, during which we have sold multiple copies of all but the rarest volumes. We have also utilized hundreds of Civil War catalogs issued by other dealers, plus auction records and private sales. Prices from these sources have been adjusted — some up, some down—to our estimate. By "full retail" we mean the price for which we would offer the title. One has to have a benchmark for prices and this is our standard. This is not to say that Civil War books cannot be purchased at a lesser price in used bookstores.

The purpose of this guide is not to tell whether a book is a $25 volume or a $30 volume. In fact, a volume listed herein at $25 might well be found for $15 in a Fourth Avenue used book store. The value of this publication is separating the $25 books from the $50 and $100 volumes. Since the prices herein are for books in good condition, we need to further define what is "good condition."

BOOK CONDITION

There's an adage in the out-of-print book trade that three factors determine the value of a book — these being CONDITION, CONDITION, CONDITION. Even very rare books in poor condition have little value. In evaluating the condition of a book, the following points should be considered.

CONDITIONS NOT AFFECTING VALUE

1. Previous owners name or inscription on front fly, unless objectionable, i.e., "From Peaches to Bull Dog," in large letters of red crayon.
2. Tasteful bookplate verso front cover.
3. Minor soiling or scuffing of cover — some wear is assumed.
4. Minor fraying of dust jacket — some wear is assumed.

CONDITIONS ADDING TO VALUE

1. Dust jacket for titles prior to 1940. These are difficult to evaluate as frequently the dust jacket is worth as much as the book.
2. Signature or presentation by author. Unless author is the Lincoln or Lee category, the additional value is probably $5 - $10.
3. Marginal notations by author or someone of knowledge, adding or correcting information in the text.
4. Related material laid in — unless newspaper clippings which have darkened the paper.

DEFECTS
Common and Forgivable — But Detracting from Value

1. Former owners name elsewhere than front fly.
2. Embossed seals — do not be a "book lover" and buy an embosser with which to damage your books. This lowers the value 30%-50%.
3. Library markings within the text — except on title page (see next category).
4. Lack of dust jacket for books after 1940, or dust jacket chipped or torn.
5. Notations or underlining in pencil.
6. More than minor wear to cover; tips of spine chipped, corners rubbed, hinges loose or cracked, fading.
7. Pages folded, foxed (brown spots from age), unevenly separated at outer edges, soiled, torn without loss of text.

DEFECTS — MAJOR

1. Rebound or lacking original covers or wraps.
2. Library markings on title page or spine.
3. Extensive underlining — non-erasable.
4. Cover or pages badly stained.

THE DEFECT — FATAL TO ALL BUT THE RAREST OF BOOKS

Loss of text via missing pages, page or any portion of a page containing written matter.

THE CIVIL WAR MARKET

~~~~

Trends

Since the last edition of this *Guide* was published in 1983, there have been some significant changes; less hair on the top of the head and more notches used in the belt. Changes have also occurred in the world of Civil War books. In short, unprecedented growth in readers, dealers, titles published, and book fairs. The pool of readers, those who buy and collect current Civil War titles for research and reading, has increased, probably five-fold in the last twenty years. However, the number of people who buy and collect old and rare Civil War books is about the same as it was twenty years ago, around 500, a number confirmed by the other dealers in Civil War out-of-print material.

Although the number of out-of-print and rare book collectors is somewhat constant, this doesn't mean the out-of-print market is stagnant, as this buyer base changes about 20% a year, with new collectors beginning and others leaving the field. However, as collections have been filled in and an ever increasing number of dealers offer books to the same number of collectors, the meteoric rise in Civil War book values has somewhat abated. Prices doubled between 1978 and 1983, with Southern regimentals leading the way. Between 1983 and 1990, overall prices increased about 30%, with Northern regimentals, medical books, and manuals closing on their Southern counterparts.

What's "Hot" And What's "Not"

~~~~

In the world of Civil War books, some subjects are "hot," i.e., eagerly collected and increasing in value, while other topics seem to languish. "Hot" and "Not" changes from time to time, but valid "hot" and"not" generalities can be made. THUS

"HOT"

Gettysburg titles — especially first-hand accounts. The peak of this collecting craze may have passed.

Cavalry — battles, soldiers, officers—Jeb Stuart, etc.

Medical — especially Southern manuals.

Blockade — particularly first person accounts.

Lee and His Generals — perennial favorites, especially first-hand accounts.

Soldier's Reminiscences — the more battles the better.

Manuals — much in demand by re-enactors. It remains to be seen if re-enacting will continue unabated, now that the 125th anniversaries have passed.

Fighting — First hand. If a volume includes personal, first-hand accounts of fighting, it's hot. The more shooting the better. If there are no shots fired within the pages of a book, it's probably "not."

"NOT"

Reconstruction — Fiction and Poetry — Politics and Politicians — General Histories — Legal — Domestic Matters — The Home Front — Finances — Diplomacy — Slavery and Abolition — Government Publications — Juveniles — Most books on Lincoln, of which there are thousands.

FACTORS AFFECTING CIVIL WAR BOOK PRICES

There are factors which may affect the value of individual titles and subjects, causing values to rise or fall in excess of the normal market trends.

A UNIQUE COPY — A previously unknown Civil War title is offered for sale. This first copy will fetch a high price — collectors and libraries vying for the best collection must have the *uniques*. However, the next copy that appears will probably be less in price — it not being *unique*. The value of the first copy falls also.

A RIP ROARING AUCTION DUEL — two old (or young) coots get into a battle royal on the auction floor over a particular volume — the end result is a sky high price. Sky high, that is, until the next copy sells at a sane price.

A CACHE IS FOUND — someone finds 100 copies of a 50-year-old $100 book. As the market absorbs the copies, the price will decrease.

CACHE ENDS — the final copies of a cache are sold and the value increases. Years ago I had 80 copies of *Micah Jenkins*, a rare pamphlet printed in 100 copies. It was especially rare because only 20 copies had ever entered the market. As I sold my copies and word of them got out, *Micah* dropped in price. When I had sold all of my copies, the price increased rapidly.

If several large Civil War collections hit the market in a short period of time, prices will temporarily depress. If time goes by without a large collection appearing, prices will increase. When the economy is up, library and personal budgets go up and, like everything else, book prices go up. And vice versa. *Please, ye powers that be, keep the Civil War book market healthy for 11 more years until my youngest is out of college.*

REFERENCE WORKS
Guides to Civil War Books & Reading

Whether you are a collector or a casual reader, reference works can be useful, enjoyable, and informative. *CAUTION. Broadfoot Publishing Company has published many Civil War reference works. Akin to the surgeon who doesn't make money unless he cuts, we don't eat unless we sell books — so, if we call a reference work "essential," you are entitled to a grain of salt.

The one essential guide is CIVIL WAR BOOKS: A CRITICAL BIBLIOGRAPHY. This two-volume set by Allen Nevins, James I. Robertson, and Bell I. Wiley, groups Civil War books into categories and evaluates them — with comments from "worthless" to "the best account." If you are interested in Stonewall Jackson, you turn to the section on Jackson and there are all the Jackson books with the wheat separated from the chaff. Though first published some twenty plus years ago, this title is even more valuable than when published, as the majority of good books on the War were published years ago and are available today via reprints more than ever before. Working under the supervision of three outstanding Civil War authorities, 15 historians selected nearly 6,000 books and wrote brief commentaries on each one. CIVIL WAR BOOKS is widely accepted as the most authoritative and comprehensive guide to books on the Civil war.

If you are interested in Confederate books, THE SOUTH TO POSTERITY by Douglas

Southall Freeman should be read and enjoyed from cover to cover. Dr. Freeman not only evaluates, but provides background information not available elsewhere — why books were written, information on the authors, public reaction to various titles, comparison of books on similar subjects — the whole panorama of Confederate writing in a very readable volume — a novel of Confederate literature. Freeman is the preeminent authority on Confederate books and this is the standard work on Confederate bibliography.

If Union books are your field, then you should have the UNION BOOKSHELF by Michael Mullins and Rowena Reed, a very able and comparative guide to Northern material. A reference source for those interested in studying books about the Civil War from the Union perspective. One hundred fourteen titles are presented with bibliographical information and annotations. Supplemental sections of unit histories and personal reminiscences listing the remainder of the books with bibliographical information are also included.

What has become the "standard" reference source for Confederacy data is John Wright's COMPENDIUM OF THE CONFEDERACY: A Bibliography of the Confederacy. The result of several decades of work, COMPENDIUM is an attempt by a noted Confederate collector and authority to gather, under one title, a listing of every book, pamphlet and article ever published relating to the Confederacy. This reference is much broader than Dornbusch's Military Bibliography of the Civil War, which does not include naval or civilian related topics, politics, or fiction. Mr. Wright also analyzed almost 200 serials for articles of Confederate content, reading most of them from start to finish, whereas Dornbusch, the standard reference for articles both North and South, searched only 50 serials. The major serials referenced, most of which have never been indexed, were read from start to finish. Each entry provides, when available, author, title, place of publication, publisher, pages, wraps or hardback, a brief note on content, and booksellers' prices with seller noted. Of major importance is the information gleaned from thousands of dealer catalogs, some dating back a hundred years.

For studying the Confederate homefront and local condition and history, you need TRAVELS IN THE CONFEDERATE STATES. If collecting books on a particular southern state or town, this is your volume — it tells what was written about Wilmington (or any other southern town or state) during the War, has a synopsis of each title's content as pertains to Wilmington, and evaluates each volume for accuracy, scope and readability.

If you collect southern books — including those printed in the South, THE CONFEDER-ATE HUNDRED and CORNERSTONES by Richard Barksdale Harwell, should be in your holdings — not only as guides but as collectibles. THE CONFEDERATE HUNDRED: A BIBLIOPHILIC SELECTION OF CONFEDERATE BOOKS, is an annotated bibliography of the hundred most important Confederate Imprints. CORNERSTONES OF CONFEDER-ATE COLLECTING is an annotated bibliography of the twenty most important Confederate Imprints, with illustrations of each cover or title page.

An invaluable reference work for Civil War books is Charles E. Dornbusch's MILITARY BIBLIOGRAPHY OF THE CIVIL WAR in four volumes. Titles are grouped under subject headings. Particularly valuable for determining what has been written for regiments, North and South. Regretfully, some of the volumes of this set are out-of-print (October 1990), however, the available volumes can be obtained from most of the Civil War dealers carrying new books (see dealer listing).

~~~~~~~~~~~~~~~

At the time this volume went to press, the above titles were available from Broadfoot Publishing Company. If you would like information on any of these titles, please call Toll Free (800) 537-5243, or write us to determine current availability and price.

BOOK TRADE ABBREVIATIONS AND TERMS

As is usual for any trade or slice of the population, those dealing in old and new books use certain terms that are baffling, unintelligible, and often maddening to the uninitiated. Adding further chaos to the situation is the fact that individual dealers, myself included, (see "crisp") throw in their own home concocted words. In order to bring some order to chaos, herein are offered definitions for most of the meaning-not-apparent words. No doubt some have been left out and we will coin others in the future. If you will bring these to our attention, we will append them to a future list.

Actually I, like most American dealers, excepting some of the double-breasted-vested literature furniture dealers, am restrained in comparison to my English counterparts. Across the sea a book measuring 6 1/4 inches in height and 4 inches in width is often described as a pott octavo, but if it gets damp and swells to 6 3/4 by 4 1/4, it becomes foolscap octavo.

AEG	All edges of pages are gilt (gold).
ALS	Autographed letter signed.
Bound by hand	Rebound by hand, preserving original margins with some attention given to matching the binding and the content.
Chipped	Small piece missing, brittle paper.
Circa (ca)	An educated guess as to date of publication.
Crisp	Better than fine, the book actually resists being opened; having never been so.
Dust jacket	Wrapper protecting the book. Wraps around the cover. May be printed or not.
Ex libris	"From a library" may have pocket, library stamp, library number on spine, or all three.
Foxing	Brown spots due to acidity of paper.
Frontis	Photograph or engraving preceding the title page.
Hinges cracked	Paper joint between inside cover and book split; a minor cosmetic defect unless the pages are loose in binding; if so, we say so.
Hinges starting	Hinges partially cracked.
ND or NP	No date or place of publication.
PB	Paperback.
Presentation (pres) copy	Inscribed and signed by author.
Reading copy	All there and that's about all.
Rebacked	New spine, otherwise original binding.
Removed	Removed from larger volume.
Shelfwear	Wear at extremities of cover.
Signature	Unit of pages within book.
Uncut	Pages never cut apart; usually a fine copy.
TEG	Top edges of pages are gilt (gold).
TLS	Typed letter signed.
Verso	Back of.
Wrapper	Dust jacket.
Wraps	Paper covers as opposed to boards or cloth.
3/4 leather	Leather spine and corners.
1/2 leather	Leather spine.

WHERE TO BUY CIVIL WAR BOOKS
NEW BOOKS.
Most general book stores carry a selection of Civil War titles, though their offering is miniscule in comparison to what is available. For a true picture of the Civil War market, a trip to a store specializing in the "late unpleasantness" is worth the effort. In addition to the dealers noted as having open shops (see listing at the beginning of this volume) most of the national Civil War parks offer a wide selection of Civil War reading material.
BUYING BY MAIL.
Probably more Civil War titles are sold by mail than through stores. Catalog sales of Civil War titles is an old, established, and trustworthy enterprise. For a listing of dealers selling Civil War books by mail see the dealer list at the first of the volume. Dealers coded "C" will be glad to send you a catalog free, or for a modest charge.
OUT-OF-PRINT AND RARE VOLUMES.
In addition to specialized stores and catalogs, out-of-print and rare Civil War books are often available at used bookshops, yard sales, library sales, and auctions.

The publication that contains the most up-to-date information on sources for Civil war books, old and new, is *Civil War News*. In addition to advertisements and announcements relating to Civil War books and events, *Civil War News* contains book reviews and essays on related topics. A free sample issue may be obtained from *Civil War News*, P.O. Box C, Arlington, MA 02174. A subscription, as of October 1990, is $15 per year.

WHERE TO SELL CIVIL WAR BOOKS
The easiest and most reliable way to sell a collection of Civil War books is through a Civil War book dealer. He knows the market and the value of the books. If selling a collection, we suggest getting several offers.

Unique books and historically important manuscript material, may fare well at auction, but over the years, I've seen very few instances where a collection at auction produced a better result than outright sale.

CIVIL WAR BOOKS AS AN INVESTMENT
Nope, no and perish the thought. If return on the dollar is your sole criterion, choose another medium. Some of my fellow dealers berate me for belittling Civil War books as a means of making money. However, I've seen enough widows whose husbands left them "bibliographic" nest eggs to stick to my guns.

ADVICE TO WIVES AND "SIGNIFICANT OTHERS"
This is not to say that a well chosen collection won't increase in value over the years, but it's like I tell my stock broker friends," If you're so smart, how come you're not rich, and if you're rich, how come the pressing need to share your largess with me?" Not bad questions to ask anyone who offers you a sure path to the golden kingdom — including book dealers.

However, before you wives and "significant others" use the above as a club to berate husband Harry about "wasting" money on Civil War books, might I say that collecting books has it's advantages, even virtues, over some of the alternatives: booze, gambling, chasing skirts, chasing pants, experimental airplanes — everything, except maybe fishing. In becoming a Civil War book collector, Harry is gaining a bit of knowledge, he's home reading the books, he's not catching anything from the books, better yet, he's not giving it to you, and he won't leave you for the books. Your marriage is, in fact, secured by the books because

Harry knows that if your union flounders, he will have to sell the books and give you half the money. So, you cohorts of collectors, be of good cheer as you step over the stacks in the hall and dust around the shelves. Books are, by far, the lesser of available evils.

CARE OF BOOKS

The first and foremost commandment in taking care of books is keep them dry. Failing this, little else matters. Normal household atmosphere, assuming heat in the winter and air-conditioning in the summer, suits books fine. If you're comfortable, they are. Protecting books from direct sunlight keeps the bindings and dust jackets from fading. Excessive heat, as in an attic, isn't desirable, though the Dead Sea Scrolls lasted thousands of years in a desert cave. Leather binding can be dressed with plain Vaseline. This keeps the leather looking good and extends the life of the hinges.

If your books should get wet, place them immediately in a freezer. The circulating cold air will dry them the same as frozen long johns on a winter clothes line. Freeze drying books came about not many years ago following one of the periodic Venetian floods. Freeze drying also works well for lawn mower instructions left in the rain and wallets that go swimming.

Mold is best removed with a terry cloth towel, after which the book should be dried to remove the cause of the mold —moisture.

Smoke. Each year we receive several calls asking how to remove smoke from books. Thus far, no satisfactory answer. If you figure this one out, give us a call.

If packing books for shipment, moving, etc., place them flat in the box. Standing them on edge, particularly on the outer edges of the covers, leads to loose bindings and broken hinges-(hinges: see terms and definitions).

Repairs. The most common book problem, loose bindings and hinges, can usually be remedied easily if the boards haven't become detached. Needed: Elmer's Glue, a slender knitting needle or similar item, and two sheets of wax paper with one straight edge each. Put the needle in the glue, insert the needle at the top of the spine, between the cloth and the pages, and spread glue the length of the spine between the spine and the pages. Before closing the book, place a piece of wax paper inside the front cover and another inside the rear cover, making sure the wax paper is snug and straight along the inner spine. The purpose of the wax paper is to prevent the glue from adhering the covers to the first page, as frequently glue will ooze from the inner seam when the volume is closed. After the glue dries, open the book slowly and easily, and the glue will flex rather than crack. If in doubt, practice on a few *Reader's Digest*.

APPRAISALS — INSURANCE — ESTATES — GIFTS

These four subjects go hand-in-hand. To insure books, or donate them and take a tax deduction, you must first know what the books are worth. For insurance purposes, you need to evaluate the books and must be able, in the event of a loss, to prove you owned the books and their value. Proof is often easy. Fire is the most common claim filed for books, and even in the worst fires, books rarely burn in their entirety. Usually the outer edges burn, but that's about it. However, burned books don't tell their condition or value prior to the fire.

For insurance purposes, you can do your own leg work. Create a file card system for your collection, a computer printout if you prefer. For each volume, note the author (last name, first name, middle initial or name), the full title of the book, place and date of publication, price you paid, and a comment on the condition (new, fine, good, fair, poor). Check your cards against this *Price Guide* and update your prices. Keep two card files in separate locations. To prove ownership and condition, make a VCR video recording of your collection, going along the shelves slowly and at close range so that the title and condition of each book is clearly shown. For the more valuable items, you may wish to picture them individually on a table against a light background. Make two copies of the tape and keep them in separate locations. In the event of a loss, the tape proves you had the books and shows the condition of your collection, the cards provide the value. Also, if you get lost, the person left behind, who usually knows nothing of books, has a checklist of your collection and an idea of individual and total values. When selling a collection, the card file and tape save time and effort all the way around. Send a file and tape to the prospective buyers. No need for anyone to rummage through the books or compile a list — though the buyer will probably want to view the collection.

If you are donating books and will be taking a tax deduction, the card file and tape prove invaluable. Someone besides you must do the appraisal. DON'T. It's forbidden by law. "The following persons cannot be qualified appraisers: The donee of the property, the person employed by or related to the above." —Department of the Treasury, Internal Revenue Service Publication 561 (Rev. Dec. 87) *Determining the Value of Donated Property.* A collector, unversed in rare book values, in IRS tax court defending an appraisal which was illegal in the first place is not a happy camper. However, your prior cataloging efforts will make the appraiser's job much less tedious and less expensive. The appraiser will have to see the books, but rather than compile bibliographic information, he can simply update the values on the cards. After the donation, keep a set of cards and tape and if the donation is called into question, the two items can go a long way towards satisfying any questions the IRS may have.

Word to the wise. If you have an appraisal for tax deduction purposes, or to settle an estate, don't badger the appraiser to make the figures low or high. Books are worth what they are worth. A top notch appraiser who is knowledgeable and fair may be able to say "I've never had an appraisal disallowed" and he'd like to keep it that way. Besides which, there are just so many Civil War titles and the same books show up over and over again in appraisals. An appraiser can't value a title for the Jones Estate at $50 and the following month put $100 on the same book which Mr. Smith is giving to the local library.

If your collection is modest, it may be included in your homeowner's policy. If large, with valuable titles, you may need a special "floater." One way to keep insurance costs down is to limit potential claims to a certain amount per book. If you have one hundred $25 titles and one $1000 item, better to take a limit of $25 per title and put the $1000 title in a bottom drawer in a plastic bag; theory being, the fire will be out before the heat melts the plastic bag which protects the book from the water which puts out the fire.

A. O. W.   See: WHEELER, A. O.

AARON, Daniel   The Unwritten War, American Writers and the Civil War.
1973   New York   25.00

ABBAZIA, Patrick   The Chickamauga Campaign. Dec. 1862 - Nov. 1863.
1988   10.00

ABBOT, Willis J.   Battle Fields and Camp Fires.
1889   New York   30.00
1890   New York   25.00
1891   New York   25.00

ABBOT, Willis J.   Blue Jackets of '61: A History of the Navy in the War of Secession.
1886   New York   35.00
1889   New York   30.00
1890   New York   30.00

ABBOT, Willis J.   The Naval History of the United States. 2 Vols.
1886   New York   75.00
1887   New York   75.00
1888   New York   75.00
1889   New York   75.00
1896   New York   60.00

ABBOTT, Allen O.   Prison Life in the South.
1865   New York   50.00

ABBOTT, Henry L.   Course of Lectures Upon the Defence of the Seacoast of the United States.   Wraps.
1888   New York   40.00

ABBOTT, Henry L.   Siege Artillery in the Campaigns Against Richmond.   Wraps.
1867   Washington, DC   175.00
1868   New York   150.00
1986   Arendtsville, PA   25.00

ABBOTT, Horace R.   My Escape from Belle Isle.   Wraps.
1889   Detroit   30.00

ABBOTT, John S. C.   History of the Civil War in America. 2 Vols.
1863-66   New York   30.00
1863-66   Springfield   30.00

ABBOTT, John S. C.   The Life of General Ulysses S. Grant.
1868   Boston   30.00
1872   Boston   25.00

ABBOTT, Lemuel A.   Personal Recollections and Civil War Diary, 1864.
1908   Burlington   75.00

ABBOTT, Martin   The Freedmen's Bureau in South Carolina 1865-1872.
1967   Chapel Hill   25.00

ABBOTT, Stephen G.   The First Regiment New Hampshire Volunteers.
1890   Keene   65.00

ABDILL, George B.   Civil War Railroads, Pictorial Story of the Iron Horse 1861-1865.
1961   New York   35.00
1961   Seattle   30.00
n.d.   New York   20.00

ABEL, Annie H.   The Slaveholding Indians. 3 Vols.
    1915-25 Cleveland   700.00
    Vol. 1   **American Indians as Slaveholder and Secessionist**   250.00
    Vol. II   **American Indians as Participant in Civil War**   350.00
    Vol. III   **American Indians Under Reconstruction**   200.00
ABEL, Parker   Uncle Tom in England or A Proof that Black's White.
    Wraps.
    (1852) New York   40.00
ABELS, Jules   Man on Fire.
    1971   New York   30.00
ABERNETHY, Alonzo   Dedication of Monuments Erected by the State
    of Iowa.
    1908   Des Moines 60.00
About the War, Plain Words to Plain People by a Plain Man.   Wraps.
    1863   Philadelphia   20.00
Abraham Lincoln Der Wiederherfteller Der Nordamerifanifchen Union.
    Wraps.
    1866   Leipzig 35.00
Abraham Lincoln Quarterly.Wraps.
    1940-52   150.00
Abraham Lincoln His Efforts to Make America a White Nation.   Wraps.
    (c.1930)   n.p.   25.00
ABRAHAM, James   With the Army of West Virginia 1861-1864, Remi-
    niscences & Letters of Lt. James Abraham, Pennsylvania Dragoons, Co.
    A, First Regiment, Virginia Cavalry.
    1974   Lancaster   Ltd-100 copies.   60.00
ABRAHAMS, Robert D.   Mr. Benjamin's Sword.
    1948   Philadelphia   20.00
    1954   n.p.   15.00
ABRAHAMS, Robert D.   The Uncommon Soldier: Major Alfred Morde-
    cai.
    1959   n.p.   20.00
ABSHIRE, David M.   The South Rejects a Prophet, the Life of Senator
    D. M. Key 1824-1900.
    1967   New York   20.00
Abstract of Infantry Tactics; Including Exercises and Maneuvres of Light-
    Infantry and Riflemen, for the Use of the Milita of the United States.
    1860   Philadelphia 75.00
Acceptance and Unveiling of the Statue of Wade Hampton.
    1929   Washington, DC   30.00
Acceptance and Unveiling of the Statues of Jefferson Davis and James Z.
    George.
    1932   Washington, DC   25.00
Acceptance of the Statues of George Washington and Robert E. Lee Pre-
    sented by the State of Virginia.
    1934   Washington, DC   30.00
An Account of the Reception Given by the Citizens of N.Y. to the Survivors
    of the Officers and Crews of the U.S. Frigates Cumberland and
    Congress.
    1862   New York   30.00
Account of the Supplies Sent to Savannah.   Wraps.
    1865   Boston   35.00

ACHESON, Sam and O'CONNELL, Julia, edited by   George Washington Diamond's Account of the Great Hanging at Gainesville, 1862.
1963   Austin   20.00
ACKER, Henry J.   Gulf Spy, Sgt. Henry J. Acker 23rd Wisconsin Vol. Inf. Wraps.
1961   Tall Timbers, MD   30.00
Acts of the General Assembly of the Commonwealth of Kentucky, Passed at the Session Which Was Begun and Held in the City of Frankfort. . . .
1864   80.00
ADAM, G. Mercer   The Life of General Robert E. Lee.
1905   New York   25.00
ADAMS, A. D.   Great Britain and the American Civil War. 2 Vols. in 1.
1958   New York   22.50
ADAMS, Charles Francis   Charles Frances Adams 1835-1915   An Autobiography.
1916   Boston   15.00
ADAMS, Charles Francis   The Confederacy and the Transvaal: A People's Obligation to Robert E. Lee.   Wraps.
1901   Boston   15.00
ADAMS, Charles Francis   A Cycle of Adams Letters 1861-1865, edited by Worthington C. Ford. 2 Vols.
1920   Boston/New York   30.0(
1921   London 2 Vols. 30.00
1969   New York   2 Vols. in one   20.00
ADAMS, Charles Francis   Lee at Appomattox.
1902   Boston and New York   20.00
1903   20.00
ADAMS, Charles Francis   Lee's Centennial: An Address Delivered at Lexington, Virginia.
(1907)   (Boston)   50.00
1948   Chicago   35.00
n.d.   Richmond   Wraps. 14.00
ADAMS, Charles Francis   Seward and the Declaration of Paris.   Wraps.
1912   Boston   30.00
ADAMS, Charles Francis   Some Phases of the Civil War.   Wraps.
1906   Cambridge   25.00
ADAMS, Charles Francis   Speech of _____ of Mass., Delivered in the House of Representatives, Jan. 31, 1861.   Wraps.
1861   Washington, DC   15.00
ADAMS, Charles Francis   Studies; Military and Diplomatic.
1911   New York   20.00
ADAMS, Charles Francis   "Tis Sixty Years Since," Address.
1913   New York   20.00
ADAMS, Charles Francis   Trans-Atlantic Historical Solidarity.
1913   Oxford   40.00
ADAMS, Ephraim D.   Great Britain and the American Civil War. 2 Vols.
1925   London   50.00
1957   New York   2 Vols. in 1 25.00
1957   Gloucester   2 Vols. in 1 25.00
1958   New York   2 Vols. in 1 20.00
1960   New York   2 Vols. in 1 20.00

ADAMS, Francis Colburn   **Siege of Washington, D.C.**
    1867   New York   75.00
ADAMS, Francis Colburn   **The Story of a Trooper.**
    1865   New York   75.00
ADAMS, Francis Colburn   **A Trooper's Adventures in the War for the Union.**
    n.d.   New York   50.00
ADAMS, George Worthington   **Doctors in Blue: The Medical History of the Union Army in the Civil War.**
    1952   New York   40.00
    1985   Dayton   17.50
    1985   Dayton   Wraps   8.95
    1987   Wraps   9.95
ADAMS, George Worthington, edited by   **Mary Logan - Reminiscence of the Civil War and Reconstruction.**
    1970   Carbondale, IL   20.00
ADAMS, Henry   **The Education of Henry Adams, an Autobiography.**
    1918   Boston   35.00
ADAMS, Henry   **The Great Secession Winter of 1860-61,** edited by George Hochfield.
    1958   New York   15.00
ADAMS, Henry C.   **Indiana at Vicksburg.**
    1911   Indianapolis   60.00
ADAMS, Herbert Lincoln   **Worcester Light Infantry 1803-1922. A History.**
    1924   Worcester   50.00
ADAMS, Jacob   **Diary of _____; Private in Company F, 21st OVI.**
    1930   Columbus   30.00
ADAMS, James Truslow   **America's Tragedy.**
    1934   New York   15.00
    1935   New York   15.00
ADAMS, John   **Elias C. Boudinot: In Memoriam.**
    n.d.   n.p.   200.00
ADAMS, John G. B.   **Reminiscences of the Nineteenth Massachusetts Regiment.**
    1899   Boston   75.00
ADAMS, John R.   **Memorial & Letters of Rev. _____ Chaplain of the Fifth Maine and the One Hundred and Twenty-first New York Regiments.**
    1890   Cambridge   100.00
ADAMS, Julia Davis   **Stonewall.**
    1931   New York   35.00
ADAMS, Michael C. C.   **Our Masters the Rebels: A Speculation on Union Military Failure in the East, 1861-1865.**
    1978   Cambridge   20.00
ADAMS, N.   **A South Side View of Slavery.**
    1855   Boston   35.00
ADAMS, Nehemiah   **The Sable Cloud: A Southern Tale, with Northern Comments.**
    1861   Boston   30.00

ADAMS, William T. ("Oliver Optic")   **Blue and Gray** series in matched
    bindings with decorated boards.
    Brother Against Brother   1894   Boston   20.00
    A Lieutenant at Eighteen   1896   Boston   20.00
    On the Staff   1897   Boston   20.00
    Our Standard Bearer   1868   Boston   20.00
    Stand by the Union   1892   Boston   20.00
    Taken by the Enemy   1888   Boston   20.00
    A Victorious Union   1894   Boston   20.00
    Within the Enemy's Lines   1890/1894   Boston   20.00
    The Yankee Middy   1875   Boston   20.00
ADAMS, William T. ("Oliver Optic")   **Fighting Joe; or The Fortunes of a
Staff Officer. A Story of the Great Rebellion.**
    1866   Boston   15.00
ADAMS, William T. ("Oliver Optic")   **The Sailor Boy. . . .**
    1893   Boston   20.00
ADAMSON, Augustus Pitt   **Brief History of the Thirtieth Georgia
Regiment. Wraps.**
    1912   Griffin, GA   750.00
    1987   Jonesboro   18.50
ADAMSON, Hans Christian   **Rebellion in Missouri 1861.**
    1961   Philadelphia   35.00
ADDEY, Markinfield   **"Old Jack" and His Foot Cavalry.**
    1864   New York   75.00
    1865   New York   65.00
ADDEY, Markinfield   **"Stonewall Jackson," Life and Military Career
of Thomas Jonathan Jackson.**
    1863   New York   90.00
**The Address of Southern Delegates in Congress to Their Constituents.
Wraps.**
    n.d.   n.p.   50.00
**The Address of the People of South Carolina Assembled in Convention to
the People of the Slaveholding States of the United States. Wraps.**
    1860   Charleston   100.00
Addresses at the Unveiling of the Bust of Matt W. Ransom. Wraps.
    1911   Raleigh   35.00
Addresses in Memory of "Murray and His Men." Wraps.
    1875   Baltimore   50.00
**Adj. Gen. Report of the State of New Hampshire, for the Year ending May
20, 1865 Vol. I.**
    1865   Concord   35.00
**Adj. Gen. Report of the State of New Hampshire, for the Year ending May
20, 1865 Vol. II.**
    1865   Concord   35.00
**Adj. Gen. Report of the State of New Hampshire, for the Year ending June
1, 1866. Vol. III.**
    1866   Concord   35.00
**Adjutant General Revised Register of the Soldiers and Sailors of New
Hampshire . . . 1861-65.**
    1895   Concord   100.00

Adjutant General, Record of Service of Michigan Volunteers in the Civil War. Vols. 1-46. 30.00 each
 1905 Kalamazoo 30.00
 Recent reprint 17.50 each
AFFLECK, C. J. and DOUGLAS, B. M. Confederate Bonds and Certificates. Wraps.
 1960 Boyce, VA 20.00
AGEE, Rucker Forrest-Streight Campaign of 1863. Wraps.
 1958 (Milwaukee) 25.00
AGEE, Rucker Let's Keep the Record Straight! Wraps.
 1963 (Birmingham) 15.00
AGER, Waldemar Oberst Heg Og Hans Gutter.
 1916 Eau Claire 145.00
AGNEW, Daniel The Spirit and Poetry of Law. Wraps.
 1866 Philadelphia 15.00
AGNUS, Felix A Woman of War and Other Stories.
 1908 Baltimore 25.00
AILSWORTH, T. S., et al, compiled by Charlotte County Rich Indeed: A History from Pre-historic Times through the Civil War.
 1979 Charlotte, VA 50.00
AIMONE, Alan Conrad Official Records of the American Civil War.
 1972 West Point 10.00
AITKEN, Roy E. The Birth of a Nation Story.
 (1965) (Middleburg, VA) 15.00
AKIN, Warren Letters of _____, Confederate Congressman, edited by Bell I. Wiley.
 1959 Athens 20.00
Alabama - Confederate Military History. See: Confederate Military History, Vol. VII (Vol. VIII, 1987 reprint ed.).
ALBAUGH, William A., III The Confederate Brass-Framed Colt & Whitney. Wraps.
 1955 Falls Church, VA Ltd. 60.00
ALBAUGH, William A., III Confederate Edged Weapons.
 1960 New York 50.00
 n.d. New York reprint 25.00
ALBAUGH, William A., III Confederate Faces.
 1970 Salona Beach, CA 125.00
ALBAUGH, William A., III More Confederate Faces.
 (1972) Washington, DC 75.00
ALBAUGH, William A., III A Photographic Supplement of Confederate Swords.
 1979 Orange, VA 35.00
ALBAUGH, William A., III Tyler, Texas, C.S.A.
 1958 Harrisburg, PA 35.00
ALBAUGH, William A., III and SIMMONS, Edward N. Confederate Arms.
 1957 Harrisburg 50.00
 1960 Harrisburg 35.00
 n.d. New York Bonanza reprint 25.00
ALBAUGH, William A., III and STEUART, Richard D. Handbook of Confederate Swords. Wraps.
 1951 Harriman 50.00

ALBAUGH, William A., III and STEUART, Richard D.   The Original
Confederate Colt.
   1953   New York   50.00

ALBAUGH, William A., III, BENET, Hugh, and SIMMONS, Edward   Confederate Handguns.
   1963   Philadelphia   50.00
   1963   New York   50.00
   1967   Philadelphia   40.00
   1969   New York   40.00
   n.d.   New York   Bonanza reprint   30.00

ALBERT, Allen D.   A Grandfather's Oft Told Tales of the Civil War.
Wraps.
   1913   Williamsport   35.00

ALBERT, Allen D., edited by   History of the 45th Regiment, Pennsylvania Veteran Volunteer Infantry.
   1912   Williamsport   85.00

ALBERT, Alphaeus H.   Buttons of the Confederacy.
   1963   Hightstown, NJ   75.00

ALBERT, Alphaeus H.   Records of American Uniform and Historical
Buttons.
   1976   Boyertown   40.00

Album of the Second Battalion Duryee Zouaves, 165th Regt. New York Volunteer Infantry.
   1906   (New York)   175.00

ALCOTT, Louisa M.   Hospital Sketches and Camp and Fireside Stories.
   1869   Boston   75.00
   1886   65.00
   1890   Boston   50.00
   1957   n.p.   20.00
   1960   Cambridge   30.00

ALDEN, Carroll Storrs   George Hamilton Perkins Commodore, U.S.N.,
His Life and Letters.
   1914   Boston   40.00

ALDEN, James   Official Memoir of Lieutenant Commander A. Boyd
Cummings, U.S.N. Wraps.
   (1862)   n.p.   35.00

ALDERMAN, Edwin Anderson and GORDON, Armistead C.   J. L. M.
Curry.
   1911   New York   30.00

ALDRICH, Bess Streeter   Song of Years.
   1939   New York   15.00

ALDRICH, Thomas M.   The History of Battery A, First Regiment
Rhode Island Light Artillery.
   1904   Providence   100.00

ALEXANDER, Augustus W.   Grant as a Soldier.
   1887   St. Louis   20.00

ALEXANDER, Edward Porter   The American Civil War.
   1908   London   100.00

ALEXANDER, Edward Porter   Military Memoirs of a Confederate
Critical Narrative.
   1907   New York   125.00
   1908   New York   80.00

1910   New York   75.00
1912   New York   75.00
1914   n.p.   75.00
1962   Bloomington 50.00
1977   Dayton 35.00
ALEXANDER, Edwin P.   **Civil War Railroads and Models.**
    1977   New York   20.00
    1989   14.98
ALEXANDER, Frederick Warren   **Stratford and the Lees Connected with Its History.**
    1912   Oak Grove, VA   25.00
ALEXANDER, Holmes M.   **Washington and Lee.**
    1966   Belmont, MA   20.00
ALEXANDER, John Brevard   **Reminiscences of the Past Sixty Years.**
    1908   Charlotte, NC   50.00
ALEXANDER, John H.   **Mosby's Men.**
    1907   New York   300.00
    1987   22.50
ALEXANDER, T., compiled by   **The 126th Pennsylvania.**
    1984   Shippensburg   25.00
ALEXANDER, T., et al   **Southern Revenge! The Civil War History of Chambersburg, PA.**
    1989   Shippensburg   28.95
ALEXANDER, Thomas B.   **Political Reconstruction in Tennessee.**
    1950   Nashville   40.00
ALEXANDER, Thomas B.   **Thomas A.R. Nelson of East Tennessee.**
    1956   Nashville   15.00
ALEXANDER, Thomas B. and **BERINGER**, Richard E., edited by   **The Anatomy of the Confederate Congress.**
    1972   Nashville   25.00
ALEXANDER, William   **Elements of Discord in Secessia.** Wraps.
    1863   New York   20.00
The "Alexandria"   **The Attorney-General versus Sillem and Others.**
    1863   Liverpool   75.00
ALFRIEND, Frank H.   **Life of Jefferson Davis.**
    1868   Cincinnati and Chicago   40.00
ALLABEN, Frank   **John Watts De Peyster.** 2 Vols.
    1908   New York   50.00
ALLAN, Elizabeth Preston   **The Life and Letters of Margaret Junkin Preston.**
    1903   Boston   60.00
ALLAN, Elizabeth Preston   **A March Past, Reminiscences of _____,** edited by Janet A. Bryan.
    1938   Richmond   100.00
ALLAN, Francis D.   **Lone Star Ballads, a Collection of Southern Patriotic Songs Made During Confederate Times.**
    1970   New York   25.00
ALLAN, Lyman Whitney   **Abraham Lincoln. A Poem.**
    1909   New York   10.00
ALLAN, William   **The Army of Northern Virginia in 1862.**
    1892   Boston   175.00
    1984   Dayton   60.00

ALLAN, William   History of the Campaign of Gen. T. J. (Stonewall) Jackson in the Shenandoah Valley of Virginia.
1880   Philadelphia   200.00
1892   Boston   150.00
1912   London entitled Stonewall Jackson's Campaign in the Shenandoah Valley 140.00
1974   Dayton   20.00
1987   Dayton   25.00
ALLAN, William   Jackson's Valley Campaign, Address. Wraps.
1878   Richmond   175.00
ALLEMAN, Mrs. Tillie Pierce   At Gettysburg, or, What a Girl Saw and Heard of the Battle.
1889   New York 80.00
1987   18.50
ALLEN, George H.   Forty-six Months with the 4th Rhode Island Volunteers.
1887   Providence   90.00
ALLEN, H. H.   Allen's Compendium of Hardee's Tactics, Elementary Instruction in the School of the Soldier, Company and Battalion with Manual of Arms. Wraps.
1861   125.00
ALLEN, Hall   Center of Conflict. Wraps.
1961   Paducah 25.00
ALLEN, Henry A.   Sergeant Allen and Private Renick A Memoir of the Eleventh Illinois Cavalry. Wraps.
1971   Galesburg, IL   25.00
ALLEN, Hervey   Action at Aquila.
1938   New York   40.00
ALLEN, Ivan   Atlanta from the Ashes.
1928   Atlanta Ltd.   25.00
ALLEN, James Lane   The Sword of Youth.
1915   New York   20.00
ALLEN, James S.   Reconstruction - The Battle for Democracy.
1937   New York   25.00
ALLEN, John   Memorial of Pickering Dodge Allen. By His Father.
1867   Boston   50.00
ALLEN, Stanton P.   A Boy Trooper with Sheridan.
1899   MA 60.00
ALLEN, Stanton P.   Down in Dixie.
1893   Boston 50.00
ALLEN, V. C.   Rhea and Meigs Counties (Tennessee) in the Confederate War.
1908   n.p. 100.00
ALLEN, Walter   "Public Duty Is My Only Master" Governor Chamberlain's Administration in South Carolina.
1888   New York   75.00
ALLEN, Walter   Ulysses S. Grant.
1901   Boston   20.00
ALLEN, William H., edited by   The American Civil War Book and Grant Album.
1894   Boston   40.00

ALLEY, Charles   Excerpts from the Civil War Diary of Lieutenant
_____, Company "C" Fifth Iowa Cavalry, edited by John S. Ezell.
Wraps.
(1951) Iowa City   35.00
ALLSOP, Fred W.   Albert Pike, A Biography.
1928   Little Rock 90.00
1982   Little Rock 40.00
ALLSOP, Fred W.   The Life and Story of Albert Pike.
1920   Little Rock 125.00
ALOE, A.   Twelfth U.S. Infantry: 1789-1919.
1919   New York   35.00
ALOTTA, Robert I.   Civil War Justice. Union Army Executions Under
Lincoln.
1989   Shippensburg   24.95
ALOTTA, Robert I.   Stop the Evil, Story of Pvt. Wm. H. Howe, 116th
Pa. Vols.
1978   San Rafael, CA   20.00
Alphabetical Index to Places of Interment of Deceased Union Soldiers in the
Various States and Territories. Wraps.
1868   Washington, DC   40.00
Alphabetical List of Graduates of the Virginia Military Institute from 1839
to 1910 with Post Office Address. Wraps.
1910   Lynchburg, VA   30.00
Alphabetical List of the Battles of the War of the Rebellion with Dates.
Wraps.
(c.1870) Philadelphia   20.00
ALSTON, J. Motte   Rice Planter and Sportsman, the Recollections of
_____ 1821-1909, edited by Arney R. Childs.
1953   Columbia, SC   30.00
ALTSHELER, Joseph A.   Before the Dawn, a Story of the Fall of Richmond.
1903   New York   30.00
ALTSHELER, Joseph A.   In Circling Camps: A Romance of the Civil
War.
1900   New York   20.00
ALTSHELER, Joseph A.   The Guns of Shiloh.
1942   New York   25.00
ALTSHELER, Joseph A.   The Rock of Chickamauga: A Story of Western Crisis.
1922   New York   20.00
ALTSHELER, Joseph A.   The Scouts of Stonewall The Story of the
Great Valley Campaign.
1914   New York   30.00
ALTSHELER, Joseph A.   The Star of Gettysburg: A Story of Southern
High Tide.
1923   New York   20.00
ALTSHELER, Joseph A.   The Sword of Antietam.
1925   New York 30.00
1942   New York 25.00

ALTSHELER, Joseph A.   The Tree of Appomattox: A Story of the Civil War's Close.
1916   New York   30.00
1926   New York   20.00

AMADON, G. F.   Rise of the Ironclads. Wraps.
1988   Missoula   9.95

AMANN, William, edited by   Personnel of the Civil War.
1961   New York   40.00
1964   New York   30.00
1968   New York   30.00

AMBLER, I. W.   "Truth Is Stranger Than Fiction," The Life of Sergeant _____.
1873   Boston   40.00
1883   Boston   35.00
1886   Boston   30.00

AMBROSE, D. Leib   History of the Seventh Regiment Illinois Volunteer Infantry.
1868   Springfield   150.00

AMBROSE, Stephen E.   Halleck: Lincoln's Chief of Staff.
1962   Baton Rouge   50.00

AMBROSE, Stephen E.   Struggle for Vicksburg.
1967   Harrisburg, PA   35.00

AMBROSE, Stephen E.   Upton and the Army.
1964   Baton Rouge   35.00

American Almanac for 1861.
1861   Boston   25.00

American Annual Cyclopedia and Register of Important Events 1861-1865. 5 Vols.
n.d.   n.p.   300.00

American Caricatures Pertaining to the Civil War.
1918   New York   50.00

American Christian Commission Doc. 1. Wraps.
1867   New York   20.00

The American Civil War: A Centennial Exhibition, Library of Congress. Wraps.
1961   Washington, DC   20.00

The American Jew in the Civil War, an Exhibit . . . Los Angeles, Dec. 10, 1962 to Jan. 11, 1963. Wraps.
n.d.   n.p.   20.00

The American Soldier in the Civil War.
1895   New York   75.00

American War Songs.
1925   Philadelphia   25.00

AMES, Adelbert   Capture of Fort Fisher, North Carolina Jan. 15, 1865. Wraps.
1897   n.p.   50.00

AMES, Blanche   Adelbert Ames, General, Senator, Governor - 1835-1933.
1964   London   30.00
1964   New York   50.00

AMES, Blanche, edited by   Chronicles from the Nineteenth Century - Family Letters of Blanche Butler and Adelbert Ames. 2 Vols.
1957   Clinton, MA   40.00

AMES, Herman V.   John C. Calhoun and Secession Movement of 1850.
Wraps.
1918   Worcester   20.00

AMES, M. C.   Ten Years in Washington Life and Scenes in the National
Capital.
1874   Cincinnati   30.00

AMES, Mary   From a New England Woman's Diary in Dixie in 1865.
1906   Springfield, MA   40.00

AMES, Nelson   History of Battery G, First Regiment New York Light
Artillery.
1900   Marshalltown, IA   100.00

AMMEN, Daniel   The Atlantic Coast. See: Campaigns of the Civil War.

AMMEN, Daniel   The Old Navy and the New.
1891   Philadelphia   60.00

AMORY, Charles B.   A Brief Record of the Army Life of _____.
1902   (Boston)   50.00

ANDERS, Curt   Fighting Confederates.
1968   New York   25.00

ANDERS, Leslie   The Eighteenth Missouri.
1968   Indianapolis   30.00

ANDERS, Leslie   The 21st Missouri From Home Guard to Union Regiment.
1975   Westport   25.00

ANDERSON, Archer   Robert Edward Lee: An Address Delivered at the
Dedication of the Monument to General Robert Edward Lee at Richmond, Va., May 29, 1890.
1890   Richmond   30.00

ANDERSON, Bern   By Sea and By River, the Naval History of the
Civil War.
1962   New York   30.00
1989   13.95

ANDERSON, Betty Baxter   Alabama Raider.
1957   Philadelphia   20.00

ANDERSON, Charles   The Cause of the War: Who Brought It On
and for What Purpose? A Speech.   Wraps.
1863   New York   20.00

ANDERSON, Charles   Letter Addressed to the Opera House Meeting,
Cincinnati. Wraps.
1863   New York   20.00

ANDERSON, Charles C.   Fighting by Southern Federals.
1912   New York   100.00

ANDERSON, E. McD.   Memoirs: Historical and Personal; Including
the Campaigns of the First Missouri Confederate Brigade.
1988   Dayton   35.00

ANDERSON, Edward   Camp Fire Stories, A Series of Sketches of the
Union Army in the Southwest.
1896   Chicago   40.00
1900   Chicago   expanded ed.   65.00

ANDERSON, Edward C.   Confederate Foreign Agent, edited by William
Stanley Hoole.
1973   Dayton 30.00
1976   University, AL   25.00

ANDERSON, Edward L.   Colonel Archibald Gracie's The Truth About
  Chickamauga. Wraps.
  n.d.   n.p.   35.00
ANDERSON, Ephraim M.   Memoirs Historical and Personal Including
  the Campaigns of the 1st Missouri Confederate Brigade.
  1868   St. Louis   700.00
  1972   Dayton   35.00
  1988   Dayton   35.00
ANDERSON, Frank Maloy   The Mystery of "A Public Man."
  1948   Minneapolis   30.00
ANDERSON, Galusha   The Story of a Border City During the Civil
  War.
  1908   Boston 35.00
  1918   Washington, DC   35.00
ANDERSON, Isabel   Under the Black Horse Flag, Annals of the Weld
  Family and Some of its Branches.
  1926   Boston   50.00
ANDERSON, J. C.   Notes on the Life of Stonewall Jackson and His
  Campaigning in Virginia.
  1904   London 150.00
  1905   London 125.00
ANDERSON, J. H.   Grant's Campaign in Virginia May 1 - June 30,
  1864.
  1908   London   90.00
ANDERSON, James H.   Life and Letters of Judge Thomas J. Anderson
  and Wife.
  1904   n.p.   50.00
ANDERSON, John   The Fifty-seventh Regiment of Massachusetts Volunteers.
  1896   Boston   65.00
ANDERSON, John H.   American Civil War The Operations in the
  Eastern Theatre from the Commencement of Hostilities to May 5, 1863,
  and in the Shenandoah Valley from April, 1861 to June, 1862.
  1912   London 100.00
ANDERSON, Mrs. John Huske   North Carolina Women of the Confederacy. Wraps.
  1926   Fayetteville 100.00
  n.d.   n.p.   Reprint 35.00
ANDERSON, John Q., edited by   Campaigning with Parsons' Texas Cavalry, C.S.A. The War Journal and Letters of the Four Orr Brothers
  12th Texas Cavalry Regiment.
  1967   Hillsboro   35.00
ANDERSON, John Q.   A Texas Surgeon in the C.S.A. See: Confederate Centennial Studies, No. 6.
ANDERSON, Joseph   History of the Soldiers' Monument in Waterbury,
  Conn.
  1886   n.p.   20.00
ANDERSON, Lee Stratton   Valley of the Shadow The Battles of
  Chickamauga and Chattanooga 1863. Wraps.
  1959   Chattanooga, TN   5.00

ANDERSON, Mabel Washbourne   The Life of General Stand Watie.
   1915   Pryor, OK   125.00
   1931   Pryor, OK   100.00
ANDERSON, Nancy S. and ANDERSON, Dwight   The Generals (Grant and Lee).
   1988   24.95
ANDERSON, Nicholas Longworth   The Letters and Journals of _____, edited by Isabel Anderson.
   1892   New York   50.00
   1942   48.00
ANDERSON, Osborne   A Voice from Harper's Ferry. A Narrative of Events . . . Incidents Prior & Subsequent to Its Capture by Captain Brown & His Men.
   1861   MA   100.00
ANDERSON, Thomas M.   The Political Conspiracies Preceding the Rebellion.
   1882   New York   25.00
ANDERSON, W. P.   Anderson Family Records.
   1936   Cincinnati   75.00
ANDERSON, William   They Died to Make Men Free. A History of the 19th Michigan in the Civil War.
   1980   25.00
ANDREW, A. Piatt   Some Civil War Letters of . . . .
   1925   Gloucester, MA   60.00
ANDREWS, Andrew J.   A Sketch of the Boyhood Days of _____ of Gloucester County, Virginia.
   1905   Richmond   125.00
ANDREWS, Christopher C.   Christopher C. Andrews . . . General in the Civil War. Recollections 1829-1922, edited by Alice E. Andrews.
   1928   Cleveland   35.00
ANDREWS, Christopher C.   History of the Campaign of Mobile.
   1867   New York   100.00
ANDREWS, E. Benjamin   A Private's Reminiscences of the First Year of the War. Wraps.
   1886   Providence   Ltd.   35.00
ANDREWS, Eliza Frances   Seven Great Battles of the Army of Northern Virginia. Wraps.
   1906   Montgomery, AL   100.00
ANDREWS, Eliza Frances   The War Time Journal of a Georgia Girl.
   1908   New York   75.00
   1960   Macon, GA   edited by Spencer Bidwell King, Jr.   25.00
   1976   Atlanta   14.95
ANDREWS, H. and NELSON, C., et al   Photographs of American Civil War Cavalry. Wraps.
   1988   E. Stroudsburg   9.95
ANDREWS, J. Cutler   The North Reports the Civil War.
   1955   Pittsburgh   Ltd. autograph. ed.   50.00
   Trade edition   40.00
ANDREWS, J. Cutler   The South Reports the Civil War.
   1970   Princeton   40.00
   1971   Princeton   25.00
   1985   Pittsburgh   20.00

ANDREWS, Marietta Minnegerode   Memoirs of A Poor Relation.
   1927   New York   35.00
   1930   22.50
ANDREWS, Marietta Minnegerode   Scraps of Paper.
   1929   New York   40.00
ANDREWS, Mary   The Counsel Assigned.
   1920   New York   15.00
ANDREWS, Mary Raymond Shipman   The Perfect Tribute.
   1907   New York   25.00
   1910   New York   25.00
   1911   New York   20.00
   1915   New York   15.00
ANDREWS, Matthew Page   The Dixie Book of Days.
   1912   Philadelphia   20.00
ANDREWS, Matthew Page   Women of the South in War Times.
   1920   Baltimore   50.00
   1923   Baltimore   40.00
   1924   Baltimore   30.00
   1927   Baltimore   30.00
ANDREWS, Richard S.   Richard Snowden Andrews, Lt. Col. Commanding the First Maryland Artillery . . . A Memoir, edited by Tunstall Smith.
   1910   Baltimore   100.00
ANDREWS, Robert W.   The Life and Adventures of Capt. Robert W. Andrews, of Sumter, South Carolina.   Wraps.
   1887   Boston   75.00
ANDREWS, Sidney   The South Since the War.
   1866   Boston   60.00
ANDREWS, W. J.   Sketch of Co. K, 23rd South Carolina Volunteers. Wraps.
   n.d.   n.p.   Reprint   25.00
ANDRUS, Michael J.   The Brooke, Farquier, Loudoun and Alexander Artillery.
   1990   16.95
ANDRUS, Onley   Civil War Letters of . . . . , edited by Fred A. Shannon.
   1947   Urbana   50.00
ANGLE, Paul M.   Abraham Lincoln His Autobiographical Writings.
   1948   New Brunswick   Ltd. & numbered   30.00
ANGLE, Paul M., edited by   Created Equal? The Complete Lincoln-Douglas Debates of 1858.
   1958   Chicago   30.00
ANGLE, Paul M.   Here I Have Lived. A History of Lincoln's Springfield 1821-1865.
   1935   Springfield   25.00
   1950   New Brunswick   15.00
ANGLE, Paul M., et al   Lincoln Day by Day. 4 Vols.
   1933-41   Springfield   50.00
ANGLE, Paul M., edited by   The Lincoln Reader.
   1947   New Brunswick   25.00
ANGLE, Paul M.   New Letters and Papers of Lincoln.
   1930   Boston   30.00

ANGLE, Paul M.   A Pictorial History of the Civil War Years.
    1967   New York   20.00
    1980   Wraps   13.00
ANGLE, Paul M.   A Shelf of Lincoln Books, A Critical, Selective Bibliography of Lincolniana.
    1946   New Brunswick   30.00
ANGLE, Paul M. and MIERS, Earl S.   A Ballad of the North and South.
    1959   Kingsport, TN   Ltd.   Boxed   30.00
ANGLE, Paul M. and MIERS, Earl S.   The Living Lincoln.
    1955   New Brunswick   25.00
ANGLE, Paul M. and MIERS, Earl S.   The Tragic Years. 2 Vols.
    1960   New York   25.00
The Annals of Harper's Ferry with Sketches of Its Founder . . . by Josephus, Junior. Wraps.
    1872   Martinsburg, WV   60.00
Annals of the War. See: McCLURE, Alexander K.
Anniversary and Reunion of the 10th New York Cavalry Association.
    37th   1898   Wraps   35.00
    57th   1913   30.00
Annual Reports.   See also: issuing organization.
Annual Report of Adjutant General of Pennsylvania.
    1863-66   Harrisburg   35.00
Annual Report of Adjutant General of Rhode Island.
    1862   Wraps   30.00
    1863   Wraps   30.00
    1865   2 Vols.   50.00
Annual Report of Quartermaster General, Ohio.
    1863-64   Wraps   40.00 each
Annual Report of the Adjutant General for the Years 1861, 1862, 1863, 1864/65. (California)
    1862-65   Sacramento   60.00 each
Annual Report of the Adjutant General of Missouri for 1864.
    1865   Jefferson City   60.00
    1866   Jefferson City   75.00
Annual Report of the Adjutant General of the State of Connecticut 1861-65.
    n.d. Hartford   30.00 each
Annual Report of the Adjutant General of the State of Maine.
    1862-67   Augusta   30.00 each
Annual Report of the Adjutant General of the State of Massachusetts. 5 Vols.
    1862-66   Boston   50.00 each
Annual Report of the Adjutant General of the State of Michigan, 1862-65.
    1863-66   Lansing   35.00 each
    1866   Lansing for years 1865-66   3 Vols.   200.00
Annual Report of the Adjutant General of the State of Minnesota for the Year Ending Dec. 1, 1866, and of Military Forces of the State from 1861-1866.
    1866   St. Paul   60.00
Annual Report of the Adjutant General of the State of West Virginia for the Year Ending Dec. 31, 1865.
    1866   Wheeling   75.00

Annual Report of the Adjutant General of the State of Wisconsin. 1861-1865.
1861-65   35.00 each
Annual Report of the Adjutant General to the Governor of the State of Ohio. Wraps.
1862-63   40.00 each
Annual Report of the Board of Military Claims of the State of Pennsylvania, for the Year 1863.
1864   Harrisburg   35.00
Annual Report of the Executive Office, Military Department of the Commonwealth of Pennsylvania. Vol. I - Year ending 1864. Vol II - Year ending 1865.
1865   Harrisburg   75.00
Annual Report of the Quartermaster General of Missouri for the Year 1863.
1864   St. Louis   60.00
Annual Report, Adjutant General, State of New York, Albany. 1863-1900.
1863-1900   35.00 each Some years were issued in multiple volumes.
Annual Reunion 47th Regiment Illinois Volunteer Infantry.
1908   Peoria   40.00
Annual Reunion of Pegram Battalion. Wraps.
1886   Richmond   160.00
ANTHONY, William   Anthony's History of the Battle of Hanover . . . Tuesday, June 30, 1863. . . .
1945   Hanover   100.00
Antietam to Appomattox with the 118th Penna. Vols., Corn Exchange Regiment. . .
1892   Philadelphia 85.00
ANTRIM, Earl   Civil War Prisons and Their Covers.
1961   New York   40.00
An Appeal for the Union. Wraps.
1860   n.p.   25.00
APPELL, George C.   The Man Who Shot Quantrill.
1957   New York   20.00
APPLEGATE, John S.   Reminiscences and Letters of George Arrowsmith of New Jersey.
1893   Red Bank, NJ   75.00
APPLER, A. C.   The Younger Brothers, Their Life and Character.
1955   New York   20.00
Appleton's Cyclopaedia of American Biography. 6 Vols., edited by James Grant Wilson and John Fiske.
1888-89 New York   150.00
APTHEKER, Herbert   The Negro in the Civil War. Wraps.
1938   New York   50.00
ARBUCKLE, John   Civil War Experiences of a Foot-Soldier Who Marched with Sherman.
1930   Columbus   80.00
ARCENEAUX, William   Acadian General, Alfred Mouton and the Civil War.
1981   Lafayette, LA   30.00
ARCHER, W.   Through Afro-America; An English Reading of the Race Problem.
1910   New York   50.00

Arkansas - Confederate Military History.   See: Confederate   Military
     History, Vol. X (Vol. XIV, 1988 reprint ed.).
ARMES, Ethel   Stratford Hall, the Great House of the Lees.
     1936   Richmond   Ltd. & signed   100.00
     Trade edition   80.00
ARMES, George A.   Ups and Downs of an Army Officer.
     1900   Washington, DC   140.00
ARMSTRONG, Nelson   Nuggets of Experience.
     1906   Los Angeles   85.00
ARMSTRONG, O. K.   Old Massas People, The Old Slaves Tell Their
     Story.
     1931   65.00
ARMSTRONG, William   Warrior in Two Camps.   Ely S. Parker, Union
     General and Seneca Chief.
     1978   25.00
ARMSTRONG, William H.   Red-Tape and Pigeon-Hole Generals.
     1864   New York   40.00
Army and Navy Official Gazette. Vols. 1 & 2, 1863-1865.
     1864-65   Washington, DC   150.00
     Vol. 1   75.00
     Vol. 2   75.00
Army Register of the Volunteer Forces of the U.S. During the Civil War. 8
     Vols.
     1987   125.00
The Army Reunion.
     1869   Chicago   60.00
ARNDT, Albert F. R.   Reminiscences of an Artillery Officer.   Wraps.
     1890   Detroit   35.00
ARNETT, Ethel Stephens   Confederate Guns Were Stacked, Greensboro,
     N.C.
     1965   Greensboro, NC   60.00
ARNOLD, Edgar   The Young Refugees.
     1912   Richmond   20.00
ARNOLD, Edwin   Land of Fadeless Stars.
     1948   Boston   20.00
ARNOLD, George   Life and Adventures of Jefferson Davis.
     1865   New Haven   40.00
ARNOLD, Isaac N.   Abraham Lincoln: A Paper.   Wraps.
     1881   Chicago   15.00
ARNOLD, Isaac N.   The History of Abraham Lincoln and the Over-
     throw of Slavery.
     1971   New York   20.00
ARNOLD, Isaac N.   The Life of Abraham Lincoln.
     1885   Chicago   15.00
ARNOLD, Isaac N.   Sketch of the Life of Abraham Lincoln.
     1869   New York   20.00
ARNOLD, Matthew   General Grant, edited by John Y. Simon.
     1966   Carbondale, IL   20.00
ARNOLD, Samuel Bland   Defense and Prison Experiences of a Lincoln
     Conspirator, Statements and Autobiographical Notes.
     1943   Hattiesburg   125.00

ARNOLD, Thomas Jackson   Early Life and Letters of General Thomas
    J. Jackson ("Stonewall").
    1916   New York   100.00
    1957   New York   50.00
    1957   Richmond   40.00
ARNOLD, William B.   The Fourth Massachusetts Cavalry in the
    Closing Scenes of the War for the Maintenance of the Union.
    (191-)   (Boston)   45.00
ARP, Bill (pseud.)   See: SMITH, Charles H.
Art Works of Scenes in the Valley of Virginia. 2 Vols.
    1897   Chicago   275.00
Artillery Tactics United States Army.
    1878   New York   40.00
ASHBROOK, Stanley B.   Some Notes on the Postal Legislation of the
    Confederate States of America 1861-1865. Wraps.
    1946   n.p.   25.00
ASHBURN, Joseph Nelson   History of the Eighty-sixth Regiment Ohio
    Volunteer Infantry.
    1909   Cleveland   140.00
ASHBY, Thomas A.   Life of Turner Ashby.
    1914   New York   250.00
    1988   20.00
ASHBY, Thomas A.   The Valley Campaigns, Being the Reminiscences of
    a Non-Combatant.
    1914   New York   150.00
ASHCRAFT, Allan C.   Texas in the Civil War: A Resume History.
    Wraps.
    1962   Austin   20.00
ASHE, S. W.   The Trial and Death of Henry Wirz, with Other Matters
    Pertaining Thereto. Wraps.
    1908   Raleigh, NC   30.00
ASHE, Samuel A.   Gen'l Robert E. Lee, The South's Peerless Soldier
    and Leader, Oration. Wraps.
    1906   Raleigh, NC   25.00
ASHE, Samuel A.   Hon. George Davis. Wraps.
    1916   Raleigh, NC   30.00
ASHE, Samuel A.   A Southern View of the Invasion of the Southern
    States and the War of 1861-65.   Wraps.
    1935   Raleigh, NC   40.00
    1938   Raleigh, NC   25.00
    1972   Wendell, NC   5.00
ASHE, Samuel A. and TYLER, Lyon G.   Secession, Insurrection of the
    Negroes, and Northern Incendiarism. Wraps.
    (1933)   n.p.   25.00
ASKEW, H. G.   2nd Texas Brigade, United Confederate Veterans.
    1916   Austin   30.00
The Assassination of Abraham Lincoln, Late President of the U.S.A. and the
    Attempted Assassination of William H. Seward and Frederick W.
    Seward.
    1866   Washington, DC   50.00
    1867   Washington, DC   20.00

ASTON, Howard   History and Roster of the Fourth and Fifth Independent Battalions and Thirteenth Regiment Ohio Cavalry Volunteers. Wraps.
    1902   Columbus   140.00

ATEN, Henry J., compiled by   A History of the Eighty-fifth Regiment Illinois Volunteer Infantry.
    1901   Hiawatha, KS   190.00

ATHEARN, Robert G.   The American Heritage New Illustrated History of the United States - The Civil War.
    1963   New York   20.00

ATHEARN, Robert G.   Forts of the Upper Missouri.
    1967   NJ   25.00

ATHEARN, Robert G.   William Tecumseh Sherman and the Settlement of the West.
    1956   OK   30.00

ATKINS, John Black   The Life of Sir William Howard Russell, The First Special Correspondent. 2 Vols.
    1911   London   75.00

ATKINS, Thomas A. and OLIVER, John W.   Yonkers in the Rebellion of 1861-1865.
    1892   New York   60.00

ATKINSON, C. F.   Grant's Campaigns of 1864 and 1865.
    1908   London   100.00

ATKINSON, Edward   Cheap Cotton by Free Labor: By a Cotton Manufacturer. Wraps.
    1861   Boston   30.00

ATKINSON, Eleanor   The Boyhood of Lincoln.
    1908   New York   15.00

Atlanta Civil War Roundtable Historical Yearbooks.   1959-1960; 1965-1966; 1966-1976.
    Atlanta   25.00 each

Atlanta in the Civil War: The Personal Perspective.
    1979   Atlanta   13.00

The Atlanta Papers, edited by Sydney C. Kerksis.
    1980   35.00
    Leatherbound   60.00

Atlantic Monthly.   See Appendix: Magazines.

Atlas of Chickamauga, Chattanooga, and Vicinity.
    1902   Washington, DC   225.00

Atlas to Accompany the Official Records of the Union and Confederate Armies See: Official Records - Atlas.

Atlas Troops Movements at the Battle of Cold Harbor. Publication No. 21, Richmond Civil War Centennial Committee.   Wraps.
    1964   Richmond   20.00

ATWATER, Dorence   List of Union Soldiers Buried at Andersonville.
    1866   New York   35.00

AUBERY, James M.   The 36th Wisconsin Volunteer Infantry.
    1900   Milwaukee   175.00

AUBIN, J. Harris, compiled by   Register of the Military Order of the Loyal Legion of the United States.
    1906   Boston   50.00

AUCHAMPAUGH, Philip Gerald   James Buchanan and His Cabinet on the Eve of Secession. Wraps.
    1926   Lancaster, PA   30.00
    1966   Boston 15.00
AUCHAMPAUGH, Philip Gerald   Robert Tyler, Southern Rights Champion 1847-1866.
    1934   Duluth, MN   40.00
Auctore Incerto. . . . (Maddox, Charles Kellogg).
    (c.1900) Atlanta   75.00
AUGHEY, John Hill   The Fighting Preacher.
    1899   Chicago 150.00
AUGHEY, John Hill   The Iron Furnace.
    1863   Philadelphia 50.00
AUGHEY, John Hill   Tupelo.
    1888   Lincoln, NE   40.00
    1905   25.00
    1971   Tupelo and New York   40.00
AUSTIN, Anne L.   The Woolsey Sisters of New York. Wraps.
    1971   Philadelphia 25.00
AUSTIN, Aurelia   Georgia Boys with "Stonewall" Jackson. Wraps.
    1967   Athens   20.00
AUSTIN, J. P.   The Blue and the Gray.
    1899   Atlanta   75.00
Autographs of Prominent Men of the Southern Confederacy and Historical Documents, E. M. Bruce Collection. Wraps.
    (c.1900) Houston, TX   50.00
AVARY, Myrta Lockett   Dixie After the War.
    1906   Richmond   50.00
    1906   New York   40.00
    1937   Boston   35.00
    1937   New York   30.00
    1946   New York   30.00
    1969   30.00
AVARY, Myrta Lockett   A Virginia Girl in the Civil War.
    1903   New York   40.00
    1906   40.00
AVERELL, William Woods   Report of _____ to Gen'l W. B. Franklin of an Inspection of State Homes for Disabled Soldiers and Sailors of the U.S. Made in Dec. 1888.
    1889   Washington, DC   35.00
AVERILL, James P., edited by   Andersonville Prison Park Report of Its Purchase and Improvement. Wraps.
    (c.1900) Atlanta   30.00
AVERY, A. C.   Memorial Address on the Life and Character of Lt. General D. H. Hill. Wraps.
    1893   Raleigh, NC   75.00
AVERY, I. M.   In Memory, Alexander Hamilton Stephens. Wraps.
    1883   Atlanta   30.00
AVERY, I. W.   The History of the State of Georgia from 1850 to 1881.
    1881   New York   100.00
AVERY, P. O.   History of the Fourth Illinois Cavalry Regiment.
    1903   Humboldt, NE   160.00

AVERY, William B.   **Gunboat Service on the James River.**   Wraps.
     1884   Providence   Ltd.   40.00

AVERY, William B.   **The Marine Artillery with the Burnside Expedition and the Battle of Camden, N. C.**   Wraps.
     1880   Providence   Ltd.   40.00

AVEY, Elijah   **Eye Witness. The Capture and Execution of John Brown.**
     1906   Chicago   50.00

AVIRETT, James B.   **The Memoirs of General Turner Ashby and His Compeers.**
     1867   Baltimore   250.00
     1904   150.00
     1984   30.00
     1987   28.50

AVIRETT, James B.   **An Oration . . . on the Occasion of Laying the Foundation Stone . . . the North Carolina Plot in the Stonewall Cemetery, Winchester, Virginia, 17th September, 1897.**   Wraps.
     (1897)   n.p.   50.00

Ayer's American Almanac.   Wraps.
     1864   Lowell, MA   25.00

AYER, I. Winslow   **The Great North-Western Conspiracy.**
     1895   Chicago   25.00

AYER, I. Winslow   **The Great Treason Plot in the North During the War. . . .**
     1895   Chicago   100.00

AYERS, James T.   **The Diary of** _____, edited by John Hope Franklin.
     1947   Springfield   20.00

BABCOCK, Bernie   **Booth and the Spirit of Lincoln.**
     1925   Philadelphia   20.00

BABCOCK, Bernie   **The Soul of Ann Rutledge   Abraham Lincoln's Romance.**
     1919   New York   20.00

BABCOCK, Willoughby M., Jr.   **Selections from the Letters and Diaries of Brevet-Brigadier General Willoughby Babcock of the 75th New York Volunteers.**   Wraps.
     1922   Albany   65.00

BACH, J. B., et al   **Ceremony of Flag Representation to Columbia University of the City of New York, May 2, 1896, and May 7, 1898.**
     1899   Astor Place   35.00

BACHE, Richard Meade   **Life of General George Gordon Meade.**
     1897   Philadelphia   30.00
     1907   30.00

BACHELDER, John B.   **Descriptive Key to the Painting of the Repulse of Longstreet's Assault at the Battle of Gettysburg (July 3, 1863) . . . painted by James Walker.**
     1870   New York   65.00

BACHELDER, John B.   **Gettysburg: What to See and How to See It.**
     1873   40.00
     1889   Boston   25.00

BACHELDER, John B.   **Maps of the Battle Field of Gettysburg.**
     1876   Boston   250.00
     1980   15.00

BACHELLER, Irving   Father Abraham.
    1925   Indianapolis   10.00
BACHELLER, Irving   A Man for the Ages, A Story of the Builders
    of Democracy.
    n.d.   New York   5.00
BACON, Edward   Among the Cotton Thieves.
    1867   Detroit   200.00
    1962   n.p. Ltd.   50.00
BACON, Georgeanna Woolsey and HOWLAND, Eliza Woolsey, edited by
    Letters of a Family During the War for the Union. 2 Vols.
    1899   np.   150.00
BACON, William Johnson   Memorial of William Kirland Bacon, Late
    Adjutant of the Twenty-sixth Regiment of New York State Volunteers.
    1863   Utica   30.00
    n.d.   Boston   30.00
BACON-FOSTER, Corra   Clara Barton Humanitarian.
    1918   Washington, DC   35.00
BADEAU, Adam   Grant in Peace. From Appomattox to Mt. McGregor.
    1887   Hartford   50.00
    1888   Philadelphia   40.00
    1971   New York   25.00
BADEAU, Adam   Military History of Ulysses S. Grant. 3 Vols.
    1868 (Vol. I)   1881   (Vols. II & III)   New York   125.00
    1882   New York   100.00
    1885   New York   100.00
BADLAM, William H.   Kearsarge and Alabama.   Wraps.
    1894   Providence   Ltd.   40.00
BAGBY, Alfred   King and Queen County, Virginia.
    1908   New York   100.00
BAGBY, George W.   The Old Virginia Gentleman and Other Sketches,
    edited by Ellen Bagby.
    1938   Richmond   20.00
BAGLEY, William Chandler   Soil Exhaustion and the Civil War.   Wraps.
    1942   Washington, DC   20.00
BAHNSON, Henry T.   The Last Days of the War.   Wraps.
    1903   Hamlet, NC   50.00
BAILEY, A. J.   Between the Enemy and Texas: Parson's Texas Cavalry
    in the Civil War.
    1989   Fort Worth   25.95
BAILEY, F. A.   Class and Tennessee's Confederate Generation.
    1987   Chapel Hill   10.00
BAILEY, George W.   A Private Chapter of the War.
    1880   St. Louis   80.00
BAILEY, Hugh C.   Notes and Documents; Disloyalty in Early Confed-
    erate Alabama.
    1957   15.00
BAILEY, Hugh C.   Hinton Rowan Helper: Abolitionist - Racist.
    1967   University, AL   15.00
BAILEY, James H.   Henrico Home Front 1861-1865.   Wraps.
    1963   Richmond   40.00
BAILEY, L. D.   Quantrell's Raid on Lawrence.
    1889   Lyndon, KS   Ltd.   125.00

BAILEY, Mahlon   Medical Sketch of the Nineteenth Regiment of Kansas Cavalry Volunteers.
   1937   n.p.   15.00
BAILEY, R. H.   Forward to Richmond, McClellan's Peninsular Campaign.
   1983   10.00
BAIN, William E., edited by   B & O in the Civil War from the Papers of Wm. Prescott Smith.
   1966   Denver   30.00
BAIRD, N. C., edited by   Journals of Amanda Virginia Edmonds, Lass of the Mosby Confederacy, 1859-1867.
   1984   Stephens City, VA   25.00
BAIRD, W. D., edited by   A Creek Warrior for the Confederacy: The Autobiography of Chief G. W. Grayson.
   1988   Norman   16.95
BAKELESS, John   Spies of the Confederacy.
   1970   Philadelphia   40.00
BAKER, Gary R.   Cadets in Gray.
   1990   Columbia, SC   21.95
BAKER, Henry H.   A Reminiscent Story of the Great Civil War, Second Paper.   Wraps.
   1911   New Orleans   250.00
BAKER, Jean H.   Mary Todd Lincoln, A Biography.
   1987   New York   19.95
BAKER, Lafayette C.   History of the U. S. Secret Service in the Late War.
   1867   Philadelphia   50.00
   1868   Philadelphia   40.00
   1869   Philadelphia   40.00
   1891   Philadelphia   40.00
BAKER, Lafayette C.   Spies, Traitors and Conspirators of the Late Civil War.
   1894   Philadelphia   30.00
BAKER, Lafayette C.   The United States Secret Service.
   1889   Philadelphia   25.00
   1900   Chicago   25.00
BAKER, Levi W.   History of the Ninth Mass. Battery.
   1888   S. Framingham   100.00
BAKER, Nina Brown   Cyclone in Calico.   The Story of Mary Ann Bickerdyke.
   1952   Boston   30.00
BAKER, Nina Brown   The Story of Abraham Lincoln.
   1952   New York   15.00
BAKER, S. T.   Fort Sumter and Its Defenders.
   1891   Buffalo   35.00
BAKER, W. W.   Memoirs of Service with John Yates Beall, C.S.N., edited by Douglas Southall Freeman.
   1910   Richmond   325.00
BAKER, William Mumford   Inside: A Chronical of Secession by George F. Harrington.
   1866   New York   60.00

BALCH, Thomas W.   **The Alabama Arbitration.**
    1900   Philadelphia   30.00
BALCH, Thomas   **International Courts of Arbitration.**
    1914   Philadelphia   50.00
BALCH, William Ralston   **The Battle of Gettysburg,   An Historical Account.**
    1885   Philadelphia   30.00
BALCH, William Ralston   **Life and Public Services of Gen. Grant.**
    1885   n.p.   15.00
BALE, Florence Gratiot   **Galena's Yesterdays.**   Wraps.
    1931   Waukegan   15.00
BALE, Florence Gratiot, compiled by   **Historic Galena, Yesterday and Today.**
    1939   Galena   10.00
BALFOUR, D.   **13th Virginia Cavalry.**
    1986   Lynchburg   Ltd.   16.50
BALL, William Watts   **The State that Forgot. South Carolina's Surrender to Democracy.**
    1932   Indianapolis   30.00
BALLARD, Colin R.   **The Military Genius of Abraham Lincoln,   An Essay.**
    1926   London   40.00
    1952   Cleveland   30.00
    1965   New York   20.00
BALLARD, M. B.   **A Long Shadow: Jefferson Davis and the Final Days of the Confederacy.**
    1987   Jackson   22.50
BALTZ, John D.   **Colonel E. D. Baker's Defense in the Battle of Ball's Bluff.**
    1888   Lancaster, PA   80.00
BALTZ, John D.   **Hon. Edward D. Baker . . . Colonel E. D. Baker's Defense in the Battle of Ball's Bluff.**
    1888   Lancaster, PA   75.00
BANCROFT, A. C., edited by   **The Life and Death of Jefferson Davis, Ex-President of the Southern Confederacy.**   Wraps.
    1889   New York   35.00
    1890   New York   30.00
BANCROFT, Frederic   **Slave-Trading in the Old South.**
    1931   Baltimore   35.00
    1967   20.00
BANCROFT, Frederic   **The Life of William H. Seward.** 2 Vols.
    1900   New York   30.00
BANCROFT, George   **Memorial Address on the Life and Character of Abraham Lincoln.**
    1866   Washington, DC   15.00
BANDY, K. and **FREELAND,** F., compiled by   **The Gettysburg Papers.** 2 Vols.
    1978   85.00
    1988   Dayton   50.00

BANES, Charles H.　　History of the Philadelphia Brigade 69th, 71st, 72nd, and 106th Pennsylvania Infantries.
　　1876　Philadelphia　125.00
　　1984　28.50
BANKS, John　　A Short Biographical Sketch of the Undersigned by Himself.
　　1936　Austell, GA　50.00
BANKS, L. A.　　Immortal Songs of Camps and Fields.
　　1898　Cleveland　50.00
BANKS, Robert W.　The Battle of Franklin　Nov. 30, 1864.
　　1908　New York　200.00
　　1982　Dayton　20.00
　　1988　Dayton　17.50
Bannerman's Military Goods Catalogues.　Wraps.
　　25.00 each
　　1945　Anniversary Catalogue　40.00
BAQUET, Camille　　History of the First Brigade, New Jersey Volunteers From 1861 to 1865.
　　1910　Trenton　135.00
　　1988　Gaithersburg　40.00
BARBEE, Muriel Culp　　A Union Forever.
　　1949　Philadelphia　15.00
BARBER, J. G.　　Alexandria in the Civil War.
　　1988　Lynchburg　16.95
BARBER, John　　The Loyal West in the Times of the Rebellion; also Before and Since Being an Encyclopedia and Panorama of the Western States, Pacific States and Territories of the Union. . . .
　　1865　250.00
BARBER, Joseph　　War Letters of a Disbanded Volunteer.　Embracing His Experiences as Honest Abe's Bosom Friend and Unofficial Adviser.
　　1864　New York　25.00
BARBER, Lucius W.　　Army Memoirs of _____ Company D, 15th Illinois Volunteer Infantry.
　　1894　Chicago　150.00
　　1984　22.00
BARBIERE, Joseph　　Scraps from the Prison Table at Camp Chase and Johnson's Island.
　　1868　Doyleston　250.00
BARCLAY, Alexander T.　　The Liberty Hall Volunteers from Lexington to Manassas.
　　1904　Lynchburg　50.00
BARDEEN, Charles W.　　A Little Fifer's War Diary.
　　1910　Syracuse, NY　100.00
BARINGER, William E.　　A House Dividing - Lincoln as President Elect.
　　1945　Springfield, IL　10.00
BARINGER, William E.　　Lincoln's Rise to Power.
　　1937　Boston　15.00
BARINGER, William E.　　Lincoln's Vandalia　A Pioneer Portrait.
　　1949　New Brunswick　15.00
BARINGER, William E., edited by　　The Philosophy of Abraham Lincoln in his Own Words.
　　1959　Indian Hills, CO　10.00

BARKER, Alan   The Civil War in America.
1961   New York   15.00

BARKER, Benedict, et al   Report Concerning the Field Relief Service of the U.S. Sanitary Commission with the Armies of the Potomac, Georgia and Tennessee. Wraps.
1865   Washington, DC   15.00

BARKER, Harold R.   History of the Rhode Island Combat Units in the Civil War, edited by A. Gurney.
1964   n.p.   35.00

BARKER, Jacob   Mr. Jacob Barker's Advocacy of Peace. New Orleans, March 21, 1864. Wraps.
1864   New Orleans   100.00

BARKER, Jacob   The Rebellion: Its Consequences, and the Congressional Committee, Denominated the Reconstruction Committee, With Their Action.
1866   New Orleans   75.00

BARKER, Lorenzo A. ("Ren")   Military History (Michigan Boys), Company "D" 66th Sharpshooters in the Civil War.
1905   Reed City, MI   100.00

BARLOW, Albert R.   Company G.   A Record of the Services of One Company of the 157th New York Volunteers.
1899   Syracuse   100.00

BARLOW, F. C.   Albany Zouave Cadets to the Rochester Union Blues.
1866   Albany   40.00

BARNARD, F. A. P.   Letter to the President of the United States by a Refugee. Wraps.
1863   New York   25.00

BARNARD, George N.   Photographic Views of Sherman's Campaign. Wraps.
1977   New York   20.00

BARNARD, Henry V.   Tattered Volunteers, The Twenty-seventh Alabama Infantry Regiment C.S.A.
1965   Northport   30.00

BARNARD, J. G.   The C.S.A. and the Battle of Bull Run.
1862   New York   100.00

BARNARD, J. G.   Eulogy on the Late Bvt. Maj. Gen. Joseph G. Totten, Chief Engineer United States Army. Wraps.
1866   Washington, DC   15.00

BARNARD, J. G.   Notes on a Sea-Coast Defence.
1861   New York   75.00

BARNARD, J. G.   The Peninsular Campaign and Its Antecedents.
1864   New York   75.00
1864   Washington, DC   50.00

BARNARD, J. G.   Report on the Defenses of Washington.
1871   Washington, DC   150.00

BARNARD, J. G. and BARRY, W. F.   Report of the Engineer and Artillery Operations of the Army of the Potomac.
1863   New York   150.00
1864   New York   125.00

BARNES, Albert   The Condition of Peace, A Thanksgiving Discourse. Wraps.
1863   Philadelphia   20.00

BARNES, David M.   The Draft Riots in New York, July 1863.   Wraps.
1863   New York   20.00

BARNES, Gilbert Hobbs   The Antislavery Impulse 1830-1844.
1957   Gloucester, MA   15.00
1964   10.00

BARNES, J. B.   Military Sketching and Map Reading.
1918   New York   20.00

BARNES, J. S.   Submarine Warfare, Offensive and Defensive, Including a Discussion of the Offensive Torpedo System. . . .
1869   New York   350.00

BARNES, James A., et al   The Eighty-sixth Regiment, Indiana Volunteer Infantry, A Narrative of Its Services in the Civil War of 1861-1865.
1895   Crawfordsville   130.00

BARNET, James, edited by   The Martyrs and Heroes of Illinois in the Great Rebellion.
1866   Chicago   80.00

BARNETT, Simeon   History of the Twenty-second Regiment Iowa Volunteer Infantry.   Wraps.
1865   Iowa City   160.00

BARNEY, Chester   Recollections of Field Service with the Twentieth Infantry Volunteers.
1865   Davenport   200.00

BARNEY, William L.   The Secessionist Impulse, Alabama and Mississippi in 1860.
1974   Princeton, NJ   17.00

BARNHART, J.   The Impact of the Civil War on Indiana.   Wraps.
1962   Indianapolis   15.00

BARNS, George C.   Denver, the Man.
1949   Wilmington, OH   35.00

BARNWELL, Robert W., Sr.   The Lines and Nature of Lincoln's Greatness.   Wraps.
1931   Columbia, SC   10.00

BARNWELL, Robert W., Sr.   Sherman and Grant Contrasted (For Historians).   Wraps.
n.d.   n.p.   15.00

BARONDESS, Benjamin   Lincoln's Cooper Institute Speech.   Wraps.
1953   New York   15.00

BARONDESS, Benjamin   Three Lincoln Masterpieces.
1954   Charleston, WV   15.00

BARR, Alwyn, edited by   Charles Porter's Account of the Confederate Attempt to Seize Arizona and New Mexico.
1964   Austin   30.00

BARR, Alwyn   Polignac's Texas Brigade.   Wraps.
1964   Houston   40.00

BARRETT, Don C.   The Greenbacks and Resumption of Specie Payments 1862-1879.
1931   Cambridge   30.00
1965   15.00

BARRETT, Edwin S.   What I Saw at Bull Run: An Address.
1886   Boston   45.00

BARRETT, Frank W. Z.   Mourning for Lincoln.
1909   Philadelphia   20.00

BARRETT, John G.   The Civil War in North Carolina.
1963   Chapel Hill, NC   25.00
1980   Chapel Hill, NC   30.95
1987   19.95
BARRETT, John G.   North Carolina as a Civil War Battleground, 1861-65.
1980   Raleigh, NC   3.00
BARRETT, John G.   Sherman's March Through the Carolinas.
1956   Chapel Hill, NC   30.00
1980   Chapel Hill, NC   20.00
1983   20.95
1988   19.95
BARRETT, Joseph O.   Life of A. Lincoln.
1865   New York   30.00
BARRETT, Joseph O.   "Old Abe" the Soldier Bird.   Wraps.
1876   Madison   50.00
BARRETT, Orvey S.   Reminiscences, Incidents, Battles, Marches and Camp Life of the Old 4th Michigan Infantry in the War of the Rebellion.
1888   Detroit   60.00
n.d. (reprint)   Detroit 25.00
BARRETT, Thomas   The Great Hanging at Gainesville, Cooke Co., Texas.
1961   Austin, TX 20.00
1985   15.00
BARRIGER, John W.   Railroads in the Civil War.   Wraps.
1966   n.p.   25.00
BARRINGER, Paul B.   The Natural Bent: The Memoirs of Dr. Paul B. Barringer.
1949   Chapel Hill, NC   25.00
BARRON, Samuel B.   The Lone Star Defenders, A Chronicle of the 3rd Texas Cavalry, Ross' Brigade.
1908   New York   1400.00
1964   Waco   30.00
1983   Washington, DC   19.95
BARROW, H. W.   Civil War Letters of Henry W. Barrow Written to John W. Fries, Salem.   Wraps.
1957   12.00
BARROW, Willie Micajah   The Civil War Diary of _____, Sept. 23, 1861 to July 13, 1862, edited by Wendell H. Stephenson and Edwin A. Davis.   Wraps.
n.d.   n.p.   25.00
BARTHELL, Edward E., Jr.   Mystery of the Merrimack.
1959   Muskegon, MI   30.00
BARTHOLOW, Roberts   A Manual of Instructions for Enlisting and Discharging Soldiers.
1863   250.00
1864   Philadelphia   200.00
BARTLESON, Frederick A.   Letters from Libby Prison, edited by Margaret W. Peelle.
1956   New York   40.00

BARTLETT, Asa W.   History of the Twelfth Regiment, New Hampshire Volunteers in the War of the Rebellion.
    1897   Concord   150.00
BARTLETT, Catherine Thom, edited by   My Dear Brother, A Confederate Chronicle.
    1952   Richmond   30.00
BARTLETT, D. W.   The Life and Public Services of Hon. Abraham Lincoln.
    1860   New York   15.00
BARTLETT, Irving H.   Wendell Phillips, Brahmin Radical.
    1961   Boston   20.00
BARTLETT, John Russell   The Literature of the Rebellion: A Catalogue of Books and Pamphlets Relating to the Civil War in the United States . . . Together with Works on American Slavery.
    1866   Providence, RI   Ltd.   400.00
BARTLETT, John Russell   Memoirs of Rhode Island Officers Who Were Engaged in the Service of Their Country During the Great Rebellion.
    1867   Providence   60.00
BARTLETT, M. L., edited by   Assault from the Sea: Essays on the History of Amphibious Warfare.
    1985   Annapolis   27.95
BARTLETT, Napier   Military Record of Louisiana.
    1875   New Orleans   600.00
    1964   Baton Rouge   edited by T. H. Williams   40.00
BARTLETT, Napier   A Soldier's Story of the War, Including the Marches and Battles of the Washington Artillery, and of Other Louisiana Troops.
    1874   New Orleans   400.00
BARTLETT, Robert F., compiled by   Roster of the Ninety-sixth Regiment, Ohio Volunteer Infantry 1862 to 1865.
    1895   Columbus   120.00
BARTLETT, Ruhl Jacob   John C. Fremont and the Republican Party.
    1930   Columbus, Ohio   35.00
BARTLETT, W. C.   An Idyl of War-Times.
    1890   New York   25.00
BARTLETT, William H.   Aunt and the Soldier Boys from Cross Creek Village, Pennsylvania, 1856-1866. Wraps.
    n.d.   CA 25.00
BARTOL, Cyrus A.   The Nation's Hour: A Tribute to Major Sidney Willard. Wraps.
    1862   Boston   15.00
BARTON, George   Angels of the Battlefield.
    1897   Philadelphia   75.00
    1898   Philadelphia   60.00
BARTON, M.   Goodmen: The Character of Civil War Soldiers.
    1981   University Park   23.00
BARTON, Thomas H.   Autobiography of _____ . . . Including a History of the 4th West Virginia Inf. Vols.
    1890   Charleston, WV   100.00

BARTON, William E.   Abraham Lincoln and His Books.
1920   Chicago   25.00
1976   25.00
BARTON, William E.   Abraham Lincoln and the Hooker Letter,   an
Address Delivered Before the Pennell Club of Philadelphia.
1928   New York   Ltd.   30.00
BARTON, William E.   Abraham Lincoln and Walt Whitman.
1928   Indianapolis 25.00
BARTON, William E.   Abraham   Lincoln,   Kentucky   Mountaineer.
Wraps.
1923   Berea, KY   Ltd.   30.00
BARTON, William E.   A Beautiful Blunder,   the True Story of Lincoln's Letter to Mrs. Lydia A. Bixby.
1926   Indianapolis Ltd.   30.00
BARTON, William E.   A Hero in Homespun.
1897   Boston   25.00
BARTON, William E.   The Influence of Chicago Upon Abraham Lincoln,   An Address.   Wraps.
1923   Chicago   10.00
BARTON, William E.   The Life of Abraham Lincoln.   2 Vols.
1924   Indianapolis 25.00
1925   Indianapolis 2 Vols. in 1   20.00
BARTON, William E.   Lincoln at Gettysburg.
1930   Indianapolis 50.00
1950   New York   30.00
BARTON, William E.   The Lineage of Lincoln.
1929   Indianapolis 25.00
BARTON, William E.   The Paternity of Abraham Lincoln.
1920   New York   40.00
BARTON, William E.   President Lincoln.   2 Vols.
1933   Indianapolis 40.00
BARTON, William E.   The Soul of Abraham Lincoln.
1920   New York   20.00
BARTON, William E.   The Women Lincoln Loved.
1927   London   50.00
1927   Indianapolis 20.00
BARUCH, M. C. and BECKMAN, E. J.   Civil   War   Union   Monuments.
Wraps.
1978   Washington, DC   10.00
BARZIZA, Decimus et Ultimus   Adventures of a Prisoner of War.
1865   Houston   3500.00
1964   Austin   25.00
BARZUN, Jacques   Lincoln the Literary Genius.
1960   Evanston, IL   50.00
BASILE, Leon, edited by   The Civil War Diary of Amos E. Stearns,   a
Prisoner at Andersonville.
1981   15.00
BASLER, Roy P.   Abraham Lincoln: His Speeches and Writings.
1946   Cleveland, OH   30.00
BASLER, Roy P.   The Collected Works of Abraham Lincoln.   8 Vols. plus
index plus supplement.
1953   New Brunswick   125.00

BASLER, Roy P., edited by   Walt Whitman's Memoranda During the War and Death of Abraham Lincoln.
    1962   Bloomington, IN   20.00

BASSETT, John S.   Running the Blockade from Confederate Ports. Wraps.
    1898   n.p.   35.00

BASSETT, M. H.   From Bull Run to Bristoe Station, Civil War Letters of a Soldier with the First Minnesota.
    1962   St. Paul   25.00

BASSLER, John H.   The Color Episode, The 149th Pennsylvania Volunteers, First Day's Flight at Gettysburg, July 1, 1863.
    1983   Baltimore   8.00

BASSO, Hamilton   Beauregard the Great Creole.
    1933   New York & London   50.00

BASSO, Hamilton   The Light Infantry Ball.
    1959   New York   10.00

The Bastille in America; or Democratic Absolutism By an Eye-Witness. Wraps.
    1861   London   20.00

BATCHELLOR, A. S.   Historical and Bibliographical Notes on the Military Annals of New Hampshire with Special Reference to Regimental Histories.
    1898   Concord   35.00

BATCHELOR, Benjamin F.   Batchelor-Turner Letters 1861-1864 Written by Two of Terry's Texas Rangers, annotated by H. J. H. Rugeley. Wraps.
    1961   Austin   50.00

BATE, W. B.   Oration by General W. B. Bate on the Occasion of the Confederate Commemoration Services at Elmwood Cemetery. . . . Wraps.
    1870   Memphis   100.00

BATES, David Homer   Lincoln in the Telegraph Office.
    1907   New York   40.00
    1939   New York   20.00

BATES, David Homer   Lincoln Stories.
    1926   New York   15.00

BATES, Edward   The Diary of Edward Bates 1859-1866, edited by Howard K. Beale in: Annual Report of the American Historical Association for 1930, Vol. IV.
    1933   Washington, DC   25.00

BATES, Finis L.   The Escape and Suicide of John Wilkes Booth.
    1907   Memphis   100.00

BATES, Ralph O. (Billy)   Billy and Dick. From Andersonville Prison to the White House.
    1910   Santa Cruz, CA   55.00

BATES, Samuel P.   The Battle of Chancellorsville.
    1882   Meadville, PA   75.00
    1883   Meadville, PA   75.00
    1986   Gaithersburg   25.00
    1987   Dayton 25.00

BATES, Samuel P.   The Battle of Gettysburg.
    1875   Philadelphia   60.00
    1987   25.00

BATES, Samuel P.   A Brief History of the One Hurdredth (sic) Regiment (Roundheads).
    1884   New Castle   150.00
BATES, Samuel P.   History of Pennsylvania Volunteers. 5 Vols.
    1869   Harrisburg   500.00
BATES, Samuel P.   Martial Deeds of Pennsylvania.
    1875   Philadelphia   75.00
    1876   Philadelphia   65.00
BATES, William C., edited by   The Stars and Stripes in Rebeldom.
    (Burnham, T. O. H. P.)
    1862   Boston   50.00
BATTEN, John M.   Reminiscences of Two Years in the United States Navy.
    1881   Lancaster, PA   75.00
BATTEY, George Magruder, Jr.   A History of Rome and Floyd County (Ga.) Vol. I (all pub).
    1922   Atlanta   85.00
BATTINE, Cecil   The Crisis of the Confederacy. A History of Gettysburg and the Wilderness.
    1905   London   100.00
    1905   New York   100.00
Battle of Antietam Centennial and Hagerstown Bicentennial Official Program and Historical Guide.   Wraps.
    1962   Hagerstown   20.00
Battle of Atlanta   Short Sketch of the Battles Around, Siege, Evacuation and Destruction of Atlanta, Ga. in 1864.   Wraps.
    1895   Atlanta   50.00
Battle of Belmont.   Wraps.
    1921   Camp Benning, GA   35.00
The Battle of Chancellorsville and the 11th Army Corps.   Wraps.
    1863   New York   50.00
Battle of Chicamauga, Ga., Sept. 19-20, 1863, Organization of the Army of the Chickamauga Cumberland and the Army of Tennessee.   Wraps.
    1893   Washington, DC   30.00
Battle of Gettysburg - 50th Anniversary of the Battle of Gettysburg, Report of the Pa. Comm. Dec. 1913.
    1915   50.00
Battle of Irish Bend   Interesting Reminiscences of that Terrible Combat, The Horrors of War Graphically Pictured. . . .   Wraps.
    1891   60.00
Battle of Mansfield, Mansfield, Louisiana, Fought April 8, 1864, Gen. Richard Taylor, Commander Confederate Forces, Gen. N. P. Banks, Commander Federal Forces.   Wraps.
    1949   Logansport, LA   25.00
Battle of Wilson's Creek.   Wraps.
    1951   Springfield, MO   20.00
BATTLE, Kemp P.   History of the University of North Carolina.   2 Vols.
    1912   Raleigh, NC   75.00
    n.d. (reprint)   n.p. 50.00
BATTLE, Kemp P.   Memories of an Old-Time Tar Heel.
    1945   Chapel Hill, NC   25.00

BATTLE, William H.   Report of Proceedings in Habeas Corpus Cases: Kerr, Moore, Also in Case of Lt. Burgen.   Wraps.
    1870   Raleigh, NC   35.00
Battlefield Markers Association, Western Division.   Wraps.
    1929   Charlottesville, VA   15.00
The Battlefield of Antietam.   Wraps.
    1906   Gettysburg, PA   35.00
Battlefields in Dixie Land and Chickamauga National Military Park. Wraps.
    (1917)   Nashville, TN   20.00
    1928   15.00
Battlefields of the South from Bull Run to Fredericksburg with Sketches of Confederate Commanders. . . .   See: CAFFEY, Thomas E.
Battles About Chattanooga, Tennessee.   Wraps.
    1932   Washington, DC   20.00
Battles and Leaders of the Civil War. See: JOHNSON, Robert U. and BUEL, Clarence C.
Battles of Atlanta.   Wraps.
    1895   Atlanta, GA   35.00
Battles of the Civil War 1861-1865,   A Pictorial Presentation.   Kurz and Allison Lithographs.
    1960   Little Rock   95.00
    1970   Little Rock   75.00
    1976   Birmingham   75.00
BAUER, Charles J.   So I Killed Lincoln, John Wilkes Booth.
    1976   New York   25.00
    1983   New York   20.00
BAUER, K. Jack   Zachary Taylor, Soldier, Planter, Statesman of the Old Southwest.
    1985   Dayton 35.00
BAUGHMAN, Theodore   Baughman, The Oklahoma Scout: Personal Reminiscences of _____.
    n.d.   Chicago   75.00
BAUMANN, Ken   Arming the Suckers 1861-1865.
    1989   29.95
BAXLEY, Henry Willis   Republican Imperialism Is Not American Liberty.   Wraps.
    (c.1862) n.p.   25.00
BAXTER, Charles N. and DEARBORN, James M.   Confederate Literature, A List of Books and Newspapers, Maps, Music, and Miscellaneous Matter Printed in the South During the Confederacy, Now in the Boston Athenaeum.
    1917   Boston   125.00
BAXTER, D. W. C.   The Volunteer's Manual.   Wraps.
    1861   Philadelphia   60.00
BAXTER, J. H.   Statistics, Medical and Anthropological, of the Provost-Marshal General's Bureau.   2 Vols.
    1875   Washington, DC   250.00
BAXTER, J. P.   The Introduction of the Ironclad Warship.
    1968   Cambridge   23.00

BAXTER, Nancy Niblack   Gallant Fourteenth. The Story of an Indiana Regiment.
   1980   Traverse City, MI   30.00
BAXTER, Nancy Niblack, edited by   Hoosier Farm Boy in Lincoln's Army The Civil War Letters of Pvt. John R. McClure.
   1971   n.p.   25.00
BAXTER, William   Pea Ridge and Prairie Grove, or Scenes and Incidents of the War in Arkansas.
   1864   Cincinnati   150.00
   1866   125.00
   1869   90.00
   1957   Van Buren   20.00
BAYARD, Samuel J.   The Life of George Dashiell Bayard.
   1874   New York   75.00
BAYLOR, George   Bull Run to Bull Run, or Four Years in the Army of Northern Virginia.
   1900   Richmond   125.00
   1983   Washington, DC   35.00
BEACH, John N.   History of the Fortieth Ohio Volunteer Infantry.
   1884   London   175.00
BEACH, William H.   The First New York (Lincoln) Cavalry.
   1902   New York   110.00
   1988   30.00
BEALE, George William   A Lieutenant of Cavalry in Lee's Army.
   1918   Boston   800.00
BEALE, Howard K.   The Critical Year - A Study of Andrew Johnson and Reconstruction.
   1930   New York   25.00
   1967   15.00
BEALE, James, compiled by   The Battle Flags of the Army of the Potomac at Gettysburg.
   1885   Philadelphia   Ltd.   1500.00
BEALE, James   Chancellorsville, A Paper Read Before the United Service Club Philadelphia, Penna. on Wednesday, February 8, 1888.
   (1888)   50.00
   1892   Philadelphia   Ltd.   30.00
BEALE, James   Tabulated Roster of the Army of the Potomac at Gettysburg, Penna. July 1, 2, 3, 1863. Wraps.
   1888   Philadelphia   40.00
BEALE, James   The Statements of Time on July 1, at Gettysburg, Pa. 1863.
   1897   Philadelphia   Ltd.   65.00
BEALE, Richard Lee Turberville   History of the Ninth Virginia Cavalry in the War Between the States.
   1899   Richmond   1000.00
   n.d.   n.p.   Reprint   Ltd.   28.00
   1981   35.00
BEALS, Charleton   War Within a War - The Confederacy Against Itself.
   1965   Philadelphia   15.00

BEAMAN, Charles C., Jr.   The National and Private "Alabama Claims"
and "Their Final and Amicable Settlement."
1871   Washington, DC   40.00
BEAN, William G.   The Liberty Hall Volunteers, Stonewall's College
Boys.
1964   Charlottesville   40.00
BEAN, William G.   Stonewall's Man, Sandie Pendleton.
1959   Chapel Hill, NC   35.00
1987   Wilmington, NC   25.00
BEAR, Henry C.   The Civil War Letters of Henry C. Bear, A Soldier in
the 116th Illinois Volunteer Infantry, edited by Wayne C. Temple.
1961   Harrogate, TN   30.00
BEARD, W. E.   The Battle of Nashville. Wraps.
1913   Nashville   75.00
BEARSS, Edwin C.   Decision in Mississippi.
1962   Jackson   75.00
1962   Little Rock   40.00
BEARSS, Edwin C.   The Fall of Fort Henry. Wraps.
1963   Dover, TN   10.00
BEARSS, Edwin C.   Forrest at Brice's Cross Roads and in North Mississippi in 1864.
1987   Dayton   30.00
BEARSS, Edwin C.   The Fort Donelson Water Batteries. Wraps.
1968   Washington, DC   40.00
BEARSS, Edwin C.   Hardluck Ironclad.
1966   Baton Rouge   30.00
1968   Baton Rouge   30.00
1980   Baton Rouge   27.50
1980   Baton Rouge   Wraps   10.00
1988   Dayton   Wraps   9.95
BEARSS, Edwin C.   Protecting Sherman's Lifeline   The Battles of
Brice's Cross Roads and Tupelo 1864. Wraps.
1971   Washington, DC   10.00
BEARSS, Edwin C.   Rebel Victory at Vicksburg.
1963   Little Rock   30.00
1989   Wilmington, NC   25.00
BEARSS, Edwin C.   Steele's Retreat from Camden and the Battle of
Jenkin's Ferry.
1967   Little Rock   40.00
n.d.   Little Rock   30.00
BEARSS, Edwin C.   Texas at Vicksburg. Wraps.
1971   Austin   20.00
BEARSS, Edwin C.   The Vicksburg Campaign. 3 Vols.
1985-86 Dayton
Vol. I   Vicksburg Is the Key   37.50
Vol. II   Grant Strikes a Fatal Blow   37.50
Vol. III   Unvexed to the Sea   37.50
BEARSS, Edwin C. and CALKINS, C.   The Battle of Five Forks.
1985   Lynchburg   17.00
1987   17.00

BEARSS, Edwin C. and **GIBSON**, A. M. **Fort Smith, Little Gibraltar on the Arkansas.**
    1969   Norman, OK   30.00
    1988   10.95
BEARSS, Margie   **Sherman's Forgotten Campaign, The Meridian Expedition.**
    1987   18.00
BEATH, Robert B.   **History of the Grand Army of the Republic.**
    1888   New York   60.00
    1889   New York   50.00
BEATIE, R. H., Jr.   **Road to Manassas.**
    1961   Cooper Square   25.00
    1968   7.00
BEATTY, John   **The Citizen-Soldier: or Memories of a Volunteer.**
    1879   Cincinnati   90.00
    1946   New York entitled **Memoirs of a Volunteer**, edited by Harvey S. Ford 30.00
BEATY, John Owen   **John Esten Cooke, Virginian.**
    1922   New York   40.00
    1965   New York   15.00
BEAUDRY (BOUDRY), Louis N.   **Historic Records of the Fifth New York Cavalry, First Ira Harris Guard.**
    1865   Albany 90.00
    1868   Albany 75.00
BEAUREGARD, P. G. T.   **A Commentary of the Campaign and Battle of Manassas of July 1861.**
    1891   New York   125.00
BEAUREGARD, P. G. T.   **General Order No. 14 to Fire on Fort Sumter, April 11, 1861.**
    1906   Boston Ltd.   30.00
Beauvoir, Jefferson Davis Shrine. Wraps.
    1945   Gulfport   15.00
BEBE, Ange C., compiled by   **An Original Collection of War Poems and War Songs of the American Civil War, 1860-1865**   **The Boys in Blue.** Wraps.
    1903   Red Wing, MN   30.00
BECHDOLT, Frederick R.   **Bold Raiders of the West.**
    1940   New York   20.00
BECK, Brandon H. and **GRUNDER**, Charles S.   **The Second Battle of Winchester, June 12-13, 1863.**
    1989   16.95
BECK, James B.   **Military Despotism to Supersede the Constitution.** Speech. Wraps.
    1871   Washington, DC   15.00
BECKER, Stephen   **When the War is Over.**
    1969   New York   20.00
BECKETT, Richard C.   **A Sketch of the Career of Company B, Armistead's Cavalry Regiment.**
    1904   Oxford   40.00
BEECHAM, Robert K.   **Gettysburg, The Pivotal Battle of the Civil War.**
    1911   Chicago   50.00

BEECHER, Harris H.   Record of the 114th Regiment, N.Y.S.V.
　1866　Norwich　110.00
BEECHER, Henry Ward   American Rebellion, Report of the Speeches of
_____.
　1864　London　20.00
BEECHER, Herbert W.   History of the 1st Light Battery Connecticut
Volunteers. 2 Vols.
　1901　New York　250.00
BEERS, Fannie A.   Memories: A Record of Personal Experience and
Adventure During Four Years of War.
　1888　Philadelphia　75.00
　1889　Philadelphia　50.00
　1891　Philadelphia　35.00
BEERS, Henry Putney   Guide to the Archives of the Government of
the Confederate States of America.
　1968　Washington, DC　25.00
BEESON, Marvin F.   Die Organization Der Negererziehung in Den
Dereinigten Staaten Von America Seit 1860.　Wraps.
　1915　Leipzig, Germany　30.00
BEFFEL, Eulalie   The Hero of Antietam.
　1943　New York　20.00
BEITZELL, Edwin W.   Point Lookout, Prison Camp for Confederates.
　1972　n.p.　20.00
　1976　n.p.　20.00
BELCHER, Wyatt Winton   The Economic Rivalry Between St. Louis
and Chicago 1850-1880.　Wraps.
　1947　New York　7.00
BELDEN, Bauman I.   War Medals of the Confederacy.　Wraps.
　1915　New York　100.00
　1957　Rochester　Ltd.　30.00
　1970　Glendale　20.00
BELDEN, David   Obsequies of President Lincoln,　An Oration Delivered
in Nevada City in 1865.　Wraps.
　n.d.　Marysville, CA　20.00
BELDEN, Thomas Graham and BELDEN, Marva Robins   So Fell the
Angels.
　1956　Boston　15.00
BELKNAP, Charles E.   History of the Michigan Organizations at
Chickamauga, Chattanooga and Missionary Ridge 1863.
　1899　Lansing　50.00
BELKNAP, William W.   History of the Fifteenth Regiment, Iowa Veteran Volunteer Infantry.
　1887　Keokuk　120.00
BELL, John T.   Tramps and Triumphs of the Second Iowa Infantry.
Wraps.
　1886　Omaha　150.00
　1961　Des Moines　25.00
BELL, John W.   Memoirs of Governor William Smith of Virginia.
　1891　New York　125.00
BELL, Landson C.   Robert E. Lee An Address.　Wraps.
　1929　n.p.　25.00

BELL, Marcus A.   Message of Love.   Southside View of Cotton is
King; and the Philosophy of African Slavery.   Wraps.
1860   Atlanta   150.00

BELL, Robert T.   The 11th Virginia Infantry.
1985   16.95

BELLAH, James Warner   Soldier's Battle: Gettysburg.
1962   New York   60.00

BELLAH, James Warner   The Valiant Virginians.
1953   New York   30.00

BELLARD, Alfred   Gone for a Soldier, The Civil War Memoirs of
_____, edited by David Herbert Donald.
1975   Boston   40.00

BELLOWS, H. W.   Speech of the Rev. _____ President of U. S. Sanitary Commission . . . 1863.   Wraps.
1863   Philadelphia   30.00

BELLOWS, H. W. and BLATCHFORD, J. S.   Circular Addressed to the
Branches and Aid Societies Tributary to the U.S Sanitary Commission,
May 15, 1865.
1865   Washington, DC   10.00

BELZ, Herman   Reconstructing the Union - Theory and Policy During
the Civil War.
1969   New York   15.00

BEMIS, George   Hasty Recognition of Rebel Belligerency and Our Right
to Complain to It.
1865   Boston   25.00

BEMIS, George   Precedents of American Neutrality.   Wraps.
1864   Boston   30.00

BENECKE, Louis   Some Light Upon a Chariton County (Missouri) Episode
of '64.
1895   Brunswick   60.00

BENEDICT, George Grenville   Army Life in Virginia: Letters from
the Twelfth Vermont Regiment.
1895   Burlington, VT   60.00

BENEDICT, George Grenville   A Short History of the 14th Vermont
Regiment.   Wraps.
1887   Bennington   50.00

BENEDICT, George Grenville   Vermont in the Civil War.   2 Vols.
1886   Burlington, VT   100.00
1908   New York   80.00
1910   New York   75.00
1912   New York   75.00
1914   n.p.   75.00
1962   Bloomington   50.00
1977   Dayton   35.00

BENEDICT, Michael L.   The American's Alternatives Series; The Fruits
of Victory: Alternatives in Restoring the Union 1865-1877.   Wraps.
1975   New York   20.00

BENEDICT, Michael L.   The Impeachment and Trial of Andrew Johnson.
1973   New York   25.00

BENET, Stephen Vincent   John Brown's Body.
    1928   Garden City, NY   40.00
    1930   25.00
    1948   New York   25.00
    1954   20.00
BENET, Stephen Vincent   A Treatise of Military Law and the Practice of Courts Martial.
    1862   New York   40.00
BENHAM, William Burton   Life of Osborn H. Oldroyd Founder and Collector of Lincoln Mementos.
    1927   Washington, DC   30.00
BENJAMIN, Judah P.   The African Slave Trade, The Secret Purpose of the Insurgents to Revive It . . . Benjamin's Intercepted Instruction to L.Q.C. Lamar. Wraps.
    1863   Philadelphia   30.00
BENJAMIN, Judah P.   Defence of the National Democracy Against the Attack of Judge Douglas - Constitutional Rights of the States, Speech. Wraps.
    1860   Washington, DC   30.00
BENJAMIN, Judah P.   Speech of _____ of Louisiana on the Right of Secession. Wraps.
    1860   Washington, DC   40.00
    1861   Washington, DC   30.00
BENJAMIN, Marcus, edited by   Washington During War Time. Wraps.
    1902   Washington, DC   30.00
BENJAMIN, Park   The United States Naval Academy.
    1900   New York   75.00
BENNER, Judith Ann   Fradulent Finance: Counterfeiting and the Confederate States 1861-1865. Wraps.
    1970   Hillsboro   10.00
BENNER, Judith Ann   Sul Ross: Soldier, Statesman, Educator.
    1983   TX   20.00
BENNETT, Andrew J.   The Story of the First Massachusetts Light Battery.
    1886   Boston   100.00
BENNETT, Charles W.   Historical Sketches of the Ninth Michigan Infantry (General Thomas' Headquarters Guards).
    1913   Coldwater   225.00
BENNETT, Edwin C.   Musket and Sword; or The Camp, March and Firing Line in the Army of the Potomac.
    1900   Boston   50.00
BENNETT, Frank M.   The Monitor and the Navy Under Steam.
    1900   Boston   75.00
BENNETT, Frank M.   The Steam Navy . . . of the . . . United States.
    1896   Pittsburgh   150.00
BENNETT, James   "Private Joe" Fifer: Members of War and Peace Imparted in His Ninety-sixth Year by Joseph Fifer at the Request of the Chicago Tribune.
    1936   Bloomington, IL   75.00
BENNETT, L. G. and HAIGH, William M.   History of the Thirty-sixth Regiment Illinois Volunteers.
    1876   Aurora   125.00

BENNETT, Lorenzo T.   Our Present Duties and Responsibilities as Christian Patriots, A Sermon. Wraps.
1861   New Haven   10.00

BENNETT, William W.   A Narrative of the Great Revival Which Prevailed in the Southern Armies.
1877   Philadelphia   200.00
1989   Harrisonburg   entitled The Great Revival in the Southern Armies.   17.50

BENSELL, Royal A.   All Quiet on the Yamhill, The Civil War in Oregon, The Journal of Corporal _____, edited by Gunter Barth.
1959   Eugene, OR   35.00

BENSON, B. K.   Bayard's Courier.
1902   New York   30.00

BENSON, B. K.   Who Goes There?
1901   New York   20.00
1902   New York   25.00

BENSON, Berry   Berry Benson's Civil War Book, edited by Susan Williams Benson.
1962   Athens, GA   60.00

BENSON, Richard and KIRSTEIN, Lincoln   Lay This Laurel.
1973   New York   40.00

BENTLEY, William H.   History of the 77th Illinois Volunteer Infantry.
1883   Peoria   175.00

BENTON, Charles E.   As Seen from the Ranks.
1902   New York   75.00

BENTON, Josiah Henry   Voting in the Field: A Forgotten Chapter of Civil War.
1915   Boston   50.00

BENTON, Thomas H.   Examination of the Dred Scott Case.
1860   New York   35.00

BENTON, Thomas H.   Thirty Years View. 2 Vols.
1856   New York   35.00

BERGERON, Arthur W., Jr.   Guide to Louisiana Confederate Military Units, 1861-1865.
1989   University, LA   24.95

BERING, John A. and MONTGOMERY, Thomas   History of the Forty-eighth Ohio Vet. Vol. Inf.
1880   Hillsboro   135.00

BERINGER, R. R., HATTAWAY, H., JONES, A. and STILL, W. N.   Why the South Lost the Civil War.
1986   Athens   29.95

BERKELEY, Henry Robinson   Four Years in the Confederate Artillery: The Diary of _____, edited by William H. Runge.
1961   Richmond   45.00
1961   Chapel Hill, NC   40.00

BERLIN, Ira   Slaves Without Masters, the Free Negro in the Antebellum South.
1974   New York   15.00

BERMAN, M.   Richmond's Jewry: Shabbat in Shockoe, 1769-1976.
1979   Charlottesville   30.00

BERN, Laurence, THUROW, Glen E., BRANN, Eva, and BRANN, Anastaplo
Abraham Lincoln, The Gettysburg Address and American Constitution-
alism. Wraps.
1976   TX   14.00
BERNARD, George S.   The Battle of the Crater in Front of Petersburg July 30, 1864 An Address. Wraps.
1890   Petersburg 50.00
1892   Petersburg 40.00
1937   n.p.   20.00
BERNARD, George S., edited by   War Talks of Confederate Veterans.
1892   Petersburg VA   75.00
1981   Dayton 40.00
BERNARD, Kenneth A.   Lincoln and the Music of the Civil War.
1966   Caldwell, Idaho   35.00
BERNARD, Mountague   A Historical Account of the Neutrality of
Great Britain During the American Civil War.
1870   London 175.00
1971   New York 35.00
BERNATH, Stuart L.   Squall Across the Atlantic, American Civil War
Prize Cases and Diplomacy.
1970   Berkeley, CA   15.00
BERRY, Chester D.   Loss of the Sultana and Reminiscences of Sur-
vivors.
1892   Lansing 125.00
BERRY, Thomas Franklin   Four Years with Morgan and Forrest.
1914   Oklahoma City   300.00
BERRYHILL, William H.   The Gentle Rebel, the Civil War Letters of 1st
Lt. William H. Berryhill, Co. D, 43rd Mississippi Volunteers.
1982   Yazoo City, MS   15.00
BESSE, S. B.   C. S. Ironclad Virginia. Wraps.
1937   Newport News, VA   20.00
BESSE, S. B.   U. S. Ironclad Monitor. Wraps.
1936   Newport News, VA   20.00
BEST, Isaac O.   History of the 121st New York State Infantry.
1921   Chicago 190.00
BETHEL, Elizabeth, edited by   War Department Collection of Confederate Records. Wraps.
1957   Washington, DC   30.00
BETTERSWORTH, John K.   Confederate Mississippi.
1943   Baton Rouge   40.00
1970   New York 30.00
1978   25.00
BETTERSWORTH, John K. and SILVER, James W., edited by Mississippi in
the Confederacy. 2 Vols.
1961   Baton Rouge Boxed   60.00
1970   New York 45.00
BETTS, Alexander Davis   Experiences of a Confederate Chaplain 1861-
1865. Wraps.
n.d. (reprint)   n.p.   150.00
BETTS, Edward E., compiled by   Atlas of Chickamauga, Chattanooga
and Vicinity.
1901   n.p.   200.00

BEVERIDGE, Albert J.   **Abraham Lincoln.** 2 Vols.
　1928　　Cambridge　35.00
　1928　　New York　35.00
　1928　　Boston　4 Vols. Manuscript ed.　100.00
BEVERIDGE, Albert J.   **Address of _____ Dedication of Indiana's Monuments April 6, 1903.**
　1903　　Indianapolis　20.00
BEVIER, Robert S.   **History of the First and Second Missouri Confederate Brigades 1861-1865.**
　1878　　300.00
　1879　　St. Louis　250.00
　1985　　Florissant, MO　24.50
BEVINS, W. E.   **Reminiscences of a Private Company "G" First Arkansas Regiment Infantry.** Wraps.
　1977　　Newport, AR　　35.00
BEYER, Walter F. and **KEYDEL**, Oscar F., edited by   **Deeds of Valor.** (Duffield, H. M.) 2 Vols.
　1905　　Detroit 75.00
　1906　　Detroit 75.00
　1907　　Detroit 60.00
BEYMER, William Gilmore   **On Hazardous Service, Scouts and Spies of the North and South.**
　1912　　New York　　30.00
Bibliography of State Participation in the Civil War 1861-1866.
　1913　　Washington, DC　100.00
　1961　　Charlottesville　50.00
A Bibliography of the American Civil War. Wraps.
　1962　　New York　　10.00
BICKHAM, W. D.   **Rosecrans' Campaign with the Fourteenth Army Corps by W.D.B.**
　1863　　Cincinnati　　100.00
BIDDLE, Ellen McGowan   **Reminiscences of a Soldier's Wife.**
　1907　　PA　100.00
BIDWELL, Frederick David   **History of the Forty-ninth New York Volunteers.**
　1916　　Albany　110.00
BIDWELL, Frederick David   **The Life of General Daniel Davidson Bidwell.**
　n.d.　　Albany　　60.00
BIERCE, Ambrose   **Ambrose Bierce's Civil War.** Wraps.
　1956　　Chicago　30.00
BIERCE, Ambrose   **Battle Sketches.**
　1930　　London　100.00
BIERCE, Ambrose   **The Best of Ambrose Bierce.**
　1946　　14.00
BIERCE, Ambrose   **The Complete Short Stories of Ambrose Bierce,** edited by Ernest Jerome Hopkins. Wraps.
　1985　　11.00
BIERCE, Ambrose   **Tales of Soldiers and Civilians.**
　1891　　San Francisco　　250.00
BIGELOW, D.   **William C. Church and the Army and Navy Journal.**
　1952　　New York　　20.00

BIGELOW, John   The Peach Orchard, Gettysburg, July 2, 1864.
　1910　Minneapolis　100.00
BIGELOW, John   Retrospections of an Active Life. 3 Vols.
　1909-13 New York　50.00
BIGELOW, John, Jr.   The Campaigns of Chancellorsville.
　1910　New Haven　500.00
　1984　250.00
　1985　200.00
BIGELOW, John, Jr.   France and the Confederate Navy.
　1888　New York　40.00
BIGELOW, John, Jr.   The Principles of Strategy Illustrated Mainly from American Campaigns.
　1891　London　150.00
　1894　Philadelphia　100.00
　1968　New York　35.00
BIGGER, David Dwight   Ohio's Silver-Tongued Orator, Life and Speeches of General William H. Gibson.
　1901　Dayton　35.00
BIGHAM, R. W.   Joe: A Boy in the War-Times.
　1890　Nashville　25.00
BILL, Alfred Hoyt   The Beleagured City Richmond 1861-1865.
　1946　New York　25.00
　1980　Westport, CT　20.00
BILL, Alfred Hoyt   Rehearsal for Conflict The War with Mexico 1846-1848.
　1947　New York　20.00
BILL, Ledyard, edited by   Lyrics, Incidents, and Sketches of the Rebellion.
　1864　New York　30.00
BILLINGS, John D.   Hard Tack and Coffee.
　A customer recently showed us an 1887 Chicago edition—the first we've ever seen. Any more out there?
　1887　Chicago　250.00
　1887　Boston　200.00
　1888　Boston　125.00
　1889　Boston　125.00
　1960　Chicago　edited by Richard Harwell 35.00
　1970　Glendale　30.00
　1974　Civil War Times ed. 23.00
　1982　30.00
　1984　23.00
BILLINGS, John D.   The History of the Tenth Massachusetts Battery of Light Artillery in the War of the Rebellion.
　1881　Boston　175.00
　1909　Boston　75.00
　1986　32.50
　1987　entitled Sleeper's Tenth Massachusetts Battery　32.50
BILLINGS, John S.   Report on Hygiene of U. S. Army.
　1974　85.00
BILLINGSLEY, A. S.   From the Flag to the Cross; or, Scenes and Incidents of Christianity in the War. . . .
　1872　Philadelphia　65.00

BILLINGTON, M. L.   The Political South in the 20th Century.
1980   9.00

BINGHAM, John A.   Reply of Judge Advocate _____ to the Defence of the Accused . . . for the Trial of Brig. Gen. William A. Hammond. Wraps.
1864   Washington, DC   20.00

BINGHAM, John A.   Trial of the Conspirators for the Assassination of President Lincoln. Wraps.
1865   Washington, DC   25.00

BINNEY, Horace   The Privilege of the Writ of Habeas Corpus Under the Constitution. Wraps.
1862   Philadelphia   25.00

A Biographical Sketch . . . John Sedgwick Major General.
1899   New York   Ltd.   50.00

Biographical Sketch of Brevet-Maj-General Thomas A. Davies.
n.d.   n.p.   75.00

Biographical Sketches and Pictures of Company B, Confederate Veterans of Nashville, Tenn. Wraps.
1902   Nashville   20.00

Biographical Supplement - Confederate Military History. See: Confederate Military History, Vol. XIII (Vol. III, 1987 reprint ed.).

BIRCHER, William A.   A Drummer Boy's Diary: Comprising Four Years of Service with the Second Regiment Minnesota Vet. Vols.
1889   St. Paul   75.00

BIRCHMORE, W. E.   Chickamauga and Chattanooga National Military Park. Wraps.
1895   Chattanooga   20.00

BIRD, Edgeworth and BIRD, Sallie   The Granite Farm Letters   The Civil War Correspondence of Edgeworth and Sallie Bird, edited by John Rozier.
1988   University, GA   24.95

BIRD, J.   Narrative of Two Perilous Adventures Recently Made into Dixie's Land, also . . . Captain S. B. Phillips' Adventures in Western Virginia since the Breaking out of the War. Wraps.
1862   75.00

BIRDSONG, James Cook   Brief Sketches of the North Carolina State Troops in the War Between the States.
1894   Raleigh, NC   250.00

BISHOP, Albert Webb   Loyalty on the Frontier; or, Sketches of Union Men in the South West, With Incidents and Adventures in Rebellion on the Border.
1863   St. Louis   125.00

BISHOP, Carter R.   "The Cockade City of the Union" Petersburg, Virginia. Wraps.
1907   n.p.   25.00

BISHOP, Jim   The Day Lincoln Was Shot.
1955   New York   15.00
1984   15.00

BISHOP, Judson W.   The Story of a Regiment, Being a Narrative of the Service of the Second Regiment Minnesota Veteran Vol. Infantry.
1890   St. Paul   160.00

BISHOP, Judson W.   Van Derveer's Brigade at Chickamauga.   Wraps.
    1903   (St. Paul)   30.00
BISSET, Johnson   The Mysteries of Chancellorsville, Who Killed
    Stonewall Jackson.   Wraps.
    1945   New York   30.00
Bits of Camplife.
    (c.1870) New York   50.00
BITTON, Davis, edited by   The Reminiscences and Civil War Letters
    of Levi Lamoni Wight.
    1970   Salt Lake City   40.00
BIVENS, Viola Cobb   Echoes of the Confederacy.
    1950   Longview, TX   20.00
The Black Horse Troop of Fauquier County.   Wraps.
    1972   Warrenton   20.00
BLACK, John Logan   Crumbling Defenses, or Memoirs and Reminiscences
    of _____.
    1960   Macon   Ltd.   75.00
BLACK, Patti C. and GRIMES, Maxyne M., compiled by   Guide to Civil
    War Source Material in the Dept. of Archives and History, State of Mis-
    sissippi.   Wraps.
    1962   Jackson   15.00
BLACK, Robert C.   The Railroads of the Confederacy.
    1952   Chapel Hill, NC   40.00
    1987   Wilmington, NC   30.00
    1987   Wilmington, NC   Wraps   12.95
BLACKBURN, J. S. and McDONALD, W. N.   A Grammar-School His-
    tory of the United States.
    1871   Baltimore   20.00
BLACKBURN, James K. P.   Reminiscences of the Terry Rangers.
    Wraps.
    1919   Austin   110.00
    1979   Austin   25.00
BLACKBURN, John   A Hundred Miles A Hundred Heartbreaks.
    1972   n.p.   25.00
BLACKERBY, H. C.   Blacks in the Blue and Gray, Afro-American
    Service in the Civil War.
    1979   AL 30.00
BLACKETT, R. J. M., edited by   Thomas Morris Chester: Black Civil
    War Correspondent.
    1989   Baton Rouge   35.00
BLACKFORD, Charles M., Jr.   Annals of the Lynchburg Home Guard.
    1891   Lynchburg   600.00
BLACKFORD, Charles M., Jr.   Campaign and Battle of Lynchburg,
    Va.   Wraps.
    1901   Lynchburg   150.00
BLACKFORD, Charles M., Jr.   The Trials and Trial of Jefferson
    Davis.
    1900   Richmond   25.00
    1901   Lynchburg   25.00
BLACKFORD, L. Minor   The Great John B. Minor and His Cousin Mary
    Face the War.   Wraps.
    1953   VA   15.00

BLACKFORD, L. Minor   Mine Eyes Have Seen the Glory.
 1954 Cambridge 25.00
 1964 25.00
BLACKFORD, Susan Leigh, compiled by   Letters from Lee's Army.
 1947 New York 30.00
 1947 New York Wraps 15.00
BLACKFORD, Susan Leigh   Memoir. Wraps.
 1959 Madison Heights 35.00
BLACKFORD, William W.   War Years with Jeb Stuart.
 1945 New York 50.00
BLACKMAN, William S.   The Boy of Battle Ford and the Man.
 1906 Marion, IL 150.00
BLACKWELL, Robert   Original Acrostics on Some of the Southern
States, Confederate Generals, and Various Other Persons and Things.
 1869 St. Louis 35.00
 1873 Baltimore 30.00
BLACKWELL, Sarah Ellen   A Military Genius Life of Anna Ella Carroll of Maryland.
 1891 Washington, DC 50.00
Blackwood's Magazine. See Appendix: Magazines.
BLAINE, James G.   Jefferson Davis - Amnesty, In the House of Representatives Monday, January 10, 1876.
 1876 Washington, DC 20.00
BLAINE, James G.   Twenty Years of Congress. 2 Vols.
 1884 Norwich 30.00
 1886 Norwich 30.00
BLAIR, Carvel Hall   Submarines of the Confederate Navy. Wraps.
 1952 Annapolis 30.00
BLAIR, Francis P.   Confiscation of Rebel Property - Speech Delivered
in the House of Representatives. Wraps.
 1864 Washington, DC 15.00
BLAIR, Maria   Matthew Fontaine Maury. Wraps.
 1981 Richmond 30.00
BLAKE, Henry N.   Three Years in the Army of the Potomac.
 1865 Boston 75.00
BLAKE, Michael   American Civil War Cavalry.
 1973 London 15.00
BLAKE, Nelson Morehouse   William Mahone of Virginia.
 1935 Richmond 75.00
BLAKE, Sarah Swan   Diaries and Letters of Francis Minot Weld, M.D.
 1925 Boston 40.00
BLAKE, W. O.   The History of Slavery and the Slave Trade, Ancient
and Modern.
 1859 Columbus 75.00
 1861 60.00
BLAKE, W. O., edited by   Pictorial National Records. 2 Vols.
 1863 75.00
 1865 Columbus, OH Vol. 1 30.00
 1866 75.00
BLAKE, Walter H.   Hand Grips. The Story of the Great Gettysburg
Reunion July 1913.
 1913 Vineland, NJ 25.00

BLAKESLEE, B. F.   History of the 16th Connecticut Volunteers.
 1875   Hartford   90.00
BLAND, T. A.   Life of Benjamin F. Butler.
 1879   Boston   20.00
BLANDENBURG, Heinrich   Die Innern Kampfe Der Nordamerifanifchen Union.
 1869   Leipzig   30.00
BLANDING, Stephen F.   In the Defences of Washington.
 1889   Providence   45.00
BLANDING, Stephen F.   Recollections of a Sailor Boy.
 1886   Providence   125.00
BLANKENSHIP, Lela McDowell   When Yesterday Was Today.
 1966   Nashville   25.00
BLATCHFORD, J. S., et al   Circular Addressed to the Branches and
Aid Societies Tributary to the U.S. Sanitary Commission, July 4, 1865.
 1865   Washington, DC   10.00
BLAY, John S.   After the Civil War   A Pictorial Profile of America
from 1865 to 1900.
 1958   New York   35.00
 1960   New York   25.00
BLAY, John S.   The Civil War, A Pictorial Profile.
 1958   New York   25.00
BLEASE, Cole L.   Destruction of Property in Columbia, S. C. by
Sherman's Army, Speech. Wraps.
 1930   Washington, DC   40.00
BLEDSOE, Albert Taylor   An Essay on Liberty and Slavery.
 1856   Philadelphia   20.00
BLEDSOE, Albert Taylor   Is Davis a Traitor; Or Was Secession a
Constitutional Right Previous to the War of 1861?
 1866   Baltimore   35.00
 1879   Lynchburg   30.00
 1907   Richmond   30.00
 1915   Lynchburg   30.00
BLEDSOE, Albert Taylor   A Theodicy; or, Vindication of the Divine
Glory, as Manifested in the Constitution. . . .
 1853   New York   65.00
BLEDSOE, Albert Taylor   The War Between the States.
 1915   Lynchburg, VA   30.00
BLEGEN, Theodore C.   Abraham Lincoln and His Mailbag.
 1964   St. Paul 10.00
BLESSINGTON, Joseph P.   The Campaigns of Walker's Texas Division
by a Private Soldier.
 1875   New York   300.00
 1968   Austin 30.00
BLOCK, Eugene B.   Above the Civil War   The Story of Thaddeus Lowe,
Balloonist, Inventor, Railway Builder.
 1966   Berkeley, CA   40.00
Blockade Runners   Pictorial Supplement III, The American Neptune.
Wraps.
 1961   Salem, MA   15.00
BLOODGOOD, John D.   Personal Reminiscences of the War.
 1893   New York   55.00

BLOOR, Alfred   Letters from the Army of the Potomac Written During the Month of May 1864 to Several of the Supply Correspondents of the US Sanitary Commission. Wraps.
1864   75.00

Blue and Grey. Wraps.
Monthly periodical of Civil War interest
20.00 per issue

BLYTHE, Vernon   A History of the Civil War in the United States.
1914   New York   60.00

BOATNER, Mark M.   The Civil War Dictionary.
1959   New York   25.00
1962   25.00
1988   29.95

BODDIE, William Willis   History of Williamsburg.
1923   Columbia   75.00

BOETHEL, Paul C.   The Big Guns of Fayette. Wraps.
1965   Austin   50.00

BOGGS, Samuel S.   Eighteen Months a Prisoner Under the Rebel Flag.
1887   Lovington, IL   35.00
1889   Lovington, IL   30.00

BOGGS, William R.   Military Reminiscences of Gen. Wm. R. Boggs, C.S.A.
1913   Durham, NC   60.00

BOHANNAN, Willis W.   Surry County at War 1861-1865. Wraps.
(1963) n.p. 25.00

BOIES, Andrew J.   Record of the Thirty-third Massachusetts Volunteer Infantry, from Aug. 1862 to Aug. 1865.
1880   Fitchburg   60.00

BOKER, George H.   The Second Louisiana.
1863   (Philadelphia)   60.00

BOKUM, Hermann   Testimony of a Refugee from East Tennessee. Wraps.
1863   Philadelphia   35.00

BOKUM, Hermann   Wanderings North and South. Wraps.
1864   Philadelphia   60.00

BOLAND, M. D.   Reinterpreting History.
1947   Tacoma, WA   20.00

BOLEY, Henry   Lexington in Old Virginia.
1936   Richmond   50.00

BOLLES, Albert S.   The Financial History of the United States from 1861-1885.
1886   New York   50.00
1894   New York   50.00

BOLLINGER, James W.   Lincoln Statesman and Logician.
1944   Davenport, IA   Ltd.   20.00

BOLTON, Horace Wilbert   Personal Reminiscences of the Late War.
1892   Chicago   80.00

BOND, Christiana   Memories of General Robert E. Lee.
1926   Baltimore   20.00

BOND, William R.   Pickett   or   Pettigrew?   An   Historical   Review. Wraps.
>1888   Weldon, NC   125.00
>(1888) Scotland Neck, NC   100.00
>1900   Scotland Neck, NC   75.00

BONEY, F. N.   John Letcher of Virginia.
>1966   University, AL   20.00

BONHAM, Milledge L.   The British Consuls in the Confederacy.
>1911   New York   75.00
>1967   New York   25.00

BONNER, James   Milledgeville. Georgia's Antebellum Capital.
>1985   Macon, GA 22.00

BONNER, James C., edited by   The Journal of a Milledgeville Girl 1861-1867. Wraps.
>1964   Athens, GA   25.00

BOOK, Janet Mae   Northern Rendezvous, Harrisburg During the Civil War.
>1951   Harrisburg   25.00

BOOKER, Richard   Abraham Lincoln in Periodical Literature.
>1941   Chicago   30.00

Books and Pamphlets Relating to the Confederate States, Confederate Imprints, Confederate Sheet Music. Wraps.
>1940   Hattiesburg, MS   50.00

BOOTH, Andrew B., compiled by   Records of Louisiana Confederate Soldiers and Louisiana Confederate Commands. 3 Vols. in 4.
>1920   New Orleans   500.00
>1984   Easley, SC   187.50
>1985   4 Vols. in 3 187.50

BOOTH, Edwin G.   In War Time. Two Years in the Confederacy and Two Years North. With Many Reminiscences of the Days Long before the War.
>1885   Philadelphia 110.00

BOOTH, George Wilson, compiled by   Illustrated Souvenir, Maryland Line, Confederate Soldiers Home, Pikesville, Maryland.
>1894   Baltimore   100.00

BOOTH, George Wilson   Personal Reminiscences of a Maryland Soldier in the War Between the States, 1861-1865.
>1898   Baltimore   500.00
>Recent reprint   22.50

BOOTH, Mary L.   The Uprising of a Great People - The United States in 1861.
>1861   New York   20.00

BOOZER, Marie   A Checkered Life Being a Brief History of the Countess Portales, Formerly Miss Marie Boozer. Wraps.
>1915   Columbia, SC   40.00

BORCKE, Heros von   At the Edge of Glory (Andes Grabes Rande). Wraps.
>1896   Berlin   150.00

BORCKE, Heros von   Memoirs of the Confederate War for Independence. 2 Vols.
>1866   Edinburgh   300.00
>1867   Philadelphia 250.00

1886   Berlin   300.00
1938   New York   70.00
1985   Gaithersburg   25.00
BORCKE, Heros von   **On the Warpath (Auf dem Kriegspfade).**   Wraps.
1895   Berlin   150.00
BORCKE, Heros von   **Zwei Jahr im Sattel.** 2 Vols. in 1.
1898   Berlin   250.00
BORCKE, Heros von and **SEIBERT**, Justus   **The Great Cavalry Battle of Brandy Station.**   In German Wraps.
1893   250.00
1976   Winston-Salem, NC   Ltd.   English, Transl. by Stuart Wright and F. D. Bridgewater.   25.00
1989   25.00
The Border Ruffian Code in Kansas.
(c.1860)   65.00
BORRESON, Ralph   **When Lincoln Died.**
1965   New York   25.00
BORTON, Benjamin   **Awhile with the Blue; or Memories of War Days.**
1898   Passaic, NJ   90.00
BORTON, Benjamin   **On the Parallels; or, Chapters of Inner History.**
1903   Woodstown   85.00
BOSANG, James N.   **Memoirs of a Pulaski Veteran.**   Wraps.
1930   Pulaski, TN   60.00
BOSBYSHELL, Oliver C.   **The 48th in the War.**
1895   Philadelphia   90.00
BOSSON, Charles P.   **History of the Forty-second Regiment Infantry, Massachusetts Volunteers.**
1886   Boston   65.00
The Boston Almanac for the Year 1862 No. XXVII.
1862   (Boston)   25.00
BOTKIN, B. A., edited by   **A Treasury of Southern Folklore.**
1949   New York   35.00
1960   New York   entitled   **A Civil War Treasury of Tales, Legends, and Folklore**   30.00
1980   17.50
BOTSFORD, T. F.   **Memories of the War of Secession.**   Wraps.
1911   Montgomery, AL   375.00
BOTTS, John Minor   **The Great Rebellion.**
1866   New York   20.00
BOTUME, Elizabeth Hyde   **First Days Amongst the Contrabands.**
1893   Boston   50.00
BOUDRY, Louis N.   See: **BEAUDRY**, Louis N.
BOURKE, John G.   **On the Border with Crook.**
1891   New York   75.00
1892   New York   60.00
1950   50.00
BOUTON, Edward   **Events of the Civil War.**   Wraps.
1906   Los Angeles   100.00
BOUTON, John Bell   **A Memoir of General Louis Bell.**
1865   New York   45.00
BOWDEN, J. J.   **The Exodus of the Federal Forces from Texas, 1861.**
1986   Austin   11.95

BOWDITCH, Henry I.   Brief Plea for an Ambulance System for the
Army of the U.S.   Wraps.
1863   100.00
BOWEN, Harold L.   Early Michigan Scrip.
n.d.   n.p.   75.00
BOWEN, James L.   History of the Thirty-seventh Regiment Mass. Volunteers in the Civil War.
1884   Holyoke   75.00
BOWEN, James L.   Massachusetts in the Civil War.
1889   Springfield   50.00
BOWEN, James R.   Regimental History of the First New York Dragoons.
1900   Lyons, MI   140.00
BOWEN, John   Civil War Days.
1987   New York   16.50
BOWEN, John   Portraits of America: Virginia.
1985   Secaucus   15.00
BOWEN, John J.   The Strategy of Robert E. Lee.
1914   New York   60.00
BOWERS, Claude G.   The Tragic Era.
1929   Cambridge   20.00
1929   New York   15.00
BOWIE, Marshall L.   A Time of Adversity and Courage, Story of Montgomery and West Point Railroad.   Wraps.
(1961)   n.p.   15.00
BOWMAN, John S.   The Civil War Almanac.
1989   9.98
BOWMAN, Col. S. M. and Lt. Col. IRWIN, R. B.   Sherman   and   His
Campaigns.
1865   New York   40.00
1868   New York   30.00
BOYCE, Charles W.   A Brief History of the Twenty-eighth Regiment
New York State Volunteers.
1896   Buffalo   135.00
BOYD, Belle   See: HARDINGE, Belle B.
BOYD, C. B.   The Devil's Den: A History of the 44th Alabama Volunteer
Infantry Regiment, C.S.A. (1862-1865).
1987   n.p.   26.95
BOYD, Cyrus F.   The Civil War Diary of _____ Fifteenth Iowa
Infantry 1861-1863, edited by Mildred Throne.   Wraps.
1953   Iowa City   40.00
1977   New York   30.00
BOYD, David French   General W. T. Sherman as College President.
Wraps.
1910   Baton Rouge   10.00
BOYD, David French   Reminiscences of the War in Virginia, edited
by T. Michael Parrish.   Wraps.
1989   6.00
BOYD, J. L. R.   John Angus Campbell, C.S.A. 1840-1933.   Wraps.
n.d.   Atlanta   25.00
BOYD, James   Marching On.
1927   New York   40.00

BOYD, James P.   The Gallant Trooper, General Philip H. Sheridan.
  1888   Philadelphia   20.00
BOYD, James P.   The Life of General William T. Sherman.
  1891   n.p.   25.00
  1892   25.00
BOYD, James P.   Military and Civil Life of General U. S. Grant.
  1887   Philadelphia   30.00
  1892   Philadelphia   25.00
BOYD, Mrs. O. B.   Cavalry Life in Tent and Field.
  1894   80.00
BOYDEN, Anna   War Reminiscences A Record of Mrs. Rebecca R. Pomroy's Experience in War-Times.
  1884   Boston   40.00
BOYER, Richard O.   The Legend of John Brown.
  1973   New York   25.00
BOYER, Samuel Pellman   Naval Surgeon Blockading the South 1862-1866. The Diary of. . . . , edited by Elinor and James Barnes.
  1963   Bloomington   35.00
BOYKIN, Burwell   Address Delivered Before the Southern Rights Association of Alabama, at Mobile. . . . Wraps.
  1850   Mobile   50.00
BOYKIN, Edward C.   Beefsteak Raid.
  1960   New York   35.00
BOYKIN, Edward C.   Congress and the Civil War.
  1955   New York   20.00
BOYKIN, Edward C.   Ghost Ship of the Confederacy: The Story of the Alabama and Her Captain, Raphael Semmes.
  1957   New York   25.00
BOYKIN, Edward C.   Sea Devil of the Confederacy, Story of the Florida.
  1959   New York   30.00
BOYKIN, Edward M.   The Falling Flag Evacuation of Richmond, Retreat and Surrender 7th South Carolina Cavalry at Appomattox.
  1874   New York   225.00
BOYKIN, Richard Manning   Captain Alexander Hamilton Boykin One of South Carolina's Distinguished Citizens.
  1942   New York Ltd.   75.00
BOYKIN, Samuel, edited by   A Memorial Volume of the Honorable Howell Cobb of Georgia.
  1870   Philadelphia   75.00
BOYLE, John Richards   Soldiers True, The Story of the One Hundred and Eleventh Regiment Pennsylvania Veteran Volunteers.
  1903   New York   100.00
BOYLES, Kate and **BOYLES**, Virgil D.   The Hoosier Volunteer.
  1914   Chicago   20.00
BOYNTON, Charles B., D.D.   The History of the Navy-During the Rebellion. 2 Vols.
  1867-68 New York   175.00
  1869-70 n.p.   100.00
BOYNTON, Edward C.   History of West Point . . . and the Origin and Progress of the U.S. Military Academy.
  1863   New York   90.00

BOYNTON, Henry V.   Chattanooga and Chickamauga. Wraps.
    1888   Washington, DC   30.00
BOYNTON, Henry V.   Dedication of the Chickamauga and Chattanooga National Military Park Sept. 18-20, 1895.
    1896   Washington, DC   40.00
BOYNTON, Henry V.   The National Military Park, Chickamauga-Chattanooga, An Historical Guide.
    1895   Cincinnati   30.00
BOYNTON, Henry V.   Organization of the Army of the Cumberland and of the Army of Tennessee. Wraps.
    1893   Washington, DC   40.00
BOYNTON, Henry V.   Sherman's Historical Raid.
    1875   Cincinnati   35.00
BOYNTON, Henry V.   Was General Thomas Slow at Nashville?
    1896   New York   Ltd.   75.00
BRACKETT, Albert G.   History of the United States Cavalry.
    1865   New York   90.00
    1965   New York   30.00
BRADBEER, William West   Confederate and Southern State Currency, Historical and Financial Data, Biographical Sketches, Descriptions, and Illustration.
    1945   Chicago   Ltd.   80.00
BRADFORD, Gamaliel, Jr.   Confederate Portraits.
    1912   Boston   40.00
    1914   Boston   35.00
    1942   Boston   30.00
    1968   Freeport   25.00
BRADFORD, Gamaliel, Jr.   Lee the American.
    1912   Boston   25.00
    1914   Boston   20.00
    1927   Boston   20.00
    1929   Boston   20.00
BRADFORD, Gamaliel, Jr.   Union Portraits.
    1916   Boston   40.00
BRADFORD, Ralph   Reprieve, A Christmas Story of 1863.
    1940   n.p.   30.00
BRADLEE, Francis B. C.   Blockade Running During the Civil War.
    1925   Salem, MA   150.00
BRADLEE, Francis B. C.   A Forgotten Chapter in Our Naval History, A Sketch of the Career of Duncan Nathaniel Ingraham. Wraps.
    1923   Salem, MA   50.00
BRADLEE, Francis B. C.   Kearsarge-Alabama Battle. Wraps.
    1921   Salem, MA   30.00
BRADLEY, C. D.   Was Jefferson Davis Disguised as a Woman When Captured? Wraps.
    1974   Hampton   10.00
BRADLEY, Erwin Stanley   Simon Cameron   Lincoln's Secretary of War.
    1968   Philadelphia   20.00
BRADLEY, George S.   The Star Corps.
    1865   Milwaukee   85.00

BRADLEY, Isaac Samuel, compiled by   A Bibliography of Wisconsin's Participation in the War Between the States.
1911   Madison   25.00

BRADLEY, James   The Confederate Mail Carrier.
1894   Mexico, MO   225.00

BRADLOW, Edna and **BRADLOW**, Frank   Here Comes the Alabama.
1958   Cape Town   25.00
1975   Birmingham   10.00

BRADY, Cyrus Townsend   As the Sparks Fly Upward.
1911   Chicago   15.00

BRADY, Cyrus Townsend   A Little Traitor to the South.
1907   New York   15.00

BRADY, Cyrus Townsend   Northwestern Fights and Fighters.
1907   New York   45.00

BRADY, Cyrus Townsend   On the Old Kearsarge: A Story of the Civil War.
1910   New York   15.00

BRADY, Cyrus Townsend   The Southerners.
1903   New York   25.00
1910   20.00

BRADY, Robert   The Story of One Regiment, The Eleventh Maine Infantry Volunteers in the War of the Rebellion.
1896   New York   85.00

BRADY, William N.   The Kedge-Anchor; or Young Sailors' Assistant, Appertaining . . . Modern Seamanship, Rigging, Knotting . . . Applicable to Ships of War and Others.
1864   New York   150.00

BRAGG, Edward S.   Address of Gen. _____ Before the Society of the Army of the Potomac at Detroit, Michigan June 14, 1882. Wraps.
1882   Washington, DC   30.00

BRAGG, Jefferson Davis   Louisiana in the Confederacy.
1941   Baton Rouge   50.00

BRAGG, Junius Newport   Letters of a Confederate Surgeon, 1861-1865, edited by Mrs. T. J. Gaughan.
1960   Camden, AR   Ltd.   60.00

BRAGG, William Harris   Joe Brown's Army: The Georgia State Line, 1862-1865.
1987   Macon   29.95

BRAGUE, S. B.   Notes on Colored Troops and Military Colonies on Southern Soil, By An Officer of the 9th Army Corps. Wraps.
1863   New York   25.00

BRAINARD, Mary G.   Campaign of the 146th Regiment of New York State Volunteers.
1915   New York   130.00

BRAMHALL, Frank J.   The Military Souvenir; A Portrait Gallery of Our Military and Naval Heroes.
1863   New York   125.00

BRANCH, Houston and **WATERS**, Frank   Diamond Head.
1948   New York   10.00

BRANCH, Mary Polk   Memoirs of a Southern Woman "Within the Lines" and a Genealogical Record.
1912   Chicago   75.00

BRANDT, J. D.   Gunnery Catechism as Applied to the Service of Naval
Ordnance.
1864   New York   150.00
BRANDT, Nat   The Town That Started the Civil War.
1990   Syracuse   29.95
BRANNON, Peter Alexander   The Organization of the Confederate
Postoffice Department at Montgomery. . . .
1960   Montgomery, AL   60.00
BRANSCOM, Alexander C.   Mystic Romances of the Blue and the
Grey.
1883   New York   80.00
BRANSON, H. C.   Salisbury Plain, A Novel of the Civil War.
1965   New York   10.00
BRANT, Jefferson E.   History of the Eighty-fifth Indiana Volunteer
Infantry.
1902   Bloomington   190.00
BRANTLEY, Rabun Lee   Georgia Journalism of the Civil War Period.
Wraps.
1929   Nashville   50.00
BRANTLEY, W. H.   Unparalleled Audacity Off Mobile Bay, Captain
Maffitt Runs 'The Florida' Through Admiral Farragut's Blockade in
Broad Daylight. Wraps.
1954   Birmingham   50.00
BRECKINRIDGE, Lucy   Lucy Breckinridge of Grove Hill, the Journal
of a Virginia Girl 1862-1864, edited by Mary D. Robertson.
1979   Kent, OH   25.00
BRECKINRIDGE, Robert J.   Our Country: Its Peril and Its Deliver-
ance. Wraps.
1861   Cincinnati   15.00
BRECKINRIDGE, William C. P.   The Ex-Confederate and What He Has
Done in Peace, An Address. Wraps.
1892   Richmond   45.00
BRECKINRIDGE, William C. P.   A Plea for a History of the Confederate War: An Address. Wraps.
1887   Louisville   40.00
BREEDEN, James O.   Joseph Jones, M.D. Scientist of the Old South.
1975   Lexington, KY   20.00
BREIHAN, Carl W.   The Killer Legions of Quantrill.
1971   Seattle   20.00
BREIHAN, Carl W.   Life of Jesse James.
n.d.   New York   15.00
BREIHAN, Carl W.   Quantrill and His Civil War Guerillas.
1959   New York   15.00
1959   Denver 10.00
BREMNER, Robert H.   The Public Good.
1980   New York   15.00
BRENT, Joseph Lancaster   Capture of the Ironclad "Indianola."
1926   New Orleans   30.00
BRENT, Joseph Lancaster   Memoirs of the War Between the States.
Wraps
1940   (New Orleans)   Ltd.   400.00

BRENT, Joseph Lancaster   Mobilizable Fortifications, and Their Controlling Influence in War.
1885   Boston   100.00
BRESLIN, Howard   A Hundred Hills.
1960   New York   15.00
BRETHAN, C. W.   Sam Hildebrand: Guerrilla. Wraps.
1984   Waumtosa   7.50
BRETT, David   My Dear Wife, The Civil War Letters of _____, Union Cannoneer 9th Massachusetts Battery.
1964   Little Rock   15.00
BREWER, Abraham T.   History Sixty-first Regiment Pennsylvania Volunteers 1861-1865.
1911   Pittsburgh   100.00
BREWER, J. H. F.   History of the 175th Infantry.
1955   Baltimore   25.00
BREWER, James H.   The Confederate Negro: Virginia's Craftsmen and Military Laborers 1861-1865.
1969   Durham, NC   25.00
BREWER, Willis   Alabama: Her History, . . . 1540-1872.
1872   Montgomery   75.00
1964   Tuscaloosa   20.00
1988   40.00
BRIANT, Charles C.   History of the 6th Regt. Indiana Volunteer Infantry.
1891   Indianapolis   150.00
BRICE, Marshall M.   Centennial Exhibition of Staunton and Augusta County During the Civil War. Wraps.
1961   Staunton   13.00
BRICE, Marshall M.   Conquest of a Valley.
1965   Charlottesville   35.00
1967   Verona, VA   30.00
1974   Verona, VA   25.00
BRICE, Marshall M.   The Stonewall Brigade Band.
1967   Verona   30.00
1982   15.00
BRICK, John   Jubilee.
1956   Garden City, NY   20.00
BRICK, John   The Richmond Raid.
1963   New York   10.00
BRIDGES, Hal, edited by   A Lee Letter on the "Lost Dispatch" and the Maryland Campaign of 1862. Wraps.
1958   Virginia   15.00
BRIDGES, Hal   Lee's Maverick General, Daniel Harvey Hill.
1961   New York   50.00
BRIDGES, Mrs. Soule Jones   A Story Founded on Fact and Verses.
1903   Memphis   50.00
A Brief and Condensed History of Parsons Texas Cavalry Brigade.
1962   Waco Ltd.   40.00
A Brief Historical Sketch of the Cuyahoga County Soldiers and Sailors Monument. Wraps.
1896   Cleveland   25.00

A Brief Historical Sketch of the "Fighting McCooks." Wraps.
   n.d.   New York   50.00
A Brief Memoir of Lt. Chas. B. Randall, Who Fell in Battle before Atlanta, Ga., Fighting for the Maintenance of Our Union. (Randall, Charles B.)
   1870   New York   55.00
Brief Suggestions in the Case of General Fitz John Porter.
   1874   Morristown, NJ   50.00
BRIER, Royce   Boy in Blue.
   1937   New York   15.00
BRIGANCE, William Norwood   Jeremiah Sullivan Black, A Defender of the Constitution and the Ten Commandments.
   1934   Philadelphia   30.00
BRIGHT, Adam S. and BRIGHT, Michael S.   Respects to All: Letters of Two Pennsylvania Boys in the War, edited by A. C. Truxall.
   1962   Pittsburgh   20.00
BRIGHT, Leslie S.   The Blockade Runner Modern Greece and Her Cargo. Wraps.
   1977   Raleigh, NC   30.00
BRIGHTWELL, J. S., et al, compiled by   Roster of the Confederate Soldiers of Georgia.
   1982   Spartanburg   30.00
BRININSTOOL, E. A.   A Trooper with Custer: and Other Historic Incidents of the Battle of the Little Big Horn.
   1926   Columbus   50.00
BRINKERHOFF, General Roeliff   Recollections of a Lifetime.
   1900   Cincinnati   75.00
   1901   Cincinnati   40.00
BRINTON, John H.   Personal Memoirs of _____ Major and Surgeon U.S.V.
   1914   New York   125.00
BRISBIN, James S.   The Lives of Ulysses S. Grant and Schuyler Colfax.
   1869   Cincinnati   20.00
BRISBIN, James S.   Winfield Scott Hancock, Major-General U.S.A., His Life. Wraps.
   1880   Philadelphia   25.00
BRISTOL, Frank Milton   The Life of Chaplain McCabe, Bishop of the Methodist Episcopal Church.
   1908   New York   35.00
BRISTOW, B. W.   Oration . . . Decoration of Soldiers' Graves at Cave Hill Cemetery. Wraps.
   1875   Washington, DC   25.00
BRISTOW, J. Q.   Tales of Old Fort Gibson.
   1961   New York   15.00
BRITTON, Wiley   The Aftermath of the Civil War.
   1924   Kansas City   20.00
   1922   25.00
BRITTON, Wiley   The Civil War on the Border . . . 1861-1862.
   1890   New York   125.00
   1891   New York   125.00
   1899   New York   80.00

BRITTON, Wiley   Memoirs of the Rebellion on the Border 1863.
1882   Chicago 125.00
1986   26.00
BRITTON, Wiley   6th Kansas Cavlary (Union).   Memoirs of the
Rebellion on the Border, 1863.
1986   26.00
BRITTON, Wiley   A Traveling Court Based on Investigation of War
Claims.
1926   Kansas City   40.00
BRITTON, Wiley   The Union Indian Brigade in the Civil War.
1922   Kansas City   125.00
BROADFOOT, Thomas and PAIR, Marianne and HUNT, Roger   Civil
War Books   A Priced Checklist.
1983   Wendell, NC   30.00
BROBST, John F.   Well Mary: Civil War Letters of a Wisconsin Volunteer, edited by Margaret B. Roth.
1960   Madison   20.00
1960   Madison   Wraps   8.50
BROCK, R. A., edited by   Gen. Robert Edward Lee - Soldier, Citizen and
Christian Patriot.
1897   Richmond   75.00
BROCK, R. A., edited by   Miscellaneous Papers, 1672-1865.
1887   Richmond   100.00
BROCK, R. A.   Paroles of the Army of Northern Viginia, SHSP, Vol.
15.
1887   Richmond   Wraps   60.00
1962   New York   entitled The Appomattox Roster.   Ltd. 50.00
BROCK, Sallie A.   See: PUTNAM, Sallie A.
BROCK, W. R.   An American Crisis - Congress and Reconstruction
1865-1867.
1963   London   20.00
BROCKETT, Linus P.   Battle-field and Hospital.
(c.1870) New York   30.00
BROCKETT, Linus P.   Men of Our Day; or, Biographical Sketches of
Patriots, Orators, Statesmen, Generals. . . .
1868   40.00
BROCKETT, Linus P.   Philanthropic Results of the War.
1864   New York   20.00
BROCKETT, Linus P.   Scouts, Spies and Heroes of the Great Civil
War.
1892   Cleveland   20.00
1892   Jersey City 20.00
1899   Washington, DC   20.00
1911   n.p.   15.00
BROCKETT, Linus P. and VAUGHAN, Mary C.   Woman's Work in the
Civil War.
✓ 1867   Philadelphia   40.00
1867   Boston   30.00
BROCKWAY, Beaman   Fifty Years in Journalism Embracing Recollections and Personal Experiences with an Autobiography.
1891   Watertown, NY   25.00

BRODIE, Fawn M.   Thaddeus Stevens.
   1959   New York   25.00

BRONAUGH, W. C.   The Youngers' Fight for Freedom.
   1906   Columbia   55.00

BROOKE, G. M.   John M. Brooke: Naval Scientist and Educator.
   1980   Charlottesville   30.00

BROOKE, John M.   The Virginia or Merrimac, Her Real Projector.
Wraps.
   1891   Richmond   35.00

BROOKES, Iveson L.   A Defense of Southern Slavery Against the
Attacks of Henry Clay and Alexander Campbell by a Southern Clergy-
man. Wraps.
   1851   Hamburg, SC   50.00

BROOKS, Aubrey Lee   Walter Clark, Fighting Judge.
   1944   Chapel Hill, NC   25.00

BROOKS, Aubrey Lee and LEFLER, Hugh Talmage   The   Papers   of
Walter Clark. 2 Vols.
   1950   Chapel Hill, NC   35.00

BROOKS, Fred Emerson   Pickett's Charge and Other Poems.
   1903   Boston   25.00

BROOKS, Gwendolyn, et al   A Portion of That Field - The Centennial
of the Burial of Lincoln.
   1967   IL   35.00

BROOKS, Noah   Abraham Lincoln.
   1900   New York   10.00
   1909   New York   10.00

BROOKS, Noah   Mr. Lincoln's Washington   The Civil War Dispatches of
_____, edited by P. J. Straudenraus.
   1967   New York   15.00
   1967   South Brunswick   15.00

BROOKS, Noah   Washington in Lincoln's Time.
   1895   New York   30.00
   1958   New York   20.00

BROOKS, R. P.   Conscription in the Confederate States of America
1862-1865. Wraps.
   1917   GA   50.00

BROOKS, Stewart   Civil War Medicine.
   1966   Springfield   75.00

BROOKS, U. R.   Butler and His Cavalry in the War of Secession 1861-
1865.
   1909   Columbia, SC   100.00

BROOKS, U. R., edited by   Stories of the Confederacy.
   1912   Columbia, SC   100.00

BROOKS, William E.   Grant of Appomattox.
   1942   Indianapolis   35.00

BROOKS, William E.   Lee of Virginia.
   1932   Indianapolis   40.00
   1932   Garden City, NY   30.00
   1942   20.00

BROSS, William   Biographical Sketch of the Late Gen. B. J. Sweet. History of Camp Douglas. Wraps.
   1878   Chicago   45.00

BROUN, Thomas L., edited by   Dr. William Leroy Broun.
1912   New York   60.00
BROWN, A. J.   History of Newton County, Mississippi From 1834-1894.
1894   Jackson, MS 125.00
BROWN, Alonzo L.   History of the Fourth Regiment of Minnesota Infantry Volunteers.
1892   St. Paul   170.00
BROWN, Augustus C.   The Diary of a Line Officer.
1906   New York   90.00
BROWN, C. O.   Battlefields Revisited, Grant's Chattanooga Campaign, a Horseback Ride from Chattanooga to Atlanta.   Wraps.
1886   Kalamazoo, MI   125.00
BROWN, D. S., edited by   Historical and Biographical Sketches of Greensville County, Virginia 1650-1967.
1968   Richmond   Ltd.   50.00
BROWN, Dee Alexander   The Bold Cavaliers, Morgan's 2nd Kentucky Cavalry Raiders.
1959   Philadelphia   40.00
BROWN, Dee Alexander   The Galvanized Yankees.
1963   Urbana, IL 30.00
1986   Wraps 7.95
BROWN, Dee Alexander   Grierson's Raid.
1954   Urbana, IL 40.00
1981   Dayton 20.00
BROWN, Edmund Randolph   The Twenty-seventh Indiana Volunteer Infantry in the War of the War of the Rebellion.
1899   Monticello 250.00
1984   35.00
1985   35.00
1986   35.00
BROWN, Ernest Francis   Raymond of the Times.
1951   New York   20.00
BROWN, Francis H.   Harvard Univ. in the War of 1861-1865. A Record of Services Rendered in the Army and Navy of the U.S. by the Graduates. . . .
1886   Boston   50.00
BROWN, Fred R.   History of the Ninth U.S. Infantry.
1909   125.00
BROWN, George W.   Reminiscences of Gov. R. J. Walker, with the True Story of the Rescue of Kansas from Slavery.
1902   Rockford, IL   30.00
1970   15.00
BROWN, George William   Baltimore and the 19th of April, 1861.
1887   Baltimore   30.00
1982   Wraps 9.95
BROWN, Henri LeFevre, compiled by   History of the Third Regiment, Excelsior Brigade 72d New York Volunteer Infantry.
1902   Jamestown   5.00
BROWN, I. C.   Michigan Men in the Civil War.   Wraps.
1959   15.00

BROWN, J. Willard   The Signal Corps, U.S.A. in the War of the Rebellion.
    1896   Boston   150.00
BROWN, James N.   Roster of Survivors of the 10th Ill. Vet. Vol. Inf.
Wraps.
    1890   60.00
BROWN, Joseph M.   Kennesaw's Bombardment   How the Sharpshooters
Woke up the Batteries.   Wraps.
    1890   Atlanta   100.00
BROWN, Joseph M.   The Mountain Campaigns in Georgia.
    1886   Buffalo, NY   35.00
    1889   New York   30.00
BROWN, Leonard   American Patriotism.
    1869   Des Moines   35.00
BROWN, Louis A.   The Salisbury Prison,   A Case Study of Confederate Military Prisons 1861-1865.
    1980   Wendell, NC   30.00
BROWN, Maud Morrow   The University Greys, Company A, Eleventh
Mississippi Regiment.
    1940   Richmond   60.00
BROWN, Norman D.   Edward Stanly: Whiggery's Tar Heel "Conqueror."
    1974   University, AL   15.00
BROWN, Philip Francis   Reminiscences   of   the   War   of   1861-1865.
Wraps.
    1912   Roanoke   250.00
    1917   Richmond   200.00
BROWN, R. Shepard   Stringfellow of the Fourth.
    1960   New York   30.00
BROWN, Spencer Kellogg   Spencer Kellogg Brown as Disclosed By
His Diary, edited by George G. Smith.
    1903   New York   35.00
BROWN, Stuart E., Jr.   The Guns of Harpers Ferry.
    1968   Berryville, VA   30.00
BROWN, Thaddeus C. S., MURPHY, Samuel J., and PUTNEY, William G.,
edited by   Behind the Guns, The History of Battery I, Second
Regiment Illinois Light Artillery.
    1965   Carbondale   Boxed   40.00
BROWN, Varina Davis   A Colonel at Gettysburg and Spotsylvania.
    1931   Columbia, SC   75.00
    1988   Baltimore   25.00
BROWN, Wilbur F.   A Tribute of Respect by Lafayette Post No. 140
. . . in Memory of Commander Richard Worsam Meade.
    1898   New York   30.00
BROWN, William Wells   The Negro in the American Rebellion   His
Heroism and His Fidelity.
    1867   Boston   75.00
BROWNE, A.   Sketch of the Official Life of John A. Andrew, as
Governor of Massachusetts.
    1868   New York   10.00
BROWNE, Francis F., edited by   Bugle-Echoes.
    1886   New York   30.00

BROWNE, Junius Henri   Four Years in Secessia.
1865   Hartford   25.00
BROWNE, Samuel T.   First Cruise of the Montauk.   Wraps.
1880   Providence   30.00
BROWNING, Orville Hickman   The Diary of _____, edited by
Theodore C. Pease and James G. Randall. 2 Vols.
1925   Springfield   45.00
BROWNLEE, Richard S.   Gray Ghosts of the Confederacy, Guerrilla
Warfare in the West.
1958   Baton Rouge   40.00
1963   Baton Rouge   35.00
1968   Baton Rouge   30.00
1975   Baton Rouge   25.00
1984   Baton Rouge   Wraps   10.00
BROWNLOW, William G.   Sketches of the Rise, Progress and Decline of
Secession.
1862   Philadelphia   40.00
BROWNSON, O. A.   The American Republic: Its Constitution, Tenden-
cies, and Destiny.
1866   New York   45.00
BRUBAKER, J. H.   The Last Capital: Danville, Virginia, and the Final
Days of the Confederacy.
1979   Danville   15.00
BRUCE, George Anson   The Capture and Occupation of Richmond.
n.d.   n.p.   45.00
BRUCE, George Anson   The Twentieth Regiment of Massachusetts
Volunteer Infantry.
1906   Boston   65.00
1988   32.50
BRUCE, Philip A.   Brave Deeds of Confederate Soldiers.
1916   Philadelphia   30.00
BRUCE, Philip A.   Robert E. Lee.
1907   Philadelphia   25.00
BRUCE, Robert V.   Lincoln and the Tools of War.
1956   New York   25.00
1956   Indianapolis   25.00
1989   Urbana   32.50
BRUNK, H. A.   Life of Peter S. Hartman.
1937   n.p.   30.00
BRUNKER, H. M. E.   Story of the Campaign in Eastern Virginia, April,
1861 to May 1863.
1910   London   75.00
BRUNSON, Joseph Woods   The Pee Dee Artillery.   Wraps.
1983   University, AL   8.00
BRYAN, Emma Lyon   A Romance of the Valley of Virginia.
1892   Harrisonburg, VA   30.00
BRYAN, George S.   The Great American Myth The True Story of Lincoln's Murder.
1940   New York   25.00
BRYAN, John Stewart   Joseph Bryan, His Times, His Family, His
Friends A Memoir.
1935   Richmond   200.00

BRYAN, Joseph, III   The Sword Over the Mantel - The Civil War and I.
   1960   New York   25.00
BRYAN, Thomas Conn   Confederate Georgia.
   1953   Athens 40.00
   1964   Athens 25.00
BRYANT, Edwin E.   History of the 3rd Regiment of Wisconsin Veteran Volunteer Infantry 1861-1865.
   1891   Madison 100.00
BRYNER, Byron Cloyd   Bugle Echoes, The Story of Illinois 47th.
   1905   Springfield   140.00
BUCHANAN, James   Mr. Buchanan's Administration on the Eve of Rebellion.
   1866   New York 25.00
BUCHANAN, Lamont   A Pictorial History of the Confederacy.
   1951   New York 25.00
   1959   New York 25.00
   1963   New York 25.00
BUCK, Charles W.   Colonel Bob and a Double Love.
   1922   Louisville, KY   20.00
BUCK, Irving A.   Cleburne and His Command.
   1908   New York and Washington, DC   300.00
   1959   Jackson   edited by Thomas R. Hay   35.00
   1985   Dayton 30.00
   1987   Dayton 30.00
BUCK, Lucy Rebecca   Sad Earth, Sweet Heaven.
   1940   n.p.   Wraps 140.00
   1973   n.p.   15.00
BUCK, Paul H.   The Road to Reunion 1865-1900.
   1937   10.00
   1938   Boston 10.00
   1947   Boston 10.00
BUCK, Samuel D.   With the Old Confeds. Actual Experiences of A Captain In The Line.
   1925   Baltimore   700.00
BUCKE, Richard M., edited by   Walt Whitman - The Wound Dresser Letters Written to His Mother from the Hospitals in Washington During the Civil War.
   1949   New York   20.00
BUCKERIDGE, J. O.   Lincoln's Choice.
   1956   Harrisburg, PA   25.00
BUCKINGHAM, J. E.   Reminiscences and Souvenirs of the Assassination of Abraham Lincoln.
   1894   Washington, DC   45.00
BUCKINGHAM, Samuel G.   The Life of William A. Buckingham The War Governor of Connecticut.
   1894   Springfield, MA   15.00
BUCKLEY, Cornelius   A Frenchman, a Chaplain, a Rebel, "The War Letters of Pere-Louis-Hippolyte Gache. S.J."
   1981   9.00
BUCKLEY, William   Buckley's History of the Great Reunion of the North and South.
   1923   Staunton, VA   35.00

BUCKLIN, Sophronia E.   In Hospital and Camp: A Woman's Record of Thrilling Incidents Among the Wounded in the Late War.
1869   Philadelphia   75.00
BUCKNER, W. P.   Calculated Tables and Ranges for Navy and Army Guns.
1865   New York   40.00
BUDDINGTON, William Ives   A Memorial of Giles F. Ward, Jr.   Late First Lieut. Twelfth N. Y. Cavalry.
1866   New York   35.00
BUEL, J. W.   The Authorized Pictorial Lives of James Gillespie Blaine and John Alexander Logan.
1884   Cincinnati   20.00
BUELL, Augustus C.   The Cannoneer, Recollections of Service in the Army of the Potomac.
1890   Washington, DC 75.00
1897   n.p.   Wraps   40.00
BUFFUM, Francis H.   A Memorial of the Great Rebellion, Being a History of the Fourteenth Regiment, N.H. Volunteers.
1882   Boston   80.00
BUFFUM, Francis H.   Sheridan's Veterans, A Souvenir of Their Two Campaigns in the Shenandoah Valley.   Wraps.
1883   Boston   55.00
BUFFUM, Francis H.   Sheridan's Veterans, No. II   A Souvenir of Their Third Campaign in the Shenandoah Valley.   Wraps.
1886   Boston   50.00
Bull Run, 1st Battle of, 1861.
1977   19.00
BULL, Rice C.   Soldiering; The Civil War Diary of _____, edited by K. Jack Bauer.
1978   San Rafael 20.00
1978   Wraps   10.00
BULLARD, F. Lauriston   Abraham Lincoln and the Widow Bixby.
1946   New Brunswick   25.00
BULLARD, F. Lauriston   Famous War Correspondents.
1914   Boston   30.00
BULLARD, F. Lauriston   A Few Appropriate Remarks   Lincoln's Gettysburg Address.
1944   Harrogate, TN   Ltd.   30.00
BULLITT, J. C.   A Review of Mr. Binney's Pamphlet on "The Privilege of the Writ of Habeas Corpus Under the Constitution."   Wraps.
1862   Philadelphia   25.00
BULLOCH, James D.   The Secret Service of the Confederate States in Europe. 2 Vols.
1883   London 300.00
1884   New York   150.00
1959   New York   Boxed   50.00
A Bummer Boy, A "Spoony" Biography.   Wraps.
1868   Washington, DC   25.00
BURCH, John P.   Charles W. Quantrell.
1923   Vega, TX   30.00

BURCHARD, Peter   One Gallant Rush, Robert Gould Shaw and His
    Brave Black Regiment.
    1965   New York   30.00
BURCKMYER, Cornelius L.   The Burckmyer Letters - March 1863 -
    June 1865.
    1926   Columbia, SC   50.00
BURDETTE, Robert J.   The Drums of the 47th.
    1914   Indianapolis   60.00
BURGE, Dolly Sumner L.   The Diary of Dolly Lunt Burge, edited by
    James I. Robertson.
    1962   Athens   30.00
BURGE, Dolly Sumner L.   A Woman's Wartime Journal.
    1918   Macon, GA   75.00
    1927   Macon, GA   50.00
BURGER, Nash K.   Confederate Spy: Rose O'Neale Greenhow.
    1967   New York   15.00
BURGER, Nash K. and BETTERSWORTH, J. K.   South of Appomattox.
    1959   New York   30.00
BURGESS, John W.   The Civil War and the Constitution. 2 Vols.
    1901   New York   50.00
    1903   New York   30.00
    1909   20.00
BURGESS, John W.   Reconstruction and the Constitution.
    1902   New York   10.00
BURGESS, Milton V.   David Gregg: Pennsylvania Cavalryman.
    1984   State College, WV   18.00
BURGESS, Milton V.   Minute Men of Pennsylvania, with a Biography
    of Their Leader in Blair, Bedford, and Cambria Counties, Col. Jacob C.
    Higgins, Including a copy of Col. Higgins' Diary of the Mexican War.
    1962   Martinsburg 50.00
BURKE, Benjamin F.   Letters of Private _____, Written While in
    the Terry's Texas Rangers, 1861-1864.   Wraps.
    1965   (Dallas)   75.00
BURKE, Robert   Escape from a Southern Prison, a Brief History of the
    Prison Life and Escape . . . from Camp Ford Prison.   Wraps.
    (c.1880) Indianapolis 120.00
BURKE, William S., compiled by   Military History of Kansas Regiments
    During the War for the Suppression of the Great Rebellion.
    1870   Leavenworth   600.00
BURLINGAME, John K.   History of the Fifth Regiment of Rhode Island
    Heavy Artillery During 3 1/2 Years of Service in North Carolina.
    1892   Providence   90.00
BURN, James Dawson   Three Years Among the Working-Classes in the
    United States During the War.
    1865   London   140.00
BURNAHM, T. O. H. P.   The Stars and Stripes in Rebeldom.   A series
    of papers written by Federal Prisoners (privates) in Richmond,
    Tuscaloosa, New Orleans, and Salisbury, NC.
    1862   Boston   75.00
BURNE, Alfred H.   Lee, Grant and Sherman.
    1938   Aldershot, Eng. 75.00
    1939   New York   60.00

BURNETT, Alfred   Incidents of the War: Humorous, Pathetic, and Descriptive.
   1863   Cincinnati   65.00

BURNETT, C.   Captain John Ericsson, Father of the "Monitor."
   1960   New York   20.00

BURNETT, W. R.   The Dark Command: A Kansas Iliad.
   1938   New York   15.00

BURNETT, William G.   Better a Patriot Soldier's Grave. The History of the Sixth Ohio Volunteer Cavalry.
   1982   20.00

BURNS, P. H.   A Brief History of the 22nd Battery, Indiana Vols. Wraps.
   1900   Knightstown   100.00

BURNS, William S.   Recollections of the 4th Missouri Cavalry (Union).
   1988   Dayton   20.00

BURNS, Zed H.   Confederate Forts.
   1977   Natchez   25.00

BURNS, Zed H.   Ship Island and the Confederacy. Wraps.
   1971   MA 14.00

BURNSIDE, Ambrose E.   The Burnside Expedition. Wraps.
   1882   Providence   Ltd.   40.00

BURR, Fearing and **LINCOLN**, George   The Town of Hingham in the Late Civil War.
   1876   Boston   50.00

BURR, Frank A.   Life and Achievements of James Addams Beaver.
   1882   Philadelphia   45.00

BURR, Frank A.   The Life and Deeds of General U.S. Grant.
   1885   Philadelphia   50.00

BURR, Frank A.   The Life of Gen. Philip H. Sheridan.
   1886   Providence   25.00
   1888   Providence   25.00
   1890   New York   25.00

BURRAGE, Henry Sweetser   Gettysburg and Lincoln.
   1906   New York   40.00

BURRAGE, Henry Sweetser   History of the Thirty-sixth Regiment Mass. Volunteers.
   1884   Boston   75.00

BURRAGE, Henry Sweetser   Thomas Hamlin Hubbard, Bvt. Brig.-Gen. U.S. Vols.
   1923   Portland   25.00

BURSON, William   A Race for Liberty: or, My Capture, Imprisonment and Escape.
   1867   Wellsville   125.00

BURT, Richard W.   War Songs, Poems and Odes, Dedicated to My Comrades of the Mexican and Civil Wars.
   1906   Peoria, IL   60.00

BURT, Silas W.   My Memoirs of the Military History of the State of New York During the War for the Union 1861-65. Wraps.
   1902   Albany   40.00

BURTON, E. Milby   **The Siege of Charleston 1861-1865.**
    1907   Columbia   40.00
    1971   Columbia   20.00
    1982   Wraps 8.00
BURTON, Elijah P.   **Diary of _____, Surgeon 7th Reg. Illinois 3rd Brigade, 2nd Div.**
    1939   Des Moines   50.00
BURTON, Joseph Q. and **BOTSWORTH,** T. F.   **Historical Sketches of the 47th Alabama Infantry, CSA.** Wraps.
    1982   University, AL   8.00
BURTON, William L.   **Descriptive Bibliography of Civil War Manuscripts in Illinois.**
    1966   Illinois   20.00
BURTON, William L.   **Melting Pot Soldiers.**
    1988   26.95
BURTSCHI, Mary   **James Hall of Lincoln's Frontier World.**
    1977   Vandalia, IL   15.00
BURTSCHI, Mary   **Vandalia: Wilderness Capital of Lincoln's Land.**
    1977   Vandalia, IL   20.00
BURWELL, Letitia M.   **A Girl's Life in Virginia Before the War.**
    1895   New York   60.00
BUSEY, John W.   **The Last Full Measure: Burials in the Soldier's National Cemetery at Gettysburg.**
    1988   Hightstown   20.00
BUSEY, John W.   **These Honored Dead: The Union Casualties at Gettysburg.**
    1988   Hightstown   24.00
BUSEY, John W. and **MARTIN,** David G.   **Regimental Strengths at Gettysburg.**
    1982   Baltimore   20.00
BUSHNELL, C. S.   **The Original U.S. Warship Monitor, Copies of Correspondence. . . .** Wraps.
    1899   55.00
BUSHNELL, Samuel C.   **The Story of the Monitor and the Merrimac.** Wraps.
    (c.1920) n.p.   30.00
BUSHONG, Millard Kessler   **General Turner Ashby and Stonewall's Valley Campaign.**
    1980   Verona, VA   35.00
BUSHONG, Millard Kessler   **A History of Jefferson County, West Virginia.**
    1941   Charles Town   50.00
BUSHONG, Millard Kessler   **Old Jube, A Biography of Jubal A. Early.**
    1955   Boyce, VA 50.00
    1961   Boyce, VA 20.00
    1985   Shippensburg, PA   19.95
    1988   24.95
BUSHONG, Millard Kessler and **BUSHONG,** Dean McK.   **Fightin' Tom Rosser, C.S.A.**
    1983   Shippensburg, PA   35.00

BUSLETT, Ole Amundson   Det Femtende Regiment Wisconsin Frivillige, Samlet Og Bearbeidet Af O. A. Buslett.
1894   Decorah, IA   100.00

BUTLER, Benjamin F.   Autobiography and Personal Reminiscences.
1892   Boston   30.00

BUTLER, Benjamin F.   Butler's Book. A Review of His Legal, Political and Military Career.
1892   Boston   40.00

BUTLER, Benjamin F.   Character and Results of the War. Wraps.
1863   Philadelphia   15.00
1863   New York   10.00

BUTLER, Benjamin F.   General Orders from Headquarters, Department of the Gulf, Issued by Major-General B. F. Butler. . . . Wraps.
1862   New Orleans   400.00

BUTLER, Benjamin F.   Private and Official Correspondence of _____ During the Period of the Civil War. 5 Vols.
1917   Norwood   350.00

BUTLER, Lorine Letcher   John Morgan and His Men.
1960   Philadelphia   50.00

BUTLER, M. C.   Address on the Life, Character and Services of General Wade Hampton. Wraps.
1903   Washington, DC   75.00

BUTLER, Marvin Benjamin   My Story of the Civil War and the Underground Railroad.
1914   Huntington   100.00

BUTLER, Pierce   Judah P. Benjamin.
1906   Philadelphia   25.00
1907   Washington, DC   20.00

BUTTERFIELD, Daniel   Camp and Outpost Duty for Infantry.
1862   New York   150.00
1863   125.00

BUTTERFIELD, Daniel   Major General Joseph Hooker and the Troops from the Army of the Potomac. Wraps.
1896   New York   20.00

BUTTERFIELD, Julia Lorrilard, edited by   A Biographical Memorial of General Daniel Butterfield.
1896   New York   Wraps   90.00
1903   New York   Ltd.   150.00
1904   New York   100.00

BUTTS, Frank B.   The Monitor and the Merrimac. Wraps.
1890   Providence   Ltd.   30.00

By-Laws and Rules of Order of George E. Pickett Camp Confederate Veterans, of Richmond, VA. Wraps.
1889   Richmond   10.00

By Laws of Company F, 13th Regiment National Greys, N.Y.S.M.
1862   75.00

BYERS, Samuel H. M.   Iowa in War Times.
1888   Des Moines   75.00

BYERS, Samuel H. M.   The March to the Sea: A Poem.
1896   Boston   20.00

BYERS, Samuel H. M.   What I Saw in Dixie: Or Sixteen Months in Rebel Prisons. Wraps.
    1868   Dansville, NY   100.00

BYERS, Samuel H. M.   With Fire and Sword.
    1911   New York   75.00

BYRD, Ethel Maddox and CASSEY, Zelda Haas   Memoirs of the War Between the States.
    1961   Richmond   30.00

BYRNE, Frank L.   Haskell of Gettysburg, A Lieutenant on the Staff of John Gibbon. Wraps.
    1989   12.50

BYRNE, Frank L. and SOMAN, J. P., edited by   Your True Marcus: The Civil War Letters of a Jewish Colonel.
    1985   Kent, OH   22.50
    Recent reprint   11.95

BYRNE, Frank L. and WEAVER, Andrew T., edited by   Haskell of Gettysburg, His Life and Civil War Papers.
    1970   Madison   35.00

CABANISS, J.   Civil War Journal and Letters of Washington Ives, 4th Fla. C.S.A. Wraps.
    1987   Ltd.   15.00

CABELL, Sears Wilson   The "Bulldog" Longstreet at Gettysburg and Chickamauga. Wraps.
    1938   Atlanta   15.00

CABLE, George Washington   The Cavalier.
    1901   New York   15.00

CABLE, George Washington   Dr. Sevier.
    1894   New York   15.00

CABLE, George Washington   Kincaid's Battery.
    1908   New York   20.00
    1911   New York   15.00

CADWALLADER, Sylvanus   Three Years with Grant, as Recalled by War Correspondent Sylvanus Cadwallader, edited by Benjamin P. Thomas.
    1955   New York   25.00
    1956   20.00
    1967   New York   20.00

CAFFEY, Thomas E.   Battlefields of the South from Bull Run to Fredericksburg with Sketches of Confederate Commanders, and Gossip of the Camps by an English Combatant. 2 Vols.
    1860   London   450.00
    1863   London   400.00
    1864   New York   300.00
    1864   London   300.00
    1984   22.00

CAIN, James M.   Mignon.
    1962   New York   15.00

CAIN, James M.   Past All Dishonor.
    1946   New York   20.00

CAIN, Marvin R.   Edward Bates of Missouri, Lincoln's Attorney General.
    1965   Columbia, MO   15.00

CAIN, Marvin R.   Lincoln's Attorney General: Edward Bates of Missouri.
   1965   22.00

CAIRNES, John E.   The Slave Power: Its Character, Career and Probable
  Designs.
   1862   60.00
   1863   New York   50.00
   1968   10.00

CALDWELL, Charles K.   The Old 6th Regiment.
   1875   New Haven   75.00

CALDWELL, David S.   Incidents of War; or Southern Prison Life.
  Wraps.
   1864   Dayton 200.00

CALDWELL, J. F. J.   The History of a Brigade of South Carolinians,
  Known First as "Gregg's" and Subsequently as "McGowan's Brigade."
   1866   Philadelphia   500.00
   1951   Marietta   40.00
   1974   Dayton 25.00
   1984   Dayton 25.00
   1987   Dayton 25.00

CALDWELL, J. F. J.   The Stranger.
   1907   New York   20.00

CALDWELL, Mrs. James E.   A Chapter from the Life of a Little Girl
  of the Confederacy.
   n.d.   Nashville   60.00

Calendar of the Jefferson Davis Postwar Manuscripts. . . . Wraps.
   1943   New Orleans   25.00

CALFEE, Mrs. B. G.   Confederate History of Culpeper County. Wraps.
   n.d.   n.p.   20.00

CALHOUN, Charles M.   Liberty Dethroned, A Concise History of Some
  of the Most Startling Events Before, During and Since the Civil War.
   (1903)   (Greenwood, SC) 500.00

CALHOUN, John C.   Mr. Calhoun's Reply to Col. Benton. Wraps.
   (c.1850) n.p.   40.00

CALHOUN, William L.   History of the 42nd Regiment, Georgia Volunteers, C.S.A. Infantry. Wraps.
   1900   Atlanta   175.00

CALIFF, Joseph M.   Record of the Services of the 7th Regiment US
  Colored Troops, from Sept. 1863 to Nov. 1866. Wraps.
   1878   Providence, RI   60.00

The California Column: Its Campaigns and Services in New Mexico, Arizona
  and Texas, During the Civil War, with Sketches of Brigadier-General
  James H. Carleton, Its Commander. Wraps.
   1908   Santa Fe   150.00

CALKINS, Christopher M.   The Battles of Appomattox Station and
  Appomattox Court House, April 8-9, 1865.
   1987   Lynchburg Ltd. to 1000 Copies   19.95

CALKINS, Christopher M.   The Final Bivouac: The Surrender Parade
  at Appomattox and the Disbanding of the Armies, April 10-May 20,
  1865.
   1988   Lynchburg   19.95

CALKINS, Christopher M.   From Petersburg to Appomattox: Tour Guide to the Routes of Lee's Withdrawal and Grant's Pursuit.   Wraps.
1983   Farmville   7.50

CALKINS, Christopher M.   Thirty-six Hours before Appomattox, April 6 and 7, 1865.   Wraps.
1980   Farmville   10.00
1989   Wraps 5.00

CALKINS, William Wirt   The History of the One Hundred and Fourth Regiment of Illinois Volunteer Infantry.
1895   Chicago 250.00

CALLAHAN, Edward W., edited by   List of Officers of the Navy of the Unted States and of the Marine Corps from 1775 to 1900. . . .
1901   New York   50.00
1988   New York   35.00

CALLAHAN, James Morton   The Diplomatic History of the Southern Confederacy.
1901   Baltimore   60.00
1957   Springfield, MA   30.00
1964   New York   40.00

CALLAWAY, Felix Richard   The Bloody Links.
1907   Shreveport, LA   300.00

CALVERT, Henry Murray   Reminiscences of a Boy in Blue.
1920   New York   55.00

Campaigns in Kentucky and Tennessee Including the Battle of Chickamauga, 1862-64.   See: Papers of Military Historical Society of Massachusetts, No. 7.

Campaigns in Virginia, 1861-1862.   See: Papers of the Military Historical Society of Massachusetts, No. 1.

Campaigns in Virginia, Maryland, Pennsylvania, 1862-1863.   See: Papers of the Military Historical Society of Massachusetts, No. 3.

Campaigns of the Civil War.   13 Vols.   Navy in the Civil War.   3 Vols. Together, 16 Vols.
1881-1905   New York   300.00
1963   New York   8 Vols.   60.00
1989   Wilmington, NC   16 Vols.   300.00

AMMEN, Daniel   The Atlantic Coast.
1883   New York   25.00
1885   New York   25.00
1989   Wilmington, NC   25.00

CIST, Henry M.   The Army of the Cumberland.
1882   New York   30.00
1885   25.00
1894   New York   25.00
1909   20.00
1989   Wilmington, NC   25.00

COX, Jacob D.   Atlanta.
1882   New York   20.00
1895   New York   20.00
1989   Wilmington, NC   25.00

COX, Jacob D.   The March to the Sea-Franklin and Nashville.
1882   New York   20.00
1886   20.00
1898   New York   20.00
1902   20.00
1989   Wilmington, NC   25.00

DOUBLEDAY, Abner   Chancellorville and Gettysburg.
1882   New York   35.00
1886   New York   30.00
1887   New York   20.00
1989   Wilmington, NC   25.00

FORCE, M. F.   From Fort Henry to Corinth.
1881   New York   20.00
1882   New York   20.00
1903   New York   25.00
1989   Wilmington, NC   25.00

GREENE, Francis Vinton   The Mississippi.
1882   New York   35.00
Many later editions   15.00
1989   Wilmington, NC   25.00

HUMPHREYS, Andrew A.   The Virginia Campaign of '64 and '65 The Army of the Potomac and the Army of the James.
1883   New York   35.00
1885   New York   30.00
1903   New York   30.00
1908   New York   30.00
1989   Wilmington, NC   25.00

MAHAN, Alfred Thayer   The Gulf and Inland Waters.
1883   New York   25.00
1989   Wilmington, NC   25.00

NICOLAY, John G.   The Outbreak of Rebellion.
1881   New York   30.00
1901   New York   25.00
1905   New York   25.00
1989   Wilmington, NC   25.00

PALFREY, Francis W.   The Antietam and Fredericksburg.
1882   New York   25.00
1885   New York   25.00
1893   New York   25.00
1906   New York   25.00
1989   Wilmington, NC   25.00

PHISTERER, Frederick   Statistical Record of the Armies of the United States.
1883   New York   25.00
1885   New York   25.00
1895   New York   25.00
1989   Wilmington, NC   25.00

POND, George E.   The Shenandoah Valley in 1864. The Campaign of Sheridan.
1883   New York   25.00
1884   New York   25.00
1886   New York   25.00

1892　New York　25.00
1989　Wilmington, NC　25.00
ROPES, John C.　**The Army Under Pope.**
1881　New York　30.00
1882　n.p.　30.00
1885　New York　30.00
1905　New York　25.00
1989　Wilmington, NC　25.00
SOLEY, J. Russell　**The Blockade and the Cruisers.**
1883　New York　25.00
1890　New York　25.00
1989　Wilmington, NC　25.00
WEBB, Alexander S.　**The Peninsula.**
1881　New York　40.00
1882　n.p. 25.00
1885　New York　25.00
1908　New York　25.00
1989　Wilmington, NC　25.00
CAMPBELL, Andrew Jackson　**The Civil War Diary of _____, edited by Jill K. Garrett. Wraps.**
1965　Columbia, TN　35.00
CAMPBELL, George　**White and Black: the Outcome of a Visit to the United States.**
1879　London　110.00
CAMPBELL, Helen Jones　**The Case for Mrs. Surratt.**
1943　New York　20.00
CAMPBELL, Helen Jones　**Confederate Courier, the Historic Trial of Johnny Surratt for the Murder of Abraham Lincoln.**
1964　New York　20.00
CAMPBELL, James Havelock　**McClellan: A Vindication of the Military Career of General George B. McClellan.**
1916　New York　65.00
CAMPBELL, John A.　**Reminiscences and Documents Relating to the Civil War During the Year 1865. Wraps.**
1887　Baltimore　100.00
CAMPBELL, Mary Emily Robertson　**The Attitude of Tennesseans Toward the Union.**
1961　New York　20.00
CAMPER, Charles and **KIRKLEY**, J. W., compiled by　**Historical Record of the First Regiment Maryland Infantry.**
1871　Washington, DC　175.00
CANBY, Courtlandt　**Lincoln and the Civil War.**
1958　New York　Wraps　5.00
1960　New York　12.00
CANDLER, Allen D.　**The Confederate Records of the State of Georgia 1860-1868. 5 Vols.** Vols. 1, 2, 3, 4, 6. (Volume 5 never published.)
1909-11 Atlanta　500.00
Individual volumes　100.00　each
CANFIELD, Cass　**The Iron Will of Jefferson Davis.**
1978　New York　15.00
1981　15.00

CANFIELD, Eugene B.   Civil War Naval Ordnance.   Wraps.
    1969   Washington, DC   13.00
CANFIELD, Eugene B.   Notes of Naval Ordnance of the American Civil
    War.   Wraps.
    1960   Washington, DC   25.00
CANFIELD, Silas S.   History of the 21st Regiment Ohio Volunteer
    Infantry in the War of the Rebellion.
    1893   Toledo   125.00
CANFIELD, William A.   A History of William A. Canfield's Experience
    in the Army.   Wraps.
    1869   Manchester   40.00
CANNON, D. D.   The Flags of the Confederacy: An Illustrated History.
    1988   Memphis, TN   30.00
    1988   Wilmington, NC   Wraps 9.95
CANNON, J. P.   Inside of Rebeldom: The Daily Life of a Private in the
    Confederate Army.   Wraps.
    1900   Washington, DC   100.00
CANNON, John   History of Grant's Campaign for the Capture of Rich-
    mond (1864 1865): With an Outline of the Previous Course of the Ameri-
    can Civil War.
    1869   London   150.00
CANNON, LeGrand B.   Personal Reminiscences of the Rebellion.
    1895   New York   75.00
CANNON, Newton   The Reminiscences of Sergeant _____, edited by
    Campbell H. Brown.   Wraps.
    1963   Franklin   30.00
CAPERS, Ellison   An Address on Memorial Day, May 20, 1890
    Greenville, S.C.   Wraps.
    1890   Greenville, SC   25.00
CAPERS, Ellison   South Carolina. See: Confederate Millitary His-
    tory, Vol. V (Vol. VI, 1987 reprint ed.).
CAPERS, Gerald M.   Occupied City, New Orleans Under the Federals
    1862-1865.
    1965   K Y   17.50
CAPERS, Gerald M.   Stephen A. Douglas Defender of the Union.
    1959   Boston   10.00
CAPERS, Henry D.   The Life and Times of C. G. Memminger.
    1893   Richmond   100.00
CAPERS, Walter B.   The Soldier-Bishop, Ellison Capers.
    1912   New York   125.00
CAPPS, Claudius Meade   The Blue and the Gray, Best Poems of the
    Civil War.
    1943   Boston   25.00
Captain Raphael Semmes and the C.S.S. Alabama.   Wraps.
    1968   Washington, DC   4.00
Captain Walter Mason Dickinson.
    1898   Amherst, ME   30.00
Captured Battle Flags.   Wraps.
    1888   n.p.   40.00
CARDOZO, J. N.   Reminiscences of Charleston.   Wraps.
    1866   Charleston   75.00
CARLETON   See: COFFIN, Charles Carleton.

CARLEY, Kenneth   Minnesota in the Civil War.
    1961   Minneapolis   30.00
CARLEY, Kenneth   The Sioux Uprising of 1862.   Wraps.
    1979   St. Paul 8.00
CARMAN, Harry J. and LUTHIN, R. H.   Lincoln and the Patronage.
    1943   New York   25.00
    1964   Gloucester, MA   20.00
    1964   New York   20.00
CARNAHAN, J. W.   Manual of the Civil War and Key to the Grand Army of the Republic.
    1899   Washington, DC   25.00
CARNAHAN, James R.   Camp Morton.   Wraps.
    1892   Indianapolis   50.00
CARNEGIE, D.   Lincoln the Unknown.
    1932   New York   15.00
    1938   New York   10.00
Carolina Rifle Club, The Presentation of the Battle Flag of the Tenth Regiment, S.C.V., C.S.A. June 12, 1875.   Wraps.
    1875   Charleston   50.00
CARPENTER, F. B.   Six Months at the White House with Abraham Lincoln.
    1866   New York   30.00
    1867   20.00
CARPENTER, George N.   History of the 8th Regiment Vermont Volunteers 1861-1865.
    1886   Boston   100.00
CARPENTER, Jesse T.   The South as a Conscious Minority 1789-1861.
    1963   Gloucester, MA   15.00
CARPENTER, John A.   Sword and Olive Branch   Oliver Otis Howard.
    1964   Pittsburg   35.00
CARPENTER, Kinchen Jahu   War Diary of _____ Company I, Fiftieth North Carolina Regiment War Between the States 1861-65, prepared by Mrs. Julie Carpenter Williams. Wraps.
    1955   Rutherfordton, NC   50.00
CARPENTER, Louis H.   Record of the Military Service of Brig.Gen. Louis Henry Carpenter . . . 1861 to 1899.
    1903   Philadelphia   Ltd.   60.00
CARPENTER, Stephen D.   Logic of History . . . Results of Slavery Agitation.
    1864   Madison, WI   110.00
CARR, Clark E.   Lincoln at Gettysburg, An Address.
    1906   Chicago   20.00
CARR, Lucien   Missouri: A Bone of Contention.
    n.d.   Boston   25.00
CARRINGTON, Henry B.   General Regulations for the Military Forces of Ohio with the Laws Pertinent Thereto.
    1861   Columbus   30.00
CARRISON, D. J.   The Navy from Wood to Steel, 1860-1890.
    1965   New York   25.00
CARROLL, Anna Ella   Miss Carroll's Claim Before Congress in Connection with the Tennessee Campaign of 1862.
    (1873)   n.p.   75.00

CARROLL, Anna Ella   The Union of the States.   Wraps.
   1856   Boston   25.00
CARROLL, Daniel B.   Henri Mercier and the American Civil War.
   1971   Princeton, NJ   20.00
CARROLL, Gordon, edited by   The Post Reader of Civil War Stories.
   1958   New York   10.00
CARROLL, J. E.   An Autobiography.
   1899   Greenville, PA   55.00
CARROLL, John F.   A Brief History of New York's Famous Seventh Regiment.
   1961   New York   40.00
CARROLL, John M.   Custer in Texas: An Interrupted Narrative.
   1975   30.00
CARROLL, John M.   List of Staff Officers of the Confederate States Army. 1861-1865.
   1983   New York   25.00
CARROLL, John M.   List of Field Officers, Regiments and Battalions in the Confederate States Army. 1861-1865.
   1983   New York   25.00
CARRUTHERS, Olive   Lincoln's Other Mary.
   1946   New York   5.00
CARSE, Robert   Blockade, The Civil War at Sea.
   1958   New York   25.00
CARSE, Robert   Department of the South: Hilton Head Island in the Civil War.
   1961   Columbia, SC   50.00
   1981   17.50
CARSON, James Petigru   Life, Letters & Speeches of James Louis Petigru.
   1920   Washington, DC   50.00
CARTER, Dan T.   When the War Was Over: The Failure of Self-Reconstruction in the South, 1865-1867.
   1985   Baton Rouge   28.00
   1985   Baton Rouge   Wraps 13.00
CARTER, Hodding   The Angry Scar, The Story of Reconstruction.
   1959   New York   25.00
CARTER, Hodding   Their Words Were Bullets, The Southern Press in War, Reconstruction, and Peace.
   1969   Athens, GA   17.00
CARTER, Howell   A Cavalryman's Reminiscences of the Civil War.
   1900   New Orleans   200.00
   1979   Baton Rouge   15.00
CARTER, Robert Goldthwaite   Four Brothers in Blue.
   1913   Washington, DC   400.00
   1978   Austin   40.00
   1979   30.00
CARTER, Samuel, III   The Final Fortress: The Campaign for Vicksburg 1862-1863.
   1980   New York   20.00
   1988   Wilmington, NC   25.00

CARTER, Samuel, III   The Last Cavaliers, Confederate and Union
    Cavalry in the Civil War.
    1979   New York   20.00
CARTER, Samuel, III   The Riddle of Dr. Mudd.
    1974   New York   15.00
CARTER, Samuel, III   The Siege of Atlanta 1864.
    1973   New York   25.00
    Recent reprint   25.00
CARTER, W. H.   Old Army Sketches.
    1906   Baltimore   35.00
CARTER, William Harding   From Yorktown to Santiago with the Sixth
    U.S. Cavalry.
    1990   Austin, TX 24.95
CARTER, William Harding   Life of Lieutenant General Chaffee.
    1917   Chicago   75.00
CARTER, William Harding   The 6th Regiment of Cavalry U.S.A.
    (c.1890) n.p.   50.00
CARTER, William Randolph   History of the 1st Regiment of Tennessee
    Volunteer Cavalry.
    1902   Knoxville   250.00
    1984   22.00
CARTLAND, Fernando G.   Southern Heroes or the Friends in War
    Time.
    1895   Cambridge 50.00
    1897   Poughkeepsie   40.00
CARTNELL, Thomas Kemp   Shenandoah Valley Pioneers and Their
    Descendants.
    n.d.   n.p.   40.00
CARVER, Willard   Fourteenth Regt. Maine Infantry. Roster of Sur-
    vivors.
    1892   n.p.   40.00
CARY, Thomas   The Life and Letters of Robert Lewis Babney.
    1903   Richmond   80.00
CASADA, James A.   History of the 48th Virginia Infantry, Hist. Soc. of
    Washington Co. Wraps.
    1969   Abingdon   15.00
The Case of the Great Britain as Laid before the Tribunal of Arbitration,
    convened at Geneva. . . . 3 Vols.
    1872   Washington, DC   150.00
CASE, Ervin T.   Battle of the Mine. Wraps.
    1879   Providence   Ltd.   50.00
CASE, Lynn M., edited by   French Opinion on the United States and
    Mexico 1860-1867.
    1936   New York and London   30.00
    1969   20.00
CASE, Lynn M. and SPENCER, Warren F.   The United States and France:
    Civil War Diplomacy.
    1970   Philadelphia   25.00
CASEY, Silas   U.S. Infantry Tactics for the Instruction Exercise and
    Maneuvres of the United States Infantry. 3 Vols.
    1862   Philadelphia   150.00

1863   New York   150.00
1985   45.00

CASH, W. T.   History of the Democratic Party in Florida; Including Biographical Sketches of Prominent Florida Democrats.
1936   Tallahassee   20.00

CASKEY, Willie Malvin   Secession and Restoration of Louisiana.
1938   Louisiana   40.00

CASKIE, J.   Life and Letters of Matthew Fontaine Maury . . . The Pathfinder of the Seas.
1928   Richmond   50.00

CASLER, John O.   Four Years in the Stonewall Brigade.
1893   Guthrie, OK   400.00
1906   Girard, KS   350.00
1951   Marietta   35.00
1971   Dayton   edited by James I. Robertson, Jr.   20.00
1971   Dayton   Ltd. and signed   75.00
1982   Dayton   25.00

CASSIDY, J. M.   Civil War Cinema: A Pictorial History of Hollywood and the War Between the States.   Wraps.
1986   Missoula   10.00

CASSIDY, Vincent H. and SIMPSON, Amos E.   Henry Watkins Allen of Louisiana.
1964   Baton Rouge   10.00

CASSIDY, Vincent H. and SIMPSON, Amos E.   The Traveling Man, the Life Story of Henry Watkins Allen.
1967   Baton Rouge   20.00

CASSO, E. J.   Francis T. Nicholls: A Biographical Tribute.
1987   Thibodaux   20.00

CASSON, Henry   "Uncle Jerry." Life of Gen. Jeremiah M. Rush.
1895   Madison, WI   30.00

CASTEL, Albert   A Frontier State at War: Kansas 1861-1865.
1958   Ithaca, NY   25.00
1979   17.50

CASTEL, Albert   General Sterling Price and the Civil War in the West.
1968   Baton Rouge   50.00

CASTEL, Albert   William Clarke Quantrill. His Life and Times.
1962   New York   30.00

CASTLE, Henry A.   The Army Mule and Other War Sketches.
1898   Indianapolis   45.00

CASTLEMAN, Alfred L.   The Army of the Potomac, Behind the Scenes.
1863   Milwaukee   100.00

CASTLEMAN, John B.   Active Service. 2nd Kentucky Cavalry, Conf.
1917   Louisville, KY   175.00

CASTLEMON, Harry   Frank Before Vicksburg.
1866   40.00
(c.1920)   Chicago   20.00

CASTLEMON, Harry   Frank on the Lower Mississippi.
1868   Philadelphia   20.00

CASTLEMON, Harry   Marcy the Blockade-Runner.
1891   Philadelphia   35.00

CASTLEN, Harriet Gift   Hope Bids Me Onward.
1945   GA   20.00

A Catalog of the Alfred Whital Stern Collection of Lincolniana in the Library of Congress.
    1960   Washington, DC   50.00

Catalog of the 6th, 7th, 8th, 9th, 10th, and 11th Regiments of Infantry, 1st Light Battery and 1st Battalion Cavalry, Connecticut Vols. 1861. Wraps.
    1862   Hartford   30.00

A Catalogue of Brady's Photographic Views of the Civil War. Wraps.
    n.d.   Watkins Glen, NY   15.00

Catalogue of Connecticut Volunteer Organizations, Infantry, Cavalry, and Artillery.
    1864   75.00
    1869   Hartford   60.00

A Catalogue of Lincolniana with an Essay on Lincoln. Wraps.
    n.d.   New York   30.00

Catalogue of Rebel Flags Captured by Union Troops Since April 19, 1861. Wraps.
    n.d.   n.p.   40.00

Catalogue of the Officers and Cadets of the North Carolina Military Inst., Charlotte, North Carolina. First Session, 1859-60. Wraps.
    1860   Charlotte   125.00

Catalogue of the Officers and Members of the Henry County Regiment, Being the 112th Regiment Illinois Volunteers. Wraps.
    1862   Geneseo   125.00

Catalogue of the 12th and 13th Regiments Connecticut Volunteers. Wraps.
    1862   Hartford   35.00

Catalogue of Valuable Miscellaneous Books & Pamphlets Relating to American History, Southern Confederacy, Scarce Trials, etc. Wraps.
    1876   Philadelphia   40.00

CATE, Wirt Armistead   Lucius Q. C. Lamar: Secession and Reunion.
    1935   Chapel Hill, NC   60.00
    1969   20.00

CATE, Wirt Armistead, edited by   Two Soldiers: The Campaign Diaries of Thomas J. Key, CSA Dec. 7, 1863-May 7, 1865 and Robert J. Campbell, USA, Jan. 1, 1864-July 21, 1864.
    1938   Chapel Hill, NC   75.00

CATHEY, James H.   Truth Is Stranger than Fiction.
    1899   n.p.   45.00
    1939   Canton, NC entitled The Genesis of Lincoln   40.00

CATTON, Bruce   America Goes to War.
    1958   Middletown, CT 20.00
    1966   20.00
    1981   10.00

CATTON, Bruce   The Army of the Potomac.
    Vol. 1   Mr. Lincoln's Army   15.00
    Vol. 2   Glory Road   15.00
    Vol. 3   A Stillness at Appomattox   15.00
    1962   New York   3 Vols.   30.00
    v.d.   Odd volumes   30.00
    1977   65.00

CATTON, Bruce   Banners at Shenandoah.
    1955   New York   15.00

CATTON, Bruce   A Bibliography of the American Civil War.   Wraps.
    1962   New York   10.00
CATTON, Bruce   The Centennial History of the Civil War.
    Vol. 1   The Coming Fury   25.00
    Vol. 2   Terrible Swift Sword   25.00
    Vol. 3   Never Call Retreat   25.00
    1961-65 Garden City, NY   3 Vols.   35.00
    v.d.   Odd volumes   15.00 each
CATTON, Bruce   Gettysburg: The Final Fury.
    1974   Garden City, NY   Boxed   25.00
CATTON, Bruce   Grant Moves South.
    1960   Boston   20.00
    1960   Boston   Wraps   14.00
CATTON, Bruce   Grant Takes Command.
    1969   Boston   20.00
CATTON, Bruce   The Meaning of the Civil War.   Wraps.
    1961   Chicago   15.00
CATTON, Bruce   Prefaces to History.
    1970   Garden City, NY   20.00
CATTON, Bruce   Reflections on the Civil War.
    1981   Garden City, NY   20.00
CATTON, Bruce   This Hallowed Ground The Story of the Union Side of
    the Civil War.
    1956   Garden City, NY   20.00
CATTON, Bruce   U. S. Grant and the American Military Tradition.
    1954   Boston   20.00
CATTON, Bruce   Waiting for the Morning Train An American Boyhood.
    1972   Garden City, NY   46.00
CATTON, Bruce   War Lords of Washington.
    1969   New York   7.00
CATTON, Bruce and KETCHUM, Richard, edited by   American
    Heritage Picture History of the Civil War.
    1960   New York 2 Vols. Boxed   30.00
    1960   New York 1 Vol. ed.   20.00
    1982   18.00
CATTON, William and CATTON, Bruce   Two Roads to Sumter.
    1963   New York 10.00
    1971   Wraps 6.00
CAUBLE, Frank P.   Biography of Wilmer McLean, May 3, 1814 - June
    5, 1882.
    1987   10.00
CAUBLE, Frank P.   The Surrender Proceedings, April 9, 1865, Appo-
    mattox Court House.
    1987   10.00
CAUTHEN, Charles E., edited by   Family Letters of Three Wade Hamp-
    tons 1782-1901.
    1953   Columbia, SC   40.00
CAUTHEN, Charles E., edited by   Journals of the South Carolina Execu-
    tive Councils of 1861 and 1862.
    1956   Columbia, SC   35.00

CAUTHEN, Charles E.　　South　Carolina　Goes　to　War　1860-1865.
　　Wraps.
　　1950　　Chapel Hill, NC　　40.00
CAVADA, Frederick F.　　Libby Life.
　　1864　　Philadelphia　　60.00
　　1865　　Philadelphia　　55.00
CAVANAGH, Michael　　Memoirs of Gen. Thomas Francis Meagher,
　　Comprising the Leading Events of His Career. . .
　　1892　　75.00
CAVANAUGH, Michael, et al, edited by　　76th Regiment Pennsylvania
　　Volunteer Infantry (Keystone Zouaves)　　The Personal Recollections,
　　1861-1865 of Sergeant John A. Porter.
　　1988　　Wilmington, NC　　25.00
CAVANAUGH, Michael and MARVEL, W.　　The Petersburg Campaign.
　　The Battle of the Crater: The Horrid Pit June 25-August 6, 1864.
　　1989　　Lynchburg Ltd.　　16.95
CAVE, Robert Catlett　　The Men in Gray.
　　1911　　Nashville, TN　　35.00
CAVELYN, Edward　　Memories of Some Courageous Southerners Before
　　and After the Civil War.
　　1940　　Boston　　65.00
Celebration of the 100th Anniversary of the Birth of Admiral Raphael
　　Semmes C.S.N. Montgomery, Alabama Sept. 27, 1898.　Wraps.
　　n.d.　　n.p.　　25.00
Century Magazine.　See Appendix: Magazines
The Century War Book.
　　1894　　New York　　75.00
　　1978　　New York　　30.00
Ceremonies and Reenactment of the One Hundredth Anniversary of the Sec-
　　ond Inauguration of Abraham Lincoln.
　　1967　　Washington, DC　　15.00
Ceremonies at Dedication of Monument of the Eighth Penna. Cavalry Regi-
　　ment at Gettysburg, September 1, 1890, with Historical Sketch of Regi-
　　ment. Wraps.
　　n.d.　　n.p.　　125.00
Ceremonies at the Dedication of the Soldiers' Monument in West Roxbury.
　　Wraps.
　　1871　　Boston　　20.00
Ceremonies at the Unveiling of the South Carolina Monument on the
　　Chickamauga Battlefield, May 27, 1901.　Wraps.
　　n.d.　　n.p.　　35.00
Ceremonies Attending the Presentation and Unveiling of the North Carolina
　　Memorial on the Battlefield of Gettysburg, Wednesday, July 3, 1929.
　　Wraps.
　　(1929)　n.p.　　35.00
Ceremonies Connected with the Inauguration of the Mausoleum and the
　　Unveiling of the Recumbent Figure of General Robert Edward Lee, at
　　Washington and Lee University. Wraps.
　　1883　　Richmond　　25.00

CHACE, Elizabeth Buffum and LOVELL, Lucy Buffum   Two   Quaker
   Sisters from the Original Diaries.
   1937   New York   40.00
CHADWICK, A. G.   Soldier's Record of the Town of St. Johnsbury,
   Vermont.
   1883   30.00
CHADWICK, French Ensor   Causes of the Civil War.
   1906   New York   10.00
CHAMBERLAIN, Joshua L.   Address of Gen. Joshua L. Chamberlain at
   the Dedication of the Maine Monuments, Battlefield of Gettysburg,
   October 3, 1889.   Wraps.
   1898   Portland   90.00
CHAMBERLAIN, Joshua L.   Five Forks.   Wraps.
   1902   75.00
CHAMBERLAIN, Joshua L.   Honor Answering Honor.
   1965   Brunswick, ME   30.00
CHAMBERLAIN, Joshua L.   The Passing of the Armies.
   1915   New York   185.00
   1974   Dayton   40.00
   1981   Dayton   30.00
   1986   Dayton   30.00
CHAMBERLAIN, W. P.   Memorandum Book of _____, 2nd Lt. Co. A,
   23rd Ohio Volunteer Infantry July 9 1863 to July 25, 1863.
   n.d.   n.p.   300.00
CHAMBERLAINE, William W.   Memoirs of the Civil War.
   1912   Washington, DC   600.00
CHAMBERLAYNE, Edwin H., Jr., compiled by   Record of the Richmond City and Henrico County Virginia Troops, Confederate States
   Army. Series 1-10.
   1879   Richmond   750.00
   Individual volumes   75.00 each
CHAMBERLAYNE, Edwin H., Jr.   War History and Roll of the Richmond
   Fayette Artillery, 38th Virginia Battalion Artillery.   Wraps.
   1883   Richmond   250.00
CHAMBERLAYNE, John Hampden   Ham Chamberlayne - Virginian
   Letters and Papers of an Artillery Officer in the War . . . 1861-1865,
   introduction and notes by his son.
   1932   Richmond Ltd.   100.00
CHAMBERLIN, George E.   Letters of George E. Chamberlin.
   1883   Springfield, IL   60.00
CHAMBERLIN, Thomas   History of the 150th Regiment Pennsylvania
   Volunteers . . . Bucktail Brigade.
   1895   Philadelphia   130.00
   1905   Philadelphia   110.00
   1980   25.00
   1986   25.00
CHAMBERLIN, William Henry   History of the Eighty-first Regiment
   Ohio Infantry Volunteers During the War of the Rebellion.
   1865   Cincinnati   150.00
CHAMBERS, H. A.   Civil War Diary of Captain Henry A. Chambers
   and Biographical Sketch, by Selby A. Daniels, edited by T. H. Pearce.
   1983   Wendell, NC   25.00

CHAMBERS, Lenoir   "Stonewall" Jackson. 2 Vols.
    1959   New York   Boxed   75.00
    1988   Wilmington, NC   60.00
CHAMBERS, Lenoir   The Whole Jackson: A Lecture Delivered in Richmond, VA, at the Stonewall Jackson Commemorative Dinner, May 1, 1963. Wraps.
    1963   Richmond   25.00
CHAMBERS, Robert W.   Ailsa Paige.
    1914   New York   10.00
CHAMBERS, Robert W.   Secret Service Operator 13.
    1934   New York   10.00
CHAMBERS, Robert W.   Smith's Battery.
    1898   New York   20.00
CHAMBERS, Robert W.   Special Messenger.
    1909   New York   10.00
CHAMBRUN, the Marquis Adolphe de   Impressions of Lincoln and the Civil War. Translated from the French by General Adelbert de Chambrun.
    1952   New York   10.00
CHANCE, Joseph   The Second Texas Infantry. From Shiloh to Vicksburg.
    1984   20.00
Chancellorsville Source Book. A Compilation of Historical Material Concerning the Campaign and Battle of Chancellorsville, 1863.
    1937   Fort Leavenworth   250.00
CHANDLER, Melbourne C.   Of Garry Owen in Glory, The History of the 7th U.S. Cavalry.
    1960   50.00
CHANNING, Steven A.   Crisis of Fear, Secession in South Carolina.
    1970   New York   20.00
CHANNING, W. E.   Slavery.
    1835   Boston   50.00
CHAPIN, Louis N.   A Brief History of the Thirty-fourth Regiment, N.Y.S.V.
    1903   New York   80.00
CHAPMAN, Horatio Dana   Civil War Diary.
    1929   Hartford   60.00
CHAPMAN, John Jay   William Lloyd Garrison.
    1913   New York   10.00
    1921   10.00
CHAPMAN, Thomas   False Reconstruction: or, The Slavery That Is Not Abolished. Wraps.
    1876   Saxonville, MA   20.00
CHARLES, Edwin F. and CHARLES, J. E., compiled by   Henry Fitzgerald Charles Civil War Record 1862-1865. Wraps.
    1969   Middleburg, PA   30.00
CHARLES, W. T.   Recollections of a Christmas During "The War" (1862-1863). Wraps.
    1959   (Montgomery)   50.00
CHARNWOOD, Lord   Abraham Lincoln.
    1917   New York   25.00

Charter, By-laws, Rules and Regulations Governing the Home for Needy Confederate Women. Wraps.
1910   Richmond   8.00

Charter, Constitution and By-Laws of the Veteran Corps, of the First Regiment Infantry, N.G. of Pa. Wraps.
1881   Philadelphia   40.00

CHASE, Edward   Memorial Life of General William Tecumseh Sherman.
1891   Chicago   25.00

CHASE, J. J.   The Charge at Day-Break: Scenes and Incidents at the Battle of the Mine Explosion near Petersburg, Va., July 30th, 1864. Wraps.
1875   Lewiston   75.00

CHASE, John A.   History of the Fourteenth Ohio Regiment O.V.V.I.
1881   Toledo   150.00

CHASE, John F.   A Short Sketch of the Battle of Gettysburg. Wraps.
n.d.   n.p.   50.00

CHASE, Peter S.   A Reunion Greeting, Together with an Historical Sketch . . . of Co. I, 2nd Regiment Vermont Volunteers.
1891   Brattleboro   50.00

CHASE, Philip H.   Basic Classification and Listing, Confederate States of America Paper Money 1861-1865. Wraps.
1936   n.p.   40.00

CHASE, Philip H.   Confederate Treasury Notes.
1947   Philadelphia   30.00

CHASE, Philip S.   Battery F, First Regiment Rhode Island Light Artillery in the Civil War, 1861-1865.
1892   Providence   Ltd.   120.00

CHASE, Salmon P.   Diary and Correspondence . . . . In: American Historical Society Annual Report for 1902, Vol. 2.
1903   Washington, DC   35.00

CHASE, Salmon P.   Inside Lincoln's Cabinet   The Civil War Diaries of _____, edited by David Donald.
1954   New York   25.00

CHASE, William C.   Story of Stonewall Jackson.
1901   Atlanta   250.00

Cheat Mountain; or, Unwritten Chapter of the Late War. By a Member of the Bar, Fayetteville, Tenn. (Carrigan, C. H. or Carrigan, Joseph G.)
1885   Nashville   750.00

CHEEK, Philip and POINTON, Mair   History of the Sauk County Riflemen known as Company "A" Sixth Wisconsin Veteran Volunteer Infantry 1861-1865.
1909   Madison   175.00
1984   25.00
1985   27.00

CHENAULT, John Cabell   Old Cane Springs: A Story of the War Between the States in Madison County, Kentucky, edited by Jonathan T. Dorris.
1936   Louisville   50.00
1937   Louisville   50.00

CHENERY, William H.   The Fourteenth Regiment Rhode Island Heavy Artillery (Colored) in the War to Preserve the Union.
1898   Providence 90.00
1969   New York   20.00
CHENEY, Newel   History of the Ninth Regiment, New York Volunteer Cavalry.
1901   Jamestown   110.00
CHESHIRE, Joseph B.   The Church in the Confederate States.
1912   New York   50.00
1914   New York   50.00
CHESNEY, C. C.   A Military View of Recent Campaigns in Virginia and Maryland.
1863   London 200.00
1864-65 London 2 Vols. 200.00
CHESNUT, Mary Boykin   A Diary from Dixie.
1905   New York   75.00
1905   London 50.00
1906   New York   30.00
1949   Boston   edited by Ben Ames Williams   30.00
1980   17.00
CHESTERMAN, W. D.   Guide to Richmond and the Battle-Fields. Wraps.
1881   Richmond   30.00
1890   Richmond   30.00
1891   Richmond   30.00
CHETLAIN, Augustus L.   Recollections of Seventy Years.
1899   Galena   80.00
CHEW, R. P.   Stonewall Jackson.   Wraps.
1912   Lexington, VA   300.00
CHIDSEY, Donald Barr   The Gentleman from New York: A Life of Roscoe Conkling.
1935   New Haven   40.00
CHILD, William   History of the Fifth Regiment New Hampshire Volunteers.
1893   Bristol 110.00
1988   35.00
CHILDE, Edward Lee   Le General Lee. Sa Vie Et Ses Campagnes. Wraps.
1874   Paris   75.00
CHILDS, George W.   Recollections of General Grant.
1890   Philadelphia   25.00
CHIPMAN, N. P.   The Tragedy of Andersonville Trial of Capt. Henry Wirz.
1911   Sacramento   60.00
1911   San Francisco   60.00
CHITTENDEN, Lucius E.   Lincoln and the Sleeping Sentinel.
1909   New York   15.00
CHITTENDEN, Lucius E.   Personal Reminiscences 1840-1890.
1893   New York   30.00
CHITTENDEN, Lucius E.   Recollections of President Lincoln and His Administration.
1891   New York   20.00

CHITTENDEN, Lucius E.   A Report of the Debates and Proceedings in the Secret Sessions of the Conference Convention . . . 1861.
  1864   New York   50.00
CHITTUM, C. H.   The Story of Finding the Coffin in Which Gen. Robert E. Lee Was Afterward Buried.
  (c.1928) Lexington   15.00
The Christian Officer. Wraps.
  n.d.   Charleston   100.00
CHRISTIAN, Frances A. and MASSIE, Susanne W., edited by   Homes and Gardens in Old Virginia.
  1931   Richmond   30.00
CHRISTIAN, George Llewellyn   Abraham Lincoln   An Address Delivered Before R. E. Lee Camp, No. 1, Confederate Veterans. . . . Wraps.
  1909   Richmond   30.00
CHRISTIAN, George Llewellyn   The Confederate Cause and Its Defenders: An Address. Wraps.
  1898   Richmond   25.00
CHRISTIAN, George Llewellyn   Official Report of the History Committee of the Grand Camp, C.V., Department of Virginia. On the Treatment and Exchange of Prisoners. Wraps.
  1902   Pulaski, VA   50.00
CHRISTIAN, George Llewellyn   Sketch of the Origin and Erection of the Confederate Memorial Institute at Richmond, Virginia. Wraps.
  (c.1925) n.p.   30.00
CHRISTEN, W., et al   Stonewall Regiment - A History of the 17th Michigan Volunteer Infantry Regiment.
  1986   Detroit 9.00
A Chronology of Indiana in the Civil War. Wraps.
  1965   Indianapolis   15.00
CHURCH, William C.   Life of John Ericsson. 2 Vols.
  1890   New York   60.00
  1891   New York   45.00
  1906   New York   40.00
  1911   n.p.   1 Vol ed.   25.00
CHURCH, William C.   Ulysses S. Grant and the Period of Preservation and Reconstruction.
  1897   New York   15.00
  1926   Garden City, NY   10.00
CHURCHILL, Franklin Hunter   Sketch of the Life of Bvt. Gen. Sylvester Churchill Inspector General U. S. Army.
  1888   New York   30.00
CHURCHILL, Winston, Sir   The American Civil War.
  1961   New York   10.00
CHURCHILL, Winston, Sir   The Crisis.
  1909   New York   15.00
  1929   Canada 10.00
CIST, Henry M.   The Army of the Cumberland. See: Campaigns of the Civil War.
Civil and Mexican Wars, 1861, 1846. See: Papers of the Military Historical Society of Massachusetts, No. 13.
The Civil War A Centennial Exhibition of Eyewitness Drawings. Wraps.
  1961   Washington, DC   15.00

The Civil War A Pictorial Guide to the Virginia Peninsula. Compiled and published by the Junior League of Hampton Roads, Va. Wraps.
  1961   Hampton Roads, VA   10.00
Civil War and Miscellaneous Papers. See: **Papers of the Military Historical Society of Massachusetts, No. 14.**
The Civil War and the Confederacy. Wraps.
  1973   New York   40.00
Civil War Battles in Winchester and Frederick County, Virginia, 1861-1865. Wraps.
  1961   Boyce   15.00
Civil War Biographical Album. (Consisting of reproductions of 50 of the little pamphlets in the "A Short History of W. Duke, Sons & Co." series.) Wraps.
  n.d.   n.p.   300.00
Civil War Centennial Commission May 1958, Vol. 1, No. 1 - June 1965, Vol. 8, No. 6 - 86 numbers.
  1965   Washington, DC   100.00
The Civil War Centennial: A Report to the Congress.
  1968   Washington, DC   15.00
Civil War History, a Quarterly Journal. Published by the Library of the State University of Iowa, Vol. I, No. 1 (March 1955) - Vol. XIV, No. 2, including cumulative index. Publication continued by Kent State University Press.
  1955-70   300.00
  Individual issues   5.00 each
  Later issues   3.00 each
The Civil War in Virginia. Wraps.
  1961   n.p.   25.00
Civil War Manuscript Songbook.
  n.d.   125.00
Civil War Maps in the National Archives.
  1964   Washington, DC   20.00
Civil War Medal of Honor Winners from Illinois. Wraps.
  1962   n.p.   10.00
Civil War Naval Chronology 1861-1865.
  1961-66 Washington, DC 6 parts Wraps 50.00
  1971   Washington, DC   40.00
Civil War Papers Read Before the Commandery of the State of Massachusetts, Mollus. 2 Vols.
  1900   Boston   100.00
Civil War Recollections of James Lemuel Clark, edited by L. D. Clark.
  1984   13.00
The Civil War Reminiscences of General M. Jeff Thompson.
  1988   24.95
Civil War Sketches and Incidents, Nebraska Commandery, Mollus. Vol. I (all pub).
  1902   Omaha   125.00
Civil War Times Illustrated (Complete run from the newspaper type issued in 1959-1979)
  1959-1979   400.00
CLACK, Louise   **Our Refugee Household.**
  1866   New York   75.00

CLAIBORNE, John Herbert   Personal Reminiscences of the "Last Days of Lee and His Paladins." Wraps.
(1890) Petersburg   15.00

CLAIBORNE, John Herbert   Seventy-five Years in Old Virginia.
1904   New York   100.00

CLAPP, Margaret   Forgotten First Citizen: John Bigelow.
1947   Boston   15.00

CLARE, Virginia   Thunder and Stars: The Life of Mildred Rutherford.
1941   Oglethorpe, GA   25.00

CLARK, Allen C.   Abraham Lincoln in the National Capital.
1925   Washington, DC   25.00

CLARK, Allen C.   Abraham Lincoln, the Mericful President, the Pardon of the Sleeping Sentinel.
1927   Washington, DC   25.00

CLARK, C.   Decoying the Yanks, Jackson's Valley Campaign.
1984   10.00

CLARK, C. W., Jr.   My Grandfather's Diary of the War, Carrol H. Clark, Co. I, 16th Regiment, Tenn. Vols. C.S.A.   Wraps.
1963   n.p.   40.00

CLARK, Charles T.   Opdycke Tigers 125th O.V.I. a History of the Regiment.
1895   Columbus   200.00

CLARK, Douglas   Rhythmic Ramblings in Battle-Scarred Manassas. Wraps.
1905   Philadelphia   15.00

CLARK, Emmons   History of the Second Company of the Seventh Regiment N.Y.S. Militia. Vol. I (all pub.)
1864   New York   55.00

CLARK, Emmons   History of the Seventh Regiment of New York 1806-1889. 2 Vols.
1890   New York   110.00

CLARK, George   A Glance Backward.
(1914) Houston   60.00

CLARK, Harvey   My Experiences with Burnside's Expedition and 18th Army Corps.
1914   Gardner   75.00

CLARK, James H.   The Iron Hearted Regiment.
1865   Albany   75.00

CLARK, James I.   The Civil War of Private Cooke A Wisconsin Boy in the Union Army. Wraps.
1955   Madison   20.00

CLARK, James S.   Life in the Middle West. Reminiscences of J. S. Clark.
1916   Chicago   90.00

CLARK, John   The True Story of the Capture of Jeff. Davis. Wraps.
1910   n.p.   45.00

CLARK, Lewis H.   Military History of Wayne County, New York: The County In The Civil War.
1883   New York   100.00

CLARK, Orton S.   The One Hundred and Sixteenth Regiment of New York State Volunteers.
    1868   Buffalo   110.00

CLARK, Peter H.   The Black Brigade of Cincinnati; Being a Report of Its Labors and a Muster Roll of Its Members, etc.   Wraps.
    1864   Cincinnati   150.00
    1969   New York   20.00

CLARK, Rufus W.   The Heroes of Albany.
    1866   Albany   50.00
    1867   Albany   40.00

CLARK, Thomas D.   The Emerging South.
    1961   New York   20.00

CLARK, Thomas D.   Pleasant Hill in the Civil War.
    1972   Lexington   20.00

CLARK, Thomas D. and KIRWAN, A. D.   The South Since Appomattox, a Century of Regional Change.
    1967   Oxford   15.00

CLARK, Thomas D., edited by   Travels in the New South.   2 Vols.
    1962   Norman, OK   150.00

CLARK, Thomas D., edited by   Travels in the Old South   A Bibliography.   Vol 3.   The Ante Bellum South, 1825-1860.
    1959   Norman, OK   30.00

CLARK, Walter   Histories of the Several Regiments and Battalions from North Carolina in the Great War 1861-1865.   5 Vols.
    1901   Goldsboro, NC   700.00
    1982   Wendell, NC   300.00

CLARK, Walter   North Carolina at Gettysburg & Pickett's Charge   A Misnomer.   Wraps.
    1921   Raleigh   40.00

CLARK, Walter A.   Under the Stars and Bars of Memories or Four Years Service with the Oglethorpes.
    1900   Augusta   500.00
    1987   17.50

CLARK, William   History of Hampton Battery F, Independent Pennsylvania Light Artillery.
    1909   Akron, PA   100.00

CLARK, William H.   Poems and Sketches with Reminiscences of the "Old 34th."   Wraps.
    1890   South Framingham   40.00

CLARK, William H.   Reminiscences of the Thirty-fourth Regiment Mass. Vol. Infantry.
    1871   Holliston   75.00

CLARKE, Asia Booth   The Unlocked Book.
    1938   New York   25.00

CLARKE, George Herbert   Some Reminiscences and Early Letters of Sidney Lanier.   Wraps.
    1907   Macon, GA   30.00

CLARKE, H. C.   See: Confederate Imprints P-5260; P-5261.

CLARKE, O. P.   The Colonel of the 10th Cavalry   A Story of the War. Wraps.
    1891   Utica, NY   35.00

CLARKSON, Charles Ervine   "A Rose of Old Virginia."
     1927   Ft. Smith, AR   15.00
CLAVREUL, H.   Diary of Reverend H. Clavreul.   Wraps.
     1910   Waterbury   45.00
CLAY, Cassius Marcellus   The Life of Cassius Marcellus Clay.   Vol. I -
     all published.
     1886   Cincinnati   125.00
CLAY, Mrs.   See: CLAY-CLOPTON, Virginia
CLAY-CLOPTON, Virginia   A Belle of the Fifties, Memoirs of Mrs.
     Clay of Alabama, edited by Ada Sterling.
     1904   New York   50.00
     1905   New York   40.00
CLAYTON, Powell   The Aftermath of the Civil War in Arkansas.
     1915   New York   60.00
     1969   New York   30.00
CLAYTON, Victoria V.   White and Black Under the Old Regime.
     1899   Milwaukee   35.00
CLAYTON, W. F.   A Narrative of the Confederate States Navy.
     1910   Weldon, NC   500.00
CLEAVES, Freeman   Meade of Gettysburg.
     1960   Norman, OK   50.00
     1980   17.50
CLEAVES, Freeman   Rock of Chickamauga: Life of Gen. George H.
     Thomas.
     1948   Norman, OK   50.00
     1959   40.00
     1974   30.00
CLEMENCEAU, Georges   American Reconstruction.
     1928   New York   20.00
CLEMENTS, Bennett A.   Memoir of Jonathan Letterman, M.D., Surgeon
     United States Army and Medical Director of the Army of the Potomac.
     Wraps.
     1909   Washington, DC   30.00
CLEMMER, Mary   Ten Years in Washington   or Inside Life and
     Scenes in Our National Capital As a Woman Sees Them.
     1882   Hartford, CT   20.00
CLEMSON, Floride   A Rebel Came Home.
     1961   Columbia, SC   40.00
CLEVELAND, H. W.   Hints to Riflemen.
     1864   95.00
CLEVELAND, Henry   Alexander H. Stephens, In Public and Private.
     1866   Philadelphia   50.00
     1866   v.p.   40.00
     n.d.   Philadelphia   30.00
CLEVELAND, Mather   New Hampshire and the Civil War. Vol. I, Nos.
     1, 2, 3, 4. Wraps.
     1962-65 Concord   35.00
CLEVELAND, Mather   New Hampshire Fights the Civil War.
     1969   New London   35.00
CLIFFORD, Deborah P.   Mine Eyes Have Seen the Glory. A Biography
     of Julia Ward Howe.
     1979   25.00

CLIFFORD, Philip Greely   Nathan Clifford, Democrat (1803-1881).
    1922   New York   25.00
CLIFT, G. Glenn, edited by   The Private War of Lizzie Hardin.
    1963   Frankfort, KY   30.00
CLIFTON, William Baldwin   Libby and Andersonville, A True Sketch.
    1910   Indianapolis   90.00
CLOWES, Walter F.   The Detroit Light Guard.
    1900   Detroit   100.00
CLUETT, William W.   History of the 57th Regiment, Illinois Volunteer
    Infantry.
    1886   Princeton   110.00
Co. A, the Campaigns of the Forty-fifth Regt. Mass Vol. Mil., the Cadet
    Regiment.
    1882   75.00
COATSWORTH, S. S.   The Loyal People of the Northwest.
    1869   Chicago   60.00
COBB, Irvin S.   Red Likker.
    1929   New York   10.00
COCHIN, Augustin   The Results of Emancipation.
    1863   Boston   25.00
COCHRAN, Hamilton   Blockade Runners of the Confederacy.
    1958   Indianapolis   30.00
    1958   New York   30.00
COCHRANE, John   The War for the Union,   Memoir of _____.
    Wraps.
    (c.1886) n.p.   40.00
COCKRELL, Monroe F., edited by   The Lost Account of the Battle of
    Corinth and the Court Martial of Gen. Van Dorn.   Wraps.
    1955   Jackson   20.00
    1987   Wilmington, NC   20.00
COCKRELL, Monroe F.   Stonewall Jackson.   Wraps.
    1955   Evanston, IL   Ltd.   60.00
COCKRUM, William M.   History of the Underground Railroad: As It
    Was Conducted by the Anti-Saloon League.
    1915   Indiana   65.00
COCO, Gregory A.   On the Bloodstained Field: 130 Human Interest
    Stories of the Campaign and Battle of Gettysburg.   Wraps.
    1987   3.95
COCO, Gregory A.   On the Bloodstained Field, II: 132 More Human
    Interest Stories.   Wraps.
    1989   5.95
COCO, Gregory A.   A Vast Sea of Misery.   A History and Guide to the
    Union and Confederate Field Hospitals at Gettysburg, July 1-November
    20, 1863.
    1988   25.00
CODDINGTON, Edwin B.   The Gettysburg Campaign.
    1968   New York   45.00
    1979   Dayton Wraps   23.00
    1983   35.00
CODY, A. E.   History of the Tennessee Division United Daughters of the
    Confederacy.
    1946   75.00

COE, Hamlin Alexander   Mine Eyes Have Seen the Glory,   Combat Diaries of Union Sergeant Hamlin Alexander Coe.
1975   Rutherford, NJ   15.00
COFFIN, Charles Carleton   Abraham Lincoln.
1892   New York   15.00
COFFIN, Charles Carleton   Drum Beat of the Nation.
1888   New York   15.00
COFFIN, Charles Carleton   Following the Flag.
1892   Boston   15.00
COFFIN, Charles Carleton   Four Years of Fighting.
1866   Boston   30.00
1881   Boston   entitled   The Boys of '61 or Four Years of Fighting.
25.00
1888   20.00
v.d.   Boston   30.00
COFFIN, Charles Carleton   Freedom Triumphant.
1891   New York   15.00
COFFIN, Charles Carleton   Marching to Victory.
1889   New York   20.00
COFFIN, Charles Carleton   My Days and Nights on the Battlefield.
1864   Boston   25.00
COFFIN, Charles Carleton   Redeeming the Republic The Third Period of the War of the Rebellion in the Year 1864.
1890   New York   25.00
1898   New York   20.00
COFFIN, Charles Carleton   Stories of Our Soldiers.   War Reminiscences by "Carleton" and by Soldiers of New England. 2 Vols.
1893   Boston   50.00
COFFIN, George H.   Three Years in the Army.   Wraps.
1925   n.p.   100.00
COFFMAN, Edward M.   The Old Army, A Portrait of the American Army in Peace Time, 1784-1898.
1986   35.00
COGGIN, J. C.   Abraham Lincoln A North Carolinian With Proof.
1927   Gastonia, NC   40.00
COGGINS, Jack   Arms and Equipment of the Civil War.
1962   Garden City, NY   20.00
1983   20.00
1987   Wilmington, NC 12.95
COGLEY, Thomas S.   History of the Seventh Indiana Cavalry Volunteers.
1876   Laporte, Indiana   160.00
COGSWELL, Leander W.   History of the Eleventh New Hampshire Regiment Volunteer Infantry.
1891   Concord   85.00
COHEN, Stanley   The Civil War in West Virginia, A Pictorial History. Wraps.
1976   Missoula   10.00
1982   Missoula   10.00
1989   Missoula   8.95
COHEN, Stanley   Hands Across the Wall: The 50th and 75th Reunions of the Gettysburg Battle. Wraps.
1982   Charleston   6.00

COHN, D. A.   Jackson's Valley Campaign.   Wraps.
1986   Washington, DC   6.98
COIT, Margaret L.   John C. Calhoun   American Portrait.
1950   Boston   25.00
COKER, Elizabeth B.   La Belle.
1959   New York   15.00
COKER, James Lide   History of Company G., Ninth S. C. Regiment, Infantry S. C. Army and Company E, Sixth S. C. Regiment, Infantry, S. C. Army.
n.d. (reprint)   n.p.   20.00
1979   Westport, CT   15.00
COLE, Arthur Charles   The Era of the Civil War 1848-1870, Centennial History of Illinois.
1919   Springfield 30.00
1987   25.00
COLE, Arthur Charles   The Irrepressible Conflict 1850-1865.
1934   New York   20.00
COLE, E.   Journal of Three Years Service with the 26th Ohio Volunteer Infantry in the Great Rebellion, 1861-64.   Wraps.
1897   60.00
COLE, G. L.   Civil War Eyewitness: An Annotated Bibliography of Books and Articles, 1955-1986.
1988   Columbia   29.95
COLE, J. R.   The Life and Public Services of Winfield Scott Hancock Major General U.S.A.
1880   Cincinnati   30.00
COLE, Jacob Henry   Under Five Commanders: or, A Boy's Experiences with the Army of the Potomac.
1906   Paterson   85.00
COLEMAN, Ann Mary Butler   The Life of John J. Crittenden with Selections from his Correspondence and Speeches. 2 Vols.
1871   Philadelphia   50.00
COLEMAN, J. Winston, Jr.   Lexington During the Civil War.
1968   Lexington Boxed   30.00
COLEMAN, J. Winston, Jr.   Slavery Times in Kentucky.
1940   Chapel Hill, NC   75.00
COLEMAN, Kenneth, edited by   Athens, 1861-65, as Seen Through Letters in the University of Georgia Libraries.   Wraps.
1969   Athens   10.00
COLEMAN, Kenneth   Confederate Athens.
1967   Athens   25.00
COLEMAN, S. B.   A July Morning with the Rebel Ram Arkansas.   Wraps.
1890   Detroit   30.00
COLES, George   History of the Eleventh Penn. Vol. Cavalry. . . .
1902   Philadelphia 100.00
COLES, George   The South Goes North, Vol. III of Children of Crisis.
1967   Boston   20.00
1971   Boston   20.00
COLLIER, Mrs. B. W.   Representative Women of the South, 1861-1920.
Vol. I.
1920   100.00

COLLIER, Calvin L.   First In - Last Out, The Capitol Guards, Arkansas Brigade in the Civil War.
  1961   Little Rock, AR   50.00
COLLIER, Calvin L.   "They'll Do to Tie To!" The Story of the Third Regiment, Arkansas Infantry, C.S.A.
  1959   Little Rock, AR   35.00
  1988   27.95
COLLIER, Calvin L.   The War Child's Children, The Story of the Third Regiment Arkansas Cavalry, Confederate States Army.
  1965   Little Rock, AR   35.00
COLLINS, George K.   An Abbreviated Account of Certain Men of Onondaga County Who Did Service in the War of 1861-65 in the 149th New York Volunteer Regiment Infantry. Wraps.
  1928   Syracuse   50.00
COLLINS, George K.   Memoirs of the 149th Regiment, N. Y. Vol. Infantry.
  1891   Syracuse   165.00
COLLINS, Loren Warren   The Story of a Minnesotan.
  n.d.   n.p.   40.00
COLLINS, R. M.   Chapters from the Unwritten History of the War Between the States.
  1893   St. Louis   275.00
  1982   Dayton   30.00
  1988   25.00
COLLINS, Richard H.   Civil War Annals of Kentucky (1861-1865), edited by Hambleton Tapp (contained in Filson Club History Quarterly July 1961 Civil War Centennial Number). Wraps.
  1961   Louisville   30.00
COLLINS, William H.   Second Address to the People of Maryland. Wraps.
  1861   Baltimore   25.00
COLLIS, Charles H. T.   Letters and Testimony Presented by Mr. Collis Defending Himself Against Accusation Made to the Mollus as to His Military Record. Wraps.
  1891   New York   65.00
COLLIS, Septima M.   A Woman's War Record 1861-1865.
  1889   New York   60.00
  1892   New York   45.00
COLTON, Matthias Baldwin   Civil War Journal and Correspondence of _____, edited by Jessie S. Colton.
  1931   Philadelphia   Ltd.   200.00
COLTON, Ray C.   The Civil War in the Western Territories.
  1959   Norman, OK   40.00
  1984   Norman, OK   Wraps   8.95
  1989   Norman, OK   Wraps   8.95
COLTRANE, Daniel Branson   The Memoirs of Daniel Branson Coltrane, Co. I, 63rd Reg., N.C. Cavalry C.S.A.
  1956   Raleigh   75.00
COLVER, A.   Mr. Lincoln's Wife.
  1943   New York   15.00
  1965   10.00

COMMAGER, Henry Steele   The Blue and the Gray. 2 Vols.   Boxed.
    1950   Indianapolis   35.00
    1950   Indianapolis   2 Vols. in 1   25.00
    1982   10.00
COMMAGER, Henry Steele, edited by   Illustrated   History   of   the
    Civil War.
    1976   New York   40.00
    1984   15.00
Compilation of Official Documents Illustrative of the Organization of the
    Army of the United States from 1789 to 1876.
    1876   Washington, DC   60.00
A Compilation of the Messages and Papers of the Confederacy Including the
    Diplomatic Correspondence 1861-1865. 2 Vols.
    1905   Nashville   50.00
Complete History of Fairfield County, Ohio 1795-1876.
    1877   Columbus   100.00
Complete History of the 46th Illinois Veteran Infantry - 1861-1866.
    1866   Freeport   150.00
    1907   125.00
Complete Roster of the Eighth Regiment, New Hampshire Volunteers.
    (189-)   Concord   40.00
Comprehensive Sketch of the Battle of Manassas.   Wraps.
    1886   65.00
    1887   Washington, DC 45.00
Comprehensive Sketch of the Merrimac and Monitor Naval Battle.   Wraps.
    1886   New York   30.00
COMPTON, James R.   Andersonville. The Story of Man's Inhumanity
    to Man.
    1887   Des Moines   65.00
COMSTOCK, Daniel   Ninth Cavalry, One Hundred and Twenty-first
    Regiment, Indiana Volunteers. Wraps.
    1890   Richmond   65.00
A Concise History of the Civil War.   Wraps.
    1961   Harrisburg, PA   10.00
CONDON, William H.   Life of Major-General James Shields.
    1900   Chicago   40.00
CONERLY, Luke Ward   Pike County, Mississippi 1698-1876.
    1909   Nashville   120.00
The Confederacy, Including Southern Poetry, . . . : The Zorn Collection.
    Wraps.
    (1936)   New York   40.00
Confederate Americana.   Wraps.
    1968   New York   25.00
Confederate Centennial Studies   William   Stanley   Hoole,   editor-in-chief.
    27 titles.   Decorated stiff wraps.
    1956-1965   Tuscaloosa, AL   Ltd. to 450 copies   1500.00
    Individual Titles:
    (No. 1) COULTER, E. Merton   Lost Generation: The Life and Death
        of James Barrow, C.S.A.
        1956   Tuscaloosa, AL   40.00

(No. 2) **MONAGHAN**, Jay   **Swamp Fox of the Confederacy: The Life and Military Services of M. Jeff Thompson.**
1956   Tuscaloosa, AL   60.00

(No. 3) **SILVER**, James W.   **Confederate Morale and Church Propaganda.**
1957   Tuscaloosa, AL   40.00
1964   Gloucester   12.50

(No. 4) **HOOLE**, William Stanley   **Vizetelly Covers the Confederacy.**
1957   Tuscaloosa, AL   35.00

(No. 5) **NICHOLS**, James L.   **Confederate Engineers.**
1957   Tuscaloosa, AL   40.00
1987   Gaithersburg   18.00

(No. 6) **ANDERSON**, John Q.   **A Texas Surgeon in the CSA.**
1957   Tuscaloosa, AL   50.00

(No. 7) **JORDAN**, Weymouth T.   **Rebels in the Making: Planters' Conventions and Southern Propaganda.**
1958   Tuscaloosa, AL   35.00

(No. 8) **YATES**, Richard E.   **The Confederacy and Zeb Vance.**
1958   Tuscaloosa, AL   35.00

(No. 9) **SCHEIBERT**, Capt. Justus   **Seven Months in the Rebel States During the North American War, 1863.**
1958   Tuscaloosa, AL   Ltd.   35.00

(No. 10) **MONTGOMERY**, Horace   **Howell Cobb's Confederate Career.**
1959   Tuscaloosa, AL   Ltd.   25.00

(No. 11) **HOOLE**, William Stanley, edited by; introduction by Allen J. Going   **Reconstruction in West Alabama: The Memoirs of John L. Hunnicutt.**
1959   Tuscaloosa, AL   30.00

(No. 12) **JONES**, Mary Sharpe and **MALLARD**, Mary Jones, edited with prologue by Haskell Monroe   **Yankees A'Coming One Month's Experience During the Invasion of Liberty County, Georgia, 1864-1865.**
1959   Tuscaloosa, AL   Ltd.   30.00

(No. 13) **HESSELTINE**, William B.   **Lincoln's Plan of Reconstruction.**
1960   Tuscaloosa, AL   30.00
1963   Gloucester   10.00

(No. 14) **MOORE**, John Preston, introduction and edited by   **"My Ever Dearest Friend" The Letters of A. Dudley Mann to Jefferson Davis, 1869-1889.**
1960   Tuscaloosa, AL   Ltd.   35.00

(No. 15) **HANNA**, Alfred J. and **HANNA**, Kathryn Abbey   **Confederate Exiles in Venezuela.**
1960   Tuscaloosa, AL   35.00

(No. 16) **HOOLE**, William Stanley   **Alabama Tories The First Alabama Cavalry, USA, 1862-1865.**
1960   Tuscaloosa, AL   40.00

(No. 17) **DAVIS**, Charles S.   **Colin J. McRae: Confederate Financial Agent.**
1961   Tuscaloosa, AL   Ltd.   30.00

(No. 18) **KEENE**, Jesse L.   **The Peace Convention of 1861.**
1961   Tuscaloosa, AL   Ltd.   30.00

(No. 19) **JONES**, Wilbur Devereux   The Confederate Rams at Birkenhead: A Chapter in Anglo-American Relations.
　　1961　　Tuscaloosa, AL　　35.00
(No. 20) **HARRIS**, William C.   Leroy Pope Walker   Confederate
Secretary of War.
　　1962　　Tuscaloosa, AL　　30.00
(No. 21) **GIRARD**, Charles   A Visit to the Confederate States of America in 1863   Memoir Addressed to His Majesty Napoleon III.
　　1962　　Tuscaloosa, AL　　Ltd.　　35.00
(No. 22) **WHITE**, William W.   The Confederate Veteran.
　　1962　　Tuscaloosa, AL　　30.00
(No. 23) **PECQUET DU BELLET**, Paul   The Diplomacy of the Con-
federate Cabinet of Richmond and Its Agents Abroad: Being
Memorandum Notes Taken in Paris During the Rebellion of the
Southern States from 1861-1865.
　　1963　　Tuscaloosa, AL　　Ltd.　　25.00
(No. 24) **HARWELL**, Richard, edited by   A Confederate Marine: A
Sketch of Henry Lea Graves with Excerpts from the Graves Family
Correspondence, 1861-1865.
　　1963　　Tuscaloosa, AL　　30.00
(No. 25) **HENDERSON**, Dwight Franklin   The Private Journal of
Georgiana Gholson Walker   1862-1865.   With Selections from the
Post-War Years, 1865-1876.
　　1963　　Tuscaloosa, AL　　30.00
(No. 26) **HOOLE**, William Stanley   Lawley Covers the Confederacy.
　　1964　　Tuscaloosa, AL　　35.00
(No. 27) **SUMMERSELL**, Charles Grayson   The Cruise of CSS
Sumter.
　　1965　　Tuscaloosa, AL　　40.00
Confederate Chronicles of Tennessee, The War Governor.
　　Vol. I　　1986　　Wraps　　15.00
　　Vol. II　　1987　　Wraps　　15.00
　　Vol. III　1989　　Wraps　　15.00
**The Confederate Cruiser "Shenandoah"   Insurance Against Capture, and the
Geneva Award.** Wraps.
　　1873　　New York　　75.00
**The Confederate Field Manual for the Use of the Officers on Ordnance
Duty.**
　　1984　　Arendtsville　　15.00
Confederate Flags. Wraps.
　　n.d.　　n.p.　　25.00
Confederate Imprint Catalog. Wraps.
　　1982　　Wendell, NC　　20.00
**Confederate Leaders and Other Citizens Request the House of Delegates to
Repeal the Resolution of Respect to Abraham Lincoln, the Barbarian.**
Wraps.
　　(1928)　　n.p.　　30.00
Confederate Medicine 1861-1865. Wraps.
　　1961　　Richmond　　30.00
**Confederate Memoirs, Alamance County Troops of the War Between the
States 1861-1865.**
　　(c.1965) n.p.　　50.00

Confederate Memorial Addresses, Monday, May 11, 1885, New Bern, N.C.
Ladies Memorial Association. Wraps.
1886   Richmond   35.00

Confederate Memorial Day at Charleston, S.C. Re-interment of the Carolina
Dead from Gettysburg, Address of Rev. Dr. Girardeau, Odes, &c. Wraps.
1871   Charleston   75.00

The Confederate Memorial Literary Society Yearbook 1908-9.
1909   Richmond   25.00

Confederate Military History, edited by Gen. Clement A. Evans.
For additional information, see Appendix: Confederate Military
History.
1899   Atlanta   12 Vols.   350.00
Vol. I   Confederate History   (J. L. M. Curry; W. R. Garrett; C. A.
Evans) 30.00
Vol. II   Maryland/West Virginia (B. T. Johnson; R. White) 40.00
extended ed.   350.00
Vol. III Virginia (J. Hotchkiss) 40.00   extended ed.   150.00
Vol. IV   North Carolina (D. H. Hill) 40.00   extended ed.   150.00
Vol. V   South Carolina (E. Capers) 40.00   extended ed.   200.00
Vol. VI   Georgia (J. T. Derry)   40.00   extended ed.   250.00
Vol. VII Alabama/Mississippi (J. Wheeler; C. E. Hooker)   40.00
extended ed.   250.00
Vol. VIII Tennessee (J. D. Porter)   40.00   extended ed.   300.00
Vol. IX   Kentucky/Missouri (J. S. Johnston; J. C. Moore)   40.00
extended ed.   1000.00
Vol. X   Louisiana/Arkansas (J. Dimitry; J. M. Harrell)   40.00
extended ed.   350.00
Vol. XI   Texas/Florida (O. M. Roberts; J. J. Dickison) 40.00
extended ed.   1200.00
Vol. XII   The Confederate States Navy   (W. H. Parker); Morale of the
Confederate Army (J. W. Jones); South Since the War (Stephen
D. Lee)   40.00
Vol. XIII Biographical Supplement   1500.00

1987-89   extended ed. Wilmington, NC   19 Vols., incl. index.   750.00
Vol. I   Confederate History 1987   50.00
Vol. II   Maryland 1987   50.00
Vol. III   West Virginia/Biographical Supplement   1987   50.00
Vol. IV   Virginia 1987   50.00
Vol. V   North Carolina   1987   50.00
Vol. VI   South Carolina   1987   50.00
Vol. VII   Georgia 1987   50.00
Vol. VIII   Alabama 1987   50.00
Vol. IX   Mississippi 1987   50.00
Vol. X   Tennessee 1987   50.00
Vol. XI   Kentucky 1988   50.00
Vol. XII   Missouri 1988   50.00
Vol. XIII   Louisiana 1988   50.00
Vol. XIV   Arkansas 1988   50.00
Vol. XV   Texas   1989   50.00

Vol. XVI   Florida   1989   50.00
Vol. XVII   The Confederate States Navy/Morale of the Confederate
       Army/South Since the War   1989   50.00
Index   2 Vols.   1987   150.00

Confederate Portrait Album   Civil War 1861-1865.
n.d.   n.p.   50.00

Confederate Receipt Book.
1960   Athens, GA   30.00
1987   Wraps   4.50

The Confederate Reveille Memorial Edition.   Wraps.
1898   Raleigh   100.00

Confederate Soldiers Home of Georgia in Memory of the Heroes in Gray 1861-1928.   Wraps.
(1928)   n.p.   55.00

Confederate Soldiers, Sailors and Civilians Who Died as Prisoners of War at Camp Douglas, Chicago, Ill. 1862-1865.   Wraps.
(c.1962) Kalamazoo, MI   25.00

Confederate States of America, Journal of the Congress 1861-1865. 7 Vols.
1904   Washington, DC   400.00
Recent reprint   n.p.   300.00

Confederate Veteran Association of Kentucky, Constitution, By-Laws and Membership, With Name, Rank, Command and Residence.
1891   n.p.   35.00

Confederate Veteran Cumulative Index. 3 Vols.
1986   Wilmington, NC   300.00
1990   Wilmington, NC   300.00

Confederate Veteran Magazine. 40 Vols. Issued monthly. Vol. I, no. 1 did not have covers.   This single issue is worth 1000.00 plus in good condition.   Caveat: Vol. I, No. 1 was reprinted with no changes—if it looks new, it is.
1892-1932   Nashville   Good condition with all covers   5000.00
1984   Wendell, NC   1500.00

Confederate Victories in the Southwest: Prelude to Defeat.
1961   Albuquerque   25.00

Confederate View of the Treatment of Prisoners. First edition in book form. March and April, 1876, numbers of *Southern Historical Society Papers*, reissued.
1876   Richmond   75.00

Confederate War Etchings.   See: VOLCK, Adelbert J.

Confederate War Journal. Vol. I, No. 1 - Vol. II, No. 12 (all published). Wraps. Monthly Journal.
Complete run   1000.00
30.00 per issue

Confederate Women of Arkansas in the Civil War, 1861-'65. Memorial Reminiscences.
1907   Little Rock 75.00

CONGDON, Charles T.   Tribune Essays, Leading Articles Contributed to NY Tribune from 1857 to 1863.
1869   New York   25.00

CONGDON, Don, edited by   Combat: The Civil War.
1967   New York   35.00
1967   New York   30.00

CONGER, Arthur L.   The Rise of U. S. Grant.
1931   New York   25.00
The Congressional Globe: Debates and Proceedings of the Second Session of the Thirty-sixth Congress Also of the Special Session of the Senate Dec. 6, 1860 - Feb. 19, 1861.
1861   Washington, DC   40.00
The Congressional Globe: Debates and Proceedings of the Second Session of the 37th Congress.
1862   Washington, DC   35.00
CONKLIN, Henry   81st New York Infantry, Through "Poverty's Vale."
1974   New York   30.00
CONN, Granville   History of the New Hampshire Surgeons in the War of the Rebellion.
1906   Concord   110.00
CONNELLEY, William E., edited by   Collections of the Kansas State Historical Society 1915-1918. . . .
1918   Topeka   50.00
CONNELLEY, William E.   The Life of Preston B. Plumb.
1913   Chicago   60.00
CONNELLEY, William E.   Quantrill and the Border Wars.
1910   Cedar Rapids, IA   150.00
1956   New York   CWBC ed.   40.00
1956   New York   Trade ed.   30.00
CONNELLY, R. W.   Biographical Sketches of the Commissioned Officers of the Confederate States Marine Corp.   Wraps.
1983   Washington, NC   10.00
CONNELLY, Thomas Lawrence   Army of the Heartland, The Army of Tennessee 1861-1862.
1967   Baton Rouge   30.00
1972   Baton Rouge   25.00
1985   25.00
CONNELLY, Thomas Lawrence   Autumn of Glory, the Army of Tennessee.
1971   Baton Rouge   30.00
1974   Baton Rouge   30.00
1982   30.00
1984   30.00
1986   30.00
1988   30.00
CONNELLY, Thomas Lawrence   Civil War Tennessee, Battles and Leaders.
1984   9.00
1984   Wraps   4.00
CONNELLY, Thomas Lawrence   The Marble Man, Robert E. Lee.
1977   New York   15.00
1978   10.00
1981   Wraps   8.00
CONNELLY, Thomas Lawrence   The Politics of Command, Factions and Ideas in Confederate Strategy.
1973   Baton Rouge   30.00

CONNELLY, Thomas Lawrence   Will Success Spoil Jeff Davis? The Last Book About the Civil War.
   1963   New York   10.00
CONNELLY, Thomas W.   History of the Seventieth Regiment from Its Organization to Its Mustering Out.   Wraps.
   1902   Cincinnati   200.00
CONNER, James   Letters of General James Conner, C.S.A., edited by Mary Conner Moffett.
   1950   Columbia   Ltd.   500.00
CONNER, Robert D. W., compiled by   Addresses at the Unveiling of the Memorial to the North Carolina Women of the Confederacy.   Wraps.
   1914   Raleigh, NC   45.00
CONNER, Robert D. W.   Memorial Day An Interpretation.   Wraps.
   1909   Raleigh, NC   35.00
CONNOLLY, Alonzo P.   A Thrilling Narrative of the Minnesota Massacre and the Sioux War of 1862-63. . . .
   1896   Chicago   300.00
CONNOLLY, James A.   Three Years in the Army of the Cumberland The Letters and Diary of _____, edited by Paul M. Angle.
   1959   Bloomington   35.00
   1969   27.50
CONNOR, Daniel Ellis   A Confederate in the Colorado Gold Fields, edited by Donald J. Berthrong and Odessa Davenport.
   1970   Norman, OK   15.00
CONNOR, George C.   Guide to Chattanooga and Lookout Mountain.   Wraps.
   (c.1885)   Chattanooga   35.00
CONNOR, Henry G.   John Archibald Campbell   Associate Justice of the U.S. Supreme Court 1853-1861.
   1920   Boston   40.00
CONRAD, August   The Destruction of Columbia, S.C. . . .   Wraps.
   1902   Roanoke, VA   75.00
CONRAD, Mary Lynn   Confederate Banners.   Wraps.
   n.d.   Harrisonburg, VA   30.00
CONRAD, Thomas N.   A Confederate Spy - A Story of the Civil War.   Wraps.
   1892   New York   135.00
   n.d. (reprint)   n.p.   15.00
CONRAD, Thomas N.   The Rebel Scout.
   1904   Washington, DC   150.00
CONRAD, W. P. and ALEXANDER, T.   When War Passed This Way.
   1982   Shippensburg   40.00
   1988   24.95
CONSTELLANO, Illion   The Hunted Unionist . . . A Record of Late Occurrences in Georgia.   Wraps.
   1864   New York   80.00
Constitution and Ordinances of the State of Mississippi. 41st Cong. 1st Sess. Ho. of Reps. Misc. Doc. 14.   Wraps.
   1869   Washington, DC   40.00
Constitution of the State of Mississippi, as Amended with the Ordinances and Resolutions Adopted by the Constitutional Convention, August, 1865.
   1865   Jackson, MS   75.00

Constitution of the State of North Carolina, Together with the Ordnances & Resolutions.
1868   Raleigh   100.00

Constitution of the State of Virginia and Ordinances Adopted by Convention . . . 13th Day of Feb., 1864. Wraps.
1864   Alexandria   35.00

Constitution, By-Laws, Roster and History of the 97th O.V.I. Regimental Association. Wraps.
n.d.   n.p.   100.00

Contributions to a History of the Richmond Howitzer Battalion.
1883-86 Richmond   500.00
No. 1   125.00
No. 2   125.00
No. 3   125.00
No. 4   125.00

CONWAY, Alan   The Reconstruction of Georgia.
1966   Minneapolis   25.00

CONWAY, Moncure D.   The Golden Hour.
1862   Boston   30.00

CONWAY, Moncure D.   The Rejected Stone: or, Insurrection vs. Resurrection in America by a Native of Virginia.
1862   Boston   40.00

CONWELL, Russell H.   Life and Public Services of Gov. Rutherford B. Hayes.
1876   Boston   25.00

CONWELL, Russell H.   Magnolia Journey.
1974   University, AL   15.00

CONYNGHAM, David P.   The Irish Brigade and Its Campaigns.
1867   New York   125.00
1869   Boston   85.00
1984   30.00
1987   30.00

CONYNGHAM, David P.   Sherman's March Through the South.
1865   New York   80.00

COOK, Adrian   The Armies of the Streets: The New York City Draft Riots of 1863.
1974   Lexington   25.00

COOK, Benjamin F.   History of the Twelfth Massachusetts Volunteers (Webster Regiment).
1882   Boston   150.00

COOK, Frederick Francis   Bygone Days in Chicago, Recollections of the "Garden City" of the Sixties.
1910   Chicago   35.00

COOK, Harvey T.   Sherman's March Through South Carolina in 1865. Wraps.
1938   Greenville, SC   25.00

COOK, J. E.   Wearing of the Gray. . . .
1988   Gaithersburg   30.00

COOK, Joel   The Siege of Richmond: A Narrative of the Military Operations of Major-General George B. McClellan During the Months of May and June 1862.
1862   Philadelphia   50.00

COOK, Roy Bird   The Family and Early Life of Stonewall Jackson.
   1924   Richmond   80.00
   1925   Richmond   65.00
   1948   Charleston, WV 40.00
   1967   Charleston, WV Wraps   30.00
COOK, Roy Bird   Lewis County in the Civil War 1861-1865.
   1924   Charleston, WV   125.00
COOK, Roy Bird   Thomas J. Jackson, A God-Fearing Soldier of the C.S.A.
   1961   Cincinnati   40.00
COOK, S. G. and **BENTON,** Charles E., edited by   The "Dutchess County Regiment" (150th Regiment of New York State Volunteer Infantry) in the Civil War.
   1907   Danbury   100.00
COOK, Walter Henry   Secret Political Societies in the South During the Period of Reconstruction, an Address. Wraps.
   (c.1900) Cleveland, OH   40.00
COOKE, Giles B.   Just Before and After Lee Surrendered to Grant. Wraps.
   (c.1922) n.p.   25.00
COOKE, John Esten   Hammer and Rapier.
   1870   New York   60.00
   1888   35.00
   1893   35.00
   1898   New York   35.00
COOKE, John Esten   Hilt to Hilt.
   1869   New York   30.00
   1890   New York   25.00
   1893   Charleston, SC   30.00
   1896   30.00
COOKE, John Esten   Leather and Silk.
   1893   Charleston, SC   35.00
COOKE, John Esten   A Life of Gen. Robert E. Lee.
   1871   New York   75.00
   1876   65.00
   1883   New York   60.00
   1887   New York   50.00
   1890   30.00
COOKE, John Esten   The Life of Stonewall Jackson. By a Virginian.
   1863   New York   100.00
   1864   New York   60.00
   1866   New York   45.00
COOKE, John Esten   Mohun or the Last Days of Lee and His Paladins.
   1869   New York   75.00
   1893   Charleston, SC   30.00
   1896   25.00
   1936   Charlottesville, VA 40.00
   1968   Ridgewood, NJ 20.00
COOKE, John Esten   Outlines from the Outpost, edited by Richard Harwell.
   1961   Chicago   30.00

COOKE, John Esten   **The Song of the Rebel.** Wraps.
  n.d.   Richmond   40.00
COOKE, John Esten   **Stonewall Jackson and the Old Stonewall Brigade,** edited by Richard Harwell.
  1954   Charlottesville, VA   40.00
COOKE, John Esten   **Stonewall Jackson: A Military Biography.**
  1866   New York   150.00
  1876   New York   125.00
COOKE, John Esten   **Surry of Eagle's Nest.**
  1866   New York   100.00
  1889   New York   40.00
  1894   New York   30.00
  1894   Chicago   30.00
  1897   New York   20.00
COOKE, John Esten   **Wearing of the Gray: Being Personal Portraits, Scenes and Adventures of the War.**
  1867   New York   125.00
  1959   Bloomington, IN edited by Philip Van Doren Stern   45.00
  1988   30.00
COOKE, Phillip St. George   **Cavalry Tactics.** 2 Vols.
  1861   Washington, DC 250.00
  1862   200.00
  1864   New York   175.00
COOLIDGE, Louis   **Ulysses S. Grant.**
  1917   Boston   25.00
  1922   Boston   20.00
  1924   20.00
COOLING, Benjamin F.   **Forts Henry and Donelson The Key to the Confederate Heartland.**
  1988   Knoxville   24.95
COOLING, Benjamin Franklin   **Jubal Early's Raid on Washington, 1864.**
  1989   22.95
COOLING, Benjamin Franklin   **Symbol, Sword, and Shield.**
  1975   Hamden, CT   20.00
COOLING, Benjamin F., and **OWEN**, W. H.   **Mr. Lincoln's Forts: The Civil War Forts of Washington, D.C.**
  1988   Shippensburg   29.95
COONS, John W., compiled by   **Indiana at Shiloh.**
  1904   Indianapolis   50.00
COOPER, Alonzo   **In and Out of Rebel Prisons.**
  1888   Oswego 75.00
  1983   22.50
COOPER, Charles R.   **Chronological and Alphabetical Record of the Engagements of the Great Civil War.**
  1904   Milwaukee   30.00
COOPER, David M.   **Obituary Discourse on Occasion of the Death of Noah Henry Ferry, Major of the 5th Michigan Cavalry, Killed at Gettysburg.** Wraps.
  1863   New York   50.00

COOPER, H. John   Chancellorsville 1863, Knight's Battles for Wargamers.
　　1973   9.00
COOPER, Peter   Reconstruction, Letter from Peter Cooper to President Johnson. Wraps.
　　n.d.   n.p.   25.00
COOPER, Samuel   A Concise System of Instructions and Regulations for the Militia and Volunteers of the U.S. Comprehending the Exercises and Movements of the Infantry. . . .
　　1860   100.00
　　Part I   **Infantry.**
　　Part II   **Cavalry.**
　　Part III   **Artillery.**
　　Part IV   **Regulations.**
COOPER, Thomas V.   Biographies of James G. Blaine . . . and John A. Logan . . . History of the Political Parties of the United States.
　　1884   10.00
COPE, Alexis   The Fifteenth Ohio Volunteers and Its Campaigns.
　　1916   Columbus   175.00
COPELAND, C.   Bravest Surrender; A Petersburg Patchwork.
　　1961   Richmond   18.00
COPELAND, P. F.   Civil War Uniforms Coloring Book. Wraps.
　　1977   3.00
COPLAND, Mary Ruffin   Confederate History of Charles City County, Virginia. Wraps.
　　1957   n.p.   35.00
COPLEY, John M.   A Sketch of the Battle of Franklin, Tenn.
　　1893   Austin   150.00
COPP, Elbridge J.   Reminiscences of the War of the Rebellion.
　　1911   Nashua   75.00
COPPEE, Henry   The Field Manual for Battalion Drill, Containing the Exercises and Manoeuvres in the School of the Battalion. Arranged in a Tabular Form. . . .
　　1863   Philadelphia   100.00
COPPEE, Henry   Field Manual of Courts-Martial.
　　1863   Philadelphia   100.00
COPPEE, Henry   General Thomas.
　　For additional information, see Appendix: Great Commander Series.
　　1883   New York   50.00
　　1893   New York   Ltd. 125.00
　　1895   New York   50.00
　　1897   New York   30.00
COPPEE, Henry   Grant and His Campaigns: A Military Biography.
　　1866   New York   25.00
COPPEE, Henry   Life and Services of Gen. U. S. Grant.
　　1868   New York   20.00
Copperhead Conspiracy in the North-West An Expose of the Treasonable Order of the "Sons of Liberty." Wraps.
　　(c.1863) New York   25.00
CORBETT, Elizabeth   Faye's Folly.
　　1941   New York   15.00

CORBIN, Diana Fontaine Maury   A Life of Matthew Fontaine Maury, USN and CSN.
1888   London   80.00
CORBIN, Richard W.   Letters of a Confederate Officer to His Family in Europe, During the Last Year of the War of Secession.   Wraps.
1865   (Paris) 1250.00
1902   Paris   1000.00
1967   Ann Arbor, MI 35.00
CORBIN, William E.   A Star for Patriotism.
1972   13.00
CORBY, William   Memoirs of Chaplain Life.
1894   Notre Dame   60.00
1893   75.00
CORELL, Philip   History of the Naval Brigade, 99th N. Y. Volunteers, Union Coast Guard, 1861-1865.
1905   New York   Ltd.   325.00
CORLEY, Florence Fleming   Confederate City, Augusta, Georgia.
1960   Columbia, SC   35.00
CORMIER, Steven A.   The Siege of Suffolk, The Forgotten Campaign April 11-May 4, 1863.
1989   19.95
CORN, James F.   Jim Witherspoon, A Soldier of the South 1862-1865. Wraps.
1962   Frankfort   30.00
CORNISH, Dudley Taylor   The Sable Arm, Negro Troops in the Union Army, 1861-1865.
1956   New York   25.00
1966   New York   20.00
CORNISH, Joseph Jenkins, III   The Air Arm of the Confederacy. Wraps.
1963   Richmond   30.00
A Correspondence Between General Early and Mahone in Regard to a Military Memoir of the Latter.   Wraps.
1871   n.p.   50.00
Correspondence on the Present Relations Between Great Britain and the United States of America.   Wraps.
1862   Boston   40.00
Correspondence Relating to the Insurrection at Harper's Ferry, Oct. 17, 1859. Wraps.
1860   Annapolis   55.00
Correspondence Relative to the Case of Messrs. Mason and Slidell.   Wraps.
1861   Washington, DC   40.00
CORRINGTON, John William   And Wait for the Night.
1964   New York   15.00
CORSAN, W. C.   Two Months in the Confederate States.
1863   London   300.00
CORT, Charles Edwin   "Dear Friends"   The Civil War Letters and Diary of _____, edited by Helen W. Tomlinson.
1962   n.p.   20.00
CORTEMANCHE, R. A.   No Need for Glory: The British Navy in American Waters, 1860- 1864.
1977   Annapolis   30.00

CORY, Charles E.   Slavery in Kansas.
    1902   n.p.   15.00
CORY, Charles E.   The Soldiers of Kansas, The 6th Kansas Cavalry
and Its Commander.   Wraps.
    1910   (Topeka)   20.00
CORY, Eugene A.   A   Private's   Recollections   of   Fredericksburg.
Wraps.
    1884   Providence   Ltd.   30.00
CORY, Marielou Armstrong   The Ladies' Memorial Association of Mont-
gomery, Alabama: Its Origin and Organization, 1860-1870.
    (1902)   Montgomery   100.00
COSTON, Martha   Signal Success,   The Work and Travels of Mrs.
Martha Coston, an Autobiography.
    1866   Philadelphia   80.00
COTTERILL, R. S.   The Old South.
    1939   Glendale   50.00
COTTON, John W.   Yours Till Death,   Civil War Letters of John W.
Cotton, edited by Lucille Griffith.
    1951   University, AL   40.00
COTTRELL, John   Anatomy of an Assassination.
    1966   New York   30.00
COTTRELL, Sue   Hoof Beats, North and South; Horses and Horsemen of
the Civil War.
    1975   New York   20.00
COULLING, Mary P.   The Lee Girls.
    1987   Winston-Salem   25.00
COULTER, E. Merton   The Civil War and Readjustment in Kentucky.
    1926   Chapel Hill, NC   75.00
    1966   Gloucester   25.00
COULTER, E. Merton   The Confederate States of America, Vol. 7 of
A History of the South.
    1950   Baton Rouge   30.00
    1968   Baton Rouge   25.00
COULTER, E. Merton   Lost Generation; The Life and Death of James
Barrow, C.S.A.   See: Confederate Centennial Studies, No. 1.
COULTER, E. Merton   Planters' Wants in the Days of the Confeder-
acy.   Wraps.
    1928   Savannah   25.00
COULTER, E. Merton   The South During Reconstruction, 1865-1877.
    1947   Baton Rouge   25.00
    1962   Baton Rouge   20.00
    1965   Baton Rouge   20.00
COULTER, E. Merton   Travels in the Confederate States.
    1948   Norman, OK   50.00
    1961   Norman, OK   40.00
    1981   Wendell, NC   25.00
COULTER, E. Merton   William G. Brownlow.
    1937   Chapel Hill, NC   40.00
    1971   Knoxville   25.00
COULTER, E. Merton   William Montague Browne.
    1967   Athens, GA   20.00

COULTER, E. Merton and STEPHENSON, Wendell Holmes   A History of the South, Vol. VII, the Confederate States of America 1861-1865.
    n.d.   n.p.   30.00

COUPER, William   Claudius Crozet, Soldier, Scholar, Educator, Engineer. Wraps.
    1936   Charlottesville   35.00

COUPER, William   One Hundred Years at Virginia Military Institute. 4 Vols.
    1939   Richmond   150.00

COUPER, William   The V.M.I. New Market Cadets.
    1933   Charlottesville   60.00

COUPER, William   Virginia Military Institute Seventy-fifth Anniversary of the Battle of New Market, May 15, 1939. Wraps.
    1939   n.p.   20.00

COUPER, William   Virginia Military Institute. Address. Wraps.
    1939   n.p.   40.00

COUPER, William   War and Work. Address. Wraps.
    1940   n.p.   40.00

COURTNEY, Patrick C.   The Seven Days Battles Around Richmond, The Civil War Round Table of London, England. Wraps.
    1960   London   20.00

COUTEMANCHE, Regis A.   No Need of Glory; The British Navy in American Waters 1860-1864.
    1977   MD 25.00

COWARD, Asbury   The South Carolinians Colonel Asbury Coward's Memoirs, edited by Natalie Jenkins Bond and Osmun L. Coward.
    1968   New York   50.00

COWDEN, Robert   A Brief Sketch of the Organization and Services of the Fifty-ninth Colored Infantry and Biographical Sketches.
    1883   Dayton 125.00

COWELL, A. T.   Tactics at Gettysburg. Wraps.
    1910   Gettysburg 40.00
    1987   15.00

COWLES, L.   History of the Fifth Massachusetts Battery, Organized Oct. 3, 1861, Mustered Out June 12, 1865.
    1902   100.00

COWLES, William H. H.   The Life and Services of Gen'l James B. Gordon, An Address. Wraps.
    1887   Raleigh, NC   50.00

COWLEY, Charles   Leaves from a Lawyer's Life: Afloat and Ashore.
    1879   Lowell, MA   40.00

COWTAN, Charles W.   Services of the Tenth New York Volunteers.
    1882   New York   110.00

COX, Earnest Sevier   Lincoln's Negro Policy.
    1972   Richmond   15.00

COX, Florence Marie Ankeny, edited by   Kiss Josey for Me.
    1974   Santa Ana, CA   30.00

COX, Jacob D.   Atlanta.   See: Campaigns of the Civil War.

COX, Jacob D.   The Battle of Franklin, Tennessee, November 30, 1864.
    1897   New York   Ltd.   125.00
    1983   30.00
    1988   30.00

COX, Jacob D.   The March to the Sea - Franklin and Nashville.   See: Campaigns of the Civil War.

COX, Jacob D.   Military Reminiscences of the Civil War. 2 Vols.
1900   New York   100.00

COX, Jacob D.   The Second Battle of Bull Run as Connected with the Fitz-John Porter Case, A Paper. Wraps.
1882   Cincinnati   60.00

COX, Jacob D.   Soldiers' Monument, Fort Stephenson Park.   Proceedings at the Unveiling of the Soldiers' Monument.
1885   75.00

COX, Lawanda and COX, John H.   Politics, Principle, and Prejudice 1865-1866.
1963   London   20.00

COX, Lawanda and COX, John H., edited by   Reconstruction, the Negro, and the New South.
1973   Columbia   20.00

COX, Robert C.   Memories of the War.   Wraps.
1893   Wellsboro, PA   50.00

COX, Samuel S.   Amnesty and the Jefferson Davis Amendment, Speech. Wraps.
1876   Washington, DC   25.00

COX, Samuel S.   Punishment or Pardon;   Force or Freedom, for the Wasted Land, Speech. Wraps.
1875   Washington, DC   25.00

COX, Samuel S.   Three Decades of Federal Legislation, 1855 to 1885.
1885   Providence   15.00

COX, William Ruffin   Address on the Life and Character of Maj. Gen. Stephen D. Ramseur. Wraps.
1891   Raleigh, NC   100.00

COX, William Ruffin   Address on the Life and Services of Gen. James H. Lane. Wraps.
1908   Richmond   75.00

COX, William Ruffin   Address on the Life and Services of General Marcus J. Wright. Wraps.
1915   Richmond   100.00

COX, William V.   The Defenses of Washington. General Early's Advance on the Capital and the Battle of Fort Stevens, July 11 and 12, 1864. Wraps.
1901   Washington, DC   40.00

COXE, Elizabeth Allen   Memories of a South Carolina Plantation During the War.
1912   n.p.   Ltd.   150.00

COYNART, R. de   Precis De La Guerre Des Etats-Unis D'Amerique. Wraps.
1867   Paris   100.00

COZZENS, Peter   No Better Place to Die: The Battle of Stones River.
1989   Urbana   24.95

CRABB, Alfred Leland   Home to Tennessee,   A Tale of Soldiers Returning.
1952   Indianapolis   25.00

CRABB, Alfred Leland   A Mockingbird Sang at Chickamauga   A Tale of Embattled Chattanooga.
1949   Indianapolis   30.00

CRAFT, David   History of the 141st Regiment Pennsylvania Volunteers.
1885   Towanda   150.00

CRAFTON, Allen   Free States Fortress, The First Ten Years of the History of Lawrence, Kansas.
1954   Lawrence   25.00

CRAFTON, Henry D.   A Treatise on the Camp and March, with Which Is Connected the Construction of Field Works and Military Bridges. . . .
1861   60.00

CRAFTS, W. A.   The Southern Rebellion. 2 Vols.
1862   Boston   100.00

Craig's Share in the War Between the States 1861-1865, Craig Chapter No. 121, U.D.C.   Wraps.
n.d.   Roanoke   30.00

CRAIG, Hugh   Grand Army Picture Book   From April 12, 1861 to April 26, 1865.
n.d.   New York   70.00

CRAIG, Reginald S.   The Fighting Parson   The Biography of Colonel John M. Chivington.
1959   Los Angeles   40.00

CRAMER, John H.   Lincoln Under Enemy Fire.
1948   Baton Rouge   20.00

CRAMER, M. J.   Ulysses S. Grant: Conversations and Unpublished Letters.
1897   New York   20.00

CRANDALL, Marjorie Lyle   Confederate Imprints. 2 Vols.
1955   Boston   75.00

CRANDALL, Warren D. and NEWELL, Isaac D.   History of the Ram Fleet and the Mississippi Marine Brigade.
1907   St. Louis   375.00

CRANE, John and KIELEY, James F.   United States Naval Academy The First Hundred Years.
1945   25.00

CRANE, Mary Powell   The Life of James R. Powell and Early History of Alabama and Birmingham.
1930   Brooklyn, NY   110.00

CRANE, Stephen   The Little Regiment and Other Episodes of the American Civil War.
1896   New York   300.00

CRANE, Stephen   The Red Badge of Courage. 1st edition, 1st state has perfect type in the last line on page 225.
1895   New York   In dust jacket   700.00
1895   New York   Without dust jacket 500.00
1896   New York   100.00
1931   Ltd. ed. of 980 copies   150.00
1944   Ltd. ed. Club   150.00

CRARY, Catherine S., edited by   Dear Belle Letters from a Cadet and Officer to His Sweetheart, 1858-1865.
  1965   Middletown, CT   30.00
CRAVEN, Avery   Civil War in the Making 1815-1860.
  1959   Baton Rouge   25.00
  1968   Baton Rouge   20.00
CRAVEN, Avery   The Coming of the Civil War.
  1942   New York 30.00
  1957   25.00
  1960   15.00
CRAVEN, Avery   Edmund Ruffin, Southerner.
  1932   New York 35.00
  1972   Baton Rouge   20.00
CRAVEN, Avery   Essays in Honor of William E. Dodd by his Former Students at the University of Chicago.
  1935   Chicago   30.00
CRAVEN, Avery   The Growth of Southern Nationalism 1848-1861.
  1953   30.00
  1962   15.00
  1964   Baton Rouge   35.00
CRAVEN, Avery   An Historian and the Civil War.
  1964   Chicago   30.00
  1964   Chicago   Wraps 10.00
CRAVEN, Avery   The Repressible Conflict 1830-1861.
  1939   Baton Rouge   25.00
CRAVEN, Avery, and VANDIVER, F.   The   American   Tragedy: The American Civil War in Retrospect.   Wraps.
  1959   Hampden-Sydney   23.00
CRAVEN, John J.   Prison Life of Jefferson Davis Embracing Details & Incidents in His Captivity.
  1866   New York   50.00
  1866   London 50.00
  1905   New York   30.00
CRAWFORD, J. Marshall   Mosby and His Men.
  1867   New York   150.00
  1987   30.00
CRAWFORD, Richard   The Civil War Songbook.   Wraps.
  1977   9.00
CRAWFORD, Samuel J.   Kansas in the Sixties.
  1911   Chicago   80.00
CRAWFORD, Samuel Wylie   The Genesis of the Civil War.
  1887   New York   50.00
  1896   New York entitled   The History of the Fall of Fort Sumter.   Wraps   30.00
  1898   New York   40.00
CRAYON, Porte   See: STROTHER, David Hunter
CREASEY, George W.   The City of Newburyport in the Civil War.
  1903   Boston   30.00
CREELMAN, James   Why We Love Lincoln.
  1909   New York   15.00
CREIGHTON, Wilbur Foster   The Life of Major Wilbur Fisk Foster.
  (1961)   (Nashville, TN)   55.00

CRENSHAW, Ollinger   The Slave States in the Presidential Election of 1860.
1945   Baltimore   25.00
1969   MA   10.00

CRESAP, Brenarr   Appomattox Commander: The Story of General E.O.C. Ord.
1981   San Diego   20.00

CRIBBEN, Henry   The Military Memoirs of Captain _____ of the 140th New York Volunteers, edited by J. Clayton Youker.
1911   Chicago 100.00

CRIPPIN, Edward   The Diary of _____, 27th Illinois Volunteers 1861-1863, edited by Robert J. Kerner.
1909   Springfield   40.00
1910   Springfield   40.00

CRISSEY, Elwell   Lincoln's Lost Speech The Pivot of His Career.
1967   New York   25.00

CRIST, Nelson   Battle of Atlanta, Story of the Cyclorama.   Wraps.
1919   n.p.   30.00

CRISWELL, Grover C.   Compendium of Paper Money, Autographs, Postal History (U.S. and Conf.), Army, Navy, Slavery, etc.   Wraps.
n.d.   5.00

CRISWELL, Grover C. and Clarence L.   Confederate and Southern State Bonds.
1961   St. Petersburg   20.00
Recent reprint   25.00

CRISWELL, Grover C. and Clarence L.   Confederate and Southern State Currency.   Plus supplement.
1957   Pass-A-Grille Beach, FL   25.00

CRITTENDEN, H. H.   The Battle of Westport.
1938   Kansas City   25.00

CRITTENDEN, H. H.   The Crittenden Memoirs.
1936   New York   60.00
1938   Kansas City   45.00

CROCKER, James F.   Gettysburg Pickett's Charge and Other War Addresses.
1915   Portsmouth   150.00

CROCKER, James F.   My Personal Experiences in Taking up Arms and in the Battle of Malvern Hill, Address.   Wraps.
1905   Portsmouth   55.00

CROFFUT, W. A. and **MORRIS**, John M.   The Military and Civil History of Connecticut . . . 1861-65.
1868   New York   75.00
1869   New York   50.00
1879   50.00

CROFTS, Daniel W.   Reluctant Confederates - Upper South Unionists in the Secession Crisis.
1989   Chapel Hill, NC   45.00

CROFTS, Thomas   History of the Service of the Third Ohio Veteran Cavalry in the War for Preservation of the Union from 1861-1865.
1910   Toledo   160.00

CROLY, David G.   Seymour and Blair Their Lives and Services.
1868   New York   35.00

CROMIE, Alice Hamilton   A Tour Guide to the Civil War.
  1965   20.00
  1975   New York   25.00
  1989   12.95
CROMWELL, G.   The Virginia Manufactory of Arms.
  1975   Charlottesville   25.00
CRONIN, David E.   The Evolution of a Life Described in the Memoirs
  of Major Seth Eyland, Late of the Mounted Rifles.
  1884   New York   75.00
CROOK, D. P.   Diplomacy During the American Civil War. Wraps.
  1975   8.00
CROOK, D. P.   The North, the South and the Powers 1861-1865.
  1974   New York   20.00
CROOK, George   General George Crook, His Autobiography, edited by
  Martin F. Schmitt.
  1946   Norman, OK   35.00
CROOK, William H.   Through Five Administrations: Reminiscences, Col.
  Wm. H. Crook, Body Guard to Lincoln.
  1910   New York   20.00
CROOKE, George   The Twenty-first Regiment of Iowa Volunteer
  Infantry.
  1891   Milwaukee   160.00
CROSBY, Alpheus   The Present Position of the Seceded States, etc.,
  An Address. Wraps.
  1865   Boston   25.00
CROSBY, Frank   Life of Abraham Lincoln.
  1865   Philadelphia   30.00
  1866   Philadelphia   25.00
CROSLAND, Charles   Reminiscences of the Sixties.
  (c.1910) Columbia   150.00
CROSS, Andrew B.   The War, Battle of Gettysburg and the Christian
  Commission. Wraps.
  1865   Baltimore   45.00
CROSS, Frederick C.   Nobly They Served the Union. Wraps.
  1976   Walnut Creek, CA   30.00
CROTTY, Daniel G.   Four Years Campaigning in the Army of the
  Potomac.
  1874   Grand Rapids   135.00
CROUCH, Howard R.   Relic Hunter, The Field Account of Civil War
  Sites, Artifacts and Hunting.
  1978   Richmond   20.00
CROW, Vernon Hugh   Storm in the Mountains: Thomas' Confederate
  Legion of Cherokee Indians and Mountaineers.
  1982   Cherokee   18.00
  1989   Wraps   8.00
CROWDER, James H.   Before and After Vicksburg. Wraps.
  1924   Dayton   120.00
CROWELL, Joseph E.   The Young Volunteer, Everyday Experiences of
  a Soldier Boy in the Civil War.
  1906   New York   50.00

CROWN, Francis J., Jr.　　Confederate Postal History.
　　1948　Lawrence, MA　55.00
　　1976　Lawrence, MA　40.00
CROWNINSHIELD, Benjamin W.　　The Battle of Cedar Creek, October 19, 1864: A Paper. . . . Wraps.
　　1879　Cambridge　60.00
CROWNINSHIELD, Benjamin W. and GLEASON, D. H. L.　　A History of the First Regiment of Massachusetts Cavalry Volunteers.
　　1891　Boston　175.00
CROZIER, Emmet　　Yankee Reporters 1861-65.
　　1956　New York　30.00
CROZIER, R. H.　　The Confederate Spy.
　　1885　Louisville　50.00
CRUIKSHANK, George L.　　Back in the Sixties. Reminiscences of the Service of Co. A, 11th Pennsylvania Regiment.　Wraps.
　　1893　Fort Dodge, IA　90.00
CRUMPTON, Washington Bryan　　A Book of Memories 1842-1920.
　　1921　Montgomery, AL　40.00
CRUSE, Mary A.　　Cameron Hall: A Story of the Civil War.
　　1867　Philadelphia　30.00
CRUSH, C. W.　　The Montgomery County Story 1776-1957.　Wraps.
　　1957　n.p.　35.00
CRUTE, Joseph H., Jr.　　Confederate Staff Officers 1861-1865.
　　1982　Powhatan　25.00
CRUTE, Joseph H., Jr.　　Units of the Confederate States Army.
　　1987　Midlothian　45.00
CUDWORTH, Warren H.　　History of the First Regiment Massachusetts Infantry.
　　1866　Boston　65.00
CUFFEL, Charles A.　　Durell's Battery . . . Independent Battery D, Pennsylvania Volunteer Artillery.
　　1900　Philadelphia　100.00
　　1903　Philadelphia entitled History of Durell's Battery　75.00
CULBRETH, David M. R.　　The University of Virginia.
　　1908　New York　80.00
CULLEN, Andrews Battle　　_____, Patriot, Orator, Soldier, Christian. Wraps.
　　(c.1905) n.p.　75.00
CULLEN, Joseph P.　　The Peninsula Campaign 1862.
　　1973　Harrisburg　25.00
　　Recent reprint　15.00
CULLEN, Joseph P.　　Where a Hundred Thousand Fell.　Wraps.
　　1966　Washington, DC　10.00
CULLOM, J. W.　　Pastoral Sketches.
　　1907　Nashville　40.00
CULLOM, Shelby M.　　Fifty Years of Public Service.
　　1911　Chicago　25.00
　　1969　15.00
CULLOP, Charles P.　　Confederate Propaganda in Europe 1861-1865.
　　1969　Coral Gables, FL　25.00

CULLUM, George W.   Biographical Register of the Officers and Graduates of the U.S. Military Academy. 2 Vols.
>   1868   New York   100.00
>   1891   7 Vols.   400.00
>   1891   Boston and New York   100.00

CULLUM, George W.   Biographical Sketch of Brigadier General Joseph G. Swift, Chief Engineer of the U.S. Army.   Wraps.
>   1877   New York   30.00

CULLUM, George W., edited and translated by   Elements of Military Art and History,   Comprising the History and Tactics of the Separate Arms. . . .
>   1863   180.00

CULLUM, George W.   Register of the Officers and Graduates of the U.S. Military Academy.
>   1850   New York   40.00

CULLUM, George W.   Systems of Military Bridges in Use by the U.S. Army . . . with Directions for the Preservation, Destruction, and Reestablishment of Bridges.
>   1863   200.00

CULP, Edward C.   The 25th Ohio Vet. Vol. Infantry in the War for the Union.
>   1885   Topeka   200.00

CULVER, Joseph Franklin   "Your Affectionate Husband, J. F. Culver": Letters Written During the Civil War.
>   1978   Iowa City   15.00

CUMMING, Kate   Gleanings from Southland. Sketches of Life and Manners of the People of the South Before, During, and After the War of Secession, with Extracts from the Author's Journal and an Epitome of the South.
>   1895   Birmingham, AL   150.00

CUMMING, Kate   A Journal of Hospital Life in the Confederate Army of Tennessee.
>   1866   Lousiville   250.00
>   1959   Baton Rouge, LA entitled   The Journal of a Confederate Nurse, edited by Richard B. Harwell   40.00
>   1975   Savannah, GA   entitled   The Journal of Kate Cumming - A Confederate Nurse, edited by Richard B. Harwell 50.00

CUMMINGS, A. Boyd   Official Memoir of Lieutenant Commander A. Boyd Cummings, edited by James Alden.   Wraps.
>   n.d.   n.p.   40.00

CUMMINGS, Charles L.   The Great War Relic, Valuable as a Curiosity of the Rebellion, Together with a Sketch of My Life, Service in the Army, and How I Lost My Feet in the War.   Wraps.
>   (188-)   Harrisburg   30.00

CUMMINGS, Charles M.   Yankee Quaker, Confederate General, the Curious Career of Bushrod Rust Johnson.
>   1971   Rutherford, NJ   35.00

CUMMINGS, Edward   Marmaduke of Tennessee.
>   1914   Chicago   15.00

CUMMINS, Archer Bernard   The Wilson-Kautz Raid.   Wraps.
>   1961   Blackstone, VA   20.00

CUNNINGHAM, D. and MILLER, W. W.   Report of The Ohio Antietam
    Battleifield Commission.
    1904   OH   60.00
CUNNINGHAM, Edward   The Port Hudson Campaign 1862-1863.
    1963   Baton Rouge   50.00
CUNNINGHAM, Frank   General Stand Watie's Confederate Indians.
    1959   San Antonio, TX Trade ed. 55.00
    1959   Signed Ltd. ed. 75.00
    1960   San Antonio, TX   40.00
CUNNINGHAM, Frank   Knight of the Confederacy   Gen. Turner
    Ashby.
    1960   San Antonio, TX   60.00
CUNNINGHAM, Horace H.   Doctors in Gray.
    1958   Baton Rouge   50.00
    1960   Baton Rouge   45.00
    1970   Gloucester, MA 20.00
CUNNINGHAM, Horace H.   Field Medical Services at the Battles of
    Manassas. Wraps.
    1968   Athens 20.00
    1987   12.50
    1988   12.50
CUNNINGHAM, John L.   Three Years with the Adirondack Regiment
    118th N. Y. Volunteers Infantry.
    1920   Norwood, MA   110.00
CURRENT, Richard N.   The History of Wisconsin; The Civil War Era
    1848-1873.
    1976   Madison 30.00
CURRENT, Richard N.   Lincoln and the First Shot.
    1963   Philadelphia 15.00
CURRENT, Richard N.   The Lincoln Nobody Knows.
    1958   New York 20.00
    1984   Wraps 7.00
CURRENT, Richard N.   Old Thad Stevens, A Story of Ambition.
    1942   Madison 15.00
CURRENT, Richard N.   The Political Thought of Abraham Lincoln.
    Wraps.
    1980   Indianapolis   15.00
CURRENT, Richard N., edited by   Reconstruction in Retrospect.
    1969   Baton Rouge   15.00
CURRIDEN, S. W., compiled by   Our Soldiers and Sailors: What They
    Said and Did on the Tenth Anniversary of the Battle of Antietam, at
    Pittsburg, Penn. . . . Wraps.
    1872   New York   40.00
CURRIE, George E.   Warfare Along the Mississippi. The Letters of
    _____, edited by Norman E. Clarke.
    1961   Mt. Pleasant, MI 20.00
CURRY, Charles   John Brown Baldwin - Lawyer, Soldier, Statesman.
    Wraps.
    1928   Staunton, VA   25.00

CURRY, J. L. M.   Civil History of the Confederate States with Some Personal Reminiscences.
1900   Richmond   40.00
1901   Richmond   30.00
CURRY, J. L. M.   The Southern States of the American Union.
1895   Richmond   20.00
CURRY, John P.   Volunteer's Camp and Field Book, Containing Useful and General Information on the Art and Science of War. . . .
1861   New York   250.00
CURRY, Leonard P.   Blueprint for Modern American, Non-Military Legislation of the First Civil War Congress.
1968   Nashville   15.00
CURRY, Richard Orr   A House Divided.
1964   Pittsburgh   15.00
CURRY, William Leontes   Four Years in the Saddle, History of the First Regiment Ohio Vol. Cavalry.
1898   Columbus   200.00
1984   35.00
CURTIS, Newton Martin   The Capture of Fort Fisher.   Wraps.
1900   Boston   40.00
CURTIS, Newton Martin   From Bull Run to Chancellorsville, The Story of the Sixteenth New York Infantry.
1906   New York   60.00
CURTIS, Orson B.   History of the Twenty-fourth Michigan of the Iron Brigade.
1891   Detroit   165.00
1984   30.00
1987   30.00
CUSHING, Caleb   The Treaty of Washington.
1873   New York   35.00
CUSSONS, John   Jack Sterry, The Jessie Scout.   Wraps.
1907   Harrisonburg   50.00
1908   Richmond   50.00
CUSSONS, John   United States "History" as the Yankee Makes and Takes It, By a Confederate Soldier.   Wraps.
1900   Glen Allen, VA   40.00
CUSTER, Elizabeth B.   "Boots and Saddles" or Life in Dakota with General Custer.
1885   New York   40.00
1974   Wraps   8.00
CUSTER, Elizabeth B.   Following the Guidon.
1966   OK 18.00
CUSTER, Elizabeth B.   Jefferson Davis, Political Soldier.
1930   New York   30.00
CUSTER, Elizabeth B.   Tenting on the Plains.
1887   New York   60.00
1889   New York   40.00
1971   OK   3 Vols.   25.00
CUSTER, George Armstrong   My Life on the Plains: Or, Personal Experiences with Indians.   Wraps.
1986   OK   7.95

CUSTER, George Armstrong   Wild Life of the Plains and Horrors of Indian Warfare.
  1883   85.00
CUSTER, Milo   Custer Genealogies.
  1979   20.00
CUTCHEON, Byron M.   The Story of the Twentieth Michigan Infantry July 15th, 1862 to May 30th, 1865.
  1904   Lansing   175.00
CUTCHINS, John A.   A Famous Command, The Richmond Light Infantry Blues.
  1934   Richmond   75.00
CUTCHINS, John A.   Richmond Light Infantry Blues, A Sketch.   Wraps.
  1910   Richmond   30.00
CUTHBERT, N. B., edited by   Lincoln and the Baltimore Plot 1861.
  1949   Los Angeles   35.00
CUTLER, Andrew Simon   Memories of _____.
  (1907)   n.p.   140.00
CUTLER, Elbridge Jefferson   Fitzhugh Birney, A Memoir.   Wraps.
  1866   Cambridge   35.00
CUTLER, Frederick M.   The Old First Massachusetts Coast Artillery in War and Peace.
  1917   Boston   60.00
CUTSHAW, Wilfred E.   The Battle Near Spotsylvania Courthouse on May 18th, 1864.   Wraps.
  1905   Richmond   80.00
CUTTER, Orlando Phelps   Our Battery: or, The Journal of Company B, 1st O.V.A.   Wraps.
  1864   Cleveland   100.00
CUTTING, Elizabeth   Jefferson Davis, Political Soldier.
  1930   New York   20.00
  1939   New York   20.00
CUTTINO, George Peddy   Saddle Bag and Spinning Wheel, Being the Civil War Letters of George W. Peddy. . . .
  1981   Macon   22.50
Cyclopedia of Eminent and Representative Men of the Carolinas of the Nineteenth Century.   2 Vols.
  1892   Madison, WI   200.00
The Cyclorama of the Battle of Gettysburg.   Wraps.
  1891   Philadelphia   30.00
D'HAMEL, Enrique B.   The Adventures of a Tenderfoot.   Wraps.
  1965   Waco   Ltd.   25.00
DABNEY, Robert L.   A Defence of Virginia.
  1867   New York   30.00
  1977   VA   25.00
DABNEY, Robert L.   Life and Campaigns of Lieut.-Gen. Thomas J. Jackson (Stonewall Jackson).
  1866   New York   75.00
  1864-66 London 2 Vols. 200.00
  1976   Harrisonburg, VA   20.00
  1983   25.00
  1988   25.00

DABNEY, Virginius   The Last Review: The Confederate Reunion, Richmond, 1932.
1984   Chapel Hill, NC   28.00
DABNEY, Virginius   The Story of Don Miff, as Told by His Friend John Bouche Whacker. A Symphony of Life.
1886   Philadelphia   30.00
DABNEY, Virginius   Virginia: The New Dominion.
1971   Garden City   20.00
DACUS, Robert H.   Reminiscences of Co. "H" 1st Arkansas Mounted Rifles. Wraps.
1972   Dayton   10.00
DAGNALL, John M.   Daisy Swain, The Flower of Shenandoah, A Tale of the Rebellion.
1865   Brooklyn, NY   35.00
DAHLGREN, John A. B.   Memoir of Ulric Dahlgren.
1872   Philadelphia   45.00
DAHLGREN, Madeleine V.   Memoir of Admiral John A. Dahlgren.
1891   125.00
DAINGERFIELD, Foxhall, Jr.   The Southern Cross   A Play in Four Acts. Wraps.
1909   Lexington, KY   15.00
DAINGERFIELD, N. G.   Frescati   A Page from Virginia History.
1909   New York   50.00
DALE, Edward Everett and LITTON, Gaston   Cherokee Cavaliers.
1939   Norman, OK   75.00
1940   Norman, OK   45.00
1969   Norman, OK   30.00
DALL, Caroline H.   Barbara Fritchie, A Study.
1892   Boston   20.00
DALTON, Kit   Under the Black Flag. Wraps.
(1914)   (Memphis)   75.00
DALY, Louise Haskell   Alexander Cheves Haskell, The Portrait of a Man.
1934   Norwood, MA   Ltd.   375.00
1989   Wilmington, NC   30.00
DALY, Maria L.   Diary of a Union Lady 1861-1865, edited by Harold Earl Hammond.
1962   New York   20.00
DALY, R. W.   How the Merrimac Won . . . The Strategic Story of C.S.S. Virginia.
1957   New York   20.00
DALY, Walter E.   The Campaign of Gettysburg.
1912   Boston   75.00
DALZELL, George W.   The Flight from the Flag.
1940   Chapel Hill, NC   25.00
DALZELL, James McCormick   Private Dalzell, His Autobiography, Poems and Comic War Papers.
1888   Cincinnati   75.00
DAME, William M.   From the Rapidan to Richmond & the Spottsylvania Campaign.
1920   Baltimore   80.00
1987   Richmond   25.00

DAMER, Eyre   When the Ku Klux Rode.
    1912   New York   40.00
DAMMANN, Gordon   A Pictorial Encyclopedia of Civil War Medical
Instruments and Equipment. Wraps.
    1987   Missoula   Vol. I 8.95
    1988   Missoula   Vol. II 8.95
DAMON, Herbert C.   History of the Milwaukee Light Guard.
    1875   Milwaukee   90.00
DANA, Charles A.   Recollections of the Civil War.
    1898   New York   30.00
    1899   New York   25.00
    1902   New York   20.00
DANA, Charles A. and **WILSON**, J. H.   The Life of Ulysses S. Grant.
    1868   Springfield, MA 25.00
    1868   Portland   25.00
DANA, Malcolm McG.   The Annals of Norwich in the Great Rebellion.
    1873   Norwich   45.00
DANDRIDGE, Danske   Historic Shepherdstown.
    1910   Charlottesville   40.00
DANIEL, Edward M.   The Speeches and Orations of John Warwick
Daniel.
    1911   Lynchburg   80.00
DANIEL, F. E.   Recollections of a Rebel Surgeon.
    1899   Austin 100.00
    1901   Chicago 50.00
DANIEL, Frederick S.   Richmond Howitzers in the War. Wraps.
    1891   Richmond 325.00
    1984   Gaithersburg   22.50
DANIEL, J. W.   A Maid of the Foot-Hills.
    1905   New York   20.00
DANIEL, J. W.   Speeches and Orations of . . . .
    1911   Lynchburg   40.00
DANIEL, John M.   The Richmond Examiner During the War; or the
Writings of John M. Daniel. With a Memoir of His Life, by His Brother,
Frederick S. Daniel.
    1868   New York   75.00
DANIEL, John W.   Campaign and Battles of Gettysburg. Address.
Wraps.
    1875   Lynchburg   75.00
DANIEL, John W.   Character of Stonewall Jackson. Wraps.
    1868   Lynchburg   60.00
DANIEL, John W.   Life and Reminiscences of Jefferson Davis by Dis-
tinguished Men of His Time.
    1890   Baltimore   60.00
DANIEL, John W.   Oration: Ceremonies Connected with the Inaugura-
tion of the Mausoleum and the Unveiling of the Recumbent Figure of
General Robert Edward Lee, at Washington and Lee University, Lexing-
ton, Va. June 28, 1883.
    1883   Lexington, VA 40.00
    1883   Lynchburg   Wraps 30.00
    1883   Richmond   25.00
    1883   Savannah   40.00

DANIEL, John W.   Oration on the Life, Services and Character of
    Jefferson Davis. Wraps.
    1890   Richmond   15.00
    1890   Baltimore   15.00
DANIEL, John W. and WILLIAMS, Robert G.   Robert Edward Lee - An
    Oration and an Address.
    1931   Strasburg, VA   20.00
DANIEL, L. J.   Cannoneers in Gray; The Field Artillery of the Army
    of Tennessee, 1861-1865.
    1984   University, AL   20.00
DANIEL, L. J. and GUNTER, R. W.   Confederate Cannon Foundries.
    1977   TN   20.00
DANIEL, Lizzie Carrie   Confederate Scrap-Book.
    1893   Richmond   30.00
DANIEL, Raleigh T.   The Unveiling of the Monument to the Confederate
    Dead of Alexandria, Va. Wraps.
    1889   Alexandria   45.00
DANIELS, Jonathan   Mosby, Gray Ghost of the Confederacy.
    1959   Philadelphia   15.00
DANIELS, Jonathan   Prince of Carpetbaggers.
    1958   Philadelphia   15.00
Danner's Pocket Guide Book of the Battlefield of Gettysburg.   Wraps.
    n.d.   Gettysburg   35.00
DANNETT, Sylvia G. L., edited by   Noble Women of the North.
    1959   New York   20.00
DANNETT, Sylvia G. L.   She Rode with the Generals.   The True and
    Incredible Story of Sarah Emma Seelye, Alias Franklin Thompson.
    1960   New York   30.00
DANNETT, Sylvia G. L.   A Treasury of Civil War Humor.
    1963   New York   25.00
DANNETT, Sylvia G. L. and BURHART, Rosamond H.   Confederate
    Surgeon: Aristides Monteiro.
    1969   New York   30.00
DANNETT, Sylvia G. L. and JONES, Katharine M.   Our   Women   of
    the Sixties. Wraps.
    1963   Washington, DC   15.00
DARBY, George W.   Incidents   and   Adventures   in   Rebeldom, Libby,
    Belle-Isle, Salisbury.
    1899   Pittsburgh   50.00
DARLING, Henry   Slavery and the War: A Historical Essay.   Wraps.
    1863   Philadelphia   20.00
DARSEY, E. W.   A War Story of a Yankee Prison.   Wraps.
    1959   Statesboro, GA   25.00
DAUCHY, George K.   The Battle of Ream's Station.   Wraps.
    1899   Chicago   30.00
DAUGHERTY, James   Lincoln's Gettysburg Address.
    1947   Chicago   15.00
DAVENPORT, Alfred   Camp   and   Field Life of the Fifth New York
    Volunteer Infantry (Duryee Zouaves).
    1879   New York   150.00
    1984   32.50

DAVENPORT, Edward A., edited by   History of the Ninth Regiment
Illinois Cavalry Volunteers.
1888   Chicago 250.00
DAVENPORT, F. Garvin   Cultural Life in Nashville on the Eve of the
Civil War.
1941   NC   20.00
DAVENPORT, Francis O., Lieut. Comm. USN   On a Man-of-War.
1878   Detroit   65.00
DAVIDSON, Donald   Lee in the Mountains and Other Poems.
1938   Boston   75.00
DAVIDSON, G.   Captain Greenlee Davidson, C.S.A., Diary and Letters,
1851-1863.
1975   Verona, VA   20.00
DAVIDSON, Henry M.   Fourteen Months in Southern Prisons.
1865   Milwaukee   100.00
DAVIDSON, Henry M.   History of Battery A, 1st Regiment Ohio Vol.
Light Artillery.
1865   Milwaukee   145.00
DAVIDSON, Homer K.   Black Jack Davidson A Cavalry Commander
on the Western Frontier.
1974   Glendale, CA   25.00
DAVIDSON, James D.   A Curiosity in Chancery in the Circuit Court
of Rockbridge. Wraps.
(1877) Lexington   60.00
DAVIDSON, John Nelson   Negro Slavery in Wisconsin And the
Underground Railroad. Wraps.
1897   Milwaukee   30.00
DAVIDSON, Laura Lee   The Services of the Women of Maryland to the
Confederate States, A Prize Essay. Wraps.
1920   Baltimore   40.00
DAVIDSON, Nora Fontaine M.   Cullings from the Confederacy 1862-
1866. Wraps.
1903   Washington, DC   30.00
DAVIDSON, William H., edited by   War Was the Place A Centennial
Collection of Confederate Soldier Letters. Wraps.
1961   n.p.   30.00
1962   Oakbowery 25.00
DAVIES, C.   Elements of Surveying, and Navigation; with a Description
of the Instruments and the Necessary Tables.
1846   New York   75.00
DAVIES, Henry E.   General Sheridan.
For additional information, see Appendix: Great Commander Series.
1895   New York   40.00
1895   New York   Ltd.   125.00
1897   New York   35.00
1918   Richmond   30.00
DAVIS, Andrew McFarland   The Origin of the National Banking System.
1910   Washington, DC   30.00
DAVIS, Andrew McFarland   Supplement to the Origin of the National
Banking System.
1911   Washington, DC   20.00

DAVIS, Archie K.   Boy Colonel of the Confederacy, the Life and Times of Henry King Burgwyn, Jr.
  1985   Chapel Hill, NC   30.00
DAVIS, Archie K.   Colonel Harry Burgwyn of the 26th North Carolina Regiment. Wraps.
  1961   Jackson, NC   75.00
DAVIS, Billy   The Civil War Journal of Billy Davis, edited by Richard S. Skidmore. Wraps.
  1989   16.95
DAVIS, Burke   Civil War: Strange and Fascinating Facts.
  1982   5.00
DAVIS, Burke   Gray Fox, Robert E. Lee and the Civil War.
  1956   New York   30.00
  1981   20.00
  1988   9.95
DAVIS, Burke   Jeb Stuart: The Last Cavalier.
  1956   New York   30.00
  1957   New York   25.00
  1958   30.00
  1963   30.00
  1988   9.95
DAVIS, Burke   The Long Surrender.
  1985   New York   20.00
DAVIS, Burke   Our Incredible Civil War.
  1960   New York   25.00
DAVIS, Burke   Sherman's March.
  1980   New York   22.00
  1988   New York   Wraps   7.95
DAVIS, Burke   They Called Him Stonewall.
  1954   New York   35.00
  1964   30.00
  1988   9.95
DAVIS, Burke   To Appomattox. Nine April Days, 1865.
  1959   New York   25.00
DAVIS, Carl L.   Arming the Union, Small Arms in the Civil War.
  1973   Port Washington, NY   25.00
DAVIS, Charles E., Jr.   Three Years in the Army. The Story of the Thirteenth Massachusetts Volunteers.
  1894   Boston   100.00
DAVIS, Charles H.   Life of Charles Henry Davis, Rear Admiral.
  1899   Boston   40.00
DAVIS, Charles S.   Colin J. McRae: Confederate Financial Agent.
  See: Confederate Centennial Studies, No. 17.
DAVIS, Edwin Adams   Fallen Guidon The Forgotten Saga off General Jo Shelby's Confederate Command.
  1962   Santa Fe   50.00
DAVIS, Evangeline and DAVIS, Burke   Rebel Raider   A Biography of Admiral Semmes.
  1966   Philadelphia   20.00
DAVIS, H.   General Sheridan.
  1895   New York   20.00

DAVIS, J. C. Bancroft   Mr. Fish and the Alabama Claims A Chapter in Diplomatic History.
1893   Boston   25.00

DAVIS, J. C. Bancroft   Mr. Sumner, the Alabama Claims, and Their Settlement, a Letter to the "New York Herald."   Wraps.
1878   New York   30.00

DAVIS, Jefferson   Jefferson Davis, Constitutionalist: His Letters, Papers and Speeches, edited by Dunbar Rowland. 10 Vols. and index.
1923   Jackson, MS   600.00

DAVIS, Jefferson   The Papers of Jefferson Davis. Vols. 1-6
1971-90 Baton Rouge   Still in publication.
Vol. 1-5   45.00 each
Vol. 6   55.00

DAVIS, Jefferson   Private   Letters   1823-1889,   edited   by   Hudson Strode.
1966   New York   25.00

DAVIS, Jefferson   The Rise and Fall of the Confederate Government.
2 Vols.
1881   New York   125.00
1938   Richmond   85.00
1958   New York   Boxed   45.00

DAVIS, Jefferson   Robert E. Lee, edited by Harold B. Simpson.
1966   Hillsboro   25.00
1983   20.00

DAVIS, Julia   Mount Up.   A True Story Based on the Reminiscences of Major E. H. McDonald of the Confederate Cavlary.
1967   New York   40.00

DAVIS, Julia   The Shenandoah.
1945   New York   25.00

DAVIS, Keith F.   George N. Barnard, Photographer of Sherman's Campaign.
n.d. University, NM   40.00
n.d. University, NM   Wraps 25.00

DAVIS, Maggie   The Far Side of Home.
1963   New York   15.00

DAVIS, Margaret B.   The Woman Who Battled for the Boys in Blue: Mother Bickerdyke.
1886   San Francisco   35.00

DAVIS, Michael   The Image of Lincoln in the South.
1971   Knoxville   20.00

DAVIS, Nicholas A.   The Campaign from Texas to Maryland, with The Battle of Fredericksburg.
For 1863 edition, see: Confederate Imprints P-4801.
1961   Austin Boxed   40.00

DAVIS, Nicholas A.   Chaplain Davis & Hood's Texas Brigade, edited by Donald E. Everett.
1962   San Antonio 35.00

DAVIS, Nora M., edited by   Military and Naval Operations in South Carolina 1860-1865. Wraps.
1959   Columbia   20.00

DAVIS, Oliver W.   The Life of David Bell Birney, Major-General, U.S. Volunteers.
    1867   New York   25.00
    1987   Gaithersburg   30.00
DAVIS, Paxton   The Battle of New Market. A Story of V.M.I.
    1963   Boston   15.00
DAVIS, Reuben   Recollections of Mississippi and Mississippians.
    1889   New York   75.00
    1890   Boston   50.00
DAVIS, Robert S.   History of the Rebel Steam Ram "Atlanta" . . . for the Benefit of the Union Volunteer Refreshment Saloon, Philadelphia. Wraps.
    1863   Philadelphia   30.00
DAVIS, Rollin V.   U. S. Sword Bayonets 1847-1865.   Wraps.
    1963   Pittsburgh   15.00
DAVIS, Samuel B.   Escape of a Confederate Officer from Prison. Wraps.
    1892   Norfolk   200.00
DAVIS, Susan Lawrence   Authentic History of the Ku Klux Klan, 1865-1877.
    1924   New York   50.00
DAVIS, Varina Howell   Jefferson Davis Ex-President of the Confederate States of America. A Memoir By His Wife. 2 Vols.
    1890   New York   150.00
DAVIS, Washington   Camp-Fire Chats of the Civil War.
    1884   Chicago   50.00
    1886   Chicago   45.00
DAVIS, William C.   Battle at Bull Run.
    1977   New York   20.00
    1985   Baton Rouge   Wraps   8.95
DAVIS, William C.   The Battle of New Market.
    1975   Garden City, NY   17.00
    1983   Wraps   10.00
DAVIS, William C.   Breckinridge, Statesman, Soldier, Symbol.
    1974   Baton Rouge   40.00
    1982   40.00
DAVIS, William C.   A Continuation of the Image of War Series. 2 Vols.
    1985   60.00
    1985   Vol. I   32.00
    1985   Vol. II   32.00
DAVIS, William C.   Duel Between the First Ironclads.
    1975   Garden City   20.00
    1981   Wraps   9.95
DAVIS, William C.   The Fighting Men of the Civil War, Rebels and Yankees.
    1989   Italy   24.98
DAVIS, William C.   Great Battles of the Civil War.
    1989   17.98
DAVIS, William C., edited by   The Image of War, 1861-1865.
    Vol. I   Shadows of the Storm. 1981   Garden City   25.00
    Vol. II   The Guns of '62. 1982   Garden City   25.00
    Vol. III The Embattled Confederacy. 1982   Garden City   25.00

Vol. IV **Fighting for Time.** 1983   Garden City   25.00
Vol. V **The South Besieged.** 1983   Garden City   25.00
Vol. VI **The End of an Era.** 1984   Garden City   25.00
DAVIS, William C.   **The Imperiled Union, 1861-1865.** 2 Vols. Vol. I -
The Deep Waters of the Proud; Vol. II - Stand in the Day of the Battle.
Vol. III- never published.
1982-83 New York   20.00 each
DAVIS, William C.   **The Orphan Brigade.**
1980   New York   25.00
1983   10.00
DAVIS, William W. H.   **History of the Doylestown Guards.**
1887   Doylestown   65.00
DAVIS, William W. H.   **History of the 104th Pennsylvania Regiment.**
1866   Philadelphia   120.00
DAVIS, William Watson   **The Civil War and Reconstruction in Florida.**
Wraps.
1913   New York   300.00
1964   Gainesville   35.00
DAWES, Rufus R.   **Service with the Sixth Wisconsin Volunteers.**
1890   Marietta   150.00
1936   Marietta   100.00
1962   Madison   50.00
1984   30.00
1985   30.00
DAWSON, Francis W.   **Our Women in the War.** Wraps.
1887   Charleston   50.00
DAWSON, Francis W.   **Reminiscences of Confederate Service 1861-**
1865.
1882   Charleston   Ltd.   3500.00
1980   Baton Rouge   25.00
1985   Baton Rouge   edited by Bell I. Wiley   17.50
1986   25.00
DAWSON, George Francis   **Life and Services of Gen. John A. Logan.**
1884   Washington, DC   30.00
1887   New York   25.00
DAWSON, J.   **Army Gen. and Reconstruction, Louisiana, 1862-1877.**
1982   25.00
DAWSON, John Harper   **Wildcat Cavalry, a Synoptic History of the**
Seventeenth Virginia Cavalry Regiment of the Jenkins-McCausland
Brigade. . . .
1982   Dayton   15.00
DAWSON, Sarah Morgan   **A Confederate Girl's Diary.**
1913   Boston & New York 75.00
1960   Bloomington, IN   edited by James Robertson, Jr.   30.00
DAY, David L.   **My Diary - Rambles with the 25th Mass. Volunteer**
Infantry.
1884   Milford   75.00
DAY, Lewis W.   **Story of the One Hundred and First Ohio Infantry.**
1894   Cleveland   175.00
DAY, Samuel Phillips   **Down South, or An Englishman's Experience**
at the Seat of the American War. 2 Vols.
1971   New York   30.00

DAY, W.   The Campaign of Gettysburg.
    1912   150.00
DAZELL, George   The Flight from the Flag.
    1940   20.00
DEADERICK, John Barron   Campaigns and Battles of America 1755-
    1865.
    1959   Boston   15.00
DEADERICK, John Barron   Shiloh, Memphis and Vicksburg. Wraps.
    1960   Memphis   15.00
DEADERICK, John Barron   Strategy in the Civil War.
    1946   Harrisburg   20.00
DEADERICK, John Barron   The Truth About Shiloh. Wraps.
    1942   Memphis   20.00
DEAN, Benjamin D.   Recollections of the 26th Missouri Infantry in the
    War for the Union.
    1892   Lamar, MO   200.00
DEAN, Henry C.   Crimes of the Civil War and Curse of the Funding Sys-
    tem.
    1868   Baltimore   50.00
    1869   Baltimore   40.00
The Death of Lee Southern Collegian, October 15, 1870. Wraps.
    1955   Atlanta   30.00
DEBOW, J. D.   Statistical View of the United States, Embracing Its
    Territory, Population, White, Free Colored, and Slave.
    1854   Washington, DC   40.00
DEBRAY, Xavier B.   A Sketch of the History of Debray's 26th Regiment
    of Texas Cavalry. Wraps.
    1884   Austin   2300.00
    1961   Waco   35.00
DECHANAL, V.   The American Army in the War of Secession.
    1894   Leavenworth   90.00
DECHANAL, V.   L'Armee Americaine.
    1872   Paris   50.00
DECKER, Eugene Donald   Kansas in the Civil War. Wraps.
    1961   n.p.   15.00
Declaration of the Immediate Causes Which Induce and Justify the Seces-
    sion of South Carolina from the Federal Union and the Ordinance of
    Secession. . . .   Counterfeit of the original 1860 publication.
    (Confederate Imprints: P-3761) Wraps.
    n.d.   Americus, GA   75.00
Decorations United States Army 1862-1926. Wraps.
    1927   100.00
Dedication of Confederate Soldiers' and Sailors' Monument, Richmond May
    30, 1894. Wraps.
    1894   Richmond   40.00
Dedication of Double Equestrian Statue: General Robert E. Lee and General
    Thomas J. (Stonewall) Jackson. Wraps.
    1948   Baltimore   20.00
Dedication of Monument . . . to Commemorate the Charge of General
    Humphries' Division . . . On Marye's Heights, Fredericksburg. Wraps.
    1908   Philadelphia   25.00

Dedication of the Equestrian Statue of Major-General John Sedgwick. Erected on the Battlefield of Gettysburg by the State of Connecticut June 19, 1913.
1913   Hartford   20.00

Dedication of the Monument at Andersonville . . . in Memory of the Men of Connecticut Who Suffered in Southern Military Prisons.
1908   Hartford   25.00

Dedication of the Monument of the 6th Penna. Cavalry "Lancers" on the Battlefield of Gettysburg. Wraps.
1889   Philadelphia   35.00

Dedication of the New York Auxiliary State Monument on the Battlefield of Gettysburg.
1926   Albany   125.00

Dedication of the Statue of . . . Lieut. Gen. Stephen Dill Lee, C.S.A.   Wraps.
1909   Vicksburg   20.00

Dedication of the Statue to Brevet Major General William Wells and the Officers and Men of the 1st Regiment Vermont Cavalry (Jackson, Horatio N.)
1914   (Burlington)   70.00

Dedicatory Ceremonies Held on the Battlefield of Manassas or 2nd Bull Run, Virginia, . . . The 5th Regt. NY Vol. Inf. "Duyree Zouaves."
1907   Brooklyn   40.00

DEERING, John R.   Lee and His Cause, or the Why and the How of the War Between the States.
1907   New York and Washington, DC   75.00

Defence of Commodore W. D. Porter Before the Naval Retiring Board. Wraps.
1863   New York   35.00

A Defense of Southern Slavery. See: BROOKES, Iveson L.

DE FONTAINE, Felix G.   Army Letters of "Personne," 1861-1865.   Nos. 1-2 (all issued). Wraps.
1896   Columbia, SC   150.00

DE FOREST, Bartholomew   Random   Sketches   and   Wandering Thoughts.
1866   Albany   75.00

DE FOREST, John William   Miss Ravenel's Conversion from Secession to Loyalty.
1867   150.00
1939   New York/London   30.00
1955   New York   20.00
1964   10.00

DE FOREST, John William   A Union Officer in the Reconstruction.
1948   New Haven, CT   40.00

DE FOREST, John William   A Volunteer's Adventures.
1946   New Haven, CT   30.00
1956   New Haven, CT   20.00

DEGLER, Carl   The Other South.
1974   v.p.   10.00

DE GRUMMOND, Lena Y. and DE GRUMMOND DELAUNE, Lynn   Jeb Stuart.
1962   New York   20.00

DEHART, William C.   Observations on Mil' ary Law and the Constitution and Practice of Courts Martial, with a summary of the Law of Evidence. . . .
    1863   New York   90.00

DELAND, Margaret Wade   The Kays.
    1926   New York   15.00

DELANEY, Caldwell   Confederate Mobile: A Pictorial History.
    1971   Mobile   35.00

DELANEY, Norman C.   Ghost Ship: The Confederate Raider Ala ama. Wraps.
    1989   Middleton   9.95

DELANEY, Norman C.   John McIntosh Kell of the Raider Alabama.
    1973   University, AL   25.00

DELANEY, Wayne Richard, and **BOWERY**, Marie E edited by   The Seventeenth Virginia Volunteer Infantry Regiment CSA. Wraps.
    1961   Washington, DC   25.00

DELAUTER, Roger U.   McNeil's Rangers.
    1986   Lynchburg Ltd.   16.45

DELAUTER, Roger U.   62nd Virginia Infantry.
    1988   16.95

DE LEEUW, Adele   Civil War Nurse, Mary Ann Bickerdyke.
    1973   New York   30.00

DE LEON, Thomas C.   Belles, Beaux and Brains of the 60's.
    1907   New York   50.00
    1909   New York   75.00

DE LEON, Thomas C.   Craig Nest A Romance of the Days of Sheridan's Ride. Wraps.
    1910   Louisville   20.00

DE LEON, Thomas C.   Four Years in Rebel Capitals.
    1890   Mobile, AL   100.00
    1892   Mobile, AL   75.00
    1983   25.00
    1988   27.50

DE LEON, Thomas C.   John Holden, Unionist.
    1893   St. Paul 25.00
    1910   New York   20.00

DE LEON, Thomas C.   Joseph Wheeler, The Man, The Statesman, The Soldier.
    1899   Atlanta 200.00
    1960   Kennesaw, GA   25.00

DELL, C.   Lincoln and the War Democrats: The Grand Erosion of Conservative Tradition.
    1975   Rutherford   20.00

DEMEISSNER, S. R.   Old Naval Days: Sketches from the Life of Rear Admiral Radford, U.S.N.
    1920   New York   45.00

DEMING, Henry C.   The Life of Ulysses S. Grant.
    1868   Hartford   20.00

The Democratic Almanac for 1866. Wraps.
    1866   New York   25.00

Democratic National Convention, Official Proceedings of, Held in 1860 - at Charleston. Wraps.
1860   Cleveland   30.00
Democratus (pseud.)   An Appeal for the Constitution: Theory and Practice of the Government. Wraps.
1862   Baltimore   35.00
The Demon of Andersonville; Or, the Trial of Wirz. Wraps.
1865   Philadelphia 100.00
DEMORET, Alfred   A Brief History of the Ninety-third Regiment Ohio Volunteer Infantry. Wraps.
1898   Ross, OH   150.00
DE MOSS, John C.   A Short History of the Soldier-Life, Capture and Death of William Francis Corbin, Captain Fourth Kentucky Cavalry, C.S.A. Wraps.
(c.1897) (Midway, KY)   200.00
DENISON, Charles Wheeler   Hancock the Superb.
1880   Philadelphia   40.00
DENISON, Charles Wheeler   Illustrated Life Campaigns and Public Services of Philip H. Sheridan (Major-General Sheridan).
1865   Philadelphia   40.00
DENISON, Charles Wheeler   Winfield, The Lawyer's Son and How He Became a Major-General.
1865   Philadelphia   30.00
DENISON, Frederic   Sabres and Spurs, The First Regiment Rhode Island Cavalry.
1876   Central Falls   150.00
DENISON, Frederic   Shot and Shell, The Third Rhode Island Heavy Artillery in the Rebellion, 1861-1865.
1879   Providence   80.00
DENISON, George T.   A History of Cavalry.
1913   London   60.00
DENISON, George T.   Modern Cavalry: Its Organization, Armament, and Employment in the War.
1868   London   150.00
DENMAN, Clarence Phillips   The Secession Movement in Alabama.
1933   Montgomery   40.00
DENNETT, John Richard   The South As It Is   1865-1866.
1965   New York   20.00
DENNETT, Tyler   John Hay: From Poetry to Politics.
1933   New York   20.00
DENNETT, Tyler, edited by   Lincoln and the Civil War in the Diaries and Letters of John Hay.
1939   New York   25.00
DENNY, J. Waldo   Wearing the Blue in the Twenty-fifth Mass. Volunteer Infantry with Burnside's Coast Division.
1879   Worcester   100.00
DE NOON, Charles E.   Charlie's Letters: the Correspondence of Charles E. De Noon, edited by Richard T. Couture. Wraps.
1982   n.p.   25.00
1989   16.95
DENSLOW, Ray V.   Civil War and Masonry in Missouri.
1930   n.p.   30.00

DENSON, Claude B.   An Address Delivered in Raleigh, N.C. on Memorial
Day May 10, 1895 . . . Memoir . . . Wm. H. C. Whiting.   Wraps.
1895   Raleigh, NC   45.00
1979   10.00
DE PEYSTER, John Watts   Address . . . Inauguration of a Monument
Erected by . . . Tivoli-Madalin to Her Defenders Who Lost Their Lives.
Wraps.
1867   New York   Ltd.   35.00
DE PEYSTER, John Watts   Battle of Oak Ridge; Wednesday, July 1,
1863, at Gettysburg July 2nd and 3rd, 1863.   After Gettysburg and at
Williamsport and Falling Waters. . . .
1987   Gaithersburg   22.50
DE PEYSTER, John Watts   The Decisive Conflicts of the Late Civil
War or Slaveholders Rebellion.
1867   New York   25.00
DE PEYSTER, John Watts   Gettysburg and After.
1987   20.00
DE PEYSTER, John Watts   Personal and Military History of Philip
Kearny, Major-General U.S. Volunteers.
1869   New York   75.00
1870   New York   45.00
1870   Elizabeth, NJ   45.00
DE PEYSTER, John Watts   Sketch of Gen. George H. Thomas   A Bio-
graphical Work.   Wraps.
n.d.   New York   85.00
DERBY, William P.   Bearing Arms in the Twenty-seventh Massachusetts
Regiment of Volunteer Infantry During the Civil War.
1883   Boston   100.00
DE ROSIER, Arthur H., Jr., edited by   Through the South with a
Union Soldier.
1969   Johnson City, TN   30.00
DERRICK, S. M.   Centennial History of South Carolina Railroad.
1930   Columbia   60.00
DERRY, Joseph T.   Georgia.   See: Confederate Military History,
Vol. VI (Vol. VII, 1987 reprint ed.).
DERRY, Joseph T.   Story of the Confederate States.
1895   Richmond   75.00
1896   Richmond   60.00
1898   Richmond   50.00
1979   New York   20.00
DERRY, Joseph T.   The Strife of Brothers   A Poem.
1903   Atlanta   45.00
1904   Atlanta   35.00
1906   40.00
DE SAUSSURE, Mrs. N. B.   Old Plantation Days Being Recollections of
Southern Life Before the Civil War.
1909   New York   50.00
A Descriptive List of the Burial Places of the Remains of Confederate Soldiers, Who Fell in the Battles of Antietam, South Mountain, Monocacy,
and Other Points in Washington and Frederick Counties, In the State of
Maryland.   Wraps.
(1868)   Hagerstown, MD   75.00

Descriptive Texts to Prang's War Pictures.
1888   Boston   40.00
Destruction of the U. S. Navy Yard at Norfolk. Wraps.
(1861) (Washington, DC)   50.00
DEUPREE, J. G.   The Noxubee Squadron of the First Mississippi Cavalry,
C.S.A. 1861-65.
1912   90.00
DE VELLING, Charles Theodore, compiled by   **History of the 17th Regiment, 1st Brigade, 3rd Division, 14th Corps, Army of the Cumberland.**
1889   Zanesville   200.00
DEVENS, Charles, Jr.   General Meade and the Battle of Gettysburg.
Wraps.
1873   Morrisania, NY   25.00
DEVEREUX, Margaret   Plantation Sketches.
1906   Cambridge   90.00
DEVLIN, B.   St. Albans Raid, Speech. Wraps.
1865   Montreal   40.00
DEW, Charles B.   Ironmaker to the Confederacy, Joseph R. Anderson and
the Tredegar Iron Works.
1966   New Haven 1st ed. 75.00
1966   Binghamton, NY   50.00
1987   Wilmington, NC   30.00
DEWITT, David Miller   The Assassination of Abraham Lincoln and Its
Expiation.
1909   New York   50.00
DEWITT, David Miller   The Impeachment and Trial of Andrew Johnson.
1903   New York   45.00
1967   Madison   15.00
DEXTER, Henry Martyn   What Ought to be Done with the Freedmen and
With the Rebels? A Sermon. Wraps.
1865   Boston   25.00
DIAL, Marshall   The Boothell Swamp Struggle. Wraps.
1961   Lilbourn, MO   25.00
**Diaries, Letters, and Recollections of the War Between the States, Va. Sol-
diers in the Civil War.** Wraps.
1955   Winchester   30.00
The Diary of a Public Man.
1945   Chicago   20.00
Diary of Edmund Ruffin. Vols. I and II.
1972   45.00 per volume
**A Diary of the 30th Regiment, Wisconsin Volunteers. A History of the
Regiment Since Its Organization.**
1864   Madison 150.00
DICEY, Edward   Spectator of America.
1971   20.00
1972   London   25.00
DICEY, Edward J.   Six Months in the Federal States. 2 Vols.
1863   London   150.00

DICKERSON, Edward   The Navy of the United States, An Exposure of Its Condition, and the Causes of Its Failure, Contained in a Speech Delivered to a Jury in the Supreme Court of the District of Columbia. . . Wraps.
1864   60.00
DICKERT, D. Augustus   History of Kershaw's Brigade.
1899   Newberry   1000.00
1973   Dayton 30.00
1988   Dayton 30.00
1990   Wilmington, NC 35.00
DICKEY, Luther S.   History of the 85th Regiment Pennsylvania Volunteer Infantry 1861-1864.
1915   New York   85.00
DICKEY, Luther S.   History of the 103d Regiment Pennsylvania Veteran Volunteer Infantry 1861-1865.
1910   Chicago   80.00
DICKEY, Thomas S. and GEORGE, Peter C.   Field Artillery, Projectiles of the American Civil War.
1980   GA   60.00
DICKINSON, Henry Clay   Diary of Capt. Henry Dickinson, C.S.A.
(191-)   Denver   Ltd.   400.00
DICKINSON, J. L.   Confederate Soldiers of Western Virginia.   Wraps.
1986   Barboursville   17.50
DICKINSON, J. L.   8th Virginia Cavalry.
1986   Lynchburg   Ltd.   16.45
DICKINSON, J. L.   Jenkins of Greenbottom: A Civil War Saga. Wraps.
1988   Charleston, WV   7.95
DICKINSON, J. L.   16th Virginia Cavalry.
1989   16.95
DICKINSON, Julian G.   The Capture of Jeff. Davis.   Wraps.
1888   Detroit   35.00
DICKINSON, Sally Bruce   Confederate Leaders.
1937   Staunton   75.00
DICKISON, J. J.   Florida.   See: Confederate Military History, Vol. XI (Vol. XVI, 1989 reprint ed.).
DICKISON, Mary Elizabeth   Dickison and His Men.
1890   Louisville, KY   375.00
1984   Jacksonville   20.00
DICKSON, Capers   John Ashton: A Story of the War Between the States.
1896   Atlanta   40.00
DIETZ, August, Sr.   The Confederate States Post-Office Department. Wraps.
1948   Richmond   30.00
1950   Richmond   20.00
DIETZ, August, Sr., edited by   Confederate States Catalog and Hand-Book of the Postage Stamps and Envelopes of the Confederate States.
1945   Richmond   40.00
1959   Richmond   25.00

DIETZ, August, Sr., edited by   The Postal Service of the Confederate
    States of America.
    1929   Richmond   350.00
    1989   75.00
DILL, Samuel P.   Journal of the Escape and Re-capture of Captain
    _____. Wraps.
    1886   Brooklyn   75.00
DIMITRY, John   Louisiana. See: Confederate Military History, Vol. X
    (Vol. XIII, 1988 reprint ed.).
DIMITRY, Adelaide Stuart   War-Time Sketches Historical and Other-
    wise.
    n.d.   New Orleans   250.00
DINKINS, James   James Dinkins 1861-65: By An Old Johnnie.
    1975   Dayton   15.00
DINKINS, James   Personal Recollections and Experiences in the Con-
    federate Army 1861 to 1865.
    1897   Cincinnati   300.00
    1975   20.00
Diplomatic Correspondence - Papers Relating to Foreign Affairs . . . 2nd
    Sess., 38th Congress. 4 Vols.
    1865   Washington, DC 100.00
DISBROW, A.   Glimpses of Chickamauga, a Complete Guide. . . .
    1895   Chicago   60.00
The Dismissal of Major Granville Haller of the Regular Army. Wraps.
    1863   Paterson, NJ   25.00
DIVINE, John   Loudoun County and the Civil War. Wraps.
    1961   Leesburg   12.00
DIX, Morgan   Memoirs of John Adams Dix. 2 Vols.
    1883   New York   40.00
DIXON, A.   The True History of the Missouri Compromise and Its
    Repeal.
    1899   Cincinnati   25.00
DIXON, Samuel H.   Robert Warren, The Texan Refugee.
    n.d.   New York   50.00
DIXON, Thomas, Jr.   The Clansman.
    1905   New York   25.00
DIXON, Thomas, Jr.   The Leopard's Spots.
    1902   New York   20.00
    1903   New York   20.00
DIXON, Thomas, Jr.   The Man in Gray.
    1921   New York   20.00
DIXON, Thomas, Jr.   The Traitor, A Story of the Fall of the Invisible
    Empire.
    1907   New York   20.00
DOAN, Isaac C.   Reminiscences of the Chattanooga Campaign. Wraps.
    1894   Richmond   50.00
DOBBINS, Austin C.   Grandfather's Journal.
    1988   24.95
DODD, D. B.   Winston: An Antebellum and Civil War History of a
    Hill County of North Alabama.
    1972   Jasper   25.00

DODD, Ephraim Shelby   Diary of _____. Wraps.
   1914   Austin   150.00
   1979   Austin   20.00
DODD, Ira S.   Song of the Rappahannock, Sketches of the Civil War.
   1898   New York   60.00
DODD, William E.   Expansion and Conflict.
   1915   New York   15.00
DODD, William E.   Jefferson Davis.
   1907   Philadelphia   25.00
DODD, William E.   Lincoln or Lee.
   1928   New York   25.00
   1964   MA   18.00
DODD, William E.   Statesmen of the Old South, or From Radicalism to Conservative Revolt.
   1929   New York   20.00
DODGE, Grenville Mellen   The Battle of Atlanta, and Other Campaigns.
   1910   Council Bluffs, IA   40.00
   1911   Council Bluffs, IA   40.00
   1965   Denver 15.00
DODGE, Grenville Mellen   Fiftieth Anniversary Fourth Iowa Veteran Volunteer Infantry, Dodge's Second Iowa Battery ... Wraps.
   1911   Council Bluffs, IA   50.00
DODGE, Grenville Mellen   Norwich University, 1819-1911 (Vermont), Her History, Her Graduates, Her Roll of Honor. 3 Vols.
   1911   125.00
DODGE, Grenville Mellen   Personal Recollections of President Abraham Lincoln, General Ulysses S. Grant, and General William T. Sherman.
   1914   Iowa   30.00
DODGE, Grenville Mellen   A Sketch of the Life and Public Services of Brigadier and Brevet Major-General James Alexander Williamson. Wraps.
   1903   Des Moines, IA   75.00
DODGE, Grenville Mellen   Sketch of the Military Service of Major General Wager Swayne. Wraps.
   1903   New York   35.00
DODGE, James H.   Across the Plains with the Ninth Wisconsin Battery in 1862, D. C. MOLLUS War Paper 23. Wraps.
   1896   n.p.   35.00
DODGE, Theodore Ayrault   A Birds-Eye View of our Civil War.
   1883   Boston 40.00
   1884   Boston 30.00
   1897   Boston 25.00
   1911   20.00
DODGE, Theodore Ayrault   The Campaign of Chancellorsville.
   1881   Boston   45.00
DODGE, William Sumner   History of the Old Second Division Army of the Cumberland.
   1864   Chicago 125.00

DODGE, William Sumner   Robert Henry Hendershot; or, the Brave Drummer Boy of the Rappahannock.
     1867   Chicago   40.00
DODGE, William Sumner   A Waif of the War: or, The History of the Seventy-fifth Illinois Infantry.
     1866   Chicago   175.00
DODSON, William C., edited by   Campaigns of Wheeler and His Cavalry.
     1899   Atlanta   125.00
Does the Country Require a National Armory and Foundry West of the Allegheny Mountains.   Wraps.
     1862   Pittsburg   30.00
DOHERTY, Herbert J., Jr.   Richard Keith Call, Southern Unionist.
     1961   Gainesville   20.00
DOLL, William H.   History of the Sixth Regiment Indiana Volunteer Infantry.
     1903   Columbus, IN   170.00
DOLLARD, Robert   Recollections of the Civil War, and Going West to Grow Up with the Country.
     1906   Scotland, SD   100.00
DONAGHY, John   Army Experiences of Captain _____, 103rd Pennsylvania Volunteers 1861-1864.
     1926   Deland, FL   110.00
DONALD, David   Charles Sumner and the Coming of the Civil War.
     1960   New York   25.00
     1961   New York   25.00
     1967   20.00
DONALD, David   Charles Sumner and the Rights of Man.
     1970   New York   25.00
     1971   20.00
DONALD, David, et al, edited by   Divided We Fought. A Pictorial History of the Civil War.
     1952   New York   25.00
     1953   New York   20.00
     1956   New York   20.00
DONALD, David   Liberty and Union. Wraps.
     1978   MA 15.00
DONALD, David   Lincoln Reconsidered.
     1956   New York   25.00
     1959   25.00
DONALD, David   Lincoln's Herndon.
     1948   New York   20.00
DONALD, David   The Politics of Reconstruction 1863-1867.
     1965   Baton Rouge   20.00
     1967   20.00
DONALD, David, edited by   Why the North Won the Civil War.
     1960   Baton Rouge   20.00
DONALD, Henderson H.   The Negro Freedman; Life Conditions of the American Negro in the Early Years after Emancipation.
     1952   25.00

DONNELLY, Ralph W.   Biographical Sketches of the Commissioned Officers of the Confederate States Marine Corps.   Wraps.
1983   Washington, NC   10.00
DONNELLY, Ralph W.   The Confederate States Marine Corps.
1989   Shippensburg   24.95
DONNELLY, Ralph W.   The History of the Confederate States Marine Corps.   Wraps.
1976   Washington, DC   Ltd.   60.00
1989   24.95
DONNELLY, Ralph W.   Service   Records   of   Confederate   Enlisted Marines.   Wraps.
1979   New Bern, NC   30.00
DONOVAN, Frank   Mr. Lincoln's Proclamation: The Story of the Emancipation Proclamation.
1964   New York   15.00
DONOVAN, Frank and CATTON, Bruce   Ironclads of the Civil War.
1961   New York   30.00
DONOVAN, William F.   Membership Roll of the 36th Illinois Veteran Volunteer Infantry.   Wraps.
1903   (Elgin)   55.00
DORF, P.   Highlights & Sidelights of the Civil War.   Wraps.
1989   Middletown   9.95
DORMAN, Lewy   Party Politics in Alabama from 1850 through 1860.
1935   Wetumpka, AL   25.00
DORNBLASER, Thomas Franklin   My Life-Story for Young and Old.
1930   Chicago   65.00
DORNBLASER, Thomas Franklin   Sabre Strokes of the Pennsylvania Dragoons, in the War of 1861-1865.
1884   Philadelphia   175.00
DORNBUSCH, Charles E.   The   Communities   of   New   York   and   the Civil War.
1962   New York   25.00
1962   New York   Wraps   8.00
DORNBUSCH, Charles E., edited by   Military Bibliography of the Civil War.   4 Vols.
1971-72   New York   3 Vols.   75.00 each
1987   Vol. 4   40.00
DORNBUSCH, Charles E., compiled by   Regimental   Publications   and Personal Narratives of the Civil War. A Checklist. (Military Bibliography of the Civil War.) Wraps.   Volume I - Northern States.
1961   Part I   Illinois   20.00
1961   Part II   New York   20.00
1961   Part III   New England States   20.00
1962   Part IV   New Jersey and Pennsylvania   20.00
1962   Part V   Indiana and Ohio   20.00
1962   Part VI   Iowa,   Kansas,   Michigan,   Minnesota   and   Wisconsin   20.00
1962   Part VII Index of Northern States   20.00
Various parts in wraps   8.00 each
DORRIS, Jonathan Truman   Pardon   and   Amnesty   Under   Lincoln   and Johnson.
1953   Chapel Hill, NC   30.00

DORSEY, R. S.   American Military Belts and Related Equipments.
Wraps.
1984   Union City   11.00
DORSEY, Sarah A.   Recollections of Henry Watkins Allen, Brig.Gen.,
C.S.A.
1866   New York   75.00
1886   New Orleans   50.00
DOTSON, Susan Merle   Who's Who of the Confederacy.
1966   TX   20.00
DOTY, Lockwood L.   Presentation of Flags of the New York Volunteer
Regiments . . . To Gov. Fenton.
1865   Albany 60.00
DOUBLEDAY, Abner   Chancellorsville and Gettysburg. See:
Campaigns in the Civil War.
DOUBLEDAY, Abner   Gettysburg Made Plain.   Wraps.
1888   New York   30.00
1987   Wraps   8.50
DOUBLEDAY, Abner   Reminiscences of Forts Sumter and Moultrie in
1860-61.
1876   New York   30.00
1976   SC   25.00
DOUBLEDAY, Abner   Reports of the Battles of Gettysburgh [sic]
July 1st, 2nd and 3rd, 1663 [sic].   Wraps.
1865   Montpelier   175.00
DOUGAN, M. B.   Confederate Arkansas. . . .
1982   15.00
DOUGLAS, Henry Kyd   The Douglas Diary: Student Days at Franklin-
Marshall College 1856-1858.
1973   Lancaster   25.00
DOUGLAS, Henry Kyd   I Rode with Stonewall.
1940   Chapel Hill, NC   30.00
1943   Chapel Hill, NC   25.00
1961   Wraps   3.00
1968   20.00
1984   17.50
1987   19.95
DOUGLAS, Lucia Rutherford, edited by   Douglas' Texas Battery, C.S.A.
1966   Tyler   40.00
DOUGLASS, Frederick   Life and Times of _____ Written By Himself.
1882   Hartford   25.00
1962   New York   15.00
DOUGLASS, Frederick   Narrative of the Life of _____ An American
Slave Written by Himself, edited by Benjamin Quarles.
1960   Cambridge, MA   20.00
DOUGLASS, H. Paul   Christian Reconstruction in the South.
1909   Boston   35.00
DOUST, Harry W. and **LAGEMANN**, Robert L.   Antietam National
Battlefield Site Maryland.   Wraps.
1958   n.p.   15.00
DOUTHAT, Robert William   Gettysburg, A Battle Ode Descriptive of
the Grand Charge of the Third Day July 3, 1863.
1905   New York/Washington, DC   100.00

DOW, Neal   The Reminiscences of Neal Dow, Recollections of Eighty Years.
    1898   Portland, ME   40.00
DOWD, Clement   Life of Zebulon B. Vance.
    1897   Charlotte, NC   30.00
DOWD, James P.   Custer Lives!
    1982   18.50
DOWD, Jerome   Life of Braxton Craven.
    1896   Raleigh   60.00
DOWDEY, Clifford   Bugles Blow No More.
    1937   Boston   25.00
    1937   New York   20.00
    1946   Boston   20.00
    1957   20.00
    1967   20.00
DOWDEY, Clifford   Death of a Nation, The Story of Lee and His Men at Gettysburg.
    1958   New York   40.00
    1988   Baltimore   25.00
    1988   Wraps   12.95
DOWDEY, Clifford   Experiment in Rebellion.
    1946   Garden City, NY   30.00
    1947   New York   25.00
DOWDEY, Clifford   The Land They Fought For.
    1955   Garden City, NY   30.00
    1956   25.00
DOWDEY, Clifford   Last Night the Nightingale.
    1962   New York   15.00
DOWDEY, Clifford   Lee's Last Campaign.
    1960   Boston   30.00
    1988   Wilmington, NC   25.00
    Recent reprint   25.00
DOWDEY, Clifford   Lee.
    1965   Boston / Toronto   30.00
    Recent reprint   20.00
DOWDEY, Clifford   The Proud Retreat.
    1953   Garden City, NY   30.00
DOWDEY, Clifford   The Seven Days: The Emergence of Lee.
    1964   Boston   30.00
    1964   New York   25.00
    1978   New York   25.00
    1988   Wilmington, NC   25.00
DOWDEY, Clifford   Tidewater.
    1943   Boston   20.00
DOWDEY, Clifford   Virginia Record.
    1961   Richmond   Confederate Centennial ed.   25.00
DOWDEY, Clifford   Where My Love Sleeps.
    1945   Boston   20.00
DOWDEY, Clifford and **MANARIN**, Louis, edited by   The Wartime Papers of R. E. Lee.
    1961   Boston   35.00

1961   New York   35.00
Recent reprint   25.00
DOWLEY, Morris Francis   History and Honorary Roll of the Twelfth
Regiment Infantry N.G. S. N. Y.
1869   New York   75.00
DOWLING, Morgan E.   Southern Prisons or, Josie the Heroine of Florence.
1870   Detroit   150.00
DOWNER, Edward T.   Stonewall Jackson's Shenandoah Valley Campaign 1862. Wraps.
1959   Lexington, VA   10.00
DOWNEY, Fairfax   Clash of Cavalry   The Battle of Brandy Station,
June 9, 1863.
1959   New York   35.00
1985   25.00
1987   25.00
DOWNEY, Fairfax   Famous Horses of the Civil War.
1959   New York   35.00
DOWNEY, Fairfax   The Guns at Gettysburg.
1958   New York   40.00
1987   25.00
DOWNEY, Fairfax   A Horse for General Lee.
1953   New York   20.00
DOWNEY, Fairfax   Sound of the Guns.
1955   New York   25.00
1956   New York   30.00
DOWNEY, Fairfax   Storming of the Gateway.
1960   New York   35.00
1960   New York   15.00
1969   Wraps   7.50
DOWNING, Alexander G.   Downing's Civil War Diary, edited by
Olynthus B. Clark.
1916   Des Moines   90.00
DOWNS, Edward C.   Four Years A Scout & Spy.
1866   Zanesville   100.00
DOWNS, Edward C.   The Great American Scout and Spy, "General
Bunker."
1868   New York   60.00
1870   New York   60.00
DOWNS, Edward C.   Perils of Scout Life, by C. L. Ruggles.
1875   New York   50.00
DOYLE, D. H.   The Social Order of a Frontier Community.
1978   13.00
DRAKE, Edwin L., edited by   The Annals of the Army of Tennessee and
Early Western History Vol I, Apr-Dec 1878.   (all published)
1878   Nashville   550.00
DRAKE, James Madison   Fast and Loose in Dixie.
1880   New York   85.00
DRAKE, James Madison   Historical Sketches of the Revolutionary and
Civil Wars.
1908   New York   65.00

DRAKE, James Madison   The History of the Ninth New Jersey Veteran
Volunteers.
1889   Elizabeth   110.00
DRAKE, James Vaulx   Life of General Robert Hatton.
1867   Nashville   200.00
DRAKE, Julia A., edited by   The Mail Goes Through, or The Civil War
Letters of George Drake.
1964   San Angelo, TX   30.00
DRAKE, Samuel Adams   The Battle of Gettysburg.
1892   Boston   60.00
1988   Wilmington, NC   20.00
DRAPER, John William   History of the American Civil War. 3 Vols.
1867-70 New York   60.00
DRAPER, William F.   Recollections of a Varied Career.
1908   Boston   35.00
1909   Boston   35.00
DREW, Benjamin   The Refugee: Or the Narratives of Fugitive Slaves
in Canada.
1856   Boston   80.00
DREWRY, W. S.   The Southampton Insurrection.
1900   Washington, DC   75.00
DRIGGS, George W.   Opening of the Mississippi, or Two Years' Campaigning in the Southwest.
1864   Madison   200.00
DRINKWATER, John   Abraham Lincoln: A Play.
1919   Boston   5.00
1921   5.00
DRINKWATER, John   American Vignettes 1860-1865.
1931   Boston   20.00
DRINKWATER, John   Robert E. Lee, A Play.
1923   London   15.00
1923   Boston   15.00
DRINKWATER, John   The World's Lincoln.
1928   New York   Ltd.   20.00
DRIVER, Robert J.   The 52nd Virginia Infantry, CSA.
1988   16.95
DRIVER, Robert J.   The 1st and 2nd Rockbridge Artillery.
1987   Lynchburg   16.50
DRIVER, Robert J.   Lexington and Rockbridge County in the Civil War.
1989   16.95
DRIVER, Robert J.   The Staunton Artillery - McClanahan's Battery.
1988   Lynchburg   19.95
DRUM, Richard C.   List of Synonyms of Organizations in the Volunteer Service of the U.S. During the Years 1861-65.
1885   Washington, DC   75.00
DUAINE, Carl L.   The Dead Men Wore Boots: An Account of the 32nd
Texas Volunteer Cavalry.
1966   Austin   20.00
DUBAY, Robert W.   John Jones Pettus, Mississippi Fire-Eater: His Life
and Times 1813-1867.
1975   Jackson   15.00

DUBERMAN, Martin B.   The Antislavery Vanguard.
1965   Princeton   25.00
DUBERMAN, Martin B.   Charles Francis Adams 1807-1886.
1961   Boston   20.00
DU BOIS, W. E. Burghardt   Black Reconstruction in America.
1935   New York   20.00
1956   10.00
DU BOIS, W. E. Burghardt   The Suppression of the African Slave
Trade to the United States of America. 1638-1870.
1954   10.00
DU BOSE, Henry K.   The History of Company B, Twenty-first Regiment
(Infantry) South Carolina Volunteers, Confederate States Provisional
Army.
1909   Columbia   500.00
DU BOSE, John W.   Alabama's Tragic Decade.
1940   Birmingham   35.00
DU BOSE, John W.   General Joseph Wheeler and the Army of Tennessee.
1912   New York   300.00
DU BOSE, John W.   Life and Times of William Lowndes Yancey.
1892   Birmingham   225.00
1942   New York   2 Vols. 50.00
DUCAT, Arthur Charles   Memoir of General A. C. Ducat.
1897   Chicago   90.00
DUDLEY, Dean, edited by   Officers of Our Union Army and Navy:
Their Lives, Their Portraits. Vol. 1 (all published).
1862   Boston   40.00
DUDLEY, Edgar S., compiled by   Roster of Nebraska Volunteers from
1861 to 1869.
1888   Hastings   100.00
DUDLEY, Henry W.   Autobiography of . . .
1914   Menasha, WI 150.00
DUDLEY, W. S.   Going South: U.S. Navy Officer Resignations & Dis-
missals on the Eve of the Civil War.   Wraps.
1981   Washington, DC   4.00
DUDLEY, William Wade   The Iron Brigade at Gettysburg.   Wraps.
1879   Cincinnati Ltd. 110.00
DUFFIELD, Henry M.   Chickamauga. Wraps.
1888   Detroit   35.00
DUFFY, Edward   History of the 159th Regiment N.Y.S. Vols. Wraps.
1890   Ltd.   200.00
DUFOUR, Charles L.   Gentle Tiger, the Gallant Life of Roberdeau
Wheat.
1957   Baton Rouge   50.00
DUFOUR, Charles L.   The Night the War Was Lost.
1960   Garden City, NY   30.00
DUFOUR, Charles L.   Nine Men in Gray.
1963   Garden City, NY   50.00
DUFUR, Simon M.   Over the Dead Line, or Tracked by Blood-Hounds.
1902   Burlington   60.00

DUGAN, M. C., edited by   Outline History of Annapolis and the
   Naval Academy.   Wraps.
   1902   Baltimore   30.00
DUGANNE, Augustine J. H.   Camps and Prisons, Twenty Months in the
   Department of the Gulf.
   1865   New York   100.00
DUGANNE, Augustine J. H.   The Quaker Soldiers - A True Story of the
   War for The Union.
   1866   65.00
   1869   New York   50.00
DUKE, Basil W.   The Great Indiana-Ohio Raid by Brig. Gen. John Hunt
   Morgan and His Men July 1863.   Wraps.
   1955   Louisville   25.00
DUKE, Basil W.   History of Morgan's Cavalry.
   1867   Cincinnati   150.00
   1906   New York/Washington, DC   100.00
   1909   entitled Morgan's Cavalry   100.00
   1960   Bloomington   edited by L. M. Holland 50.00
DUKE, Basil W.   Reminiscences of General Basil W. Duke, C.S.A.
   1911   New York   125.00
   1969   New York   45.00
DUKE, Basil W. and KNOTT, R. W.   The Southern Bivouac: A Monthly
   Literary and Historical Magazine. Vol. I.
   1885-86 Louisville   50.00
DUKE, Basil W. and KNOTT, R. W.   The Southern Bivouac: A Monthly
   Literary and Historical Magazine. Vol. II.
   1886-87 Louisville   50.00
DUKE, John K.   History of the Fifty-third Regiment Ohio Volunteer
   Infantry.
   1900   Portsmouth   200.00
DUMOND, Dwight L.   Anti-slavery.   The Crusade for Freedom in
   America.
   1939   Ann Arbor 25.00
   1961   25.00
DUMOND, Dwight L.   Anti-slavery Origins of the Civil War in the
   United States.
   1939   Ann Arbor 35.00
   1959   Ann Arbor 25.00
   1966   25.00
DUMOND, Dwight L.   The Secession Movement 1860-1861.
   1931   New York   25.00
DUMOND, Dwight L., edited by   Southern Editorials on Secession.
   1931   New York   35.00
   1964   30.00
DUNAWAY, Wayland Fuller   Reminiscences of a Rebel.
   1913   New York   150.00
DUNCAN, Alexander Mc.   Roll of Officers and Members of the Georgia Hussars and of the Cavalry Companies.
   1906   Savannah   350.00
DUNCAN, George W.   John Archibald Campbell.   Wraps.
   1905   Montgomery, AL   25.00

DUNCAN, Louis C.   The Medical Department of the United States Army in the Civil War.   Wraps.
(1910)   Washington, DC   40.00
1985   28.50
1987   28.50

DUNCAN, R. H.   The Captain and Submarine C.S.S. H. L. Hunley.
1965   Memphis   Ltd.   20.00

DUNCAN, Robert Lipscomb   Reluctant General: The Life and Times of Albert Pike.
1961   New York   40.00

DUNCAN, Thomas D.   Recollections of _____, A Confederate Soldier.   Wraps.
1922   Nashville   200.00

DUNGLISON, R.   Medical Lexicon, A Dictionary of Medical Science.
1858   150.00

DUNHAM, Chester Forrester   The Attitude of the Northern Clergy Toward the South 1860-1865.   Wraps.
1942   Chicago   15.00
1974   15.00

DUNKELMAN, M. and WINEY, M.   The Hardtack Regiment.   An Illustrated History of the 154th NYV.
1981   New York   22.50

DUNKLE, John J.   Prison Life During the Rebellion   By Fritz Fuzzlebug.   Wraps.
1869   Singer's Glen, VA   70.00

DUNLAY, Thomas W.   Wolves for the Blue Soldiers: Indian Scouts and Auxiliaries with the U.S. Army 1860-90.
1982   25.00
1982   Wraps   9.00

DUNLOP, W. S.   Lee's Sharpshooters.
1899   Little Rock, AR   200.00
1983   Dayton 35.00
1988   Dayton 35.00

DUNN, Ballard S.   Brazil, the Home for Southerners: or, a Practical Account of What the Author, and Others, Who Visited that Country, for the Same Objects, Saw and Did While in that Empire.   By . . . Rector of St. Phillip's Church, New Orleans. . . .
1866   New York and New Orleans   100.00

DUNN, Byron A.   On General Thomas's Staff.
1899   Chicago   50.00
1912   Chicago   40.00

DUNN, Byron A.   The Young Missourians Series.   With Lyon in Missouri.
1910   Chicago   20.00

DUNNING, William Archibald   The British Empire and the United States.
1969   New York   25.00

DUNNING, William Archibald   Essays on the Civil War.
1898   New York   25.00
1931   New York   20.00
1969   MA   15.00

DU PONT, Henry A.   The Campaign of 1864 in the Valley of Virginia and the Expedition to Lunchburg.
1925   New York   75.00
DU PONT, Henry A.   Rear Admiral Samuel Francis Du Pont.
1926   New York   60.00
DU PONT, Samuel Francis   Official Dispatches and Letters of Rear Admiral Du Pont, U.S. Navy 1846-48 1861-63.
1883   Wilmington, DE   400.00
DU PONT, Samuel Francis   Samuel Francis Du Pont, A Selection from His Civil War Letters, edited by John D. Hayes. 3 Vols.
1969   Ithaca   75.00
Vol. I   The Mission: 1860-1862.
Vol. II   The Blockade: 1862-1863.
Vol. III   The Repulse: 1863-1865.
DUPRE, Louis J.   Fagots from the Camp Fire.
1881   Washington, DC   30.00
DUPUY, Ernest and DUPUY, Trevor N.   The Compact History of the Civil War.
1960   New York   25.00
DUPUY, Trevor N.   The Military History of the Civil War Land Battles.
1960   New York   25.00
DURDEN, Robert F.   The Gray and the Black.
1972   Baton Rouge   20.00
DURHAM, Walter T.   Nashville, The Occupied City.
1985   19.00
DURKIN, Joseph T.   Confederate Navy Chief: Stephen R. Mallory.
1987   21.95
DURKIN, Joseph T.   General Sherman's Son.
1959   New York   25.00
DURKIN, Joseph T.   John Dooley, Confederate Soldier, His War Journal.
1945   New York   50.00
1945   Washington, DC   50.00
DURKIN, Joseph T.   Stephen R. Mallory, Confederate Navy Chief.
1954   Chapel Hill, NC   40.00
1987   Columbia   24.95
DURST, Ross C.   Garrett County Maryland and the Civil War.
1961   Oakland   20.00
DUSSAUCE, Professor H.   A Practical Treatise on the Fabrication of Matches, Gun Cotton, Colored Fires and Fulminating Powders.
1864   Philadelphia   150.00
DUVERGIER DE HAURANNE, Ernest   A Frenchman in Lincoln's America. 2 Vols.
1974   Chicago   35.00
✓DUYCKINCK, Evert A.   A National History of the War for the Union, Civil, Military and Naval. 3 Vols.
1861   New York   75.00
1868   New York   75.00
DWIGHT, Allan   Linn Dickson Confederate.
1934   New York   25.00

DWIGHT, Charles Stevens   A South Carolina Rebel's Recollections. Wraps.
    1919   Columbia   Ltd.   225.00

DWIGHT, Theodore F., edited by   Campaigns in Virginia, 1861-1862 / The Virginia Campaign of 1862 Under General Pope / Campaigns in Virginia, Maryland, Pennsylvania, 1862-1863.   See: Papers of the Military Historical Society of Massachusetts, Nos. 1, 2, and 3.

DWIGHT, Wilder   Life and Letters of _____ Lieut. Col. Second Mass. Inf. Vols., edited by Elizabeth A. Dwight.
    1868   Boston   75.00

DYE, John S.   History of the Plots and Crimes of the Great Conspiracy to Overthrow Liberty in America.
    1866   New York   30.00
    1969   New York   30.00

DYER, Elisha   Official Register of Rhode Island Officers and Men Who Served in the U.S. Army & Navy from 1861 to 1866. 2 Vols.
    1893-95 Providence   125.00

DYER, Frederick H.   A Compendium of the War of the Rebellion.
    1908   Des Moines   1 Vol. ed.   175.00
    1959   New York   3 Vols.   150.00
    1959   New York   3 Vols. Ltd. ed. of 50 sets in leather   300.00
    1978   125.00
    1987   125.00

DYER, John P.   From Shiloh to San Juan, The Life of "Fightin' Joe" Wheeler.
    1941   Baton Rouge   50.00
    1961   Baton Rouge   40.00
    1989   30.00

DYER, John P.   The Gallant Hood.
    1950   Indianapolis   40.00

DYER, John Will   Reminiscences or Four Years in the Confederate Army.
    1898   Evansville   275.00

EAKLOR, V. L.   American Antislavery Songs: A Collection and Analysis.
    1988   Westport   65.00

EARLE, David M.   History of the Excursion of the Fifteenth Massachusetts Regiment and Its Friends to Battlefield of Gettysburg . . . 1886.
    1886   Worcester   35.00

EARLE, Peter   Robert E. Lee.
    1973   New York   20.00

EARLE, Pliny   Memoirs of _____, M.D. with Extracts from His Diary and Letters, edited by F. B. Sanborn.
    1898   Boston   40.00

Early History of the Department of Massachusetts G.A.R. from 1866 to 1880.
    1895   25.00

The Early Life, Campaigns, and Public Services of Robert E. Lee.
    1871   New York   55.00

EARLY, Jubal A.   Address Contained in Proceedings of the Third Annual Meeting of the Survivor's Association of the State of South Carolina. Wraps.
1872   Charleston   40.00
EARLY, Jubal A.   Campaigns of Gen. Robert E. Lee. Wraps.
1872   Baltimore   125.00
EARLY, Jubal A.   The Heritage of the South.
1915   Lynchburg   50.00
EARLY, Jubal A.   Jackson's Campaign Against Pope in August, 1862, An Address . . . Before the First Annual Meeting of Assoc. of Maryland Line. Wraps.
(1883)   n.p.   125.00
EARLY, Jubal A.   Lieutenant General Jubal Anderson Early, C.S.A. Autobiographical Sketch and Narrative of the War Between the States.
1912   Philadelphia   200.00
1960   Bloomington   entitled War Memoirs   50.00
1989   Wilmington, NC   35.00
EARLY, Jubal A.   A Memoir of the Last Year of the War for Independence in the Confederate States of America. Wraps.
1866   Toronto   150.00
1867   Lynchburg   100.00
1867   Augusta, GA   100.00
1867   New Orleans   100.00
EARLY, Jubal A.   The Relative Strength of the Armies of Generals Lee and Grant. Wraps.
1870   n.p.   70.00
EARNSHAW, William   History of the National Home for Disabled Volunteer Soldiers.
1875   Dayton 35.00
EASBY-SMITH, Anne   William Russell Smith of Alabama: His Life and Works.
1931   Philadelphia   25.00
EASUM, Chester Verne   The Americanization of Carl Schurz.
1929   Chicago   15.00
EATON, Clement   The Growth of Southern Civilization 1790-1860.
1961   New York   25.00
EATON, Clement   Henry Clay and the Art of . . . Politics.
1957   New York   20.00
EATON, Clement   A History of the Southern Confederacy. Wraps.
1954   New York   20.00
1959   New York   20.00
Recent reprint   12.95
EATON, Clement   Jefferson Davis.
1977   New York   25.00
EATON, Clement   The Mind of the Old South.
1964   20.00
1969   Baton Rouge   20.00
EATON, E. B.   Original Photographs Taken on the Battlefields During the Civil War of the United States. . . .
1907   Hartford   150.00
EATON, J. H.   Army Paymaster's Manual.
1864   Washington, DC   125.00

EATON, John   Grant, Lincoln and the Freedmen.
   1907   New York   40.00
EATON, William   History of the Richardson Light Guard, of Wakefield,
   Massachusetts 1851-1901.
   1901   Wakefield   60.00
EBY, Cecil D., Jr.   Porte Crayon, The Life of David Hunter Strother.
   1960   Chapel Hill, NC   25.00
   1973   15.00
EBY, Henry Harrison   Observations of an Illinois Boy in Battle, Camp
   and Prisons 1861-1865.
   1910   Mendota   60.00
Echoes from the Marches of the Famous Iron Brigade, 1861-1865.   Wraps.
   1988   Gaithersburg   10.00
Echoes from the South.   See: ESTVAN, Bela
ECKEL, Alexander   History of the Fourth Tennessee Cavalry, U.S.A.
   War of the Rebellion 1861-65 . . . All of Which I Saw and Part of Which
   I Was.
   1929   (Knoxville)   750.00
ECKENRODE, H. J.   Jefferson Davis.
   1923   New York   30.00
   1930   New York   20.00
ECKENRODE, H. J.   Life of Nathan B. Forrest.
   1918   Richmond   40.00
ECKENRODE, H. J.   The Political History of Virginia During the
   Reconstruction.
   1904   Baltimore   30.00
   1966   20.00
ECKENRODE, H. J. and CONRAD, Bryan   George B. McClellan.
   1941   Chapel Hill, NC   30.00
   1987   Wilmington, NC   25.00
ECKENRODE, H. J. and CONRAD, Bryan   James Longstreet, Lee's War
   Horse.
   1936   Chapel Hill, NC   60.00
   1986   19.95
ECKERT, Edward K.   Fiction Distorting Fact; Prison Life Annotated
   by Jefferson Davis.
   1987   Macon   39.95
ECKERT, Edward K. and AMATO, Nicholas J.   10 Years in the Saddle. The Memoirs of William Woods Averell, 1851-1862.
   1978   25.00
ECKERT, Ralph Lowell   John Brown Gordon: Soldier, Southerner,
   American.
   1989   Baton Rouge   32.50
EDDY, Richard   History of the Sixtieth Regiment New York State Volunteers.
   1864   Philadelphia   75.00
EDDY, Thomas M.   The Patriotism of Illinois. 2 Vols.
   1865-66 Chicago   175.00
EDEN, Robert C.   The Sword and Gun. A History of the 37th Wisconsin Volunteer Infantry.
   1865   Madison   80.00

EDGE, Frederick M.   Major General McClellan and the Campaign on the Yorktown Peninsula.
    1865   London 140.00
    1868   75.00

EDMONDS, David C.   The Guns of Port Hudson.   2 Vols.
    1983   Lafayette, LA   Vol. I   The River Campaign 17.00
    1984   Lafayette, LA   Vol. II The Investment, Siege and Reduction 17.95

EDMONDS, David C.   Yankee Autumn in Acadiana.
    1979   Lafayette, LA   20.00
    1987   19.95

EDMONDS, Franklin Spencer   Ulysses S. Grant.
    1915   Philadelphia   20.00

EDMONDS, George (pseud.)   See: **MERIWETHER**, Elizabeth A.

EDMONDS, Howard O.   Owen-Edmonds, Incidents of the American Civil War 1861-1865.
    1928   Chicago   50.00

EDMONDS, Sara Emma E.   Nurse and Spy in the Union Army.
    1865   Hartford   30.00

EDMONDS, Sara Emma E.   Unsexed; or, The Female Soldier.
    1864   Philadelphia   35.00

EDMONDSTON, Catherine Ann Devereux   Journal of a Secesh Lady: The Diary of _____ 1860-1866, edited by Beth Crabtree and James W. Patton.
    1979   Raleigh, NC   30.00

EDMONDSTON, Catherine Ann Devereux   The Journal of _____ 1860-1866, edited by Margaret Mackay Jones.
    1954   Mebane, NC   Ltd.   75.00

EDMUNDS, P. W.   Virginians Out Front.
    1972   Richmond   23.00

EDWARDS, E. M. H.   Commander W. B. Cushing of the U. S. Navy.
    1898   New York   60.00

EDWARDS, John   Shelby's Expedition to Mexico.
    1964   Austin   Boxed   55.00

EDWARDS, John Ellis   The Confederate Soldier, Being a Memorial Sketch of George N. and Bushrod W. Harris.
    1868   New York   250.00

EDWARDS, John Frank   Army Life of Frank Edwards, Confederate Veteran.
    1911   La Grange   350.00

EDWARDS, John N.   Biography, Memoirs, Reminiscences and Recollections, compiled by Jennie Edwards.
    1889   Kansas City   125.00

EDWARDS, John N.   Noted Guerrillas, or Warfare of the Border.
    1877   St. Louis   125.00
    1976   Dayton   20.00

EDWARDS, John N.   Shelby and His Men.
    1897   Kansas City   75.00
    1867   Cincinnati   125.00

EDWARDS, Mrs. J. Griff and **ANDREWS**, Matthew P., edited by   Echoes From Dixie, Old Time Southern Songs.
    1918   New York   50.00

EDWARDS, Ward   Lion-Hearted Luke;   or, The Plan to Capture Mosby, War Library Vol. 7, No. 235.   Wraps.
    1887   New York   50.00
EDWARDS, William B.   Civil War Guns: The Complete Story of Federal and Confederate Small Arms.
    1962   Harrisburg, PA 40.00
EDWARDS, William B.   The Story of Colt's Revolver   The Biography of Col. Samuel Colt.
    1953   Harrisburg, PA 75.00
    1957   Harrisburg, PA 45.00
EFLOR, Oram   Chain-Shot; or Mosby and His Men, War Library Vol. 2, No. 35.   Wraps.
    1883   New York   30.00
EGAN, Ferol   Fremont - Explorer for a Restless Nation.
    1977   New York   30.00
EGAN, J. B. and DESMOND, A. W.   The Civil War.   Its Photgraphic History.
    1941   Wellesley Hills   30.00
EGAN, Michael   The Flying Gray-Haired Yank.
    1888   Philadelphia   75.00
    n.d.   n.p.   60.00
EGGLESTON, George Cary   The History of the Confederate War: Its Causes and Its Conduct. 2 Vols.
    1910   New York   100.00
EGGLESTON, George Cary   A Rebel's Recollections.
    1875   New York   75.00
    1889   New York   75.00
    1897   New York   75.00
    1959   Bloomington   35.00
EGGLESTON, George Cary   Recollections of a Varied Life.
    1910   New York   40.00
EGGLESTON, George Cary   Southern Soldier Stories.
    1898   New York   50.00
EGGLESTON, George Cary   The Warrens of Virginia.
    1908   New York   15.00
EGGLESTON, Joseph William   Tuckahoe.
    1903   New York   50.00
EGLE, William H.   Life and Times of Andrew Gregg Curtin.
    1896   Philadelphia 25.00
EHLE, John   Time of Drums.
    1970   New York   10.00
EHRLICH, Leonard   God's Angry Man.
    1932   15.00
EHRMANN, Bess V.   The Missing Chapter in the Life of Abraham Lincoln.
    1938   Chicago   Ltd.   30.00
The 18th (Eighteenth) Regiment Connecticut Volunteer Infantry in the War of the Rebellion 1862-1865.   Wraps.
    1889   Hartford   40.00
The Eighty-sixth Regiment Indiana Volunteer Infantry.
    1895   Crawfordsville   150.00

EISENSCHIML, Otto   The Celebrated Case of Fitz John Porter.
   1950   Indianapolis   30.00
   1950   New York   30.00
EISENSCHIML, Otto   The Fifty-fifth Illinois at Shiloh.   Wraps.
   (1963)   n.p.   30.00
EISENSCHIML, Otto   The Hidden Face of the Civil War.
   1961   Indianapolis   25.00
   1961   New York   25.00
EISENSCHIML, Otto   Historian Without an Armchair.
   1962   Indianapolis   25.00
   1963   25.00
EISENSCHIML, Otto   In the Shadow of Lincoln's Death.
   1940   New York   30.00
EISENSCHIML, Otto   Reviewers Reviewed.   Wraps.
   1940   Ann Arbor   15.00
EISENSCHIML, Otto   The Story of Shiloh.
   1946   Chicago   40.00
EISENSCHIML, Otto   Why the Civil War?
   1958   Indianapolis   35.00
   1958   New York   35.00
EISENSCHIML, Otto   Why Was Lincoln Murdered?
   1937   Boston   30.00
   1937   New York   30.00
EISENSCHIML, Otto   Without Fame The Romance of a Profession.
   1942   Chicago   25.00
   1942   New York   25.00
EISENSCHIML, Otto and LONG, E. B.   As Luck Would Have It.
   1948   Indianapolis   30.00
   1958   Indianapolis   20.00
EISENSCHIML, Otto and NEWMAN, Ralph   The American Iliad The
   Epic Story of the Civil War as Narrated by Eyewitnesses and Contemporaries.
   1947   Indianapolis   20.00
   1947   Indianapolis   Ltd. signed & boxed   60.00
   1947   New York   20.00
   1956   New York   entitled The Civil War 2 Vols. 25.00
   1985   10.00
ELDER, W.   Debt and Resources of the United States, and the Effect of
   Secession Upon the Trade and Industry of the Loyal States.   Wraps.
   1863   Philadelphia   25.00
ELDERKIN, James D.   Biographical Sketches and Anecdotes of a Soldier of Three Wars.
   1899   Detroit   90.00
ELDREDGE, Daniel   The Third New Hampshire and All About It.
   1893   Boston   130.00
ELDRIDGE, Shalor Winchell   Recollections of Early Days in Kansas -
   Contained in Pub. of Kansas State Historical Society.
   1920   Topeka   35.00
Elements of Discord in Secessia.   See: ALEXANDER, William
Eleven Days in the Militia During the War of the Rebellion; Being a Journal
   of the "Emergency" Campaign of 1862. By a Militiaman.
   1883   Philadelphia   35.00

ELIOT, Ellsworth, Jr.   Theodore Winthrop.
1938   New Haven   30.00
ELIOT, Ellsworth, Jr.   West Point in the Confederacy.
1941   New York   50.00
ELIOT, Ellsworth, Jr.   Yale in the Civil War.
1932   New Haven   50.00
ELIOT, George Fielding   Caleb Pettengill, U.S.N.
1956   New York   15.00
ELLICOTT, Charles Winslow   Winfield Scott, The Soldier and the Man.
1937   New York   40.00
ELLICOTT, John M.   The Life of John Ancrum Winslow, Rear Admiral, USN.
1905   New York   40.00
ELLINGER, Esther Parker   The Southern War Poetry of the Civil War.
1918   Philadelphia   50.00
ELLINGTON, Charles G.   The Trial of U.S. Grant; The Pacific Coast Years, 1852-1854.
1987   Glendale   27.50
ELLIOTT, James Cantey   Lieutenant General Richard Heron Anderson: Lee's Noble Soldier.
1985   Dayton   20.00
ELLIOTT, James Carson   The Southern Soldier Boy.   Wraps.
1907   Raleigh, NC   100.00
1979   Wendell, NC   10.00
ELLIOTT, James W.   Transport to Disaster (The Sultana).
1962   New York   15.00
ELLIOTT, Joseph Taylor   The Sultana Disaster.   Wraps.
1913   Indianapolis   70.00
ELLIS, D. R.   The Monitor of the Civil War.
(c.1908) n.p.   65.00
ELLIS, Daniel   Thrilling Adventures of Daniel Ellis.
1867   New York   60.00
1971   New York   20.00
1974   Kingsport, TN   Ltd.   15.00
ELLIS, Edward S.   The Campfires of General Lee.
1886   Philadelphia   40.00
ELLIS, Helen H.   Michigan in the Civil War, A Guide to the Material in Detroit Newspapers 1861-1866.   Wraps.
1962   50.00
1965   Lansing   35.00
1966   25.00
ELLIS, Thomas T.   Leaves from the Diary of an Army Surgeon.
1863   New York   110.00
ELLISON, Mary   Lancashire and the American Civil War.
1972   Chicago   25.00
ELLSWORTH, E. E.   The Zouave Drill, Being a Complete Manual of Arms. . . .   Wraps.
1861   Philadelphia   115.00
ELSON, H. W.   Civil War Through the Camera.
1912   New York   50.00
1912   Springfield, MA   60.00
1912   New York   16 parts, each in wraps   100.00

ELWOOD, John William   **Elwood's Stories of the Old Ringgold Cavalry.**
    1914   Coal Center 100.00
    Recent reprint   Wraps   20.00
ELY, Alfred   **Journal of** _____, edited by Charles Lanman.
    1862   New York   60.00
ELY, Ralph   **Diary of Capt.** _____ **of the 8th Michigan Infantry,** edited by Geo. M. Blackburn.   **Wraps.**
    1965   Mt. Pleasant   10.00
ELZAS, Barnett A.   **The Jews of South Carolina.**
    1905   Philadelphia 150.00
EMANUEL, S.   **Historical Sketch of the Georgetown Rifle Guards.** **Wraps.**
    1909   Georgetown   100.00
The Embattled Confederacy.   See: **DAVIS**, William C.   **The Image of War, 1861-1865.**
EMBICK, Milton A.   **Military History of the Third Division, Ninth Corps Army of the Potomac.**
    1913   Harrisburg   45.00
EMBICK, Milton A.   **Proceedings of the Reunion of the Third Division Ninth Corps, Army of the Potomac.** Wraps.
    1892   Harrisburg   60.00
EMERSON, Bettie Alder Calhoun   **Historic Southern Monuments.**
    1911   New York   150.00
EMERSON, Edward W.   **Life and Letters of Charles Russell Lowell.**
    1907   Boston   50.00
    1971   New York   50.00
EMILIO, Luis F.   **The Assault on Fort Wagner, July 18, 1863. The Memorable Charge of the 54th Massachusetts Vols.**   Wraps.
    1887   Boston   50.00
EMILIO, Luis F.   **History of the Fifty-fourth Regiment of Massachusetts Volunteer Infantry 1863-1865.**
    1891   Boston   100.00
    1894   Boston   75.00
    1969   25.00
EMILIO, Luis F.   **Roanoke Island Its Occupation, Defense and Fall.** **Wraps.**
    1891   New York   50.00
EMMERTON, James A.   **A Record of the Twenty-third Regiment Mass Vol. Infantry.**
    1886   Boston   100.00
EMPSON, William H.   **A Story of Rebel Military Prison.**
    n.d.   Lockport, NY   175.00
EMPSON, William H.   **Let Us Forgive, But Not Forget,   or What I Saw and Suffered.**   Wraps.
    n.d.   New York   150.00
EMURIAN, Ernest K.   **Living Stories of Favorite Songs.**
    1958   Boston   25.00
EMURIAN, Ernest K.   **Stories of Civil War Songs.**
    1960   Natick, MA   20.00
EMURIAN, Ernest K.   **The Sweetheart of the Civil War.**
    1962   Natick, MA   20.00

Encounter at Hanover: Prelude to Gettysburg.
   1963   Hanover   40.00
   1985   Shippensburg   edited by G. R. Prowell 18.00
The End of an Era.   See: **DAVIS**, William C. **The Image of War, 1861-1865.**
ENGEL, L.   **Panorama Views of Chattanooga and all the Battlefields.** Wraps.
   1914   Chattanooga   30.00
EPLER, Percy H.   **The Life of Clara Barton.**
   1915   New York   30.00
EPPES, Susan Bradford   **Through Some Eventful Years.**
   1926   Macon, GA   100.00
   1968   Gainesville   15.00
EPSTEIN, Samuel and EPSTEIN, Beyl   **The Andrews Raid.**
   1956   New York   25.00
The Equestrian Statue of Major General Joseph Hooker, Erected and Dedicated by the Commonwealth of Massachusetts.
   1903   Boston   25.00
ERVING, Annie Priscilla   **Reminiscences of the Life of a Nurse in Field, Hospital and Camp During the Civil War.** Wraps.
   1904   New York   75.00
ESCOTT, Paul D.   **After Secession.**
   1978   Baton Rouge   18.00
ESCOTT, Paul D.   **Slavery Remembered. A Record of Twentieth Century Slave Narratives.**
   1979   Chapel Hill, NC   25.00
   1979   Chapel Hill, NC   Wraps 10.00
ESKEW, G. L.   **Williard's of Washington: The Epic of a Capital Caravansary.**
   1954   New York   23.00
ESPOSITO, Vincent J., edited by   **West Point Atlas of American Wars, 1689-1953.** 2 Vols.
   1959   New York   50.00
   1962   New York   50.00
   1964   50.00
   1967   50.00
ESTABROOK, Charles E., edited by   **Records and Sketches of Military Organizations.**
   1914   Milwaukee   60.00
ESTABROOKS, Henry L.   **Adrift in Dixie: Or, A Yankee Officer Among the Rebels.**
   1866   New York   45.00
ESTES, Claud, edited by   **List of Field Officers, Regiments and Battalions in the Confederate States Army 1861-1865.**
   1912   Macon, GA   125.00
ESTVAN, Bela   **Echoes from the South.**
   1866   New York   35.00
ESTVAN, Bela   **War Pictures from the South.**
   1863   New York   50.00
   1863   London   2 Vols. 250.00
Eulogy on Comrade H. G. Palmer, Co. "G" 15th O.V.V.I. Wraps.
   1910   n.p.   25.00

EVANS, Augusta J. (pseud.)   See: WILSON, Augusta Jane Evans

EVANS, Clement A., edited by   Confederate Military History.
    See: Confederate Military History.

EVANS, Clement A.   "Contributions of the South to the Greatness of the American Union." Wraps.
    1895   Richmond   50.00

EVANS, Eli N.   Judah P. Benjamin, The Jewish Confederate.
    1988   New York   24.00
    1988   Wraps   12.95

EVANS, N. W.   In Memoriam: A Tribute of Respect to the Memory of the Deceased Soldiers of Adams County, Ohio. Wraps.
    1902   Portsmouth   30.00

EVANS, Robley D.   A Sailor's Log.
    1901   New York   40.00
    1902   New York   30.00

EVANS, Samuel M.   Allegheny County, Penna. in the War . . . Roll of Honor.
    1924   Pittsburgh   75.00

EVANS, W. A.   Mrs. Abraham Lincoln A Study of Her Personality and Her Influence on Lincoln.
    1932   New York   60.00

EVANS, W. McKee   Ballots and Fence Rails.
    1967   Chapel Hill, NC   20.00

EVANS, W. McKee   To Die Game, The Story of the Lowry Band, Indian Guerillas of Reconstruction.
    1971   Baton Rouge   20.00
    1977   Baton Rouge   20.00

EVE, F. Edgeworth   Address Delivered Before the Confederate Survivors' Association . . . on Memorial Day, April 27th, 1896. Wraps.
    1896   Augusta, GA   35.00

EVERETT, Edward   Address of _____, at the Consecration of the National Cemetery at Gettysburg.
    1864   Boston   75.00

EVERETT, Edward   The Great Issues Now Before the Country, An Oration. Wraps.
    1861   New York   25.00

EVERETT, Frank E., Jr.   Brierfield, Plantation Home of Jefferson Davis.
    1979   (reprint)   20.00

EVERETT, Lloyd T.   For Maryland's Honor A Story of the War for Southern Independence.
    1922   Boston   30.00

EVERETT, Lloyd T.   Patrick R. Cleburne, Prophet. Wraps.
    1946   DeLand   30.00

EVERETT, Lloyd T.   Was It Anti-Slavery. Wraps.
    1916   Ballston, VA   15.00

EWELL, Richard S.   The Making of a Soldier: Letters of General R. S. Ewell, edited by Captain Percy G. Hamlin.
    1935   Richmond   40.00

EWER, James K.   The Third Massachusetts Cavalry in the War for the Union.
    1903   Maplewood   75.00

EWING, E. W. R.   Northern Rebellion and Southern Secession.
    1904   Richmond   60.00
EWING, Elmore Ellis   Bugles and Bells; or Stories Told Again.
    1899   Cincinnati   80.00
An Excursion in Southern History Briefly Set Forth in the Correspondence Between Senator A. J. Beveridge and David Rankin Barbee. Wraps.
    1928   Asheville   15.00
Executive and Congressional Directory of the Confederate States 1861-1865. Wraps.
    1899   Washington, DC   25.00
Executive Documents, House of Representatives, Third Session of the 37th Congress, 1862-1863.
    1863   60.00
Exercises at the Dedication of the Monument to Colonel Robert Gould Shaw, etc.
    1897   Boston   25.00
Exercises Connected with the Unveiling of the Ellsworth Monument at Mechanicville, May 27, 1874.
    1875   Albany   30.00
An Exhibition of Miniatures Owned in South Carolina and Miniatures of South Carolinians Owned Elsewhere. . . . Wraps.
    1936   Charleston   5.00
An Extraordinary Collection of Engraved Portraits and Views Relating to the Civil War in America Belonging to the Hon. James T. Mitchell. Wraps.
    1910   Philadelphia   40.00
FAGAN, W. D., edited by   Southern War Songs.
    1890   New York   100.00
FAHRNEY, Ralph Ray   Horace Greeley and the Tribune in the Civil War.
    1936   Cedar Rapids, IA   50.00
FAIRCHILD, Charles B.   History of the 27th Regiment N. Y. Vols.
    1888   Binghamton   110.00
Fairfax County and the War Between the States. Wraps.
    1961   Vienna   15.00
    1987   7.00
FAIRMAN, Charles   Mr. Justice Miller and the Supreme Court 1862-1890.
    1939   Cambridge   50.00
FALLER, Leo W. and FALLER, John I.   Dear Folks at Home, The Civil War Letters of _____, edited by Milton E. Flower.** Wraps.
    1963   Carlisle   30.00
FALLON, John T.   List of Synonyms of Organizations in the Volunteer Service of the United States.
    1885   Washington, DC   50.00
FALLOWS, Alice Katharine   Everybody's Bishop: Being the Life and Times of the Right Reverend Samuel Fallows.
    1927   New York   25.00
False Reconstruction; Or, The Slavery That Is Not Abolished. Wraps.
    1876   Saxonville, MA   20.00

Famous Adventures and Prison Escapes of the Civil War.
    1893   New York   50.00
    1898   New York   40.00
    1909   40.00

FARBER, James   Fort Worth in the Civil War.
    1960   Belton   20.00

FARBER, James   Texas, C.S.A. A Spotlight on Disaster.
    1947   New York   35.00

FARLEY, Joseph Pearson   Three Rivers The James, The Potomac, The Hudson.
    1910   New York/Washington, DC   70.00

FARLEY, Joseph Pearson   West Point in the Early Sixties. Wraps.
    1902   Troy, NY   50.00

FARMER, H. H.   Virginia Before and During the War. Wraps.
    1892   Henderson, KY   50.00

FARR, Finis   Margaret Mitchell of Atlanta, The Author of Gone With The Wind.
    1965   New York   30.00

FARRAGUT, Loyall   The Life of David Glasgow Farragut, First Admiral of the U.S. Navy.
    1879   New York   35.00
    1882   New York   20.00

FARRAR, C. C. S.   The War Its Causes and Consequences.
    1864   Cairo   35.00

FARRAR, Samuel Clark   The Twenty-second Pennsylvania Cavalry and the Ringgold Battalion 1861-1865.
    1911   Pittsburgh   120.00

FARROW, Edward   Farrow's Military Encyclopedia. 3 Vols.
    1895   New York   250.00

FAULK, Odie   General Tom Green: 'Fightin' Texan. Introduction by Rupert N. Richardson. Wraps.
    1963   Waco, TX   40.00
    Limited bound edition   75.00

FAULKNER, Joseph   The Life of Philip Henry Sheridan.
    1888   New York   20.00

FAULKNER, William   The Unvanquished.
    1938   New York   300.00   one of 250 signed   750.00
    1960   London   30.00
    1965   New York   20.00

FAUST, Drew Gilpin   The Creation of Confederate Nationalism: Ideology and Identity in the Civil War South.
    1988   Baton Rouge   19.95

FAUST, Drew Gilpin   A Sacred Circle, the Dilemma of the Intellectual in the Old South, 1840-1860.
    1977   Baltimore   12.00

FAVILL, Josiah M.   The Diary of a Young Officer.
    1909   Chicago   140.00

FAY, Edwin H.   "This Infernal War," The Confederate Letters of Sgt. Edwin H. Fay, edited by Bell I. Wiley and Lucy E. Fay.
    1958   Austin   50.00

FAY, Frank B.   War Papers of Frank B. Fay, edited by William H. Reed.
    1911   Boston   35.00
FEARN, Frances, edited by   Diary of a Refugee.
    1910   New York   75.00
FEATHERSTON, John C.   Battle of the Crater, an Address.   Wraps.
    (1906)   n.p.   60.00
FEATHERSTONHAUGH, G. W.   Excursion Through the Slave States.
    1844   New York 1 Vol. ed.   75.00
    1844   London 2 Vols.   200.00
Federal and Confederate Commanders.   See: Papers of the Military Historical Society of Massachusetts, No. 10.
FEHRENBACHER, Don E.   Abraham Lincoln   A Documentary Portrait Through His Speeches and Writings.
    1964   Stanford, CA   20.00
FEHRENBACHER, Don E.   Chicago Giant: A Biography of "Long John" Wentworth.
    1957   25.00
FEHRENBACHER, Don E.   The Dred Scott Case,   Its Significance in American Law and Politics.
    1978   New York   20.00
FEHRENBACHER, Don E.   Prelude to Greatness, Lincoln in the 1850's.
    1962   Stanford, CA   15.00
FELLMAN, Michael   Inside War: The Guerrilla Conflict in Missouri During the American Civil War.
    1989   24.95
    1990   Wraps   9.95
FENNER, Earl   The History of Battery H, First Regiment Rhode Island Light Artillery.
    1894   Providence   80.00
FENTON, E. B.   From the Rapidan to Atalnta   Leaves from the Diary of _____.   Wraps.
    1893   Detroit   40.00
FERGUSON, Edwin L.   Sumner County, Tennessee in the Civil War.
    1972   Tompkinsville   25.00
FERGUSON, John L., compiled and edited by   Arkansas   and   the   Civil War.
    1964   Little Rock   35.00
FERGUSON, Joseph   Life-struggles in Rebel Prisons.
    1865   Philadelphia   60.00
FERGUSON, Robert   American During and After the War.
    1866   London   65.00
FERGUSON, W. J.   I Saw Booth Shoot Lincoln.
    1930   Boston   25.00
FERRI-PISANI, Camille   Prince Napoleon in America, 1861.
    1959   Bloomington, IN   25.00
FERRIS, Norman B.   Desperate Diplomacy.
    1976   Knoxville   25.00
FERRIS, Norman B.   The Trent Affair,   A Diplomatic Crisis.
    1977   Knoxville   20.00
FERTIG, James W.   The Secession and Reconstruction of Tennessee.
    1898   Chicago   60.00

FESSENDEN, Francis   Life and Public Services of William Pitt Fessenden: United States Senator from Maine 1854-1864. . . . 2 Vols.
    1907   Boston and New York   30.00
FEUERLICHT, Roberta Strauss   Andrews' Raiders.
    1967   New York   20.00
A Few Historic Records of the Church in the Diocese of Texas During the Rebellion, Together with a Correspondence Between Rt. Rev. Alexander Gregg and the Rev. Charles Gillette. Wraps.
    1865   New York   50.00
FICKLEN, John Rose   History   of   Reconstruction   in   Louisiana. Wraps.
    1910   Baltimore   75.00
    1966   MA   20.00
FIEBEGER, G. J.   The Campaign and Battle of Gettysburg.
    (c.1915)   n.p.   35.00
    1984   PA Wraps   13.00
FIEBEGER, G. J.   Campaigns of the American Civil War.
    1910   West Point   25.00
    1914   West Point   20.00
FIELD, Charles D.   Three Years in the Saddle from 1861 to 1865, Memoirs of _____. Wraps.
    1898   Goldfield, IA   90.00
FIELD, Henry M.   Bright Skies and Dark Shadows.
    1890   New York   25.00
FIELDER, Herbert   A Sketch of the Life and Times and Speeches of Joseph E. Brown.
    1883   Springfield, MA   30.00
FIELDS, Joseph E.   Robert E. Lee's Farewell Order. Wraps.
    1949   New York   25.00
Fifty-second Anniversary and Reunion of the Tenth New York Cavalry at Gettysburg July 1, 2, 3, 1913.
    1913   Washington, DC   125.00
FIGG, Royall W.   "Where Men Only Dare to Go!" or The Story of a Boy Company (C.S.A.)
    1885   Richmond   175.00
Fighting for Time.   See: DAVIS, William C. The Image of War, 1861-1865.
FILLER, Louis   The Crusade Against Slavery 1830-1869, edited by Henry S. Commager and Richard B. Morris.
    1960   London   20.00
FIORE, J. D.   Massachusetts in the Civil War: Vol. II. The Year of Testing and Trial, 1861-1862. Wraps.
    1961   Boston   12.50
First Anniversary of the Proclamation of Freedom in South Carolina, held at Beaufort. S.C., January 1, 1864. (Higginson, Thomas Wentworth, et al).
    1864   Beaufort, SC   200.00
The First Hundred Years of Company I, Seventh Regiment N.G.N.Y. 1838-1938.
    (c.1938)   n.p.   40.00
First Maine Cavalry, Proceedings at Annual Reunions. Wraps.
    1876-1882   25.00 each

The First Manassas, Correspondence Between Generals R. S. Ewell and G. T. Beauregard, etc. Wraps.
 1885   Nashville   75.00
 1907   n.p. Ltd.   15.00
 1970   Wraps   15.00
First Ohio Volunteer Heavy Artillery, Company M, by Its Members.
 1914   Toledo, OH 250.00
First Regiment of Infantry Massachusetts Volunteer Militia Col. Robert Cowdin, Commanding.
 1903   Boston   30.00
FISCHER, LeRoy H.   Lincoln's Gadfly, Adam Gurowski.
 1964   Norman   25.00
FISCHER, LeRoy H. and GILLI, J.   Confederate Indian Forces Outside of Indian Territory. Wraps.
 1969   Oklahoma City   10.00
FISCHER, LeRoy H. and RAMPP, L. C.   Quantrill's Civil War Operations in Indian Territory. Wraps.
 1968   Oklahoma City   10.00
FISCHER, LeRoy H., edited by   Western Territories in the Civil War. Wraps.
 1977   Manhattan, KS 10.00
FISH, Carl Russell   The American Civil War.
 1937   London and New York   25.00
FISHER, George Adams   The Yankee Conscript.
 1864   Philadelphia   25.00
FISHER, Horace   A Staff Officer's Story.
 1960   Boston   40.00
FISHER, Hugh D.   The Gun and the Gospel.
 1896   Chicago   60.00
 1902   Kansas City   50.00
FISHER, Margaret   Utah and the Civil War.
 1929   n.p.   75.00
FISHER, Richard Swainson   A Chronological History of the Civil War in America.
 1863   New York   75.00
FISHWICK, Marshall   General Lee's Photographer: The Life & Work of Michael Miley.
 1954   Chapel Hill, NC   40.00
FISHWICK, Marshall   Lee After the War.
 1963   New York   25.00
FISHWICK, Marshall   The Life and Work of Michael Miley, Gen. Lee's Photographer.
 1954   Chapel Hill, NC   30.00
FISK, Joel C. and BLAKE, William H. D.   A Condensed History of the 56th Regiment New York Veteran Volunteer Infantry.
 1906   Newburgh   90.00
FISK, Wilbur and ROSENBLATT, Ruth and Emil   Anti-Rebel, Civil War Letters.
 1983   26.00
FISKE, Ethel F.   Letters of John Fiske.
 1940   New York   25.00

FISKE, John   The Mississippi Valley in the Civil War.
   1900   Boston 40.00
   1901   Cambridge 30.00
   1902   Boston 20.00
FISKE, Joseph E.   War Letters, of Capt. Joseph E. Fiske, Written to His Parents During the War of the Rebellion. . . .
   (190-)   Wellesley   75.00
FISKE, Samuel Wheelock   Mr. Dunn Browne's Experiences in the Army.
   1866   Boston   40.00
FITCH, John   Annals of the Army of the Cumberland.
   1863   Philadelphia   100.00
   1864   Philadelphia   75.00
FITCH, Michael H.   The Chattanooga Campaign.
   1911   Madison 50.00
FITCH, Michael H.   Echoes of the Civil War as I Hear Them.
   1905   New York 90.00
FITE, Emerson David   The Presidential Campaign of 1860.
   1911   New York 20.00
   1967   10.00
FITE, Emerson David   Social and Industrial Conditions in the North During the Civil War.
   1910   New York 35.00
   1930   New York 20.00
   1963   10.00
FITZGERALD, Oscar P.   John B. McFerrin, A Biography.
   1888   Nashville 30.00
FITZHUGH, Lester N.   Terry's Texas Rangers, 8th Texas Cavalry, C.S.A. Wraps.
   1958   Dallas   25.00
FITZHUGH, Lester N., compiled by   Texas Batteries, Battalions, Regiments, Commanders and Field Officers, C.S.A. 1861-1865. Wraps.
   1959   Midlothian   25.00
FITZPATRICK, Marion Hill   Letters to Amanda . . . 1862-1865.
   1976   Culloden, GA   25.00
   1982   25.00
Five Points in the Record of North Carolina in the Great War of 1861-1865. Wraps.
   1904   Goldsboro   75.00
FLADELAND, Betty L.   James Gillespie Birney: Slaveholder to Abolitionists.
   1955   5.00
FLAGLER, D. W.   A History of the Rock Island Arsenal from Its Establishment in 1863 to December, 1876.
   1877   Washington, DC   200.00
Flags of the Army of the United States Carried During the War of the Rebellion.
   1887   Philadelphia   500.00
   1888   325.00
Flags of the Confederate Armies Returned to the Men Who Bore Them by the U.S. Govt. Wraps.
   1905   St. Louis   50.00

The Flags of the Confederate States of America.   Wraps.
  1907   n.p.   20.00
FLANDERS, Ralph Betts   Plantation Slavery in Georgia.
  1967   CosCob, CT   30.00
FLEET, Betsy and FULLER, John, edited by   Green Mount,   A Virginia
  Plantation Family During the Civil War.
  1962   Lexington   25.00
  1977   20.00
FLEHARTY, Stephen F.   Our Regiment, A History of the 102nd Illinois
  Infantry Volunteers.
  1865   Chicago   200.00
FLEISCHMANN, S. M.   The Memorial Tablet Published Under the
  Auspices of Buckley Post 12, GAR.
  1883   Akron   20.00
FLEMING, Andrew M.   A Soldier of the Confederacy.
  1934   Boston   40.00
FLEMING, C. S.   Memoir of Capt. C. Seton Fleming . . . Illustrative of
  the History of the Florida Troops in Virginia During the War Between
  the States.
  1985   Alexandria   20.00
FLEMING, Francis P.   Memoir of Capt. C. Seton Fleming 2nd Florida
  Inf., C.S.A.
  1884   Jacksonville, FL   750.00
  1985   VA   28.00
FLEMING, George Thornton, edited by   Life and Letters of Alexander
  Hays.
  1919   Pittsburgh   225.00
FLEMING, Vivian Minor   Battles of Fredericksburg and Chancellorsville,
  Virginia.
  1921   Richmond   75.00
FLEMING, Vivian Minor   Campaigns of the Army of Northern Virginia
  Including the Jackson Valley Campaign, 1861-1865.
  1928   Richmond   100.00
FLEMING, Vivian Minor   The Wilderness Campaign.   Wraps.
  1922   Richmond   40.00
FLEMING, Walter L.   Civil War and Reconstruction in Alabama.
  1905   New York   200.00
  1911   Cleveland   100.00
  1949   New York   40.00
  1978   Spartanburg   30.00
FLEMING, Walter L.   Documentary History of Reconstruction.
  1906-07 Cleveland   2 Vols. 250.00
  1950   New York   2 Vols. in 1 50.00
FLEMING, Walter L., edited by   General W. T. Sherman as College
  President.
  1912   Cleveland   25.00
FLEMING, Walter L.   Jefferson Davis at West Point.   Wraps.
  1910   Baton Rouge   18.00
FLEMING, Walter L.   Louisiana State University 1860-1863.
  1936   Baton Rouge   35.00

FLEMING, Walter L.   **The Sequel of Appomattox.**
  1921   New Haven   25.00
  (1929)   20.00
FLETCHER, Daniel C.   **Reminiscences of California and the Civil War.**
  1894   Ayer, MA   125.00
FLETCHER, Elliott H.   **A Civil War Letter of _____, edited by J. H.**
  Atkinson. Wraps.
  1963   Little Rock   35.00
FLETCHER, John Gould   **Arkansas.**
  1947   Chapel Hill, NC   35.00
FLETCHER, Samuel H.   **The History of Company A, Second Illinois
  Cavalry.**
  1912   Chicago   250.00
FLETCHER, William Andrew   **Rebel Private Front and Rear: Experiences and Observations.**   Most of the edition was destroyed by fire.
  Surviving copies are usually smoked. Price is for a good copy.
  1908   Beaumont   1000.00
  1954   Austin   40.00
  1983   Washington, DC   20.00
FLINN, Frank M.   **Campaigning with Banks in Louisiana, '63 and '64
  and with Sheridan in the Shenandoah Valley.**
  1887   Lynn   50.00
  1889   Boston   45.00
FLINT, H. M.   **Life of Stephen A. Douglas to Which Are Added His
  Speeches and Reports.**
  1863   Philadelphia   25.00
FLIPPIN, Percy Scott   **Herschel V. Johnson of Georgia.**
  1931   Richmond   40.00
FLOAN, Howard R.   **The South in Northern Eyes 1831-1861.**
  1958   Austin   25.00
FLOOD, Charles   **Lee, the Last Years.**
  1981   Boston   22.50
Florida - Confederate Military History.   See: **Confederate Military History,**
  Vol. XI (Vol. XVI, 1989 reprint ed.).
Florida in the Civil War 1860 through Reconstruction. Wraps.
  1961   Pensacola, FL   25.00
FLOURNOY, Mary H.   **Side Lights on Southern History.**
  1939   Richmond   30.00
FLOWER, Frank Abial   **Edwin McMasters Stanton.**
  1905   Boston   30.00
  1905   Akron   30.00
FLOWER, Frank Abial   **Old Abe, The Eighth Wisconsin War Eagle.**
  1885   Madison   55.00
FLOYD, David Bittle   **History of the 75th Regiment of Indiana
  Infantry Volunteers.**
  1893   Philadelphia   160.00
FLOYD, Fred C.   **History of the Fortieth (Mozart) Regiment New York
  Volunteers.**
  1909   Boston   100.00
FLUKER, Anne and **FLUKER**, Winifred   **Confed'ric Gol!**
  1926   Macon, GA   30.00
  1984   entitled   **Confederate Gold**   20.00

FLYNN, Frank J.   The "Fighting Ninth" for Fifty Years and the Semi-Centennial Celebration.
1911   n.p.   35.00

FOERING, John O.   Register of the Members of the "Artillery Corps Washington Grays" of the City of Philadelphia Who Served in the War of the Rebellion 1861-1865.
1912   Philadelphia   50.00

FOLSOM, William R.   Vermonters in Battle and Other Papers.
1953   Burlington   30.00

FOLTZ, Charles S.   Surgeon of the Seas.
1931   Indianapolis   50.00

FONER, Eric   Politics and Ideology in the Age of the Civil War.
1980   New York   15.00

FONERDEN, Clarence A.   Brief History of the Military Career of Carpenter's Battery.
1911   New Market   300.00
1983   Gaithersburg   15.00

FONTAINE, Francis   Etowah. A Romance of the Confederacy.
1887   Atlanta   35.00

FONTAINE, Lamar   My Life and My Lectures.
1908   New York   190.00

FONTAINE, Lamar   The Prison Life of Major Lamar Fontaine: One of the Immortal Six Hundred Confederate Officers, Prisoners of War, on Prison Ship Crescent City, on Morris Island, Fort Pulaski and Hilton Head, S.C., 1864-1865. Wraps.
1910   Clarksdale, MS   90.00

FOOTE, Caleb and WILDER, Mary   Reminiscences and Letters, edited by Mary Wilder Tileston.
1918   Boston   25.00

FOOTE, Corydon Edward and HORMEL, Olive Deane   With Sherman to the Sea, A Drummer's Story of the Civil War.
1960   New York   25.00

FOOTE, Henry S.   Casket of Reminiscences.
1874   Washington, DC   150.00

FOOTE, Henry S.   War of the Rebellion.
1866   New York   50.00

FOOTE, Kate   Harriet Ward Foote Hawley.
(c.1890)   n.p.   35.00

FOOTE, Shelby   The Civil War: A Narrative. 3 Vols.
1958-74   New York   85.00
Individual volumes   25.00   each

FOOTE, Shelby, edited by   The Night Before Chancellorsville and Other Civil War Stories. Wraps.
1957   New York   30.00

FOOTE, Shelby   Shiloh.
1952   New York   15.00

For Love of a Rebel.
1964   40.00

FORAKER, Joseph Benson   Notes of a Busy Life.
1916   Cincinnati   60.00
1917   Cincinnati   50.00

FORBES, Edwin   An Artist's Story of the Great War.
  1890   New York   4 Vols.   125.00
  1890   New York   20 parts in wraps   500.00
FORBES, Edwin   A Civil War Artist at the Front: Edwin Forbes' Life
  Studies of the Great Army.
  1957   New York   20.00
FORBES, Edwin   Life Studies of the Great Army.   40 copper plate etch-
  ings.
  1876   New York   1000.00
FORBES, Mrs. Ida B.   General Wm. T. Sherman, His Life and Battles.
  1886   New York   25.00
FORBES, John Murray   Letters   and   Recollections,   edited   by   Sarah
  Forbes Hughes. 2 Vols.
  1899   Boston   30.00
  1900   Boston   20.00
FORBES, Robert B.   Personal Reminiscences.
  1878   Boston   45.00
FORCE, Manning Ferguson   From Fort Henry to Corinth.   See:
  Campaigns of the Civil War.
FORCE, Manning Ferguson   General Sherman.
  For additional information, see Appendix: Grat Commanders Series.
  1899   New York   35.00
  1899   New York   Ltd.   125.00
FORD, Andrew E.   The Story of the Fifteenth Regiment Massachusetts
  Volunteer Infantry.
  1898   Clinton   75.00
FORD, Arthur P.   Life in the Confederate Army, Being Personal
  Experiences of a Private Soldier in the Confederate Army.   Published
  and bound with **FORD**, Marion Johnstone - Some Experiences and
  Sketches of Southern Life.
  1905   New York   150.00
FORD, Jesse Hill   The Raider.
  1975   Boston/Toronto   20.00
FORD, Sally Rochester   Raids and Romance of Morgan and His Men.
  1864   New York   75.00
  1865   New York   75.00
FORMBY, John   The American Civil War. 2 Vols.
  1910   London 60.00
  1910   New York   50.00
FORNEY, John W.   Anecdotes of Public Men. 2 Vols.
  1881   New York   30.00
FORNEY, John W.   Letter from Europe.
  1867   PA   45.00
FORNEY, John W.   Life and Military Career of Winfield Scott Hancock.
  1880   Philadelphia   20.00
FORREST, D. F.   Odyssey in Gray; A Diary of Confederate Service,
  1863-1865.
  1979   Richmond   18.00
FORRESTER, Izola   This One Mad Act . . . The Unknown Story of
  John Wilkes Booth and His Family.
  1937   Boston   30.00

FORRESTER, Rebel C.   Glory and Tears, Obion County, Tennessee
1860-1870.
1966   Union City   20.00
FORSYTH, George A.   Thrilling Days in Army Life.
1900   New York   100.00
Fort Pillow Massacre.
1864   Washington, DC   100.00
Fort Sumter Memorial. The Fall of Fort Sumter, edited by Frank Moore.
Replacing the Flag Upon Sumter. Adapted by F. Milton Willis and General Robert Anderson. By Ed. S. Cornell.
1915   New York   Ltd.   65.00
FORT, Kate Haynes   Memoirs of the Fort and Fannin Families.
1903   Chattanooga 150.00
FORTEN, Charlotte L.   The Journal of Charlotte L. Forten, edited by
Ray Allen Billington.
1953   New York   20.00
FORTIER, James J. A., edited by   Carpet-Bag Misrule in Louisiana.
Wraps.
1938   New Orleans   30.00
FOSDICK, Charles   Five Hundred Days in Rebel Prisons.
1887   Bethany, MO   75.00
1887   Chicago   65.00
FOSDICK, Charles   A Rebellion in Dixie.
1897   (Philadelphia)   20.00
FOSDICK, Charles   Rodney the Overseer.
1892   Philadelphia 20.00
FOSDICK, Charles   Rodney the Partisan.
1890   Philadelphia 20.00
FOSS, W. O.   The United States Navy in Hampton Roads.   Wraps.
1984   Norfolk   17.00
FOSTER, Alonzo   Reminiscences and Record of the 6th New York
V.V. Cavalry.
1892   Brooklyn   190.00
FOSTER, B. G.   Abraham Lincoln Inventor.   Wraps.
1928   n.p.   10.00
FOSTER, G. A.   Lincoln's World.
1944   New York   30.00
FOSTER, G. A.   The Eyes and Ears of the Civil War.
1963   New York   40.00
FOSTER, John T.   Rebel Sea Raider, The Story of Raphael Semmes.
1965   New York   20.00
FOSTER, John Watson   War Stories for My Grandchildren.
1918   Washington, DC   100.00
FOSTER, John Young   New Jersey and the Rebellion.
1868   Newark   160.00
FOSTER, Lillian   President Johnson.
1866   New York   20.00
FOSTER, Samuel T.   One of Cleburne's Command, the Civil War Reminiscences and Diary of Capt. _____, Granbury's Texas Brigade, edited by Norman D. Brown.
1980   Austin   40.00

FOSTER, Stephen   A Treasury of Stephen Foster.
    1946   New York   20.00

FOSTER, William Lovelace   Vicksburg: Southern City Under Siege, William Lovelace Foster's Letter Describing the Defense and Surrender of the Confederate Fortress on the Mississippi, edited by Kenneth T. Urquhart.
    1980   New Orleans   15.00

FOULKE, William Dudley   Lucius B. Swift, A Biography.
    1930   Indianapolis   25.00

FOUT, Frederick W.   The Dark Days of the Civil War, 1861 to 1865.
    1904   St. Louis   175.00

FOUT, Frederick W.   Die Schweisten Tage Des Burgerkrieges Von 1864 Und 1865. Der Feldzug Unter Schofield Und Thomas Gegen Hood in Tennessee. Die Schlachten Von Franklin Und Nashville. Erinnerungen Von Frederick W. Fout, Herausgegeben Von Albert E. Fout.
    1902   St. Louis   150.00

FOWLE, George   Letters to Eliza from a Union Soldier 1863-1865, edited by Margery Greenleaf.
    1970   Chicago   25.00

FOWLER, James A. and **MILLER**, Miles M.   History of the Thirtieth Iowa Infantry.
    1908   Mediapolis   150.00

FOWLER, William Chauncey   The Sectional Controversy.
    1862   New York   25.00
    1863   New York   25.00

FOX, Charles B.   Record of the Service of the Fifty-fifth Regiment of Massachusetts Volunteer Infantry.
    1868   Cambridge   Wraps   90.00
    1971   Freeport, NY   30.00

FOX, Charles K., edited by   Gettysburg.
    1969   New York   15.00
    1969   Wraps   6.00

FOX, Gustavus Vasa   Confidential Correspondence of _____, Assistant Secretary of the Navy during the Civil War, edited by R. M. Thompson & Richard Wainright.
    1918   New York   Ltd. Boxed   75.00
    1920   75.00

FOX, John A.   The Capture of Jefferson Davis.   Wraps.
    1964   New York   20.00

FOX, John, Jr.   The Little Shepherd of Kingdom Come.
    1911   New York   5.00

FOX, Simeon M.   The Early History of the Seventh Kansas Cavalry. Wraps.
    1910   Topeka   20.00

FOX, Simeon M.   The 7th Kansas Cavalry: Its Service in the Civil War. An Address.   Wraps.
    1908   Topeka   25.00

FOX, Simeon M.   The Story of the Seventh Kansas.   Wraps.
    1902   Topeka   30.00

FOX, Thomas Bailey   Memorial of Henry Ware Hall, Adjutant 51st Regiment Infantry Volunteers, An Address.   Wraps.
    1864   Boston   40.00

FOX, Wells B.   What I Remember of the Great Rebellion.
   1892   Lansing   140.00
FOX, William F.   New York Monuments Commission for the Battlefields of Gettysburg and Chattanooga. Final Report on the Battlefield of Gettysburg. 3 Vols. (New York at Gettysburg).
   1902   Albany   150.00
FOX, William F.   Regimental Losses in the American Civil War 1861-1865.
   1889   Albany   100.00
   1893   Albany   75.00
   1974   Dayton   45.00
   1985   Dayton   50.00
FRAMPTON, Roy   Inscriptions and Locations of the Gettysburg Battlefield Memorials. 2 Vols. Wraps.
   1987   58.00
FRANCINE, Albert Philip   Louis Raymond Francine, Brevet Brigadier-General U.S. Volunteers 1837-1863.
   1910   n.p.   Ltd.   50.00
FRANCIS, Augustus T.   History of the 71st Regiment N.G.N.Y.
   1919   New York   90.00
FRANCIS, Charles L.   Narrative of a Private Soldier in the Volunteer Army of the United States.
   1879   Brooklyn   90.00
Frank Leslie's Illustrated Famous Leaders. . . . See: LESLIE, Frank
Frank Leslie's Illustrated History. . . .   See: LESLIE, Frank
Frank Leslie's Illustrated Newspaper. . . . See: LESLIE, Frank
Frank Leslie's Pictorial History. . . . See: LESLIE, Frank
Frank Leslie's Scenes and Portraits. . . . See: LESLIE, Frank
FRANK, John P.   Lincoln as a Lawyer.
   1961   Urbana, IL   10.00
FRANKLIN, Charles H.   Study on Project of Publication, The War of the Rebellion.
   1931   Washington, DC   25.00
FRANKLIN, John Hope   The Emancipation Proclamation. Wraps.
   1963   New York   8.00
FRANKLIN, John Hope   From Slavery to Freedom A History of Negro Americans.
   1947   New York   30.00
   1956   New York   30.00
   1967   New York   30.00
   1980   New York   30.00
FRANKLIN, John Hope   The Militant South 1800-1861.
   1956   Cambridge   20.00
   1970   10.00
FRANKLIN, John Hope   Reconstruction After the Civil War.
   1961   Chicago   15.00
   1961   Chicago   Wraps   8.00
FRANKLIN, John Hope   A Southern Odyssey: Travels in the Antebellum North.
   1976   Baton Rouge   15.00
FRANKLIN, Samuel R.   Memories of a Rear-Admiral.
   1898   New York   40.00

FRANKLIN, William B.   Reply to the Report of the Joint Committee of
Congress on the Conduct of the War.   Wraps.
1863   New York   50.00
FRANKS, Kenneth A.   Stand Watie and the Agony of the Cherokee
Nation.
1979   Memphis   25.00
FRANTZ, Mabel Goode   Full Many a Name, The Story of Sam Davis,
Scout and Spy, C.S.A.
1961   Jackson   25.00
FRASSANITO, William A.   Antietam,   the Photographic Legacy of
America's Bloodiest Day.
1978   New York   20.00
1978   London   20.00
1979   New York   Wraps 13.00
FRASSANITO, William A.   Gettysburg, A Journey in Time.
1975   New York   30.00
FRASSANITO, William A.   Grant and Lee: The Virginia Campaigns,
1864-1865.
1983   New York   35.00
1986   27.50
1986   Wraps   15.95
FRAZIER, John W.   Reunion of the Blue and Gray, Philadelphia
Brigade and Pickett's Division July 2, 3, 4, 1887 and September 15, 16,
17, 1906. Wraps.
1906   Philadelphia   95.00
FREDERIC, Harold   Marsena and Other Stories of the Wartime.
1894   New York   25.00
FREDERIC, Harold   The Copperhead and other Stories of the North
During the American War.
1894   25.00
FREDERICK, Gilbert   The Story of a Regiment Being a Record of
the Military Services of the 57th New York State Volunteer Infantry.
1895   Chicago   130.00
FREDERICKSON, George M.   The Inner Civil War.
1965   New York   15.00
FREEHLING, William W.   Prelude to Civil War: The Nullification Controversy in South Carolina 1816-1836.
1965   New York   15.00
1966   New York   15.00
FREEMAN, Andrew A.   Abraham Lincoln Goes to New York.
1960   New York   20.00
FREEMAN, Benjamin H.   The Confederate Letters of _____, edited by
Stuart Wright.
1974   New York   15.00
FREEMAN, Douglas Southall   An Address April 1950, Appomattox Court
House Virginia. Wraps.
1964   n.p.   35.00
FREEMAN, Douglas Southall   Automobile Tour of Principal Battlefields
Near Richmond.
1969   Richmond   15.00

FREEMAN, Douglas Southall   A Calendar of Confederate Papers.
  1908   Richmond   Ltd.   75.00
  1969   New York   40.00

FREEMAN, Douglas Southall   The Confederate Tradition of Richmond.
  Wraps.
  1957   Univ. of Iowa   18.00

FREEMAN, Douglas Southall   The Cornerstones of Stratford, An Address. Wraps.
  (1935)   n.p.   30.00

FREEMAN, Douglas Southall   Douglas Southall Freeman, May 1886-June 1953. Wraps.
  (1953)   (Richmond)   35.00

FREEMAN, Douglas Southall   The Last Parade.
  1932   Richmond   Ltd.   300.00

FREEMAN, Douglas Southall   The Last Review, The Confederate Reunion, Richmond, 1932, by Virginius Dabney, and including The Last Parade and The Confederate Tradition of Richmond, by Freeman.
  1984   Chapel Hill   30.00

FREEMAN, Douglas Southall   Lee of Virginia.
  1958   New York   25.00

FREEMAN, Douglas Southall   Lee's Lieutenants. 3 Vols.
  1942-44   New York   150.00
  1946   New York Arlington Edition   200.00
  1966   New York   90.00
  Recent reprint Vol. I Wraps   17.95
  Recent reprint Vol. II Wraps   17.95
  Recent reprint Vol. III Wraps   18.95

FREEMAN, Douglas Southall   The Lengthening Shadow of Lee. Wraps.
  1936   Richmond   75.00

FREEMAN, Douglas Southall   Publicity and the Public Mind Annual Address Delivered at the Seventy-first Annual Meeting of the American Medico-Psychological Association, Old Point Comfort, Va., May 11-14, 1915. Wraps.
  1915   35.00

FREEMAN, Douglas Southall   R. E. Lee. 4 Vols.
  1934-35 New York   225.00
  1936   New York Pulitzer Prize ed.   175.00
  Issued hereafter about once a year in New York   150.00

FREEMAN, Douglas Southall   Robert E. Lee and the Ladies. October and November issues, Scribners Magazine.
  1925   50.00

FREEMAN, Douglas Southall   The South to Posterity.
  1939   New York   65.00
  1951   New York   40.00
  1983   Wendell, NC   30.00

FREEMAN, Douglas Southall and McWHINEY, G., edited by   Lee's Dispatches, Unpublished Letters of General Robert E. Lee to Jefferson Davis . . . 1862-1865.
  1915   New York   90.00
  1957   New York   45.00

FREEMAN, G.   Washington.   Wraps.
  1968   19.00
FREEMAN, Walker Burford   Memoirs of Walker Burford Freeman, 1843-
  1935.
  1978   Richmond   35.00
FREESE, Jacob R.   Secrets of the Late Rebellion.
  1882   Philadelphia   15.00
FREIDEL, Frank   Francis Lieber: Nineteenth-Century Liberal.
  1947   Baton Rouge   25.00
FREIDEL, Frank, edited by   Union Pamphlets of the Civil War.   2 Vols.
  1957   Cambridge   30.00
  1967   30.00
FREITAG, Alfred J.   Detroit in the Civil War.   Wraps.
  1951   Detroit   20.00
FREMANTLE, Arthur J. L.   Three Months in the Southern States.
  1863   Edinburgh   250.00
  1863   London   200.00
  1863   New York   125.00
  For 1864 edition, see: **Confederate Imprints** P-5392.
  1904   Boston   50.00
  1954   Boston   entitled **The Fremantle Diary,** edited by Walter Lord
        25.00
  1956   London   30.00
  1970   20.00
  1984   20.00
FREMANTLE, Arthur J. L. and HASKELL, Frank   Two Views of Gettys-
  burg, edited by Richard Harwell.
  1964   Chicago   30.00
FREMONT, Jessie Benton   The Story of the Guard.
  1863   Boston   75.00
FRENCH, "Chester" S. Bassett   Centennial Tales, Memoirs of _____,
  edited by Glenn C. Oldaker.
  1962   New York   25.00
FRENCH, Samuel G.   Two Wars: An Autobiography.
  1901   Nashville   140.00
FRENCH, Samuel L.   The Army of the Potomac from 1861 to 1863.
  1905   New York   75.00
  1906   New York   60.00
FRENCH, William H. et al   Instruction for Field Artillery.
  1860   Philadelphia   150.00
  1861   Philadelphia   100.00
  1863   Phildelphia   75.00
  1968   New York   30.00
FROHMAN, Charles   Rebels on Lake Erie.
  1956   Columbus   50.00
  1965   40.00
  1975   20.00
FROST, Griffin   Camp and Prison Journal, Embracing Scenes in Camp,
  on the March, and in Prisons. . . .
  1867   Quincy, IL   1500.00

FROST, Holloway H.   Union Joint Operations Along the Confederate
    Coast in the Civil War. Wraps.
    1932   Washington, DC   Ltd.   100.00
FROST, J. B., compiled by   The Rebellion in the United States: or,
    the War of 1861. . . .
    1862   Hartford   30.00
FROST, Lawrence A.   The Court-Martial of General George Arm-
    strong Custer.
    1968   Norman, OK   25.00
FROST, Lawrence A.   The Custer Album,   A Pictorial Biography of
    General George A. Custer.
    1964   Seattle   30.00
    1984   15.00
FROST, Lawrence A.   Custer's 7th Cavalry and the Campaign of
    1873.
    1986   45.00
FROST, Lawrence A.   General Custer's Libbie.
    1976   Seattle   Ltd.   50.00
FROST, Lawrence A.   The Phil Sheridan Album.
    1968   Seattle   25.00
    1978   25.00
FROST, Lawrence A.   U. S. Grant Album, A Pictorial Biography.
    1966   New York   20.00
    1966   Seattle   15.00
    Recent reprint   27.50
FROST, M. O.   Regimental History of the Tenth Missouri Volunteer
    Infantry.
    1892   Topeka   350.00
FROST, Robert W.   Picket Pins and Sabers.
    1971   13.00
FRY, James B.   The Conkling and Blaine-Fry Controversy in 1866.
    1893   New York   15.00
FRY, James B.   The History and Legal Effect of Brevets in the Armies
    of the U.S. and Great Britain from Their Origin in 1692 to the Present
    Time.
    1877   125.00
FRY, James B.   McDowell and Tyler in the Campaign of Bull Run 1861.
    Wraps.
    1884   New York   40.00
FRY, James B.   Military Miscellanies.
    1889   New York   50.00
FRY, James B.   Operations of the Army Under Buell from June 10th to
    October 30th, 1862.
    1884   New York   80.00
FRY, Smith D.   Lincoln and Lee A Patriotic Story.   Wraps.
    1922   Washington, DC   5.00
FRYE, Dennis E.   12th Virginia Cavalry.
    1988   Lynchburg   16.95
FRYE, James Albert   From Headquarters.
    1893   Boston   40.00
FUESS, Claude M.   Carl Schurz: Reformer (1829-1906).
    1932   15.00

FUESS, Claude M.　　　Daniel Webster. 2 Vols.
　　1930　30.00
FUESS, Claude M.　　　The Life of Caleb Cushing. 2 Vols.
　　1923　New York　50.00
FULD, George and FULD, Melvin　　　Patriotic Civil War Tokens.
　　1965　Lincoln, MA　30.00
　　1981　Lincoln, MA　Wraps　10.00
FULKERSON, H. S.　　　A Civilian's Recollections of the War Between the
　　States, edited by P. O. Rainwater.
　　1939　Baton Rouge　Ltd.　190.00
FULLAM, George Townley　　　The Journal of _____, edited by Charles
　　G. Summersell.
　　1973　University, AL　30.00
FULLER, Claud E.　　　Confederate Currency and Stamps 1861-1865.
　　1949　Nashville　75.00
FULLER, Claud E.　　　The Rifled Musket.
　　1958　Harrisburg　40.00
FULLER, Claud E., edited by　　　Springfield Muzzle-Loading Shoulder Arms.
　　1930　New York　100.00
　　1968　75.00
FULLER, Claud E. and STEUART, R. D.　　　Firearms of the Confederacy.
　　1944　Huntington, WV　100.00
　　1977　60.00
FULLER, J. F. C.　　　Decisive Battles of the U.S.A.
　　1942　New York　20.00
　　1953　New York　15.00
FULLER, J. F. C.　　　The Generalship of Ulysses S. Grant.
　　1929　New York　40.00
　　1929　London 45.00
　　1958　Bloomington, IN　30.00
FULLER, J. F. C.　　　Grant and Lee.
　　1933　New York　40.00
　　1933　London 45.00
　　1957　Bloomington, IN　25.00
　　1982　30.00
　　1982　Wraps　11.00
FULLER, Richard F.　　　Chaplain Fuller.
　　1863　Boston　25.00
　　1864　Boston　20.00
FULLER, Richard J.　　　History of the Trials and Hardships of the
　　Twenty-fourth Indiana Volunteer Infantry.　Wraps.
　　1913　250.00
FULTON, William Frierson II　　　Family Record and War Reminiscences.
　　(c.1910)　n.p.　500.00
FUNK, Arville L.　　　The Battle of Corydon.　Wraps.
　　1976　IN　5.00
FURBISH, Julia A. M., editor & illustrator　　　The Flower of Liberty.
　　1869　Boston　60.00
FURMAN, G.　　　The Medical Register of the City of New York for the
　　Year 1864.
　　1864　175.00

FURNAS, J. C.   Goodbye to Uncle Tom.
    1956   New York   10.00
FURNAS, J. C.   The Road to Harpers Ferry.
    1959   New York   15.00
FUTCH, Ovid L.   History of Andersonville Prison.
    1968   Gainesville, FL   20.00
    1978   10.00
FUTRELL, Robert Frank   Economic Readjustment in Mississippi
    During Reconstruction, 1865-1875. Wraps.
    1939   University, MS   75.00
FUZZLEBUG, Fritz (pseud.)   See: DUNKLE, John J.
GACHE, P. L. H.   A Frenchman, A Chaplain, A Rebel: The War Let-
    ters of Pere Louis Hippolyte Gache, S. J.
    1981   Chicago   13.00
GAFF, Alan D.   Brave Men's Tears: The Iron Brigade at Brawner's
    Farm.
    1985   Dayton   17.50
    1988   Dayton   19.95
GAGE, Moses D.   From Vicksburg to Raleigh, or a Complete History of
    the 12th Regiment Indiana Volunteer Infantry.
    1865   Chicago   200.00
GAINES, Francis Pendleton   Lee, The Final Achievement.
    1933   New York   Ltd. Signed   40.00
    1933   n.p. Wraps   30.00
GAINES, W. C.   The Confederate Cherokees: John Drew's Regiment of
    Mounted Rifles.
    1989   Baton Rouge   19.95
GAINES, William H., Jr.   Biographical Register of Members Virginia
    State Convention of 1861, 1st Sess. Wraps.
    1969   Richmond   10.00
GALBREATH, C. B.   General Keifer Honored. Wraps.
    1926   OH   30.00
GALLAGHER, Gary W., edited by   Antietam: Essays on the 1862
    Maryland Campaign.
    1989   Ltd.   17.50
GALLAGHER, Gary W., edited by   Fighting for the Confederacy.
    The Personal Recollections of General Edward Porter Alexander.
    1989   Chapel Hill, NC   34.95
GALLAGHER, Gary W.   Stephen Dodson Ramseur. Lee's Gallant Gen-
    eral.
    1986   Chapel Hill, NC   20.00
GALLAHER, De Witt Clinton   A Diary Depicting the Experiences of
    DeWitt Clinton Gallaher in the War Between the States. Wraps.
    1945   Charleston, SC   30.00
GALLAWAY, B. P., edited by   Dark Corner of the Confederacy, Accounts
    of Civil War Texas.
    1968   Dubuque   20.00
GALLAWAY, B. P.   The Ragged Rebel: A Common Soldier in W. H.
    Parson's Texas Cavalry, 1861-1865.
    1988   Austin   22.50

GALLOWAY, C. B.   The South and the Negro: An Address Delivered at the Seventh Annual Conference for Education in the South. . . .   Wraps.
1904   New York   23.00
GALLOWAY, G. Norton   The Ninety-fifth Pennsylvania Volunteers in the Sixth Corps. Wraps.
1884   Philadelphia 100.00
GALLOWAY, Richard   One Battle Too Many. The Writings of Simon Bolivar Hulbert, Private, Company E, 100th New York Volunteers.
1987   28.00
GALWEY, Thomas Francis   The Valiant Hours, edited by W. S. Nye.
1961   Harrisburg   35.00
GAMBLE, Thomas   Savannah Duels and Duelists 1733-1877. Wraps.
1923   Savannah   30.00
GAMMAGE, W. L.   The Camp, The Bivouac, and the Battle Field. Being a History of the 4th Arkansas Regiment.
1958   Little Rock   50.00
GAMMONS, John G.   The Third Massachusetts Regiment Volunteer Militia in the War of the Rebellion 1861-1863.
1906   Providence   65.00
GANNON, Michael V.   Rebel Bishop, The Life and Era of Augustin Verot.
1964   Milwaukee   25.00
GANTT, E. W.   Address: Brigadier General E. W. Gantt, C.S.A.
1860   Little Rock   175.00
(c.1863) (Philadelphia)   75.00
GARBER, Mrs. A. W., edited by   In Memoriam Sempiternam, Confederate Memorial Literary Society.
1896   Richmond   20.00
GARBER, J. A.   Robert E. Lee. Wraps.
1930   Washington, DC   10.00
GARD, R. Max   Morgan's Raid into Ohio.
1963   Lisbon, OH   25.00
GARDINER, Asa Bird   Argument on Behalf of Lieut. Gen. Philip H. Sheridan . . . Before the Court of Inquiry: The Battles of "Gravelly Run," "Dinwiddie Court House," and "Five Forks," Va. 1865. Wraps.
1881   Washington, DC   75.00
1881   Chicago   60.00
GARDINER, F. E.   Cyrus Edward's Stories of Early Days.
1940   75.00
GARDNER, Alexander   Original Photographs Taken on the Battlefields During the Civil War.
1907   Hartford   150.00
GARDNER, Alexander   Photographic Sketchbook of the Civil War. 2 Vols.
(1865-66)   Washington, DC   100 Plates   20,000.00
1959   New York   25.00
GARDNER, James B.   Massachusetts Memorial to Her Soldiers and Sailors Who Died in the Department of North Carolina Dedicated at New Bern . . . 1908.
1909   Boston   50.00

GARDNER, W.   Life of Stephen A. Douglas.
1905   Boston   25.00
GARESCHE, Louis   Biography of Lieut. Col. Julius P. Garesche.
1887   Philadelphia   125.00
GARFIELD, James A.   The Wild Life of the Army: Civil War Letters
of _____, edited by Frederick D. Williams.
1964   Chapel Hill, NC   15.00
GARLAND, Hamlin   Trail-Makers of the Middle Border.
1926   New York   25.00
GARLAND, Hamlin   Ulysses S. Grant His Life and Character.
1898   New York   35.00
1920   New York   20.00
GARLINGTON, J. C.   Men of the Time.
1902   Spartanburg 100.00
GARNER, James Wilford   Reconstruction in Mississippi.
1901   New York   125.00
1964   22.50
1968   Baton Rouge Wraps 15.00
GARNETT, John J.   Gettysburg, A Complete Historical Narrative of
the Battle. Wraps.
1888   New York   50.00
GARNETT, Theodore S.   J. E. B. Stuart . . . An Address.
1907   New York   85.00
GAROFALO, Robert and ELROD, Mark   A Pictorial History of Civil
War Era Musical Instruments and Military Bands. Wraps.
1985   Missoula   10.00
1987   10.00
GARRETT, David R.   The Civil War Letters of _____, Detailing the
Adventures of the 6th Texas Cavalry, edited by Max Lale & Hobart
Key, Jr. Wraps.
1964   Marshall   Ltd. 30.00
GARRETT, Jill K., edited by   Confederate Soldiers and Patriots of
Maury County Tenn.
1970   Columbia   30.00
GARRETT, Jill K., and LIGHTFOOT, Marise P. The Civil War in Maury
County, Tennessee.
1980   n.p.   40.00
GARRISON, Fielding H.   John Shaw Billings, A Memoir.
1915   New York   50.00
GARTH, David   Gray Canaan.
1947   New York   15.00
GASKILL, Joseph W.   Footprints Through Dixie.
1919   Alliance 100.00
GASPARIN, Agenor de   America Before Europe Principles and Interests.
1862   New York   35.00
GASPARIN, Agenor de   The Uprising of a Great People.
1861   New York   30.00
1861   Paris entitled Les Etats-Unis En 1861 Un Grande Peuple Qui
Se Releve. Wraps.   35.00
1862   25.00

GASTON, John Thomas   Confederate War Diary of _____, edited by Allifaire (Allie) Gaston Walden. Wraps.
  1960   Columbia   40.00
GASTON, Paul M.   The New South Creed.
  1970   New York   15.00
GASTON, Robert H. & William H.   "Tyler To Sharpsburg" The War Letters of _____, edited by Robert Glover. Wraps.
  1960   Waco   25.00
GATES, Paul W.   Agriculture and the Civil War.
  1965   New York   30.00
GATES, Theodore B.   The "Ulster Guard" (20th N. Y. State Militia) and the War of the Rebellion.
  1879   New York   140.00
GATES, Theodore B.   War of the Rebellion.
  1884   New York   100.00
GAUCH, Patricia Lee   Thunder at Gettysburg.
  1975   New York   20.00
GAULT, W. P.   See: Ohio at Vicksburg.
GAUSE, Isaac   Four Years with Five Armies.
  1908   New York   125.00
GAVIN, William G.   Accoutrement Plates, North and South 1861-1865.
  1963   Philadelphia   50.00
  1975   New York   40.00
GAVIN, William G.   Campaigning with the Roundheads: The History of the Hundredth Pennsylvania Veteran Volunteer Infantry Regiment 1861-65.
  1989   Dayton   40.00
GAVRONSKY, Serge   The French Liberal Opposition and the American Civil War.
  1968   New York   15.00
GAY, George H.   A Few Remarks on the Primary Treatment of Wounds. Wraps.
  1862   Boston   50.00
GAY, Mary A. H.   Life in Dixie During the War.
  1892   Atlanta   125.00
  1894   Atlanta   100.00
  1897   Atlanta   75.00
  1901   Atlanta   60.00
  1982   Decatur   25.00
GAY, Mary A. H.   The Transplanted, A Story of Dixie Before the War.
  1907   New York/Washington, DC   60.00
GEER, John J.   Beyond the Lines.
  1863   Philadelphia   80.00
  1864   Philadelphia   75.00
GEER, Walter   Campaigns of the Civil War.
  1926   New York   100.00
GELMAN, Barbara, edited by   The Wood Engravings of Winslow Homer.
  1969   New York   30.00
GENCO, James G.   Arming Michigan's Regiments. Wraps.
  1982   10.00

GENCO, James G.   To the Sound of Musketry and Tap of the Drum. A History of Michigan's Battery D Through the Letters of Artificer Harold J. Bartlett 1861-1864.
1983   Rochester, MI   25.00
General Grant's Tour Around the World.
1879   Chicago   20.00
General Order No. 27, HQ Dept. of the Ohio.
1861   Louisville, KY   50.00
General Plan of Gettysburg National Military Park. . . .
1935   20.00
General Regulations for the Military Forces of the State of New York.
1858   Albany   65.00
The General Scott Maps of the War, A Campaign Pocket Atlas.
1861   200.00
General Washington and General Jackson on Negro Soldiers. Wraps.
1863   Philadelphia   40.00
Generals and Battles of the Civil War.
1891   Canton, OH   125.00
GENOVESE, Eugene D.   Roll, Jordan, Roll, the World the Slaves Made.
1974   New York   20.00
GENTRY, Claude   The Battle of Brice's Crossroads. Wraps.
1968   Baldwyn, MS   15.00
1971   10.00
GENTRY, Claude   Private John Allen.
1951   Decatur   35.00
GEORG, K. R. and **BUSEY**, J. W.   Nothing but Glory: Pickett's Division at Gettysburg.
1987   Hightstown   40.00
GEORGE, G. Jasper   William Newby, Alias "Dan Benton," Alias "Rickety Dan," Alias "Crazy Jack."
1893   Cincinnati   60.00
GEORGE, Henry   History of the Third, Seventh, Eighth, and Twelfth Kentucky, C.S.A.
1911   Louisville   225.00
1970   Lyndon   Ltd.   35.00
GEORGE, James Z.   Political History of Slavery in the United States.
1915   New York   75.00
Georgia - Confederate Military History.   See: Confederate Military History, Vol. VI (Vol. VII, 1987 reprint ed.).
GERNON, Blaine Brooks   The Lincolns in Chicago.
1934   Chicago   15.00
GERRISH, Theodore   Army Life.
1882   Portland   40.00
GERRISH, Theodore   Will Newton The Young Volunteer.
1884   Maine   20.00
GERRISH, Theodore and **HUTCHINSON**, J. S.   The Blue and the Gray.
1883   Portland   50.00
1884   Bangor   35.00
GERSON, Noel B.   The Trial of Andrew Johnson.
1977   New York   15.00
Gettysburg and Adjacent Portions of Adams County, Penn., 1-4, July, 1863.
1963   Alexandria   35.00

Gettysburg Battle Views.
    n.d.   n.p.   25.00
Gettysburg Blue Book of the Geological Field Excursion from New York to Gettysburg. Wraps.
    1926   New York   30.00
Gettysburg. A Comprehensive Description of the Greatest Work of the Celebrated French Artist Paul Philippoteaux Battle of Gettysburg. Wraps.
    (1933) (Chicago)   30.00
The Gettysburg Guide. Wraps.
    1987   8.95
Gettysburg: Historical Articles of Lasting Interest. Wraps.
    1989   Dayton   4.95
Gettysburg Memorial Commission, Report of.
    1887   Columbus   Wraps   30.00
    1914   Harrisburg 30.00
Gettysburg National Military Park, Annual Reports to the Secretary of War.
    1900   Washington, DC 1893-1899   40.00
    1902   Washington, DC 1893-1901   40.00
    1905   Washington, DC 1893-1904   40.00
Gettysburg Sources, Vol. I.
    1987   Baltimore   20.00
Gettysburg Sources, Vol. II.
    1987   Baltimore   23.50
GHERST, M. A.   A History of a Trip Across the Plains Made by Company A, 14th Pennsylvania Cavalry. Wraps.
    1893   Pittsburgh   30.00
GIBBES, James G.   Who Burnt Columbia?
    1902   Newberry, SC   100.00
GIBBON, John   An Address on the Unveiling of the Statue of Maj. Gen. George G. Meade in Philadelphia. Wraps.
    1887   Philadelphia   30.00
GIBBON, John   The Artillerist's Manual.
    1863   New York   150.00
    1970   Glendale   75.00
    1971   Westport, CT   50.00
GIBBON, John   Personal Recollections of the Civil War.
    1928   New York   100.00
    1978   30.00
    1988   30.00
GIBBONS, A. R.   The Recollections of an Old Confederate Soldier: A. R. Gibbons. Wraps.
    n.d.   Shelbyville, MO   35.00
GIBBONS, T.   Warships and Naval Battles of the Civil War.
    1989   New York   24.98
GIBBS, James M.   History of the First Battalion Pennsylvania Six Months Volunteers and 187th Regiment Pennsylvania Volunteer Infantry.
    1905   Harrisburg   80.00
GIBSON, Florence E.   The Attitudes of the New York Irish towards State and National Affairs 1848-1892.
    1951   New York   12.00

GIBSON, James Monroe   Memoirs of J. M. Gibson: Terrors of the Civil War and Reconstruction Days, edited by James G. Alverson & James, Jr.
1929   Houston, TX   65.00
1966   n.p.   20.00
GIBSON, John M.   Soldier in White, The Life of Gen. George Miller Sternberg.
1958   18.00
GIBSON, John M.   Those 163 Days.
1961   New York   25.00
GIBSON, Joseph T., edited by   History of the 78th Pennsylvania Volunteer Infantry.
1905   Pittsburgh   65.00
GIBSON, Randall Lee   Shiloh, Equestrian Monument Erected by the Veterans of the Army of Tennessee. Wraps.
1887   New Orleans   25.00
GIBSON, Ronald, edited by   Jefferson Davis and the Confederacy.
1977   Dobbs Ferry, NY   15.00
GIBSON, William H.   Ohio's Silver-Tongued Orator, Life and Speeches of General William H. Gibson.
1901   Dayton   60.00
GIDDINGS, Joshua   The Exiles of Florida.
1858   Columbus   115.00
GILBERT, Alfred W.   Col. A. W. Gilbert, Citizen Soldier of Cincinnati, edited by W. E. Smith and O. D. Smith.
1934   Cincinnati   80.00
GILBERT, C. E.   Two Presidents: Abraham Lincoln, Jefferson Davis. Wraps.
1927   Houston, TX   30.00
GILBERT, J. Warren   Battle of Gettysburg Made Plain, Historical Guide-Book. Wraps.
(c.1890) Gettysburg   30.00
GILBERT, J. Warren   The Blue and Gray. Wraps.
1922   n.p.   25.00
GILCHRIST, Robert C.   The Confederate Defence of Morris Island. Wraps.
1884   Charleston, SC   50.00
GILDERSLEEVE, Basil L.   The Creed of the Old South 1865-1915.
1915   Baltimore   50.00
GILES, Leonidas B.   Terry's Texas Rangers.
1911   Austin   1000.00
1967   Austin   50.00
GILES, Val C.   Rags and Hope: The Memoirs of _____, Four Years with Hood's Brigade, Fourth Texas Infantry 1861-1865, edited by Mary Lasswell.
1961   New York   35.00
GILHAM, William   Manual of Instruction for the Volunteers and Militia of the United States.
1861   Philadelphia   125.00
GILL, John   Reminiscences of Four Years as a Private Soldier in the Confederate Army.
1904   Baltimore   450.00

GILLESPIE, Ira   From Michigan to Murfreesboro: The Diary of the
_____ of the Eleventh Michigan Infantry, edited by Daniel B. Weber.
Wraps.
1965   Mt. Pleasant, MI   10.00
GILLESPIE, Samuel L.   A History of Co. A, First Ohio Cavalry 1861-
1865 A Memorial Volume.
1898   Washington Courthouse   250.00
GILLETTE, William   Retreat from Reconstruction. Wraps.
1979   Baton Rouge   10.00
GILLMORE, Q. A.   Engineer and Artillery Operations Against the
Defenses of Charleston Harbor in 1863.
1862   New York   125.00
1865   New York   100.00
1868   New York   100.00
GILLMORE, Q. A.   Official Report to the United States Engineer
Department, of the Siege and Reduction of Fort Pulaski, Georgia,
February, March and April, 1862.
1862   New York   100.00
Recent reprint   35.00
Recent reprint   Wraps 8.95
GILLS, Mary Louise   It Happened at Appomattox. Wraps.
1948   Richmond   10.00
GILMAN, Bradley   Robert E. Lee.
1915   New York   15.00
GILMER, Morgan   Shockley's Alabama Escort Company, with Nathan
Bedford Forrest. Wraps.
1983   8.00
GILMOR, Harry   Four Years in the Saddle.
1866   New York   100.00
1866   London   125.00
1985   25.00
1987   Baltimore   25.00
GILMORE, George C.   Manchester Men: Soldiers and Sailors in the
Civil War 1861-1866.
1898   Concord   25.00
GILMORE, James Roberts   Among the Guerillas.
1866   New York   20.00
GILMORE, James Roberts   Among the Pines; or, South in Secession-
Time.
1862   New York   25.00
1865   New York   25.00
GILMORE, James Roberts   Down in Tennessee.
1864   New York   35.00
GILMORE, James Roberts   Life in Dixie's Land: Or, South in Seces-
sion-Time.
1863   London   100.00
GILMORE, James Roberts   My Southern Friends.
1863   New York   30.00
GILMORE, James Roberts   On the Border.
1867   Boston   25.00
GILMORE, James Roberts   Patriot Boys and Prison Pictures.
1866   Boston   25.00

GILMORE, James Roberts   Personal Recollections of Abraham Lincoln
and the Civil War.
    1898   Boston   25.00
    1899   London   25.00
GILMORE, Pascal P.   Civil War Memories.
    1928   Bangor   50.00
GILSON, John H., compiled by   Concise History of the 126th Regiment
Ohio Volunteer Infantry.
    1883   Salem   225.00
GIRARD, Charles   A Visit to the Confederate States of America in
1863. . . .   See: Confederate Centennial Studies, No. 21.
GIRARD, Charles   Les Etats Confederes d'Amerique Visites en 1863.
    1864   Paris   100.00
GITTINGS, John C.   Personal Recollections of Stonewall Jackson.
    1899   Cincinnati   300.00
GLASGOW, Ellen   The Battle-Ground.
    1946   10.00
GLASS, Paul and SINGER, Louis C.   Singing Soldiers: A History of the
Civil War in Song.
    1968   New York   30.00
    1988   13.95
GLASSELL, W. T.   W. T. Glassell and the Little Torpedo Boat "David."
    1937   Los Angeles   30.00
GLATTHAAR, J. T.   Forged in Battle: Civil War Alliance of Black Sol-
diers and White Officers.
    1989   New York   25.00
GLATTHAAR, J. T.   The March to the Sea and Beyond; Sherman's
Troops in the Savannah and Carolinas Campaigns.
    1985   New York   28.00
GLAZIER, Willard   Battles for the Union.
    1875   Hartford   30.00
    1878   Hartford   30.00
GLAZIER, Willard   The Capture, The Prison Pen and the Escape.
    1866-70 Various editions   25.00 each
GLAZIER, Willard   Three Years in the Federal Cavalry.
    1870   New York   40.00
    1873   New York   30.00
    1874   New York   30.00
GLEASON, David King   Virginia Plantation Homes.
    1989   39.95
GLEASON, William J.   History of the Cuyahoga County Soldiers' and
Sailor's Monument.
    1894   Cleveland   40.00
GLENN, William Wilkins   Between North and South: A Maryland Jour-
nalist Views the Civil War, the Narrative of _____ 1861-1869, edited
by B. E. Marks and M. N. Schatz.
    1976   Rutherford, NJ   30.00
GLICKSBERG, Charles I., edited by   Walt Whitman and the Civil War,
A Collection of Original Articles and Manuscripts.
    1933   Philadelphia   30.00
    1963   Wraps   5.00

Glimpses of the Nation's Struggle, Papers Read Before the Minnesota Commandery, Mollus. 6 Vols.
   Individual Volumes   75.00   each
   1887-1909   St. Paul   500.00
GLOVER, Edwin A.   **Bucktailed Wildcats.**
   1960   New York   35.00
GLOVER, W.   **Abraham Lincoln and the Sleeping Sentinel of Vermont.**
   1936   Montpelier   20.00
GLYNDON, Howard (pseud.)   See: SEARING, Laura C. R.
GODDARD, Henry P.   **14th Connecticut Volunteers, Regimental Reminiscences of the War.**   Wraps.
   1877   Middletown   40.00
GODDARD, Henry P.   **Memorial of Deceased Officers of the 14th Regiment Connecticut Vols.**   Wraps.
   1872   Hartford   30.00
GODDARD, Joseph A.   **A Brief Autobiography of Joseph A. Goddard.**
   1929   Muncie   60.00
GODDARD, Samuel A.   **Letters on the American Rebellion.**
   1870   London   65.00
GODFREY, Carlos E.   **Sketch of Major Henry Washington Sawyer, First Regiment Cavalry, New Jersey Volunteers.**   Wraps.
   1907   Trenton   40.00
GOEBEL, Dorothy Burne and **GOEBEL,** Jr. Julius   **Generals in the White House.**
   1945   New York   20.00
GOEN, C. C.   **Broken Churches, Broken Nation; Denominational Schisms and the Coming of the Civil War.**   Wraps.
   1985   Macon   15.00
GOETZMANN, William H.   **Army Exploration in the American West, 1803-1863.**
   1979   Lincoln, NE   32.00
   1979   Lincoln, NE   Wraps   7.95
GOFF, Richard D.   **Confederate Supply.**
   1969   Durham, NC   25.00
GOLD, Thomas D.   **History of Clarke County, Virginia and Its Connections with the War Between the States.**
   1914   Berryville   165.00
   1962   Berryville   40.00
GOLDSBOROUGH, Edward Yerbury   **Early's Great Raid.**   Wraps.
   1898   n.p.   100.00
GOLDSBOROUGH, William W.   **Index to the Maryland Line in the Confederate Army 1861-1865.**   Wraps.
   1944   Annapolis   30.00
GOLDSBOROUGH, William W.   **The Maryland Line in the Confederate States Army.**
   1869   Baltimore   250.00
   1900   Baltimore   200.00
   1972   Port Washington, NY   40.00
   1983   35.00
   1987   35.00

GOLDSMITH, M. A Report on Hospital Gangrene, Erysipelas and Pyaemia, as Observed in the Departments of the Ohio and the Cumberland. . . .
1863   Louisville   150.00

GOLDSTON, Robert Coming of the Civil War.
1972   10.00

GOLTZ, Carlos W. Incidents in the Life of Mary Todd Lincoln. Wraps.
1928   Sioux City   20.00

GOOD, John J. Cannon Smoke: Letters of Captain John J. Good, Good-Douglas Texas Battery, C.S.A., edited by Lester N. Fitzhugh.
1971   Hillsboro   60.00

GOODALE, Katherine Behind the Scenes with Edwin Booth.
1931   Boston 35.00

GOODE, John Recollections of a Lifetime.
1906   New York & Washington, DC   75.00

GOODHART, Briscoe History of the Independent Loudoun Virginia Rangers, U.S. Volunteer Cavalry (Scouts).
1896   Washington, DC   250.00
1985   Gaithersburg   25.00

GOODHUE, Benjamin W. Incidents of the Civil War.
1890   Chicago   80.00

GOODLOE, Albert T. Confederate Echoes, A Voice from the South in the Days of Secession and of the Southern Confederacy.
1907   Nashville   200.00
1983   Washington, DC   30.00

GOODLOE, Albert T. Some Rebel Relics from the Seat of War.
1893   Nashville   275.00

GOODMAN, Thomas M. A Thrilling Record, edited by Thomas R. Hooper. Wraps.
1960   Maryville, MO   Ltd.   25.00

GOODRICH, Frank B. The Tribute Book.
1865   New York   30.00

GOODRICH, Frederick E. The Life and Public Services of Winfield Scott Hancock.
1880   Indianapolis   25.00
1880   Boston 25.00
1886   Boston 20.00

GOODWIN, Thomas S. The Natural History of Secession.
1864   New York   50.00

GORDON, Armistead C. Figures from American History; Jefferson Davis.
1918   New York   40.00

GORDON, Armistead C. In the Picturesque Shenandoah Valley.
1930   Richmond   50.00

GORDON, Armistead C. Memories and Memorials of William Gordon McCabe. 2 Vols.
1925   Richmond   100.00

GORDON, Armistead C. William Fitzhugh Gordon, A Virginian of the Old School.
1909   New York   45.00

GORDON, Armistead C.   William Gordon McCabe A Brief Memoir.
  1920   Richmond   30.00
GORDON, Caroline   None Shall Look Back.
  1937   New York   25.00
  1971   New York   25.00
GORDON, George H.   Brook Farm to Cedar Mountain in the War of
the Great Rebellion 1861-62.
  1883   Boston 80.00
  1885   Boston 70.00
GORDON, George H.   History of the Campaign of the Army of Virginia, Under John Pope.
  1880   Boston   110.00
  1889   100.00
GORDON, George H.   History of the Second Massachusetts Regiment
of Infantry. Wraps.
  1875   Boston   55.00
GORDON, George H.   A War Diary of Events of the War of the
Great Rebellion.
  1882   Boston   75.00
GORDON, John B.   Reminiscences of the Civil War.
  1903   New York   100.00
  1904   New York   60.00
  1905   New York   50.00
  1985   Dayton   30.00
GORDON, Marquis Lafayette   M. L. Gordon's Experiences in the Civil
War, edited by Donald Gordon.
  1922   Boston   125.00
GORDY, Wilbur F.   Abraham Lincoln.
  1918   New York   20.00
GORE, Henry W.   The Independent Corps of Cadets of Boston, Mass.
  1888   Boston   Ltd.   100.00
GORE, James Howard   My Mother's Story.
  1923   Philadelphia   40.00
GORGAS, Josiah   The Civil War Diary of _____, edited by Frank E.
Vandiver.
  1947   University, AL   60.00
GORHAM, George C.   Life and Public Services of Edwin M. Stanton.
2 Vols.
  1899   Boston   60.00
GORMAN, John C.   Lee's Last Campaign With an Accurate History of
Stonewall Jackson's Last Wound.
  1866   Raleigh, NC 600.00
GOSNELL, H. Allen   Guns on the Western Waters.
  1949   Baton Rouge   35.00
GOSS, Warren Lee   Jed. A Boy's Adventures in the Army of '61-'65.
  1889   New York   20.00
GOSS, Warren Lee   Recollections of a Private A Story of the Army of
the Potomac.
  1890   New York   40.00
  1984   20.00

GOSS, Warren Lee   The Soldier's Story of His Captivity at Andersonville, Belle Isle, and Other Rebel Prisons.
1866   Boston   50.00
1867   Boston   40.00
Various editions 30.00 each

GOSS, Warren Lee   Tom Clifton or Western Boys of Grant's and Sherman's Army '61-'65.
1894   20.00

GOTTSCHALL, Irwin   A Bibliography of Maps of the Civil War Battlefield Areas. Geological Survey Circular 462.   Wraps.
1962   Washington, DC   25.00

GOUGH, J. E.   Fredericksburg and Chancellorsville.
1913   London   180.00

GOULD, Alta Isadore   The Veteran's Bride and Other Poems.
1894   Grand Rapids   15.00

GOULD, Edward K.   Major General Hiram G. Berry.
1899   Rockland   75.00

GOULD, John Mead   History of the First-Tenth-Twenty-ninth Maine
Regiment.
1871   Portland   165.00

GOULD, John Mead   Joseph K. F. Mansfield, A Narrative of Events
Connected with His Mortal Wounding at Antietam Sept. 17, 1862.
1895   Portland   40.00

GOULD, Joseph   The Story of the Forty-eighth.
1908   Philadelphia   80.00

GOVAN, Gilbert E. and **LIVINGOOD**, James W.   The Chattanooga Country
1540-1976.
1977   Knoxville   18.00

GOVAN, Gilbert E. and **LIVINGOOD**, James W.   Chattanooga Under Military Occupation 1863-1865.   Wraps.
1952   New York   20.00

GOVAN, Gilbert E., and **LIVINGOOD**, James W.   A Different Valor   The
Story of Gen. Joseph E. Johnston, C.S.A.
1956   New York   50.00
1973   Westport   30.00

GRABER, William Henry   The Life Record of H. W. Graber, A Terry
Texas Ranger.
1916   n.p.   900.00
1987   Austin   22.50

GRACEY, Samuel L.   Annals of the Sixth Pennsylvania Cavalry.
1868   Philadelphia   120.00

GRACIE, Archibald   The Truth About Chickamauga.
1911   Boston   115.00
1987   40.00

GRADY, John C. and **FELMLY**, Bradford K.   Suffering to Silence, 29th
Texas Cavalry, CSA.
1975   Quanah   35.00

GRAEBNER, Norman A., edited by   Politics and the Crisis of 1860.
1961   Urbana, IL   15.00

GRAFTON, Henry D.   A Treatise on the Camp and March, with
Which Is Connected the Construction of Field Works and Military
Bridges with an Appendix of Artillery Ranges. . . .
1861   60.00
GRAGG, Rod   Civil War Quiz and Fact Book.   Wraps.
1985   New York   9.00
GRAHAM, C. R.   Under Both Flags.
1896   Philadelphia   25.00
GRAHAM, James A.   The James A. Graham Papers 1861-1864, edited by
H. M. Wagstaff.   Wraps.
1928   Chapel Hill, NC   30.00
GRAHAM, M. J.   Concerning the Battle of Antietam, Letter of Lt. M. J.
Graham to Col. Rush C. Hawkins, 9th New York Volunteers.   Wraps.
1894   New York   30.00
GRAHAM, Martin F. and SKOCH, George F.   Mine Run, A Campaign of
Lost Opportunities October 21, 1863, May 1, 1864.
1988   16.95
GRAHAM, Matthew J.   The Ninth Regiment New York Volunteers
(Hawkins' Zouaves).
1900   New York   140.00
GRAHAM, W. A.   Abstract of the Official Record of Proceedings of the
Reno Court of Inquiry, Convened at Chicago, Illinois. . . .
1954   Harrisburg   65.00
GRAHAM, Ziba B.   On to Gettysburg   Ten Days from My Diary of
1863.   Wraps.
1893   Detroit   35.00
GRAINGER, Gervis D.   Company I, 6th Kentucky Infantry . . . Four
Years with the Boys in Gray.   Wraps.
1972   Dayton   20.00
Grand Army of the Republic (G.A.R.), Proceedings at Encampments.
1st-10th   25.00 each   thereafter 15.00 each.
GRANGER, J. T.   A Brief Biographical Sketch of the Life of Major-
General Grenville M. Dodge.   Wraps.
1893   New York   40.00
GRANGER, Moses Moorhead   The Official War Record of the 122nd
Regiment of Ohio Infantry from Oct. 8, 1862 to June 26, 1865.   Wraps.
1912   Zanesville   125.00
The Grant Memorial in Washington.
1924   Washington, DC   25.00
GRANT, A. F.   Sharpshooter and Spy; or, The Terrible Panic at Bull
Run. War Library Vol. 7, No. 242.   Wraps.
n.d.   n.p.   20.00
GRANT, A. F.   The War Detective; or Secret Service in the Rebellion.
The War Library, Vol. 7, No. 232.   Wraps.
n.d.   n.p.   20.00
GRANT, Jesse R.   In the Days of My Father, General Grant.
1925   New York   20.00
GRANT, Joseph W.   The Flying Regiment. Journal of the Campaign of
the 12th Regiment Rhode Island Volunteers.
1865   Providence   65.00
GRANT, Joseph W.   My First Campaign.
1863   Boston   60.00

GRANT, Julia Dent   The Personal Memoirs of Julia Dent Grant (Mrs. Ulysses S. Grant).
1975   New York   25.00
1988   edited by John Y. Simon 19.95
1988   Wraps   10.95
GRANT, Nicholas B.   The Life of a Common Soldier, 1862-1865.   Wraps.
(c.1927) LaFollette, TN   400.00
GRANT, Ulysses S.   Letters of Ulysses S. Grant to his Father and His Youngest Sister 1857-78.
1912   15.00
GRANT, Ulysses S.   The Papers of Ulysses S. Grant, edited by John Y. Simon. 10 Vols.
1967-82 Carbondale, IL
Vols. 1-4   25.00 each
Vol. 5   32.50
Vol. 6   36.00
Vols. 7-8   40.00 each
Vols. 9-16   47.50 each
GRANT, Ulysses S.   Personal Memoirs of U. S. Grant.   2 Vols.
✓1885-86 New York   55.00
Recent reprints 40.00
GRANT, Ulysses S.   Report of Lieut. Gen. U. S. Grant, of the Armies of the United States, 1864-65.   Wraps.
1865   Washington, DC   100.00
GRANT, Ulysses S.   [Subscription Salesman's Order Book for the Personal Memoirs of U.S. Grant.]
1885   New York   30.00
GRANT, Ulysses S., III   Ulysses S. Grant: Warrior and Statesman.
1969   New York   20.00
GRAVES, Henry Lea   A Confederate Marine: A Sketch of Henry Lea Graves with Excerpts from the Graves Family Correspondence, 1861-1865.   See: Confederate Centennial Studies, No. 24.
GRAVES, Joseph A.   The History of the Bedford Light Artillery. Wraps.
1903   Bedford City   250.00
1983   Gaithersburg   17.00
GRAY, Amy   The Lily of the Valley.
1868   Baltimore   25.00
GRAY, John Chipman and ROPES, John Codman   War Letters 1862-1865.
1927   New York   40.00
1927   Boston   40.00
1927   Cambridge   40.00
GRAY, John Gordon   Lieut.-Colonel Robert Burns Beath, Memoir. Wraps.
(1915)   Philadelphia   30.00
GRAY, John S.   Centennial Campaign. The Sioux War of 1876.   Wraps.
1988   University, OK   14.95
GRAY, Wood   The Hidden Civil War.
1942   New York   25.00
GRAYDON, Nell S.   Another Jezebel.
1958   Columbia, SC   20.00

The Grayjackets.   See: McCABE, James D., Jr.

GRAYSON, A. J.   "The Spirit of 1861" History of the Sixth Indiana Regiment in the Three Months Campaign in Western Virginia. Wraps.
    1875   Madison, IN   100.00

GRAYSON, William   James Louis Petigru.
    1866   New York   80.00

Great Battles of the Civil War. Wraps.
    1961   New York   10.00

Great Commanders Series. See individual authors and titles; for additional information, see Appendix: Great Commanders Series.

The Great Impeachment and Trial of Andrew Johnson, President of the U.S.
    1868   Philadelphia   25.00

The Great Panic: Being Incidents Connected with Two Weeks of the War in Tennessee. By an Eye-witness. (McKee, John Miller). Wraps.
    1862   Nashville   500.00

GREBNER, Constantin   "Die Neuner." Eine Schilderung Der Kriegsjahre, Des 9 Ten Regiments Ohio Vol. Infanterie, vom 17, April 1861 bis 7 June, 1864.
    1897   Cincinnati   200.00

GREBNER, Constantin   We Were the Ninth A History of the Ninth Regiment, Ohio Volunteer Infantry. . . .
    1987   26.50

GRECIAN, Joseph   History of the Eighty-third Regiment, Indiana Volunteer Infantry.
    1865   Cincinnati   200.00

GREELEY, Horace   The American Conflict. 2 Vols.
    1864   Hartford   65.00
    1866   50.00
    Many later editions 30.00

GREELEY, Horace   Recollections of a Busy Life.
    1868   New York   20.00
    1869   New York   20.00

GREELEY, Horace and CLEVELAND, John, edited by   A Political Text-Book for 1860.
    1860   New York   30.00

GREELY, A. W.   Reminiscences of Adventure and Service.
    1927   New York   75.00

GREEN, Anna Maria   The Journal of a Milledgeville Girl 1861-1867, edited by James A. Bonner. Wraps.
    1964   Athens, GA   20.00

GREEN, Charles R.   A Historical Pamphlet, Wakeman, Ohio, Lives of the Volunteers in the Civil War.
    1914   Olathe, KS   40.00

GREEN, Horace   General Grant's Last Stand A Biography.
    1936   New York   35.00

GREEN, Horace   Triumph, General Grant's Final Victory.
    1941   New York   15.00

GREEN, John W.   Johnny Green of the Orphan Brigade: The Journal of a Confederate Soldier, edited by A. D. Kirwan.
    1956   Lexington   40.00

GREEN, Robert M.   History of the One Hundred and Twenty-fourth Regiment Pennsylvania Volunteers 1862-1863.
1907   Philadelphia   125.00

GREEN, Thomas W.   The Artillery of the Civil War, Civil War Round Table of London, England.   Wraps.
1959   London   25.00

GREEN, Thomas W.   Ironclads of the Sixties.   Wraps.
1959   London   25.00

GREEN, Thomas W.   Major Caleb Huse, C.S.A.   A Memoir.   Wraps.
1966   London   35.00

GREEN, Wharton J.   Recollections and Reflections.
1906   Raleigh   75.00

GREENBERG, Martin H., edited by   Civil War Stories.
1985   10.00

GREENBIE, Marjorie Barstow   Lincoln's Daughters of Mercy.
1944   New York   15.00

GREENBIE, Marjorie Barstow   My Dear Lady   The Story of Anna Ella Carroll.
1940   New York   30.00

GREENBIE, Sydney and GREENBIE, Marjorie B.   Anna Ella Carroll and Abraham Lincoln   A Biography.
1952   Manchester, ME   30.00

GREENE, Albert R.   From Bridgeport to Ringgold by Way of Lookout Mountain.   Wraps.
1890   Providence Ltd.   40.00

GREENE, Francis Vinton   The Mississippi.   See: Campaigns of the Civil War.

GREENE, Homer   A Lincoln Conscript.
1909   Boston   15.00

GREENE, Jacob L.   General William B. Franklin and the Operations of the Left Wing at the Battle of Fredericksburg Dec. 13, 1862.
1900   Hartford   50.00

GREENE, Jerome A.   U. S. Army Uniforms and Equipment, 1889.   Wraps.
1986   University, NE   9.95

GREENE, John W.   Camp Ford Prison and How I Escaped.
1893   Toledo   225.00

GREENE, Laurence   The Raid, A Biography of Harper's Ferry.
1953   New York   15.00

GREENHOW, Rose   My Imprisonment and the First Year of the Abolition Rule at Washington.
1863   London   250.00

GREENLEAF, Charles R., M.D.   A Manual for the Medical Officers of the United States Army.
1864   250.00

GREER, Jack Thorndyke   Leaves from a Family Album, edited by Jane Judge Greer.
1975   Waco, TX   15.00

GREER, James K.   Louisiana Politics 1845-1861.
1930   Baton Rouge   25.00

GREGG, David McM.   The Second Cavalry Division of the Army of the Potomac in the Gettysburg Campaign.   Wraps.
1907   Philadelphia   35.00

GREGG, John Chandler   Life in the Army in the Departments of Virginia and the Gulf.
    1868   Philadelphia   40.00

GREGORY, T. W.   Reconstruction and the Ku Klux Klan, A Paper Read Before the Arkansas and Texas Bar Associations.   Wraps.
    1906   Austin, TX   75.00

GREINER, H. C.   General Phil Sheridan as I Knew Him, Playmate-Comrade-Friend.
    1908   Chicago   60.00

GRESHAM, Matilda   Life of Walter Quinton Gresham 1832-95.   2 Vols.
    1919   Chicago   65.00

GRESHAM, Otto   The Greenbacks,   or, The Money that Won the Civil War.
    1927   Chicago   65.00

GRIERSON, Alice Kirk   The Colonel's Lady on the Western Frontier, edited by Shirley Anne Leskie.
    1989   University, NE   25.95
    1989   University, NE   Wraps 9.95

GRIERSON, Francis   The Valley of Shadows.
    1948   Boston   15.00

GRIESS, T. E., edited by   The American Civil War.
    1987   West Point   25.00

GRIESS, T. E., edited by   Atlas for the American Civil War.   Wraps.
    n.d.   20.00

GRIFFITH, P.   Battle in the Civil War: Generalship and Tactics in America, 1861-65.   Wraps.
    1986   Nottinghamshire   14.95

GRIFFITH, P.   Battle Tactics of the Civil War.
    1989   24.95

GRIGSBY, Melvin   The Smoked Yank.
    1888   Sioux Falls   50.00
    1911   Sioux Falls   65.00

GRIMES, Bryan Extracts of Letters of Major-General Grimes to His Wife Written While in Active Service in the Army of Northern Virginia . . . , compiled by Pulaski Cowper.   Wraps.
    1883   Raleigh, NC   200.00
    1884   Raleigh, NC   125.00
    1986   Wilmington, NC   edited by Gary Gallagher   20.00

GRIMES, Messr.   The Navy in Congress.   Wraps.
    1865   Washington, DC   100.00

GRIMM, Herbert L. and **ROY**, Paul L.   Human Interest Stories of the Three Days' Battles at Gettysburg.   Wraps.
    1927   Gettysburg   35.00

GRIMSLEY, Daniel A.   Battles in Culpeper County, Virginia.   Wraps.
    1900   Culpeper   100.00
    Recent reprint   15.00

GRISWOLD, Anna   Colonel Griswold.
    1866   Brookline   35.00

GRISWOLD, B. Howell, Jr.   The Spirit of Lee and Jackson.
    1927   Baltimore   45.00

GROENE, Bertram   Tracing Your Civil War Ancestry.
    1973   Winston-Salem   15.00

GROSE, Parlee C.   The Case of Private Smith and the Remaining Mysteries of the Andrews Raid.   Wraps.
1963   McComb, OH   20.00

GROSE, William   The Story of the Marches, Battles and Incidents of the 36th Regiment Indiana Volunteer Infantry.
1891   New Castle   140.00

GROSS, George J.   The Battle-field of Gettysburg.
1866   125.00

GROSS, Luelja Zearing   Sketch of the Life of Major James Roberts Zearing and Civil War Letters.
1922   Springfield, IL   40.00

GROSSMAN, Julian   Echo of a Distant Drum   Winslow Homer and the Civil War.
(1974)   New York   25.00

GRUBB, Davis   A Dream of Kings.
1955   New York   10.00

GUESS, George W.   Civil War Letters of Colonel _____ to Mrs. Sarah Horton Cockrell.
1946   n.p. Ltd.   125.00

Guide to Civil War Records in the North Carolina State Archives.   Wraps.
1966   Raleigh   20.00

GUILD, George B.   A Brief Narrative of the Fourth Tennessee Cavalry Regiment.
1913   Nashville   275.00

GUILD, Thelma S. and CARTER, Harvey L.   Kit Carson: A Pattern for Heroes.
1984   Lincoln, NE   19.00

GULICK, William O.   Journal and Letters of _____.
1942   n.p.   50.00

GUNDERSON, Robert G.   Old Gentleman's Convention: The Washington Peace Conference of 1861.
1961   Madison, WI   15.00

GUNN, Jane Augusta   Memorial Sketches of Doctor Moses Gunn.
1889   Chicago   100.00

GUNN, Ralph White   24th Virginia Infantry.
1987   Lynchburg   16.45

The Guns of '62.   See: DAVIS, William C. The Image of War, 1861-1865.

GUNTER, Archibald C.   Billy Hamilton.
1898   New York   15.00

GURGANUS, A.   The Oldest Living Confederate Widow Tells All.
1989   New York   21.95

GUROWSKI, Adam   Diary. . . . 3 Vols.
1862-66   Boston   125.00
Vol. I   Diary from March 4, 1861 to Nov. 12, 1862.
1862   Boston   25.00
Vol. II   Diary from Nov. 18, 1862 to Oct. 18, 1863.
1864   New York   25.00
Vol. III   Diary: 1863 - '64-'65.
1866   Washington, DC   25.00

GUROWSKI, Adam   Slavery in History.
1860   New York   150.00

HAAS, Ralph, edited by   The Ringgold Cavalry. The Rest of the Story.
    1988   25.00
HABERSHAM, Josephine Clay   Ebb Tide As Seen Though the Diary of
    _____, edited by Spencer Bidwell King, Jr.
    1958   Athens, GA 20.00
    1987   Macon, GA Wraps 8.95
HACKETT, Horatio B.   Christian Memorials of the War.
    1864   Boston   20.00
HACKLEY, F. W.   A Report on Civil War Explosive Ordnance. Wraps.
    1960   Indian Head, MD   20.00
HACKLEY, Woodford B.   The Little Fork Rangers A Sketch of Com-
    pany "D" Fourth Virginia Cavalry.
    1927   Richmond   75.00
HADLEY, Amos   Life of Walter Harriman.
    1888   Boston   30.00
HADLEY, John V.   An Indiana Soldier in Love and War: The Civil
    War Letters of _____, edited by James I. Robertson, Jr.
    1963   Indianapolis   30.00
HADLEY, John V.   Seven Months a Prisoner. Wraps.
    1868   Indianapolis   190.00
    1898   New York   50.00
HAERRER, William   With Drum and Gun in '61. Wraps.
    1908   Greenville, PA   130.00
HAFEN, LeRoy R.   The Overland Mail, 1849-1869: Promoter of Settle-
    ment.
    1976   Lincoln, MA   25.00
HAFENDORFER, Kenneth   Perryville. Battle for Kentucky.
    1981   Owensboro, KY   45.00
HAGAN, John W.   Confederate Letters of _____, edited by Bell I.
    Wiley. Wraps.
    1954   Athens   25.00
HAGEMANN, J.   The Heritage of Virginia: The Story of Place Names
    in the Old Dominion. Wraps.
    1986   Norfolk   8.95
HAGER, Ira P.   Blue and Gray Battlefields.
    1978   13.00
HAGERMAN, Edward   The American Civil War and the Origins of
    Modern Warfare: Ideas, Organization, and Field Command.
    1988   Bloomington   37.50
HAGOOD, Johnson   Meet Your Grandfather.
    n.d.   n.p.   100.00
HAGOOD, Johnson   Memoirs of the War of Secession.
    1910   Columbia, SC   150.00
    1989   30.00
HAGUE, Parthenia Antoinette   A Blockaded Family.
    1888   Boston and New York   75.00
    1889   Boston   50.00
    1894   Boston   50.00
HAHN, George W., edited by   The Catawba Soldier of the Civil War, A
    Sketch of Every Soldier from Catawba County.
    1911   Hickory   300.00

HAIGHT, Theron Wilbur   Three Wisconsin Cushings   A Sketch of the Lives of Howard B., Alonzo H., and William B. Cushing, Children of a Pioneer Family of Waukesha County.
 1910   (Madison)   25.00
HAINES, Alanson A.   History of the Fifteenth Regiment, New Jersey Volunteers.
 1883   New York   175.00
 1987   30.00
HAINES, William P.   History of the Men of Co-F, with Description of the Marches and Battles of the 12th New Jersey Vols.
 1897   Mickleton   140.00
HAINES, Zenas T.   Letters from the Forty-fourth Regiment, M.V.M. . . . in the Department of North Carolina in 1862-3.
 1863   Boston   100.00
HALDERMAN, Cyrus S.   A True Romance of the Rebellion.
 1886   Boston   20.00
HALE, Donald R.   They Called Him Bloody Bill, The Missouri Bad-man Who Taught Jesse James Outlawry.   Wraps.
 1975   Clinton, MO   10.00
HALE, Donald R.   We Rode with Quantrill.   Wraps.
 1975   Independence, MO   15.00
HALE, Edward E., edited by   Stories of War Told by Soldiers.
 1879   Boston   20.00
HALE, John P.   Report on Abandonment of Pensacola and Norfolk Navy Yards.
 1861   Washington, DC   35.00
HALE, Laura Virginia   Belle Boyd, Southern Spy of the Shenandoah.   Wraps.
 n.d.   Front Royal, VA   15.00
HALE, Laura Virginia   Four Valiant Years in Lower Shenandoah Valley 1861-1865.
 1968   Strasburg, VA   50.00
 1969   50.00
 1973   Strasburg, VA   40.00
 1986   40.00
HALE, Laura Virginia   Memories in Marble: The Story of the Four Confederate Monuments at Front Royal, Va.   Wraps.
 1956   n.p.   15.00
HALE, Laura Virginia and PHILLIPS, Stanley S.   History of the Forty-ninth Virginia Infantry C.S.A. "Extra Billy Smith's Boys."
 1981   Lanham   35.00
HALE, Laura Virginia, et al   Warren County Civil War Centennial Commemoration, Battle of Front Royal, Virginia, May 19-20, 1862.   Wraps.
 1962   Front Royal   20.00
HALE, Will T.   History of DeKalb County Tennessee.
 1969   McMinnville   25.00
HALE, William Harlan   Horace Greeley, Voice of the People.
 1950   New York   10.00
HALEY, J.   Evetts, George W. Littlefield, Texan, 1842-1920, 8th Texas Cavalry, C.S.A.   Wraps.
 1972   8.00

HALEY, J. W.   The Rebel Yell & the Yankee Hurrah; the Civil War
Journal of a Maine Volunteer.
  1985   Camden   23.00
Hall's Journal of Health.   Wraps.
  1862   65.00
HALL, Charles B.   Military Records of General Officers of the Confederate States of America.
  1898   New York   Ltd.   2500.00
  1960   100.00
  1963   Austin   Boxed   100.00
HALL, Clifton R.   Andrew Johnson - Military Governor of Tennessee.
  1916   Princeton   50.00
HALL, Courtney Robert   Confederate Medicine, Medical Life, Sept 1935.
Wraps.
  1935   n.p.   45.00
HALL, Florence Howe   Memories Grave and Gay.
  1918   New York   25.00
HALL, Florence Howe   The Story of the Battle Hymn of the Republic.
  1916   New York   15.00
HALL, Granville Davisson   Lee's Invasion of Northwest Virginia in
1861.
  1911   Chicago   75.00
HALL, Harry H.   A Johnny Reb Band from Salem: The Pride of
Tarheelia.   Wraps.
  1963   Raleigh   35.00
  1980   New York   25.00
HALL, Isaac   History of the Ninety-seventh Regiment, New York Volunteers (Conkling Rifles).
  1890   Utica   165.00
HALL, James E.   Diary of a Confederate Soldier, edited by Ruth W.
Dayton.
  1961   Charleston   30.00
HALL, John Leslie   Half-Hours in Southern History.
  1907   Richmond   35.00
HALL, Martin Hardwick   The Confederate Army of New Mexico.
  1978   Austin   45.00
HALL, Martin Hardwick   Sibley's New Mexico Campaign.
  1960   Austin   60.00
HALL, Newman   The American War   A Lecture to Working Men Delivered in London Oct 20, 1862.   Wraps.
  1863   New York   35.00
HALL, Sam S.   Wild Bill, The Union Scout of Missouri, War Library
Vol. 6, No. 282.   Wraps.
  1888   New York   30.00
HALL, W. W.   Soldier-Health.
  1863   New York   125.00
HALL, Wade H.   Reflections of the Civil War in Southern Humor.
Wraps.
  1962   Gainesville, FL   10.00

HALL, Winchester   The Story of the 26th Louisiana Infantry in the Service of the Confederate States.
(1890)   n.p.   1100.00
1984   Gaithersburg   28.00

HALLECK, H. W.   Elements of Military Art and Science; or Course of Instruction in Strategy, Fortification, Tactics of Battle. . . .
1863   New York   125.00

HALLENBECK, Wynkoop   History of the 18th Regiment of Cavalry Pa. Volunteers (163rd Rgt. of the Line) 1862-65.
1909   New York   115.00

HALLOWELL, Norwood Penrose   The Negro as a Soldier in the War of the Rebellion: An Address Delivered on Memorial Day, May 30, 1896.
1896   Boston   125.00

HALLUM, John   Reminiscences of the Civil War. Vol. 1   (all pub.)
1903   Little Rock   85.00

HALPINE, Charles G.   Baked Meats of the Funeral, Collection of Essays, Poems, Speeches Histories by Miles O'Reilly.
1866   New York   25.00

HALPINE, Charles G.   The Life and Adventures Songs, Services and Speeches of Private Miles O'Reilly.
1864   New York   30.00

HALSEY, Ashley, Jr.   Who Fired the First Shot?
1963   New York   15.00

HALSEY, Don P.   Historic and Heroic Lynchburg.
1935   Lynchburg   50.00

HALSEY, Don P.   A Sketch of the Life of Capt. Don P. Halsey of the Confederate States Army.   Wraps.
1904   Richmond   35.00

HALSTEAD, Murat   Caucuses of 1860.   A History of the National Political Conventions of the Current Presidential Campaign.
1860   Columbus   75.00

HAMAND, Lavern M., edited by   Coles County in the Civil War.   Wraps.
1961   Charleston, IL   20.00

HAMBLIN, Deborah   Brevet Major General Joseph Eldridge Hamblin, 1861-1865.
1902   Boston   50.00

HAMERSLY, Lewis R.   Records of Living Officers of the U.S. Navy and Marine Corps.
1870   Philadelphia   90.00
1878   Philadelphia   90.00
1884   Philadelphia   90.00
1890   Philadelphia   90.00

HAMIL, H. M.   Sam Davis, A True Story of a Young Confederate Soldier.   Wraps.
1912   Griffin, GA   80.00
1959   Kennesaw, GA   10.00

HAMILTON, A. J.   Address . . . to the People of Texas.   Wraps.
1864   New Orleans   300.00

HAMILTON, A. J.   Speech . . . at the War Meeting at Faneuil Hall, April 1863.   Wraps.
1863   Boston   100.00

HAMILTON, Andrew G.   Story of the Famous Tunnel Escape from Libby Prison.   Wraps.
    1893   Chicago   40.00

HAMILTON, Charles and **OSTENDORF**, Lloyd   Lincoln in Photographs.
    1963   Norman, OK   40.00
    1985   40.00
    1985   Leatherbound   150.00

HAMILTON, D. H.   History of Company M, First Texas Volunteer Infantry, Hood's Brigade.
    1962   Waco   Ltd.   50.00

HAMILTON, Frank Hastings, M.D.   A Treatise on Military Surgery and Hygiene.
    1865   New York   225.00

HAMILTON, H. S.   The Dixie Jacket.   Wraps.
    1935   n.p.   20.00

HAMILTON, H. S.   Reminiscences of a Veteran.
    1897   Concord, NH   150.00

HAMILTON, Holman   Prologue to Conflict - The Crisis and Compromise of 1850.
    1964   Lexington, KY   15.00

HAMILTON, J. G. de R., edited by   The Papers of Randolph Abbott Shotwell.   See: **SHOTWELL**, Randolph Abbott.

HAMILTON, J. G. de R., edited by   The Papers of Thomas Ruffin.   4 Vols.
    1918   Raleigh, NC   100.00

HAMILTON, J. G. de R.   Reconstruction in North Carolina.
    1914   New York   150.00
    1964   Gloucester   30.00

HAMILTON, J. G. de R. and **HAMILTON**, Mary T.   The Life of Robert E. Lee, For Boys and Girls.
    1917   Boston   10.00

HAMILTON, James   The Battle of Fort Donelson.
    1968   South Brunswick   50.00
    1968   New York   40.00

HAMILTON, Nolman   The Three Kentucky Presidents: Lincoln, Taylor, Davis.
    1978   Lexington, KY   7.00

HAMILTON, Peter   The Reconstruction Period, being Vol. 16 in Lee and Thorpe's History of North America.
    (1905)   Philadelphia   100.00

HAMILTON, Peter Joseph   A Little Boy in Confederate Mobile.
    1947   Mobile, AL   Ltd.   50.00

HAMILTON, William Douglas   Recollections of a Cavalryman of the Civil War After Fifty Years 1861-1865.
    1915   Columbus   175.00

HAMLIN, Augustus Choate   The Battle of Chancellorsville.
    1896   Bangor, ME   75.00

HAMLIN, Augustus Choate   Martyria: or, Andersonville Prison.
    1866   Boston   60.00

HAMLIN, Charles   Brief Sketch of the Battle of Gettysburg.   Wraps.
    1898   Portland   70.00

HAMLIN, Percy Gatling   The Making of a Soldier. Letters of General R. S. Ewell.
1935   35.00

HAMLIN, Percy Gatling   Old Bald Head (General R. S. Ewell).
1940   Strasburg, Virginia   150.00

HAMLIN, Percy Gatling   Richard Stoddert Ewell - Old Bald Head and Making of a Soldier.
1988   35.00

HAMMETT, Hugh B.   Hilary Abner Herbert: A Southerner Returns to the Union. Wraps.
1976   Philadelphia   20.00

HAMMOCK, John C.   With Honor Untarnished: The Story of the First Arkansas Infantry Regiment, C.S.A.
1961   Little Rock   30.00

HAMMOND, Bray   Sovereignty and an Empty Purse, Banks and Politics in the Civil War.
1970   Princeton, NJ   20.00

HAMMOND, William A.   A Treatise on Hygiene with Special Reference to the Military Service.
1863   Philadelphia   200.00

Hampton Legion Survivors, Minutes of the Proceedings of the Reunion, Held in Columbia, S. C. Wraps.
1875   Charleston   40.00

HAMPTON, Wade   Address on the Life and Character of Gen. Robert E. Lee. Wraps.
1871   Baltimore   50.00
1872   Baltimore   50.00

HANABURGH, David H.   History of the One Hundred and Twenty-eighth Regiment, New York Volunteers.
1894   Poughkeepsie   100.00

HANCHETT, William   Irish, Charles G. Halpine in Civil War America.
1970   New York   25.00

HANCHETT, William   The Lincoln Murder Conspiracies.
1985   Champaign, IL   23.00
1985   Champaign, IL   Wraps   10.00

HANCOCK, Albert Elmer   Henry Bourland.
1901   New York   10.00

HANCOCK, Cornelia   The South After Gettysburg: Letters of Cornelia Hancock, edited by Henrietta S. Jaquette.
1937   Philadelphia   30.00
1956   New York   30.00

HANCOCK, H. I.   Life at West Point. The Making of the American Army Officer: His Studies, Discipline, and Amusements.
1902   New York   20.00

HANCOCK, Harold Bell   Delaware During the Civil War, A Political History.
1961   Wilmington, DE   35.00

HANCOCK, Richard R.   Hancock's Diary; or, A History of the 2nd Tennessee Cavalry. 2 Vols. in 1.
1887   Nashville   250.00

HANCOCK, Mrs. Winfield Scott   Reminiscences of Winfield Scott Hancock.
    1887   New York   75.00

Hand-Book of the Tenth Annual Reunion, of the Seventh Association Held at Valparaiso, Indiana, September 7th and 8th, 1892. Wraps.
    1892   Valparaiso, IN   75.00

HANDERSON, Henry E.   Yankee in Gray: The Civil War Memoirs of _____.
    1962   Cleveland   35.00

HANDLIN, Oscar and Lilian   Abraham Lincoln and the Union.
    1980   Boston   10.00

HANDLIN, W. W.   American Politics, a Moral and Political Work, Treating of the Causes of the Civil War . . . and the Necessity for Reform.
    1864   New Orleans   75.00

HANDY, Isaac W. K.   United States Bonds.
    1874   Baltimore   150.00

HANEY, M. L.   The Story of My Life An Autobiography.
    1904   Normal, OK   125.00

HANIFEN, Michael   History of Battery B, First New Jersey Artillery.
    1905   Ottawa, IL   130.00

HANKINS, Samuel W.   Simple Story of a Soldier.
    1912   Nashville   100.00

HANLY, J. Frank   Andersonville.
    1912   Cincinnati   30.00

HANLY, J. Frank   Dedication of the Indiana Monuments at Vicksburg, Mississippi, December 29, 1908.
    1908   Cincinnati   25.00

HANNA, Alfred Jackson   Flight into Oblivion.
    1938   Richmond   40.00
    1959   Bloomington   30.00

HANNA, Alfred Jackson and HANNA, Kathryn A.   Confederate Exiles in Venezuela.   See: Confederate Centennial Studies, No. 15.

HANNAFORD, E.   The Story of a Regiment: A History of the Campaigns and (6th Infantry) Associations in the Field of the Sixth Regiment Ohio Volunteer Infantry.
    1868   Cincinnati   150.00

HANSON, John W.   Historical Sketch of the Old Sixth Regiment of Massachusetts Volunteers.
    1866   Boston   60.00

HANSON, Joseph Mills   Bull Run Remembers. Wraps.
    1952   Manassas   20.00
    1953   Manassas   20.00
    1957   Manassas   17.50

HAPGOOD, Norman   Abraham Lincoln.
    1900   New York   25.00

HAPPEL, Ralph   Jackson. Wraps.
    1971   Richmond   15.00

HARCOURT, William   Letters by Historicus on Some Questions of International Law.
    1863   London   50.00

HARD, Abner   History of the Eighth Cavalry Regiment, Illinois Volunteers.
  1868   Aurora   250.00
  1984   Dayton   40.00
HARDEE, William Joseph   Rifle and Light Infantry Tactics.
  1861   Philadelphia   2 Vols.   75.00
  1861   New York   1 Vol. ed.   Wraps   50.00
  1907   Glendale   40.00
HARDEMAN, Nicholas P.   Shucks, Shocks, and Hominy Blocks.
  1981   20.00
HARDEMAN, Nicholas P.   Wilderness Calling.
  1977   University, TN   22.00
HARDEN, Henry O.   History of the 90th Ohio Volunteer Infantry in the War of the Rebellion.
  1902   Stoutsville   225.00
HARDEN, Samuel   Those I Have Met.
  1888   Anderson, IN   80.00
HARDESTY, Jesse   Killed and Died of Wounds, In the Union Army During the Civil War.   Wraps.
  1915   San Jose   45.00
HARDIE BROS., Proprietors   Descriptive Catalogue of Lookout Mountain War Relic Museum.   Wraps.
  (1893)   Chattanooga   40.00
HARDIN, Albert N.   The American Bayonet, 1776-1964.
  1964   55.00
HARDIN, Bayless   Brigadier General John Hunt Morgan of Kentucky "Thunderbolt of the Confederacy."   Wraps.
  (1938)   Frankfort, KY   40.00
HARDIN, Martin D.   History of the 12th Regiment Pennsylvania Reserve Volunteer Corps.
  1890   New York   110.00
HARDING, George   The Miscellaneous Writings of . . . .
  1882   Indianapolis   55.00
HARDINGE, Belle B.   Belle Boyd in Camp and Prison.
  1865   London   2 Vols.   250.00
  1865   New York   2 Vols. in 1   100.00
  1867   New York   2 Vols. in 1   100.00
  1968   New York   edited by C. C. Davis   15.00
HARGIS, O. P.   Thrilling Experiences of a First Georgia Cavalryman in the Civil War. Special Scout Under General Wheeler. . . .   Wraps.
  n.d.   Rome, GA   750.00
HARGRETT, L., compiled by   An Unrivalled Collection of Confederate Louisiana Secession Laws, Legislative Journals and Related Documents, Offered for Sale by the Owner.   Wraps.
  (1961)   Tallahassee   25.00
HARLOW, Alvin F.   Brass-Pounders, Young Telegraphers of the Civil War.
  1962   Denver   20.00
HARMON, George D.   Confederate Migrations to Mexico.   Wraps.
  1938   Bethlehem, PA   25.00

HARMON, George D.   **Political Aspects of Slavery and the Civil War.** Wraps.
  1952   Bethlehem, PA   25.00
HARNDEN, Henry   **The Capture of Jefferson Davis.**
  1898   Madison   60.00
HARNSBERGER, Caroline Thomas   **The Lincoln Treasury.**
  1950   New York   20.00
  Recent reprint   Chicago   20.00
Harper's Magazine. See Appendix: Magazines.
Harper's Pictorial History of the Great Rebellion. 2 Vols.
  1866   New York   150.00
  1866   New York   2 Vols. in 1   125.00
  1866   Chicago   2 Vols.   100.00
  1894   Chicago   2 Vols.   125.00
  1896   Chicago   2 Vols.   125.00
  n.d. (reprint)   New York   2 Vols. 50.00
Harper's Weekly 1861-1865.
  Bound in 5 Vols.   2000.00
  Same in individual issues   2400.00
  1961-65   Shenandoah, IA   300.00
HARPER, HAMMOND, SIMMS, and **DEW**   **The Pro-Slavery Argument as Maintained by the Most Distinguished Writers of the Southern States.**
  1853   Philadelphia   40.00
HARPER, R. S.   **Lincoln and the Press.**
  1951   New York   30.00
Harpers Ferry Invasion, The Report to Congress.
  1860   Washington, DC   40.00
HARRELL, John M.   **Arkansas.** See: **Confederate Military History, Vol. X** (Vol. XIV, 1988 reprint ed.).
HARRELL, John M.   **The Brooks and Baxter War, A History of the Reconstruction Period in Arkansas.**
  1893   St. Louis   110.00
HARRILL, Lawson   **Reminiscences of 1861-1865.** Wraps.
  1910   Statesville   200.00
HARRINGTON, Fred Harvey   **Fighting Politician Major General N. P. Banks.**
  1948   Philadelphia   40.00
  1973   n.p.   20.00
HARRINGTON, George F. (pseud.)   See: **BAKER**, William Mumford
HARRIS, Charles   **Civil War Relics of the Western Campaigns 1861-1865,** designed and produced by Michael O'Donnell.
  1987   29.95
HARRIS, Cicero W.   **The Sectional Struggle.**
  1902   Philadelphia   35.00
HARRIS, Gertrude   **A Tale of Men Who Knew Not Fear.** Wraps.
  1935   San Antonio   45.00
HARRIS, Harry L. and **HILTON**, John T., edited by   **A History of the Second Regiment, Second N.J. Volunteers, Fifth New Jersey Infantry.**
  1908   Peterson   40.00
HARRIS, Joel Chandler   **A Little Union Scout.**
  1904   New York   50.00

HARRIS, Joel Chandler   On the Plantation: A Story of a Georgia Boy's Adventures during the War.
  1892   New York   25.00
  1981   Wraps   8.00
HARRIS, Joel Chandler   On the Wings of Occasions.
  1900   New York   75.00
  1969   New York   20.00
HARRIS, Joel Chandler   The Shadow Between His Shoulder Blades.
  1907   Boston   75.00
HARRIS, Joel Chandler   Tales of the Home Folks in Peace and War.
  1898   Boston   100.00
HARRIS, Leon and BEALS, Frank   Look Away Dixieland.
  1937   New York   20.00
HARRIS, N. E.   Autobiography: The Story of an Old Man's Life.
  1925   Macon   50.00
HARRIS, N. E.   The Civil War, Its Results and Lessons: An Address. Wraps.
  1906   Macon   20.00
HARRIS, Samuel   Personal Reminiscences.
  1897   Chicago   120.00
HARRIS, Samuel   A Story of the Civil War, Why I Was Not Hung. Wraps.
  n.d.   60.00
HARRIS, Thomas L.   The Trent Affair.
  1896   Indianapolis   35.00
HARRIS, Thomas Maley   Assassination of Lincoln.
  1892   Boston   60.00
HARRIS, V. S., compiled by   History of Pulaski and Bleckley Counties, Georgia, 1808-1956. 2 Vols.
  1957-58   Hawkinsville   50.00
HARRIS, William C.   Leroy Pope Walker   Confederate Secretary of War. See: Confederate Centennial Studies, No. 20.
HARRIS, William C.   Prison Life in the Tobacco Warehouse at Richmond.
  1862   Philadelphia   80.00
HARRISON, Mrs. Burton   Recollections Grave and Gay.
  1912   London   45.00
  1911   New York   50.00
  1912   New York   45.00
HARRISON, Ida Withers   Beyond the Battle's Rim.
  1917   New York   50.00
  1918   New York   50.00
HARRISON, Ida Withers   Memoirs of William Temple Withers.
  1924   Boston   50.00
HARRISON, Lowell H.   The Civil War in Kentucky.
  1975   Lexington   25.00
  1987   Lexington   12.00
HARRISON, Walter   Pickett's Men: A Fragment of War History.
  1870   New York   80.00
  1984   Gaithersburg   25.00

HARROLD, John   Libby, Andersonville, Florence, The Capture, Imprisonment, Escape and Rescue of _____.
1870   Philadelphia   50.00
1892   Atlantic City, NJ   40.00
HART, Albert Bushnell   Salmon Portland Chase.
1899   Boston   20.00
1980   Wraps   7.00
HART, B. H. Liddell   Sherman The Genius of the Civil War.
1930   (London)   50.00
HART, E. Marvin   The 15th Regiment Connecticut Volunteers A History.
1889   Hartford   60.00
HART, H. M.   Tour Guide to Old Western Forts.
1980   23.00
HART, Scott   Eight April Days.
1949   New York   20.00
HART, Scott   From Sayler's Creek to Appomattox. Wraps.
(1965) (Farmville, VA)   5.00
HARTER, Eugene C.   The Lost Colony of the Confederacy. Wraps.
1988   University, MS   9.95
HARTJE, Robert G.   Van Dorn, the Life and Times of a Confederate General.
1967   Nashville   35.00
HARTLEY, Marcellus   _____, A Brief Memoir.
1903   New York   60.00
HARTMAN, P. S.   Reminiscences of the Civil War; with a Biography of Peter S. Hartman by H. A. Brunk. Wraps.
1964   Lancaster   18.00
HARTPENCE, William Ross   History of the Fifty-first Indiana Veteran Volunteer Infantry.
1894   Cincinnati   175.00
HARTWIG, D. S., compiled by   The Maryland Campaign and the Battle of Antietam: A Bibliography.
1989   Westport   45.00
HARTZLER, Daniel David   Confederate Presentation & Inscribed Swords & Revolvers.
1988   35.00
HARTZLER, Daniel David   Medical Doctors of Maryland in the C.S.A. Wraps.
1988   Gaithersburg   20.00
Harvard Memorial Biographies. 2 Vols.
1866   Cambridge   135.00
1867   Cambridge   135.00
HARVEY, A. M.   The Twenty-second Kansas Volunteer Infantry. Wraps.
1935   Topeka   30.00
HARVEY, Paul, Jr.   Old Tige: General William L. Cabell, C.S.A.
1970   Hillsboro   25.00
1970   Hillsboro   Wraps   18.00
HARWELL, Richard Barksdale   A Confederate Diary of the Retreat from Petersburg. Wraps.
1953   Atlanta   25.00

HARWELL, Richard Barksdale   The Confederate Hundred   A Bibliophilic Selection of Confederate Books.
1964   Urbana, IL   50.00
1982   Wendell, NC   Ltd. ed. - 500 copies   20.00
1982   Wendell, NC   Ltd., signed ed.   40.00

HARWELL, Richard Barksdale, edited by   Confederate Imprints in the University of Georgia Libraries.   Wraps.
1964   Athens, GA   20.00

HARWELL, Richard Barksdale   A Confederate Marine: A Sketch of Henry Lea Graves with Excerpts from the Graves Family Correspondence, 1861-1865.   See: Confederate Centennial Studies, No. 24.

HARWELL, Richard Barksdale   Confederate Music.
1950   Chapel Hill, NC   50.00

HARWELL, Richard Barksdale   The Confederate Reader.
1957   New York   25.00
1962   Chapel Hill, NC   35.00
1962   Richmond   35.00
1979   20.00
1984   15.00

HARWELL, Richard Barksdale   Cornerstones of Confederate Collecting.   Wraps.
1952   Charlottesville, VA   50.00
1953   Charlottesville, VA   50.00
1982   Wendell, NC   Ltd. ed.   20.00
1982   Wendell, NC   Ltd., signed ed.   40.00

HARWELL, Richard Barksdale   In Tall Cotton: The 200 Most Important Books for the Reader, Researcher, and Collector.
1978   Austin   100.00

HARWELL, Richard Barksdale   Lee,   an Abridgement of the set by Douglas Southall Freeman.
1961   New York   30.00

HARWELL, Richard Barksdale, edited by   Louisiana Burge: The Diary of a Confederate College Girl.   Wraps.
1952   Georgia   25.00

HARWELL, Richard Barksdale   A Military Tourist: Colonel Fremantle and His Confederate Travels.   Wraps.
1954   Chicago   10.00

HARWELL, Richard Barksdale   The Mint Julep.
1985   Charlottesville   8.00

HARWELL, Richard Barksdale   More Confederate Imprints.   2 Vols.   Wraps.
1957   Richmond   40.00

HARWELL, Richard Barksdale, edited by   Songs of the Confederacy.
1951   New York   75.00

HARWELL, Richard Barksdale, compiled by   The Sweep of American History.   Wraps.
1957   n.p.   20.00

HARWELL, Richard Barksdale   The Union Reader.
1958   New York   30.00
1984   10.00

HARWELL, Richard Barksdale   The War They Fought.   Confederate Reader and Union Reader in 1 Vol.
    1960   New York   30.00

HASKELL, Frank A.   The Battle of Gettysburg.
    1908   Boston   50.00
    1908   Madison   50.00
    1910   Madison   40.00
    1958   Cambridge   edited by Bruce Catton   25.00

HASKELL, John Cheves   The Haskell Memoirs, edited by G. Govan and J. Livingood.
    1960   New York   30.00

HASKIN, William L.   The History of the First Regiment of Artillery, from its Organization in 1821 to January 1st 1876.
    1879   Portland, ME   150.00

HASSLER, Warren W., Jr.   Commanders of the Army of the Potomac.
    1962   Baton Rouge   30.00

HASSLER, Warren W., Jr.   Crisis at the Crossroads.
    1970   25.00
    1986   Gaithersburg   25.00

HASSLER, Warren W., Jr.   General George B. McClellan.
    1957   Baton Rouge   40.00

HASSLER, William Woods   A. P. Hill Lee's Forgotten General.
    1957   Richmond   45.00
    1962   Chapel Hill, NC   35.00
    1962   Richmond   35.00
    1979   Chapel Hill, NC   20.00
    1984   15.00

HASSLER, William Woods   Colonel John Pelham, Lee's Boy Artillerist.
    1960   Richmond   30.00
    1986   14.95
    1987   14.95

HASSON, B. F.   Escape from the Confederacy.
    1900   Bryant, OH   50.00

HATCH, Carl E., edited by   Dearest Susie: A Civil War Infantryman's Letters to His Sweetheart.
    1971   New York   15.00

HATCHER, Edmund N.   The Last Four Weeks of the War.
    1891   Columbus   50.00
    1892   Columbus   40.00

HATCHER, William E.   Along the Trail of the Friendly Years.
    1910   New York   20.00

HATHAWAY, John L.   General Philip H. Sheridan - US Army. Wraps.
    1891   Milwaukee   25.00

HATTAWAY, Herman   General Stephen D. Lee.
    1976   Jackson 30.00
    1988   Wraps 12.95

HATTAWAY, Herman and **JONES**, Archer   How the North Won: A Military History of the Civil War.
    1983   Champaign, IL   35.00

HAUPT, Herman   Military Bridges.
    1864   New York   150.00

HAUPT, Herman   Reminiscences of General Herman Haupt.
1901   Milwaukee   Ltd., signed ed.   165.00

HAUPT, L. M.   The Topographer, His Instruments and Methods.
1883   New York   45.00

HAVENS, Lewis C.   Historical Sketch of the 136th New York Infantry, 1862-1865.   Wraps.
1934   Dalton   50.00

HAWES, Jesse   Cahaba, A Story of Captive Boys in Blue.
1888   New York   150.00

HAWK, Emory Q.   Economic History of the South.
1934   New York   25.00

HAWKINS, John Parker   Memoranda Concerning Some Branches of the Hawkins Family and Connections.
1913   Indianapolis   75.00

HAWKINS, M. L.   Sketch of the Battle of Winchester, September 19, 1864, a Paper.   Wraps.
1884   Cincinnati   35.00

HAWKINS, Rush C.   An Account of the Assassination of Loyal Citizens of North Carolina for Having Served in the Union Army Which Took Place at Kingston in the Months of February and March 1864.   Wraps.
1897   100.00

HAWKS, E. H.   A Woman Doctor's Civil War . . . , edited by Gerald Schwartz.
1984   Columbia   18.00

HAWN, William   All Around the Civil War, or Before and After.
(1908)   New York   50.00

HAY, David and Joan   The Last of the Confederate Privateers.
1977   n.p.   20.00

HAY, John   Letters of John Hay and Extracts from Diary.   3 Vols.
1908   Washington, DC   325.00

HAY, Thomas Robson   Braxton Bragg and the Southern Confederacy.   Wraps.
1925   Savannah   50.00

HAY, Thomas Robson   Hood's Tennessee Campaign.
1929   New York   125.00
1976   Dayton 20.00

HAYDEN, Howard K.   Billy Yank Soldier of the North.
(1965)   Long Branch, NJ   30.00

HAYDON, F. Stansbury   Aeronautics in the Union and Confederate Armies.   Vol. 1 (all pub.)
1941   Baltimore   150.00

HAYES, Jim   War Between the States: Autographs and Biographical Information.
1989   James Island   50.00

HAYES, John D., edited by   Samuel Francis DuPont, A Selection from His Civil War Letters. 3 Vols.
1969   Ithaca, NY   50.00

HAYES, M.   Mr. Lincoln Runs for President.
1960   New York   15.00

HAYES, Rutherford B.   Remarks of Gen. _____ at the Annual
  Reunion of the 23rd Regiment, Ohio Vet. Vol. Inf. at Youngstown, Ohio
  Sept 17, 1879.
  (1879)   n.p.   30.00
HAYES, Rutherford B.   Remarks of General _____ at the Reunion of
  the 23rd Ohio Veterans, Canton, Sept. 1, 1880.
  n.d.   n.p.   30.00
HAYNES, Draughton Stith   The Field Diary of a Confederate Soldier.
  1963   Darien, GA   Ltd.   40.00
HAYNES, Edwin M.   A History of the 10th Regiment Vermont Vols.
  1870   Lewiston   75.00
  1894   Rutland   70.00
HAYNES, George H.   Charles Sumner.
  1909   Philadelphia   20.00
HAYNES, Martin A.   A History of the Second Regiment, New Hampshire
  Volunteer Infantry in the War of the Rebellion.
  1865   Manchester   125.00
  1896   Lakeport   90.00
HAYNES, Martin A., compiled by   Muster Out Roll of the Second
  New Hampshire Regiment in the War of the Rebellion.
  1917   Lakeport   Ltd.   35.00
HAYNIE, J. Henry   The Nineteenth Illinois, A Memoir of a Regiment.
  1912   Chicago   130.00
HAYS, Alexander   General Alexander Hays at the Battle of Gettys-
  burg.
  1913   Pittsburgh   45.00
HAYS, Ebenezer Z., edited by   History of the Thirty-second Regiment
  Ohio Veteran Volunteer Infantry.
  1896   Columbus   180.00
HAYS, Gilbert Adams, compiled by   Under the Red Patch: Story of
  the 63rd Regiment Pennsylvania Volunteers 1861-1865.
  1908   Pittsburgh   75.00
HAYS, Helen Ashe   The Antietam and Its Bridges The Annals of an
  Historic Stream.
  1910   New York and London   45.00
HAYTHORNTHWAITE, Philip John   Uniforms of the Civil War 1861-
  1865.
  1976   New York   23.00
  1986   Wraps   12.00
HAYWARD, J. Henry   Poetical Pen-Pictures of the War; Selected
  from Our Union Poets.
  1863   New York   25.00
HAZELTON, Joseph P. (pseud.)   See: BROCKETT, Linus P.
HAZEN, William B.   A Narrative of Military Service.
  1885   Boston   90.00
HAZLETT, James C., OLMSTEAD, Edwin and PARKS, M. Hume   Field
  Artillery Weapons of the Civil War.
  1988   45.00
HAZZARD, George   Hazzard's History of Henry County, Indiana 1822-
  1906 Military Edition Vols. I & II.
  1905-1906   New Castle   175.00

HEAD, Thomas A.   Campaigns and Battles of the 16th Regiment Tennessee Volunteers.
1885   Nashville   150.00
1961   McMinnville   50.00
HEADLEY, J. T.   Farragut and Our Naval Commanders.
1867   New York 50.00
1880   45.00
HEADLEY, J. T.   Grant and Sherman.
1865   New York 25.00
1866   New York 25.00
HEADLEY, J. T.   The Great Rebellion.
1863   Hartford   2 Vols. in 1   25.00
1864   Hartford   2 Vols. 30.00
1866   Hartford   2 Vols. 30.00
1898   Washington, DC 2 Vols. 30.00
HEADLEY, J. T.   The Great Riots of New York 1712 to 1873.
1873   New York 30.00
HEADLEY, J. T.   The Life and Travels of General Grant.
1881   Philadelphia   15.00
1897   Philadelphia   15.00
HEADLEY, J. T.   The Life of U. S. Grant.
1868   New York 20.00
1885   New York 15.00
HEADLEY, John W.   Confederate Operations in Canada and New York.
1906   New York 150.00
1984   22.50
HEADLEY, P. C.   The Life and Campaigns of Lieut.-Gen. U. S. Grant.
1866   New York 30.00
HEADLEY, P. C.   Life and Military Career of Major-General Philip Henry Sheridan.
1865   New York 15.00
1889   Boston 15.00
HEADLEY, P. C.   Life and Naval Career of Vice-Admiral David Glasgow Farragut.
1865   New York 25.00
HEADLEY, P. C.   Massachusetts in the Rebellion.
1866   Boston   75.00
HEADSPETH, W. Carroll   The Battle of Staunton River Bridge. Wraps.
1949 South Boston, VA   30.00
HEADSPETH, W. Carroll   Halifax Volunteers in the Confederate Army. Wraps.
(1939) n.p.   60.00
HEAGNEY, H. J.   Blockade Runner: A Tale of Adventure Aboard the Robt. E. Lee. Wraps.
1952   Chicago   25.00
HEALY, Laurin Hall and KUTNER, Luis   The Admiral.
1944   Chicago   20.00
HEAPS, Willard A. and PORTER, W.   The Singing Sixties.
1960   Norman, OK   30.00
HEARTMAN, Charles F.   What Constitutes a Confederate Imprint? Preliminary Suggestions for Bibliographers and Catalogers. Wraps.
1939   Hattiesburg, MS   Ltd.   50.00

HEARTSILL, William W.   Fourteen Hundred and 91 Days in the Confederate Army.
>   1876   Marshall, TX   9000.00
>   1954   Jackson edited by Bell I. Wiley 50.00
>   1987   Wilmington, NC   Ltd. ed.   500.00
>   1987   Wilmington, NC   30.00

The Hebe Skirmish Centennial and the Fort Fisher Visitor Center - Museum Groundbreaking Program. Wraps.
>   1963   Wilmington, NC   15.00

HEBERT, Walter H.   Fighting Joe Hooker.
>   1944   Indianapolis   50.00
>   1987   30.00

HECK, Frank H.   The Civil War Veteran.
>   1941   Oxford, OH   60.00

HECK, Frank H.   Proud Kentuckian, John C. Breckinridge 1821-1875.
>   1976   Lexington, KY   10.00

HEDLEY, Fenwick Y.   Marching Through Georgia.
>   1885   Chicago   30.00
>   1887   Chicago   30.00
>   1895   Chicago   25.00

HEDRICK, Mary A.   Incidents of the Civil War.
>   1888   Lowell, MA   30.00

HEER, George W.   Episodes of the Civil War, Nine Campaigns in Nine States.
>   1890   San Francisco   200.00

HEG, E. Biddle   Stephen O. Himoe, Civil War Physician. Norwegian-American Studies and Records. Vol. XI.
>   1940   Northfield   35.00

HEG, Hans Christian   The Civil War Letters of Colonel _____, edited by T. C. Blegen.
>   1936   Northfield   35.00

HEGARTY, Lela Whitton   Father Wore Gray.
>   1963   San Antonio   30.00

HEIN, O. L.   Memories of Long Ago.
>   1925   New York   70.00

HEITMAN, Francis B.   Historical Register and Dictionary of the United States Army.
>   1890   Washington, DC   1 Vol. ed.   75.00
>   1903   Washington, DC   2 Vols.   125.00
>   1965   Urbana   50.00
>   1988   2 Vols.   45.00

HELM, Katherine   The True Story of Mary, Wife of Lincoln.
>   1928   New York   35.00

HELPER, Hinton Rowan   Compendium of the Impending Crisis of the South. Wraps.
>   1859   New York   80.00
>   1860   New York   75.00

HELPER, Hinton Rowan   The Impending Crisis of the South: How to Meet It.
>   1857   New York   80.00
>   1859   New York   75.00
>   1860   75.00

1909   Miami 20.00
1957   15.00
1968   Cambridge 30.00
HELPER, Hinton Rowan   **Nojoque: A Question for a Continent.**
1867   New York 30.00
HEMMERLEIN, Richard F.   **Prisons and Prisoners of the Civil War.**
1934   Boston   75.00
HENDERSON, Dwight Franklin, edited by   **The Private Journal of Georgiana Gholson Walker 1862-1865.** See: **Confederate Centennial Studies, No. 25.**
HENDERSON, George F. R.   **The Campaign of Fredericksburg, Nov. - Dec., 1862.**
    1886   London   200.00
    1888   London   175.00
    1908   London   175.00
    1984   20.00
HENDERSON, George F. R.   **The Civil War. A Soldier's View,** edited by Jay Luvaas.
    1958   Chicago   35.00
    1959   Chicago   25.00
HENDERSON, George F. R.   **The Science of War.**
    1905   London   150.00
    1908   75.00
    1912   New York   75.00
    1913   75.00
    1916   London   75.00
HENDERSON, George F. R.   **Stonewall Jackson and the American Civil War. 2 Vols.**
    1898   London   200.00
    1898   New York   175.00
Many later editions 1899-   50.00
    1932   London   45.00
    1949   New York   2 Vols. in 1 40.00
    1961   40.00
    1968   Gloucester   40.00
    1986   16.50
    1988   22.98
HENDERSON, Harry McCorry   **Texas in the Confederacy.**
1955   San Antonio 40.00
HENDERSON, Lillian, compiled by   **Roster of the Confederate Soldiers of Georgia 1861-1865. 6 Vols.**
1959-64   Hapeville, GA 250.00
HENDERSON, Lindsey P., Jr.   **The Oglethorpe Light Infantry. Wraps.**
1961   Savannah   60.00
HENDERSON, William D.   **The Road to Bristoe Station: Campaigning with Lee and Meade, August 1- October 20, 1863.**
1987   Lynchburg   Ltd. 1000 Copies.   16.95
HENDRICK, Burton J.   **The Lees of Virginia.**
1935   Boston   60.00
HENDRICK, Burton J.   **Lincoln's War Cabinet.**
1946   Boston   25.00

HENDRICK, Burton J.   Statesmen of the Lost Cause.
    1939   New York   25.00
HENKELS, Stan V., edited by   Valuable Collection of Engraved Por-
    traits Belonging to the Hon. James T. Mitchell Embracing the Portion
    Relating to the Civil War. Wraps.
    1910   Philadelphia   25.00
HENNESSY, Dorothy, edited by   Civil War The Years Asunder.
    1973   Waukesha, WI   30.00
HENNESSY, John   The First Battle of Manassas, An Era to Inno-
    cence, July 18-21, 1861.
    1989   Lynchburg   Ltd.   16.95
HENRY, F. A.   Captain Henry of Geauga, A Family Chronicle.
    1942   60.00
HENRY, Guy V.   Military Record of Civilian Appointments in the US
    Army. 2 Vols.
    1869-73   New York   80.00
HENRY, H. F.   Souvenir of the Battlefield of Bull Run.   Wraps.
    1900   Manassas   30.00
HENRY, Robert Selph, edited by   As They Saw Forrest, Some Recollec-
    tions and Comments of Contemporaries.
    1956   Jackson, TN   40.00
    1987   Wilmington, NC   30.00
HENRY, Robert Selph   First with the Most Forrest.
    1944   Indianapolis   45.00
    1969   Jackson, TN   40.00
    1974   35.00
    1987   Wilmington, NC   30.00
    1987   Wraps   11.95
HENRY, Robert Selph   The Story of Reconstruction.
    1938   New York   25.00
    1963   Gloucester   15.00
HENRY, Robert Selph   The Story of the Confederacy.
    1931   Indianapolis   35.00
    1931   Garden City   25.00
    1936   New York   20.00
    1989   14.95
HENRY, Will   Journey to Shiloh.
    1960   New York   10.00
HENSEL, W. U.   Robert E. Lee - As a Citizen, Soldier and Statesman.
    Wraps.
    1909   Lancaster   20.00
HENSHAW, Sarah Edwards   Our Branch and Its Tributaries, Being a
    History of the Work of the Northwestern Sanitary Commission and Its
    Auxiliaries.
    1868   Chicago   35.00
HENTY, G. A.   With Lee in Virginia.
    n.d.   London   20.00
    n.d.   New York   15.00
HEPWORTH, George H.   The Whip, Hoe and Sword.
    1864   Boston   40.00
    1971   25.00

HERBERT, George B., edited by   Anecdotes of the Rebellion.   Wraps.
   1894   Springfield, OH   25.00

HERBERT, George B.   The Popular History of the Civil War in America.
   1884   (New York)   20.00

HERBERT, Hilary A.   History of the 8th Alabama Volunteer Regiment C.S.A. by the Colonel of the Regiment.
   1977   60.00

HERBERT, Hilary A., et al   Why the Solid South?   or, Reconstruction and Its Results.   Wraps.
   1890   Baltimore   35.00
   1969   19.00

HERBST, Frank   The Lone Sentinel of Fort Fisher.   Wraps.
   (c.1920) n.p.   30.00

HERDEGEN, Lance and BEAUDOT, William J. K.   In the Bloody Railroad Cut at Gettysburg.
   1990   Dayton   29.95

HERGESHEIMER, Joseph   The Limestone Tree.
   1931   New York   25.00

HERGESHEIMER, Joseph   Sheridan: A Military Narrative.
   1931   New York   40.00
   1931   Boston   Ltd.   150.00

HERGESHEIMER, Joseph   Swords and Roses.
   1929   New York   25.00
   1972   New York   25.00

HERMANN, Isaac   Memoirs of a Veteran.
   1911   Atlanta   250.00
   1974   Lakemont, GA   Ltd.   30.00

HERNDON, Dallas T.   Letters of David O. Dodd with Biographical Sketch.   Wraps.
   (c.1920) n.p.   35.00

HERNDON, William H. and WEIK, Jesse W.   Abraham Lincoln. 2 Vols.
   1893   New York   35.00

HERNDON, William H. and WEIK, Jesse W.   Herndon's Life of Lincoln.
   1942   Cleveland   15.00
   1943   15.00
   1983   edited by Paul Angle   Wraps   11.00

HERNDON, William H. and WEIK, Jesse W.   Herndon's Lincoln: The True Story of a Great Life, The History and Personal Recollections of Abraham Lincoln. 3 Vols.
   1889   Chicago   100.00

HERNON, Joseph M., Jr.   Celts, Catholics and Copperheads: Ireland Views the American Civil War.
   1968   Ohio State   15.00

The Heroes in Gray.   By a Confederate Soldier. (Robert B. Stratton).   Wraps.
   1894   Lynchburg   250.00

HERR, John K. and WALLACE, Edward S.   The Story of the U.S. Cavalry 1775-1942.
   1953   Boston   50.00

HERR, Pamela   Jessie Benton Fremont, A Biography.   Wraps.
   1988   University, OK   14.95

HERRING, Ethel and WILLIAMS, Carolee   Fort Caswell in War and Peace.
    1983   Wendell, NC   12.00
HERTZ, Emanuel   Abraham Lincoln, A New Portrait. 2 Vols.
    1931   New York   20.00
HERTZ, Emanuel   Abraham Lincoln, the Tribute of the Synagogue.
    1927   New York   25.00
HERTZ, Emanuel   The Hidden Lincoln.
    1938   New York   15.00
HESS, Earl J., edited by   A German Yankee in the Fatherland. The Civil War Letters of Henry A. Kircher.
    1983   24.00
HESS, George   The Maryland Campaign from Sept. 1st to Sept. 20th, 1862. Wraps.
    1890   Hagerstown, MD   45.00
HESSELTINE, William B.   Civil War Prisons.
    1930   Columbus, OH   50.00
    1962   Kent, OH   30.00
    1964   New York   30.00
    1972   30.00
    1977   30.00
    1978   New York   30.00
HESSELTINE, William B.   Confederate Leaders in the New South.
    1950   Baton Rouge   35.00
HESSELTINE, William B.   Lincoln and the War Governors.
    1948   New York   25.00
    1955   New York   15.00
    1972   15.00
HESSELTINE, William B.   Lincoln's Plan of Reconstruction.   See: Confederate Centennial Studies, No. 13.
HESSELTINE, William B., edited by   Three Against Lincoln, Murat Halstead Reports the Caucuses of 1860.
    1960   Baton Rouge   20.00
HESSELTINE, William B.   The Tragic Conflict - the Civil War and Reconstruction.
    1962   New York   20.00
HESSELTINE, William B.   Ulysses S. Grant, Politician.
    1935   New York   20.00
    1948   New York   15.00
    1957   New York   15.00
HESSELTINE, William B. and WOLF, Hazel C.   The Blue and the Gray on the Nile.
    1961   Chicago   30.00
HETH, Henry   The Memoirs of Henry Heth, edited by James L. Morrison.
    1974   Westport   30.00
HETRICH, G. and GUTTAG, Julius   Civil War Tokens and Tradesmen's Store Cards.
    1924   New York   75.00
HEUMAN, William   Custer, Man and Legend.
    1968   New York   35.00

HEWITT, Lawrence L.   Port Hudson: Confederate Bastion on the Mississippi.
1987   Baton Rouge   19.95
HEWITT, William   History of the Twelfth West Virginia Volunteer Infantry. Wraps.
1892   Steubenville   125.00
HEYMAN, Max   The Prudent Soldier.
1959   Glendale   40.00
HEYSINGER, Isaac W.   Antietam and the Maryland and Virginia Campaigns of 1862.
1912   New York   80.00
1987   30.00
HEYWARD, Dubose   Peter Ashley.
1932   New York   35.00
HEYWARD, Dubose and SASS, Herbert Ravenel   Fort Sumter.
1938   New York   35.00
HIBBEN, Paxton   Henry Ward Beecher: An American Portrait.
1927   New York   10.00
HICKEN, Victor   Illinois in the Civil War.
1966   Urbana   30.00
HICKERSON, Thomas Felix   Echoes of Happy Valley.
1962   Durham, NC   25.00
HICKS, Irl   The Prisoner's Farewell to Johnson's Island; or Valedictory Address to the Young Men's Christian Association of Johnson's Island, Ohio. A Poem. Wraps.
1872   St. Louis   100.00
HIGDON, Hal   The Union vs. Dr. Mudd.
1964   Chicago   15.00
HIGGINS, William C.   Scaling the Eagle's Nest: Life of Russell H. Conwell.
1889   Springfield   30.00
HIGGINSON, Mary   Thomas Wentworth Higginson; the Story of his Life.
1914   Boston and New York   15.00
HIGGINSON, Thomas Wentworth   Army Life in a Black Regiment.
1870   Boston   75.00
1882   75.00
1960   Lansing   30.00
HIGGINSON, Thomas Wentworth   Cheerful Yesterdays.
1898   Boston   25.00
HIGGINSON, Thomas Wentworth   Harvard Memorial Biographies.   2 Vols.
1866   Cambridge   50.00
HIGGINSON, Thomas Wentworth   Letters and Journals of Thomas Wentworth Higginson, 1846-1906.
1921   Boston   30.00
HIGGINSON, Thomas Wentworth   Massachusetts in the Army and Navy During the War. 2 Vols.
1896   Boston   75.00
HIGH, Edwin W.   History of the Sixty-eighth Regiment Indiana Volunteer Infantry 1862-1865.
1902   Metamora   150.00

HIGHT, John J.   History of the 58th Regiment of Indiana Volunteer Infantry. . . .
    1895   Princeton   175.00
HILDEBRAND, Samuel S.   Autobiography of _____, edited by James W. Evans and A. Wendell Keith.
    1870   Jefferson City   125.00
HILDEBRAND, V. M.   The Sharpsburg Rifles, 1st Maryland Regiment Potomac Home Brigade Maryland Volunteers. (U.S.A.).   Wraps.
    (c.1960) n.p.   25.00
HILL, A. F.   John Smith's Funny Adventures on a Crutch.
    1869   Philadelphia   20.00
HILL, Alfred J.   History of Company E of the Sixth Minnesota Regiment of Volunteer Infantry.
    1899   St. Paul   125.00
HILL, Alonzo   In Memoriam   A Discourse . . . on Lieut. Thomas Jefferson Spurr.
    1862   Boston   25.00
HILL, Archibald F.   Our Boys.
    1864   Philadelphia   40.00
    1865   Philadelphia   40.00
    1890   Philadelphia   35.00
HILL, Benjamin H., Jr.   Senator Benjamin H. Hill of Georgia.
    1893   Atlanta   30.00
HILL, Daniel Harvey   Bethel to Sharpsburg. 2 Vols.
    1926   Raleigh   150.00
HILL, Daniel Harvey   North Carolina.   See: Confederate Military History, Vol. IV (Vol. V, 1987 reprint ed.).
HILL, Daniel Harvey   The Old South,   An Address . . . at Ford's Grand Opera House . . . June 6, 1887. . . .   Wraps.
    1887   Baltimore   50.00
HILL, Frederick   Lincoln the Lawyer.
    1906   New York   10.00
HILL, Herbert E.   Campaign in the Shenandoah Valley 1864, A Paper. Wraps.
    1886   Boston   35.00
HILL, Jim Dan   Sea Dogs of the Sixties.
    1935   Minneapolis   35.00
HILL, John Wesley   If Lincoln Were Here.
    1925   New York   15.00
HILL, Louise B.   Governor Brown and the Confederacy.   Wraps.
    1938   Nashville   25.00
HILL, Louise B.   Joseph E. Brown and the Confederacy.
    1939   Chapel Hill, NC   40.00
    1972   Westport, CT   30.00
    1974   30.00
HILL, Louise B.   State Socialism in the Confederate States of America. Wraps.
    1936   Charlottesville, VA   10.00
HILL, Richard Taylor and **ANTHONY,** William Edward   Confederate Longarms and Pistols.
    1978   Charlotte, NC   50.00

HILL, Sarah Jane Full   Mrs. Hill's Journal - Civil War Reminiscences, edited by Mark M. Krug.
1980   Chicago   30.00
HILLARD, G. S.   Life and Campaigns of George B. McClellan.
1864   Philadelphia   35.00
HILLEARY, William M.   The Diary of 1864-1866 A Webfoot Volunteer, edited by H. B. Nelson and P. E. Onstad.
1965   Corvallis   35.00
HILLIARD, Sam Bowers   Atlas of Antebellum Southern Agriculture.
1984   28.00
1984   Wraps   9.00
HILLMAN, Benjamin J.   Monuments to Memories Virginia's Civil War Heritage in Bronze and Stone. Wraps.
(1961-65)   Richmond   10.00
HILLS, Alfred C.   MacPherson, The Confederate Philosopher.
1864   New York   60.00
Hillsborough Military Academy, Hillsborough, North Carolina, General R. E. Colston, Superintendent. Wraps.
(1866)   (Hillsborough)   100.00
HINDS, Thomas   Tales of War Times.
1904   Watertown, NY   150.00
HINKLEY, Julian Wisner   A Narrative of Service with the Third Wisconsin Infantry.
1912   Madison   60.00
HINKLEY, Julian Wisner   Some Experiences of a Veteran in the Rear. Wraps.
1893   Minneapolis   35.00
HINMAN, Wilbur F.   Corporal Si Klegg and His "Pard."
1887   Cleveland   30.00
1888   Cleveland   30.00
1889   Cleveland   30.00
1892   Cleveland   30.00
1895   30.00
HINMAN, Wilbur F.   The Story of the Sherman Brigade.
1897   Alliance 225.00
HINSDALE, Harriet   Confederate Gray: The Story of Traveller.
1963   Peterborough, NH   25.00
HINTON, Richard J.   John Brown and His Men.
1894   New York   25.00
HINTON, Richard J.   Rebel Invasion of Missouri and Kansas.
1865   Chicago 100.00
HIRSHON, Stanley P.   Grenville M. Dodge, Soldier, Politician, Railroad Pioneer.
1967   Bloomington   40.00
Historic Points of Interest in Richmond, Virginia Official Publication No. 24, Richmond Civil War Centennial Committee. Wraps.
(1965) Richmond   10.00
Historic Views of America's Greatest Battlefield Gettysburg. Wraps.
(c.1920) np.   45.00
Historic Virginia: Her Sixteen Immortals. Wraps.
(c.1925) Fredericksburg   8.00

Historical Base Map; Part of the Master Plan, Kennesaw Mountain National Battlefield Park.
　　1941　25.00
Historical Data on Major General John H. Forney, CSA, Vol. 1. Wraps.
　　1961　n.p.　50.00
Historical Sketch of the Chicago Board of Trade Battery, Horse Artillery, Illinois Volunteers.
　　1902　Chicago　150.00
Historical Sketch: Dedication of Monument . . . 150th New York Volunteer Infantry, Gettysburg, Sept. 17, 18, 1889.
　　1889　New York　35.00
Historical Times Illustrated Encyclopedia of the Civil War, edited by Patricia L. Faust.
　　1986　New York　30.00
HISTORICUS　See: HARCOURT, William
History and Reminiscences of Dougherty County, Georgia.
　　1924　Albany　50.00
History and Roster of Maryland Volunteers, War of 1861-5. Vol. I.
　　1898　75.00
History and Roster of the 130th Infantry Regiment Illinois Volunteers. Wraps.
　　1893　Greenville　100.00
History and Roster of the Seventh Pa. Cavalry. Wraps.
　　1904　Pottsville　160.00
History of Antietam National Cemetery Including a Descriptive List of all the Loyal Soldiers Buried . . . and Address on the Occasion of the Dedication of the Grounds, September 17th, 1867.
　　1869　Baltimore　75.00
History of Battle-Flag Day, September 17, 1879.
　　1879　Hartford　40.00
History of General Leonidas Polk.
　　1888　Park Place, NY　40.00
History of Greene County, Missouri.
　　1883　St. Louis　150.00
History of Henry and St. Clair Counties, Missouri.
　　1968　Clinton　30.00
A History of the Confederate Monumental Association and Roster of Forbes Bivouac.
　　1893　Clarksville　125.00
History of the Confederated Memorial Associations of the South.
　　1903　New Orleans　40.00
　　1904　New Orleans　35.00
　　1904　Washington, DC　40.00
History of the DeWitt Guard Co. A 50th Regiment, NG NY.
　　1866　Ithaca　50.00
History of the Eighteenth Regiment of Cavalry, Pennsylvania Volunteers (163rd Regiment of the Line).
　　1909　New York　125.00
History of the Eighth Cavalry Regiment, Illinois Volunteers, During the Great Rebellion.
　　1868　Aurora, IL　300.00

History of the Eighty-eighth Indiana Volunteers Infantry.
    1895   Fort Wayne   160.00
History of the Eleventh Pennsylvania Volunteer Cavalry.
    1902   Philadelphia 125.00
History of the Fifth Massachusetts Battery.
    1902   Boston   80.00
History of the Fifty-seventh Regiment, Pennsylvania Veteran Volunteer Infantry.
    1904   Meadville   150.00
History of the Forty-sixth Regiment Indiana Volunteer Infantry September 1861 to September 1865.
    1888   Logansport   135.00
History of the Great Western Sanitary Fair.
    1864   Cincinnati   30.00
History of the Hampton Battery in the Civil War 1861-65.
    1909   50.00
History of the Life of Rev. Wm. Mack Lee Body Servant of General Robert E. Lee. Wraps.
    1918   Norfolk   50.00
History of the North-Western Soldiers' Fair.
    1864   Chicago   25.00
History of the One Hundred and Seventeenth Regiment, N.Y. Volunteers (Fourth Oneida) . . . August, 1862 . . . June, 1865.
    1866   Hartford   75.00
History of the One Hundred and Twenty-fifth Regiment, Pa. Vols. 1862-1863.
    1906   Philadelphia   125.00
    1907   Philadelphia   75.00
History of the 121st Regiment Penn. Vols.
    1893   Philadelphia   125.00
    1906   Philadelphia   100.00
History of the 127th Regiment Pennsylvania Volunteers Familiarly Known as the "Dauphin County Regiment."
    1902   Lebanon   80.00
History of the Organization of the First Light Infantry Veteran Association of Providence, R.I. with a Roster of the Association. Vol. I. (all pub).
    1870   (Providence)   35.00
History of the Ram Fleet and the Mississippi Marine Brigade. . . .
    1907   St. Louis   400.00
History of the Reunion Society of the 23rd Regiment N.J. Volunteers.
    1890   Philadelphia   75.00
History of the Second Battalion, Duryee Zouaves, 165th Regiment New York Volunteer Infantry.
    1905   New York   100.00
History of the Seventy-ninth Regiment Indiana Volunteer Infantry in the Civil War of Eighteen Sixty-one.
    1899   Indianapolis 130.00
History of the Seventy-third Indiana Volunteers in the War of 1861-65.
    1909   Washington, DC   160.00
A History of the Seventy-third Regiment of Illinois Infantry Volunteers . . . (The Preacher Regiment, 1862-65).
    1890   Springfield   150.00

History of the Sixth New York Cavalry (Second Ira Harris Guard).
1908   Worcester   150.00

History of the Third Division, Ninth Corps, Army of the Potomac.
1892   Harrisburg   30.00

History of the Third Pennsylvania Cavalry, 60th Regiment Pennsylvania Volunteers.
1905   Philadelphia   125.00

History of the Thirty-fifth Regiment Massachusetts Volunteers.
1884   Boston   60.00

History of the Thirty-sixth Regiment Massachusetts Volunteers.
1884   Boston   75.00

A History of the U. S. Signal Corps.
1961   New York   35.00

HITCHCOCK, Benjamin   **Hitchcock's Chronological Record of the American Civil War.** Wraps.
1868   New York   30.00

HITCHCOCK, Caroline Hanks   **Nancy Hanks The Story of Abraham Lincoln's Mother.**
1900   New York   50.00

HITCHCOCK, Ethan Allen   **Fifty Years in Camp and Field**, edited by W. A. Croffut.
1909   New York   55.00

HITCHCOCK, Frederick L.   **War from the Inside; or, Personal Experiences, Impressions and Reminiscences of One of the 'Boys' in the War of the Rebellion.**
1904   Philadelphia   100.00
1985   25.00

HITCHCOCK, Henry   **Marching with Sherman, Passages from the Letters and Campaign Diaries.**
1927   New Haven, CT   75.00

HOADLEY, John C., edited by   **Memorial of Henry Sanford Gansevoort, Captain Fifth Artillery.**
1875   Boston   50.00

HOAR, George F.   **Autobiography of Seventy Years.** 2 Vols.
1903   New York   50.00

HOAR, Jay S.   **New England's Last Civil War Veterans.** Wraps.
1976   9.00

HOAR, Jay S.   **The South's Last Boys in Gray.**
1986   Bowling Green   39.95
Recent reprint   Wraps   19.95

HOBART, E. L.   **The Truth about Shiloh, with Roster of Survivors.**
(c.1890) n.p.   90.00

HOBART-HAMPDEN, Augustus C.   **Hobart Pasha: Blockade-Running, Slaver Hunting, and War Sports in Turkey**, edited by Horace Kephart.
1915   New York   100.00

HOBART-HAMPDEN, Augustus C.   **Never Caught.**
1867   London   350.00
1908   New York   125.00
1967   Carolina Beach   Wraps   25.00

HOBART-HAMPDEN, Augustus C.   **Sketches from My Life.**
1886   London   250.00
1887   New York   200.00

HOBBS, Charles Albert   Vicksburg, A Poem.
    1880   Chicago   55.00

HOBBS, Thomas Hubbard   **The Journals of _____,** edited by Faye Acton Axford.
    1976   University, AL   15.00

HOBEIKA, John E.   **Lee, The Soul of Honor.**
    1932   Boston   15.00

HOBEIKA, John E.   **A Tribute to the Confederate Soldier An Address.** Wraps.
    1930   n.p.   15.00

HOBSON, Charles and **SHANKMAN,** Arnold   **Colonel of the Bucktails: Civil War Letters of Charles Frederick Taylor.** Wraps.
    1973   n.p.   20.00

HOBSON, H. S.   **The Famous Cruise of the Kearsarge.**
    1895   Bonds Village, MA   60.00

HODGE, George Baird   **Sketch of the First Kentucky Brigade.** Wraps.
    1874   Frankfort, KY   175.00

HODGES, William R.   **Lest We Forget.** Wraps.
    1912   St. Louis   25.00

HODGKINS, William H.   **The Battle of Fort Stedman (Petersburg, Virginia) Mar. 25, 1865.** Wraps.
    1889   Boston   75.00

HODGMAN, Stephen A.   **The Nation's Sin and Punishment.**
    1864   New York   20.00

HODGSON, Joseph   **The Cradle of the Confederacy: Or, The Times of Troup, Quitman and Yancey.**
    1876   Mobile   100.00
    1975   Spartanburg   25.00

HOEHLING, A. A.   **Damn the Torpedoes! Naval Incidents of the Civil War.**
    1989   Winston-Salem   19.95

HOEHLING, A. A.   **Last Train From Atlanta.**
    1958   New York   25.00

HOEHLING, A. A.   **Thunder at Hampton Roads.**
    1976   Englewood Cliffs, NJ   15.00

HOEHLING, A. A.   **Vicksburg, 47 Days of Siege, May 18-July 4, 1863.**
    1969   Englewood Cliffs, NJ   30.00

HOEHLING, A. A. and **HOEHLING,** Mary   **The Day Richmond Died.**
    1981   New York   25.00

HOEHLING, A. A. and **HOEHLING,** Mary   **The Last Days of the Confederacy: An Eyewitness Account of the Fall of Richmond. . . .**
    1986   New York   15.00

HOEHLING, Mary   **Girl Soldier and Spy - Sarah Emma Edmundson.**
    1959   New York   30.00

HOEHLING, Mary   **Thaddeus Lowe, America's One-Man Air Corps.**
    1958   Chicago   27.50

HOFFMAN, Wickham   **Camp, Court and Siege.**
    1877   New York   40.00

HOFFMANN, John   **Confederates at Missionary Ridge The Confederate Collapse at the Battle of Missionary Ridge: The Reports of James Patton Anderson and his Brigade Commanders.**
    1985   Dayton   15.00

HOFMANN, J. William   Remarks on the Battle of Gettysburg.   Wraps.
    1880   Philadelphia   45.00
HOGAN, John Joseph   On the Mission in Missouri 1857-1888.
    1892   Kansas City, MO   80.00
HOGE, Mrs. A. H.   The Boys in Blue.
    1867   New York   30.00
HOGE, Peyton H.   Moses Drury Hoge: Life and Letters.
    1899   Richmond   65.00
HOGG, A. M., edited by   Virginia Cemeteries: A Guide to Resources.
Wraps.
    1986   Charlottesville   9.95
HOIT, T. W.   The Right of American Slavery. Southern and Western edition. Wraps.
    1860   St. Louis   200.00
HOKANSON, Nels   Swedish Immigrants in Lincoln's Time.
    1942   New York   75.00
HOKE, Jacob   Reminiscences of the War   or Incidents Which Transpired in and About Chambersburg, During the War of the Rebellion.
    1884   Chambersburg, PA   80.00
HOKE, Jacob   The Great Invasion of 1863.
    1887   Dayton   75.00
    1888   75.00
    1913   Dayton   60.00
    1959   New York   40.00
HOLBROOK, William C.   A Narrative of the Officers & Enlisted Men of the 7th Regiment Vermont Volunteers.
    1882   New York   60.00
HOLCOMB, Richmond C.   A Century with Norfolk Naval Hospital, 1830-1930.
    1930   Portsmouth, VA   Ltd.   65.00
HOLCOMBE, R. I.   History of the First Regiment Minnesota Volunteer Infantry 1861-1864.
    1987   30.00
HOLCOMBE, R. I. and ADAMS   An Account of the Battle of Wilson's Creek.
    1883   Springfield   140.00
    1961   Springfield   25.00
HOLDEN, Leverett   My First and Last Fights, Fredericksburg to Gettysburg, Memories of the Civil War. Wraps.
    1914   50.00
HOLDEN, W. W.   Memoirs of W. W. Holden.
    1911   Durham   45.00
HOLIEN, K. B.   Battle at Ball's Bluff; Leesburg, Virginia, October 21, 1861. Wraps.
    1989   Alexandria   20.00
HOLLAND, Cecil Fletcher   Morgan and His Raiders.
    1942   New York   65.00
    1943   40.00
HOLLAND, J. G.   Das Leben Abraham Lincoln's.
    1866   (Springfield, MA)   15.00
HOLLAND, J. G.   The Life of Abraham Lincoln.
    1866   Springfield   25.00

HOLLAND, Lynwood M.   **Pierce M. B. Young,   The Warwick of the South.**
    1964   Athens, GA   20.00
HOLLAND, Mary H.   **Our Army Nurses.**
    1895   Boston 90.00
    1897   Boston 75.00
HOLLIDAY, F. W. M.   **In Memoriam - General Robert E. Lee,   Oration.   Wraps.**
    1871   Winchester   45.00
HOLLIDAY, John Hampden   **Indianapolis and the Civil War.   Wraps.**
    1972   Indianapolis   15.00
HOLLINGSWORTH, Alan M. and **COX,** James M.   **The   Third   Day   at Gettysburg: Pickett's Charge.   Wraps.**
    1959   New York   20.00
HOLLIS, John J.   **Reminiscences of John J. Hollis.   Wraps.**
    1913   Sandy Creek, NY   40.00
HOLLIS, John Porter   **The Early Period of Reconstruction in South Carolina.   Wraps.**
    1905   Baltimore   30.00
HOLLISTER, John J., edited by   **Chickamauga   and   Chattanooga,   On Your Own.   Wraps.**
    1981   3.00
HOLLISTER, Ovando J.   **Boldly   They   Rode: History   of   1st   Colorado Regiment of Volunteers.**
    1949   Lakewood   45.00
HOLLISTER, Ovando J.   **Colorado   Volunteers   in   New   Mexico   1862, edited by Richard Harwell.**
    1962   Chicago   35.00
HOLLOWAY, Laura C.   **Howard: The Christian Hero.**
    1885   New York   20.00
HOLLOWELL, J. M.   **War-Time   Reminiscences   and   Other   Selections. Wraps.**
    1939   Goldsboro   80.00
HOLLYDAY, Frederic B. M., edited by   **Running the Blockade: Henry Hollyday Joins the Confederacy.   Wraps.**
    (c.1947) n.p.   25.00
HOLMES, Anne Middleton   **Southern Relief Association of New York City 1866-67.   Wraps.**
    1926   New York   20.00
    1928   New York   20.00
HOLMES, Clay W.   **The Elmira Prison Camp.**
    1912   New York   225.00
HOLMES, Emma   **The Diary of Miss Emma Holmes, 1861-1866.**
    1979   Baton Rouge   35.00
HOLMES, Fred L.   **Abraham Lincoln Traveled This Way.**
    1930   Boston   15.00
HOLMES, John Haynes   **The Life and Letters of Robert Collyer 1823-1912.   2 Vols.**
    1917   New York   35.00
HOLMES, Mary J.   **Rose Mather.**
    1868   New York   15.00

HOLMES, Mead   A Soldier of the Cumberland: Memoir of _____.
Wraps.
1864   Boston   55.00
HOLMES, Oliver Wendell, Jr.   Touched with Fire, Civil War Letters and
Diary of _____ 1861-1864.
1946   Cambridge   30.00
1969   Jersey City   20.00
HOLMES, Oliver Wendell, Sr.   John Lothrop Motley A Memoir.
1879   15.00
HOLMES, Robert M.   Kemper County Rebel.   The Civil War Diary of
_____ Co. I, 24th Miss. Vols., C.S.A., edited by Frank A. Dennis.
1973   Jackson   25.00
HOLMES, T. S.   April Tragedy: The Assassination of Abraham Lincoln.
1986   Gaithersburg   25.00
HOLMES, T. S.   Horse Soldiers in Blue.
1984   28.00
HOLSTEIN, Mrs. W. H.   Three Years in Field Hospitals of the Army of
the Potomac.
1867   Philadelphia   80.00
HOLT, Joseph   An Address to the People of Kentucky.   Wraps.
1861   New York   30.00
HOLZMAN, Robert S.   Adapt or Perish.   The Life of General Roger
A. Pryor, C.S.A.
1976   New York   22.00
HOLZMAN, Robert S.   Stormy Ben Butler.
1954   New York   35.00
1976   New York   20.00
Home of the Mothers, Widows, and Daughters of Confederate Soldiers,
Charleston, S.C. Proceedings of the Fourth Anniversary.   Wraps.
1872   Charleston   15.00
Home of the Mothers, Widows, and Daughters of Confederate Soldiers,
Charleston, S.C. Proceedings of the Sixth Anniversary.   Wraps.
1874   Charleston   15.00
Home of the Mothers, Widows, and Daughters of Confederate Soldiers,
Charleston, S.C. Seventh Annual Report.   Wraps.
1875   Charleston   10.00
HONIG, Donald   Walk Like a Man.
1961   New York   15.00
Honor Roll of Confederate Veterans of Chester County from 1861-1865.
Wraps.
(c.1900) Chester, SC   50.00
HOOD, Mrs. B. H. and DOZIER, Mrs. W. S.   Records and Reminscences
of Confederate Soldiers in Terrell County (Georgia).   Wraps.
1914   Dawson, GA   250.00
HOOD, John Bell   Advance and Retreat - Personal Experiences in the
U.S. and Confederate States Armies.
1880   New Orleans, LA   175.00
1880   Philadelphia   150.00
1959   Bloomington, IN   edited by Richard N. Current   25.00
1977   35.00
1981   35.00
1985   20.00

HOOKER, Charles E.   Mississippi.   See: Confederate Military History, Vol. VII (Vol. IX, 1987 reprint ed.).

HOOLE, William Stanley   Four Years in the Confederate Navy: The Career of Captain John Low on the C.S.S. Fingal, Florida, Alabama, Tuscaloosa and Ajax.
1964   Athens   30.00

HOOLE, William Stanley, edited by   Confederate Centennial Studies
See: Confederate Centennial Studies.

HOPE, A. J. B. Beresford   A Popular View of the American Civil War. Wraps.
1861   London   25.00

HOPKIN, J. H.   Scriptural, Ecclesiastical and Historical View of Slavery.
1864   New York   50.00

HOPKINS, C. F.   The Andersonville Diary and Memoirs of Charles Hopkins.
1988   Kearny   33.00

HOPKINS, Charles A.   The March to the Sea.
1885   Providence   Ltd.   40.00

HOPKINS, Garland Evans   The First Battle of Modern Naval History.
1943   Richmond   Ltd. and signed ed.   75.00

HOPKINS, Luther W.   From Bull Run to Appomattox, A Boy's View.
1908   Baltimore   75.00
1911   n.p.   60.00
1914   Baltimore   50.00

HOPKINS, Owen J.   Under the Flag of the Nation, edited by Otto F. Bond.
1961   Columbus   15.00

HOPKINS, William P.   The Seventh Regiment, Rhode Island Volunteers.
1903   Providence   75.00

HOPLEY, Catherine Cooper   Life in the South, From the Commencement of the War . . . to August, 1862, By a Blockaded British Subject.   2 Vols.
1863   London   300.00
1971   80.00

HOPLEY, Catherine Cooper   "Stonewall" Jackson, Late General of the Confederate States Army.   A Biographical Sketch, and an Outline of His Virginian Campaigns.
1863   London   250.00
Recent reprint   15.00

HOPPER, George C.   The Battle of Groveton, or, Second Bull Run. Wraps.
1893   Detroit   35.00

HOPPIN, James Mason   Life of Andrew Hull Foote, Rear-Admiral United States Navy.
1874   New York   60.00

HOPSON, Ella Lord   Memoirs of Dr. Winthrop Hopson.
1887   Cincinnati   75.00

HORAN, James D.   Confederate Agent.
1954   New York   30.00
1960   New York   30.00

HORAN, James D.   Desperate Women.
    1952   New York   30.00
HORAN, James D.   Mathew Brady, Historian with a Camera.
    1955   New York   30.00
    1959   New York   25.00
    Recent reprint   20.00
HORAN, James D.   The Pinkertons: The Detective Dynasty That Made History.
    1969   New York   20.00
HORAN, James D.   Timothy O'Sullivan, America's Forgotten Photographer.
    1966   New York   35.00
HORGAN, Paul   Citizen of New Salem.
    1961   New York   15.00
HORN, Stanley F.   The Army of Tennessee.
    1941   Indianapolis   60.00
    1952   Norman   40.00
    1953   Norman   30.00
    1953   Indianapolis   30.00
    1955   Norman   30.00
    1987   Wilmington, NC   30.00
HORN, Stanley F.   The Battle of Stone's River.   Wraps.
    1972   Harrisburg   15.00
HORN, Stanley F.   The Boy's Life of Robert E. Lee.
    1935   New York   20.00
HORN, Stanley F.   The Decisive Battle of Nashville.
    1956   Baton Rouge   40.00
    1957   Baton Rouge   35.00
    1968   Knoxville   30.00
    1984   17.00
    1986   14.50
HORN, Stanley F.   Gallant Rebel. The Fabulous Cruise of the C.S.S. Shenandoah.
    1947   New Brunswick, NJ   30.00
HORN, Stanley F.   Invisible Empire, The Story of the Ku Klux Klan.
    1939   Boston   60.00
    1969   Cos Cob, CT   45.00
    1973   30.00
HORN, Stanley F.   The Robert E. Lee Reader.
    1949   Indianapolis   35.00
HORN, Stanley F., compiled and edited by   Tennessee's War 1861-65 Described by Participants.
    1965   Nashville   30.00
    1973   25.00
    1985   30.00
HORN, Stanley, edited by   Union Army Operations in the Southwest.
    1961   Albuquerque   45.00
HORNBECK, Betty   Upshur Brothers of the Blue and Gray.
    1967   Parsons, WV   35.00
HORNER, Dan   The Blockade-Runners: True Tales of Running the Yankee Blockade of the Confederate Coast.
    1968   New York   30.00

HORNER, Harlan H.   Lincoln and Greeley.
 1953   Urbana, IL   10.00
HORRALL, Spillard F.   History of the Forty-second Indiana Volunteer
   Infantry.
 1892   Chicago 125.00
HORROCKS, James   My Dear Parents.   The Civil War Seen by an
   English Union Soldier.
 1982   New York   20.00
HORSFORD, E. N.   The Army Ration.   Wraps.
 1864   New York   40.00
 1961   n.p.   15.00
HORST, Samuel   Mennonites in the Confederacy.
 1967   Scottdale   25.00
HORTON, Joshua H.   A History of the Eleventh Regiment (Ohio).
 1866   Dayton 175.00
HORTON, Louise   Samuel Bell Maxey: A Biography.
 1974   Austin, TX   25.00
HORTON, R. G.   The Life and Public Services of James Buchanan.
 1971   New York   25.00
HORTON, R. G.   A Youth's History of the War of 1861.
 1867   New York   20.00
HOSMER, Francis   A Glimpse of Andersonville and Other Writings.
   Wraps.
 1896   Springfield   60.00
HOSMER, G. W.   As We Went Marching On: A Story of the War.
 1885   New York   25.00
 1900   New York   25.00
HOSMER, James Kendall   The American Civil War. 2 Vols.
 1913   New York   30.00
HOSMER, James Kendall   The Appeal to Arms 1861-1863.
 1907   New York   25.00
HOSMER, James Kendall   The Color Guard: Being a Corporal's Notes
   of Military Service in the Nineteenth Army Corps.
 1864   Boston   50.00
HOSMER, James Kendall   Outcome of the Civil War 1863-1865.
 1935   New York   15.00
HOSMER, James Kendall   The Thinking Bayonet.
 1865   Boston   25.00
Hospital Transports   See: OLMSTED, Frederick Law.
HOTCHKISS, Jedediah   Make Me a Map of the Valley: The Civil War
   Journal of Jackson's Topographer, edited by Archie P. McDonald.
 1973   Dallas 35.00
 1981   35.00
 1988   12.95
HOTCHKISS, Jedediah   Virginia.   See: Confederate Military History,
   Vol. III (Vol. IV, 1987 reprint ed.).
HOTCHKISS, Jedediah and ALLEN, William   The Battle Fields of Virginia . . . Chancellorsville.
 1867   New York 1000.00
 1984   50.00

HOTZE, Henry   Three Months in the Confederate Army, edited by Richard Harwell. Wraps.
    1952   University, AL   35.00

HOUCK, Peter W.   Confederate Surgeon. The Personal Recollections of E. A. Craighill.
    1989   16.95

HOUCK, Peter W.   A Prototype of a Confederate Hospital Center in Lynchburg, Virginia.
    1986   Lynchburg   15.00

HOUGH, Alfred L.   Soldier in the West, The Civil War Letters of _____, edited by Robert G. Athearn.
    1957   Philadelphia   25.00

HOUGH, Franklin   History of Duryee's Brigade, During the Campaign in Virginia Under Gen. Pope, and in Maryland Under Gen. McClellan.
    1864   Albany Ltd.   250.00

HOUGHTON, Edwin B.   The Campaigns of the Seventeenth Maine.
    1866   Portland   155.00
    1987   30.00

HOUGHTON, William R. and **HOUGHTON,** Mitchell B.   Two Boys in the Civil War and After.
    1912   Montgomery 225.00

HOUK, Eliza P. T.   A Tribute to General Gates Phillips Thruston.
    1914   Nashville   40.00

HOUSER, M. L.   The Books that Lincoln Read. Wraps.
    1929   Peoria, IL   15.00

HOUSTON, Henry C.   The Thirty-second Maine Regiment of Infantry Volunteers.
    1903   Portland   100.00

HOVEY, Carl   Stonewall Jackson.
    1900   Boston   50.00

HOWARD, Charles Wallace   An Address: The Women of the Late War. Wraps.
    1875   Charleston   25.00

HOWARD, F. K.   Fourteen Months in American Bastiles. Wraps.
    1863   Baltimore   75.00

HOWARD, Frances Thomas   In and Out of the Lines.
    1905   New York and Washington, DC   130.00

HOWARD, James H. W.   Bond and Free.
    1886   Harrisburg   35.00

HOWARD, McHenry   Recollections of a Maryland Confederate Soldier and Staff Officer Under Johnston, Jackson, and Lee.
    1914   Baltimore   225.00
    1975   Dayton edited by J. I. Robertson 20.00

HOWARD, Oliver Otis   Autobiography. 2 Vols.
    1907   New York   200.00
    1908   175.00

HOWARD, Oliver Otis   Fighting for Humanity.
    1898   London   30.00

HOWARD, Oliver Otis   General Taylor.
    1892   New York   Trade ed.   30.00
    L.P. ed., Ltd.   75.00

HOWARD, Oliver Otis   Who Burnt Columbia? . . .   See: Who Burnt Columbia? . . .

HOWARD, Philip E.   The Life Story of Henry Clay Trumbull.
1905   Philadelphia   25.00

HOWARD, Richard L.   History of the 124th Regiment Illinois Infantry Volunteers.
1880   Springfield   175.00

HOWARD, Robert M.   Reminiscences.
1912   Columbus, GA   80.00

HOWARD, Samuel M.   The Illustrated Comprehensive History of the Great Battle of Shiloh.
1931   Gettysburg and Kansas City   150.00

HOWARD, Wiley C.   Sketch of Cobb Legion Cavalry and Some Incidents and Scenes Remembered.
(c.1949) Marietta, GA   15.00
1901   25.00

HOWARD, William F.   The Gettysburg Death Roster, The Federal Dead at Gettysburg.
1990   Dayton   22.50

HOWBERT, Abraham R.   Reminiscences of the War.
1888   Springfield   45.00

HOWE, Daniel Wait   Civil War Times 1861-1865.
1902   Indianapolis   50.00

HOWE, Daniel Wait   Political History of Secession.
1914   New York   25.00

HOWE, Henry   The Times of the Rebellion in the West, A Collection of Miscellanies, Showing the Part Taken in the War by Each Western State. . . .
1867   Cincinnati   110.00

HOWE, Henry Warren   Passages from the Life of _____ Consisting of Diary and Letters Written During the Civil War 1861-1865.
1899   Lowell   80.00

HOWE, Mark DeWolfe   Justice Oliver Wendell Holmes, The Shaping Years, 1841-1870.
1957   Cambridge   35.00

HOWE, Thomas H.   Adventures of an Escaped Union Prisoner from Andersonville. Wraps.
1886   San Francisco   60.00

HOWE, Thomas J.   Wasted Valor, The Petersburg Campaign June 15-18, 1864.
1988   16.95

HOWE, W. W.   Kinston, Whitehall and Goldsboro Expedition.
1890   New York   150.00

HOWELL, Edgar M.   United States Army Headgear, 1855-1902.
1980   Washington, DC   22.50
1975   Wraps   13.00

HOWELL, H. Grady, Jr.   Going to Meet the Yankees, a History of the "Bloody Sixth" Mississippi Infantry, C.S.A.
1981   Jackson   50.00

HOWELL, Helena A.   Chronicles of the One Hundred Fifty-first Regiment New York State Volunteer Infantry.
1911   Albion   85.00

HOWELLS, W. D.   Life of Abraham Lincoln.
1960   Bloomington, IN   10.00
HOWLAND, Edward   Grant as a Soldier and Statesman.
1868   Hartford   15.00
HOY, P. C.   A Brief History of Bradford's Battery, Confederate Guards Artillery.
(1932)   (Pontotoc, MS)   150.00
HOYT, Edward Jonathon   Buckskin Joe, Memoirs of.
1966   10.00
HUBBARD, Charles Eustis   The Campaign of the Forty-fifth Regiment Massachusetts Volunteer Militia "The Cadet Regiment."
1882   Boston   75.00
HUBBARD, John Milton   Notes of a Private.
1909   Memphis   100.00
1911   St. Louis   75.00
1913   St. Louis   60.00
1973   n.p.   25.00
HUBBELL, Raynor   Confederate Stamps, Old Letters and History.
n.d.   n.p.   55.00
HUBERT, Charles F.   History of the 50th Regiment Illinois Volunteer Infantry in War of the Union.
1894   Kansas City   275.00
HUBNER, Charles W., edited by   War Poets of the South and Confederate Camp-Fire Songs.
n.d.   (Atlanta)   85.00
HUDDLESTON, Ed   The Civil War in Middle Tennessee.
1965   Nashville   30.00
HUDSON, E. M.   The Second War of Independence in America.   Wraps.
1863   London   50.00
HUDSON, Henry N.   A Chaplain's Campaign with General Butler. Wraps.
1865   New York   30.00
HUDSON, Joshua Hilary   Sketches and Reminiscences.
1903   Columbia   75.00
HUDSON, T.   Soldier Boys in Gray: A History of the 59th Georgia Volunteer Infantry Regiment. 5 issues.   Wraps.
1979-84   Atlanta   45.00
HUEBNER, Henry Richard   Civil War Artillery Manual.   Wraps.
1962   Indianapolis   25.00
HUEY, Pennock   A True History of the Charge of the Eighth Pennsylvania Cavalry at Chancellorsville.
1883   Philadelphia   100.00
1885   Philadelphia   80.00
1888   Philadelphia   70.00
HUFF, Sarah   My 80 Years in Atlanta.   Wraps.
1937   Atlanta   75.00
HUFFMAN, James   Ups and Downs of a Confederate Soldier.
1940   New York   50.00
HUGHES, N. Collin   Hendersonville in Civil War Times   1860-1865. Wraps.
1936   Hendersonville, NC   65.00

HUGHES, Nathaniel Cheairs, Jr.   **General William J. Hardee, Old Reliable.**
    1965   Baton Rouge   40.00
    1987   Wilmington, NC 30.00
HUGHES, Robert M.   **General Johnston.**
    For additional information, see Appendix: Great Commanders Series.
    1893   New York   Trade ed.   40.00
    1883   New York   Ltd.   125.00
HUGHES, W. J.   **Rebellious Ranger, Rip Ford and The Old Southwest. Wraps.**
    1964   Norman   80.00
HUIDEKOPER, Henry S.   **Orations by General _____ at the Reunion of the Survivors of the 150th Regiment Pa. Vols. (Bucktails) at Gettysburg. Wraps.**
    1894   n.p.   35.00
HUIDEKOPER, Henry S.   **A Short Story of the First Day's Fight at Gettysburg. (Reprinted after revision.) Wraps.**
    1906   Philadelphia   45.00
HULBERT, S. B.   **One Battle Too Many. . . .**
    1987   Alexandria   28.50
HULL, Augustus   **The Campaigns of the Confederate Army.**
    1901   Atlanta   140.00
HULL, Edward A.   **The Burnside Breech Loading Carbines.**
    1986   Lincoln, RI   16.00
HULL, Susan R.   **Boy Soldiers of the Confederacy.**
    1905   New York   150.00
HUME, Edgar Erskine   **Colonel Heros Von Borcke. Wraps.**
    1935   Charlottesville, VA   30.00
HUME, Edgar Erskine   **Colonel Theodore O'Hara, Author of the Bivouac of the Dead. Wraps.**
    1936   Charlottesville   20.00
HUMES, Thomas William   **The Loyal Mountaineers of Tennessee.**
    1888   Knoxville   100.00
HUMPHREY, Willis   **The Great Contest: A History of Military and Naval Operations. . . .**
    1886   Detroit   40.00
HUMPHREYS, Andrew A.   **From Gettysburg to the Rapidan   The Army of the Potomac July 1863 to April 1864.**
    1883   New York   75.00
    1987   Baltimore   17.50
HUMPHREYS, Andrew A.   **The Virginia Campaign of 1864 and 1865.**
    See: **Campaigns of the Civil War.**
HUMPHREYS, Charles A.   **Field, Camp, Hospital and Prison in the Civil War 1863-1865.**
    1918   Boston   50.00
    1971   Freeport, NY   30.00
HUMPHREYS, David   **Heroes and Spies of the Civil War.**
    1903   New York   100.00
HUMPHREYS, Henry H.   **Andrew Atkinson Humphreys; A Biography.**
    1924   Philadelphia   75.00
    1988   35.00

HUMPHREYS, Henry S., edited by   Songs of the Confederacy, Civil
War Song-Anthology.   Wraps.
   1961   20.00
   1966   Cincinnati   20.00
HUMPHREYS, M. W.   Capt. Thomas A. Bryan, Bryan's Battery, 13th
Battalion Virginia Artillery, C.S.A., 1862-65.   Wraps.
   (c.1910)   350.00
HUNDLEY, Daniel R.   Prison Echoes of the Great Rebellion.
   1874   New York   450.00
HUNDLEY, Daniel R.   Social Relations in Our Southern States.
   1979 (reprint)   Baton Rouge   28.00
HUNGERFORD, Edward   The Story of the Baltimore & Ohio Railroad
1827-1927. 2 Vols.
   1928   New York   125.00
HUNNICUTT, John L.   Reconstruction in West Alabama, The Memoirs
of _____.   See: Confederate Centennial Studies, No. 11.
HUNT, Aurora   The Army of the Pacific.
   1951   Glendale   100.00
HUNT, Aurora   Major General James H. Carleton.
   1958   Glendale   60.00
HUNT, Cornelius R.   The Shenandoah: or The Last Confederate
Cruiser.
   1867   New York   90.00
HUNT, Gaillard, edited by   Israel, Elihu and Cadwallader Washburn:
A Chapter in American Biography.
   1925   New York   30.00
HUNT, Grace Lea   Some Old Southern Letters.   Wraps.
   1924   n.p.   30.00
HUNT, H. Draper   Hannibal Hamlin of Maine.   Lincoln's First Vice
President.
   1969   Syracuse   30.00
HUNTER, A. F.   A Year on a Monitor and the Destruction of Fort
Sumter.
   1987   Columbia   21.95
HUNTER, Alexander   Johnny Reb and Billy Yank.
   1905   New York   275.00
HUNTER, Alexander   The Women of the Debatable Land.
   1912   Washington, DC   150.00
HUNTER, Alfred G.   History of the Eighty-second Indiana Volunteer
Infantry.
   1893   Indianapolis   125.00
HUNTER, David   Report of the Military Services of _____ During
the War of the Rebellion.   Wraps.
   1892   New York   35.00
HUNTER, John Warren   A Story of the Civil War Period.   Heel-Fly
Time in Texas.   Wraps.
   (191-)   Bandera, TX   750.00
   1931   Bandera, TX   75.00
HUNTER, Martha T.   A Memoir of Robert M. T. Hunter.
   1903   Washington, DC   80.00
HUNTER, Robert   Sketches of War History 1861-1865, Vol. II.
   1888   OH   50.00

HUNTER, Robert M. T.   Correspondence of R. M. T. Hunter, edited by
Charles H. Ambler In: Annual Report of the American Historical Association 1916 Vol. II.
1918   Washington, DC   40.00
1971   20.00
HUNTINGTON, James Freeman   The   Battle   of   Chancellorsville.
Wraps.
1897   n.p.   40.00
HUNTLEY, Elizabeth Valentine   Peninsula Pilgrimage.
1941   Richmond   35.00
1974   25.00
HUNTON, Eppa   Autobiography of Eppa Hunton.
1933   Richmond   Ltd.   4000.00
4500.00 in dust jacket. Dust jacket is plain cream-colored wrapper.
HURLBERT, William Henry   Gen. McClellan and the Conduct of the
War.
1864   New York   40.00
HURLBURT, J. S.   History of the Rebellion in Bradley County, East
Tennessee.
1866   Indianapolis 110.00
HURN, Ethel Alice   Wisconsin Women in the War Between the States.
1911   Madison   40.00
Hurrah for the Texans: Civil War Letters of George W. Ingram. (Ingram,
George W.)   Wraps.
1974   College Station, TX   75.00
HURST, M. B.   History of the 14th Alabama Volunteers.   Wraps.
1982   University, AL   8.00
HURST, Samuel H.   Journal-History of the Seventy-third Ohio Volunteer Infantry.
1866   Chillicothe   160.00
HUSE, Caleb   The Supplies for the Confederate Army.   Wraps.
1904   Boston   100.00
1907   Houston   75.00
1976   Dayton   5.00
HUSSEY, George A. and TODD, William   History of the Ninth Regiment
NYSM, NGSNY (Eighty-third N. Y. Volunteers).
1889   New York   125.00
HUTCHENS, Jane   John Brown's Cousin.
1940   New York   5.00
HUTCHINS, E. R., edited by   The War of the Sixties.
1912   New York   160.00
HUTCHINS, James S.   Horse Equipment and Cavalry Accoutrements.
Ordnance Memoranda No. 29.
1984   15.00
HUTCHINSON, John G.   Roster Fourth Regiment New Hampshire Volunteers.
1896   Manchester   60.00
HUTCHINSON, Nelson V.   History of the Seventh Massachusetts Volunteer Infantry in the War of the Rebellion.
1890   Taunton 200.00
HUTCHINSON, W. T.   Cyrus Hall McCormick. 2 Vols.
1930-35   Ltd. 1025 copies   45.00

HUTCHINSON, William F.　　　The Bay Fight　A Sketch of the Battle of
　　Mobile Bay.　Wraps.
　　1879　　Providence　Ltd.　　35.00
HUTTON, P. A.　　　Phil Sheridan and His Army.
　　1985　　35.00
　　1985　　Wraps　15.00
HUYETTE, Miles Clayton　　　The Maryland Campaign and the Battle of
　　Antietam.
　　1915　　Buffalo　80.00
HUYETTE, Miles Clayton　　　Reminiscences of a Soldier in the Ameri-
　　can Civil War.　Wraps.
　　1908　　60.00
HYDE, Solon　　　A Captive of War.
　　1900　　New York　　65.00
HYDE, Thomas W.　　　Following the Greek Cross.
　　1894　　Boston　　60.00
　　1988　　25.00
HYDE, William L.　　　History of the 112th Regt. N.Y. Vols.
　　1866　　Fredonia, NY　　125.00
HYLTON, J. D.　　　The Bride of Gettysburg,　An Episode of 1863.
　　1878　　Palmyra, NJ　30.00
HYMAN, Harold M.　　　Era of the Oath.
　　1954　　Philadelphia　10.00
　　1978　　20.00
HYMAN, Harold M.　　　A More Perfect Union,　the Impact of the Civil
　　War and Reconstruction on the Constitution.
　　1973　　New York　　15.00
HYMAN, Harold M., edited by　　　Heard Around the World　The Impact
　　Abroad of the Civil War.
　　1969　　New York　　30.00
HYMAN, Harold M., edited by　　　New Frontiers of the American Recon-
　　struction.
　　1966　　Urbana, IL　　25.00
HYNDMAN, William　　　History of a Cavalry Company, a Complete Record
　　of Company A, 4th Penna Cavalry.
　　1872　　Philadelphia　　140.00
ICKIS, Alonzo Ferdinand　　　Bloody Trails Along the Rio Grand:　The
　　Diary of _____, edited by Nolie Mumey.
　　1958　　Denver　Ltd.　　110.00
Illinois at Vicksburg.
　　1907　　Chicago　50.00
Illinois Commandery.　Memorials of Deceased Companions May 8th, 1879-
　　Dec. 31st, 1922.　3 Vols.
　　n.d.　　n.p. 115.00
Illinois Military Units in the Civil War.　Wraps.
　　1962　　Springfield　20.00
Illustrated Catalogue of Arms and Military Goods: Regulations for the Uni-
　　form of the Army, Navy, Marine and Revenue Corps of the United
　　States.　Wraps.
　　1864　　New York　80.00
　　1961　　45.00

Illustrated Catalogue of the A. E. Brooks's Collection of Antique Guns, Pistols, Etc. of Hartford, Conn. . . . Guns Used in Both Armies During the Civil War. . . . Wraps.
   1899   CT   100.00
Illustrated Guide to Richmond, the Confederate Capital, Together with a Facsimile Reprint of the City Intelligencer of 1862. Wraps.
   1960   Richmond   15.00
Illustrated Life, Services, Martyrdom, and Funeral of Abraham Lincoln.
   1865   Philadelphia   30.00
Illustrated London News. Jan. 1861 - Dec. 1866. 5 Vols.
   Bound   1500.00
   Unbound   1700.00
IMHOLTE, John Q.   The First Minnesota Volunteers.
   1963   Minneapolis   25.00
   1969   Minneapolis   20.00
The Immortal Autograph Letters, Documents, Manuscripts, Portraits, Personal Relics and Other Lincolniana.
   1952   New York   50.00
In Memoriam. Abner Doubleday 1819-1893 and John Cleveland Robinson 1817-1897.
   1918   Albany   45.00
In Memoriam, Alexander Stewart Webb, 1835-1911 (Webb and His Brigade at the Angle).
   1916   Albany   70.00
In Memoriam: Charles Ewing By His Youngest Corporal.
   1888   Philadelphia   50.00
In Memoriam. George Sears Greene, Brevet Major-General United States Volunteers 1801-1899.
   1909   Albany   40.00
In Memoriam. Major-General Winfield Scott Hancock, United States Army.
   n.d.   n.p.   30.00
In Memoriam. William T. Sherman Proceedings of the Senate and Assembly of the State of N. Y.
   1892   Albany   20.00
Inauguration of the Jackson Statue. Address of Gov. Kemper and . . . Rev. Hoge . . . Oct. 26, 1875. Wraps.
   1875   Richmond   25.00
Indicents in the Life of William A. Moffitt A Memorial. Wraps.
   (c.1920) n.p.   75.00
Incidents of Life in a Southern City During the War. A Series of Sketches Written for the Rutland Herald by a Vermont Gentleman. . . . Wraps.
   (1880's) (Rutland, VT)   500.00
Indiana at Antietam, Report of the Indiana Antietam Monument Commission and Ceremonies at the Dedication of the Monument.
   1911   Indianapolis   40.00
Indiana at Chickamauga 1863-1900 Report of the Indiana Commissioners Chickamauga National Military Park.
   1900   Indianapolis   25.00
Indiana at Vicksburg.
   1911   Indianapolis   30.00

INGERSOLL, Charles   A Letter to a Friend in a Slave State by a Citizen of Pennsylvania. Wraps.
    1862   Philadelphia   60.00
INGERSOLL, Charles   An Undelivered Speech on Executive Arrests. Wraps.
    1862   Philadelphia   25.00
INGERSOLL, Lurton Dunham   A History of the War Department of the United States.
    1879   Washington, DC   75.00
    1880   75.00
INGERSOLL, Lurton Dunham   Iowa and the Rebellion.
    1866   Philadelphia   70.00
INGHAM, William H.   Iowa Northern Border Brigade, Annals of Iowa, Vol. V. No. 7. Wraps.
    1902   Des Moines   50.00
INGLESBY, Charles   Historical Sketch of the First Regiment of South Carolina Artillery. Wraps.
    n.d.   Charleston   200.00
INGRAHAM, Charles A.   Elmer E. Ellsworth and the Zouaves of '61. Wraps.
    1925   Chicago   35.00
INGRAHAM, Prentiss   The Two Flags; or, Love for the Blue, Duty for the Gray.
    1897   New York   50.00
Instruction for Field Artillery.
    1863   New York   150.00
    1968   New York   30.00
Instruction for Heavy Artillery.
    1863   New York   150.00
Instructions for Making Muster Rolls, Mustering into Service, Periodical Payments, and Discharging from Service Volunteers or Militia.
    1863   50.00
Instructions for Making Quarterly Returns of the Ordnance Stores as Prescribed by the Gen Regs of the Army. . . .
    1863   60.00
Instructions for Officers and Non-Commissioned Officers on Outpost and Patrol Duty. Wraps.
    1862   Washington, DC   50.00
IOBST, Richard W., et al   The Bloody Sixth   The Sixth N. C. Regt. C.S.A. Wraps.
    1965   Raleigh   50.00
    1987   35.00
Iowa Commissioners' Report to Locate the Position of Iowa Troops in the Siege of Vicksburg. Wraps.
    1902   Des Moines   35.00
IRBY, Richard   The Captain Remembers: The Papers of Captain Richard Irby, edited by V. F. Jordan. Wraps.
    1975   n.p.   20.00
IRBY, Richard   Historical Sketches of the Nottoway Grays. Usually lacks frontis and illustrations.
    1878   Richmond   175.00
    1983   19.00

IRWIN, Richard B.   History of the Nineteenth Army Corps.
    1892   New York   125.00
    1893   New York   100.00
    1987   35.00
ISHAM, A. Chapman   Autobiography of Asa Brainerd Isham, M.D. 1844-
1912. Wraps.
    1957   MI   30.00
ISHAM, Asa B.   Experience in Rebel Prisons.
    1890   Cincinnati   75.00
ISHAM, Asa B.   An Historical Sketch of the Seventh Regiment Michigan Volunteer Cavalry.
    1893   New York   175.00
ISHAM, Asa B., DAVIDSON, Henry M., and FURNESS, Henry B. Prisoners of War and Military Prisons.
    1890   Cincinnati   200.00
IZLAR, William Valmore   A Sketch of the War Record of the Edisto Rifles 1861-1865. This title is usually quite stained, probably due to a mishap in storage after printing.
    1914   Columbia   125.00
JACKMAN, Lyman   History of the Sixth New Hampshire Reg. in the War for the Union, by Capt._____, and edited by Amos Hadley.
    1891   Concord   165.00
JACKSON, Alto Loftin, edited by   So Mourns the Dove, Letters of a Confederate Infantryman.
    1965   New York   30.00
JACKSON, B.   A Course of Military Surveying; Including Instructions for Sketching in the Field, Plan Drawing, Levelling, Military Reconnaisance, etc. . . .
    1838   London   135.00
JACKSON, Donald   Custer's Gold: The United States Cavalry Expedition of 1874. Wraps.
    1966   5.00
JACKSON, Edgar Allan, BRYANT, James F., and WILLS, Irvin C.   Three Rebels Write Home.
    1955   Franklin, VA   40.00
JACKSON, Harry F. and O'DONNELL, Thomas F., edited by   Herman Clark and His Letters.
    1965   Syracuse   15.00
JACKSON, Henry R.   Letter from _____ of Georgia to Ex-Senator Allen G. Thurman. Wraps.
    1887   Atlanta   25.00
JACKSON, Horatio Nelson   Dedication of the Statue to Brevet Major-General William Wells. etc.
    1914   np.   40.00
JACKSON, Isaac   Some of the Boys . . . Civil War Letters of _____, edited by Joseph O. Jackson.
    1960   Carbondale   40.00
JACKSON, John Collins   Grant's Strategy and Other Addresses.
    1910   Ohio   20.00
JACKSON, Mary Anna   Julia Jackson Christian.
    1910   Charlotte, NC   50.00

JACKSON, Mary Anna   Life and Letters of General Thomas J. Jackson by His Wife.
    1892   New York   125.00
    1895   Louisville   Enlarged ed. entitled **Memoirs of Stonewall Jackson** 175.00
    1976   Dayton 50.00
JACKSON, Oscar Lawrence   The Colonel's Diary: Journals Kept Before and During the Civil War.
    1922   Sharon, PA   175.00
JACKSON, Samuel M.   Diary of General _____ for the Year 1862. Wraps.
    1925   Apollo   70.00
JACOBS, Michael   Notes on the Rebel Invasion of Maryland and Pennsylvania and the Battle of Gettysburg.
    1864   Philadelphia   50.00
    1884   Gettysburg Wraps 40.00
    1909   Gettysburg Wraps 25.00
JACOBS, Thornwell   When For the Truth.
    1950   Charleston   15.00
JAFFA, Harry V.   Crisis of the House Divided: An Interpretation of the Issues in the Lincoln-Douglas Debates.
    1959   New York   10.00
    1982   10.00
JAGO, Federick West   The Twelfth New Jersey Volunteers 1862-1865.
    1967   Gloucester   20.00
    1976   Wraps 4.00
JAHNS, Patricia   Matthew Fontaine Maury and Joseph Henry: Scientists of the Civil War.
    1961   New York   30.00
James Conner. In Memoriam.
    1883   Charleston   200.00
The James E. Taylor Sketchbook: With Sheridan Up the Shenandoah Valley in 1864.
    1989   85.00
JAMES, Bushrod Washington   Echoes of Battle.
    1895   Philadelphia   30.00
JAMES, Frederick Augustus   Civil War Diary, edited by Jefferson Hammer.
    1973   Rutherford   25.00
JAMES, Henry B.   Memories of the Civil War.
    1898   New Bedford   60.00
JAMES, Marquis   The Raven. The Life Story of Sam Houston.
    1929   New York   20.00
JAMES, Martha Elizabeth McArthur   A Mixed Up Family. Wraps.
    1955   Clinton, NC   60.00
JAMES, Powhatan W.   George W. Truett, a Biography.
    1939   New York   50.00
JAMISON, Matthew H.   Recollections of Pioneer and Army Life.
    1911   135.00
JARRELL, Hampton M.   Wade Hampton and the Negro.
    1949   Columbia, SC   50.00

Jefferson Davis and "Stonewall" Jackson.
  1866   Philadelphia   50.00
  1885   Philadelphia   35.00
JEFFREY, William H.   Richmond Prisons, 1861-1862.
  1893   St. Johnsbury, VT   60.00
JEFFRIES, Charlie C.   Terry's Rangers.
  1961   New York   35.00
JENKINS, Brian   Fenians and Anglo-American Relations During Reconstruction.
  1969   London   20.00
JENKINS, Paul B.   The Battle of Westport.
  1906   Kansas City   60.00
JENKINS, William Sumner   Pro-Slavery Thought in the Old South.
  1960   10.00
JENNINGS, Janet   The Blue and the Gray.
  1910   Madison, WI   25.00
JENNINGS, N. A.   A Texas Ranger.
  1959   Austin, TX   Boxed   40.00
JENNISON, Keith W.   The Humorous Mr. Lincoln.
  1965   New York   10.00
JENSEN, Oliver, edited by   Bruce Catton's America.
  1979   25.00
JEROME, Edward S.   Edwin McMasters Stanton: The Great War Secretary. Wraps.
  1909   n.p.   10.00
JERVEY, Theodore D.   Charleston During the Civil War.   Wraps.
  1915   Washington, DC   30.00
JERVEY, Theodore D.   The Elder Brother.
  1905   New York   40.00
JERVEY, Theodore D.   The Railroad the Conquerer.   Wraps.
  1913   Columbia, SC   45.00
JERVEY, Theodore D.   The Slave Trade.
  1925   Columbia, SC   50.00
JEWELL, Jacob   Heroic Deeds of Noble Master Masons During the Civil
  War.
  1916   CO   30.00
JEWETT, Albert Henry Clay   A Boy Goes to War.
  1944   Bloomington   30.00
JILLSON, Willard Rouse   Lincoln Back Home.
  1932   Lexington   15.00
JIMERSON, Randall C.   The Private Civil War: Popular Thought During the Sectional Conflict.
  1988   Baton Rouge   24.95
JOEL, Joseph A. and STEGMAN, Lewis R.   Rifle   Shots   and   Bugle
  Notes.
  1884   New York   30.00
JOHANNSEN, Robert W.   Stephen A. Douglas.
  1973   New York   20.00
JOHANNSEN, Robert W.   The Lincoln-Douglas Debates.   Wraps.
  1965   9.00

JOHANNSEN, Robert W.   To The Halls of the Montezumas. The Mexican War.
   1985   30.00
JOHN, Evan   Atlantic Impact 1861.
   1952   Kingswood, England   25.00
   1952   New York   20.00
JOHNS, George S.   Philip Henson, The Southern Union Spy. Wraps.
   1887   St. Louis   80.00
JOHNS, Henry T.   Life with the Forty-ninth Massachusetts Volunteers.
   1864   Pittsfield   60.00
   1890   Washington, DC   60.00
JOHNS, Jane Martin   Personal Recollections of Early Decatur, Abraham
Lincoln, Richard J. Oglesby.
   1912   Decatur   30.00
JOHNS, John E.   Florida During the Civil War.
   1963   Gainesville   35.00
   1989   22.50
JOHNSON, Adam Rankin   The Partisan Rangers of the Confederate
States Army, edited by William J. Davis.
   1904   Louisville   300.00
   1979   25.00
JOHNSON, Allen   Stephen A. Douglas. A Study in American Politics.
   1908   20.00
   1970   55.00
JOHNSON, Andrew   The Papers of _____, edited by Leroy Graf and
Ralph W. Haskins. 3 Vols.
   1967   Knoxville, TN   50.00
JOHNSON, Ben C.   A Soldier's Life: The Civil War Experiences of
_____, Originally Entitled "Sketches of the Sixth Regiment Michigan
Infantry," edited by Alan S. Brown. Wraps.
   1962   Kalamazoo   15.00
JOHNSON, Bradley T.   Address of Gen'l Bradley T. Johnson Before
the Association of Confederate Soldiers and Sailors of Maryland, June
10, 1874.
   1874   Baltimore   40.00
JOHNSON, Bradley T.   An Address Delivered at the Dedication of the
Confederate Memorial Hall, Richmond, Va., February 22, 1896. Wraps.
   1896   Richmond   75.00
JOHNSON, Bradley T.   Maryland. See: Confederate Military History,
Vol. II.
JOHNSON, Bradley T.   The First Maryland Campaign, An Address . . .
4th Annual Re-Union of the Assoc. of the Maryland Line. Wraps.
   1886   Baltimore   50.00
JOHNSON, Bradley T.   The Maryland Confederates. An Address . . .
before the Confederate Society of St. Mary's at Leonardtown. March,
1894. Wraps.
   (1894)   Baltimore   50.00
JOHNSON, Bradley T., edited by   A Memoir of the Life and Public Service of Joseph E. Johnston.
   1891   Baltimore   75.00
   1894   Baltimore   60.00

JOHNSON, Byron Berkeley   Abraham Lincoln and Boston Corbett with Personal Recollections of Each.
1914   Waltham, MA   25.00
JOHNSON, Charles Beneulyn   Muskets and Medicine.
1917   Philadelphia 150.00
JOHNSON, Charles F.   The Long Roll.
1911   New York Ltd.   130.00
1986   30.00
JOHNSON, Clifton   Battleground Adventures.
1915   Boston and New York   25.00
JOHNSON, Fletcher   Life of William Tecumseh Sherman.
1891   Edgewood   17.50
JOHNSON, George Kinney   The Battle of Kernstown, March 23, 1862. Wraps.
1890   Detroit   35.00
JOHNSON, Gerald W.   The Secession of the Southern States.
1933   New York   30.00
JOHNSON, Gerald W.   The Undefeated.
1927   New York   15.00
JOHNSON, Guion   Ante-Bellum North Carolina: A Social History.
1937   Chapel Hill   75.00
JOHNSON, H. L., compiled by   Souvenir Roster, 1895, of the 371 Living Members of the Sixteenth Regiment New Hampshire Volunteers.
1895   Washington, DC   35.00
JOHNSON, Hannibal A.   The Sword of Honor.   Wraps.
1903   Providence   Ltd.   30.00
1906   Worcester   30.00
1906   Hallowell   30.00
JOHNSON, James Ralph and BILL, Alfred Hoyt   Horsemen Blue and Gray: a Pictorial History.
1960   New York   20.00
JOHNSON, John   The Defense of Charleston Harbor.
1890   Charleston, SC   175.00
1970   Freeport   40.00
JOHNSON, John   Fort Sumter.   Wraps.
1899   Charleston, SC   25.00
JOHNSON, John Lipscomb   Autobiographical Notes.
1958   n.p.   Ltd.   75.00
JOHNSON, John Lipscomb   The University Memorial Biographical Sketches of Alumni of the University of Virginia Who Fell in the Confederate War.
1871   Baltimore   5 Vols. in 1   65.00
JOHNSON, L.   Contraband Trade During the Last Year of the Civil War.   Wraps.
1963   Lincoln   10.00
JOHNSON, Lewis Warren   First Independent Battery, Ohio Light Artillery, The Thornless Rose.
1910   n.p.   75.00
JOHNSON, Ludwell H.   Red River Campaign.
1958   Baltimore   40.00
1986   25.00

JOHNSON, Reverdy   A Reply to the Recent Speech of Sir Roundell
   Palmer on the Washington Treaty, and the Alabama Claims. Wraps.
   1871   Baltimore   50.00
JOHNSON, Richard W.   Memoir of Maj. Gen. George H. Thomas.
   1881   Philadelphia   75.00
JOHNSON, Richard W.   A Soldier's Reminiscences in Peace and War.
   1886   Philadelphia   75.00
   1961   Chapel Hill, NC   25.00
JOHNSON, Robert Erwin   Rear Admiral John Rodgers 1812-1882.
   1967   Annapolis   30.00
JOHNSON, Robert U.   Remembered Yesterdays.
   1923   Boston   40.00
JOHNSON, Robert U. and BUEL, C. C., edited by   Battles and Leaders
   of the Civil War . . . Being for the Most Part Contributions by Union
   and Confederate Officers. 4 Vols.
   1884-88   New York   200.00
   1887   New York   Vols. 1-4 in 32 parts. Wraps   125.00
   Recent reprint   50.00
   1887-88   4 Vols.   175.00
   1894   New York   Century War Book People's Pictorial edition
               Wraps   20 parts   150.00
   1956   New York   4 Vols.   Boxed   100.00
   1956   New York   Bound in full morocco   200.00
   1956   New York   edited by Ned Bradford   1 Vol. condensed edition
               20.00
JOHNSON, Rossiter   Campfire and Battle-field   An Illustrated History
   of the Campaigns and Conflicts of the Great Civil War.
   1894   Boston   100.00
   1894   New York   100.00
   1896   New York   100.00
   1960   New York   30.00
JOHNSON, Rossiter   The Fight for the Republic.
   1917   New York   35.00
JOHNSON, Rossiter   A Short History of the War of Secession.
   1888   Boston   30.00
   1910   New York   20.00
JOHNSON, Sidney Smith   Texans Who Wore the Gray. Vol. I (all
   pub).
   1907   Tyler   300.00
JOHNSON, Thomas Cary   The Life and Letters of Benjamin Morgan
   Palmer.
   1903   Richmond   60.00
   1906   Richmond   45.00
JOHNSON, Thomas Cary   The Life and Letters of Robert Lewis
   Dabney.
   1903   Richmond   50.00
JOHNSON, Virginia Weisel   The Unregimented General   A Biography
   of Nelson A. Miles.
   1962   Boston   30.00
JOHNSON, W. Fletcher   Life of William Tecumseh Sherman.
   1891   Philadelphia   25.00

JOHNSON, William J.   **Abraham Lincoln, the Christian.**
1913   New York   15.00
JOHNSON, Zachary T.   **The Political Policies of Howell Cobb.**
1929   Nashville   25.00
JOHNSTON, Adam S.   **The Soldier Boy's Diary Book.**
1867   Pittsburgh   75.00
JOHNSTON, Albert S.   **Captain Beirne Chapman and Chapman's Battery. An Historical Sketch.** Wraps.
1903   Union, WV   375.00
JOHNSTON, Angus James   **Virginia Railroads in the Civil War.**
1961   Chapel Hill, NC   35.00
JOHNSTON, David E.   **A History of the Middle New River Settlements and Contiguous Territory.**
1906   Huntington, WV   125.00
JOHNSTON, David E.   **The Story of a Confederate Boy in the Civil War.**
1914   Portland   100.00
1980   20.00
JOHNSTON, Gertrude K.   **Dear Pa - And So It Goes.**
1971   Harrisburg   25.00
JOHNSTON, Isaac N.   **Four Months in Libby and the Campaign Against Atlanta.** Wraps.
1864   Cincinnati   150.00
1893   Cincinnati   125.00
JOHNSTON, J. Ambler, compiled by   **The Civil War, 1861-1865, in Arkansas and Missouri.** Wraps.
1967   Richmond   40.00
1968   Virginia State Penitentiary Wraps 40.00
JOHNSTON, J. Ambler   **Echoes of 1861-1961.**
1970   Richmond   60.00
1971   Milwaukee Wraps 45.00
JOHNSTON, J. Stoddard   **Kentucky.** See: **Confederate Military History,** Vol. IX (Vol. XI, 1988 reprint ed.).
JOHNSTON, J. W.   **The True Story of "Jennie" Wade, a Gettysburg Maid.**
1917   Rochester   100.00
JOHNSTON, Joseph E.   **Narrative of Military Operations, Directed During the Late War.**
1874   New York   125.00
1959   Bloomington   50.00
1969   New York   40.00
1981   50.00
JOHNSTON, Mary   **Cease Firing.**
1912   Boston   20.00
1912   Boston Ltd. signed edition 50.00
JOHNSTON, Mary   **The Long Roll.**
1911   Boston and New York   30.00
1911   Boston Ltd. signed edition 60.00
JOHNSTON, Mary   **To Have and to Hold.**
1900   Boston   25.00

JOHNSTON, Mary and **LIPSCOMB**, Elizabeth Johnston **Amelia Gayle Gorgas A Biography.**
    1978   University, AL   15.00

JOHNSTON, Richard Malcolm   **Autobiography.**
    1900   Washington, DC   40.00

JOHNSTON, Richard Malcolm and **BROWNE**, William H.   **Life of Alexander H. Stephens.**
    1878   Philadelphia   50.00

JOHNSTON, Robert M.   **Bull-Run, Its Strategy and Tactics.**
    1913   Boston   75.00

JOHNSTON, William Preston   **The Life of Gen. Albert Sidney Johnston.**
    1878   New York   125.00
    1879   New York   100.00

JOHNSTONE, H. W.   **Truth of the War Conspiracy of 1861.**   Wraps.
    1921   Curryville, GA   25.00

JOHNSTONE, W. J.   **Robert E. Lee the Christian.**
    1933   New York   45.00

JOINVILLE, Prince Francois F. P. L. M. de   **Album of Paintings by the Prince de Joinville 1861-1862.**
    1964   New York   In slipcase   35.00

JOINVILLE, Prince Francois F. P. L. M. de   **The Army of the Potomac.** Wraps.
    1862   New York   35.00

JOINVILLE, Prince Francois F. P. L. M. de   **Campagne de L'Armee Du Potomac.** Wraps.
    1862   New York   35.00

JOLLY, Ellen Ryan   **Nuns of the Battlefield.**
    1927   Providence   35.00

JOMINI, Baron de   **The Art of War.**
    1854   New York   35.00
    1854   New York   40.00
    1862   Philadelphia   35.00
    1864   Philadelphia   35.00
    1965   Harrisburg entitled **Jomini and His Summary of the Art of War** (condensed version), edited by J. D. Hittle   5.00

JONES, Adoniram J.   **A Private of the Cumberland, Memoirs and Reminiscences of the Civil War.**
    n.d.   n.p.   75.00

JONES, Archer   **Confederate Strategy, From Shiloh to Vicksburg.**
    1961   Baton Rouge   30.00

JONES, Archer   **Tennessee and Mississippi: Joe Johnston's Strategic Problem.** Wraps.
    1959   Tennessee   20.00

JONES, Benjamin Washington   **Battle Roll of Surry County, Virginia in the War Between the States.**
    1913   Richmond   300.00

JONES, Benjamin Washington   **Under the Stars and Bars.**
    1909   Richmond   500.00
    1975   Dayton edited by Lee A. Wallace, Jr.   25.00
    1980   20.00

JONES, Beuhring H.   **The Sunny Land; or Prison Prose and Poetry.**
  1868   Baltimore   25.00
JONES, C. W.   **In Prison at Point Lookout.** Wraps.
  (c.1890) Martinsville   40.00
JONES, Charles C., Jr.   **An Address Delivered Before the Confederate Survivor's Association, In Augusta, Georgia.** Wraps.
  1881   Augusta, GA   30.00
  1890   20.00
  1891   20.00
JONES, Charles C., Jr.   **Battle of Honey Hill: An Address.** Wraps.
  1885   Augusta, GA   35.00
JONES, Charles C., Jr.   **Brigadier General Robert Toombs. An Address . . . April 26, 1886.** Wraps.
  1886   Augusta, GA   25.00
JONES, Charles C., Jr.   **Defence of Battery Wagner, July 18th, 1863, Addresses Delivered Before the Confederate Survivors' Association.** Wraps.
  1892   Augusta, GA   60.00
JONES, Charles C., Jr.   **The Evacuation of Battery Wagner, and the Battle of Ocean Pond . . . An Address.** Wraps.
  1888   Augusta, GA   40.00
JONES, Charles C., Jr.   **Funeral Oration Pronounced . . . In Honor of President Jefferson Davis.** Wraps.
  1889   Augusta, GA   35.00
JONES, Charles C., Jr.   **General Sherman's March from Atlanta to the Coast . . . An Address.** Wraps.
  1884   Augusta, GA   40.00
JONES, Charles C., Jr.   **Georgians During the War . . . An Address.** Wraps.
  1889   Augusta, GA   40.00
JONES, Charles C., Jr.   **Historical Sketch of the Chatham Artillery During the Confederate Struggle for Independence.**
  1867   Albany   225.00
JONES, Charles C., Jr.   **The Life and Services of Commodore Josiah Tattnall.**
  1878   Savannah   140.00
JONES, Charles C., Jr.   **Military Lessons Inculcated on the Coast of Georgia During the Confederate War: An Address.** Wraps.
  1883   Augusta, GA   35.00
JONES, Charles C., Jr.   **Military Operations in Georgia During the War Between the States, An Address.** Wraps.
  1893   Augusta, GA   35.00
JONES, Charles C., Jr.   **The Old South, An Address.** Wraps.
  1887   Augusta, GA   20.00
JONES, Charles C., Jr.   **Post-Bellum Mortality Among Confederates, Address Delivered Before the Confederate Survivors' Association.** Wraps.
  1887   Augusta, GA   30.00
JONES, Charles C., Jr.   **The Siege and Evacuation of Savannah, Ga. Dec. 1864, An Address.** Wraps.
  1890   Augusta, GA   40.00

JONES, Charles C., Jr.   The Siege of Savannah in December, 1864.
Wraps.
1874   Albany   75.00
Recent reprint   17.50

JONES, Charles C., Jr.   Sons of Confederate Veterans.   An Address.
Wraps.
1891   Augusta, GA   25.00

JONES, Charles C., Jr. and **CUMMING, J. B.**   Address Delivered Before
the Confederate Survivors' Ass'n. in Augusta, Georgia. . . . Wraps.
1893   Augusta, GA   30.00

JONES, Charles Edgeworth   **Georgia in the War 1861-1865.** Wraps.
1909   Atlanta   80.00
1988   15.00

JONES, Charles Edgeworth   **In Memoriam Col. Charles C. Jones, Jr.**
Wraps.
1893   Augusta, GA   20.00

JONES, Douglas C.   **The Court-martial of George Armstrong Custer.**
1976   New York   15.00

JONES, Edgar DeWitt   **Lincoln and the Preachers.**
1948   New York   15.00

JONES, Edward Smyth   **The Sylvan Cabin,   A Centenary Ode on the
Birth of Lincoln.**
1911   Boston   15.00

JONES, Evan Rowland   **Four Years in the Army of the Potomac.**
1881   London   100.00

JONES, Evan Rowland   **Lincoln,   Stanton   and   Grant   Historical
Sketches.**
1875   London   40.00

JONES, Frank J.   **Personal Recollections of Some of the Generals in
Our Army During the Civil War.**
(1913)   n.p.   40.00

JONES, J. William   **Army of Northern Virginia Memorial Volume.**
1880   Richmond   100.00
1976   Dayton   17.50

JONES, J. William   **Christ in the Camp.**
1887   Richmond   75.00
1888   Richmond   50.00
1904   Atlanta   45.00
1986   24.00

JONES, J. William   **The Davis Memorial Volume.**
1890   Richmond   30.00
1890   Atlanta   25.00

JONES, J. William   **Life and Letters of Robert Edward Lee.**
1906   New York and Washington, DC   75.00
1978   20.00
1986   16.95

JONES, J. William   **Personal Reminiscences, Anecdotes and Letters of
Gen. Robert E. Lee.**
1874   New York   1st edition   75.00
1875   New York   75.00

JONES, James P.   Black Jack,   John A. Logan and Southern Illinois in the Civil War Era.
1967   Tallahassee   25.00
JONES, James P. and KEUCHEL, Edward F.   Civil War Marine, A Diary of the Red River Expedition, 1864.
1975   Washington, DC   20.00
JONES, James Pickett   Yankee Blitzkrieg: Wilson's Raid Through Alabama and Georgia.
1976   Athens 20.00
1988   Wraps   13.95
JONES, Jenkin Lloyd   An Artilleryman's Diary   Private, Sixth Wisconsin Battery.
1914   np.   75.00
JONES, John Beauchamp   A Rebel War Clerk's Diary, edited by Earl Schenck Miers. 2 Vols.
1866   Philadelphia 250.00
1866   Philadelphia 2 Vols. in 1   200.00
1935   New York 2 Vols., edited by Howard Swiggett   50.00
1958   New York 1 Vol., edited by Earl Schenck Miers 30.00
1982   45.00
JONES, John Beauchamp   Wild Southern Scenes, A Tale of Disunion and Border War.
1859   Philadelphia 50.00
JONES, John Sills   History of the 174th O.V.I.   Wraps.
1894   Marysville   130.00
JONES, Joseph   Medical and Surgical Memoirs; Containing Investigations on the Geographical Distribution, Causes, Nature, Relations and Treatment of Various Diseases. Vol. II
1887   New Orleans   175.00
JONES, Joseph   Researches upon "Spurious Vaccination," or the Abnormal Phenomena Accompanying and Following Vaccination in the Confederate Army. . . . Wraps.
1867   Nashville   250.00
JONES, Katharine M., edited by   Heroines of Dixie.
1955   Indianapolis 40.00
JONES, Katharine M.   Heroines of Dixie: Spring of High Hopes. Wraps.
1983   3.00
JONES, Katharine M.   Heroines of Dixie: Winter of Desperation. Wraps.
1979   3.00
JONES, Katharine M.   Ladies of Richmond.
1962   Indianapolis 30.00
JONES, Katharine M., edited by   New Confederate Short Stories.
1954   Columbia, SC   30.00
JONES, Katharine M.   The Plantation South.
1957   Indianapolis 20.00
JONES, Katharine M.   When Sherman Came: Southern Women and the "Great" March.
1964   New York   40.00
JONES, Mabel Cronise   Gettysburg.
1902   Syracuse, NY   5.00

JONES, Mary Sharpe and MALLARD, Mary Jones   Yankees A'Coming.
See: Confederate Centennial Studies, No. 12.
JONES, Paul   The Irish Brigade.
    1969   Washington, DC   30.00
JONES, Robert H.   The Civil War in the Northwest.
    1960   Norman   35.00
    1961   Norman   35.00
JONES, Robert H.   Disrupted Decades. The Civil War and Reconstruction.
    1973   New York   25.00
JONES, S. B., edited by   Twenty Favorite Songs for the Grand Army of the Republic. Wraps.
    1882   Omaha   25.00
JONES, Samuel   The Siege of Charleston and The Operations on the South Atlantic Coast in the War Among the States.
    1911   New York   200.00
JONES, Samuel Calvin   Reminiscences of the Twenty-second Iowa Volunteer Infantry.
    1907   Iowa City   160.00
JONES, Sarah L. (pseud.)   See: HOPLEY, Catherine Cooper
JONES, Terry L.   Lee's Tigers The Louisiana Infantry in the Army of Northern Virginia.
    1987   Baton Rouge and London   30.00
JONES, Thomas A.   J. Wilkes Booth.
    1893   Chicago   150.00
    n.d.   n.p.   Wraps   20.00
JONES, Thomas B.   Complete History of the 46th Illinois Volunteer Infantry.
    (1907)   Freeport   175.00
JONES, Thomas G.   Last Days of the Army of Northern Virginia An Address. Wraps.
    1893   Richmond   140.00
JONES, Tilghman   Five Days to Glory: Letters of _____, edited by Glenn W. Sunderland.
    1970   S. Brunswick and New York   25.00
JONES, Tom   Hood's Texas Brigade Sketch Book.
    1988   Ltd.   20.00
JONES, Virgil Carrington   The Civil War at Sea.
    1960-62 New York   3 Vols.   125.00
    Vol. I   The Blockaders.
    Vol. II   The River War.
    Vol. III   The Final Effort.
    Odd volumes   40.00 each
    1990   Wilmington, NC   3 Vols.   90.00
JONES, Virgil Carrington   Eight Hours Before Richmond.
    1957   New York   40.00
JONES, Virgil Carrington   Gray Ghosts and Rebel Raiders.
    1956   New York   45.00
    1959   25.00
JONES, Virgil Carrington   Ranger Mosby.
    1944   Chapel Hill, NC   50.00
    1987   Wraps   14.95

JONES, Walter Burgwyn, edited by   Confederate War Poems.
1959   Montgomery, AL   10.00

JONES, Walter Burgwyn   The South Faces History Unafraid,   An Address. Wraps.
(1945)   Montgomery, AL   10.00

JONES, Walter Burgwyn   War Poems of the Southern Confederacy,   An Address. Wraps.
1946   n.p.   20.00

JONES, Wilbur Devereux   The Confederate Rams at Birkenhead: A Chapter in Anglo-American Relations.   See: Confederate Centennial Studies, No. 19.

JONES, Mrs. Wilbur Moore, edited by   Historic Beauvoir, Souvenir Booklet of Beauvoir-on-the-Gulf, Harrison County, Mississippi.   Wraps.
1921   Hattiesburg   10.00

JONES, Winfield   Knights of the Ku Kux Klan.
1941   New York   75.00

JORDAN, Charles Edward   A Letter from _____ to His Family and Friends.
1932   (Charlottesville)   125.00

JORDAN, D. M.   Winfield Scott Hancock: A Soldier's Life.
1988   Bloomington   29.95

JORDAN, Donaldson and PRATT, Edwin J.   Europe and the American Civil War.
1931   Boston   35.00

JORDAN, E. L.   Charlottesville and the University of Virginia in the Civil War.
1988   Lynchburg   16.95

JORDAN, E. L. and THOMAS, H. A.   19th Virginia Infantry.
1987   Lynchburg   16.45

JORDAN, Jan   Dim the Flaring Lamps, A Novel of the Life of John Wilkes Booth.
1972   Englewood Cliffs, NJ   15.00

JORDAN, Robert Paul   The Civil War.
1969   New York   20.00

JORDAN, Thomas and PRYOR, John P.   The Campaigns of Lieut. Gen. N. B. Forrest and of Forrest's Cavalry.
1868   New Orleans   225.00
1868   St. Louis and Cincinnati   175.00
1869   New Orleans   175.00
1973   Dayton 30.00
1977   35.00
1988   Dayton 45.00

JORDAN, Weymouth T., Jr.   The Battle of Bentonville. Wraps.
1990   Wilmington, NC   4.95

JORDAN, Weymouth T., Jr.   North Carolina Troops, Vol. 12. See: North Carolina Troops.

JORDAN, Weymouth T., Jr.   Rebels in the Making: Planters' Conventions and Southern Propaganda. See: Confederate Centennial Studies, No. 7.

JORDAN, William B., compiled by   Maine in the Civil War: Bibliographical Guide. Wraps.
1976   Portland   15.00

Joseph Bryan His Times His Family His Friends.
n.d.   n.p.   35.00
JOSEPH, J. M.   War on the Rapidan. Wraps.
1988   Orange   15.00
JOSEPHUS, Junior   See: Annals of Harper's Ferry.
Journal and Proceedings of the Missouri State Convention, Held at Jefferson City, and St. Louis, March 1861.
1861   St. Louis   40.00
Journal of Confederate History, Vol. 2, No. 1. Wraps.
1989   12.00
A Journal of Incidents Connected with the Travels of the 22nd Regiment Connecticut Volunteers for Nine Months, in Verse by an Orderly Sergeant.
1863   Hartford   20.00
Journal of Southern History.
1935-   n.p.   400.00
Journal of the Confederate Historical Society. Wraps.
1962-72   Essex, England   5.00 each
Journal of the Congress of the Confederate States of America 1861-1865. 7 Vols.
1904-05   Washington, DC   500.00
Journal of the Fifty-fifth National Encampment of the Republic.
1922   Washington, DC   35.00
Limited to 1500 copies.
Journal of the Proceedings and Debates in the Constitutional Convention of the State of Mississippi, August, 1865.
1865   Jackson, MS   100.00
Journal of the Secession Convention of Texas 1861. Wraps.
1912   Austin   40.00
JOYCE, John A.   A Checkered Life.
1883   Chicago   50.00
JOYCE, John A.   Jewels of Memory.
1895   Washington, DC   50.00
1896   Washington, DC   40.00
JUDD, David W.   The Story of the Thirty-third N.Y.S. Vols.
1864   Rochester   125.00
Judge Jenkins History of Miller County Missouri Through the Civil War. Wraps.
1971   n.p.   30.00
JUDSON, Amos M.   History of the 83rd Regiment Pennsylvania Volunteers.
1865   Erie   150.00
1985   Dayton   20.00
1986   Dayton   30.00
JUERGENSEN, Hans   Major General George Henry Thomas. A Summary in Perspective. Wraps.
1980   Tampa, FL   5.00
Julius Shakespeare Harris, Born February 17, 1845, Died March 19, 1936. Wraps.
(c.1940) n.p.   100.00

JUNKIN, D. X. and NORTON, Frank H.   Life of Winfield Scott Hancock.
 1880 New York 35.00
JUNKIN, G. Political Fallacies.
 1863 New York 20.00
JURGEN, R. and KELLER, A. Major General John Sedgwick, U.S. Volunteers (1813-64). Wraps.
 1964 25.00
KAJENCKI, Francis C. Star on Many a Battlefield. Brevet Brigadier General Joseph Karge in the American Civil War.
 1980 22.00
KAKUSKE, Herbert P. A Civil War Drama. The Adventures of a Union Soldier in Southern Imprisonment.
 1970 New York 20.00
KALMAN, James and PATTERSON, C. Meade A Pictorial History of U.S. Single Shot Martial Pistols.
 (1957) New York 50.00
KAMM, S. R. The Civil War Career of Thomas A. Scott.
 1940 50.00
KANE, Harnett T. Bride of Fortune.
 1948 New York 15.00
KANE, Harnett T. The Gallant Mrs. Stonewall.
 1957 New York 15.00
 1978 New York 13.00
KANE, Harnett T. Gentlemen, Swords and Pistols.
 1951 New York 20.00
KANE, Harnett T. Gone Are the Days.
 1960 New York 25.00
KANE, Harnett T. An Illustrated History of the Old South: Gone are the Days.
 1960 15.00
KANE, Harnett T. The Lady of Arlington: A Novel based on the Life of Mrs. Robert E. Lee.
 1953 New York 15.00
KANE, Harnett T. Natchez on the Mississippi.
 1947 15.00
KANE, Harnett T. The Romantic South.
 1961 New York 10.00
KANE, Harnett T. The Smiling Rebel: A Novel based on the Life of Belle Boyd.
 1955 New York 25.00
KANE, Harnett T. Spies for the Blue and Gray.
 1954 Garden City, NY 30.00
 1954 Garden City, NY Southern ed. signed by author 40.00
Kansas Historical Society Collection, 1915-1918. Vol. XIV
 1918 Topeka 85.00
KANTOR, MacKinlay Andersonville.
 1955 New York 40.00
KANTOR, MacKinlay Arouse and Beware.
 1936 New York 15.00
KANTOR, MacKinlay Gettysburg.
 1952 New York 20.00

KANTOR, MacKinlay   **The Jaybird.**
    1932   New York   15.00
KANTOR, MacKinlay   **Long Remember.**
    1934   New York   15.00
KARPINSKI, L. C., compiled by   **Early Maps of Carolina and Adjoining Regions, from the Collection of Henry P. Kendall. Wraps.**
    1937   n.p.   10.00
KATCHER, Philip R. N.   **American Civil War Armies (1): Confederate Artillery, Cavalry and Infantry.**
    1989   London   9.95
KATCHER, Philip R. N.   **American Civil War Armies (2): Union Artillery, Cavalry and Infantry.**
    1988   London   9.95
KATCHER, Philip R. N.   **American Civil War Armies (3): Staff, Specialist and Maritime Services.**
    1986   London   9.95
KATCHER, Philip R. N.   **American Civil War Armies (4): State Troops.**
    1988   London   9.95
KATCHER, Philip R. N.   **Army of Northern Virginia. Wraps.**
    1988   London   9.95
KATCHER, Philip R. N.   **Army of the Potomac. Wraps.**
    1975   Berkshire, Great Britain 10.00
KATZ, D. Mark   **Custer in Photographs.**
    1985   Gettysburg   75.00
KATZ, Irving I.   **The Jewish Soldier from Michigan in the Civil War. Wraps.**
    1962   Detroit   20.00
KAUTZ, August V.   **The Company Clerk.**
    1863   Philadelphia   75.00
    1864   75.00
KEAN, Robert G. H.   **Inside the Confederate Government the Diary of _____, edited by Edward Younger.**
    1957   New York   35.00
    1957   New York   Autographed edition.   45.00
KEARNY, Thomas   **General Philip Kearny.**
    1937   New York   55.00
KEARSEY, Alexander H. C.   **A Study of the Strategy and Tactics of the Shenandoah Valley Campaign, 1861-65. Wraps.**
    (c.1918) 55.00
    1953   London   50.00
KEELER, William Frederick   **Aboard the USS Florida: 1863-65, the Letters of Paymaster to His Wife, edited by Robert W. Daly.**
    1968   Annapolis   25.00
KEELER, William Frederick   **Aboard the USS Monitor 1862 The Letters of _____, edited by Robert W. Daly.**
    1964   Annapolis   25.00
KEEN, Joseph S.   **Experiences in Rebel Military Prisons at Richmond, Danville, Andersonville, and Escape from Andersonville.**
    1890   Detroit   90.00

KEEN, Newton A.   Living and Fighting with the Texas 6th Cavalry, compiled by Mary Lou Barnes Lawlis.
1982   19.00
1986   Gaithersburg   18.50
KEENE, Harry S.   History of the Sixth Wisconsin Battery with Roster of Officers and Members.
1879   Lancaster   110.00
KEENE, Jesse L.   The Peace Convention of 1861.   See: Confederate Centennial Studies, No. 18.
KEESY, William Allen   Roster of Richmond Soldiers and History of Richmond Township, Tiffin Ohio.
1908   n.p.   45.00
KEESY, William Allen   War as Viewed From the Ranks.
1898   Norwalk   90.00
KEIFER, Joseph Warren   A Forgotten Battle: Sailor's Creek April 6, 1865.   Wraps.
1888   Cincinnati   40.00
KEIFER, Joseph Warren   Slavery and Four Years of War. 2 Vols.
1900   New York   100.00
KEIL, Frederick W.   35th Ohio, A Narrative of Service, August 1861 to 1864.
1894   Fort Wayne   225.00
KEILEY, A. M.   In Vinculis, or, the Prisoner of War.
1866   New York   125.00
1866   Petersburg, VA   100.00
KEIM, DeB. Randolph   William T. Sherman: A Memorial in Art, Oratory and Literature by the Society of the Army of Tennessee.
1904   Washington, DC   25.00
KELEHER, William A.   Turmoil in New Mexico 1846-1868.
1952   Santa Fe, NM   40.00
Recent reprint   18.95
KELL, John McIntosh   Recollections of a Naval Life.
1900   Washington, DC   150.00
KELLER, Allan   Morgan's Raid.
1961   Indianapolis   40.00
1961   New York   40.00
KELLER, Allan   Thunder at Harper's Ferry.
1958   Englewood Cliffs, NJ   40.00
KELLER, Morton   The Art and Politics of Thomas Nast.
1968   New York   25.00
KELLEY, Daniel G.   What I Saw and Suffered in Rebel Prisons.   Wraps.
1866   Buffalo   50.00
1868   Buffalo   40.00
KELLEY, Dayton   General Lee and Hood's Texas Brigade at the Battle of the Wilderness.   Wraps.
1969   Waco, TX   25.00
KELLEY, Dayton   The Texas Brigade at the Wilderness, May 6, 1864.
n.d.   Gatesville   Ltd.   30.00
KELLEY, Duren F.   The War Letters of _____ 1862-1865, edited by R. S. Offenberg and R. R. Parsonage.
1967   New York   25.00

KELLEY, Evelyn O.   Seeded Furrows.
1957   Daytona Beach   10.00
KELLEY, William D.   Lincoln and Stanton.
1885   New York   20.00
KELLOGG, J. J.   The Vicksburg Campaign and Reminiscences . . . From Milliken's Bend to July 4, 1863. Wraps.
1913   (Washington, IA) 100.00
KELLOGG, John Azor and SPENCER, R. H.   Capture and Escape. A Narrative of Army and Prison Life. Wraps.
1896   Algona, IA 50.00
1908   Madison   50.00
KELLOGG, Robert H.   Life and Death in Rebel Prisons.
1865   Hartford   35.00
1866   Hartford   35.00
1867   Hartford   25.00
KELLOGG, Sanford C.   The Shenandoah Valley and Virginia 1861 to 1865.
1903   New York   100.00
KELLY, Henry B.   Port Republic. Wraps.
1886   Philadelphia 200.00
KELSEY, Albert Warren   Autobiographical Note and Memoranda.
1911   Baltimore Ltd. 100.00
KELSEY, D. M.   Deeds of Daring by Both Blue and Gray.
1883   Philadelphia 25.00
1899   Chicago 20.00
KELSO, Isaac   The Stars and Bars.
1863   Boston   60.00
1864   Boston   40.00
KEMBLE, Frances Anne   Journal of a Residence on a Georgian Plantation in 1838-1839.
1863   New York   55.00
1984   Wraps 10.00
KEMPER, G. W. H.   A Medical History of the State of Indiana.
1911   Chicago 50.00
KEMPF, Edward J.   Abraham Lincoln's Philosophy of Common Sense. 3 Vols.
1965   New York Boxed   50.00
KENDRICK, Benjamin B.   The Journal of the Joint Committee of Fifteen on Reconstruction, 39th Cong 1865-1867. Wraps.
1914   New York   40.00
KENDRICKEN, Paul Henry   Memoirs.
1910   Boston   70.00
KENNARD, Martin P.   Address . . . On Presentation to the Town of a Memorial Portrait of the Late Brig. Gen. Edward Augustus Wild.
1894   Brookline, MA   10.00
KENNAWAY, John H.   On Sherman's Track or the South After the War.
1867   London 100.00
KENNEDY, Elijah R.   The Contest for California in 1861; how Colonel E. D. Baker saved the Pacific States to the Union.
1912   Boston   60.00

KENNEDY, Elijah R.   John B. Woodward, A Biographical Memoir.
1897   New York   40.00
KENNY, Thomas Moore   Two Graves.
1902   Baltimore   15.00
KENT, Arthur A., edited by   3 Years with Co. K, 13th Massachusetts Regiment.
1976   23.00
KENT, Charles N.   History of the Seventeenth Regiment, New Hampshire Volunteer Infantry.
1898   Concord   75.00
KENT, Will Parmiter   The Story of Libby Prison. Also Some Perils and Sufferings of Certain of Its Inmates. Compiled from Personal Narratives. . . . Wraps.
1890   Chicago   150.00
Kentucky - Confederate Military History.   See: Confederate Military History, Vol. IX (Vol. XI, 1988 reprint ed.).
KEPLER, William   History of the Three Months' and Three Years' Service . . . Fourth Regiment Ohio Volunteer Infantry.
1886   Cleveland   190.00
KERBEY, J. O.   The Boy Spy.
1889   Chicago   25.00
1890   Chicago   20.00
1898   Washington, DC Wraps   15.00
KERBEY, J. O.   On the War Path. A Journey Over the Historic Grounds of the Late Civil War.
1890   Chicago   25.00
KERBY, Robert L.   Confederate Invasion of New Mexico and Arizona.
1958   Los Angeles, CA   Ltd.   50.00
1981   17.50
KERBY, Robert L.   Kirby-Smith's Confederacy: The Trans-Mississippi South 1863- 1865.
1972   New York   35.00
KERCHEVAL, Samuel   A History of the Valley of Virginia.
1925   Strasburg   55.00
KERKSIS, Sydney C., edited by   The Atlanta Papers.
1980   Dayton   35.00
KERKSIS, Sydney C.   Heavy Artillery Projectiles of the Civil War.
1972   Kennesaw, GA   40.00
KERKSIS, Sydney C.   Plates and Buckles of the American Military 1795-1874.
1974   Kennesaw, GA   50.00
1987   39.95
KERKSIS, Sydney C. and DICKEY, Thomas S.   Field Artillery Projectiles of the Civil War 1861-1865.
1968   Atlanta   40.00
KERN, Albert, compiled by   History of the First Regiment Ohio Vol. Infantry in the Civil War.
1918   Dayton   100.00
KERNER, Otto   Journal of the Illinois State Historical Society. Wraps.
1963   IL   20.00
KERR, Homer   Fighting with Ross' Texas Cavalry Brigade, C.S.A.
1976   Hillsboro   50.00

KERR, John Leeds   The Story of a Southern Carrier,   The Louisville and Nashville R.R.
   1933   New York   35.00
KERR, William S. R.   The Confederate Secession.
   1864   Edinburgh   110.00
KERRIGAN, Evans E.   American War Medals and Decorations.
   (1964)   New York   25.00
KERSHAW, Miss C. D., compiled by   Richard Kirkland, C.S.A.   Wraps.
   1910   Camden   80.00
KERSHAW, John   Address Delivered Before the Ladies' Memorial Association and Citizens of Charleston.   Wraps.
   1893   Charleston, SC   25.00
KERWOOD, Asbury L.   Annals of the Fifty-seventh Regiment Indiana Volunteers, Marches, Battles, and Incidents of Army Life.
   1868   Dayton   250.00
KERWOOD, Asbury L.   Military History of Delaware County, Ind.
   1909   n.p.   40.00
KETCHUM, Hiram   General McClellan's Peninsula Campaign. Review of the Report of the Committee on the Conduct of the War Relative to the Peninsula Campaign. Wraps.
   1864   n.p.   20.00
KETTELL, Thomas P.   History of the Great Rebellion.
   1865   Hartford   35.00
KETTELL, Thomas P.   Southern Wealth and Northern Profits.
   1860   New York   75.00
   1965   University, AL   22.50
KEY, William   The Battle of Atlanta and the Georgia Campaign.
   1958   New York   20.00
   1981   Wraps   10.00
KEYES, Charles M., edited by   Military History of the 123rd Regiment of Ohio Vol. Inf.
   1874   Sandusky   130.00
KEYES, Dwight W.   The First Wisconsin Infantry U.S. Vols. Its Organization, and Move to the Front.
   1896   Milwaukee   40.00
KEYES, E. D.   Fifty Year's Observations of Men and Events, Civil and Military.
   1884   New York   50.00
KEYES, Edward L.   Lewis Atterbury Stimson, M.D.
   1918   New York   40.00
KIBBY, Leo P.   Book Review Reference for a Decade of Civil War Books, 1950-1960.   Wraps.
   1961   San Jose, CA   40.00
KIBLER, Lillian Adel   Benjamin F. Perry, South Carolina Unionist.
   1946   Durham   25.00
KIDD, James H.   Address of _____ at the Dedication of Michigan Monuments upon the Battlefield of Gettysburg Jun 12, 1889.
   n.d.   n.p.   45.00
KIDD, James H.   The Michigan Cavalry Brigade in the Wilderness. Wraps.
   1889   Detroit   50.00

KIDD, James H.   **Personal Recollections of a Cavalryman.**
1908   Ionia   225.00
1969   Grand Rapids   40.00
1983   30.00
KIDD, Reuben Vaughan   **Soldier of the Confederacy.**
1947   Petersburg   40.00
KIEFER, William R.   **History of the 153rd Regiment Pennsylvania Volunteer . . . Infantry Northampton County.**
1909   Easton   80.00
KIEFFER, Henry M.   **The Recollections of a Drummer-Boy.**
1883   Boston   40.00
1888   Boston   35.00
1889   Boston   30.00
1890   30.00
1911   Boston   30.00
KIELL, Norman, edited by   **Psychological Studies of Famous Americans, The Civil War Era.**
1964   New York   10.00
KIMBALL, Moses   **A Discourse Commemorative of Major Charles Jarvis of the 9th Vermont Volunteers.**
1864   New York   20.00
KIMBALL, Orville S.   **History and Personal Sketches of Company I, 103 N.Y.S.V., 1862-1864.**
1900   Elmira   75.00
KIMBALL, William J., edited by   **Richmond in Time of War.**   Wraps.
1960   Boston   25.00
KIMBELL, Charles Bill   **History of Battery "A," First Illinois Light Artillery Volunteers.**
1899   Chicago   160.00
KIMBERLY, Robert L. and **HOLLOWAY**, E. S.   **The 41st Ohio Veteran Volunteer Infantry in the War of the Rebellion 1861-1865.**
1897   Cleveland   225.00
KIMMEL, Stanley   **The Mad Booths of Maryland.**
1940   Indianapolis   40.00
KIMMEL, Stanley   **Mr. Davis's Richmond.**
1958   New York   25.00
KIMMEL, Stanley   **Mr. Lincoln's Washington.**
1957   New York   15.00
KINCAID, Robert L.   **Kentucky in the Civil War.**   Wraps.
1947   n.p.   20.00
KINCHEN, Oscar A.   **Confederate Operations in Canada and the North.**
1970   N. Quincy, MA   25.00
KINCHEN, Oscar A.   **Daredevils of the Confederate Army.**
1959   Boston   25.00
KINCHEN, Oscar B.   **General Bennett H. Young, Confederate Raider and a Man of Many Adventures.**
1981   11.00
KINER, Frederick F.   **One Year's Soldiering, Embracing the Battles of Fort Donelson and Shiloh.**
1863   Lancaster, PA   100.00
KING, Alvy   **Louis T. Wigfall, Southern Fire-Eater.**
1970   Baton Rouge   15.00

KING, Charles   Between the Lines.
     1888   25.00
     1889   New York   25.00
KING, Charles   A Broken Sword: A Tale of the Civil War.
     1905   New York   10.00
KING, Charles   Campaigning with Crook.
     1890   New York   50.00
KING, Charles   Gainsville, August 28th, 1862. Wraps.
     1903   Milwaukee   40.00
KING, Charles   The General's Double: A Story of the Army of the Potomac.
     1898   Philadelphia   20.00
KING, Charles   In Spite of Foes or Ten Years Trial.
     1901   Philadelphia   25.00
KING, Charles   The Iron Brigade A Story of the Army of the Potomac.
     1902   New York   10.00
KING, Charles   Kitty's Conquest.
     1893   10.00
KING, Charles   A Knight of Columbia: A Story of the War.
     1904   New York   10.00
KING, Charles   Norman Holt A Story of the Army of the Cumberland.
     1901   New York   15.00
KING, Charles   The Rock of Chickamauga.
     1907   New York   15.00
KING, Charles   A War-Time Wooing.
     1888   New York   15.00
KING, David H., compiled by   History of the Ninety-third Regiment, New York Volunteer Infantry 1861-1865.
     1895   Milwaukee   125.00
KING, Edward   The Great South.
     1875   Hartford   100.00
     1972   Baton Rouge   30.00
KING, Grace   Memories of a Southern Woman of Letters.
     1932   New York   40.00
KING, Horatio C.   The Army of the Potomac, Sketch and the Phantom Column, Poem. Wraps.
     (1898)   New York   20.00
KING, Horatio C.   Turning on the Light.
     1895   Philadelphia   25.00
KING, James   War Eagle: Life of General Eugene A. Carr.
     1963   NE   50.00
KING, John H.   Three Hundred Days in a Yankee Prison.
     1904   Atlanta   200.00
     1959   Kennesaw, GA   20.00
KING, John R.   A Brief History of the Sixth Regiment Maryland Infantry Volunteers, Second Brigade, Third Division, Sixth Army Corps. Wraps.
     1915   Baltimore   75.00

KING, Josias Ridgate   The Battle of Bull Run, A Confederate Victory Obtained, But Not Achieved. Wraps.
    1907   n.p.   35.00

KING, Spencer B.   Darien. The Death and Rebirth of a Southern Town.
    1981   14.00

KING, Spencer B.   Sound of Drums: Selected Writings of Spencer B. King from His Civil War Centennial Columns Appearing in the Macon (Georgia) Telegraph News, 1960-65.
    1984   Macon   25.00

KING, W. C. and DERBY, W. P., edited by   Camp-Fire Sketches and Battle-field Echoes of the Rebellion.
    1887   Springfield 45.00
    1888   Cleveland   40.00
    1889   Springfield 40.00

KING, Willard L.   Lincoln's Manager David Davis.
    1960   Cambridge, MA   10.00

KINGSBURY, Allen A.   The Hero of Medfield; Containing the Journal and Letters of. . . .
    1862   Boston   35.00

KINNEAR, John R.   History of the Eighty-sixth Regiment Illinois Volunteer Infantry.
    1866   Chicago 175.00

KINSLEY, D. A.   Favor the Bold, Custer: The Civil War Years.
    1967   New York 25.00
    1967-68 2 Vols. 30.00

KIRCHER, Henry A.   A German in the Yankee Fatherland: The Civil War Letters of Henry A. Kircher, edited by Earl J. Hess.
    1983   Kent   20.00

KIRK, Charles H., compiled by   History of the 15th Pennsylvania Volunteer Cavalry.
    1906   Philadelphia   100.00
    1916   85.00

KIRK, Hyland C.   Heavy Guns and Light: History of the 4th New York Heavy Artillery.
    1890   New York   125.00

KIRKE, Edmund (pseud.)   See: GILMORE, James

KIRKLAND, Charles P.   The Destiny of our Country. Wraps.
    1864   New York   25.00

KIRKLAND, Charles P.   A Letter to Peter Cooper, On "The Treatment to Be Extended to the Rebels Individually," and the Mode of Restoring the Rebel States to the Union. Wraps.
    1865   New York   30.00

KIRKLAND, Charles P.   Liability of the Government of Great Britain for the Depredations of Rebel Privateers on the Commerce of the United States Considered. Wraps.
    1863   New York   35.00

KIRKLAND, Edward Chase   The Peacemakers of 1864.
    1927   New York   15.00

KIRKLAND, Frazar   The Pictorial Book of Anecdotes and Incidents of
the War of the Rebellion.
1866   Hartford   25.00
1887   St. Louis   20.00
KIRKLAND, Frazar   Reminiscences of the Blue and Gray, '61-'65.
1866   Hartford   50.00
1895   Chicago   45.00
KIRKPATRICK, George Morgan   42nd Indiana. The Experiences of a
Private Soldier in the Civil War. Wraps.
1973   Carmel   30.00
KIRWAN, Albert D., edited by   The Confederacy.
1959   New York   25.00
1961   25.00
KIRWAN, Albert D.   John J. Crittenden, The Struggle for the Union.
1962   Lexington   15.00
KIRWAN, Thomas and SPLAINE, Henry   Memorial History of the Seventeenth Regiment Massachusetts Volunteer Infantry . . . 1861-1865.
1911   Salem   75.00
KITCHENS, Ben E.   Gunboats and Cavalry, A History of Eastport, Mississippi. Wraps.
1985   Florence   10.00
KITCHING, J. Howard   More Than Conqueror or Memorials of Col. J.
Howard Kitching, edited by Theodore Irving.
1873   New York   35.00
KITTINGER, Joseph   Diary 1861-1865, 23rd New York Independent Battery. Wraps.
n.d.   New York   40.00
KITTREDGE, Walter   Tenting on the Old Camp Ground.
1891   Troy, NY   50.00
KITTRELL, Norman G.   Ned: Nigger an' Gentlman; A Story of War
and Reconstruction.
1907   New York   60.00
KLEIN, Frederic S.   Just South of Gettysburg. Carroll County Maryland in the Civil War.
1963   Westminster 40.00
1974   Lancaster   30.00
KLEIN, Maury   Edward Porter Alexander.
1971   Athens   30.00
KLEMENT, Frank L.   The Copperheads in the Middle West.
1960   Chicago   30.00
KLEMENT, Frank L.   Dark   Lanterns: Secret   Political   Societies,
Conspiracies, and Treason Trials in the Civil War. Wraps.
1989   Baton Rouge   9.95
KLEMENT, Frank L.   The Limits of Dissent.
1970   Lexington, KY   22.00
KLEMENT, Frank L.   Wisconsin and the Civil War. Wraps.
1963   Madison   10.00
KLOTTER, James C.   The Breckinridges of Kentucky, 1760-1981.
1986   Lexington, KY   35.00
KNAPP, David   The Confederate Horseman.
1966   New York   40.00

KNAPP, David   The Magnificent Rebels. Wraps.
  1967   Mobile   25.00
KNAPP, F. N.   Extracts from the Quarterly Special Relief Report of the U.S. Sanitary Commission. Wraps.
  1865   Washington, DC   10.00
Knapsack and Rifle or Life in the Grand Army.
  1888   Philadelphia   25.00
KNAUSS, William H.   The Story of Camp Chase.
  1906   Nashville   150.00
KNIFFIN, Gilbert C.   Assault and Capture of Lookout Mountain.
  1895   Washington, DC   160.00
  1898   Chattanooga   50.00
KNIGHT, Josephine Augusta Clarke   Symbols of the South.
  1941   Richmond   30.00
KNIGHT, Lucian Lamar   Alexander H. Stephens. Wraps.
  1930   n.p.   15.00
KNIGHT, Lucian Lamar   Stone Mountain.
  1923   Atlanta   10.00
KNIGHT, Wilfred   Red Fox: Stand Watie's Civil War Years in Indian Territory.
  1988   Glendale   27.50
KNOLES, George Harmon, edited by   The Crisis of the Union 1860-1861.
  1965   Baton Rouge   15.00
KNOTTS, R. J. and STEVENS, R. E.   Calhoun County in the Civil War.
  1982   WV   25.00
KNOWLES, David   The American Civil War - A Brief Sketch.
  1926   Oxford   25.00
KNOX, Rose B.   Gray Caps.
  1933   Garden City, NY   20.00
KNOX, Thomas W.   Boy's Life of General Grant.
  1899   Akron   10.00
KNOX, Thomas W.   Camp-Fire and Cotton-Field.
  1865   New York   65.00
KNOX, Thomas W.   The Lost Army.
  1894   New York   25.00
  1899   New York   25.00
KOCHER, A. Lawrence and BEARSTYNE, Howard   Shadows in Silver, Virginia 1850-1900, People, Plantations, Towns, and Cities, a Pictorial Record.
  1954   New York   60.00
KOEHLER, Leroy Jennings   The History of Monroe County, Penna. During the Civil War.
  1950   Monroe County   35.00
KOMROFF, M.   Photographing History: Mathew Brady.
  1962   Chicago   20.00
KORN, Bertram W.   American Jewry and the Civil War.
  1951   Philadelphia   40.00
  1957   Philadelphia   35.00
KORNGOLD, Ralph   Thaddeus Stevens.
  1955   New York   35.00
KORNGOLD, Ralph   Two Friends of Man.
  1950   Boston   25.00

KOUNTZ, John S.   Record of the Organizations Engaged in the Campaign, Siege and Defense of Vicksburg.   Wraps.
    1901   Washington, DC   65.00
KRAMER, Samuel   Maryland and the Glorious Old Third in the War for the Union, Reminiscences in the Life of Her Militant Chaplain and Major Samuel Kramer. Wraps.
    1882   125.00
KRANZ, Henry B.   Abraham Lincoln A New Portrait.
    1959   New York   10.00
KREMER, Wesley P.   100 Great Battles of the Rebellion.
    1906   Hoboken, NJ   30.00
KREUTZER, William   Notes and Observations Made During Four Years Service with Ninety-eighth New York Volunteers.
    1878   Philadelphia 85.00
KRICK, Robert E. L.   40th Virginia Infantry.
    1985   Lynchburg   17.00
KRICK, Robert K.   The Fredericksburg Artillery.
    1986   Lynchburg   16.50
KRICK, Robert K.   The Gettysburg Death Roster, The Confederate Dead at Gettysburg.
    1985   Dayton   17.50
KRICK, Robert K.   Lee's Colonels, A Biographical Register of the Field Officers of the Army of Northern Virginia.
    1979   Dayton   30.00
    1984   Dayton   40.00
KRICK, Robert K.   Maxcy Gregg Political Extremist and Confederate General. Wraps.
    1973   Kent, OH   6.00
KRICK, Robert K.   Neale Books, An Annotated Bibliography.
    1977   Dayton   25.00
KRICK, Robert K.   9th Virginia Cavalry.
    1982   Lynchburg 17.00
KRICK, Robert K.   Parker's Virginia Battery, C.S.A.
    1975   Berryville   30.00
    1989   Wilmington, NC   30.00
KRICK, Robert K.   Stonewall Jackson at Cedar Mountain.
    1990   Chapel Hill, NC   29.95
KRICK, Robert K.   30th Virginia Infantry.
    1983   Lynchburg 17.00
Ku Klux Conspiracy.   13 Vols.
    1872   Washington, DC   450.00
    Ku Klux Conspiracy - Report of the Joint Select Committee to Inquire into . . . the Insurrrectionary States.   40.00
    Ku Klux Conspiracy - Testimony Taken by the Joint Select Committee to Inquire into . . . the Insurrectionary States.   40.00
    Ku Klux Conspiracy - Testimony Taken by the Joint Select Committee to Inquire into . . . the Insurrectionary States, SC. 3 Vols.   100.00
    Ku Klux Conspiracy - Testimony Taken by the Joint Select Committee to Inquire into . . . the Insurrectionary States, GA. 2 Vols.   75.00
    Ku Klux Conspiracy - Testimony Taken by the Joint Select Committee to Inquire into . . . the Insurrectionary States, AL. 3 Vols.   100.00

Ku Klux Conspiracy - Testimony Taken by the Joint Select Committee to Inquire into . . . the Insurrectionary States, MS. 2 Vols.   60.00

Ku Klux Conspiracy - Testimony Taken by the Joint Select Committee to Inquire into . . . the Insurrectionary States, Misc. and FL.   40.00

KUNE, Julian   **Reminiscences of an Octogenarian Hungarian Exile.**
  1911   Chicago   75.00

KUNHARDT, Dorothy M. and **KUNHARDT**, Phillip   **Twenty Days.**
  1965   New York   25.00

KURTZ, Lucy F. and **RITTER**, Benny   **A Roster of Confederate Soldiers Buried in Stonewall Cemetery, Winchester, Virginia.** Wraps.
  1962   (Winchester, VA)   12.00
  1984   12.50

KURTZ, Wilbur G.   **Atlanta and the Old South.** Wraps.
  1969   Atlanta   9.00

KURTZ, Wilbur G.   **The Atlanta Cyclorama, the Story of the Famed Battle of Atlanta.** Wraps.
  1954   Atlanta   15.00

KURZ and ALLISON   See: Battles of the Civil War.

LABOULAYE, Edouard R. L. de   **Les Etats-Unis Et La France.** Wraps.
  1862   Paris   50.00

LABOULAYE, Edouard R. L. de   **Upon Whom Rests the Guilt of the War?** Wraps.
  1863   New York   20.00

LA BREE, Ben, edited by   **Camp Fires of the Confederacy.**
  1898   Louisville   150.00
  1899   Louisville   100.00

LA BREE, Ben, edited by   **The Confederate Soldier in the Civil War.**
  1895   Louisville   150.00
  1897   Louisville   100.00
  1959   New York   50.00
  1977   New York   35.00

LACIAR, J. D.   **Patriotism of Carbon County.**
  1867   Mauch Chunk   55.00

LAFRAMBOISE, L. W.   **History of the Artillery, Cavalry, & Infantry Branch of Service Insignia.**
  1976   Steelville   50.00

LAIR, John   **Songs Lincoln Loved.** Wraps.
  1954   New York   5.00

LAKE, Harry F. and **FARNUM**, George R.   **The Great Debate Between Abraham Lincoln and Stephen A. Douglas in 1858. Those of His Contemporaries.** Wraps.
  1941   Norwood, MA   25.00

LAMAR, Joseph R.   **The Private Soldier of the Confederacy.** Address. Wraps.
  1902   New York   75.00

LAMB, Sarah Anne Chaffee   **Letters from the Colonel's Lady: Correspondence of Mrs. (Col.) William Lamb written from Fort Fisher, N.C., C.S.A. . . . Dec. 1861 to Jan. 1865,** edited by Cornelius M. D. Thomas, Clarendon Imprint No. 7.
  1965   Wilmington, NC   50.00

LAMB, William   Colonel Lamb's Story of Fort Fisher: The Battles Fought Here in 1864 and 1865. Wraps.
    1966   Carolina Beach, NC   15.00
LAMB, William   The Battle of Fort Fisher, North Carolina 1861-1865. Wraps.
    n.d.   n.p.   15.00
    1966   15.00
LAMBERT, William H.   George Henry Thomas, Oration Before the Society of the Army of the Cumberland . . . 1884.
    1884   Philadelphia   40.00
LAMBERT, William H.   Major General Winfield Scott Hancock, Oration at the National Cemetery, Gettysburg May 29, 1886. Wraps.
    1886   Philadelphia   Ltd.   40.00
LAMERS, William M.   The Edge of Glory, A Biography of General William S. Rosecrans.
    1961   New York   40.00
LAMON, Ward Hill   The Life of Abraham Lincoln from His Birth to His Inauguration as President.
    1872   Boston   50.00
LAMON, Ward Hill   Recollections of Abraham Lincoln 1847-1865.
    1895   Chicago   30.00
LAMPREY, L.   Days of the Leaders.
    1925   New York   25.00
LANARD, Thomas S.   One Hundred Years with the State Fencibles: A History of the First Company.
    1913   Philadelphia   50.00
LANCASTER, Bruce   Night March.
    1958   Boston   15.00
LANCASTER, Bruce   No Bugles Tonight.
    1948   Boston   10.00
LANCASTER, Bruce   Roll Shenandoah.
    1956   Boston   15.00
LANCASTER, Bruce   The Scarlet Patch.
    1947   Boston   15.00
The Land We Love. 6 Vols.
    Vols. 1-6, May 1866-March 1869 Charlotte, NC
    Complete set   Bound   750.00
    Complete set   Wraps 800.00
    Individual volumes   75.00
LANDIS, Robert W.   The Duty and Obligations of American Citizens in Relations to the Union, An Oration. Wraps.
    1860   Somerset   30.00
LANDRUM, J. B. O.   History of Spartanburg County.
    1954   Spartanburg   35.00
LANE, J. Robert   A Political History of Connecticut During the Civil War. Wraps.
    1941   Washington, DC   25.00
LANE, Miles   Marching Through Georgia.
    1978   New York   25.00

LANE, Walter P.   The Adventures and Recollections of General Walter P. Lane, A San Jacinto Veteran. . .
    1928   Marshall, TX   50.00
    1970   Austin 20.00
LANG, H. Jack   Lincoln's Fireside Reading.
    1965   Cleveland   10.00
LANG, H. Jack   The Wit and Wisdom of Abraham Lincoln as Reflected in His Briefer Letters and Speeches.
    1944   OH   25.00
LANG, Theodore F.   Loyal West Virginia from 1861 to 1865.
    1895   Baltimore   150.00
LANGHEIN, Eric   Jefferson Davis Patriot.
    1962   New York   15.00
LANGSDORF, Edgar   Price's Raid and the Battle of Mine Creek. Wraps.
    1964   Topeka   15.00
LANGWORTHY, Daniel Avery   Reminiscences of a Prisoner of War and His Escape.
    1915   Minneapolis   50.00
LANIER, Sidney   Poems of Sidney Lanier, edited by His Wife.
    1884   New York   35.00
    1892   New York   25.00
    1893   New York   25.00
    Various later editions   20.00
LANKFORD, N. D., edited by   An Irishman in Dixie: Thomas Connelly's Diary of the Fall of the Confederacy.
    1988   Columbia   24.95
LANMAN, C.   Dictionary of the U. S. Congress.
    1864   Washington, DC   35.00
LANMAN, Charles   The Red Book of Michigan, A Civil, Military, and Biographical History.
    1862   New York   30.00
    1871   Detroit   30.00
LANUX, Pierre De   Sud.   Wraps.
    1932   Paris   60.00
LANZA, Conrad H.   Fort Henry and Fort Donelson Campaigns, February 1862.
    1923   Ft. Leavenworth   100.00
LAPHAM, William B.   My Recollections of the War of the Rebellion.
    1892   Augusta   75.00
LARKE, Julian K.   General Grant and His Campaigns.
    1864   New York   15.00
LATANE, Lucy Temple   A Short Sketch of James Allen Latane.
    1949   Richmond   35.00
LATHROP, David   The History of the Fifty-ninth Regiment Illinois Volunteers.
    1865   Indianapolis   200.00
LATHROP, George Parsons   History of the Union League of Philadelphia.
    1884   Philadelphia   30.00
LATHROP, H. W.   The Life and Times of Samuel J. Kirkwood.
    1893   Iowa City   25.00

LATIMER, E.   Idyls of Gettysburg.
   1872   Philadelphia   10.00
LATTA, James W.   History of the 1st Regiment Infantry National
   Guard . . . (Gray Reserves).
   1912   Philadelphia   75.00
LATTA, James W.   Was Secession Taught at West Point?   Wraps.
   1909   n.p.   30.00
LATTIMORE, Ralston B., edited by   The Story of Robert E. Lee.
   1964   Philadelphia   25.00
   1964   Philadelphia   Wraps 55.00
LAUGEL, Auguste   Les   Etats-Unis   Pendant   La   Guere   1861-1865.
   Wraps.
   1866   Paris   35.00
LAUGEL, Auguste   The United States During the War.
   1866   New York   45.00
   1961   Bloomington, IN   entitled   The United States During the Civil
          War, edited by Allen Nevins 35.00
   1969   New York   25.00
LAUGHLIN, Clara   The Death of Lincoln.
   1909   New York   40.00
LAURENCE, Robert   The George Walcott Collection of Used Civil War
   Patriotic Covers.
   1893   n.p.   125.00
   1934   New York   65.00
LAVENDER, John W.   The War Memories of . . . , C.S.A., edited by
   Ted R. Worley.
   1956   Pine Bluff, AR   50.00
LAW, Tom   Citadel Cadets, The Journal of Cadet Tom Law.
   1942   Clinton, SC   75.00
LAWRENCE, Alexander A.   James Moore Wayne. Southern Unionist.
   1943   Chapel Hill, NC   25.00
LAWRENCE, Alexander A.   Johnny Leber and the Confederate Major.
   1962   Darien, GA   Ltd.   35.00
LAWRENCE, Alexander A.   Present for Mr. Lincoln - The Story of
   Savannah From Secession to Sherman.
   1961   Macon   35.00
LAWRENCE, Catherine L.   Autobiography: Sketch of Life and Labors
   of. . . .
   1893   Albany   50.00
LAWRENCE, F. Lee and GLOVER, Robert W.   Camp Ford, C.S.A.
   1964   Austin   225.00
LAWRENCE, George Alfred   Border and Bastille.
   n.d.   New York   40.00
LAWRENCE, William   Life of Amos A. Lawrence.
   1888   Boston   20.00
Laws of War, and Marital Law.   Wraps.
   1863   Boston   40.00
LAWTON, Eba Anderson   Major Robert Anderson and Fort Sumter, 1861.
   1911   New York   35.00

The Lay of John Haroldson.   Wraps.
  1866   Philadelphia   Ltd.   125.00
LEACH, Eugene Walter   Racine County Militant, an Illustrated Narrative of War Times and a Soldier's Roster.
  1915   Racine   75.00
LEARNED, Marion Dexter   Abraham Lincoln.
  1909   Philadelphia   Ltd.   50.00
L'ECLAIR   Lenare: A Story of the Southern Revolution and Other Poems.
  1866   New Orleans   70.00
LECOMTE, Ferdinand   Guerre De La Secession.   3 Vols.   Wraps.
  1866-67 Paris   150.00
LECONTE, Emma   When the World Ended: The Diary of Emma LeConte, edited by Earl Schenck Miers.
  1957   New York   35.00
LECONTE, Joseph   The Autobiography of _____, edited by William Dallam Armes.
  1903   New York   100.00
LECONTE, Joseph   'Ware Sherman,   A Journal of Three Months' Personal Experience in the Last Days of the Confederacy.
  1937   Berkeley   35.00
  1938   Berkeley   30.00
LEDFORD, Preston L.   Reminiscences of the Civil War 1861-1865.   Wraps.
  1909   Thomasville   75.00
LEDUC, William G.   Recollections of a Civil War Quartermaster: Autobiography of LeDuc.
  1963   St. Paul   15.00
LEE, Agnes   The Journal of Agnes Lee,   Growing Up in the 1850's, edited by Mary Custis Lee de Butts.
  1984   12.00
LEE, Baker P.   Confederate Memorial Address, Delivered at Elmwood Cemetery, Norfolk, Va. May 19, 1887.   Wraps.
  1887   Richmond   30.00
  1888   Richmond   25.00
LEE, Basil Leo   Discontent in New York City 1861-1865 A Dissertation.   Wraps.
  1943   Washington, DC   20.00
LEE, Cazenove Gardner   Lee Chronicles   Studies of the Early Generations of the Lees of Virginia.
  1957   New York   30.00
LEE, Charles Robert, Jr.   The Confederate Constitutions.
  1963   Chapel Hill, NC   35.00
LEE, Edmund Jennings   Lee of Virginia 1642-1892.
  1895   Philadelphia   200.00
  1974   Baltimore   30.00
LEE, F. D. and AGNEW, J. L.   Historical Record of the City of Savannah.
  1869   Savannah   75.00
LEE, Fitzhugh   Chancellorsville: Address Before Virginia Division of the Army of Northern Virginia.
  1879   Richmond   125.00

LEE, Fitzhugh   **General Lee.**
 For additional information, see Appendix: Great Commanders Series.
 1894   New York   35.00
 1894   New York   Ltd.   150.00
 1895   New York   30.00
 1897   New York   35.00
 1899   New York   35.00
 1905   New York   30.00
 1989   Wilmington, NC   30.00
LEE, Guy Carleton   **The True History of the Civil War.**
 1903   Philadelphia   15.00
LEE, Laura Elizabeth   **Forget-Me-Nots of the Civil War.**
 1909   St. Louis   125.00
LEE, Richard M.   **General Lee's City: An Illustrated Guide to the Historic Sites of Confederate Richmond.**   Wraps.
 1987   McLean   16.95
LEE, Richard M.   **Mr. Lincoln's City: An Illustrated Guide to the Civil War Sites of Washington.** Wraps.
 1981   McLean   15.00
LEE, Robert E.   **"To Markie": The Letters of Robert E. Lee to Martha Custis Williams,** edited by Avery Craven.
 1933   Cambridge   50.00
 1934   50.00
LEE, Robert E.   **General Order Number Nine.**   Wraps.
 (1955)   Chicago   30.00
LEE, Robert E.   **Glimpses of the Past, Letters of Robert E. Lee to Henry Kayser 1838-1846.** Wraps.
 1936   St. Louis   15.00
LEE, Robert E.   **Recollections and Letters of General Robert E. Lee.**
 1904   New York   45.00
 1905   New York   40.00
 1924   New York   35.00
 1988   Wilmington, NC   25.00
 1988   Wilmington, NC   Wraps   8.95
LEE, Robert E.   **Reconstruction.   Testimony of Gen. Robert E. Lee Before the Congressional Committee.** Wraps.
 1866   New York   50.00
LEE, Robert E., Jr.   **My Father, General Lee.**
 1960   Garden City, NY   15.00
LEE, Susan P.   **Memoirs of William Nelson Pendleton.**
 1893   Philadelphia   200.00
LEE, William Mack   **History of the Life of Rev. Wm. Mack Lee, Body Servant of General Robert E. Lee.**   Wraps.
 1918   Newport News, VA   100.00
LEECH, Margaret   **The Garfield Orbit.**
 1978   New York   15.00
LEECH, Margaret   **Reveille in Washington.**
 1941   New York   20.00
 1945   New York   20.00
LEECH, Samuel Vanderlip   **The Raid of John Brown at Harper's Ferry as I Saw It.**
 1909   Washington, DC   35.00

LEEPER, Wesley Thurman   **Rebels Valiant, Second Arkansas Mounted Rifles (Dismounted).**
1964   Little Rock, AR   40.00
LEFLER, Hugh Talmage   **Hinton Rowan Helper,   Advocate of "White America."** Wraps.
1935   Charlottesville, VA   15.00
A Legal View of the Seizure of Messrs. Mason and Slidell. Wraps.
1861   New York   25.00
LEGEAR, Clara, compiled by   **The Hotchkiss Map Collection.** Wraps.
1951   Washington, DC   10.00
Legends of the Operations of the Army of the Cumberland. Wraps.
1869   Washington, DC   80.00
LEGRAND, Julia   **The Journal of _____**, edited by Kate Mason Rowland and Mrs. Morris L. Croxall.
1911   Richmond   100.00
LEIB, Charles   **Nine Months in the Quartermaster's Department.**
1862   Cincinnati   70.00
LEIGH, Egbert G., Jr.   **An Appreciation of Colonel Archer Anderson, Late President of the Tredegar Company.** Wraps.
1918   n.p.   40.00
LELAND, Charles Godfrey   **Memoirs.**
1893   New York   30.00
LELAND, John A.   **A Voice from South Carolina.**
1879   Charleston, SC   100.00
LENFEST, Solomon A.   **The Diary of _____ Co. G, Sixth Massachusetts Infantry While Stationed at Suffolk, Virginia August 29, 1862 to May 29, 1863.** Wraps.
1975   Suffolk   20.00
LENTZ, Perry   **The Falling Hills.**
1967   New York   15.00
LEON, Louis   **Diary of a Tar Heel Confederate Soldier.**
1913   Charlotte   100.00
LEONARD, Albert C.   **The Boys in Blue of 1861-65.**
1904   Lancaster   30.00
LESLIE, Frank   **Frank Leslie's Illustrated Famous Leaders and Battle Scenes of the Civil War**, edited by Louis S. Moat.
1896   New York   125.00
Recent reprint   35.00
LESLIE, Frank   **Frank Leslie's Illustrated History of the Civil War**, edited by Louis S. Moat.
1895   New York   150.00
LESLIE, Frank   **Frank Leslie's Illustrated Newspaper 1861-65.**
5 Vols.   bound   1200.00
Individual volumes   175.00
LESLIE, Frank   **Frank Leslie's Pictorial History of the Civil War**, edited by Ephraim Squire. 2 Vols.
1861-62 New York   100.00
LESLIE, Frank   **Frank Leslie's Scenes and Portraits of the Civil War.**
10 parts in 1 Vol.
1894   New York   110.00
LESTER, C. Edwards   **Life and Public Services of Charles Sumner.**
1874   New York   25.00

LESTER, Frank A.   Society of the Ninth Michigan Infantry Veteran Volunteers Semi-Centennial Roster.   Wraps.
    1911   Lansing   60.00
LESTER, John C. and **WILSON**, D. L.   Ku Klux Klan, Its Origin, Growth and Disbandment.
    1905   New York   175.00
LESTER, Richard I.   Confederate Finance and Purchasing in Great Britain.
    1975   Charlottesville   16.00
LETFORD, W., et al   Location and Classification and Dates of Military Events in Alabama, 1861-1865.   Wraps.
    1961   University, AL   20.00
Letter from Secretary of War . . . Relative to Military Service Rendered by the Missouri Militia. 38th Cong. 1st Sess. Ho. of Reps. Doc. 59. Wraps.
    1864   Washington, DC   30.00
Letter from the Secretary of War . . . Missouri Troops in Service During the Civil War. 57th Cong. 1st Sess. Senate Doc. 412.
    1902   Washington, DC   75.00
Letter to the President by a Refugee. See: BARNARD, F. A. P.
LETTERMAN, Jonathan   Medical Recollections of the Army of the Potomac.
    1866   New York   100.00
LEVEY, William T.   The Blue and the Gray, a Sketch of Soldier Life in Camp and Field in the Army of the Civil War.   Wraps.
    1904   50.00
LEVIN, A. L.   This Awful Drama: General Edwin Gray Lee, C.S.A. and His Family.
    1987   New York   14.95
LEWIS, Berkeley R.   Notes on Ammunition of the American Civil War **1861-1865.** Wraps.
    1959   Washington, DC   25.00
LEWIS, Berkeley R.   Notes on Cavalry Weapons of the American Civil War. Wraps.
    1961   Washington, DC   25.00
LEWIS, Berkeley R.   Small Arms and Ammunition in the U.S. Service **1776-1865.**
    1956   Washington, DC   35.00
LEWIS, Charles Bertrand   Field, Fort and Fleet.
    1885   Detroit   70.00
LEWIS, Charles Edward   War Sketches.
    1897   London   100.00
LEWIS, Charles Lee   Admiral Franklin Buchanan.
    1929   Baltimore   40.00
LEWIS, Charles Lee   David Glasgow Farragut, Our First Admiral.
    1943   Annapolis   40.00
LEWIS, Charles Lee   David Glasgow Farragut. 2 Vols.
    1941-43 Annapolis   50.00
LEWIS, Charles Lee   Matthew Fontaine Maury, Pathfinder of the Seas.
    1927   Annapolis   30.00
LEWIS, Emmanuel R.   Seacoast Fortifications of the United States from Colonial Times to World War II.   Wraps.
    1986   9.95

LEWIS, George   The History of Battery E, First Regiment Rhode Island Light Artillery.
1892   Providence   90.00
LEWIS, George W.   The Campaigns of the 124th Regiment Ohio Volunteer Infantry.
1894   Akron   175.00
LEWIS, John Howard   Recollections from 1860 to 1865.   Wraps.
1895   Washington, DC   750.00
1983   Dayton 15.00
1983   Dayton Wraps   10.00
LEWIS, Lloyd   Captain Sam Grant.
1950   Boston   25.00
LEWIS, Lloyd   Letters from Lloyd Lewis Showing Steps in the Research for His Biography of U.S. Grant.
1950   Boston   20.00
LEWIS, Lloyd   Myths After Lincoln.
1929   New York   15.00
1941   New York   15.00
1973   14.00
LEWIS, Lloyd   Sherman, Fighting Prophet.
1932   New York   30.00
1958   New York   25.00
LEWIS, Montgomery S.   Legends That Libel Lincoln.
1946   New York   10.00
LEWIS, Oscar   The War in the Far West: 1861-1865.
1961   New York   25.00
LEWIS, Osceola   History of the 138th Regiment, Pennsylvania Volunteer Infantry.
1866   Norristown   75.00
LEWIS, Paul   Yankee Admiral A Biography of David Dixon Porter.
1968   New York   20.00
LEWIS, Richard   Camp Life of a Confederate Boy, of Bratton's Brigade, Longstreet's Corps, C.S.A. . . .
1983   Gaithersburg   25.00
LEWIS, Samuel E.   Surgeon General Samuel Preston Moore and the Officers of the Medical Depts. of the Confederate States.   Wraps.
1911   n.p.   60.00
LEWIS, Samuel E.   The Treatment of Prisoners-of-War 1861-65.   Wraps.
1910   Richmond   20.00
LEWIS, T. H.   History of Company E of the Sixth Minnesota Regiment of Volunteer Infantry.
1899   St. Paul   125.00
LEWIS, Thomas A.   The Guns of Cedar Creek.
1988   New York   24.95
LEWIS, Virgil A.   How West Virginia was made, proceedings of the First Convention of the People of Northwestern Virginia at Wheeling.
1909   Charleston   30.00
LEWIS, William T.   The Centennial History of Winston County, Mississippi.   Wraps.
1972   Pasadena, TX   25.00

The Libby Chronicle. Devoted to Facts and Fun.
    1889   Albany, NY   80.00
Library of the Late Charles D. Richmond . . . ; Catalogue of the Portion Relating to the War of the Rebellion and to Slavery. . . . Wraps.
    1899   New York   50.00
Licking County's Gallant Soldiers, Who Died in Defence of Our Glorious Union. Wraps.
    1874   Newark   30.00
LIDDELL HART, Basil H.   Sherman: Soldier, Realist, American.
    1929   New York   25.00
    1930   New York   25.00
    1958   New York   20.00
LIDDELL HART, Basil H.   Sherman: The Genius of the Civil War.
    1930   London   35.00
LIDDELL, St. John R.   Liddell's Record, edited by N. C. Hughes.
    1985   Dayton   20.00
LIEBER, Francis   Guerrilla Parties Considered with Reference to the Laws and Usages of War. Wraps.
    1862   New York   60.00
LIEBER, Francis   Instructions for the Government of Armies of the United States in the Field. Wraps.
    1863   New York   40.00
LIEBER, Francis   No Party Now, But All For Our Country: An Address. Wraps.
    1863   Philadelphia   10.00
    1864   New York   10.00
LIEBER, Francis   On Civil Liberty and Self-Government.
    1859   Philadelphia   40.00
The Lieutenant Willis Jefferson Dance, Junior, Memorial Lectures Delivered at the Virginia Military Institute, Lexington, Virginia 1952-1963.
    1965   Lexington   50.00
Life and Campaigns of Lieut. Gen. Thomas J. Jackson (Stonewall Jackson). See: DABNEY, Robert L.
Life and Character of William Allan Late Principal of McDonogh School. Wraps.
    1889   McDonogh   25.00
The Life and Public Services of Major-General Benjamin F. Butler. Wraps.
    1864   Philadelphia   40.00
Life and Reminiscences of General William T. Sherman by Distinguished Men of His Time.
    1891   n.p.   35.00
Life in the South.   See: HOPLEY, Catherine Cooper.
Life of James W. Jackson, The Alexandria Hero, The Slayer of Ellsworth, the First Martyr in the Cause of Southern Independence. Wraps.
    1985   Falls Church   Ltd.   7.00
Life of John C. Calhoun. Presenting a Condensed History of Political Events from 1811 to 1843. Wraps.
    1843   New York   100.00
Life of Stephen A. Douglas.
    1860   New York   15.00
The Life, Campaigns and Battles of General Ulysses S. Grant.
    1868   New York   10.00

The Life, Campaigns, and Public Services of General McClellan.
1864   Philadelphia   20.00
The Life, Trial and Execution of Capt. John Brown.
1859   New York   50.00
The Light and Dark of the Rebellion.
1863   Pennsylvania   40.00
LIGHTFOOT, Robert M., Jr., edited by   The   Lincoln   Collections   of
Bradley University.   Wraps.
1962   Peoria, IL   15.00
LIGHTSEY, Ada Christine   **The Veteran's Story: Dedicated to the**
Heroes Who Wore the Gray.
1899   Meridian, MS   200.00
Lincoln and His America with the Words of Abraham Lincoln, arranged by
David Plowden.
1970   New York   25.00
LINCOLN, Abraham   **Abraham Lincoln's Letter to Major General Joseph**
Hooker, dated January 26, 1863.
1942   Chicago   40.00
LINCOLN, Abraham   **Addresses and Letters of _____,** edited by Charles
W. Moore.
1914   New York   10.00
LINCOLN, Abraham   **Complete Works of Abraham Lincoln,** edited by
John G. Nicolay and John Hay.   12 Vols.
(1894)   Lincoln Memorial Univ.   125.00
1905   New York   12 Vols.   125.00
1907   New York   2 Vols.   25.00
LINCOLN, Abraham   **A House Divided Against Itself Cannot Stand.**
1936   Chicago   Ltd.   20.00
LINCOLN, Abraham   **Lincoln Letters (The Bibliophile Society).**
1913   n.p.   10.00
LINCOLN, Abraham   **Lincoln's Ellsworth Letter.**
1916   New York   Ltd.   30.00
LINCOLN, Abraham   **Lincoln's Last Speech in Springfield in the Cam-**
paign of 1858.
1925   Chicago   25.00
LINCOLN, Abraham   **Uncollected Letters of . . . ,** edited by Gilbert A.
Tracy.
1916   Boston   Ltd.   20.00
1917   Boston   Ltd.   20.00
LINCOLN, Abraham   **The Writings of Abraham Lincoln,** edited by
Arthur Brooks Lapsley.   8 Vols.
1905   New York   35.00
LINCOLN, Charles P.   **"Engagement at Thompson Station, Tenn."**
Wraps.
1893   n.p.   25.00
LINCOLN, Levi   **A Memorial of William Sever Lincoln.**
1899   Worcester   30.00
LINCOLN, William S.   **Life with the Thirty-fourth Mass. Infantry.**
1879   Worcester   75.00
Lincoln-Douglas Debates.   See: Political Debates. . . .

LINDEMAN, Jack, edited by   The Conflict of Convictions, American Writers Report the Civil War.
1968   Philadelphia   20.00
LINDERMAN, G. F.   Embattled Courage: The Experience of Combat in the American Civil War.
1987   New York   27.95
LINDQUIST, Orville A.   Common Fallacies Regarding United States History. Wraps.
1953   Richmond   5.00
LINDSEY, T. J.   Ohio at Shiloh: Reports of the Commission.
1903   Cincinnati   40.00
LINDSLEY, J. Frank   Pilgrimage of the Fifteenth Regiment New Jersey Volunteers' Veteran Assoc. to White Oak Church Camp Grounds and Battlefields of Fredericksburg, Va. & Vicinity May 22 to 26, 1906.
1906   Newark   70.00
LINDSLEY, John B.   Military Annals of Tennessee, Confederate.
1886   Nashville   175.00
LINK, Arthur S. and REMBERT, W. Patrick, edited by   Writing Southern History, Essays in Historiography in Honor of Fletcher M. Green.
1967   Baton Rouge   10.00
LIPPITT, Francis   A Treatise on Intrenchments.
1866   New York   90.00
List of Staff Officers of the Confederate States Army.   Wraps.
1891   Washington, DC   125.00
List of Synonyms of Organizations in the Volunteer Service of the United States.
1885   Washington, DC   75.00
A List of the Awards of the Congressional Medal of Honor . . . Under the Authority of the Congress of the United States 1862-1926. Wraps.
1927   Washington, DC   30.00
LITTLE, George and MAXWELL, James R.   History of Lumsden's Battery, C.S.A. Wraps.
(c.1905) Tuscaloosa   100.00
LITTLE, Henry F. W.   The Seventh Regiment New Hampshire Volunteers in the War of the Rebellion.
1896   Concord   70.00
LITTLE, R. H.   A Year of Starvation and Plenty.
(c.1900) Belton, TX   300.00
1966   Belton, TX   30.00
LITTLETON, William G.   The Battle Between the Alabama and the Kearsarge, Off Cherbourg, France, Sunday June 19, 1864 An Address. Wraps.
1932   n.p.   35.00
LITWACK, Leon F.   Been in the Storm So Long, the Aftermath of Slavery.
1979   New York   25.00
LIVELY, Robert A.   Fiction Fights the Civil War.
1957   Chapel Hill, NC   30.00
LIVERMORE, Mary A.   My Story of the War.: A Woman's Narrative.
1888   Hartford   40.00
1889   Hartford   30.00

1890   Hartford   30.00
1891   Hartford   30.00
1972   40.00

LIVERMORE, Mary A.   **The Story of My Life.**
1897   Hartford   30.00   ARTIST SIGNED
1898   Hartford   30.00

LIVERMORE, Thomas L.   **Days and Events 1860-1866.**
1920   Boston   70.00

LIVERMORE, Thomas L.   **History of the Eighteenth New Hampshire Volunteers.**
1904   Boston   65.00

LIVERMORE, Thomas L.   **Numbers and Losses in the Civil War - 1861-1865.**
1901   Boston   25.00
1957   Bloomington   25.00
1969   New York   25.00
1986   20.00

Lives of Jefferson Davis and Stonewall Jackson.
1890   New York   30.00

Lloyd's Battle History of the Great Rebellion Complete in One Volume.
1866   New York   30.00

LLOYD, John Uri   **Felix Moses, the Beloved Jew of Stringtown on the Pike.**
1930   Cincinnati   50.00

LLOYD, John Uri   **Stringtown on the Pike   A Tale of Northernmost Kentucky.**
1901   New York   10.00

LLOYD, John Uri   **Warwick of the Knobs   A Story of Stringtown County, Kentucky.**
1901   New York   10.00

LLOYD, William P.   **History of the First Regiment Pennsylvania Reserve Cavalry.**
1864   Philadelphia 100.00

The Location of the Monuments, Markers and Tablets on the Battlefield of Gettysburg.   Wraps.
1921   60.00

LOCKE, David R.   **Divers Views, Opinions and Prophecies of Petroleum V. Nasby.**
1867   Cincinnati   20.00

LOCKE, E. W.   **Three Years in Camp and Hospital.**
1870   Boston   40.00
1871   Boston   40.00
1872   Boston   30.00

LOCKE, William H.   **The Story of the Regiment.**
1868   Philadelphia 110.00

LOCKRIDGE, Ross, Jr.   **Raintree County.**
1948   Boston   10.00

LOCKWOOD, James D.   **Life and Adventures of a Drummer-Boy.**
1893   Albany   75.00

LOCKWOOD, John   **Our Campaign Around Gettysburg.**
1864   Brooklyn   75.00

LOEHR, Charles T.   War History of the Old First Virginia Infantry Regiment. Wraps.
    1884   Richmond   700.00
    1970   Dayton 10.00
    1978   12.50
LOFTON, John   Denmark Vesey's Revolt: The Slave Plot that Lit a Fuse to Fort Sumter. Wraps.
    1983   10.00
LOGAN, H. C.   Cartridges, a Pictorial Digest of Small Arms Ammunition.
    1954   Huntington   25.00
LOGAN, India W. P.   Kelion Franklin Peddicord of Quirk's Scouts, Morgan's Kentucky Cavalry, C.S.A.
    1908   New York   300.00
LOGAN, John A.   The Great Conspiracy.
    1886   New York   30.00
LOGAN, John A.   The Logan Monument Memorial (edited by George Francis James.)
    1898   Chicago   30.00
LOGAN, John A.   Speech on the Fitz-John Porter Case Dec. 29, 1882 and Jan. 2-3 1883.
    1883   Washington, DC   30.00
LOGAN, John A.   The Volunteer Soldier of America.
    1887   Chicago   50.00
    1979   20.00
LOGAN, Mrs. John A.   Reminiscences of a Soldier's Wife.
    1913   New York   30.00
LOGAN, Kate Virginia Cox   My Confederate Girlhood, Memoirs, edited by Lily L. Morrill.
    1932   Richmond   45.00
LOGAN, T. M.   Oration Delivered at the Reunion of the Hampton Legion in Columbia, S.C. July 21, 1875. Wraps.
    1875   Charleston   30.00
LOMASK, Milton   Andrew Johnson: President on Trial.
    1960   New York   15.00
LOMAX, Elizabeth Lindsay   Leaves from an Old Washington Diary, 1854-1863, edited by Lindsay Lomax Wood.
    1943   New York   25.00
LONDON, H. A.   Memorial Address on the Life and Services of General Bryan Grimes, etc. Wraps.
    1886   Raleigh, NC   90.00
LONG, A. L. and **WRIGHT**, Marcus J., edited by   Memoirs of Robert E. Lee, His Military and Personal History.
    1877   New York   100.00
    1886   New York   75.00
    1887   New York   50.00
    1983   Secaucus, NJ   10.00
LONG, E. B.   The Saints and the Union, Utah Territory During the Civil War.
    1981   Urbana   20.00

LONG, E. B. and LONG, Barbara   The Civil War Day by Day, An Almanac 1861-1865.
1971   Garden City, NY   30.00
Recent reprint Wraps 19.95
LONG, Ellen Call   Florida Breezes; or, Florida, New and Old.
1962   Gainesville   25.00
LONG, H. W.   The Story of the Battle as the Field is Marked Today, Gettysburg, as the Battle Was Fought. Wraps.
1927   n.p.   20.00
LONG, James T.   Gettysburg: How the Battle Was Fought. Wraps.
1890   Harrisburg 35.00
1890   Harrisburg 35.00
1891   35.00
LONG, James T., edited by   . . . Gettysburg Souvenir . . . Compliments of . . . Hotel Gettysburg. Wraps.
(c.1890)   Gettysburg   20.00
LONG, James T.   The Sixteenth Decisive Battle of the World . . . Gettysburg. Wraps.
1906   Gettysburg 30.00
1911   Gettysburg 20.00
LONG, Lessel   Twelve Months in Andersonville.
1886   Huntington, IN   100.00
1965   25.00
LONG, N. M.   Address on General Robert E. Lee.
1920   20.00
LONG, Walter E.   Andrew Davidson Long, Stonewall's Foot Cavalryman.
1965   Austin   30.00
LONGACRE, Edward G.   The Cavalry at Gettysburg; A Tactical Study of Mounted Operations During the Civil War's Pivotal Campaign 9 June-14 July, 1863.
1986   Rutherford   39.95
LONGACRE, Edward G.   From Antietam to Fort Fisher. The Civil War Letters of Edward King Wightman, 1862-1865.
1985   40.00
LONGACRE, Edward G.   From Union Stars to Top Hat: Biography of General James Harrison Wilson.
1972   Harrisburg   35.00
LONGACRE, Edward G.   The Man Behind the Guns, a Biography of General Henry Jackson Hunt.
1977   South Brunswick 20.00
LONGACRE, Edward G.   Mounted Raids of the Civil War.
1975   South Brunswick 25.00
LONGACRE, Edward G.   To Gettysburg and Beyond: The Twelfth New Jersey, II Corps, Army of the Potomac, 1862-1865.
1988   Hightstown   36.00
LONGMORE, T. A.   Treastise on Gunshot Wounds, Authorized and Adopted by Surgeon General of U.S. Army., etc.
1863   Philadelphia   275.00
LONGSTREET, Helen D.   Lee and Longstreet at High Tide.
1904   Gainesville, GA   125.00
1905   Gainesville, GA   100.00

1969   New York   45.00
1981   31.00
1989   Wilmington, NC   30.00
LONGSTREET, James   From Manassas to Appomattox.
✓1896   Philadelphia   200.00
1903   Philadelphia   125.00
1912   100.00
1960   Bloomington, edited by James I. Robertson   50.00
1976   Millwood, NY   30.00
1984   35.00
1985   30.00
LONN, Ella   Desertion During the Civil War.
1928   New York   60.00
1966   Gloucester   20.00
LONN, Ella   Foreigners in the Confederacy.
1940   Chapel Hill, NC   75.00
1965   Gloucester   25.00
LONN, Ella   Foreigners in the Union Army and Navy.
1951   Baton Rouge   50.00
1965   Gloucester   30.00
1969   35.00
LONN, Ella   Reconstruction in Louisiana After 1868.
1918   New York   50.00
1967   22.50
LONN, Ella   Salt as a Factor in the Confederacy.
1933   New York   90.00
1965   University, AL   30.00
LOOMIS, John S.   Report of . . . Expedition of Surgeons and Nurses . . . to Vicksburg and Memphis for Relief of Sick and Wounded Soldiers. Wraps.
1863   Springfield, IL   20.00
LORANT, Stefan   Lincoln, A Picture Story of His Life.
1952   New York   25.00
1957   New York   20.00
LORANT, Stefan   Lincoln, His Life in Photographs.
1941   New York   20.00
1954   20.00
LORD, Edward O., edited by   History of the Ninth Regiment New Hampshire Volunteers.
1895   Concord   75.00
LORD, Francis A.   Civil War Collector's Encyclopedia, Arms, Uniforms, and Equipment of the Union and Confederacy.
1963   Harrisburg   30.00
Various later printings   25.00
Recent reprint   19.95
LORD, Francis A.   Civil War Collector's Encyclopedia. Vol. 2
1975   n.p.   25.00
LORD, Francis A.   Civil War Collector's Encyclopedia. Vol. 3
1979   West Columbia, SC   25.00
LORD, Francis A.   Civil War Collector's Encyclopedia. Vol. 4
1984   Columbia, SC   25.00

LORD, Francis A.   Civil War Sutlers and their Wares.
 1969 New York 35.00
LORD, Francis A.   Lincoln's Railroad Man: Herman Haupt.
 1969 Rutherford 25.00
LORD, Francis A.   They Fought for the Union.
 1960 Harrisburg 30.00
 1969 New York 25.00
 1988 New York 12.98
LORD, Francis A. and **WISE**, Arthur Bands and Drummer Boys of the Civil War.
 1966 New York 25.00
LORD, Francis A. and **WISE**, Arthur Uniforms of the Civil War.
 1970 New York 30.00
LORD, George A.   A Short Narrative and Military Experience of Corp. _____. Wraps.
 1864 Troy 65.00
LORD, John Frontier Dust.
 1926 Hartford Ltd. 60.00
LORD, Theodore A. A Summary of the Case of General Fitz-John Porter. Wraps.
 1883 San Francisco 35.00
LORING, Charles G., et al Correspondence on the Present Relations Between Great Britain and the United States.
 1862 Boston 30.00
LORING, Charles G. England's Liability for Indemnity: Remarks on the Letter of "Historicus" Dated Nov. 4, 1863. Wraps.
 1864 Boston 25.00
LORING, Charles G. Neutral Relations of England and the United States.
 1863 New York 20.00
 1863 Boston 20.00
LORING, W. W. A Confederate Soldier in Egypt.
 1884 New York 100.00
LOSSEN, Christopher Tennessee Forgotten Warriors, Frank Cheatham and His Confederate Division.
 1989 University, TN 24.95
LOSSING, Benson J. A History of the Civil War. Wraps 16 parts.
 1912 New York 75.00
 1912 New York 1 Vol. edition 65.00
 1927 1 Vol. 75.00
LOSSING, Benson J. The League of States.
 1863 New York 15.00
LOSSING, Benson J. The Life, Campaigns and Battles of General Ulysses S. Grant.
 1868 New York 15.00
LOSSING, Benson J. Memoir of Lieut.-Col. John T. Greble.
 1870 Philadelphia 35.00
LOSSING, Benson J. The Pictorial Field Book of the Civil War. 3 Vols.
 1878 New Haven 75.00
 Many other editions 75.00

LOSSING, Benson J.   **Pictorial History of the Civil War.** 3 Vols.
  1866-68 Philadelphia   75.00
  1876   Hartford   75.00
  Many later editions   40.00
LOSSON, C.   **Tennessee's Forgotten Warriors: Frank Cheatham and His Confederate Division.**
  1989   Knoxville   24.95
LOTHROP, Charles H.   **A History of the First Regiment Iowa Cavalry Veteran Volunteers.**
  1890   Lyons   240.00
LOTHROP, Thornton K.   **William Henry Seward.**
  1896   Boston and New York   10.00
  1899   Boston   10.00
LOUGHBOROUGH, Mrs. James (Mary Ann)   **My Cave Life in Vicksburg . . . By a Lady.**
  1864   New York   150.00
  1881   100.00
  1882   Little Rock 100.00
  1882   St. Louis   100.00
  1976   Spartanburg, SC   30.00
  1989   Wilmington, NC   24.95
Louisiana - Confederate Military History.   See: **Confederate Military History, Vol. X** (Vol. XIII, 1988 reprint ed.).
Louisiana in the Civil War A Bibliography, compiled by Edith T. Atkinson. Wraps.
  1962   Baton Rouge   10.00
LOVE, John   **Report of Major General Love, of the Indiana Legion.**
  1863   Indianapolis   45.00
LOVE, William DeLoss   **Wisconsin in the War of the Rebellion.**
  1866   Chicago   75.00
The Love-Life of Brig. Gen. Henry M. Naglee Consisting of a Correspondence on Love, War and Politics.
  1867   n.p.   15.00
LOWELL, Charles Russell   **Memoirs of the War of '61 and Cousins. . . .**
  1920   Boston   35.00
LOWERY, Roland   **The Story of Battery I First Regiment Ohio Volunteer Light Artillery 1861-1865.** Wraps.
  1971   Cincinnati   20.00
  1972   Cincinnati   20.00
LOWREY, Grosvenor P.   **English Neutrality. Is the Alabama a British Pirate?** Wraps.
  1863   Philadelphia   75.00
  1863   New York   75.00
LOWRY, Terry   **September Blood: The Battle of Carnifex Ferry.** Wraps.
  1985   Charleston   10.00
Loyalist's Ammunition. Wraps.
  1863   Philadelphia   10.00
LOZIER, John Hogarth   **Forty Rounds, From Fighting Chaplain.**
  n.d.   Mt. Vernon, IA Wraps   30.00
Lt.-Col. Charles Lyon Chandler A Memorial.
  1864   Cambridge   25.00

LUBBOCK, Francis R.   Six Decades in Texas   or, Memoirs of Francis Richard Lubbock, Governor of Texas in War Time 1861-1863, edited by C. W. Raines.
1900   Austin   250.00
LUCAS, Daniel B.   Memoir of John Yates Beall: His Life, Trial; Correspondence; Diary.
1865   Montreal   450.00
LUCAS, Daniel R.   New History of the 99th Indiana Infantry.
1900   Rockford, IL   175.00
LUCAS, Marion Brunson   Sherman and the Burning of Columbia.
1976   College Station, TX   25.00
1988   Wraps   11.95
LUCKE, Jerome B., L.L.B.   History of the New Haven Grays from Sept. 13, 1816, to Sept. 13, 1876.
1876   New Haven   60.00
LUCKE, Wilbert   Journey to Honey Hill. Wraps.
1976   Washington, DC   10.00
LUDLOW, William   The Battle of Allatoona October 5, 1864.   Wraps.
n.d.   Michigan   25.00
LUDWIG, Emil   Lincoln.
1930   Boston   10.00
LUFKIN, Edwin B.   History of the Thirteenth Maine Regiment.
1898   Brighton   140.00
LUNT, Dolly Sumner   See: **BURGE,** Dolly Sumner L.
LUNT, George   The Origin of the Late War.
1866   New York   45.00
1867   New York   35.00
LUSK, William Thompson   War Letters of _____ Captain, Assistant Adjutant-General U.S. Vols. 1861-1863.
1911   New York   65.00
LUTHIN, Reinhard H.   The First Lincoln Campaign.
1944   Cambridge   10.00
1964   10.00
LUTHIN, Reinhard H.   The Real Abraham Lincoln.
1960   Englewood Cliffs, NJ   20.00
LUVAAS, Jay   The Military Legacy of the Civil War: The European Inheritance.
1959   Chicago   35.00
LUVAAS, Jay and **NELSON,** Harold W.   The Gettysburg Guide.   Wraps.
1987   8.95
LUVAAS, Jay and **NELSON,** Harold W., edited by   The U.S. Army War College Guide to the Battle of Antietam: The Maryland Campaign of 1862.
1987   Carlisle   21.95
LUVAAS, Jay and **NELSON,** Harold W., edited by   The U.S. Army War College Guide to the Battle of Gettysburg.
1986   25.00
LUVAAS, Jay and **NELSON,** Harold W.   The War College Guide to Chancellorsville and Fredericksburg.
1988   21.95
1989   Wraps   8.95

LYLE, William W.   Lights and Shadows of Army Life.
    1865   Cincinnati   135.00
LYMAN, Theodore   Meade's Headquarters 1863-65 Letters of Col.
    Theodore Lyman from the Wilderness to Apomattox, edited by George
    'R. Agassiz.
    1922   Boston   50.00
    1970   Freeport   30.00
    1987   29.95
LYNCH, Charles H.   The Civil War Diary 1862-1865 of _____ 18th
    Conn. Volunteers.
    1915   Hartford   45.00
LYNCH, John R.   The Facts of Reconstruction.
    1913   New York   60.00
    1979   New York   10.00
LYON, James A.   A Lecture on Christianity and the Civil Laws.   Wraps.
    1859   Columbus, MS   30.00
LYON, Mattie H.   My Memoirs of the War Between the States. Wraps.
    1960   n.p.   35.00
LYON, William Penn   Reminiscences of the Civil War Compiled from the
    War Correspondence of Col. _____, edited by William P. Lyon, Jr.
    1907   San Jose, CA   110.00
LYONS, W. F.   Brigadier-General Thomas Francis Meagher.
    1870   New York   60.00
    1879   50.00
    1886   New York   50.00
Lyrics, Incidents, and Sketches of the Rebellion.   See: **BILL**, Ledyard
LYSTER, Henry Francis LeHunte   Recollections of the Bull Run
    Campaign. Wraps.
    1888   Detroit   35.00
LYTLE, Andrew N.   Bedford Forrest and His Critter Company.
    1931   New York   75.00
    1938   London   75.00
    1960   New York   40.00
    1984   18.00
LYTLE, Andrew N.   The Long Night.
    1936   Indianapolis   40.00
MACALUSO, G. J.   The Fort Pillow Massacre: The Reason Why.
    1989   New York   11.95
MACARTNEY, Clarence Edward   Grant and His Generals.
    1953   New York   30.00
MACARTNEY, Clarence Edward   Highways and Byways of the Civil
    War.
    1926   Philadelphia   40.00
    1938   Pittsburgh   30.00
MACARTNEY, Clarence Edward   Lincoln and His Cabinet.
    1931   New York   15.00
MACARTNEY, Clarence Edward   Lincoln and His Generals.
    1925   Philadelphia   25.00
    1926   Philadelphia   25.00
    1970   17.50

MACARTNEY, Clarence Edward   Mr. Lincoln's Admirals.
   1950   New York   30.00
   1956   New York   30.00
MacBRIDE, Robert   Civil War Ironclads.
   1962   Philadelphia   25.00
MacBRIDE, Van Dyk   Confederate Patriotic Covers. Wraps.
   1943   Federalsburg, MD   25.00
MacCAULEY, Clay   Through Chancellorsville Into and Out of Libby Prison. Wraps.
   1904   n.p.   40.00
MacDONALD, Helen G.   Canadian Public Opinion on the American Civil War. Wraps.
   1926   New York   30.00
MacDONALD, Rose Mortimer Elizey   Mrs. Robert E. Lee.
   1939   Boston 35.00
   1973   25.00
MacDUFF, J. R.   The Soldier's Text-Book: or, Confidence in Time of War. Wraps.
   (c.1861) New York   40.00
MACHEN, Arthur W.   Letters of _____ with Biographical Sketch, edited by Arthur W. Machen, Jr.
   1917   Baltimore   20.00
MACK, Charles   First City Zouaves and City Grays, History of Harrisburg's Leading Military Organizations 1861-1913. . . .
   1914   60.00
MACKALL, William W.   A Son's Recollections of His Father.
   1930   300.00
MacKENZIE, Robert   America and Her Army.
   1865   London   50.00
MACLAY, Edgar Stanton   A History of the United States Navy from 1775 to 1902. 3 Vols.
   1894-1901   New York   75.00
MACLAY, Edgar Stanton   Reminiscences of the Old Navy (1800-1875).
   1898   New York   Ltd.   75.00
MacLEAN, David   Prisoner of the Rebels in Texas. The Civil War Narrative of Aaron T. Sutton, Corporal, 83rd OVI.
   1978   45.00
MacLEOD, George H. B., M.D.   Notes on the Surgery of the War in the Crimea, with Remarks on the Treatment of Gunshot Wounds.
   1862   Philadelphia 350.00
MacNAMARA, Daniel G.   History of the Ninth Regiment Massachusetts Volunteer Infantry.
   1899   Boston 80.00
MacNAMARA, Michael H.   The Irish Ninth in Bivouac and Battle.
   1867   Boston 75.00
MACON, Nathaniel   Letters to Charles O'Connor - The Destruction of the Union Is Emancipation. Wraps.
   1862   Philadelphia 25.00
MACON, Thomas J., compiled by   Life Gleanings.
   1913   Richmond   70.00

MACON, Thomas J.   Reminiscences of the First Company of Richmond Howitzers.
(1909)   Richmond   125.00
1913   Richmond   100.00
MACRAE, David   The Americans at Home.
1952   New York   25.00
MACY, Jesse   Jesse Macy, an Autobiography, edited by Katharine M. Noyes.
1933   Springfield, IL   50.00
1933   Menash, WI   50.00
MADAUS, Howard Michael   The Battle Flags of the Confederate Army of Tennessee.   Wraps.
1976   Milwaukee   30.00
MADDEX, Jack P., Jr.   The Virginia Conservatives 1867-1879.
1970   Chapel Hill, NC   15.00
MADDOCKS, Elden B.   History of the Twenty-sixth Maine Regiment.
1899   Bangor 125.00
MADISON, Lucy Foster   Lincoln. 2 Vols.
1928   New York   Boxed   40.00
MAFFITT, Emma Martin   The Life and Services of John Newland Maffitt.   Seldom found in good condition: the cover is usually speckled. Evidently the Neale warehouse suffered water damage as many of the Neale titles are speckled and water damaged.
1906   New York   250.00
MAFFITT, John N.   Nautilus, Or Cruising Under Canvas.
1871   New York   250.00
Magazine of Albemarle County History, Civil War Issue.   Wraps.
1964   Charlottesville   20.00
MAGEE, Harvey White   The Story of My Life.
1926   Albany   30.00
MAGILL, Mary Tucker   Women or Chronicles of the Late War.
1871   Baltimore   40.00
MAGILL, Robert M.   Co. "F," 39th Georgia Infantry.
1907   Richmond   150.00
MAGILL, Robert M.   Magill Family Record.
1907   Richmond   100.00
MAGLATHLIN, Henry B.   Company I, Fourth Massachusetts Regiment, Nine Months Volunteers in Service 1862-3.   Wraps.
1863   Boston   35.00
MAGNER, Blake A. and CAVANAUGH, Michael A.   A Photo Guide to Gettysburg Battlefield Commanders.   Wraps.
1988   6.95
MAHAN, Alfred Thayer   Admiral Farragut.
For additional information, see Appendix: Great Commanders Series.
1892   New York   80.00
1892   New York   Ltd.   125.00
1893   New York   75.00
1897   New York   75.00
1905   40.00
MAHAN, Alfred Thayer   From Sail to Steam.
1907   New York   50.00
1968   New York   23.00

MAHAN, Alfred Thayer The Gulf and Inland Waters.   See: Campaigns of the Civil War.

MAHAN, Alfred Thayer   Letter of Alfred Thayer Mahan to Samuel A'Court Ashe (1858-59.)
  1931   Durham, NC   125.00

MAHAN, Alfred Thayer   The Navy in the Civil War.
  1898   New York   35.00

MAHAN, Alfred Thayer   Some Neglected Aspects of War.
  1907   Boston   75.00

MAHAN, Asa   A Critical History of the Late American War.
  1877   New York   75.00

MAHAN, D. H.   An Elementary Course in Civil Engineering; for the Use of Cadets of the U.S. Military Academy.
  1856   New York   50.00

MAHAN, D. H.   An Elementary Treatise on Advanced Guard, Outpost and Detachment Service of Troops.
  1861   New York   40.00

MAHAN, D. H.   Summary of the Course of Permanent Fortification. . . .
  1860   West Point   300.00

MAHAN, D. H.   A Treatise on Field Fortifications.
  1846   New York   40.00
  1860   35.00
  1861   New York   35.00
  1968   17.50

MAHAN, J. C.   Memoirs of James Curtis Mahan.
  1919   Lincoln   75.00

MAHONE, William   The Battle of the Crater.   Wraps.
  n.d.   Petersburg   125.00

MAHONY, D. A.   The Prisoner of State.
  1863   New York   30.00

MAHOOD, W.   The Plymouth Pilgrims: A History of the Eighty-fifth New York Infantry in the Civil War.
  1989   Hightstown   30.00

MAILE, John Levi   "Prison Life in Andersonville."
  1912   Los Angeles   Ltd.   60.00

MAIN, Edwin M.   The Story of the Marches, Battles, and Incidents of The Third United States Colored Cavalry.
  1970   New York   35.00

Maine at Gettysburg. Report of the Maine Commissioners.
  1898   Portland   80.00

Major General Henry W. Lawton of Fort Wayne, Indiana.   Wraps.
  1954   Fort Wayne   10.00

MAJOR, Duncan K. and FITCH, Roger S.   Supply of Sherman's Army During the Atlanta Campaign.
  1911   Ft. Leavenworth   60.00

MALET, William Wyndham   An Errand to the South in the Summer of 1862.
  1863   London   200.00

MALKUS, Alida Sims   We Were There at the Battle of Gettysburg.
  1955   New York   25.00

MALLARD, R. Q.   Plantation Life Before Emancipation.
  1892   Richmond   35.00

MALONE, Bartlett Yancey   Whipt 'em Everytime, The Diary of _____
Co. H, 6th N. C. Regiment, edited by William Whatley Pierson, Jr.
1960   Jackson 30.00
1987   Wilmington, NC   25.00
MALONE, Dumas   The Pen of Douglas Southall Freeman.   Wraps.
1957   n.p.   40.00
MALONE, Thomas H.   Memoir of _____.
1928   Nashville   175.00
MALTBY, Charles   The Life and Public Services of Abraham Lincoln.
1884   Stockton, CA   50.00
The Man Without a Country.   Wraps.
1865   Boston   250.00
MANAKEE, Harold R.   Maryland in the Civil War.
1961   n.p.   50.00
1969   Baltimore   35.00
MANARIN, Louis H.   A Guide to Military Organizations and Installa-
tions North Carolina 1861-1865.   Wraps.
1961   Raleigh   20.00
MANARIN, Louis H.   North Carolina Troops.   See: North Carolina
Troops.
MANARIN, Louis H., edited by   Richmond at War.
1966   Chapel Hill, NC   35.00
MANARIN, Louis H. and DOWDEY, C.   The   History   of   Henrico
County.
1984   Charlottesville   15.00
MANARIN, Louis H. and WALLACE, Lee A., Jr.   Richmond Volunteers.
1969   Richmond   40.00
MANDERSON, Charles F.   The Twin Seven-Shooters.
1902   New York   50.00
MANDEVILLE, James de, compiled by   History of the 13th Regiment,
N.G., S.N.Y.
1894   New York   70.00
MANIGAULT, Arthur Middleton   A Carolinian Goes to War: The Civil
War Narrative of Arthur Middleton Manigault, Brigadier General, C.S.A.
1983   Columbia   25.00
MANIGAULT, Edward   Siege Train, the Journal of a Confederate
Artilleryman in the Defense of Charleston.
1986   Columbia   24.95
MANIGAULT, G.   The United States Unmasked.
1879   London   25.00
MANLY, Marline   The Old Knapsack; or, Longstreet's Mad Charge at
Knoxville.   Wraps.
n.d.   n.p.   30.00
MANN, A. Dudley   "My Ever Dearest Friend" The Letters of A. Dud-
ley Mann to Jefferson Davis.   See: Confederate Centennial Studies,
No. 14.
MANN, Albert W.   History of the Forty-fifth Regiment Massachusetts
Volunteer Militia.
1908   Boston   65.00
MANN, B. D.   They Were Heard from: VMI Alumni in the Civil War.
Wraps.
1986   Lexington, VA   4.50

MANN, J. T.   A Confederate Spy.   A Thrilling Story About His Escape from Choking Dead on the End of a Rope.   An Authentic Narrative. Wraps.
1908   Fitzgerald, GA   400.00

MANNING, J. F.   Epitome of the Geneva Award Contest in the Congress of the U.S.
1882   New York   25.00

MANNIX, D. P. and COWLEY, M.   Black Cargoes: A History of the Atlantic Slave Trade 1518 to 1865.
1963   New York   20.00

MANSFIELD, Edward D.   The Life and Military Services of Lieut.-General Winfield Scott.
1861   New York   20.00

MANSFIELD, Edward D.   A Popular and Authentic Life of Ulysses S. Grant.
1868   Cincinnati   20.00

MANTELL, Martin E.   Johnson, Grant, and Reconstruction Politics.
1973   New York   20.00

Manual of Military Telegraphy for the Signal, Service, United States Army, Embracing Permanent and Field Lines.
1872   Washington, DC   100.00

The Manual of the . . . National Guard N. Y.
1868   New York   30.00

Manual of the Panorama of the Battle of Shiloh.
1885   Chicago   25.00

Map of the Battlefield of Fredericksburg.
1866   Lynchburg, VA   300.00

MAPP, Alf J., Jr.   Frock Coats and Epaulets.
1963   New York   25.00

Maps of the Battlefield of Antietam.
(1959)   n.p.   30.00

Maps of the Battlefield of Chickamauga, Sept. 19, and 20, 1863.
1889   Washington, DC   65.00

MARBAKER, Thomas D.   History of the Eleventh New Jersey Volunteers.
1898   Trenton   140.00

MARBURG, Theodore   In the Hills.
1895   n.p.   25.00

MARCHAND, John B.   Charleston Blockade: The Journals of John B. Marchand, US Navy, 1861-1862.   Wraps.
1976   Newport   10.00

MARCHAND, S. A.   Forgotten Fighters 1861-65 (From Ascension Parrish, Louisiana).
1966   Donaldsonville, LA   40.00

MARCOT, Roy M.   Col. Hiram Berdan.
1989   59.95
Deluxe Edition   125.00

MARCOT, Roy M.   Spencer Repeating Firearms.
1989   59.95

MARCOT, Roy M.   Spencer Rimfire Cartridges, The Complete History and Development of Ammunition for Spencer Repeating Firearms. Wraps.
1983   9.00

MARCY, Randolph B.   Border Reminiscences.
   1872   New York   100.00
MARDER, William and ESTELLE, Anthony   The Man, The Company,
   The Cameras, An American Photographic Pioneer, edited by Robert G.
   Duncan.
   1982   75.00
Marietta College in the War of Secession, 1861-65. Wraps.
   1878   Cincinnati   50.00
MARK, Penrose G.   Red, White and Blue Badge Pennsylvania Veteran
   Volunteers.
   1911   Harrisburg   75.00
MARKEY, Morris   The Band Plays Dixie.
   1927   New York   15.00
MARKHAM, Jerald H.   The Botetourt Artillery.
   1986   Lynchburg   Ltd.   16.45
MARKS, Bayly Ellen and SHATZ, M. Norton   Between North and South.
   1976   20.00
MARKS, James Junius   The Peninsular Campaign in Virginia.
   1864   Philadelphia   75.00
   1874   Philadelphia   50.00
MARQUIS, Thomas B.   Custer, Cavalry and Crows.
   1975   20.00
MARQUIS, Thomas B.   Keep the Last Bullet for Yourself, True Story
   of Custer's Last Stand.
   1976   25.00
   1984   Wraps   15.00
MARSHAL, Francis   The Battle of Gettysburg.
   1987   30.00
MARSHALL, Albert O.   Army Life from a Soldier's Journals.
   1883   Joliet   65.00
   1884   Joliet   65.00
MARSHALL, Charles   Address Delivered Before the Lee Monument
   Association at Richmond, Virginia. Wraps.
   1888   Baltimore   30.00
MARSHALL, Charles   Address of Col. Charles Marshall. Wraps.
   1875   Richmond   40.00
MARSHALL, Charles   An Aide-De-Camp of Lee, Being the Papers of
   Colonel Charles Marshall, edited by Sr. Frederick Maurice.
   1927   Boston   40.00
MARSHALL, D. Porter   Company K, 155th Pa. Volunteer Zouaves.
   1888   n.p.   150.00
MARSHALL, H. Snowden   Address Delivered at the Opening of the
   Building of the Confederate Memorial Institute at Richmond, Va. on
   May 3, 1921. Wraps.
   1921   Richmond   40.00
   1925   Richmond   25.00
MARSHALL, John A.   American Bastile.
   1871   Philadelphia   35.00
   1875   Philadelphia   30.00
   1876   Philadelphia   30.00
   1885   Philadelphia   25.00

MARSHALL, Park   A Life of William B. Bate.
1908   Nashville   100.00
MARSHALL, Thomas B.   History of the 83rd Ohio Volunteer Infantry, The Greyhound Regiment.
1912   Cincinnati   225.00
MARSHALL-CORNWALL, James   Grant as Military Commander.
1970   London   30.00
MARSZALEK, J. F.   Sherman's Other War: The General and the Civil War Press.
1981   Memphis   15.00
MARTIN, Bessie   Desertion of Alabama Troops from the Confederate Army.
1932   New York   80.00
1966   New York   30.00
MARTIN, C. S.   Seventy Five Years with the 10th Regiment, Infantry N.Y. N.G. (177th New York Volunteer Infantry 1860-1935).
n.d.   n.p.   40.00
MARTIN, David G.   Carl Bornemann's Regiment: The Forty-first New York Infantry (DeKalb Regt.) in the Civil War.
1987   Hightstown   Ltd. 500 copies   23.95
MARTIN, David G.   Confederate Monuments at Gettysburg. . . .
1986   Hightstown   24.95
MARTIN, David G., edited by   The Monocacy Regiment: A Commemorative History of the Fourteenth New Jersey Infantry in the Civil War, 1862-1865.
1987   Hightstown   30.00
MARTIN, David G.   The Shiloh Campaign.
1987   9.98
1987   Wraps   7.95
MARTIN, John A.   Addresses . . . Delivered in Kansas.
1888   Topeka   60.00
MARTIN, John Henry, compiled by   Columbus, Georgia, from Its Selection as a "Trading Town" in 1827, to Its Partial Destruction by Wilson's Raid. 2 Vols.
1874   GA   150.00
MARTIN, Robert Hugh   A Boy of Old Shenandoah.
1977   Parsons, WV   10.00
MARTIN, Thomas Ricaud   The Great Parliamentary Battle and Farewell Addresses of the Southern Senators on the Eve of the Great Civil War.
1905   New York   50.00
MARTYN, Carlos   Wendell Phillips: the Agitator.
1890   New York   14.00
The Martyr's Monument Being the Patriotism and Political Wisdom of Abraham Lincoln as Exhibited in Speeches. . . .
1865   New York   20.00
MARVEL, William   The First New Hampshire Battery, 1861-1865. Wraps.
1985   S. Conway   7.00
MARVEL, William   Race of the Soil: The Ninth New Hampshire Regiment in the Civil War.
1988   Wilmington, NC   35.00

MARVIN, Abijah P.   History of Worcester in the War of the Rebellion.
  1870   Cleveland   60.00
  1870   Worcester   60.00
MARVIN, Edwin E.   The Fifth Regiment, Connecticut Volunteers, a History.
  1889   Hartford   75.00
MARX, Karl and ENGLES, Frederick   The Civil War in the United States, Works of Marxism-Leninism.
  1937   New York   35.00
  1940   New York   25.00
Maryland - Confederate Military History.   See: Confederate Military History, Vol. II.
Maryland Historical Magazine.   Wraps.
  1964   Baltimore   10.00
Maryland Remembers: A Guide to Historic Places and People of the Civil War in Maryland.   Wraps.
  1961   Hagerstown   18.00
MASON, Amos Lawrence, edited by   Memoir and Correspondence of Charles Steedman, Rear-Admiral United States Navy with His Autobiography and Private Journals 1811-1890.
  1912   Harvard   Ltd.   75.00
MASON, Emily V.   Popular Life of Gen. Robert E. Lee.
  1874   Baltimore   35.00
MASON, Emily V., edited by   The Southern Poems of the War.
  1867   Baltimore   50.00
  1878   Baltimore   40.00
MASON, Frank Holcomb   The Forty-second Ohio Infantry.
  1876   Cleveland   250.00
MASON, George   Illinois at Shiloh: Report of the Illinois Shiloh Battlefield Commission.
  1905   Chicago   40.00
MASON, H. N.   Official Program 61st and Final Reunion United Confederate Veterans and 56th General Convention. . . .   Wraps.
  1951   20.00
MASON, Virginia   The Public Life and Diplomatic Correspondence of James M. Mason with Some Personal History.
  1906   New York   50.00
  1906   Roanoke, VA   50.00
Massachusetts in the Army and Navy 1861-1865.   2 Vols.
  1896   Boston   55.00
Massachusetts Report of the Commission on Andersonville Monument.
  1902   Boston   20.00
Massachusetts Soldiers, Sailors, and Marines in the Civil War.   8 Vols. & Index.
  1931-35 Norwood   375.00
MASSEY, John E.   Autobiography of _____, edited by Elizabeth H. Hancock.
  1909   New York   75.00
MASSEY, Mary Elizabeth   Bonnet Brigades, American Women and The Civil War.
  1966   New York   35.00

MASSEY, Mary Elizabeth   Ersatz in the Confederacy.
   1952   Columbia, SC   60.00
MASSEY, Mary Elizabeth   Refugee Life in the Confederacy.
   1964   Baton Rouge   40.00
MASSIE, James William   America: The Origin of Her Present Conflict.
   1864   London   80.00
MASTERS, Edgar Lee   Lee, A Dramatic Poem.
   1926   New York   40.00
MASTERS, Edgar Lee   Lincoln the Man.
   1931   New York   20.00
   1931   London   20.00
MASTERS, Edgar Lee   The Tide of Time.
   1937   New York   10.00
MATHENY, Herman E.   Wood County, West Virginia, in Civil War Times. With an Account of the Guerrilla Warfare in the Little Kanawha Valley.
   1987   Parkersburg   30.00
MATHENY, Herman E.   Major General Thomas Maley Harris.
   1963   Parsons   25.00
MATHES, J. Harvey   General Forrest.
   For additional information, see Appendix: Great Commanders Series.
   1902   New York   100.00
   1902   New York   Ltd. 225.00
   1976   Memphis   35.00
   1987   30.00
MATHES, J. Harvey   The Old Guard in Gray.
   1897   Memphis   125.00
   Reprint   enlarged ed.   40.00
MATHEWS, B. H.   The McCook-Stoneman Raid.
   1976   Philadelphia   23.00
MATHEWS, W. H.   Harry: Being the Recollections of an English Boy Who Served in the Union Army.
   1927   Iowa City   75.00
MATHIAS, Frank E.   Incidents and Experiences in the Life of Thomas W. Parsons.
   1975   18.00
MATLOFF, Maurice, edited by   The Civil War: A Concise History of the War Between the States.
   1978   7.00
MATTER, William D.   If It Takes All Summer. The Battle of Spotsylvania.
   1988   Chapel Hill, NC   30.00
MATTHEWS, Byron H., Jr.   The McCook-Stoneman Raid.
   1976   Philadelphia   30.00
MATTHEWS, Joseph J., edited by   The Capture and Wonderful Escape of General John H. Morgan. Wraps.
   1947   Atlanta   20.00
MATTHEWS, W.   Harry, Being the Recollections of an English Boy who Served Four Years in the Union Army During the Civil War.
   1927   125.00

MAULL, D. W.　　　The Life and Military Services of the Late Brigadier General Thomas A. Smyth.
　　1870　　Wilmington, DE　　50.00
MAURICE, Frederick　　　Robert E. Lee, The Soldier.
　　1925　　Boston　30.00
　　1925　　London 30.00
　　1925　　New York　30.00
　　1930　　New York　15.00
MAURICE, Frederick　　　Statesmen and Soldiers of the Civil War.
　　1926　　Boston　35.00
MAURY, Ann　　　Intimate Virginia.
　　1941　　Richmond　18.00
MAURY, Dabney Herndon　　　Recollections of a Virginian in the Mexican, Indian and Civil Wars.
　　1894　　New York　75.00
　　1897　　New York　45.00
MAURY, Richard L.　　　The Battle of Williamsburg and the Charge of the 24th Virginia, of Early's Brigade.　Wraps.
　　1880　　Richmond　250.00
　　1960　　Williamsburg　25.00
MAURY, Richard L.　　　A Brief Sketch of the Work of Matthew Fontaine Maury During the War 1861-1865.　Wraps.
　　1915　　Richmond　125.00
MAUZY, James H.　　　Historical Sketch of the Sixty-eighth Regiment Indiana Volunteers.
　　1887　　Rushville　150.00
MAXFIELD, Albert and BRADY, Robert, Jr.　　　Roster and Statistical Record of Company D, of the Eleventh Regiment Maine Infantry Volunteers.　Wraps.
　　1890　　New York　40.00
MAXSON, William P.　　　Camp Fires of the Twenty-third. By Pound Sterling.
　　1863　　New York　60.00
MAXWELL, William Quentin　　　Lincoln's Fifth Wheel: The Political History of the U.S. Sanitary Commission.
　　1956　　New York　35.00
MAY, George S.　　　Michigan and the Civil War Years, 1860-1866:　A Wartime Chronicle.　Wraps.
　　1966　　Lansing　20.00
MAY, George S., edited by　　　Michigan Civil War History . . . An Annotated Bibliography.　Wraps.
　　1961　　Detroit　20.00
MAY, George S., compiled by　　　Michigan Civil War Monuments.　Wraps.
　　1965　　Lansing　23.00
MAY, John Amasa and FAUNT, Joan Reynolds　　South Carolina Secedes.
　　1960　　Columbia　35.00
MAY, Robert E.　　　John A. Quitman, Old South Crusader.
　　1985　　Baton Rouge　40.00
　　1985　　Wraps　20.00
MAY, Samuel J.　　　Some Recollections of our Antislavery Conflict.
　　1869　　Boston　20.00

MAYER, Brantz   The Emancipation Problem in Maryland.   Wraps.
1862   Baltimore   25.00
MAYES, Edward   Lucius Q. C. Lamar: His Life, Times and Speeches,
1825-1893.
1896   Nashville   60.00
MAYO, Perry   The Civil War Letters of Perry Mayo, edited by Robert
W. Hodge.   Wraps.
1967   East Lansing   25.00
McADAMS, Francis Marion   Every-day Soldier Life: or, A History of
the 113th Ohio Volunteer Infantry.
1884   Columbus   145.00
McALEXANDER, U. G.   History of the Thirteenth Regiment United
States Infantry.
1905   (Fort McDowell, CA)   100.00
McALLISTER, J. Gray   Sketch of Captain Thompson McAllister, Citizen, Soldier, Christian.   Wraps.
1896   Petersburg   100.00
McALLISTER, Robert   Civil War Letters of General Robert McAllister,
edited by James I. Robertson.
1965   New Brunswick 40.00
McARTHUR, Henry C.   The Capture and Destruction of Columbia,
South Carolina February 17, 1865.
1911   Washington, DC   45.00
McAULAY, John D.   Carbines of the Civil War, 1861-1865.   Wraps.
1981   Union City   8.95
McBRIDE, John Randolph   History of the Thirty-third Indiana Veteran Volunteer Infantry.
1900   Indianapolis 140.00
McBRIDE, Robert E.   In the Ranks; From the Wilderness to Appomattox
Courthouse.
1881   Cincinnati   80.00
McBRIDE, Robert W.   Lincoln's Body Guard, The Union Light Guard
of Ohio.   Wraps.
1911   Indianapolis   90.00
McBRIEN, Joe Bennett   The Tennessee Brigade.
1977   Chattanooga   50.00
McBRYDE, Randell W.   The Historic "General"   A Thrilling Episode of
the Civil War.
1904   Chattanooga   50.00
1967   n.p.   Wraps   15.00
McCABE, James D., Jr.   The Grayjackets . . . By a Confederate.
1867   Richmond   150.00
McCABE, James D., Jr.   The Great Republic.
1871   Toledo   25.00
McCABE, James D., Jr.   Life and Campaigns of General Robert E. Lee.
1866   St. Louis   75.00
1867   New York   75.00
1870   75.00
McCABE, William Gordon   Annual Reunion of Pegram Battalion Association in the Hall of House of Delegates, Richmond, Va., May 21st,
1886. . . . Wraps.
1886   Richmond   50.00

McCABE, William Gordon   Brief Sketch of Andrew Reid Venable, Jr.
Wraps.
1909   Richmond   30.00
McCABE, William Gordon   Captain Robert E. Lee, Jr.   Wraps.
1915   Richmond   50.00
McCABE, William Gordon   Col.   John   Barry   Purcell   1849-1916.
Wraps.
1971   n.p.   30.00
McCABE, William Gordon   George Ben Johnston, M.D. of Richmond
1853-1916. Wraps.
1918   n.p.   30.00
McCABE, William Gordon   Joseph Bryan. A Brief Memoir.
1909   Richmond   65.00
McCABE, William Gordon   Major-General George Washington Custis
Lee. Wraps.
1914   Washington, DC   50.00
McCABE, William Gordon   Speech of Capt. _____. Wraps.
1900   Nashville   50.00
McCAFFREY, James   This Band of Heroes.
1985   Austin   25.00
McCAGUE, James   The Second Rebellion: The Story of the New York
City Draft Riots of 1863.
1968   New York   15.00
McCALL, Samuel W.   Thaddeus Stevens.
1899   Boston   25.00
McCALLISTER, Anna   Ellen Ewing, Wife of General Sherman.
1936   New York   35.00
McCALLUM, J. H.   Martin County During the Civil War, Including a
Roster of Troops from Martin County.
1971   Williamston   40.00
McCALMONT, Alfred B.   Extracts from Letters Written By Alfred B.
McCalmont, Late Lt. Col., 142nd Regt.
1908   Franklin, PA   90.00
McCANN, Thomas H.   The Campaigns of the Civil War.
1915   New York   45.00
McCANTS, E. C.   One of the Grayjackets and Other Stories.
1908   Columbia   70.00
McCARLEY, J. Brett   The Atlanta Campaign. Wraps.
1989   9.95
McCARTHY, Carlton   Detailed Minutiae of Soldier Life in the Army
of Northern Virginia.
1882   Richmond   125.00
1884   Richmond   100.00
1888   Richmond   100.00
1899   Richmond   60.00
1982   35.00
McCARTHY, Carlton   Walks About Richmond. . . .
1870   Richmond   100.00
McCARTHY, Charles H.   Lincoln's Plan of Reconstruction.
1901   New York   100.00
1966   19.00

McCARTY, Burke   The Suppressed Truth About the Assassination of
Abraham Lincoln.
1924   PA 35.00
McCASH, William B.   Thomas R. R. Cobb: The Making of a Southern
Nationalist.
1983   Macon   20.00
McCLELLAN, Carswell   General Andrew A. Humphreys at Malvern
Hill. Wraps.
1888   St. Paul   30.00
McCLELLAN, Carswell   The Personal Memoirs and Military History of
U.S. Grant Versus the Record of the Army of the Potomac.
1887   Boston   20.00
McCLELLAN, George B.   Letter of the Secretary of War, Transmitting
Report of the Organization of the Army of the Potomac, and Its Cam-
paigns. . . .
1864   Washington, DC   30.00
McCLELLAN, George B.   Manual of Bayonet Exercise.
1862   Philadelphia   60.00
McCLELLAN, George B.   McClellan's Own Story. The War for the
Union.
1887   New York   60.00
McCLELLAN, George B.   Regulations and Instructions for the Field Service of the U.S. Cavalry in Time of War, The Basis of Instruction for
the U.S. Cav. from the Authorized Tactics. . . .
1961   250.00
McCLELLAN, George B.   Report on the Organization and Campaigns of
the Army of the Potomac.
1864   New York 35.00
1864   Washington, DC 35.00
1864   Boston 35.00
McCLELLAN, Henry B.   The Life and Campaigns of Major General J.
E. B. Stuart.
1885   Boston   200.00
1958   Bloomington entitled I Rode with Jeb Stuart, edited by Burke
        Davis 50.00
1969   New York 35.00
1987   39.95
McCLENDON, W. A.   Recollections of War Times.
1973   San Bernardino, CA   40.00
McCLERNAND, John A.   Battle Report of Columbus, Kentucky to General U. S. Grant (Fieldpress printing).
1861   Camp Cairo, IL   500.00
McCLURE, Alexander K.   "Abe" Lincoln's Yarns and Stories.
1901   n.p.   35.00
McCLURE, Alexander K.   Abraham Lincoln and Men of War-Times.
1892   Philadelphia 25.00
McCLURE, Alexander K.   The Annals of the War Written by Leading
Participants North and South.
1879   Philadelphia 75.00
1974   Philadelphia 35.00
1988   35.00

McCLURE, Alexander K.   The Life and Services of Andrew G. Curtin.
1895   Harrisburg   15.00
McCLURE, Alexander K.   Recollections of a Half a Century.
1902   Salem, MA   25.00
McCLURE, J. B.   Stories and Sketches of General Grant at Home and Abroad.
1879   Chicago   10.00
McCOLL, Nellie Thomas   Old Folks at Home.
1921   n.p.   40.00
McCOLLOM, Albert O.   The War Time Letters of _____ Confederate Soldier, edited by Walter J. Lemke.   Wraps.
1961   Fayetteville, AR   45.00
McCONKEY, Harriet E. B.   Dakota War Whoop: or Indian Massacres and War in Minnesota, of 1862-3.
1864   St. Paul   60.00
1965   Chicago   30.00
McCONNELL, Roland C.   Negro Troops of Antebellum Louisiana.
1969   Baton Rouge   25.00
McCORD, Simeon   Letters Home 1861-1865. Camp and Campaign Life of a Union Artilleryman.
n.d.   n.p.   50.00
McCORD, William B.   Battle of Corinth, The Campaigns Preceding and Leading Up to This Battle and Its Results.   Wraps.
n.d.   n.p.   30.00
McCORDOCK, Robert Stanley   The Yankee Cheese Box.
1938   Philadelphia   40.00
McCORKLE, John   Three Years with Quantrill: A True Story by O. S. Barton.
(c.1914) Armstrong, MO 200.00
1967   New York   30.00
McCORMICK, David Isaac, compiled by   Indiana Battle Flags and Record of Indiana Organizations in the Mexican, Civil and Spanish-American Wars . . . , edited by Mrs. Mindwell C. Wilson.
1928   Indianapolis   125.00
1929   110.00
McCORMICK, John Gilchrist   Personnel of the Convention of 1861 and Legislation of the Convention of 1861.   Wraps.
1900   Chapel Hill, NC   30.00
McCORMICK, Robert R.   The War Without Grant.
1950   New York   35.00
McCORMICK, Robert R.   Ulysses S. Grant, the Great Soldier of America.
1934   New York   30.00
1950   30.00
McCORVEY, T. C.   Alabama Historical Sketches.
1971   Charlottesville   15.00
McCOWAN, Archibald   The Prisoners of War.
1901   New York   45.00
McCRADY, Edward   Formation, Organization, Discipline and Characteristics of the Army of Northern Virginia: An Address.   Wraps.
1886   Richmond   45.00

McCRADY, Edward   Gregg's Brigade of South Carolinians in the Second
Battle of Manassas, an Address.   Wraps.
1885   Richmond   80.00
McCRADY, Louis DeB.   General Edward McCrady.   Wraps.
1905   Charleston   50.00
McCREA, Tully   Dear Belle,   Letters from a Cadet and Officer to His
Sweetheart 1858-1865, edited by Catherine S. Crary.
1965   Middletown, CT   30.00
McCULLOCH, Hugh   Men and Measures of Half a Century: Sketches
and Comments.
1888   New York   25.00
McCULLOCH, L. W.   Card Photographs, a Guide to Their History and
Value.
1981   30.00
McCURDY, Charles M.   Gettysburg, A Memoir.   Wraps.
1929   Pittsburgh   60.00
McDANIEL, H. Pleasants   War Poems 1861-1865.
1901   New York   25.00
McDERMOTT, Anthony Wayne   A Brief History of the 69th Regiment
Pennsylvania Veteran Volunteers.
1889   Philadelphia   100.00
Recent reprint   37.50
McDONALD, Mrs. Cornelia   A Diary with Reminiscences of the War
and Refugee Life in the Shenandoah Valley 1860-1865. Annotated and
supplemented by Hunter McDonald.
1935   Nashville   125.00
McDONALD, J.   Great Battles of the Civil War.
1988   New York   39.95
McDONALD, John W.   A Soldier of Fortune.
1888   New York   40.00
McDONALD, William N.   A History of the Laurel Brigade.
1907   Baltimore   300.00
1969   Arlington   35.00
1987   30.00
1988   Gaithersburg   30.00
McDONOUGH, James Lee   Chattanooga - A Death Grip on the Confederacy.
1985   Knoxville   20.00
McDONOUGH, James Lee   Schofield: Union General in the Civil War
and Reconstruction.
1972   Tallahassee   20.00
McDONOUGH, James Lee   Shiloh - In Hell Before Night.
1977   Knoxville   20.00
1980   Knoxville   20.00
1985   Wraps   8.95
1987   19.95
McDONOUGH, James Lee   Stones River - Bloody Winter in Tennessee.
1980   Knoxville   20.00
1982   19.95
Wraps   8.95

McDONOUGH, James Lee and CONNELLY, Thomas L.   Five   Tragic Hours. The Battle of Franklin.
1983   Knoxville   25.00

McDONOUGH, James Lee, and JONES, J. P.   War So Terrible: Sherman and Atlanta.
1987   New York   19.95

McDOUGAL, Henry Clay   Recollections 1844-1909.
1910   Kansas City   75.00

McDOWELL, Amanda and BLANKENSHIP, Lela McDowell   Fiddles in the Cumberlands.
1943   New York   40.00

McDOWELL, Robert Emmett   City of Conflict, Louisville in the Civil War 1861-65.
1962   Louisville   30.00
1962   Louisville   15.00

McELROY, John   Andersonville, a Story of Rebel Military Prisons.
1879   Toledo   50.00
1899   Washington, DC   2 Vols. Wraps 30.00

McELROY, John   Further Haps and Mishaps to Si Klegg and Shorty. Wraps.
1898   Washington, DC   20.00

McELROY, John   The Red Acorn A Romance of the War.   Wraps.
1883   Washington, DC   25.00

McELROY, John   Si Klegg: His Transformation from a Raw Recruit to a Veteran. Wraps.
1910   Washington, DC   30.00
1915   Washington, DC   25.00

McELROY, John   Si, "Shorty" and Boys on "the March to the Sea." Wraps.
1902   Washington, DC   30.00

McELROY, John   The Struggle for Missouri.
1909   Washington, DC   50.00
1913   Washington, DC   40.00

McELROY, John   This Was Andersonville, edited by Roy Meredith.
1957   New York   25.00
1958   New York   25.00

McELROY, Joseph C.   The Battle of Chickamauga Historical Map and Guide Book. Wraps.
(c.1900) Chatttanooga, TN   25.00

McELROY, Joseph C.   Chickamauga, Record of the Ohio Chickamauga and Chattanooga National Park Commission.
1896   Cincinnati   40.00

McELROY, Robert   Jefferson Davis, the Unreal and the Real.
1937   New York   2 Vols. Boxed   75.00
1969   New York   2 Vols. in 1 35.00

McFARLAND, Louis B.   Memoirs and Addresses.
(1922)   n.p.   250.00

McFARLAND, Robert White   The   Surrender   of   Cumberland   Gap, September 9, 1863.   Wraps.
1898   Columbus   55.00

McFEELY, William S.   Grant A Biography.
1981   New York   20.00

McFEELY, William S.　　　Yankee Stepfather.　Gen. O. O. Howard and the Freedmen.
1968　New Haven　20.00

McGAVOCK, Randal W.　　Pen and Sword,　The Life and Journals of Randal W. McGavock, Colonel CSA, edited by Hershel Gower and Jack Allen.
1959　Nashville　40.00
1960　Nashville　35.00

McGEE, Benjamin F.　　History of the 72nd Indiana Volunteer Infantry of the Mounted Lightning Brigade.
1882　Lafayette　225.00

McGEEHAN, Albert H.　　My Country and Cross.　The Civil War Letters of John Anthony Wilterdink, Company I, 25th Michigan Infantry.
1982　40.00

McGEHEE, J. O.　　Causes That Led to the War Between the States.
1915　Atlanta　20.00

McGEHEE, Thomasine　　Journey Proud.
1939　New York　10.00

McGIFFIN, Lee　　Swords, Stars and Bars.
1959　New York　25.00

McGINTY, Garnie W.　　Louisiana Redeemed:　The Overthrow of Carpetbag Rule 1876-1880.
1941　New Orleans　30.00

McGOODWIN, Bessie Ware　　War-Time Memories of the Southland.
n.d.　n.p.　35.00

McGRATH, Franklin　　The History of the 127th New York Volunteers.
(1898)　n.p.　110.00

McGREGOR, Charles　　History of the Fifteenth New Hampshire Volunteers 1862-1863.
1900　Concord　75.00

McGREGOR, James C.　　The Disruption of Virginia.
1921　New York　50.00
1922　New York　40.00

McGUIRE, Hunter　　Address by _____ Medical Director 2nd Army Corps (Stonewall Jackson's), Army of Northern Virginia.　Wraps.
1897　Lynchburg　60.00

McGUIRE, Hunter　　An Address on Stonewall Jackson.　Wraps.
1897　Richmond　100.00
1899　Richmond　50.00

McGUIRE, Hunter and CHRISTIAN, George L.　　The Confederate Cause and Conduct in the War Between the States.
1907　Richmond　60.00
1911　Richmond　50.00

McGUIRE, Judith W.　　Diary of a Southern Refugee During the War　By a Lady of Virginia.
1867　New York　100.00
1867　Richmond　100.00
1868　New York　75.00
1889　Richmond　75.00
1972　New York　35.00
1986　35.00

McGUIRE, Ruth Robertson   Stuart McGuire: An Autobiographical Sketch.
   1956   Richmond   20.00
McGUIRE, Stuart   Hunter Holmes McGuire, M.D., L.L.D.   Wraps.
   1938   New York   35.00
McHATTON-RIPLEY, Eliza   From Flag to Flag: A Woman's Experiences in the South During the War, in Mexico, and in Cuba.
   1889   New York   85.00
McHENRY, George   The Cotton Trade . . . in Connection with . . . Negro Slavery in the Confederate States.
   1863   London   125.00
McILVAINE, Mabel   Reminiscences of Chicago During the Civil War.
   1967   New York   15.00
McILWAINE, Richard   Memories of Three Score Years and Ten.
   1908   New York and Washington, DC   75.00
McINTIRE, John Jackson   As I Saw It.
   1902   San Francisco   50.00
McINTOSH, David Gregg   The Campaign of Chancellorsville.   Wraps.
   1915   Richmond   150.00
McINTOSH, David Gregg   Review of the Gettysburg Campaign.
   1984   Falls Church   20.00
McINTYRE, B. F.   Federals on the Frontier: Diary of _____ 1862-1864, edited by Nannie M. Tilley.
   1963   Austin   30.00
McINVALE, Morton R.   The Battle of Pickett's Mill, "Foredoomed to Oblivion."   Wraps.
   1977   Atlanta   15.00
McKAY, Mrs. C. W.   Stories of Hospital and Camp.
   1876   Philadelphia   75.00
McKAY, Martha Nicholson   When the Tide Turned in the Civil War.
   1929   Indianapolis   35.00
McKEE, Irving   "Ben-Hur" Wallace.
   1947   Berkeley, CA   40.00
McKEE, Ivan N.   Lost Family - Lost Cause, a Story of the McKee Family. . . .
   1978   25.00
McKEE, James Cooper   Narrative of the Surrender of a Command of U. S. Forces at Fort Fillmore.
   1960   Houston   Ltd.   30.00
McKEE, James H.   Back "In War Times" History of the 144th Regiment New York Volunteer Infantry.
   1903   Unadilla, NY   70.00
McKEE, W. Reid and MASON, M. E., Jr.   Civil War Projectiles II Small Arms and Field Artillery.
   1980   n.p.   30.00
   1989   29.95
McKEEN, Silas   Heroic Patriotism Sermon Delivered . . . in the Presence of the Bradford Guards . . . 1st Regt. of Vermont Vols.   Wraps.
   1861   Windsor   25.00
McKELVEY, Blake, edited by   Rochester in the Civil War.
   1944   New York   35.00

McKIM, Randolph H.　　　A Soldier's Recollections, Leaves from the Diary of a Young Confederate.
1910　New York　100.00
1911　New York　75.00
1921　New York　50.00
1983　25.00

McKIM, Randolph H.　　　The Motives and Aims of the Soldiers of the South in the Civil War.　Wraps.
(1904)　n.p.　75.00

McKIM, Randolph H.　　　The Numerical Strength of the Confederate Army.
1912　New York　125.00

McKIM, Randolph H.　　　The Soul of Lee.
1918　New York　50.00

McKINNEY, E. P.　　Life in Tent and Field 1861-1865.
1922　Boston　60.00

McKINNEY, Francis F.　　Education in Violence. The Life of George H. Thomas and the Army of the Cumberland.
1961　Detroit　75.00

McKINNEY, T.　　The Civil War in Fayette County, West Virginia.
1988　Charleston　16.00

McKITRICK, Eric L.　　Andrew Johnson and Reconstruction.
1960　Chicago　20.00
1970　Chicago　Wraps　20.00

McKITRICK, Eric L.　　Slavery Defended: The Views of the Old South.
1963　NJ　20.00
1963　NJ　10.00

McLAUGHLIN, Jack　　Gettysburg, the Long Encampment.
1963　New York　15.00

McLAUGHLIN, James Fairfax　　The American Cyclops, the Hero of New Orleans, and Spoiler of Silver Spoons. Dubbed LL.D. by Pasquino. (Volck, Adelbert J.)
1868　Baltimore　125.00

McLAUGHLIN, William　　Ceremonies Connected with the Unveiling of the Bronze Statue of Gen. Thomas J. (Stonewall) Jackson at Lexington, VA July 21, 1891. Wraps.
1891　Baltimore　40.00

McLEAN, J. L.　　Cutler's Brigade at Gettysburg.
1987　Baltimore　Ltd. 300 copies.　30.00

McLEAN, J. L., compiled by　　Gettysburg Sources. Vol. I.
1986　Baltimore　Ltd. 750 copies.　20.00

McLEAN, J. L., compiled by　　Gettysburg Sources. Vol. II.
1987　Baltimore　Ltd. 750 copies　23.50

McLEAN, William E.　　The Forty-third Regiment of Indiana Volunteers.
1903　Terre Haute　125.00

McLEARY, A. C.　　Humorous Incidents of the Civil War.　Wraps.
(c.1903)　n.p.　75.00

McLEOD, Martha N.　　Brother Warriors　The Reminiscences of Union and Confederate Veterans.
1940　Washington, DC　50.00

McLOUGHLIN, Emmett   An Inquiry into the Assassination of Abraham Lincoln.
1963   New York   30.00

McMAHON, Martin T.   General John Sedgwick, An Address.   Wraps.
1880   Rutland   20.00

McMANUS, Howard Rollins   The Battle of Cloyds Mountain.   The Virginia-Tennessee Railroad Raid, April 29-May 19, 1864.
1989   16.95

McMASTER, John B.   History of the People of the United States During Lincoln's Administration.
1927   New York   30.00

McMEEKIN, Isabel McLennan   Robert E. Lee: Knight of the South.
1950   New York   25.00

McMILLAN, Malcolm C.   The Alabama Confederate Reader.
1963   University   50.00

McMILLAN, Malcolm C.   The Disintegration of a Confederate State.
1986   16.95

McMORRIES, Edward Young   History of the First Regiment Volunteer Infantry C.S.A.
1904   Montgomery, AL   175.00
1970   25.00

McMURRAY, William Josiah   History of the 20th Tennessee Regiment Volunteer Infantry, C.S.A.
1904   Nashville   150.00
1976   Nashville   30.00

McMURRY, Richard M.   John Bell Hood and the War for Southern Independence.
1982   Lexington   25.00

McMURRY, Richard M.   Two Great Rebel Armies.
1989   Chapel Hill, NC   19.95

McMURTY, R. Gerald   Ben Hardin Helm: "Rebel" Brother-in-Law of Abraham Lincoln.
1943   Chicago   Ltd.   75.00

McNAMAR, J. B.   Official Souvenir & Program of Monument, 1st Conn. Heavy Artillery.
1902   Hartford   60.00

McNEILY, J. S.   Barksdale's Mississippi Brigade at Gettysburg.   Wraps.
1987   Gaithersburg   10.00

McPHERSON, Edward   Political History of the United States During the Great Rebellion.
1864   Washington, DC   50.00
1865   Washington, DC   30.00
1876   Washington, DC   entitled The Political History of the U.S.A. During the Civil War.   30.00
1880   Washington, DC   30.00

McPHERSON, Edward   A Political Manual for 1866.
1866   Washington, DC   30.00

McPHERSON, James M.   Battle Cry of Freedom: The Civil War Era.
1988   Oxford   30.00

McPHERSON, James M.   The Negro's Civil War.
1965   New York   25.00

McPHERSON, James M.   The Struggle for Equality.
1964   Princeton, NJ   25.00
McSWAIN, J. J.   The Causes of Secession: An Essay. Wraps.
1917   Greenville, SC   25.00
McWHINEY, Grady   Braxton Bragg and Confederate Defeat, Vol. 1
Field Command.
1969   New York   25.00
McWHINEY, Grady, edited by   Grant, Lee, Lincoln and the Radicals -
Essays on Civil War Leadership.
1964   n.p.   30.00
McWHINEY, Grady   Southerners and Other Americans.
1973   New York   20.00
McWHINEY, Grady and JAMIESON, Perry D.   Attack and Die, Civil War
Military Tactics and the Southern Heritage.
1982   Heritage, AL   25.00
1984   Wraps   11.00
McWILLIAMS, Carey   Ambrose Bierce: A Biography.
1929   New York   40.00
McWILLIAMS, John   Recollections of John McWilliams: His Youth
Experiences in California and the Civil War.
(1921)   Princeton   75.00
MEACHAM, Henry H.   The Empty Sleeve; or, the Life and Hardships
of Henry H. Meacham. . . . Wraps.
1869   Springfield   30.00
MEAD, F.   Heroic Statues in Bronze of Abraham Lincoln.
1932   Fort Wayne   Ltd.   35.00
MEAD, Homer   The 8th Iowa Cavalry in the Civil War.
1927   Augusta, IL   80.00
MEADE, G. G.   Gettysburg. Wraps.
1988   York   7.95
MEADE, George   Battle of Gettysburg. Wraps.
1924   Ambler, PA   20.00
MEADE, George   Did General Meade Desire to Retreat at the Battle of
Gettysburg? Wraps.
1883   Philadelphia   40.00
MEADE, George   General Meade's Letter on Gettysburg. Wraps.
1886   Philadelphia   35.00
MEADE, George   The Life and Letters of George Gordon Meade. 2 Vols.
1913   New York   200.00
MEADE, George   With Meade at Gettysburg.
1930   Philadelphia   50.00
MEADE, Richard W.   Forty-five Years of Active Service. Wraps.
1896   New York   25.00
MEADE, Robert Douthat   Judah P. Benjamin Confederate Statesman.
1943   New York   40.00
1944   40.00
MEANEY, P. J.   The Prison Ministry of Father Peter Whelan, Georgia
Priest and Confederate Chaplain. Wraps.
1987   4.00
MEANS, Alexander   Diary for 1861. Wraps.
1949   Atlanta   30.00

MEARNS, David C.   Largely Lincoln.
  1961   New York   10.00
MEARNS, David C.   The Lincoln Papers.
  1948   Garden City, NY   2 Vols. Boxed   30.00
  1969   New York   2 Vols. in 1   20.00
MEBANE, John   Books Relating to the Civil War.
  1963   New York   25.00
MECKLIN, John M.   The Ku Klux Klan   A Study of the American
  Mind.
  1924   50.00
  1963   New York   20.00
MECUR, J.   Elements of the Art of War, Prepared for the use of the
  Cadets of the U.S. Military Academy.
  1889   New York   35.00
Medal of Honor 1863-1968 "In the Name of the Congress of the United
  States."
  1968   Washington, DC   15.00
The Medal of Honor of the United States Army.
  1948   Washington, DC   25.00
Medal of Honor Recipients 1863-1963.   Wraps.
  1964   Washington, DC   40.00
Medical and Surgical History of the War of Rebellion. 6 Vols. Arranged in
  a most confusing fashion. 3 medical volumes and 3 surgical volumes.
  1870-88 Washington, DC 1200.00
  Individual Vols. 125.00 each
  For Prospectus See: Reports of the Extent . . . .
Medical Report Upon the Uniform and Clothing of the Soldiers of the U.S.
  Army, Surgeon General's Office.   Wraps.
  1868   75.00
Meeting of the Pilot Knob Memorial Association on the 40th Anniversary of
  the Battle of Pilot Knob, Sept. 27, 1904.   Wraps.
  1904   St. Louis   50.00
MEIER, Heinz K., edited by   Memoirs of a Swiss Officer in the American Civil War.
  1972   Switzerland   40.00
MELIGAKES, N. A.   The Spirit of Gettysburg.
  1950   Gettysburg   20.00
  1950   n.p. 15.00
MELLON, James, edited by   The Face of Lincoln.
  1979   New York   75.00
  1982   15.00
MELTON, Maurice   The Confederate Iron Clads.
  1968   New York   20.00
MELVILLE, Herman   Battle-Pieces and Aspects of the War.
  1866   New York   25.00
  1963   New York   entitled   The Battlepieces of Herman Melville,
          edited by Hennig Cohen. 15.00
  1964   New York   10.00
MEMMINGER, Christopher G.   Address of _____, Special Commissioner from the State of South Carolina Before . . . State of Virginia
  Jan 19, 1860.   Wraps.
  1860   Richmond   40.00

MEMMINGER, Christopher G.　　　The Mission of South Carolina to Virginia. Wraps.
　　n.d.　　n.p.　　50.00
Memoir of George Boardman Boomer.
　　1864　　Boston　　30.00
Memoir of James Allen Hardie, Inspector-General, United States Army.
　　1877　　Washington, DC　　45.00
Memoir of Lieut. Edward Lewis Mitchell Who Fell at the Battle of Shiloh, Aged Twenty-two Year.
　　1864　　New York　　25.00
A Memoir - Rufus R. Dawes, Born July 4, 1838, Died August 1, 1899.
　　(1900)　　New York　　150.00
Memoirs for the History of the War in Texas, translated by Wallace Woolsey.
　　1985　　20.00
Memoirs of Georgia. 2 Vols.
　　1895　　Atlanta　　160.00
Memorandum Relative to the General Officers Appointed by the President in the Armies of the Confederate States 1861-1865. Wraps.
　　1905　　Washington, DC　　Ltd.　　50.00
　　1908　　Washington, DC　　30.00
Memorial Addresses on the Life and Character of Ambrose Burnside.
　　1882　　Washington, DC　　20.00
Memorial Addresses on the Life and Character of Andrew Johnson.
　　1876　　Washington, DC　　20.00
Memorial Addresses on the Life and Character of John Warwick Daniel.
　　1911　　Washington, DC　　20.00
Memorial Addresses on the Life and Character of William H. F. Lee Delivered in the House of Representatives.
　　1892　　Washington, DC　　30.00
Memorial Day Annual 1912　The Causes and Outbreak of the War Between the States 1861-1865. Wraps.
　　1912　　Richmond　　15.00
Memorial of Benjamin Dana Fearing. Wraps.
　　1881　　n.p.　　100.00
Memorial of Capt. Jacob V. Marshall.
　　n.d.　　Staunton, VA　　30.00
A Memorial of Charles Sumner.
　　1874　　Boston　　20.00
Memorial of Colonel John Stanton Slocum, First Colonel of the 2nd Rhode Island Vols. Who Fell in the Battle of Bull Run, Va. July 21, 1861.
　　1886　　Providence　　35.00
Memorial of Gen. J. K. F. Mansfield, Who Fell in Battle at Sharpsburg.
　　1862　　Boston　　20.00
Memorial of Joel Parker.
　　1889　　Freehold, NJ　　20.00
A Memorial of Lt. Daniel Perkins Dewey of the Twenty-fifth Regiment Connecticut Volunteers.
　　1864　　Hartford　　30.00
Memorial of Margaret E. Breckinridge.
　　1865　　Philadelphia　　40.00

A Memorial of Paul Joseph Revere and Edward H. R. Revere.
1874   Boston   50.00
1913   Clinton   30.00
A Memorial of Philip Henry Sheridan from the City of Boston.
1889   Boston   20.00
Memorial to Brevet Major General Galusha Pennypacker.
1934   Philadelphia   15.00
Memorial to Civil War Soldiers, 1861 to 1866 . . . Kinsman Post No. 7,
    G.A.R., Des Moines, Iowa.   Wraps.
1942   Des Moines   50.00
Memorial to Confederate Soldiers Elmwood Cemetery, Shepherdstown, W.
    Va. Unveiled September 18, 1937.   Wraps.
n.d.   n.p.   40.00
The Memorial to Major General George Gordon Meade in Washington, D.C.
1927   n.p.   15.00
Memorial to Samuel K. Zook, Brevet Major-General.
1889   Philadelphia   30.00
A Memorial: Soldier Spirit of Waterville, Ohio, A Souvenir.
1899   n.p.   45.00
Memorials of Deceased Companions of the Commandery of the State of Illi-
    nois, Military Order of the Loyal Legion of the United States.
1901   IL   75.00
MENCKEN, August, edited by   By the Neck A Book of Hangings.
1942   New York   20.00
MENDE, Elsie and PEARSON, Henry   An American Soldier and Diplomat, Horace Porter.
1927   New York   30.00
MENDELL, G. H.   A Treatise on Military Surveying, Theoretical and
Practical Including a Description of Surveying Instruments.
1864   150.00
MENEELY, Alexander Howard   The War Department 1861: A Study in
    Mobilization and Administration.
1928   New York and London   25.00
MERCER, Charles   Enough Good Men.
1960   New York   25.00
MERCER, Philip   The Life of the Gallant Pelham.
1929   Macon, GA   175.00
1958   Kennesaw, GA   40.00
MERCHANT, Thomas E.   Eighty-fourth Regiment, Pennsylvania Volunteers.
1890   Philadelphia   75.00
MEREDITH, Roy   The American Wars. A Pictorial History from
    Quebec to Korea.
1955   New York   20.00
MEREDITH, Roy   The Face of Robert E. Lee in Life and Legend.
1947   New York   30.00
1981   New York   25.00
MEREDITH, Roy   Mr. Lincoln's Camera Man, Mathew B. Brady.
1946   New York   30.00
1976   15.95
1976   Wraps   12.00

MEREDITH, Roy   **Mr. Lincoln's Contempories: An Album of Portraits by Mathew B. Brady.**
    1951   New York   25.00
MEREDITH, Roy   **Mr. Lincoln's General: Ulysses S. Grant.**
    1959   New York   25.00
    1981   15.00
MEREDITH, Roy   **Storm Over Sumter.**
    1957   New York   20.00
MEREDITH, Roy   **The World of Mathew Brady Portraits of the Civil War Period.**
    1976   Los Angeles   20.00
MERIDETH, Lee   **Civil War Times and Civil War Times Illustrated 30 Year Comprehensive Index.** Wraps.
      29.95
MERIWETHER, Colyer   **Raphael Semmes.**
    1913   Philadelphia   40.00
MERIWETHER, Elizabeth Avery   **Facts and Falsehoods Concerning the War on the South.** Wraps.
    1904   Memphis, TN   75.00
MERIWETHER, Elizabeth Avery   **Recollections of 92 Years 1824-1916.**
    1958   Nashville   35.00
MERK, F.   **Slavery and the Annexation of Texas.**
    1972   New York   25.00
MERLI, Frank J.   **Great Britain and the Confederate Navy 1861-1865.**
    1970   Bloomington   25.00
MERRELL, William H.   **Five Months in Rebeldom: or Notes from the Diary of Bull Run Prisoner at Richmond.** Wraps.
    1862   Rochester   60.00
MERRICK, Caroline E.   **Old Times in Dixie Land.**
    1901   New York   35.00
MERRILL, J. M.   **DuPont, The Making of an Admiral.**
    1986   21.95
MERRILL, James M.   **Battle Flags South.**
    1970   Cranbury, NJ   25.00
MERRILL, James M.   **The Rebel Shore.**
    1957   Boston   25.00
MERRILL, James M.   **Spurs to Glory, The Story of the U.S. Cavalry.**
    1966   Chicago   25.00
MERRILL, James M.   **William Tecumseh Sherman.**
    1971   Chicago   35.00
MERRILL, Julian W.   **Records of the 24th Independent Battery, New York Light Artillery.**
    1870   New York   110.00
MERRILL, Samuel   **The Seventieth Indiana Volunteer Infantry in the War of the Rebellion.**
    1900   Indianapolis   160.00
MERRILL, Samuel Hill   **The Campaigns of the First Maine and First District of Columbia Cavalry.**
    1866   Portland   80.00
The Merrimac and Monitor Naval Engagement. Wraps.
    n.d.   Baltimore   30.00

MERRITT, Elizabeth   James Henry Hammond 1806-1864.   Wraps.
   1923   Baltimore   20.00
MERWIN, John W.   Roster and Monograph, 161st Regt. N.Y.S. Volunteer Infantry.
   1902   Elmira   60.00
MESERVE, Frederick Hill   Grant in the Wilderness.   Wraps.
   1914   New York   Ltd.   50.00
MESERVE, Frederick Hill and SANDBURG, Carl   The Photographs of Abraham Lincoln.
   1944   New York   80.00
MESERVE, William N.   Meserve Civil War Record, edited by Richard A. Huebner.
   1988   25.00
METCALF, K. N. and BEESON, L.   Effects of the Civil War on Manufacturing in Michigan.   Wraps.
   1966   Lansing   8.00
METZ, Helen Hart   Lincoln Herald Analytical Index   1937-1949.   Wraps.
   1954   Harrogate, TN   30.00
MEYER, Henry C.   Civil War Experiences Under Bayard, Gregg, Kilpatrick, Custer Raulston, and Newberry.
   1911   New York   140.00
MEYER, Howard N.   Colonel of the Black Regiment.
   1967   New York   25.00
MEYER, Howard N.   Let Us Have Peace,   The Story of Ulysses S. Grant.
   1966   New York   10.00
MEYER, J. A.   William Glaze and the Palmetto Armory.   Wraps.
   1982   Columbia   10.00
MEYER, Leland Winfield   The Life and Times of Colonel Richard M. Johnson of Kentucky.
   1932   New York   50.00
MICHAEL, William H.   Cooperation Between General Grant and Commodore Foote and Between General Grant and Admiral Porter . . . Address.   Wraps.
   1904   n.p.   50.00
MICHIE, Peter S.   General McClellan.
   For additional information, see Appendix: Great Commanders Series.
   1901   New York   30.00
   1901   New York   125.00
MICHIE, Peter S.   The Life and Letters of Emory Upton.
   1885   New York   60.00
   1979   27.50
Michigan at Gettysburg, July 1, 2, and 3, 1863, Proceedings Incident to the Dedication of the Michigan Monuments upon the Battlefield of Gettysburg.
   1889   Detroit   110.00
Michigan at Shiloh Report of the Michigan Shiloh Soldiers' Monument Commission.   Wraps.
   1920   Lansing   20.00
Michigan Civil War Centennial Observance Commission   5.00 each

Michigan Soldiers and Sailors Alphabetical Index.
　1984　　Okemos, MI　　Ltd.　　50.00
Michigan Women in the Civil War.　Wraps.
　1963　　Lansing　　15.00
MIDDLETON, Alicia Hopton　　Life in Carolina and New England During the Nineteenth Century.
　1929　　Briston, RI　　75.00
MIERS, Earl Schenck　　The American Civil War.
　1961　　New York　　35.00
MIERS, Earl Schenck　　Billy Yank and Johnny Reb.
　1961　　New York　　20.00
MIERS, Earl Schenck, edited by　　The Fundamental Creed of Abraham Lincoln.　Wraps.
　1956　　Newark, DE　　10.00
MIERS, Earl Schenck　　The General Who Marched to Hell, William Tecumseh Sherman.
　1951　　New York　　30.00
MIERS, Earl Schenck　　The Great Rebellion.
　1958　　Cleveland　　35.00
MIERS, Earl Schenck　　The Last Campaign . . . Grant Saves the Union.
　1972　　Philadelphia　　10.00
　1972　　New York　　10.00
MIERS, Earl Schenck, edited by　　Lincoln Day by Day.　3 Vols.
　1960　　Washington, DC　　45.00
MIERS, Earl Schenck　　New Jersey and the Civil War.
　1964　　New Brunswick　　30.00
MIERS, Earl Schenck　　Robert E. Lee, A Great Life in Brief.
　1956　　New York　　30.00
　1964　　New York　　30.00
　1967　　New York　　30.00
MIERS, Earl Schenck　　The Web of Victory.　Grant at Vicksburg.
　1955　　New York　　20.00
　1984　　Wraps　　9.00
MIERS, Earl Schenck and BROWN, Richard A., edited by　　Gettysburg.
　1948　　New Brunswick　　30.00
MILES　　See: DALY, Walter E.
MILES, J.　　Georgia Civil War Sites:　A Comprehehsive Guide to 300 Civil War Battlefields, Forts, Museums, and Cemeteries in Georgia.　Wraps.
　1987　　7.95
MILES, Nelson A.　　Personal Recollections and Observations.
　1896　　Chicago　　85.00
　1897　　Chicago　　75.00
MILES, Nelson A.　　Serving the Republic.
　1911　　New York　　45.00
MILHAM, Charles G.　　Gallant Pelham: American Extraordinary.
　1959　　Washington, DC　　60.00
　1985　　Gaithersburg　　25.00

MILHOLLEN, Hirst D. and JOHNSON, James Ralph   Best   Photos   of
the Civil War.
1961   New York   25.00
1969   New York   20.00
MILHOLLEN, Hirst D. and MUGRIDGE, Donald H., compiled by   Civil
War Photographs 1861-1865.   Wraps.
1961   Washington, DC   10.00
MILHOLLEN, Hirst D., JOHNSON, James Ralph and BILL, Alfred
Horsemen Blue and Gray.
1960   New York   30.00
Military Despotism: Suspension of the Habeas Corpus: Curses Coming Home
to Roost!   Wraps.
1863   New York   15.00
Military History and Reminiscences of the Thirteenth Regiment of Illinois
Volunteer Infantry.
1892   Chicago   175.00
Military History of Ohio.
1886   Toledo   Montgomery County ed.   60.00
1886   Toledo   Stark County ed.   60.00
1887   Toledo   Franklin County ed.   60.00
1888   Toledo   Morgan County ed.   60.00
1889   Toledo   Mahoning County ed.   60.00
Military Map Referring to the Campaigns of the Army of the Potomac in
Virginia, Maryland, and Pennsylvania.
1865   New York   200.00
Military Map Showing the Marches of the United States Forces Under
Command of Maj.Gen. W.T. Sherman, U.S.A., During the Years, 1863,
1864, 1865.
1865   St. Louis   150.00
Military Map N.E. Virginia and Vicinity of Washington.
1862   n.p.   200.00
Military Operations in Jefferson County Virginia (and West Va.) 1861-1865.
Jefferson County Camp, U.C.V.
1911   (Charles Town, WV)   75.00
A Military Record of Battery D, First Ohio Veteran Volunteer Light
Artillery.
1908   Oil City, PA   140.00
Military Uniforms in America, Vol. III - Long Endure: The Civil War
Period, 1852-1867.
1988   Novato   40.00
MILLBROOK, Minnie Dubbs   A Study in Valor   Michigan Medal of
Honor Winners in the Civil War.   Wraps.
1966   Lansing   15.00
MILLBROOK, Minnie Dubbs, edited by   Twice Told Tales of Michigan
and Her Soldiers in the Civil War.   Wraps.
1966   Lansing   15.00
Milledgeville and Baldwin County Civil War Centennial.   Wraps.
1961   Milledgeville   15.00
MILLER, Alonzo   Diaries and Letters Written by Pvt. Alonzo Miller,
Co. A, 12th Wisconsin Infantry.
1958   Marietta, GA   40.00

MILLER, Charles D.   "Old Abe" the War Eagle in Report of the Great
Re-Union of the Veteran Soldiers and Sailors of Ohio.
1878   Newark   40.00
MILLER, Charles D.   Report of the Great Re-Union of the Veteran Soldiers and Sailors of Ohio Held at Newark July 22, 1878.
1879   Newark   60.00
MILLER, Delevan S.   Drum Taps in Dixie, Memories of a Drummer Boy
1861-1865.
1905   Watertown, NY   50.00
MILLER, Delavan S.   A Drum's Story and Other Tales.
1909   Watertown, NY   25.00
MILLER, E. M.   U.S.S. Monitor: The Ship that Launched a Modern
Navy.
1978   Annapolis   35.00
MILLER, Edward G.   Captain Edward Gee Miller of the 20th Wisconsin,
His War 1861-1865, edited by W. J. Lemke.   Wraps.
1960   Fayetteville   30.00
MILLER, Edwin J.   The Adventures of Ned Minton.
1904   45.00
MILLER, Emily Van Dorn, edited by   A Soldier's Honor with Reminiscences of Major General Earl Van Dorn.
1902   New York   325.00
MILLER, Francis T., edited by   The Photographic History of the Civil
War.   10 Vols.
1911-12   New York   300.00
1957   New York   10 Vols. in 5   Boxed   75.00
1970   100.00
1987   74.50
MILLER, Francis T.   Portrait Life of Lincoln.
1910   Chicago   25.00
1910   Springfield 25.00
MILLER, George   Missouri's Memorable Decade 1860-1870.
1898   Missouri   50.00
MILLER, Helen Topping   Christmas with Robert E. Lee.
1958   New York   10.00
MILLER, James Hervey   My War Experiences.
n.d.   Gardner, MA   45.00
MILLER, James N.   The Story of Andersonville and Florence.   Wraps.
1900   Des Moines   40.00
MILLER, Stephen Franks   Ahab Lincoln: A Tragedy of the Potomac.
1958   Chicago   15.00
MILLER, William Bluffton   "I Soldiered for the Union" The Civil War
Diary of William Bluffton Miller, edited by Robert J. Willey.   Wraps.
(1982) n.p.   30.00
MILLIGAN, John D.   Gunboats Down the Mississippi.
1965   Annapolis   15.00
MILLIGAN, John D., edited by   From the Fresh-Water Navy: 1861-64.
1975   Annapolis   20.00
MILLS, Anson   My Story.
1918   Washington, DC   35.00

MILLS, C. J.   Through Blood and Fire; The Civil War Letters of Maj. Charles J. Mills, 1862-1865.
    1982   Gettysburg   Ltd.   28.00

MILLS, J. Harrison   Chronicles of the Twenty-first Regiment, N. Y. State Vols.
    1867   Buffalo 200.00
    1887   Buffalo 90.00

MILLS, Lewis E.   General Pope's Virginia Campaign of 1862.   Wraps.
    1870   Cincinnati   40.00

MILTON, George Fort   Abraham Lincoln and the Fifth Column.
    1942   New York   20.00

MILTON, George Fort   The Age of Hate.   Andrew Johnson and the Radicals.
    1930   New York   30.00

MILTON, George Fort   Conflict.   The American Civil War.
    1941   New York   20.00

MILTON, George Fort   The Eve of Conflict.
    1934   Boston   15.00
    1963   15.00

MIMS, Edwin   The Advancing South, Stories of Progress and Reaction.
    1926   Garden City and New York   35.00

MIMS, Edwin   Sidney Lanier.
    1905   Boston   25.00

MIMS, Wilbur F.   War History of the Prattville Dragoons.   Wraps.
    n.d.   Thurber, TX   125.00
    n.d.   n.p.   35.00

Miniature Biographies of Civil War Generals.   50 biographies issued, copyrighted 1888 by Knapp & Company, Lithographers and Printers, Park Place, New York.   For issue with individual packages of Duke's Cigarettes.   Colored photo likeness on cover; scene or symbol on rear cover.   Approx. 15 pp each for biography.   Frontis: facsimile signature.   Beautifully boxed, labeled.   The Lakeside Press, Chicago.   Each issue approx. 7 cm.
    1888   New York   750.00

Minnesota in the Civil War and Indian Wars 1861-1865.   2 Vols.
    1890-93   St. Paul   100.00

MINNICH, J. W.   Inside and Outside of Rock Island Prison, from December, 1863, to June, 1865.
    1908   Nashville   200.00

MINNIGERODE, Charles   Jefferson Davis. A Memorial Address . . . Wraps.
    1890   Richmond   40.00

MINNIGH, Luther W.   Gettysburg.   Wraps.
    1892   n.p.   35.00
    1917   Gettysburg   25.00
    1920   n.p.   25.00
    1924   n.p.   25.00

MINOR, Benjamin Blake   The Southern Literary Messenger 1834-1864.
    1905   New York   80.00

MINOR, Charles L. C.   The Real Lincoln, edited by Kate Mason Rowland.   Wraps.
    1901   Richmond   20.00

MINOR, Kate Pleasants   **Southern Historical Society Papers Index.**
  1970   Dayton   15.00
  1978   Dayton   13.00
MINOR, Kate Pleasants, edited by   **From Dixie.**
  1893   Richmond   35.00
Minutes of Proceedings of . . . Annual Reunion Survivors of Seventy-third Illinois Volunteer Infantry. Wraps.
  1894   n.p.   20.00
  1904   Springfield   20.00
  1905   Farmer City   20.00
Mississippi Historical Society, Publications of. Vols. 1-11.
  1898-1910   Oxford   50.00 each
  1916-1921   Centenary Series   Vols. 1-4   50.00 each
The Mississippi Valley, Tennessee, Georgia, Alabama, 1861-1864.   See: **Papers of the Military Historical Society of Massachusetts, No. 8.**
Mississippi - Confederate Military History.   See: **Confederate Military History, Vol. VII** (Vol. IX, 1987 reprint ed.).
Missouri - Confederate Military History.   See: **Confederate Military History, Vol. IX** (Vol. XII, 1988 reprint ed.).
MITCHEL, Cora   **Reminiscences of the Civil War.**
  n.d.   Providence   20.00
MITCHEL, F. A.   **Ormsby MacKnight Mitchel, Astronomer and General.**
  1887   Boston   40.00
MITCHELL, Mrs. A. L., edited by   **Songs of the Confederacy and Plantation Melodies.** Wraps.
  1901   Cincinnati   30.00
MITCHELL, B. L.   **Edmund Ruffin, a Biography.**
  1981   Bloomington   20.00
MITCHELL, D. W.   **Ten Years in the United States.**
  1862   London   70.00
MITCHELL, Frederick W.   **"A Conundrum of the Days of '64,"** D.C. Mollus War Paper 5. Wraps.
  1890   n.p.   25.00
MITCHELL, Joseph B.   **The Badge of Gallantry.**
  1968   New York   20.00
MITCHELL, Joseph B.   **Decisive Battles of the Civil War.**
  1955   New York   25.00
  1955   New York   Wraps   5.00
MITCHELL, Joseph B.   **Military Leaders in the Civil War.**
  1972   New York   15.00
MITCHELL, Joseph B. and **HART**, Scott, edited by   **1st Manassas (Bull Run) and the War Around It.** Wraps.
  1961   Manassas   20.00
MITCHELL, Margaret   **Gone With the Wind.**
  1936   NY 1st Edition 1st issue (May)   600.00
  1936   not 1st ed.   40.00
  1960   30.00
  1961   35.00
  1968   New York   2 Vols. Limited Editions Club   85.00
  Many later editions   25.00

MITCHELL, Margaret   Margaret Mitchell's Gone with the Wind, Letters 1936-1949, edited by Richard Harwell.
    1976   New York   30.00

MITCHELL, Mary H.   Hollywood Cemetery, the History of a Southern Shrine.
    1985   Richmond   25.00

MITCHELL, Memory F.   Legal Aspects of Conscription and Exemption in North Carolina 1861-1865. Wraps.
    1965   Chapel Hill   25.00

MITCHELL, R.   Civil War Soldiers: Their Expectations and Their Experiences.
    1988   New York   19.95

MITCHELL, S. Weir   In War Time.
    1885   Boston   20.00

MITCHELL, S. Weir   Westways: A Village Chronicle.
    1913   New York   10.00

MITCHELL, Stewart   Horatio Seymour of New York.
    1938   Cambridge   20.00

MITCHELL, T. K.   Autobiography of Dr. T. K. Mitchell, Sr.   Wraps.
    1914   Atlanta   40.00

MITCHELL, William   General Greeley, The Story of a Great American.
    1936   New York   30.00

MITGANG, Herbert, edited by   Lincoln as They Saw Him.
    1956   New York   10.00

MITGANG, Herbert, edited by   Washington in Lincoln's Time.
    1958   New York   10.00

MIXSON, Frank M.   Reminiscences of a Private.
    1910   Columbia   350.00

MOAT, Louis Shepheard   See: LESLIE, Frank

MOEHRING, E. and KAYLIN, Arleen, edited by   The Civil War Extra.
    1975   New York   30.00

MOGELEVER, Jacob   Death to Traitors.
    1960   New York   30.00

MOHR, J. C., edited by   The Cormany Diaries: A Northern Family in the Civil War.
    1982   Pittsburgh   33.00

M.O.L.L.U.S.   Military Order of the Loyal Legion. 45-50 volumes. At press time of this volume we are trying to identify all the MOLLUS volumes so that we may reprint them. Individual titles are listed in this guide under author or title.

MONAGHAN, Jay   Civil War on the Western Border 1854-1865.
    1955   New York   40.00
    1955   Boston   40.00
    Recent reprint   25.00

MONAGHAN, Jay   Custer - The Life of General George Armstrong Custer.
    1959   Boston   50.00

MONAGHAN, Jay   Diplomat in Carpet Slippers   Abraham Lincoln Deals with Foreign Affairs.
    1945   Indianapolis   15.00

MONAGHAN, Jay   Lincoln Bibliography 1839-1939. 2 Vols.
    1943   Springfield   50.00

MONAGHAN, Jay   The Man Who Elected Lincoln.
1956   Indianapolis   10.00
MONAGHAN, Jay   Swamp Fox of the Confederacy: The Life and Military Services of M. Jeff Thompson.   See: Confederate Centennial Studies No. 2.
MONJO, F. N.   Gettysburg, Tad Lincoln's Story.
1976   New York   17.50
MONNETT, Howard N.   Action Before Westport 1864.
1964   Kansas City   Ltd.   30.00
Monograph on the Monitor, The First Monitor and Its Builders.   Wraps.
1884   Poughkeepsie, NY   40.00
MONROE, J.   The Company Drill of the Infantry of the Line.
1862   New York   50.00
MONSELL, Helen A.   Boy of Old Virginia: Robert E. Lee.
1937   Indianapolis   10.00
MONTAGUE, Ludwell Lee   Gloucester County in the Civil War. Wraps.
1965   Gloucester   15.00
MONTEIRO, Aristides   War Reminiscences by the Surgeon of Mosby's Command.   Wraps.
1890   Richmond   175.00
1984   Gaithersburg   25.00
MONTFORT, Elias R.   From Grafton to McDowell Through Tygart's Valley.   Wraps.
1886   Cincinnati   35.00
MONTFORT, Elias R., FURNESS, H. B. and ALMS, Fred H.   G.A.R. War Papers, Papers Read Before Fred C. Jones Post No. 401. . . .
1891   Cincinnati   250.00
MONTFORT, Theodorick W.   Rebel Lawyer: Letters of _____ 1861-1862, edited by Spencer B. King, Jr.   Wraps.
1965   Athens   25.00
MONTGOMERY, Franklin A.   Reminiscences of a Mississippian in Peace and War.
1901   Cincinnati   150.00
MONTGOMERY, Horace   Howell Cobb's Confederate Career.   See: Confederate Centennial Studies, No. 10.
MONTGOMERY, Horace   Johnny Cobb Confederate Aristocrat.   Wraps.
1964   Athens, GA   25.00
1981   25.00
MONTGOMERY, Horace   A Union Officer's Recollections of the Negro as a Soldier.   Wraps.
1961   PA   30.00
MONTGOMERY, James Stuart   The Shaping of a Battle: Gettysburg.
1959   Philadelphia   40.00
MONTGOMERY, M. W.   History of Jay County, Indiana.
(1864)   Chicago   90.00
MONTGOMERY, Walter A.   Address and Poem Delivered at the Unveiling of the Monument Erected to the Memory of the Confederate Dead of Warren County, N. C.   Wraps.
1906   Raleigh   35.00

MOODY, Claire N.　　　Battle of Pea Ridge or Elkhorn Tavern March 7-8, 1862. Wraps.
1956　Little Rock　20.00

MOODY, Granville　　A Life's Retrospect, Autobiography of Rev. Granville Moody, edited by Rev. Sylvester Weeks.
1890　Cincinnati　45.00

MOODY, Loring　　The Destruction of Republicanism the Object of the Rebellion.
1863　Boston　15.00

MOON, H. L.　　　Balance of Power: The Negro Vote.
1948　New York　20.00

Historical Significance of Brown's Gap in the War Between the States. Wraps.
1937　Waynesboro　25.00

MOORE, Albert B.　　　Conscription and Conflict in the Confederacy.
1924　New York　50.00
1963　New York　30.00

MOORE, Alison　　The Louisiana Tigers or The Two Louisiana Brigades of the Army of Northern Virginia 1861-1865.
1961　Baton Rouge　75.00

MOORE, Alison　　Old Bob Wheat, High Private. Wraps.
1957　Baton Rouge　30.00

MOORE, Avery C.　　Confederate California.
1956　Sonora, CA　35.00

MOORE, Avery C.　　Destiny's Soldier (Gen. Albert Sidney Johnston). Wraps.
1958　San Francisco　30.00

MOORE, Charles, edited by　　Lincoln's Gettysburg Address and Second Inaugural.
1927　Boston　Ltd.　25.00

MOORE, Claude Hunter　　Thomas Overton Moore: A Confederate Governor.
1960　Clinton, NC　20.00

MOORE, Edward A.　　The Story of a Cannoneer Under Stonewall Jackson. In all of the untrimmed copies we have seen, the first few pages vary in size from the rest of the book.
1907　New York and Washington, DC　200.00
1910　Lynchburg　125.00
1971　Freeport　20.00
1983　New York　25.00

MOORE, Frank　　Anecdotes, Poetry and Incidents of the War: North and South 1860-1865.
1867　New York　30.00

MOORE, Frank　　The Civil War in Song and Story.
1882　New York　25.00
1889　New York　25.00
1970　New York　42.00

MOORE, Frank, edited by　　The Portrait Gallery of the War, Civil, Military and Naval. A Biographical Record.
1865　New York　100.00

MOORE, Frank　　Rebel Rhymes and Rhapsodies.
1864　New York　35.00

MOORE, Frank, edited by   The Rebellion Record. 12 Vols.
1862-69   New York   450.00
1977   400.00
MOORE, Frank, edited by   Songs of the Soldiers.
1864   New York   30.00
MOORE, Frank   Women of the War.
1866   Hartford   35.00
1867   Hartford   30.00
MOORE, George Ellis   A Banner in the Hills, West Virginia's State-
hood.
1963   New York   20.00
MOORE, George H.   Notes on the History of Slavery in Massachusetts.
1866   New York   35.00
MOORE, Glover   William Jemison Mims, Soldier and Squire.
1966   Birmingham   35.00
MOORE, Guy W.   The Case of Mrs. Surratt.
1954   Norman, OK   20.00
MOORE, J. Staunton   Reminiscences, Letters, Poetry and Miscellanies.
1903   Richmond   100.00
MOORE, James   A Complete History of the Great Rebellion: or The
Civil War in the United States, 1861-1865.
1866   New York   15.00
MOORE, James   History of the Cooper Shop Volunteer Refreshment
Saloon.
1866   60.00
MOORE, James   Kilpatrick and Our Cavalry.
1865   New York   75.00
MOORE, John C.   Missouri.   See: Confederate Military History, Vol.
IX (Vol. XII, 1988 reprint ed.).
MOORE, John Hammond   The Juhl Letters to the Charleston Courier - A
View of the South 1865-1871.
1974   GA   20.00
MOORE, John Hampton   Baker at Ball's Bluff, An Address of _____
. . . Oct. 21, 1911. Wraps.
n.d.   n.p.   50.00
MOORE, John Henry   The Horizon and Zenith of the Great Rebel-
lion, or the Kansas Troubles, and the Taking of Vicksburg. . . .
1870   Cincinnati   400.00
MOORE, John Preston, edited by "My Ever Dearest Friend"   The Letters of
A. Dudley Mann to Jefferson Davis, 1869-1889.   See: Confederate
Centennial Studies, No. 14.
MOORE, John W.   Roster of North Carolina Troops in the War
Between the States. 4 Vols.
1882   Raleigh, NC   400.00
MOORE, Robert A.   A Life for the Confederacy . . . Diaries of _____
Co. G, 17th Mississippi Regiment, edited by James N. Silver.
1959   Jackson   40.00
1987   Wilmington, NC   25.00
MOORE, Samuel J. T., Jr.   Moore's Complete Civil War Guide to
Richmond. Wraps.
1978   Richmond   10.00

MOORE, Ward   Bring the Jubilee.
1953   New York   15.00
MOORS, John F.   History of the Fifty-second Regiment Massachusetts Volunteers.
1893   Boston   75.00
MORAN, Benjamin   The Journal of _____ 1857-1865, edited by Sarah A. Wallace and Frances E. Gillespie. 2 Vols.
1948-49   Chicago   45.00
MORAN, Frank E.   Bastiles of the Confederacy.
1890   Baltimore   35.00
MORAN, Frank E.   A Thrilling History of the Famous Underground Tunnel of Libby Prison. Wraps.
1893   New York   135.00
MORDECAI, S.   Richmond in By-Gone Days. . . .
1856   Richmond   100.00
1946   Richmond   25.00
MORFORD, Henry   The Days of Shoddy.
1863   Philadelphia   30.00
MORFORD, Henry   Red-Tape and Pigeon-Hole Generals. By a Citizen-Soldier.
1864   New York   35.00
MORFORD, Henry   Shoulder-Straps   A Novel of New York and the Army.
1863   Philadelphia   35.00
MORGAN, A. T.   Yazoo; or, On the Picket Line of Freedom in the South.
1884   Washington, DC   75.00
MORGAN, James Norris   Recollections of a Rebel Reefer.
1917   Boston   150.00
1918   London   200.00
MORGAN, John Hunt   The Great Indiana-Ohio Raid. Wraps.
n.d.   Louisville, KY   25.00
MORGAN, Julia   How It Was: Four Years Among the Rebels.
1892   Nashville   150.00
MORGAN, Murray   Dixie Raider: The Saga of the C.S.S. Shenandoah.
1948   New York   30.00
MORGAN, William H.   A Narrative of the Service of Company D, First Massachusetts Heavy Artillery.
1907   Boston   75.00
MORGAN, William H.   Personal Reminiscences of the War of 1861-65.
1911   Lynchburg, VA   100.00
1971   35.00
MORHOUS, Henry C.   Reminiscences of the 123rd Regiment, N.Y.S.V.
1879   Greenwich   110.00
MORLEY, Christopher, edited by   The Blue and the Gray   or War Is Hell.
1930   Garden City, NJ   15.00
MORRILL, Lily Logan   A Builder of the New South.
1940   Boston   35.00
MORRIS, George and FOUTZ, Susan   Lynchburg in the Civil War. The City - The People - The Battle.
1984   17.00

MORRIS, Gouverneur   The History of a Volunteer Regiment . . . Known as Wilson's Zouaves.
1891   New York   125.00
MORRIS, Richard B.   Voices of America's Past, A House Divided: The Civil War. Wraps.
1976   New York   6.00
MORRIS, William S.   History 31st Regiment Illinois Volunteers.
1902   Evansville, IN   165.00
MORROW, D. F.   Then and Now, Reminiscences and Historical Romance 1856-1865.
1926   Macon, GA   30.00
MORROW, Honore W.   Forever Free: A Novel of Abraham Lincoln.
1927   New York   10.00
MORROW, Honore W.   Great Captain.
n.d.   New York   10.00
MORROW, Honore W.   The Last Full Measure.
1930   New York   10.00
MORROW, Honore W.   Mary Todd Lincoln.
1928   New York   10.00
MORROW, Honore W.   With Malice Toward None.
1935   10.00
MORROW, Josiah   Life and Speeches of Thomas Corwin.
1896   Cincinnati   20.00
MORROW, Maude E.   Recollections of the Civil War. Wraps.
1901   Lockland, OH   30.00
MORROW, Ralph E.   Northern Methodism and Reconstruction.
1956   5.00
MORSE, Charles F.   History of the Second Massachusetts, Regiment of Infantry, Gettysburg. Wraps.
1882   Boston   35.00
MORSE, Charles F.   Letters Written During the Civil War 1861-1865.
1898   Boston   50.00
MORSE, Charlotte Ingersoll, compiled by   The Unknown Friends A Civil War Romance / Letters of My Father and My Mother.
1948   Chicago   35.00
MORSE, Francis W.   Personal Experiences in the War of the Great Rebellion.
1866   Albany   75.00
MORSE, John T.   Abraham Lincoln. 2 Vols.
1893   Boston   20.00
1898   20.00
MORTON, Frederic   The Story of Winchester in Virginia.
1925   Strasburg   55.00
MORTON, John Watson   The Artillery of Nathan Bedford Forrest's Cavalry.
1909   Nashville   200.00
1962   Kennesaw   75.00
1988   28.00
MORTON, Joseph W., Jr., edited by   Sparks from the Campfire, or Tales of the Old Veterans.
1890   Philadelphia   35.00
1899   Philadelphia   35.00

MORTON, Oliver T.   The Southern Empire.
    1892   Boston   25.00
MORTON, Oren F.   A History of Rockbridge County, Virginia.
    1920   Staunton, VA   50.00
MOSBY, John S.   The Letters of John S. Mosby.
    1989   32.50
MOSBY, John S.   The Memoirs of _____, edited by Charles W. Russell.
    1917   Boston   200.00
    1959   Bloomington   40.00
    1975   New York   25.00
    1987   Gaithersburg   35.00
MOSBY, John S.   Mosby's War Reminiscences & Stuart's Cavalry Cam-
    paigns. Wraps.
    1887   New York   100.00
    1887   Boston   75.00
    1898   New York   75.00
    1958   New York   30.00
    1984   25.00
    1987   25.00
MOSBY, John S.   Stuart's Cavalry in the Gettysburg Campaign.
    1908   New York   100.00
    1984   30.00
    1987   25.00
MOSES, Belle   The Gray Knight, The Story of Robert E. Lee.
    1936   New York   20.00
MOSGROVE, George Dallas   Kentucky Cavaliers in Dixie.
    1895   Louisville   250.00
    1957   Jackson, TN edited by Bell I. Wiley 40.00
    1987   30.00
MOSS, Lemuel   Annals of the United States Christian Commission.
    1868   Philadelphia   55.00
MOSS, W., compiled by   Confederate Broadside Poems: A Bibliography.
    1989   Westport   44.50
MOTLEY, John Lothrop   The   Causes   of   the   American   Civil   War.
    Wraps.
    1861   New York   15.00
MOTLEY, John Lothrop   The Correspondence of John Lothrop Motley.
    2 Vols.
    1889   New York   20.00
MOTT, Smith B.   The Campaigns of the 52nd Regiment Penn. Volunteer
    Infantry, First Known as "The Luzerne Regiment."
    1911   Philadelphia   75.00
MOTT, Valentine, M.D.   Pain and Anesthetic: An Essay.
    1862   60.00
MOTTELAY, Paul F. and CAMPBELL-COPELAND, T., edited by   The
    Soldier in our Civil War. 2 Vols.
    1884-85 New York   125.00
    1890   75.00
MOULTON, C. H.   Fort Lyon to Harper's Ferrry: On the Border of
    North and South with Rambling 'Jour,' the Civil War Letters and News-
    paper Dispatches of. . . .
    1987   Shippensburg   19.95

MOWRER, George H., compiled by　　　History of the Organization and Service of Co. A, 14th Pennsylvania Cavalry.
(189-)　n.p.　140.00
MOWRIS, James A.　　　History of the 117th Regiment N. Y. Volunteers (4th Oneida).
1866　Hartford　75.00
n.d.　n.p.　60.00
MOWRY, William A.　　Camp Life in the Civil War Eleventh R. I. Infantry. Wraps.
1914　Boston　40.00
MOYER, Henry P., compiled by　　　History of the 17th Regt. Penna. Volunteer Cavalry.
1911　Lebanon　115.00
Mr. Buchanan's Administration on the Eve of Rebellion.
1866　New York　25.00
MUDD, Joseph A.　　　With Porter in North Missouri:　A Chapter in the History of the War Between the States.
1909　Washington, DC　160.00
MUDD, Nettie, edited by　　The Life of Dr. Samuel A. Mudd.
1906　New York　150.00
1955　Marietta, GA　30.00
1975　Linden, TN　25.00
MUFFLY, Joseph W.　　Fort Sumter, A Paper.　Wraps.
1897　Des Moines　35.00
MUFFLY, Joseph W., edited by　　　Story of Our Regiment; History of the 148th Pennsylvania Volunteers.
1904　Des Moines　125.00
MUGRIDGE, Donald H., compiled by　　The American Civil War　A Selected Reading List.　Wraps.
1960　Washington, DC　5.00
MUHLENFELD, Elisabeth　　　Mary Boykin Chesnut　A Biography.
(1981)　Baton Rouge and London　　25.00
MULHOLLAND, St. Clair A.　　The American Volunteer.
1909　Philadelphia　40.00
MULHOLLAND, St. Clair A.　　A Military Order Congress Medal of Honor Legion of the United States.
1905　Philadelphia　75.00
MULHOLLAND, St. Clair A.　　The Story of the 116th Regiment Pennsylvania Infantry.
1899　Philadelphia　90.00
1903　Philadelphia　75.00
MULLER, William F.　　War Papers of the Confederacy.　Wraps.
1961　Charlottesville, VA　15.00
MULLINS, Michael and REED, Rowena　　The Union Bookshelf:　A Selected Civil War Bibliography.
1982　Wendell, NC　20.00
MULVIHILL, M. J.　　First Mississippi Regiment - Its Foundation, Organization and Record.　Wraps.
(1931)　Vicksburg　50.00
MULVIHILL, M. J.　　Vicksburg and Warren County, Mississippi . . . Civil War Veterans.
1931　Vicksburg　35.00

MULVIHILL, M. J.　　　Vicksburg, Fort St. Peter, Fort Snyder.　Wraps.
　　1931　Vicksburg　　15.00
MUNDEN, Kenneth W. and **BEERS**, Henry P.　　　Guide to Federal Archives
　　Relating to the Civil War.
　　1962　Washington, DC　　30.00
MUNDIE, J. A.　　　The Confederate Generals Buried in Louisiana.　Wraps.
　　1987　New Orleans　　　5.00
MUNFORD, Beverley B.　　　Virginia's Attitude Toward Slavery and Seces-
　　sion.
　　1909　New York　　30.00
　　1910　New York　　30.00
　　1914　Richmond　　25.00
　　1915　Richmond　　25.00
　　1969　New York　　20.00
MUNFORD, George Wythe　　　The Jewels of Virginia:　A Lecture . . . .
　　Wraps.
　　1867　Richmond　　30.00
MUNFORD, Robert B., Jr.　　　Richmond Homes and Memories.
　　1936　Richmond　　40.00
MUNHALL, Leander W.　　　The Chattanooga Campaign.　Wraps.
　　1902　Philadelphia　35.00
MUNK, Joseph A.　　　Activities of a Lifetime.
　　1924　Los Angeles　90.00
MUNROE, James P.　　　A Life of Francis Amasa Walker.
　　1923　New York　　20.00
　　1934　New York　　20.00
MUNSON, John W.　　　Reminiscences of a Mosby Guerrilla.
　　1906　New York　　100.00
　　1983　Washington, DC　　20.00
MURDOCK, Eugene C.　　　One Million Men:　The Civil War Draft in the
　　North.
　　1971　Madison　25.00
MURDOCK, Eugene C.　　　Patriotism Limited 1862-1865　The Civil War
　　Draft and the Bounty System.
　　1967　n.p.　20.00
MURFIN, James V.　　　The Gleam of Bayonets.
　　1965　New York　　35.00
　　1968　New York　　30.00
　　Recent reprint　　30.00
　　Recent reprint　　Wraps　10.00
MURFREE, Mary (Charles Egbert Craddock)　　　The　Storm　Centre:　A
　　Novel.
　　1905　New York　　15.00
MURPHEY, Thomas G.　　　Four Years in the War.　The History of the
　　First Regiment of Delaware Veteran Volunteers.
　　1866　Philadelphia　150.00
MURPHY, James B.　　　L. Q. C. Lamar　Pragmatic Patriot.
　　1973　Baton Rouge　　15.00
MURPHY, John M.　　　Confederate Carbines and Musketoons.
　　1986　Dallas　　45.00

MURRAY, Alton J.   South Georgia Rebels . . . True War Time Experiences of the 26th Regiment Georgia Volunteer Infantry, Lawton-Gor-
don-Evans Brigade, C.S.A. 1861-1865.
1976   Jacksonville, FL   35.00
MURRAY, Elizabeth Dunbar   My Mother Used to Say.
1959   Boston   30.00
MURRAY, George W.   A History of George W. Murray and His Long
Confinement at Andersonville, Ga.   Wraps.
(186-)   Hartford   75.00
MURRAY, John Ogden   The Immortal Six Hundred.
1905   Winchester   150.00
1911   Roanoke   80.00
1986   29.95
MURRAY, John Ogden   Three Stories in One.
1911   Roanoke   75.00
1915   n.p.   45.00
MURRAY, Thomas H.   History of the 9th Regiment, Connecticut Volunteer Infantry, "The Irish Regiment."
1903   New Haven   85.00
Muster Roll of First Regiment Georgia Volunteers 1861.   Wraps.
1890   Atlanta   125.00
Muster Roll of New Orleans Vol. Infantry U.S. Army, June 13, 1864 to 31st
August, 1864. Wraps.
n.d.   n.p.   75.00
Muster Roll of the 22nd Reg. Connecticut Vols., 28 February 1863 to 7th
Day July 1863.
1863   65.00
MYERS, Frank M.   The Comanches: A History of White's Battalion.
1871   Baltimore   750.00
1956   Marietta   40.00
1985   27.50
1987   Gaithersburg   35.00
MYERS, Frank M.   Soldiering in Dakota, Among the Indians in 1863-
64-65.   Wraps.
1936   Pierre, SD   30.00
1975   17.50
MYERS, John C.   A Daily Journal of the 192nd Regiment Pennsylvania
Volunteers.
1864   Philadelphia   90.00
MYERS, Raymond E.   The Zollie Tree.
1964   Louisville, KY   25.00
MYERS, Robert Manson, edited by   The Children of Pride,   a True
Story of Georgia and the Civil War.
1972   New Haven   40.00
1973   New York   40.00
1984   New Haven   35.00
MYERS, William Starr   The Maryland Constitution of 1864.   Wraps.
1901   Baltimore   25.00
MYERS, William Starr   The Mexican War Diary of General George B.
McClellan.
1972   Jersey City   23.00

MYERS, William Starr   The Self-Reconstruction of Maryland.   Wraps.
    1909   Baltimore   35.00
MYERS, William Starr   A Study in Personality: General George Brinton
   McClellan.
    1934   New York   35.00
NACHTIGALL, H.   History of the 75th Pennsylvania Infantry.   Wraps.
    1987   Riverside, IL   12.00
NAGEL, Charles   A Boy's Civil War Story.
    1934   St. Louis   40.00
    1937   Philadelphia   35.00
NAGLEE, H. M.   The Secret History of the Peninsular Campaign Letter
   of _____ About General McClellan.   A Message from Old Soldiers to
   the Army . . . by the McClellan Legion. Wraps.
    (c.1864) n.p.   30.00
NAISAWALD, L. Van Loan   Grape and Canister.
    1960   New York   45.00
    1983   29.50
NALTY, Bernard C.   The US Marines in the Civil War.   Wraps.
    1958   Washington, DC   30.00
Names of Officers and Soldiers Found on the Battle-fields of the Wilderness
   and of Spotsylvania Courthouse, VA.   Wraps.
    1865   Washington, DC   35.00
Names of Soldiers Who Died in Defence of the American Union, Interred in
   the National Cemeteries at Fortress Monroe and Hampton, Virginia.
   Wraps.
    1866   Washington, DC   60.00
Names of Soldiers Who Died in Defense of the American Union, Interred in
   the National Cemeteries at Memphis, Tennessee, and Chalmette, (Near
   New Orleans), Louisiana. Wraps.
    1869   Washington, DC   75.00
Names of Soldiers Who Died in Defense of the American Union, Interred in
   the National Cemeteries at Washington, D.C. from August 3, 1861, to
   June 30, 1865. Wraps.
    1865   Washington, DC   75.00
Names of Soldiers Who Died in Defense of The Union, Interred in the
   National Cemeteries at Vicksburg, Mississippi and New Albany, Indiana.
   Wraps.
    1869   Washington, DC   75.00
NANKIVELL, John H.   History of the Military Organizations of the
   State of Colorado.
    1935   Denver   80.00
NANKIVELL, John H.   History of the 25th Regiment, U.S. Infantry,
   1829-1926.
    1969   New York   20.00
NANZIG, Thomas P.   3rd Virginia Cavalry.
    1989   16.95
Napoleon's Maxim's of War.
    1861   125.00
Narrative of Privations and Sufferings of United States Officers and Sol-
   diers While Prisoners of War in the Hands of the Rebel Authorities.
   Wraps.
    1864   Philadelphia   45.00

1864   Boston   35.00
1865   Boston   30.00
NASBY, Petroleum (pseud.)   See: LOCKE, David R.
NASH, Charles Edward   **Biographical Sketches of Gen. Pat Cleburne and General T. C. Hindman.**
   1898   Little Rock 450.00
   1977   Dayton 20.00
NASH, Eugene A.   **A History of the 44th Regiment New York Volunteer Infantry.**
   1911   Chicago 125.00
   1988   40.00
NASH, Howard P., Jr.   **Andrew Johnson.**
   1972   15.00
NASH, Howard P., Jr.   **A Naval History of the Civil War.**
   1973   New York   20.00
NASH, Howard P., Jr.   **Stormy Petrel: The Life and Times of General Benjamin F. Butler 1818-1893.**
   1969   Rutherford   20.00
NASON, Elias   **The Life and Public Services of Henry Wilson.**
   1876   Boston   20.00
NASON, Elias   **The Life and Times of Charles Sumner.**
   1874   Boston   20.00
NASON, George W.   **History and Complete Roster of the Massachusetts Regiments. Minute Men of '61.**
   1910   Boston   50.00
NASON, W. A.   **With the Ninth Army Corps in East Tennessee.**
   1891   Providence   Ltd.   35.00
NATHANS, Elizabeth S.   **Losing the Peace. Georgia Republicans and Reconstruction 1865-1871.**
   1968   Baton Rouge   20.00
The National Tribune Scrap Book. Stories of the Camp, March, Battle, Hospital and Prison Told by Comrades. 3 Vols. Wraps.
   n.d.   Washington, DC   75.00
The National Tribune Soldier's Handbook, Pension, Increase. Plus Supplement. Wraps.
   1898   Washington, DC   20.00
National Union Convention, Proceedings Held in Phila., Pa. . . . 1966. Wraps.
   1866   Washington, DC   35.00
Naval Actions.   See: **Papers of the Military Historical Society of Massachusetts, No. 11.**
Naval Actions and History, 1799-1898.   See: **Papers of the Military Historical Society of Massachusetts, No. 12.**
NAYLOR, Colin T., Jr.   **Civil War Days in a Country Village.**
   1961   Peekskill, NY   30.00
NEAGLES, J. C.   **Confederate Research Sources: A Guide to Archive Collections. Wraps.**
   1986   Salt Lake City   13.00
NEAL, John R.   **Disunion and Restoration in Tennessee.**
   1971   12.00

NEAL, Lois S., compiled by   Genealogical Index to North Carolina Volume of Confederate Military History. Expanded portion of N. C. volume. Wraps.
  1975   Raleigh   5.00
NEAL, Lois S., compiled by   A Personal Name Index to the Expanded Edition of Jedediah Hotchkiss' Virginia (Vol. 3) of Confederate Military History. Wraps.
  1976   Raleigh , NC   6.00
NEAL, M. J.   The Journal of Eldress Nancy; Kept at the South Union, Kentucky Shaker Colony. . . .
  1963   Nashville   35.00
NEAL, W. A., edited by   An Illustrated History of the Missouri Engineer & the 25th Infantry Regiments.
  1889   Chicago   200.00
NEALE, Walter   The Sovereignty of the States.
  1910   New York   75.00
NEELY, Mark E.   The Abraham Lincoln Encyclopedia. Wraps.
  n.d.   New York   17.50
NEELY, Mark E., et al   The Confederate Image, Prints of the Lost Cause.
  1987   Chapel Hill, NC   32.50
  1987   Chapel Hill, NC   Wraps   14.95
NEELY, Mark E. and McMURTY, R. Gerald   The Insanity File (Mary Todd Lincoln).
  1986   19.95
NEESE, George M.   Three Years in the Confederate Horse Artillery.
  1911   New York   350.00
  1983   Dayton   22.00
  1988   35.00
NEFF, Robert O,   Tennessee's Battered Brigadier. The Life of General Joseph B. Palmer. Wraps.
  1988   10.00
NEIL, Henry M.   A Battery at Close Quarters: A Paper Read Before the Ohio Commandery of the Loyal Legion, Oct 6, 1909.
  n.d.   n.p.   40.00
NEILSON, Eliza Lucy Irion   Lucy's Journal.
  1967   Greenwood, MS   40.00
NEIMAN, S. I.   Judah Benjamin.
  1963   New York   35.00
NELSON, Alanson H.   The Battles of Chancellorsville and Gettysburg.
  1899   Minneapolis   65.00
NELSON, C. P.   Abe The War Eagle. Wraps.
  1903   Lynn   30.00
NELSON, Horatio   If I am Killed on This Trip, I Want My Horse Kept for My Brother. Wraps.
  1980   Manassas   15.00
NELSON, Henry   Uniforms of the United States Army.
  1959   New York   50.00
NELSON, Larry E.   Bullets, Ballots, and Rhetoric, Confederate Policy for the United States Presidential Contest of 1864.
  1980   University, AL   15.00

NELSON, Truman   The Old Man - John Brown at Harpers Ferry.
   1973   New York   30.00

NEMO   Remarks on the Policy of Recognizing the Independence of Southern States of North America, and the Struggle in that Continent. Wraps.
   1863   London   75.00

NEPVEUX, Ethel S.   George Alfred Trenholm and Company that Went to War 1861-1865.
   1973   Charleston   40.00

NESBIT, John W.   General History of Company D, 149th Pennsylvania Volunteers.
   1908   Oakdale, CA   135.00

NEVILLE, Edmund   Rebellion and Witchcraft - A Thanksgiving Sermon. Wraps.
   1861   Newark, NJ   20.00

NEVIN, D.   The Road to Shiloh, Early Battles in the West.
   1984   10.00

NEVINS, Allan   The Emergence of Lincoln. 2 Vols.
   1950   New York   Boxed   25.00

NEVINS, Allan   Fremont, Pathmaker of the West. 2 Vols.
   1961   50.00

NEVINS, Allan, edited by   Lincoln and the Gettysburg Address Commemorative Papers.
   1964   Urbana, IL   15.00

NEVINS, Allan   Ordeal of the Union. 2 Vols. Boxed.
   1947   New York   30.00

NEVINS, Allan   Statesmanship of the Civil War.
   1953   New York   25.00

NEVINS, Allan   The War for the Union. 4 Vols.
   Vol. 1   The Improvised War.
   Vol. 2   War Becomes Revolution.
   Vol. 3   The Organized War 1863-1864.
   Vol. 4   The Organized War to Victory 1864-1865.
   1959-71   New York   70.00

NEVINS, Allan, ROBERTSON, James I., Jr. and WILEY, Bell I., edited by Civil War Books: A Critical Bibliography. 2 Vols.
   1967   Baton Rouge   60.00
   1970   Wendell, NC   60.00
   1989   Wilmington, NC   60.00

New Light on Lincoln's Character. Wraps.
   n.d.   n.p.   15.00

New Market Day at V.M.I. Wraps.
   1903   n.p.   30.00

The New Reign of Terror in the Slaveholding States for 1859-1860.
   1860   New York   45.00

New York at Andersonville, Dedication of Monument Erected by the State of New York at Andersonville, Georgia 1914.
   1916   Albany   60.00

New York at Antietam, Dedication of the New York State Monument on the Battlefield of Antietam.
   1923   Albany   35.00

New York at Chattanooga.
    1928   New York   35.00
New York at Gettysburg, N. Y. Monuments Commission . . .   3 Vols.
    1900   Albany   150.00
    1902   125.00
New York Monument Commission - In Memoriam: Henry Warner Slocum,
    1826-1894.
    1904   Albany   60.00
New York Monument Commission - Major Gen. Francis C. Barlow at Gettys-
    burg and Other Battlefields.
    1923   Albany   40.00
New York Monument Commission - Major General James S. Wadsworth at
    Gettysburg and Other Fields.
    1916   50.00
New York State and the Civil War. Wraps.
    1961-63   24 numbers   60.00
New York State Soldier's Depot, Report of the Board of Managers. Wraps.
    1864   Albany   40.00
New York Times.
    1861-65 (Complete run)   1500.00
    200.00 per year
New York, Monuments Commission Fiftieth Anniversary of the Battle of
    Gettysburg.
    1916   Albany   50.00
NEWBERRY, J. S.   The U. S. Sanitary Commission in the Valley of
    the Mississippi During the War of the Rebellion.
    1871   Cleveland   60.00
NEWCOMB, M. A.   Four Years of Personal Reminiscences of the War.
    1893   Chicago   50.00
NEWCOMB, Rexford   In the Lincoln Country Journeys to the Lincoln
    Shrines.
    1928   Philadelphia   10.00
NEWCOMB, Simon   A Critical Examination of our Financial Policy
    During the Southern Rebellion.
    1865   New York   30.00
NEWCOMER, C. Armour   Cole's Cavalry, or Three Years in the Saddle in
    the Shenandoah Valley.
    1895   Baltimore   175.00
    1970   New York   35.00
NEWELL, Joseph Keith   "Ours," Annals of the 10th Regiment Mas-
    sachusetts Volunteers.
    1875   Springfield   75.00
NEWHALL, F. C.   How Lee Lost the Use of His Cavalry Before the
    Battle of Gettysburg. Wraps.
    1878   Philadelphia   60.00
NEWHALL, Frederick C.   With General Sheridan in Lee's Last Campaign.
    1866   Philadelphia   60.00
NEWHALL, Walter S.   A Memoir.
    1864   Philadelphia   50.00

NEWLIN, William H.   Account of the Escape of Six Federal Soldiers from Prison at Danville, Va.   Wraps.
1886   Cincinnati   90.00
1887   Cincinnati   70.00
1889   Cincinnati   50.00
NEWLIN, William H.   A History of the Seventy-Third Regiment of Illinois Infantry Volunteers.
1890   Springfield   120.00
NEWMAN, H. W.   Maryland and the Confederacy.
1976   Annapolis Ltd.   50.00
NEWMAN, Ralph G., edited by   Abraham Lincoln, His Story in His Own Words.
1975   New York   15.00
NEWMAN, Ralph G., edited by   Lincoln for the Ages.
1960   New York   20.00
1960   New York   Ltd.   35.00
NEWMAN, Ralph G. and LONG, E. B.   A Basic Civil War Library A Bibliographical Essay.   Wraps.
1964   Springfield, IL   20.00
NEWMAN, Ralph G. and LONG, E. B.   The Civil War Digest.
1960   New York   15.00
NEWSOME, Edmund   Experience in the War of the Great Rebellion.
1880   Cardondale   150.00
NEWTON, A. H.   Out of the Briars: An Autobiography and Sketch of the 29th Conn. Regiment of Volunteers.
1910   Philadelphia   80.00
1969   Miami   30.00
NEWTON, James K. A Wisconsin Boy in Dixie, The Selected Letters of . . . , edited by Stephen Ambrose.
1961   Madison   25.00
NEWTON, Joseph Fort   Lincoln and Herndon.
1910   Cedar Rapids, IA   25.00
NEWTON, Thomas Wodehouse   Lord Lyons; a Record of British Diplomacy.   2 Vols.
1913   New York   75.00
NEWTON, Virginius   The Confederate States Ram Merrimac or Virignia.   Wraps.
1892   Richmond   40.00
1907   Richmond   30.00
NEY, James W.   The Issues Raised by the Rebellion, the Status of the Seceded States . . . Speech.   Wraps.
1866   Washington, DC   25.00
NICHOLAS, Alexander F., edited by   Second Brigade of the Pennsylvania Reserves at Antietam . . . Reports & Ceremonies at Dedication of the Monuments.
1908   Harrisburg   25.00
NICHOLS, Alice   Bleeding Kansas.
1954   New York   25.00
NICHOLS, Edward J.   Toward Gettysburg, A Biography of General John F. Reynolds.
1958   State College, PA   50.00
1986   30.00

NICHOLS, George Ward   Major Soule, A Memorial of Alfred B. Soule.
   1866   Salem   35.00
NICHOLS, George Ward   The Sanctuary: A Story of the Civil War.
   1866   New York   25.00
NICHOLS, George Ward   The Story of the Great March.
   1865   New York   35.00
   1866   New York   35.00
   1972   20.00
NICHOLS, George Washington   A Soldier's Story of His Regiment.
   1898   Jessup, GA   750.00
   1961   Kennesaw, GA   25.00
NICHOLS, Isaac T.   Historic Days in Cumberland County, New Jersey, 1855-1865. Political and War Time Reminiscences.
   1907   Bridgeton, NJ   125.00
NICHOLS, James L.   Confederate Engineers.   See: Confederate Centennial Studies, No. 5.
NICHOLS, James L.   The Confederate Quartermaster in the Trans-Mississippi.
   1964   Austin, TX   20.00
NICHOLS, James M.   Perry's Saints or The Fighting Parson's Regiment.
   1886   Boston   75.00
NICHOLS, Roy F.   The Disruption of American Democracy.
   1948   New York   15.00
NICHOLS, Samuel Edmund   "Your Soldier Boy Samuel" Civil War Letters of Lt. _____.
   1929   Buffalo Ltd.   55.00
NICHOLSON, J. W.   Stories of Dixie.
   1966   Baton Rouge   8.00
NICHOLSON, John Page   Catalogue of Library of Brevet Lieutenant-Colonel John Page Nicholson, U.S. Vols. Relating to the War of the Rebellion.
   1914   Philadelphia   200.00
NICKELSON, B. C.   Brief Sketch of the Life of a Confederate Soldier. Wraps.
   1928   Dallas   40.00
NICKERSON, Ansel D.   A Raw Recruit's War Experiences.
   1888   Providence Ltd.   50.00
NICOLAY, Helen   Lincoln's Secretary: A Biography of John G. Nicolay.
   1949   New York   20.00
NICOLAY, Helen   Personal Traits of Abraham Lincoln.
   1912   New York   10.00
NICOLAY, John George   The Outbreak of Rebellion.   See: Campaigns of the Civil War.
NICOLAY, John George and HAY, John   Abraham Lincoln A History. 10 Vols.
   1890   New York   75.00
   1914   New York   50.00
NICOLL, Fancher   Seventh Regiment Centennial.
   1906   New York   60.00

NIEBAUM, John H.   History of the Pittsburgh Washington Infantry. 102nd (Old 13th) Regiment Pennsylvania Veteran Volunteers.
1931   Pittsburgh   80.00
Ninety-second Illinois Volunteers.
1875   Freeport   160.00
Ninth Cavalry, 121st Regiment Indiana Volunteers.   Wraps.
1890   135.00
Ninth Reunion of the 37th OVVI, St. Marys, Ohio Sept. 10 and 11, 1889.
1890   Toledo   90.00
NISBET, James Cooper   Four Years on the Firing Line.
(1914)   Chattanooga   500.00
1963   Jackson, TN   edited by Bell I. Wiley   40.00
1987   Wilmington, NC   30.00
NIVEN, Alexander, compiled by   Civil War Day by Day 1861   A Chronology of the Principal Events of the War's First Year, edited by Arthur W. Monk.   Wraps.
1961   Cambridge   5.00
NIVEN, John   Connecticut for the Union.
1965   New Haven   30.00
NIVEN, John   Gideon Welles, Lincoln's Secretary of the Navy.
1973   New York   25.00
NIVEN, John   John C. Calhoun and the Price of Union.
1988   Baton Rouge   24.95
NIXDORFF, Henry M.   Life of Whittier's Heroine Barbara Fritchie.
1906   Frederick, MD   25.00
NOBLE, Glenn   John Brown and the Jim Lane Trail.
1977   Nebraska   15.00
NOBLE, Hollister   Woman with a Sword, Biographical Novel of Anna Ella Carroll of Maryland.
1948   New York   15.00
1954   15.00
NOBLIN, Stuart   Leonidas LaFayette Polk, Agrarian Crusader.
1949   Chapel Hill, NC   45.00
NOEL, Baptist Wriothesley   The Rebellion in American.
1863   London   60.00
NOEL, L. P.   John Hunt Morgan.   Wraps.
1933   Paducah   40.00
NOEL, Theophilus   Autobiography and Reminiscences of _____.
1904   Chicago   140.00
NOEL, Theophilus   A Campaign from Santa Fe to the Mississippi, edited by Martin Hall & Edwin Davis.
1961   Houston   40.00
NOFI, Albert A., edited by   The Bloody Struggle: The Civil War in the East, 1862.
1988   New York   9.95
NOFI, Albert A., edited by   Opening Guns: Fort Sumter to Bull Run, 1861.
1988   New York   9.95

NOLAN, Alan T.   The Iron Brigade.
    1961   New York   40.00
    1975   Madison 30.00
    1983   20.00
    1985   20.00
NOLL, Arthur Howard, edited by   Doctor Quintard, Chaplain C.S.A. . . . Being His Story of the War. (1861-1865).
    1905   Sewanee, TN   200.00
    1906   entitled Bishop Quintard's Memoirs of the War Wraps. 200.00
NOLL, Arthur Howard   General Kirby-Smith.
    1907   Sewanee, TN   Ltd.   300.00
NORMAN, William M.   A Portion of My Life, Being A Short and Imperfect History Written While a Prisoner of War on Johnson's Island 1864.
    1959   Winston-Salem   25.00
The North and South (or) Slavery and Its Contrasts.
    1852   Philadelphia   35.00
North Carolina - Confederate Military History.   See: Confederate Military History, Vol. IV (Vol. V, 1987 reprint ed.).
North Carolina Troops, edited by Louis H. Manarin and W. T. Jordan, Jr. 12 Vols.
    1966-90   Raleigh, NC   400.00
    1989-90   Reprint Vol. 1-7   35.00 each
    Individual volumes 35.00
NORTH, S. N. D. and NORTH, Ralph H.   Simeon North, First Official Pistol Maker of the United States.
    1913   Concord, NH   60.00
NORTH, Thomas   Five Years in Texas.
    1870   Cincinnati 300.00
    1871   Cincinnati 150.00
NORTHROP, Henry Davenport   Life and Deeds of General Sherman.
    (c.1880) Brooklyn   25.00
    1891   Waukesha, WI   25.00
NORTHROP, John Worrell   Chronicles from the Diary of a War Prisoner in Andersonville and Other Military Prisons of the South in 1864.
    1904   Wichita 75.00
Northumberland Historical Society, Bulletin of . . . Civil War Centennial Issue, Vol. 1, No. 1. Wraps.
    1965   n.p. 25.00
NORTON, Andre   Ride Proud, Rebel!
    1961   Cleveland   10.00
NORTON, Henry   Deeds of Daring: or History of the Eighth N. Y. Volunteer Cavalry.
    1889   Norwich   150.00
NORTON, Herman   Rebel Religion.
    1961   St. Louis   45.00
NORTON, Oliver Willcox   Army Letters 1861-1865   Being Extracts from Private Letters.
    1903   Chicago 200.00
    Recent reprint 29.95

NORTON, Oliver Willcox   Strong Vincent and His Brigade at Gettysburg July 2, 1863.
1909   Chicago   80.00
NORTON, Oliver Willcox   The Attack and Defense of Little Round Top.
1913   New York   100.00
1983   25.00
NORVELL, Stevens T.   New Mexico in the Civil War.   Wraps.
1903   (Washington, DC)   35.00
NORWOOD, Thomas Manson   A True Vindication of the South.
1917   Savannah, GA   25.00
NOTT, Charles C.   Sketches in Prison Camps.   A Continuation of Sketches of the War.
1865   New York   50.00
NOTT, Charles C.   Sketches of the War: A Series of Letters to the North Moore Street School of New York.
1863   New York   75.00
1865   New York   75.00
1911   New York   35.00
Now and Then Club of '63: "Minutes" of its Organization and Thirteen Nightly Meetings. "By the Scribe." Wraps.
1923   Louisville   75.00
NOYES, George F.   The Bivouac and the Battle-Field.
1863   New York   40.00
1864   New York   30.00
NUNN, W. C.   Escape from Reconstruction.
1956   Fort Worth, TX   30.00
NUNN, W. C., edited by   Ten More Texans in Gray - Ford, Green, Johnston, Maxey, McCulloch, Roberts, Ross, Sibley, Terry, Throckmorton.
1980   Hillsboro, TX   15.00
NUNN, W. C., edited by   Ten Texans in Gray.
1968   Hillsboro, TX   25.00
NYE, Elwood   Marching with Custer: A Day-by-day Evaluation of the Uses, Abuses, and Conditions of the Animals on the Ill-fated Expedition of 1876.
1964   Glendale Ltd. 300 copies.   75.00
NYE, Russel B.   George Bancroft: Brahmin Rebel.
1944   20.00
NYE, Russel B.   William Lloyd Garrison and the Humanitarian Reformers.
1955   Boston   7.00
NYE, Wilbur Sturtevant   Here Come the Rebels!
1965   Baton Rouge   50.00
1988   Dayton   25.00
OAKLEY, Daniel   History of the Second Massachusetts Regiment of Infantry, Beverly Ford.   Wraps.
1884   Boston   35.00
OATES, Stephen B.   Confederate Cavalry West of the River.
1961   Austin, TX   75.00
OATES, Stephen B.   Our Fiery Trial, Abraham Lincoln, John Brown, and the Civil War Era.
1979   Amherst, MA   15.00

OATES, Stephen B.   Visions of Glory: Texas on the Southwestern Frontier.
    1970   Norman   15.00
OATES, Stephen B.   With Malice Toward None, the Life of Abraham Lincoln.
    1977   New York   15.00
OATES, William C.   Speech . . . On the Battles of Chickamauga and Chattanooga. Wraps.
    1895   Montgomery, AL   30.00
OATES, William C.   The War Between the Union and the Confederacy.
    1905   New York/Washington, DC   250.00
    1974   Dayton 35.00
    1985   35.00
OATS, Sergeant (pseud.)   See: VAUGHTER, John B.
OBERHOLTZER, Ellis P.   Abraham Lincoln.
    1904   Philadelphia   10.00
OBERHOLTZER, Ellis P.   Jay Cooke, Financier of the Civil War. 2 Vols.
    1907   Philadelphia   50.00
O'BRIEN, John Emmet   Telegraphing in Battle.
    1910   Scranton, PA   80.00
OBREITER, John   The 77th Pennsylvania at Shiloh.
    1905   Harrisburg 65.00
    1908   Harrisburg 50.00
Obsequies of Abraham Lincoln in the City of New York.
    1866   New York   20.00
O'CONNOR, Richard   Company Q.
    1957   New York   10.00
O'CONNOR, Richard   Guns of Chickamauga.
    1955   New York   10.00
O'CONNOR, Richard   Hood: Cavalier General.
    1949   New York   60.00
O'CONNOR, Richard   Sheridan the Inevitable.
    1953   Indianapolis   50.00
    1954   New York   35.00
O'CONNOR, Richard   Thomas; Rock of Chickamauga.
    1948   New York   35.00
O'CONNOR, T. P., Mrs.   My Beloved South.
    1914   New York   35.00
O'CONNOR, Thomas H.   The Disunited States - The Era of Civil War and Reconstruction. Wraps.
    1978   New York   20.00
O'CONNOR, Thomas H.   Lords of the Loom.
    1968   New York   15.00
OEMLER, Marie Conway   Johnny Reb.
    1929   New York   25.00
O'FERRALL, Charles Triplett   Forty Years of Active Service.
    1904   New York   75.00
Officers in the Confederate States Navy, 1861-65. Wraps.
    1898   Washington, DC   65.00
Official Army Information Digest, August, 1961. The Lesson and the Legacy. Wraps.
    1961   Washington, DC   15.00

Official Army Register for 1861.
1861   n.p.   40.00
Official Army Register of the Volunteer Force of the U.S. Army for the Years 1861, '62, '63, '64, '65. 8 parts.
1865   Washington, DC   250.00
1987   9 Vols.   200.00
Official Documents of the Post Office Department of the Confederate States of America. 2 Vols.
1979   Holland, MI   65.00
Official Documents Relating to a "Chaplain's Campaign (Not) with General Butler," but in New York. Wraps.
1865   Lowell   20.00
Official Military Atlas of the Civil War.
1983   New York   75.00
Official Program 71st General Convention Sons of Confederate Veterans. Wraps.
1966   Charleston   8.00
Official Programme of Festival and Tournament, Benifit of Beauregard Monument Asociation. . . . Wraps.
(1902)   (New Orleans)   50.00
Official Records - Atlas.   175 plates in 35 parts.
For additional information, see Appendix: Atlas to Accompany the Official Records.
1891-95 Washington, DC   Bound   700.00
1958   New York   1 Vol.   75.00
1978   New York   1 Vol.   75.00
Official Records of the Union and Confederate Armies, War of the Rebellion. 128 Vols.
For additional information and checklist, see Appendix: Official Records of the Union and Confederate Armies.
1880-1901   Washington, DC 1500.00
Leather bound edition   4000.00   Value of a set in fine condition.   If worn, value is the same as cloth edition.
Index only   100.00
1972   1800.00
1987   2500.00
Official Records of the Union and Confederate Navies, War of the Rebellion. 30 Vols. and index.   Series I Vols. 1-27, Series II Vols. 1-3.
1894-1922   Washington, DC   600.00
1987   Reprint 620.00
Official Register of the Officers and Cadets of the U.S. Military Academy, West Point, NY.   Wraps.
1864   New York   30.00
1865   New York   20.00
Official Reports Relative to the Conduct of Federal Troops in Western Louisiana During the Invasions of 1863 and 1864. . . .
1939   Baton Rouge   50.00
Official Roster of the Soldiers of the State of Ohio in the War of the Rebellion and in the War with Mexico. 12 Vols.
1886-95   Akron, Cincinnati, Norwalk   450.00
Individual volumes   30.00 each

Official Souvenir Program, V.M.I. Cadets - U.S. Marines Re-enacting the Battle of New Market, 1864-1923. Wraps.
    1923   Roanoke   15.00
O'FLAHERTY, Daniel   General Jo Shelby: Undefeated Rebel.
    1954   Chapel Hill, NC   45.00
    1987   Wilmington, NC   30.00
OGLESBY, T. K.   The Britannica Answered and the South Vindicated. Wraps.
    1891   Montgomery   30.00
Ohio at Antietam, Report of the Ohio Antietam Battlefield Commission.
    1904   Springfield   40.00
Ohio at Shiloh, Report of the Commission.
    1903   Cincinnati   35.00
Ohio at Vicksburg, Report of Ohio Vicksburg Battlefield Commission. (Gault, W. P.).
    1906   Columbus   50.00
Ohio Boys in Dixie: The Adventures of 22 Scouts Sent By Gen. O. M. Mitchell to Destroy a Railroad. Wraps.
    1863   New York   45.00
OLBRICH, Emil   The Development of Sentiment on Negro Suffrage to 1860.
    1912   Wisconsin   25.00
OLCUTT, Mark   The Civil War Letters of Lewis Bissell. Wraps.
    1981   Washington, DC   15.00
The Old Capitol and Its Inmates.
    1867   New York   50.00
The Old Flag and the New Nation or Paul Wyman's Experience. Wraps.
    1901   n.p.   60.00
The Old Flag Camp Ford, Tyler, Smith Co., Texas Feb. 17, Mar. 1, Mar. 13, 1864.
    1864   n.p.   225.00
The Old Guard. Wraps.
    Monthly periodical   10.00 per issue
Old Jack and His Foot Cavalry, or, A Virginian Boy's Progress to Renown. (Bradburn, John)
    1864   New York   50.00
Old Johnie   See: DINKINS, James
OLDROYD, Osborn H.   A Soldier's Story of the Siege of Vicksburg with Confederate Accounts from Authentic Sources and an Introduction by Bvt. Maj. M. F. Force.
    1885   Springfield   100.00
OLDROYD, Osborn H.   The Assassination of Abraham Lincoln.
    1901   Washington, DC   50.00
    1907   Washington, DC   40.00
    1917   Washington, DC   30.00
OLDROYD, Osborn H.   The Lincoln Memorial: Album-Immortelles.
    1882   Boston   30.00
OLDROYD, Osborn H., edited by   The Poets' Lincoln.
    1915   Washington, DC   15.00
OLDROYD, Osborn H.   The Words of Lincoln.
    1895   Washington, DC   5.00

The Oliver R. Barrett Lincoln Collection, Public Auction Sale . . .
   1952   New York   30.00

OLMSTEAD, Charles H.   The Memoirs of _____, edited by Lilla Mills
Hawes' Collections of Georgia Historical Society Vol. XIV.
   1964   Savannah   30.00

OLMSTEAD, Charles H.   Reminiscences of Services with the First Volunteer Regiment of Georgia, Charleston Harbor, in 1863. Wraps.
   1879   Savannah   125.00

OLMSTED, Frederick Law   The Cotton Kingdom. 2 Vols.
   1861   London   250.00
   1953   New York   35.00
   1966   20.00

OLMSTED, Frederick Law   Hospital Transports, a Memoir of the
Embarkation of the Sick and Wounded from the Peninsula of Virginia
in the Summer of 1862.
   1863   Boston   50.00

OLMSTED, Frederick Law   A Journey in the Back Country In the
Winter of 1853-'54. 2 Vols.
   1907   New York and London   100.00
   1970   New York   25.00

OLMSTED, Frederick Law   A Journey in the Seaboard Slave States.
   1856   New York   75.00
   1859   New York   60.00
   1979   20.00

OLMSTED, Frederick Law   A Report to the Secretary of War of the
Operations of the Sanitary Commission. . . . Wraps.
   1861   Washington, DC   28.00

OLSEN, Otto H.   Carpetbagger's Crusade: The Life of Albion Winegar
Tourgee.
   1965   Baltimore   20.00

OLSON, Kenneth E.   Music and Musket: Bands and Bandsmen of the
American Civil War.
   1981   Westport   25.00

OLSZEWSKI, G. J.   Historic Structures Report: Restoration of Ford's
Theatre, Washington, D.C. Wraps.
   1963   Washington, DC   18.00

O'NEAL, Cothburn   Untold Glory.
   1957   New York   10.00

O'NEALL, John Belton and CHAPMAN, John A.   The Annals of Newberry in Two Parts.
   1892   Newberry, SC   120.00

O'NEILL, Charles   Wild Train.
   1956   New York   40.00

Operations on the Atlantic Coast, 1861-1865, Virginia in 1862, 1864 and
Vicksburg.   See: Papers of the Military Historical Society of
Massachusetts, No. 9.

OPIE, John N.   A Rebel Cavalryman with Lee, Stuart, and Jackson.
All copies we have seen lack the second page of the table of contents.
   1899   Chicago   200.00
   1972   Dayton   25.00

OPTIC, Oliver (pseud.)   See: ADAMS, William T.

Orange County, Virginia in the Civil War, 1861-1865. Wraps.
 1979   Orange, VA   15.00
Orange Court House, 1861-1865. Wraps.
 1979   Orange, VA   18.00
Organization and Status of Missouri Troops (Union and Confederate) in Service During the Civil War.
 1902   Washington, DC   100.00
Organization of the Lee Monument Association and the Association of the Army of Northern Virginia. Wraps.
 1870   Richmond   40.00
 1871   Richmond   35.00
Original Muster Roll of the 1st Rhode Island Artillery.
 n.d.   n.p.   65.00
ORME, W. W. Civil War Letters of Brigadier General William Ward Orme, 1862- 1866. Wraps.
 1930   Springfield   30.00
ORTON, Richard H., compiled by Records of California Men in the War of the Rebellion.
 1890   Sacramento   200.00
 1979   Detroit   75.00
ORVIN, Maxwell Clayton In South Carolina Waters 1861-1865.
 1961   Charleston, SC   40.00
ORWIG, Joseph R. History of the 131st Pennsylvania Volunteers.
 1902   Williamsport   90.00
OSBON, Bradley S. Cruise of the U.S. Flag-Ship Hartford, 1862-1863; Being a Narrative of All Her Operations Since Going into Commission, in 1862, Until Her Return to New York in 1863. . . . Wraps.
 1863   New York   75.00
OSBORN, Hartwell The Eleventh Army Corps, Western Reserve Bulletin. Wraps.
 1913   n.p.   30.00
OSBORN, Hartwell Trials and Triumphs: The Record of the Fifty-fifth Ohio Volunteer Infantry.
 1904   Chicago   150.00
OSBORN, T. W. The Fiery Trail: A Union Officer's Account of Sherman's Last Campaigns, edited by Richard Harwell and Philip N. Racine.
 1986   Knoxville   22.50
OSBORNE, Arthur D. The Capture of Fort Fisher by Maj. Gen. Alfred H. Terry. Wraps.
 1911   New Haven   50.00
OSBORNE, William H. The History of the Twenty-ninth Regiment of Massachusetts Volunteer Infantry.
 1877   Boston   75.00
OSOFSKY, Gilbert, edited by Puttin' on Ole Massa, the Slave Narratives of Henry Bibb, William Wells Brown, and Solomon Northup.
 1969   New York   15.00
OSTENDORF, Lloyd Mr. Lincoln Came to Dayton. Wraps.
 1959   Dayton   10.00
OSTERWEIS, Rollin G. Judah P. Benjamin, Statesman of the Lost Cause.
 1933   New York   35.00

OSTERWEIS, Rollin G.   The Myth of the Lost Cause, 1865-1900.
1973   Hamden   13.00

OSTRANDER, Alson B.   An Army Boy of the Sixties.
1926   New York   25.00

OTIS, George A.   A Report on Excisions of the Head of the Femur for Gunshot Injury. Wraps.
1869   Washington, DC   100.00

OTIS, George H.   History of the Second Wisconsin.
1984   Dayton   25.00

OTIS, George H.   The Second Wisconsin Infantry, edited by Alan Gaff.
1984   25.00

OULD, Robert   The Argument of Robert Ould in the "Salt Cases" in the Court of Appeals in Virginia. Wraps.
n.d.   n.p.   25.00

Our Acre and Its Harvest, Historical Sketch of the Soldiers' Aid Society of Northern Ohio.
1869   Cleveland   25.00

Our Confederate Dead, Souvenir, Ladies' Hollywood Memorial Assoc., Richmond, Va. Wraps.
1896   Richmond   40.00

Our Living and Our Dead, Vol. 1 through Vol. 4, No. 1, Sept. 1874 - Mar. 1876. (all published). Wraps.
Raleigh, NC   750.00
Individual issues   10.00 each

Our Village in War-Time.
1864   New York   30.00

Our War Songs North and South.
1887   Cleveland, OH   30.00

Our Women in the War.
1885   Charleston, SC   50.00

OVERHOLSER, James F.   Diary of _____ Co. D, 81st Ohio Infantry. Three Years with the Union Army.
(1937)   n.p.   145.00

OVERMILLER, Howard   York, Pennsylvania in the Hands of the Confederates June 28-30 1863. Wraps.
n.d.   n.p.   25.00

OVIATT, George A.   Memorial Address Delivered at the Funeral of Capt. Samual B. Hayden at Windsor Locks. Wraps.
1863   Hartford   20.00

OWEN, Mrs. A. L.   "Elmwood" During the War, and My Old Battered Canteen. Wraps.
(1896)   (Richmond)   50.00

OWEN, Narcissa   Memoirs of _____ 1831-1907.
1907   Washington, DC   70.00

OWEN, Thomas James   The Letters and Diary of Thomas James Owen, Fiftieth New York Volunteer Engineer Regiment During the Civil War. Wraps.
1985   Washington, DC   8.50

OWEN, Thomas McAdory   Minutes of the 11th Annual Reunion of the United Sons of Confederate Veterans.
1907   TN   60.00

OWEN, William Miller   In Camp and Battle with the Washington Artillery of New Orleans.
    1885   Boston   265.00
    1964   New Orleans Ltd.   75.00
    1983   Gaithersburg   32.50
    1985   30.00
OWENS, Harry P. and COOKE, James J.   The Old South in the Crucible of War. Wraps.
    1983   Jackson, MS   8.00
OWENS, Ira S.   Greene County in the Late War.
    1872   Dayton   125.00
OWENS, Ira S.   Greene County Soldiers in the Late War - Together with Sketches. . . .
    1884   Dayton 250.00
OWENS, John Algernon   Sword and Pen, or Ventures & Adventures of Willard Glazier.
    1880   Philadelphia   30.00
    1881   Philadelphia   30.00
    1882   Philadelphia   30.00
    1883   Philadelphia   30.00
    1889   Philadelphia   30.00
OWENS, Leslie Howard   This Species of Property - Slave Life and Culture in the Old South. Wraps.
    1977   New York   10.00
OWSLEY, Frank Lawrence   The C.S.S. Florida   Her Building and Operations.
    1965   Philadelphia   25.00
    1987   15.95
OWSLEY, Frank Lawrence   King Cotton Diplomacy: Foreign Relations of the Confederate States.
    1931   Chicago   30.00
    1959   Chicago   30.00
    1969   30.00
OWSLEY, Frank Lawrence   Plain Folk of the Old South.
    1982   23.00
    1982   Wraps   7.00
OWSLEY, Frank Lawrence   The South: Old and New Frontiers, Selected Essays, edited by Harriet Chappell Owsley.
    1969   Athens, GA   15.00
OWSLEY, Frank Lawrence   State Rights in the Confederacy.
    1925   Chicago 40.00
    1931   Chicago 30.00
    1961   Gloucester, MA   30.00
OXLEY, J. MacDonald   Baffling the Blockade.
    1896   London   40.00
PADOVER, Saul K.   Karl Marx on America and the Civil War. Wraps.
    n.d.   New York   30.00
PAGE, Charles A.   Letters of a War Correspondent, edited by James R. Gilmore.
    1899   Boston   60.00

PAGE, Charles D.   History of the 14th Regiment, Connecticut Volunteer Infantry.
1906   Meriden, CT 100.00
1987   30.00
PAGE, Elwin L.   Cameron for Lincoln's Cabinet. Wraps.
1954   Boston   25.00
PAGE, James Madison   The True Story of Andersonville Prison.
1908   New York and Washington, DC   90.00
PAGE, Richard Channing Moore   Sketch of Page's Battery; or, Morris Artillery, 2nd Corps, Army of Northern Virginia, by One of the Company. Wraps.
1885   New York   425.00
PAGE, Rosewell   The Iliads of the South.
1932   Richmond   25.00
PAGE, Rosewell   Thomas Nelson Page A Memoir of a Virginia Gentleman.
1923   New York   35.00
1923   New York   Ltd. ed.   40.00
1969   New York   20.00
PAGE, Thomas Nelson   Among the Camps.
1891   New York   50.00
1899   New York   35.00
PAGE, Thomas Nelson   The Burial of the Guns and Other Stories.
1894   London   30.00
PAGE, Thomas Nelson   A Captured Santa Claus.
1902   New York   15.00
PAGE, Thomas Nelson   Gordon Keith.
1910   15.00
PAGE, Thomas Nelson   Meh Lady, a Story of the War.
1893   25.00
1909   New York   20.00
PAGE, Thomas Nelson   Red Rock, A Chronicle of Reconstruction.
1900   New York   15.00
1903   10.00
PAGE, Thomas Nelson   Robert E. Lee, Man and Soldier.
1909   London   35.00
1911   New York   30.00
1912   30.00
PAGE, Thomas Nelson   Robert E. Lee, The Southerner.
1908   New York   25.00
1909   New York   20.00
PAGE, Thomas Nelson   Two Little Confederates.
1888   New York   75.00
1908   New York   25.00
1909   New York   25.00
1924   New York   20.00
1942   15.00
1954   20.00

PAGE, Thomas Nelson   The Works of Thomas Nelson Page.
Plantation edition. 18 Vols.
1906   New York   175.00
Vol. I   In Ole Virginia.
Vol. II   The Burial of the Guns.
Vol. III On Newfound River.
Vol. IV   Red Rock I.
Vol. V   Red Rock II.
Vol. VI   Gordon Keith I.
Vol. VII   Gordon Keith II.
Vol. VIII   The Black Stock & Santa Claus's Partner.
Vol. IX   Bred in the Bone.
Vol. X   Pastime Stories & Poems.
Vol. XI   Two Little Confederates & Among the Camps.
Vol. XII   The Old South & Essays.
Vol. XIII   The Old Dominion.
Vol. XIV   Under the Crust & Tommy Trot's Visit to Santa Claus.
Vol. XV   John Marvel, Assistant I.
Vol. XVI   John Marvel, Assistant II.
Vol. XVII   Robert E. Lee I.
Vol. XVIII   Robert E. Lee II.
PAKULA, Marvin H.   Centennial Album of the Civil War.
1960   New York   20.00
PALFREY, Francis Winthrop   The Antietam and Fredericksburg.   See:
Campaigns of the Civil War.
PALFREY, Francis Winthrop   Memoir of William Francis Bartlett.
1878   Boston   40.00
1879   Boston   30.00
PALMER, Abraham J.   The History of the Forty-eighth Regiment,
New York State Volunteers.
1885   New York   80.00
PALMER, Benjamin Morgan   The Present Crisis and Its Issues.   Wraps.
1872   Lexington, VA   20.00
PALMER, Benjamin Morgan and **LEACOCK**, W. T.   The Rights of the
South Defended in the Pulpits.   Wraps.
1860   Mobile   150.00
PALMER, Bruce   Chancellorsville, Disaster in Victory.
1967   New York   20.00
PALMER, Bruce   First Bull Run, the Nation Wakes to War.
1965   New York   15.00
PALMER, Donald McN.   Four Weeks in the Rebel Army.   Wraps.
1865   New London   500.00
PALMER, Edwin Franklin   The Second Brigade, or Camp Life by a
Volunteer.
1864   Montpelier   50.00
PALMER, George Thomas   A Conscientious Turncoat: The Story of
John M. Palmer, 1817-1900.
1941   New Haven   50.00
PALMER, H. R., edited by   In Dixie Land, Stories of the Reconstruction Era.
1926   New York   25.00

PALMER, Jewett   Historical Sketch of Company B, 18th Regiment Ohio Infantry.   Wraps.
    1911   Marietta   65.00
PALMER, Jewett   Roster of Survivors, 36th Ohio Infantry.
    1912   Marietta   75.00
PALMER, John M.   Personal Recollections of John M. Palmer, the Story of an Earnest Life.
    1901   Cincinnati   65.00
PALMER, Loomis T.   The Life of General U. S. Grant.
    1885   Chicago   30.00
    1885   New Haven, CT 25.00
    1888   25.00
PALMER, S. A.   The Story of Aunt Becky's Army-Life.
    1867   New York   65.00
    1868   50.00
PALMER, William J.   Letters, 1853-1868, compiled by Isaac H. Clothier.
    1906   Philadelphia   90.00
PALUDAN, Philip Shaw   A People's Contest. Impact of Civil War on the North.
    1988   27.95
PALUDAN, Phillip Shaw   Victims, a True Story of the Civil War.
    1981   Knoxville   15.00
PALUMBO, Frank   George Henry Thomas. The Dependable General.
    1985   25.00
Panorama of the Battle of Gettysburg on Exhibition . . . Chicago.
    1884   Chicago   20.00
Papers of the Military Historical Society of Massachusetts.
    1895-1918   14 Vol. set   1000.00
    1989   Wilmington, NC   15 Vols. including index   450.00
    (No. 1)   **Campaigns in Virginia, 1861-1862,** edited by T. F. Dwight.
    1895   Boston and New York   150.00
    1989   Wilmington, NC   30.00
    (No. 2)   **The Virginia Campaign of 1862 Under General Pope,** edited by T. F. Dwight.
    1895   Boston and New York   150.00
    1989   Wilmington, NC   30.00
    (No. 3)   **Campaigns in Virginia, Maryland, Pennsylvania, 1862-1863,** edited by T. F. Dwight.
    1903   Boston   150.00
    1989   Wilmington, NC   30.00
    (No. 4)   **The Wilderness Campaign, May-June, 1864.**
    1905   Boston   150.00
    1989   Wilmington, NC   30.00
    (No. 5)   **Petersburg, Chancellorsville, and Gettysburg.**
    1906   Boston   150.00
    1989   Wilmington, NC   30.00
    (No. 6)   **The Shenandoah Campaigns of 1862 and 1864, and the Appomattox Campaign.**
    1906   Boston   150.00
    1989   Wilmington, NC   30.00

(No. 7) Campaigns in Kentucky and Tennessee Including the Battle of Chickamauga 1862-64.
  1908   Boston   150.00
  1989   Wilmington, NC   30.00
(No. 8) The Mississippi Valley, Tennessee, Georgia, Alabama, 1861-1864.
  1910   Boston   150.00
  1989   Wilmington, NC   30.00
(No. 9) Operations on the Atlantic Coast, 1861-1865, Virginia in 1862, 1864 and Vicksburg.
  1912   Boston   150.00
  1989   Wilmington, NC   30.00
(No. 10) Federal and Confederate Commanders.
  1895   Boston   150.00
  1989   Wilmington, NC   30.00
(No. 11) Naval Actions and Operations Against Cuba and Porto [sic] Rico 1593-1918.
  1901   Boston   100.00
  1990   Wilmington, NC   30.00
(No. 12) Naval Actions and History, 1799-1898.
  1902   Boston   100.00
  1990   Wilmington, NC   30.00
(No. 13) Civil and Mexican Wars, 1861, 1846.
  1913   Boston   100.00
  1990   Wilmington, NC   30.00
(No. 14) Civil War and Miscellaneous Papers.
  1918   Boston   100.00
  1990   Wilmington, NC   30.00
(No. 15) Papers of the Military Historical Society. . . .   Index.
  1990   Wilmington, NC   100.00
The Papers of U. S. Grant.
  1967   Vol. I   1837-1861   25.00
  1969   Vol. II   April-September, 1861   25.00
  1970   Vol. III October, 1861-January, 1862   25.00
  1972   Vol. IV January-March, 1862   25.00
  1973   Vol. V   April-August, 1862   32.50
  1977   Vol. VI September-December, 1862   35.00
  1979   Vol. VII   December, 1862-March, 1863   40.00
  1979   Vol. VIII April-July, 1863   45.00
  1982   Vol. IX   July-December, 1863   47.50
  1982   Vol. X   January-May, 1864   47.50
  1984   Vol. XI   June 1-August 15, 1864   47.50
  1984   Vol. XII   August 16, 1864-November 15, 1864   47.50
  1985   Vol. XIII November 16, 1864-February 20, 1865   47.50
  1985   Vol. XIV February 21, April 30, 1865   47.50
  1988   Vol. XV   May 1-December 31, 1865   47.50
  1989   Vol. XVI 1866   47.50
PAQUETTE, W.   United States Colored Troops from Lower Tidewater in the Civil War.   Wraps.
  1982   Portsmouth   35.00
PARIS, Comte de   The Battle of Gettysburg.
  1886   Philadelphia   40.00
  1987   30.00

PARIS, Comte de   History of the Civil War in America. 4 Vols.
    1876-88 Philadelphia   160.00
PARISH, Peter J.   The American Civil War.
    1975   New York   15.00
PARK, Clyde W.   Morgan the Unpredictable.
    1959   n.p.   50.00
PARK, Robert Emory   Sketch of the 12th Alabama Infantry of Bat-
    tle's Brigade, Rhodes' Division, Early's Corps, of the Army of Northern
    Virginia. Wraps.
    1906   Richmond   250.00
PARKER, Arthur C.   The Life of General Ely S. Parker: Last Sachem
    of the Iroquois and General Grant's Military Secretary.
    1919   Buffalo   75.00
PARKER, B. and SHERMAN, S., compiled by   In   Commemoration   of
    Joshua Lawrence Chamberlain: A Guide- Bibliography. Wraps.
    1978   Augusta   20.00
PARKER, David B.   A Chautauqua Boy in '61 and Afterward, edited by
    Torrance Parker.
    1912   Boston   55.00
PARKER, Foxhall A.   The Battle of Mobile Bay.
    1878   Boston   175.00
PARKER, Francis J.   The Story of the Thirty-second Regiment Mas-
    sachusetts Infantry.
    1880   Boston   75.00
PARKER, Joel   The Character of the Rebellion, and the Conflict of
    the War. Wraps.
    1862   Cambridge   15.00
PARKER, Joel   Habeas Corpus, and Martial Law A Review. Wraps.
    1861   Cambridge   20.00
PARKER, Joel   The Right of Secession. A Review of the Message . . .
    of Jefferson Davis. Wraps.
    1861   Cambridge   15.00
PARKER, John A.   What Led to the War or the Secret History of the
    Kansas-Nebraska Bill. Wraps.
    1886   Washington, DC   25.00
PARKER, John L. and CARTER, Robert G.   Henry   Wilson's   Regiment
    History of the Twenty-second Massachusetts Infantry.
    1887   Boston   125.00
PARKER, Thomas H.   History of the 51st Regiment of Pennsylvania
    Volunteers and Veteran Volunteers.
    1869   Philadelphia 100.00
PARKER, William Harwar   Instruction   for   Naval   Light   Artillery,
    Afloat or Ashore. Wraps.
    1861   Annapolis   80.00
    1862   75.00
PARKER, William Harwar   Recollections   of   a   Naval   Officer,   1861-
    1865.
    1883   New York   100.00
    1885   New York   100.00
    1985   Annapolis   23.95
PARKHURST, John G.   Recollections of Stone's River. Wraps.
    1890   Detroit   35.00

PARKS, George E.   "The Long Winter" Being a Factual Narrative of One Story of the "Unusual" 109th Regiment Volunteer Infantry of State of Illinois. Wraps.
    1963   n.p.   40.00
PARKS, Joseph H.   Gen. Edmund Kirby Smith, C.S.A.
    1954   Baton Rouge   75.00
    1962   Baton Rouge   40.00
PARKS, Joseph H.   General Leonidas Polk, C.S.A. The Fighting Bishop.
    1962   Baton Rouge   50.00
PARKS, Joseph H.   John Bell of Tennessee.
    1950   Baton Rouge   20.00
PARKS, Joseph H.   Joseph E. Brown of Georgia.
    1977   Baton Rouge   40.00
PARRAMORE, T. C., JOHNSON, F. R. and STEPHENSON, E. R., edited by Before the Rebel Flag Fell.
    1968   Murfreesboro   10.00
PARRISH, Randall   Love Under Fire.
    1911   Chicago   15.00
PARRISH, Randall   My Lady of the North.
    1905   15.00
PARRISH, Randall   My Lady of the South A Story of the Civil War.
    1909   Chicago   15.00
    1911   15.00
PARRISH, Randall   The Red Mist: A Tale of Civil Strife.
    1914   Chicago   15.00
PARRISH, T. Michael and WILLINGHAM, Robert M., Jr.   Confederate Imprints. A Bibliography of Southern Publications from Secession to Surrender.
    1987   Austin, TX and Katonah, NY   95.00
PARRISH, Tom Z.   The Saga of the Confederate Ram Arkansas.
    1987   17.50
PARRISH, William E.   The Civil War. Wraps.
    1978   6.00
PARRISH, William E.   Missouri Under Radical Rule, 1865-1870.
    1965   Columbia   26.00
PARRISH, William E.   Turbulent Partnership, Missouri and the Union 1861-1865.
    1963   Columbia   25.00
Partial Chronology of the Rebellion, War Department, Adjutant General's Office December 1860-65.
    1866   Washington, DC   30.00
PARTON, James   General Butler in New Orleans.
    1864   Boston   30.00
    1864   New York   30.00
    1892   Boston   20.00
PARTRIDGE, Charles A.   History of the Ninety-sixth Regiment Illinois Volunteer Infantry.
    1887   Chicago   165.00
PARTRIDGE, Warren Graham   Life of Frederick H. Alms.
    1904   Cincinnati   60.00
PASHA, Admiral Hobart   See: HOBART-HAMPDEN, Augustus Charles

PASQUINO (pseud.)   See: McLAUGHLIN, James Fairfax
PATCH, Joseph Dorst   The Battle of Ball's Bluff, edited by Fitzhugh
 Turner.
 1958 Leesburg 25.00
 1958 Leesburg Wraps 10.00
PATRICK, Marsena Rudolph   Inside Lincoln's Army, the Diary of
 _____, edited by David S. Sparks.
 1964 New York 30.00
PATRICK, Rembert W.   The Fall of Richmond.
 1960 Baton Rouge 25.00
PATRICK, Rembert W.   Florida Under Five Flags.
 1945 Gainesville 35.00
PATRICK, Rembert W.   Jefferson Davis and His Cabinet.
 1944 Baton Rouge 30.00
 1961 Baton Rouge 40.00
PATRICK, Robert   Reluctant Rebel.   The Secret Diary of _____
 1861-65, edited by F. Jay Taylor.
 1959 Baton Rouge 55.00
 1961 30.00
PATRICK, Robert W.   Knapsack and Rifle.
 1887 Chicago 15.00
The Patriot's Offering: or the Life Services, Military Career of the Noble
 Trio, Ellsworth, Lyon and Baker.
 1862 New York 15.00
The Patriotic Glee Book.
 1863 Chicago 40.00
PATTEN, G. W.   Voices of the Border; Comprising Songs of the Field,
 Songs of the Bower, Indian Melodies, and Promiscuous Poems.
 1867 New York 30.00
PATTEN, George   Patten's Army Manual.
 1862 New York 100.00
PATTEN, George   Patten's Infantry Tactics, Bayonet Drill, etc.
 Wraps.
 1862 New York 125.00
PATTERSON, Edmund DeWitt   Yankee Rebel Civil War Journal of
 _____ 9th Alabama Infantry, edited by John G. Barrett.
 1966 Chapel Hill, NC 35.00
PATTERSON, Robert   A Narrative of the Campaign in the Valley of
 the Shenandoah in 1861.
 1865 Philadelphia 100.00
PATTON, James Welch, edited by   Minutes of the Proceedings of the
 Greenville Ladies Association in Aid of Volunteers of the Confederate
 Army.   Wraps.
 1937 Durham 20.00
PATTON, James Welch   Unionism and Reconstruction in Tennessee
 1860-69.
 1934 Chapel Hill, NC 50.00
 1966 Gloucester 20.00
PATTON, John S.   Jefferson, Cabell and the University of Virginia.
 1906 New York 70.00
PATTON, Joseph T.   Personal Recollections of Four Years in Dixie.
 1892 Detroit 35.00

PAUL, William G., compiled by   Wisconsin's   Civil   War   Archives.
Wraps.
1965   Madison   10.00
PAVER, John M.   What I Saw from 1861 to 1864 Personal Recollections
of _____. Wraps.
1906   Indianapolis   145.00
PAXSON, Frederic L.   The Civil War.
1911   New York   15.00
PAXSON, Lewis C.   Diary of Lewis C. Paxson, Stockton, N.J., 1862-
1865.
1908   Bismarck   75.00
PAXTON, Elisha Franklin   Memoir and Memorials Elisha Franklin
Paxton, arranged by his son, John G. Paxton.
1905   n.p.   350.00
1907   New York   325.00
PAXTON, Frank   The Civil War Letters of General Frank "Bull" Paxton,
C.S.A., edited by John Gallatin Paxton.
1978   Hillsboro, TX   35.00
PAXTON, John R.   Sword and Gown, edited by Calvin D. Wilson.
1926   New York   35.00
PAYNE, Edwin W.   History of the Thirty-fourth Regiment of Illinois
Infantry, Sept. 7, 1861 - July 12, 1865.
1902   Clinton, IA   160.00
PEABODY, Andrew P.   Lessons from our Late Rebellion. An Address.
Wraps.
1867   Boston   10.00
PEARCE, Haywood J.   Benjamin H. Hill.
1928   Chicago   30.00
PEARCE, Thilbert H.   They Fought, The Story of Franklin County,
N. C. Men in the Years 1861-65.
1969   Franklinton   20.00
PEARL, Cyril   Rebel Down Under.
1970   Melbourne   25.00
PEARSALL, Uri B.   Official Reports of Building the "Red River Dam"
at Alexandria, LA.
1896   Lansing   35.00
PEARSON, Elizabeth W.   Letters from Port Royal Written at the Time
of the Civil War.
1906   Boston   50.00
PEARSON, Henry Greenleaf   James S. Wadsworth of Geneseo.
1913   New York   40.00
PEARSON, Henry Greenleaf   The Life of John A. Andrew, War Governor of Mass., 1861-65.   2 Vols.
1904   Boston   40.00
PEAVEY, James Dudley, compiled and edited by   Confederate   Scout:
Virginia's Frank Stringfellow.   Wraps.
1956   Onacock   30.00
PECK, Eli Nelson, compiled by   Supplement to the History of the 13th
Regiment Vermont Volunteers.
1911   n.p.   70.00

PECK, George W.   How Private George W. Peck Put Down the Rebellion.
    1887   Chicago   25.00
    1900   Chicago   20.00
PECK, Taylor   Round-Shot to Rockets,   A History of the Washington Navy Yard and U.S. Naval Gun Factory.
    1949   Annapolis   30.00
PECK, Theodore S., compiled by   Revised Roster of Vermont Volunteers . . . During the War of the Rebellion.   All copies we have seen (15+) were waterstained. Price is for a good copy. Waterstained copy   50.00.
    1892   Montpelier   100.00
PECKHAM, James   Gen. Nathaniel Lyon, and Missouri in 1861.
    1866   New York   35.00
PECQUET DU BELLET, Paul   The Diplomacy of the Confederate Cabinet of Richmond and Its Agents Abroad. . . .   See: Confederate Centennial Studies, No. 23.
Pee Dee Artillery.   Wraps.
    1983   8.00
PEET, Frederick Tomlinson   Civil   War   Letters   and   Documents   of _____ with the 7th New York.
    1917   Newport Ltd.   325.00
PEET, Frederick Tomlinson   Personal Experiences in the Civil War.
    1905   New York Ltd.   325.00
PEGRAM, John C.   Recollections of the U.S. Naval Academy.   Wraps.
    1891   Providence Ltd.   40.00
PEIRSON, Charles Lawrence   A Monograph, Ball's Bluff: An Episode and Its Consequences to Some of Us.
    1913   Salem   45.00
PELLET, Elias P.   History of the 114th Regiment New York State Volunteers.
    1866   Norwich   90.00
PELLETAN, Eugene   Adresse Au Roi Coton.   Wraps.
    1863   New York   25.00
PEMBER, Phoebe Yates   A Southern Woman's Story.
    1897   New York   250.00
    1959   Jackson edited by Bell I. Wiley   25.00
    1979   30.00
    1987   Wilmington, NC   30.00
PEMBERTON, John C.   Pemberton, Defender of Vicksburg.
    1942   Chapel Hill, NC   60.00
    1945   Chapel Hill, NC   40.00
    1987   Wilmington, NC   30.00
PENDER, William Dorsey   The General to His Lady . . . The Civil War Letters of . . . to Fanny Pender, edited by William W. Hassler.
    1965   Chapel Hill, NC   35.00
PENDERGRAST, J. E.   An Account of the 19th Annual Reunion of the Seventh Georgia Regimental Association . . . Manassas, Va., July 21, 1902.   Wraps.
    1902   Newman, GA   200.00
PENDLETON, Louis   Alexander H. Stephens.
    1908   Philadelphia   40.00

PENDLETON, William Frederic   **Confederate Diary Capt. _____ January to April 1865.** Wraps.
    1957   Bryn Athyn, PA   40.00
PENDLETON, William Frederic   **Confederate Memoirs . . . ,** edited by Constance Pendleton.
    1958   Bryn Athyn, PA   90.00
PENICK, Charles Clifton   **Our Dead: Our Memories: Our Lessons: Our Duties: An Oration.** Wraps.
    1888   Louisville   20.00
PENNELL, Joseph Stanley   **The History of Rome Hanks and Kindred Matters.**
    1944   New York   8.00
    1982   New York   15.00
PENNELL, Orrin Henry, edited by   **Religious View of Abraham Lincoln.** Wraps.
    1899   Alliance, OH   20.00
Pennsylvania at Andersonville, Ga., Ceremonies at the Dedication of the Memorial.
    1905   n.p.   25.00
    1909   Harrisburg   20.00
Pennsylvania at Antietam, Reports and Ceremonies at the Monuments.
    1906   Harrisburg   25.00
Pennsylvania at Chickamauga and Chattanooga.
    1897   Harrisburg   40.00
    1900   Harrisburg   35.00
    1901   Harrisburg   35.00
Pennsylvania at Cold Harbor Dedication of the Monument.
    1912   Harrisburg   25.00
Pennsylvania at Culpeper Report of the Culpeper Monument Commission.
    1914   Harrisburg   25.00
Pennsylvania at Gettysburg, Battlefield Commission. 4 Vols.
    1893-1939   125.00
    Individual volumes   30.00 each
Pennsylvania at Salisbury, N. C., Ceremonies at the Dedication of the Memorial.
    1910   Harrisburg   20.00
PENNYPACKER, Isaac R.   **General Meade.**
    For additional information, see Appendix: Great Commanders Series.
    1901   New York   40.00
    1901   New York   Ltd.   125.00
    1987   Gaithersburg   30.00
Peoria County, Illinois Monuments, Love's Labor.
    1906   Peoria, IL   60.00
PEPPER, George W.   **Personal Recollections of Sherman's Campaigns in Georgia and the Carolinas.**
    1866   Zanesville   150.00
PEPPER, George W.   **Under Three Flags, or The Story of My Life.**
    1899   Cincinnati   50.00
PEREYRA, Lillian A.   **James Lusk Alcorn, Persistant Whig.**
    1966   Baton Rouge   15.00
PERKERSON, M. F.   **White Columns in Georgia.**
    1952   New York   20.00

PERKINS, Dexter   The Monroe Doctrine 1820-1867.
1933   Baltimore   40.00
PERKINS, Fred B., edited by   The Picture and the Men: Being Biographical Sketches of President Lincoln and His Cabinet.
1867   New York   10.00
PERKINS, George   A Summer in Maryland and Virginia, or Campaigning with the 149th Ohio Volunteer Infantry.
1911   Chillicothe   125.00
PERKINS, George H.   Letters of Capt. George H. Perkins, USN 1856-1880, edited by George E. Belknap.
1886   Concord, NH   50.00
1908   Concord, NH   40.00
PERKINS, Howard Cecil, edited by   Northern Editorials on Secession. 2 Vols.
1942   New York   65.00
1964   50.00
PERKINS, Jacob R.   Trails, Rails and War.   The Life of Gen. G. M. Dodge.
1929   Indianapolis   35.00
Permanent Fortifications and Sea-Coast Defenses. Report 86, 37th Congress, 2nd Session, House of Reps.
1862   Washington, DC   55.00
PERRY, Benjamin Franklin   Reminiscences of Public Men.
1889   Greenville, SC   25.00
PERRY, Bliss   Life and Letters of Henry Lee Higginson. 2 Vols.
1921   Boston Ltd.   40.00
1922   n.p.   30.00
PERRY, Bliss   Little Masterpieces - Abraham Lincoln.
1915   New York   20.00
PERRY, Henry Fales   History of the Thirty-eighth Regiment Indiana Volunteer Infantry.
1906   Palo Alto, CA   85.00
PERRY, John G.   Letters from a Surgeon of the Civil War, compiled by Martha D. Perry.
1906   Boston   80.00
PERRY, Milton F.   Infernal Machines: The Story of Confederate Submarine and Mine Warfare.
1965   Baton Rouge   35.00
1985   Wraps   8.95
PERRY, Oran   Recollections of the Civil War. Wraps.
1924   n.p.   75.00
PERSICO, Joseph E.   My Enemy, My Brother Men and Days of Gettysburg.
1977   New York   20.00
Personal Memoirs of Major-General D. S. Stanley, U.S.A.
1987   25.00
Personal Narratives of the Rebellion Rhode Island Soldiers and Sailors Historical Society. Wraps.
1st-7th Series   1878-1915   Ltd. 100 numbers   2000.00
Also bound into volumes. Individual volumes   150.00 each
See author, title listing for individual numbers.

Personal Recollections of the War of the Rebellion: Addresses Delivered Before the New York Commandery, Mollus. 4 Vols.
1891-1912   60.00 per volume
Personal Reminiscences and Experiences by Members of the 103rd Ohio Volunteer Infantry.
1900   Oberlin   150.00
PERSONNE   See: De FONTAINE, Felix G.
PETERS, M. T., compiled by A Guidebook to Virginia's Historical Markers. Wraps.
1987   Charlottesville   9.95
Petersburg, Chancellorsville, and Gettysburg.   See: Papers of the Military Historical Society of Massachusetts, No. 5.
PETERSEN, Frederick A.   Military Review of the Campaign in Virginia and Maryland. Parts 1 and 2. Wraps.
1862-63 New York   150.00
Individual volumes   50.00 each
PETERSEN, Svend   The Gettysburg Address, the Story of Two Orations.
1963   New York   10.00
PETERSON, C. Stewart   Admiral John A. Dahlgren; Father of U.S. Naval Ordnance. Wraps.
1945   New York   15.00
PETERSON, C. Stewart   Last Civil War Veteran in Each State. Wraps.
1951   Baltimore   20.00
PETERSON, Cyrus A.   Narrative of the Capture and Murder of Major James Wilson. Wraps.
1906   St. Louis   100.00
PETERSON, Cyrus A. and HANSON, Joseph M.   Pilot Knob.
1914   New York   100.00
1964   Cape Girardeau   25.00
PETERSON, Harold L.   Notes on Ordnance of the American Civil War. Wraps.
1959   Washington, DC   25.00
PETERSON, Harold L.   Round Shot and Rammers.
1969   Harrisburg, PA   30.00
PETERSON, Mendel L.   The Journals of Daniel Noble Johnson 1822-1863 United States Navy. Wraps.
1959   Washington, DC   20.00
PETERSON, S.   The Gettysburg Addresses: The Story of Two Orations.
1963   New York   15.00
PETICOLAS, A. B.   Rebels on the Rio Grande; The Civil War Journal of _____.
1985   Albuquerque   20.00
PETROFF, Peter   Ante-Mortem Depositions of Peter Petroff.
1895   San Francisco   25.00
PETTENGILL, Samuel B.   The College Cavaliers.
1883   Chicago   35.00
PETTIS, George H.   The California Column. Its Campaign and Services in New Mexico, Arizona and Texas, During the Civil War. Wraps.
1908   Santa Fe   275.00

PETTIS, George H.   Frontier Service During the Rebellion, or a History of Company K, 1st Infantry California Volunteers. Wraps.
1885   Providence   Ltd.   160.00
PETTIS, George H.   Kit Carson's Fight with the Comanche and Kiowa Indians. Wraps.
1878   Providence   Ltd.   175.00
1908   Santa Fe   175.00
PETTIT, Ira S.   The Diary of a Dead Man: Letters and Diary of _____, edited by J. P. Ray.
1972   n.p.   30.00
1976   n.p.   20.00
PETTY, A. Milburn   History of the 37th Regiment, New York Volunteers.
1937   New York   50.00
PETTY, Elijah P.   Journey to Pleasant Hill, the Civil War Letters of _____, Walker's Texas Division, edited by Norman D. Brown.
1982   San Antonio   45.00
Collector's ed.   Ltd.   Boxed   75.00
PEYTON, John Lewis   The American Crisis; or Pages from the Note-Book of a State Agent During the Civil War. 2 Vols. in 1.
1867   London   150.00
PEYTON, John William   The Diaries of _____, 1862-1865, transcribed by Robert A. Hodge. Wraps.
1978   VA   35.00
PFANZ, Harry   Gettysburg, the Second Day.
1987   34.95
PHELPS, Charles A.   Life and Public Services of General Ulysses S. Grant.
1868   Boston   15.00
PHELPS, Mrs. Lincoln, edited by   Our Country, In Its Relations to the Past, Present and Future.
1864   Baltimore   20.00
PHELPS, Mary Merwin   Kate Chase, Dominant Daughter; The Life Story of a Brilliant Woman and Her Famous Father.
1935   New York   25.00
PHILIPPOTEAUX, Paul   Battle of Gettysburg. Wraps.
1866   Boston   20.00
1889   Boston   15.00
PHILLIPS, Christopher   Damned Yankee, The Life of General Nathaniel Lyon.
1990   University, MO   26.00
PHILLIPS, Elizabeth B.   Matthew Fontaine Maury. Wraps.
1921   40.00
PHILLIPS, Isaac N., edited by   Abraham Lincoln   By Some Men Who Knew Him.
1910   Bloomington   10.00
PHILLIPS, John Wilson   The Civil War Diary of _____, edited by Robert G. Athearn. Wraps.
1954   VA   25.00
PHILLIPS, S. K.   Immortelles and Other Memorial Poems.
1890   Chattanooga   25.00

PHILLIPS, Stanley S.　　　Civil War Corps Badges and Other Related Awards, Badges, Medals of the Period. Including a Section on Post-Civil War and Spanish-American War Corps Badges.
　　1982　　Marceline, MO　　60.00
PHILLIPS, Stanley S.　　　Excavated Artifacts from Battlefields and Campsites of the Civil War.
　　1975　　(Lanham, MD)　30.00
　　1977　　(Lanham, MD)　30.00
　　1986　　30.00
PHILLIPS, Ulrich B.　　　American Negro Slavery; Survey of the Supply, Employment and Control of Negro Labor as Determined by the Plantation Regime.
　　1918　　New York　　35.00
　　1959　　12.00
　　1985　　Wraps　11.00
PHILLIPS, Ulrich B., edited by　　　The Correspondence of Robert Toombs, Alexander H. Stephens and Howell Cobb, AHA Report 1911.
　　1913　　Washington, DC　30.00
　　1970　　New York　　20.00
PHILLIPS, Ulrich B.　　　The Course of the South to Secession, edited by E. Merton Coulter.
　　1958　　Gloucester, MA　　15.00
PHILLIPS, Ulrich B.　　　Georgia and State Rights. (Annual Report of American Historical Assoc. . . . 1901).
　　1902　　Washington, DC　30.00
PHILLIPS, Ulrich B.　　　Life and Labor in the Old South.
　　1929　　Boston　　30.00
　　1929　　New York　　20.00
　　1937　　20.00
　　1941　　n.p.　　20.00
PHILLIPS, Ulrich B.　　　The Life of Robert Toombs.
　　1913　　New York　　40.00
PHILLIPS, Ulrich B.　　　The Slave Economy of the Old South: Selected Essays in Economic and Social History, edited by Eugene D. Genovese. Wraps.
　　1985　　10.00
PHILLIPS, Ulrich B. and DILLON, Merton L.　　　U. B. Phillips, Historian of the Old South.
　　1985　　20.00
PHILLIPS, Wendell　　　Speeches, Lectures and Letters.
　　1863　　Boston　　10.00
　　1880　　Boston　　10.00
　　1905　　Boston　　10.00
　　(196-)　　12.00
PHILLIPS, William　　　The Conquest of Kansas, Missouri and Her Allies.
　　1856　　Boston　　30.00
PHILPOTT, William Bledsoe　　　The Sponsor Souvenir Album and History of the United Confederate Veterans.
　　1895　　Houston　125.00

PHINNEY, Mary (Baroness von Olnhausen)   Adventures of an Army Nurse in Two Wars, Edited from the Diary and Correspondence of Mary Phinney, Baroness von Olnhausen, by James P. Munroe.
1903   Boston   75.00
1904   Boston   50.00
PHISTERER, Frederick   Assoc. of Survivors, Regular Brigade 14th Corps, Army of the Cumberland.
1898   Columbus   60.00
PHISTERER, Frederick, compiled by   New York in the War of the Rebellion 1861-1865. 5 Vols. & Index.
1890   Albany   75.00
1912   Albany   250.00
PHISTERER, Frederick   The Regular Brigade of the 14th Army Corps, Army of the Cumberland in the Battle of Stone River, or Murfreesboro, Tenn.
1883   95.00
PHISTERER, Frederick   Statistical Record of the Armies of the United States.   See: Campaigns of the Civil War.
Photography and the Civil War.   Wraps.
(1962)   Binghamton, NY   15.00
PIATT, Donn   General George H. Thomas, A Critical Biography.
1893   Cincinnati   50.00
PIATT, Donn   Memories of the Men Who Saved the Union.
1887   New York   20.00
PICKERILL, William N.   History of the Third Indiana Cavalry.
1906   Indianapolis   150.00
PICKERILL, William N., compiled by   Indiana at the Fiftieth Anniversary of the Battle of Gettysburg. . . .
1913   n.p.   150.00
The Picket Line and Camp Fire Stories.
(c.1880) New York   20.00
The Picket.
1862   Philadelphia   30.00
PICKETT, Charles E.   The Existing Revolution; Its Causes and Results.   Wraps.
1861   Sacramento   150.00
PICKETT, George E.   The Heart of a Soldier: As Revealed in the Intimate Letters of Gen. Geroge E. Pickett, CSA.
1913   New York   30.00
PICKETT, George E.   Soldier of the South, Gen. Pickett's War Letters to His Wife, edited by Arthur C. Inman.
1928   Boston   40.00
PICKETT, LaSalle Corbell   Across My Path: Memories of People I Have Known.
1916   New York   25.00
PICKETT, LaSalle Corbell   The Bugles of Gettysburg.
1913   Chicago   20.00
PICKETT, LaSalle Corbell   Pickett and His Men.
1899   Atlanta   45.00
1900   Atlanta   40.00
1909   Atlanta   40.00
1913   Philadelphia   40.00

PICKETT, LaSalle Corbell   What Happened to Me.
    1917   New York   35.00
PICKETT, Thomas E.   A Soldier of the Civil War by a Member of the
    Virginia Hist. Society.
    1900   Cleveland   Ltd.   150.00
PICKETT, W.   The Negro Problem   A. Lincoln's Solution.
    1909   New York   10.00
PIERCE, Charles F.   History and Camp Life of Company C, Fifty-first
    Regiment Mass. Vol. Militia.
    1886   Worcester   75.00
PIERCE, Edward L.   Memoirs and Letters of Charles Sumner. 4 Vols.
    1893   Boston 50.00
    n.d.   London 40.00
PIERCE, F. M.   The Battle of Gettysburg, the Crest-Wave of the
    American Civil War. By Francis Marshall (pseud.)
    1987   Gaithersburg   30.00
PIERCE, Gerald S.   Texas Under Arms.
    1969   Austin Ltd.   50.00
PIERCE, Lyman B.   History of the 2nd Iowa Cavalry.
    1865   Burlington   170.00
PIERCE, Solon W.   Battle Fields and Camp Fires of the Thirty-eighth.
    1866   Milwaukee   175.00
PIERCE, Thomas Jefferson   Letters Home, compiled by Ellen K. Korb-
    itz. Wraps.
    1957   Burlington, IA   20.00
PIERCE, Wendell E.   The Acadia A Blockade Runner 1865. Wraps.
    1973   n.p.   30.00
PIERREPONT, Alice V. D.   Reuben Vaughan Kidd: Soldier of the
    Confederacy.
    1947   Petersburg   175.00
PIKE, Albert   State or Province? Bond or Free? Wraps.
    1861   Little Rock   100.00
PIKE, James   The Scout and Ranger.
    1865   Cincinnati   500.00
PIKE, James S.   First Blows of the Civil War.
    1879   New York   50.00
PIKE, James S.   The Prostrate State.   South Carolina Under Negro
    Government.
    1874   80.00
    1935   New York   30.00
The Pilgrim's Book Containing the Articles of Constitution of the Pilgrims
    to the Battlefields of the Rebellion.
    1911   Philadelphia   60.00
PILLSBURY, Parker   Acts of the Anti-Slavery Apostles.
    1883   Concord, NH   25.00
PILSEN, John   Reply to Emil Schalk's Criticisms of the Campaign in
    the Mountain Department Under Maj-Gen. Fremont. Wraps.
    1863   New York   35.00
PINCHON, Edgcumb   Dan Sickles.
    1945   Garden City, NY   20.00

PINKERTON, Allan   History and Evidence of the Passage of Abraham Lincoln from Harrisburg, Pa. to Washington, D.C. on . . . 1861.
 1906 New York 30.00
PINKERTON, Allan The Spy of the Rebellion.
 1883 Hartford 40.00
 1884 Boston 40.00
 1884 Toronto 30.00
 1885 Cincinnati 40.00
 1885 Hartford 40.00
 1886 Hartford 40.00
 1886 New York 30.00
 1888 New York and Philadelphia 30.00
 1989 Wraps 15.95
PINKOWSKI, Edward Pills, Pen and Politics.
 1974 Wilmington, DE 15.00
PISTON, W. G. Lee's Tarnished Lieutenant: James Longstreet and His Place in Southern History.
 1987 Athens 24.95
PITKIN, T. M. The Captain Departs: Ulysses S. Grant's Last Campaign.
 1973 Carbondale 15.00
PITMAN, Benn The Assassination of President Lincoln and the Trial of the Conspirators.
 1865 New York 75.00
 1954 New York 40.00
PITMAN, Benn The Trials for Treason at Indianapolis.
 1865 Cincinnati 100.00
 1865 Salem, IN 75.00
PITTARD, Pen Lile and WATTS, W. C. Alexander County's Confederates. Wraps.
 n.d. NC 50.00
PITTENGER, William Capturing a Locomotive.
 1882 Philadelphia 35.00
 1883 Philadelphia 25.00
 1885 Washington, DC 25.00
 1905 Washington, DC Wraps 20.00
PITTENGER, William Daring and Suffering: A History of the Andrews Railroad Raid into Georgia. . . .
 1863 Philadelphia 50.00
 1864 Philadelphia 40.00
 1887 New York Wraps 40.00
 1916 35.00
 1929 Philadelphia entitled The Great Locomotive Chase 35.00
 1982 25.00
PITTENGER, William In Pursuit of the General, A History of the Civil War Railroad Raid.
 1965 San Marino, CA 30.00
PITTMAN, Samuel Emlen The Operations of Gen. Alpheus S. Williams and His Command in the Chancellorsville Campaign. Wraps.
 1888 Detroit 30.00
PITTS, Charles F. Chaplains in Gray.
 1957 Nashville 35.00

PIVANY, Eugene   Hungarians in the American Civil War.   Wraps.
1913   Cleveland   35.00
PLAKE, Kate   The Husband Outwitted by His Wife.
1868   Philadelphia   50.00
PLANK, W.   Banners and Bugles: A Record of Ulster County in the Civil War.   Wraps.
1963   Marlborough   35.00
1972   Marlborough   25.00
PLEASANTS, Henry   The Tragedy of the Crater.
1938   Boston   100.00
PLEASANTS, Henry, Jr. and STRALEY, George H.   Inferno at Petersburg.
1961   Philadelphia   20.00
PLEASANTS, Samuel Augustus   Fernando Wood of New York.
1948   New York   20.00
PLOWDEN, John Covert   The   Letters   of   Private _____ 1862-1865, edited by Henry B. Rollins.   Wraps.
1970   Sumter   35.00
PLUM, William R.   The Military Telegraph During the Civil War in the U.S.   2 Vols.
1882   Chicago   200.00
1974   New York   2 Vols. in 1   Wraps   75.00
PLUM, William R.   The Sword and the Soul.
1917   New York   50.00
PLUMMER, Albert   History of the Forty-eighth Regiment M.V.M.
1907   Boston   60.00
POAGUE, William Thomas   Gunner with Stonewall.   Reminiscences of _____, edited by Monroe F. Cockrell.
1957   Jackson, TN   50.00
1987   Wilmington, NC   30.00
1987   Wilmington, NC   Wraps   7.95
1989   Wilmington, NC   30.00
1989   Wilmington, NC   Wraps   10.95
POCHE, Felix Pierre   A Louisiana Confederate, Diary of _____, edited by Edwin C. Bearss.
1972   Natchitoches, LA   40.00
POE, Clarence   True Tales of the South at War.
1961   Chapel Hill, NC   15.00
1961   Chapel Hill, NC   Confederate Descendants ed.   25.00
POE, David   Personal Reminiscences of the Civil War.   Wraps.
1911   Buckhannon, WV   525.00
POE, Orlando Metcalf   Personal Recollections of the Occupation of East Tennessee and the Defense of Knoxville.   Wraps.
1889   Detroit   30.00
POINDEXTER, C.   Richmond, an Illustrated Hand-Book and Guide with Notices of the Battle-fields.   Wraps.
1896   Richmond   35.00
1907   Richmond   30.00
POINDEXTER, James E.   Address on the Life and Services of Gen. Lewis A. Armistead.   Wraps.
1909   Richmond   100.00

POLAND, Charles A.   Army Register of Ohio Volunteers in the Service of the United States, April 1862.   Wraps.
1862   Columbus   50.00
POLE, J. R.   Abraham Lincoln.
1964   London   10.00
Political Debates Between Hon. Abraham Lincoln and Hon. Stephen A. Douglas, in the Celebrated Campaign of 1858.
1860   Columbus   75.00
1908   Springfield, IL   entitled   The Lincoln-Douglas Debates of 1858, edited by Edwin Erle Sparks 25.00
POLK, J. M.   Memories of the Lost Cause, Stories and Adventures of a Confederate Soldier.   Wraps.
1905   Austin   60.00
POLK, J. M.   The North and South American Review.   Wraps.
1912   Austin   60.00
1914   60.00
POLK, James K.   Correspondence of _____, edited by Herbert Weaver and Paul H. Bergeron.   2 Vols.
1969   Nashville   20.00 each
POLK, William M.   Leonidas Polk, Bishop and General.   2 Vols.
1893   New York   300.00
1894   New York   300.00
1915   New York   250.00
POLLARD, Edward A.   La Cause Perdue,   Histoire de la Guerre des Confederes.
1867   Nouvelle-Orleans   60.00
POLLARD, Edward A.   Lee and His Lieutenants.
1867   New York   125.00
1870   New York   entitled   The Early Life, Campaigns, and Public Services of R. E. Lee   75.00
1871   New York   75.00
POLLARD, Edward A.   The First Year of the War.
1863   New York   35.00
1863   London   75.00
1863   Toronto   50.00
1864   New York   35.00
POLLARD, Edward A.   The Last Year of the War.
1866   New York   40.00
POLLARD, Edward A.   Letters of the Southern Spy in Washington and Elsewhere.   Wraps.
1861   Baltimore   125.00
POLLARD, Edward A.   Life of Jefferson Davis,   With a Secret History of the Southern Confederacy.
1869   Philadelphia   30.00
POLLARD, Edward A.   The Lost Cause.
1866   New York   75.00
1867   New York   50.00
POLLARD, Edward A.   The Lost Cause Regained.
1868   New York   50.00
POLLARD, Edward A.   The Second Year of the War.
1864   New York   40.00

POLLARD, Edward A.   Southern History of the War. 2 Vols.
   1866   New York   75.00
POLLARD, Edward A.   The Third Year of the War.
   1865   New York   40.00
POLLARD, Henry Robinson   Memoirs and Sketches of the Life of
   _____ An Autobiography.
   1923   Richmond   50.00
POLLARD, Josephine   Our Hero - General U. S. Grant.
   1885   New York   20.00
POLLEY, Joseph B.   Hood's Texas Brigade.
   1910   New York / Washington, DC 800.00
   1976   Dayton 22.50
   1988   Dayton 30.00
POLLEY, Joseph B.   A Soldier's Letters to Charming Nellie.
   1908   New York   450.00
   1984   Baltimore   25.00
POMPEY, Sherman Lee   Keep the Home Fires Burning: A History of
   the 7th Regt. Missouri State Militia Cavalry in the Civil War.   Wraps.
   1962   Warrensburg, MO   30.00
POND, Cornelia Jones   Life on a Liberty County Plantation,   The
   Journal of _____, edited by Josephine Bacon Martin.
   1974   Darien, GA   Ltd.   30.00
POND, George E.   The Shenandoah Valley in 1864.   The Campaign of
   Sheridan.   See: Campaigns of the Civil War.
POOL, John   Admission of Georgia, Speech . . . in the Senate . . . April
   15, 1870.   Wraps.
   1870   Washington, DC   25.00
POORE, Ben Perley   The Life and Public Services of Ambrose E. Burn-
   side.
   1882   Providence   35.00
POORE, Ben Perley   Perley's Reminiscences of Sixty Years in the
   National Metropolis. 2 Vols.
   1886   Philadelphia   40.00
POORE, Ben Perley and TIFFANY, O. H.   Life of U. S. Grant.
   1892   New York   20.00
POPE, John   The Campaign in Virginia, of July and August, 1862.
   Wraps.
   1863   Milwaukee   75.00
POPPENHEIM, Mary B. Merchant, McKINNEY, Maude, FARIS, May M.,
   et al   The History of the United Daughters of the Confederacy.
   2 Vols. in 1.
   1938   Richmond   40.00
   1956   Raleigh, NC   35.00
PORTER, A. Toomer   Led on: Step by Step.
   1898   New York   45.00
PORTER, Burton B.   One of the People, His Own Story.
   1907   Colton, CA   50.00
PORTER, Charles H.   The Fifth Corps at the Battle of Five Forks.
   1889   50.00

PORTER, David D.   Incidents and Anecdotes of the Civil War.
    1885   New York   35.00
    1886   New York   35.00
    1891   35.00
PORTER, David D.   Memoir of Commodore David Porter.
    1875   Albany   55.00
PORTER, David D.   The Naval History of the Civil War.
    1886   New York   125.00
    1890   New York   50.00
    1970   Glendale   25.00
    1984   40.00
PORTER, Duval   Lyrics of the Lost Cause.
    1914   Danville, VA   50.00
PORTER, Fitz-John   Appeal to President of U. S. for Re-Examination of Proceedings of General Court Martial in His Case. Wraps.
    1869   Morristown, NJ   60.00
PORTER, Fitz-John   Gen'l Fitz John Porter's Reply to Hon. Z. Chandler's Speech in the U.S. Senate, Feb. 21, 1870. Wraps.
    1870   Morristown, NJ   40.00
PORTER, Fitz-John   General Fitz John Porter's Statement of the Services of the Fifth Army Corps, in 1862, in North Carolina. Wraps.
    1878   New York   60.00
PORTER, Fitz-John   General Porter's Appeal. Wraps.
    1874   n.p.   35.00
PORTER, Horace   Campaigning with Grant.
    1897   New York   40.00
    1906   New York   30.00
    1907   New York   30.00
    1961   Bloomington   30.00
    1981   22.50
    1984   18.00
PORTER, James D. Tennessee.   See: Confederate Military History, Vol. VIII (Vol. X, 1987 reprint ed.).
PORTER, John W. H.   A Record of Events in Norfolk County, Virginia, from April 19th 1861 to May 10th 1862.
    1892   Portsmouth   125.00
PORTER, Mary W.   The Surgeon in Charge.
    1949   Concord, NH   30.00
PORTER, Valentine M.   History of Battery "A" of St. Louis.
    1904   85.00
    1905   St. Louis   75.00
PORTER, William D.   State Sovereignty and the Doctrine of Coercion . . . Together with a Letter from Hon. J. K. Paulding.
    (c.1860)   Charleston, SC   75.00
Portland Soldiers and Sailors in the War of the Rebellion. Wraps.
    1884   Portland   30.00
The Portrait Monthly   Containing Sketches of Departed Heroes, and Prominent Personages of the Present Time,   Interesting Stories, etc. Vol. I.
    1864   New York   150.00

POST, Marie Caroline   The Life and Memoirs of Comte Regis de Trobriand Major-General in the Army of the United States.
1910   New York   75.00

POSTELL, William   The Health of the Slaves on Southern Plantations.
1970   12.00

POTTER, David M.   The Impending Crisis 1848-1861.
1973   New York   25.00
1976   New York   15.00
Wraps   10.00

POTTER, David M.   Lincoln and His Party in the Secession Crisis.
1942   New Haven   25.00

POTTER, David M.   The South and the Sectional Conflict.
1968   Baton Rouge   30.00
1973   28.00

POTTER, John   Reminiscences of the Civil War in the United States.
1897   Oskaloosa   135.00

POTTER, John Mason   Thirteen Desparate Days.
1964   New York   30.00

POTTER, Orlando B.   Oration of Hon. _____ on the Dedication of the Monument Erected by the 9th Regiment, N.G.S.N.Y.
1888   n.p.   30.00

POTTER, Theodore Edgar   The Autobiography of Theodore Edgar Potter.
1978   25.00

POTTS, Frank   The Death of the Confederacy: The Last Week of the Army of Northern Virginia as Set Forth in a Letter of April 1865. Wraps.
1928   Richmond   250.00

POWELL, Edward   Nullification and Secession in the United States.
1897   New York   30.00
1898   New York   30.00

POWELL, J. W.   Yankee Cavalrymen: Through the Civil War with the Ninth Pennsylvania Cavalry.
1985   Knoxville   23.95

POWELL, Lawrence N.   New Masters Northern Planters During the Civil War and Reconstruction.
1980   New Haven   15.00

POWELL, William H.   The Fifth Army Corps.
1896   New York   Ltd.   125.00
1984   60.00

POWELL, William H.   List of Officers of the Army of the U. S. from 1779-1900.
1900   New York   50.00
1967   Detroit   30.00

POWELL, William H., edited by   Officers of the Army and Navy (Regular and Volunteer) Who Served in the Civil War.
1894   Philadelphia   175.00

POWELL, William H., edited by   Officers of the Army and Navy (Volunteer) Who Served in the Civil War.
1893   Philadelphia   110.00

POWELL, William H.   Records of Living Officers of the U. S. Army.
1890   Philadelphia   50.00

POWELL, William H. and SHIPPEN, Edward, edited by   Officers of the Army and Navy (Regular) Who Served in the Civil War.
1892   Philadelphia   100.00
POWELSON, Benjamin F.   History of Company K of the 140th Regiment Pennsylvania Volunteers.
1906   Steubenville   150.00
POWER, John Carroll   Abraham Lincoln, His Life, Public Service, Death of, Great Funeral Cortage.
1889   Chicago   50.00
POWER, John Hatch   Anatomy of the Arteries of the Human Body.
1863   Philadelphia   275.00
POWERS, Elvira J.   Hospital Pencillings, Being a Diary While in Jefferson Gen. Hospital.
1866   Boston   50.00
POWERS, George W.   The Story of the Thirty-eighth Regiment of Massachusetts Volunteers.
1866   Cambridge   125.00
POWHANKA, B. C.   Distant Thunder: A Photographic Essay on the American Civil War.
1988   Charlottesville   37.50
PRATT, Fletcher   The Civil War.
1955   Garden City, NY   25.00
PRATT, Fletcher   Civil War in Pictures.
1955   New York   25.00
1957   Garden City, NY   15.00
PRATT, Fletcher   Civil War on Western Waters.
1956   New York   25.00
PRATT, Fletcher   The Compact History of the United States Navy.
(1957)   New York   25.00
PRATT, Fletcher   Ordeal by Fire.
1935   New York   35.00
1948   New York   30.00
PRATT, Fletcher   Stanton - Lincoln's Secretary of War.
1953   New York   20.00
PRATT, Harry E., edited by   Concerning Mr. Lincoln.
1944   Springfield, IL   5.00
PRATT, Harry E.   The Personal Finances of Abraham Lincoln.
1943   Springfield, IL   5.00
PRAUS, A., compiled by   Confederate Soldiers and Sailors Who Died as Prisoners of War at Camp Butler, Illinois, 1862-1865.   Wraps.
(c.1960) Kalamazoo   35.00
PRAY, Mrs. R. F.   Dick Dowling's Battle.
1936   San Antonio   25.00
PREBLE, George H.   Henry Knox Thatcher Rear Admiral U.S. Navy. Wraps.
1882   Boston   75.00
PREBLE, George H.   The Chase of the Rebel Steamer of War Oreto, Commander J. N. Maffit, C.S.N. . . . Sept 4 1862.   Wraps.
1862   Cambridge   200.00
PRENTIS, Noble Lovely   Kansas Miscellanies.
1889   Topeka   80.00

Presentation of Regimental Colors to the Legislature, State of New York.
Wraps.
   1863   n.p.   35.00
Presidents, Soldiers, Statesmen. 2 Vols.
   1894   New York   75.00
PRESSLY, Thomas J.   Americans Interpret Their Civil War.
   1954   Princeton   30.00
   1962   New York   8.00
PRESTON, Francis W.   Port Hudson: A History of the Investment, Siege and Capture. Wraps.
   1892   Brooklyn   70.00
PRESTON, Margaret J.   Beechenbrook.
   1866   Baltimore   30.00
   1867   Baltimore   30.00
   1872   Peoples ed.   30.00
PRESTON, Margaret J.   Semi-Centennial Ode for the Virginia Military Institute, Lexington, Virginia 1839-1889. Wraps.
   1889   New York   30.00
PRESTON, Noble D.   History of the Tenth Regiment of Cavalry New York State Volunteers.
   1892   New York   225.00
PRESTON, Randolph   Lee at Lexington, An Address. Wraps.
   1935   n.p.   7.00
   1936   n.p.   7.00
PRESTON, Walter C.   Lee, West Point and Lexington.
   1934   Yellowsprings, OH   45.00
PRICE, George F.   Across the Continent with the Fifth Cavalry.
   1883   New York   200.00
   1959   New York   Ltd.   65.00
PRICE, Isaiah   History of the Ninety-seventh Regiment, Pennsylvania Volunteer Infantry, During the War of the Rebellion 1861-65.
   1875   Philadelphia   90.00
PRICE, Isaiah   Reunion of the 97th Regiment Pa. Vols. Oct. 29th, 1884 . . . West Chester, Pa.
   1884   Philadelphia   40.00
PRICE, William   Memorials of Edward Herndon Scott, M.D. Wraps.
   1874   Wytheville, VA   20.00
PRICE, William H.   The Civil War Centennial Handbook. Wraps.
   1961   Arlington   8.00
PRIEST, John M.   Antietam: The Soldier's Battle.
   1989   Shippensburg   34.95
PRINGLE, Cyrus   The Record of a Quaker Conscience, Cyrus Pringle's Diary.
   1918   New York   40.00
   1962   Lebanon   Wraps 5.00
PRINGLE, Elizabeth W.   The Chronicles of Chicora Wood.
   1922   New York   45.00
   1923   New York   40.00
   1940   New York   30.00

Proceedings and Report of the Board of Army Officers Convened by Special Orders No. 78, Headquarters of the Army . . . In the Case of Fitz-John Porter. . . . 3 Parts.
1879   n.p.   100.00

Proceedings at the Dedication of the Monumental Shaft . . . Erected Upon the Field of the Cavalry Engagement . . . Battle of Gettysburg. Wraps.
1885   Philadelphia   30.00

Proceedings, Findings, and Opinions of the Court of Inquiry. . . In the Case of Gouverneur K. Warren. 3 Parts.
1883   Washington, DC   125.00

Proceedings in Congress on the Occasion of the Reception and Acceptance of the Statue of General Ulysses S. Grant.
1901   Washington, DC   25.00

Proceedings of Reunions of 55th Illinois Veteran Volunteer Infantry. Wraps.
7th & 8th   30.00
11th   30.00
12th   30.00
13th   30.00
15th   30.00
16th   30.00

Proceedings of the Albany Bar on the Occasion of the Death of Col. Lewis Benedict of Albany.
1864   Albany   20.00

Proceedings of the Constitutional Convention of South Carolina.
1868   Charleston   100.00

Proceedings of the 1st and 2nd Reunions of the 7th Vermont Veteran Volunteers.
1883   New York   40.00

Proceedings of the 48th Annual Reunion of the 15th Ohio Regimental Assoc. Held at Mansfield, Ohio Sept. 26 and 27, 1912. Wraps.
n.d.   Mansfield   35.00

Proceedings of the Meeting of the Georgetown Rifle Guard, at Steel's Opera House, Georgetown, SC, January 10, 1896, on the Occasion of the Presentation of a Testimonial to Mr. Sol Emanuel. Wraps.
1896   Charleston   75.00

Proceedings of the Officers and Soldiers of the Indiana Regiments in the Army of the Cumberland.
1863   Indianapolis   65.00

Proceedings of the Reunion . . . Association of Survivors of the Seventh Illinois Regiment. 2 Vols. 1898-1911; 1912-1917.
n.d.   n.p.   250.00

Proceedings of the Reunion Society of Vermont Officers.
1885   Burlington   30.00

PROCTER, Ben H.   Not Without Honor - The Life of John H. Reagan.
1962   Austin, TX   30.00

Provisional Record of Confederate Medical Officers. Wraps.
(c.1890) (Wilmington, NC)   50.00

PROWELL, George R.   History of the 87th Regiment Pennsylvania Volunteers.
1901   York   110.00

PRUCHA, Francis Paul   A Guide to the Military Posts of the United
States 1789-1895.
1964   Madison, WI   25.00
PRUETT, Jakie L., edited by   Civil War Letters.
1985   Austin, TX   16.00
PRUTSMAN, Christian Miller   A Soldier's Experience in Southern
Prisons.
1901   New York   65.00
PRYOR, Mrs. Roger A.   My Day. Reminiscences of a Long Life.
1909   New York   35.00
1924   New York   30.00
PRYOR, Mrs. Roger A.   Reminiscences of Peace and War.
1904   New York   50.00
1905   New York   25.00
1908   New York   20.00
Public Ceremonies in Connection with the War Memorials of the Washington
Light Infantry with the Orations of Hampton, Simonton, and Porter.
Wraps.
1894   Charleston   35.00
PULA, James S.   The History of a German Polish Civil War Brigade.
Wraps.
1976   CA   65.00
PULESTON, Capt. W. D.   Mahan.
1946   New Haven, CT   100.00
PULLEN, John J.   Comic Relief. The Life and Laughter of Artemus
Ward.
1983   25.00
PULLEN, John J.   A Shower of Stars. The Medal of Honor and the
27th Maine.
1966   Philadelphia/New York   30.00
PULLEN, John J.   The Twentieth Maine, A Volunteer Regiment in
the Civil War.
1957   Philadelphia   50.00
1983   Dayton   19.95
1983   Dayton   Wraps   12.00
PUNTENNEY, George H.   History of the Thirty-seventh Regiment of
Indiana Infantry Volunteers.
1896   Rushville, IN   160.00
PURDUE, Howell and PURDUE, Elizabeth   Pat Cleburne. Confederate General A Definitive Biography.
1973   Hillsboro   50.00
1977   Tuscaloosa   35.00
1987   Gaithersburg   35.00
PUTNAM, Elizabeth C.   Memoirs of the War of '61.
1920   Boston   30.00
PUTNAM, G.   Address Spoken at the Funeral of Brig. Gen. Charles
Russell Lowell. Wraps.
1865   Cambridge, MA   10.00
PUTNAM, George Haven   Abraham Lincoln, the Great Captain Personal
Reminiscences by a Veteran of the Civil War.
1928   Oxford   12.00

PUTNAM, George Haven   **Memories of My Youth 1844-1865.**
1914   New York   40.00
PUTNAM, George Haven   **A Prisoner of War in Virginia 1864-5.**
1912   New York   50.00
1914   New York   40.00
PUTNAM, George Haven   **Some Memories of the Civil War.**
1924   New York   25.00
1928   New York   20.00
PUTNAM, Mildred Patterson, edited by   **Day Book of I. Frank Patterson, July 22, 1864 to April 30, 1865.**   Wraps.
1962   n.p.   Ltd.   35.00
PUTNAM, Sallie A.   **Richmond During the War.**
1867   New York   60.00
1961   New York   entitled   **In Richmond During the Confederacy**
25.00
PUTNAM, Samuel H.   **The Story of Company A, Twenty-fifth Regiment, Massachusetts Volunteers.**
1886   Worcester   Ltd.   140.00
PYNE, Henry R.   **The History of the First New Jersey Cavalry.**
1871   Trenton   160.00
PYNE, Henry R.   **Ride to War, The History of the First New Jersey Cavalry,** edited by Earl S. Miers.
1961   New Brunswick   30.00
QUAD, M. (pseud.)   See: **LEWIS**, Charles Bertrand
QUAIFE, Milo M., edited by   **Absalom Grimes: Confederate Mail Runner.**
1926   New Haven   50.00
QUARLES, Benjamin   **Frederick Douglass.**
1948   Washington, D.C.   30.00
QUARLES, Benjamin   **Lincoln and the Negro.**
1962   New York   15.00
QUARLES, Benjamin   **The Negro in the Civil War.**
1953   Boston   15.00
1968   New York   15.00
QUICK, Herbert   **Vandermark's Folly.**
1922   Indianapolis   10.00
QUIEN, George   **Reminiscences of the Service and Experience of Lieut. _____ Co. K, 23rd Conn. Vols.**
1906   Waterbury   60.00
QUINCY, Samuel M.   **History of the Second Massachusetts Regiment of Infantry; A Prisoner's Diary.**   Wraps.
1882   Boston   30.00
QUINCY, Samuel M.   **A Manual of Camp and Garrison Duty. By Colonel ... 73d United States Colored Infantry. ...**   Wraps.
(1865)   New Orleans   300.00
QUINER, Edwin B.   **The Military History of Wisconsin.**
1866   Chicago   100.00
QUINN, S. J.   **The History of the City of Fredericksburg, Virginia.**
1908   Richmond   75.00
QUINT, Alonzo H.   **The Potomac and the Rapidan.**
1864   Boston   50.00

QUINT, Alonzo H.　　The Record of the Second Massachusetts Infantry.
　　1867　　Boston　　80.00
　　1867　　Boston　　Ltd.　160.00
QUINTARD, Charles T.　　Doctor Quintard, Chaplain C.S.A., edited by Arthur H. Noll.
　　1905　　Sewanee　300.00
RACINE, J. Polk　　Recollections of a Veteran; or, Four Years in Dixie.
　　1894　　Elkton　　250.00
RADCLIFFE, George L.　　Governor Thomas H. Hicks of Maryland and the Civil War.
　　1901　　Baltimore　30.00
　　1965　　Baltimore　15.00
Radical Rule: Military Outrage in Georgia. Arrest of Columbus Prisoners: With Facts Concerning Their Imprisonment and Release.
　　1868　　Louisville　150.00
RADLEY, Kenneth　　Rebel Watchdog: The Confederate States Army Provost Guard.
　　1989　　Baton Rouge　　29.95
RAGAN, Robert A.　　Escape from East Tennessee to the Federal Lines.
　　1910　　Washington, DC　60.00
RAINS, George W.　　History of the Confederate Powder Works.
　　1882　　Augusta, GA　　125.00
　　1882　　Newburgh, NY　75.00
　　Later ed., undated, Wendell, NC　　Wraps　7.00　　Printed by a young publisher who didn't have sense enough to put a date on his reprints.
RAINWATER, Percy Lee　　Mississippi: Storm Center of Secession 1856-1861.
　　1938　　Baton Rouge　Ltd. 125.00
　　1969　　Jersey City　25.00
　　1985　　Baton Rouge　　33.00
RAMAGE, James A.　　Rebel Raider, the Life of Gen. John Hunt Morgan.
　　1986　　Lexington　　25.00
RAMEY, Emily and **GOTT,** John, compiled by　　The Years of Anguish: Fauquier County, Virginia 1861-1865.
　　1965　　Warrenton　25.00
　　1987　　20.00
RAMEY, Sanford W.　　Kings of the Battlefield.
　　1885　　Philadelphia　20.00
RAMPP, Larry C. and **RAMPP,** Donald L.　　The Civil War in the Indian Territory.
　　1975　　Austin　　35.00
RAMSDELL, Charles W.　　Behind the Lines in the Southern Confederacy, edited by Wendell H. Stephenson.
　　1944　　Baton Rouge　　35.00
　　1973　　Greenwood　　25.00
RAMSDELL, Charles W., edited by　　Laws and Joint Resolutions of the Last Session of the Confederate Congress (Nov. 7, 1964 - March 1865).
　　1941　　Durham, NC　　75.00
　　1965　　New York　　40.00
RAMSDELL, Charles W.　　Reconstruction in Texas.　Wraps.
　　1910　　New York　　150.00
　　1964　　Magnolia, MA　　30.00

RAMSEY, Grover C.   Confederate Postmasters in Texas. Wraps.
  1963   Waco Ltd.   30.00
RAMSEY, J. G. M.   Dr. J. G. M. Ramsey, Autobiography and Letters.
  1954   Nashville   40.00
RANCK, James Byrne   Albert Gallatin Brown - Radical Southern
  Nationalist.
  1937   New York   25.00
RAND, Clayton   Sons of the South.
  1961   New York   20.00
RANDALL, J. G.   Constitutional Problems Under Lincoln.
  1926   New York   20.00
  1951   Urbana, IL 15.00
RANDALL, J. G.   Lincoln and the South.
  1946   Baton Rouge   15.00
RANDALL, J. G.   Lincoln The Liberal Statesman.
  1947   New York   15.00
RANDALL, J. G.   Lincoln the President. 4 Vols.
  1945-55   New York   40.00
  1952   New York   1 Vol.   25.00
  1953   New York   1 Vol.   25.00
  1955   New York   1 Vol.   25.00
RANDALL, J. G.   Living with Lincoln and Other Essays.
  1949   Decatur, IL   10.00
RANDALL, J. G.   Mr. Lincoln, edited by R. Current.
  1957   New York   20.00
RANDALL, J. G. and DONALD, David   The Civil War and Reconstruction.
  1937   Boston 25.00
  1953   Boston 25.00
  1966   Boston 25.00
RANDALL, J. G. and DONALD, David   The Divided Union.
  1961   Boston   20.00
RANDALL, Ruth Painter   Colonel Elmer Ellsworth.
  1960   Boston   30.00
RANDALL, Ruth Painter   The Courtship of Mr. Lincoln.
  1957   10.00
RANDALL, Ruth Painter   Lincoln's Sons.
  1955   Boston   20.00
RANDALL, Ruth Painter   Mary Lincoln: Biography of a Marriage.
  1953   Boston   15.00
RANDEL, William P.   The Ku Klux Klan.
  1965   Philadelphia   25.00
RANDLE, E. H.   Characteristics of the Southern Negro.
  1910   New York   80.00
RANDOLPH, Hollins N.   Address Delivered at the Annual Convention
  UDC, Savannah, Ga., Nov. 19, 1924. Wraps.
  (1924)   (Savannah, GA)   25.00
RANDOLPH, Isham   Gleanings from a Harvest of Memories.
  1937   Columbia, MO   50.00
RANDOLPH, Sarah Nicholas   Life of Gen. Thomas J. Jackson.
  1876   Philadelphia 175.00

RANKIN, G. W.   William Dempster Hoard.
    1925   Fort Atkinson   50.00
RANKIN, Henry B.   Personal Recollections of Abraham Lincoln.
    1916   New York   10.00
RANKIN, R. H.   Uniforms of the Sea Services, a Pictorial History.
    1962   Annapolis   28.00
RANKIN, Richard C.   History of the Seventh Ohio Volunteer Cavalry. Wraps.
    1881   Ripley   160.00
RANKIN, Thomas   The 37th Virginia Infantry.
    1987   Lynchburg, VA 16.50
RANKINS, Walter   Morgan's Cavalry and the Home Guard at Augusta, Kentucky An Account of the Attack . . . Sept. 27, 1862. Wraps.
    1953   Louisville   30.00
RANSOM, John L.   Andersonville Diary, Escape, and List of the Dead.
    1881   Auburn, NY   75.00
    1883   Philadelphia   50.00
    1963   New York   entitled John Ransom's Diary. 30.00
    1986   17.50
RAPHAEL, Morris   The Battle in the Bayou Country.
    1975   Detroit   20.00
Rare Autograph Letters and Manuscripts Collected by the Late Charles M. Wallace. . . . Wraps.
    n.d.   n.p.   35.00
Rare Confederate Books and Pamphlets. Wraps.
    (1913) n.p.   45.00
RATCHFORD, J. W.   Some Reminiscences of Persons and Incidents of the Civil War.
    n.d.   Austin   Boxed   40.00
RATHBURN, Julius G.   Trip of the First Regiment C.N.G. to Yorktown, Va. and Charleston, S.C.
    1882   Hartford   30.00
RAUCH, William H., compiled by   Pennsylvania Reserve Volunteer Corps: "Round-Up."
    1903   Philadelphia 25.00
RAUM, Green B.   The Existing Conflict Between Republican Government and Southern Oligarchy.
    1884   Washington, DC   40.00
RAUP, Hallock F.   Letters from a Pennsylvania Chaplain at the Seige of Petersburg 1865. Wraps.
    1961   Kent, OH   25.00
RAUS, E. J.   A Generation on the March - The Union Army at Gettysburg.
    1987   Lynchburg   19.95
RAUS, Edward   A Generation on the March.
    1988   19.95
RAUSCHER, Frank   Music on the March 1862-65 With the Army of the Potomac 114th Regt. P.V. Collis' Zouaves.
    1892   Philadelphia 125.00
RAVENEL, Henry William   The Private Journal of _____ 1859-1887, edited by Arney Robinson Childs.
    1947   Columbia, SC   30.00

RAWLE, William Brooke   Gregg's Cavalry Fight at Gettsyburg . . .
Address. Wraps.
1884   Philadelphia   140.00

RAWLE, William Brooke   History of the Third Pennsylvania Cavalry,
Sixteenth Regiment.
1905   Philadelphia   130.00

RAWLE, William Brooke   The Right Flank at Gettysburg, An Account of
the Operations of General Gregg's Cavalry Command.
1878   Philadelphia   60.00

RAWLE, William Brooke   With Gregg in the Gettysburg Campaign.
Wraps.
1884   Philadelphia   60.00

RAWLEY, James A.   Edwin D. Morgan 1811-1883.
1955   17.00

RAWLEY, James A.   The Politics of Union: Northern Politics During
the Civil War.
1980   Lincoln, NE   19.00
1980   Lincoln, NE   Wraps 10.00

RAWLEY, James A.   Race and Politics - "Bleeding Kansas" and the
Coming of the Civil War.
1969   Philadelphia   10.00
1979   Lincoln, NE   Wraps 7.00

RAWLEY, James A.   Turning Points of the Civil War.
1966   Lincoln, NE   20.00
1976   13.00
1976   Wraps 6.00

RAWLING, Charles J.   History of the First Regiment Virginia
Infantry.
1887   Philadelphia   125.00

RAWLINGS, Mary, edited by   Early Charlottesville. Recollections of
James Alexander 1828- 1874. Wraps.
1942   25.00

RAY, Frederick E.   Alfred R. Waud Civil War Artist.
1974   New York   15.00

RAY, Frederick E.   Gettysburg Sketches   A Concise and Illustrated
History of the Battle of Gettysburg. Wraps.
n.d.   Gettysburg, PA   20.00

RAYMOND, Henry J.   History of the Administration of President
Lincoln.
1864   New York   20.00

RAYMOND, Henry J.   The Life and Public Services of Abraham Lincoln.
1865   New York   20.00

RAYMOND, Henry J. and SAVAGE, John   The Life of Abraham Lincoln,
and of Andrew Johnson.
n.d.   New York   20.00

RAYMOND, Samuel   The Record of Andover During the Rebellion.
1875   Andover   30.00

REA, Ralph R.   Sterling Price.
1959   Little Rock   60.00

READ, Opie and PIXLEY, Frank   The Carpet-Bagger.
1899   Chicago   10.00

READ, Thomas Buchanan   Sheridan's Ride A Poem.
    n.d.   n.p.   5.00
READ, Thomas Buchanan   A Summer Story.
    1865   Philadelphia   10.00
READER, Frank S.   History of the Fifth West Virginia Cavalry.
    1890   New Brighton   100.00
REAGAN, John H.   Memoirs, with Special Reference to Secession and the Civil War.
    1906   New York   175.00
    1958   Austin 20.00
    1968   Austin/New York   20.00
The Rebellion in Tennessee, Observations on Bishop Otey's Letter to the Hon. William H. Seward by a Native of Virginia. Wraps.
    1862   Washington, DC   40.00
Rebellion Record: The Battle of Bull Run, or Stone Bridge. Wraps.
    1861   New York   30.00
The Rebuke of Secession Doctrines by Southern Statesmen. Wraps.
    1863   Philadelphia   25.00
Recognition of the Southern Confederacy. Wraps.
    1863   London   75.00
Recollections of the Early Days of the National Guard . . . of the Famous Seventh Regiment New York Militia.
    1868   New York   30.00
The Record of Athol, Massachusetts, in Suppressing the Great Rebellion.
    1866   Boston   50.00
The Record of Hon. C. L. Vallandigham on Abolition, the Union and the Civil War. Wraps.
    1863   Columbus, OH   20.00
Record of Massachusetts Volunteers, 1861-65. 2 Vols.
    1868-70   Boston   200.00
Record of Officers and Men of New Jersey in the Civil War. 2 Vols.
    1876   Trenton 275.00
Record of Service of Michigan Volunteers in the Civil War 1861-1865.
    1907   Kalamazoo   60.00
Record of Service of the Connecticut Men in the Army and Navy of the War of the Rebellion.
    1889   Hartford   100.00
Record of the Commissioned Officers, Non-Commissioned Officers and Privates of the Regiments . . . New York. 8 Vols.
    1864-68   Albany 350.00
A Record of the Dedication of the Statue of Major General William Francis Bartlett: A Tribute of the Commonwealth of Massachusetts May 27, 1904.
    1905   Boston   30.00
The Record of the Democratic Party, 1860-1865. Wraps.
    (c.1870)   n.p.   25.00
Record of the Ninety-fourth Regiment Ohio Volunteer Infantry.
    (189-)   Cincinnati   140.00
Record of the Proceedings at the Dedication of the Monument . . . Gettysburg by the Survivors of the Tammany Regiment. Wraps.
    1892   New York   35.00

Record of the Procession and of the Exercises at the Dedication of the Monument . . . Erected by the People of Hanover, Mass. . . . In Grateful Memory of the Soldiers and Sailors . . . Who Died in the War for the Preservation of the Union. Wraps.
1878   Boston   20.00

Record of the Service of the Forty-fourth Massachusetts Volunteer Militia in North Carolina.
1887   Boston   115.00

Records of Living Officers of the United States Army.
1884   125.00

Red-Tape and Pigeon-Hole Generals.   See: MORFORD, Henry

REDDEN, Laura C.   See: SEARING, Laura C. R.

REDFIELD, I. F.   Judge Redfield's Letter to Senator Foot (Vermont). Wraps.
1865   New York   20.00

REDINGTON, E. D., and HODGKINS, W. H.   Military Record of the Sons of Dartmouth.
1907   Boston   30.00

REDPATH, James   Public Life of Capt. John Brown.
1860   Boston   25.00

REDWAY, G. W.   Fredericksburg, A Study in War.
1906   New York   40.00

REDWAY, G. W.   The War of Secession.
1910   London   40.00

REDWAY, Maurine Whorton   Marks of Lee on our Land.
1972   San Antonio   15.00

REDWAY, Maurine Whorton and BRACKEN, Dorothy Kendall   Marks of Lincoln on Our Land.
1957   New York   15.00

REDWING, Morris   Mosby's Trail, or Guerrillas of the Potomac, War Library, Vol. 3, No. 55.   Wraps.
1883   New York   30.00

REED, Charles W. and HARLOW, Louis K.   Bits of Camp Life.
1886   Munich and New York   40.00

REED, David Wilson   The Battle of Shiloh and the Organizations Engaged.
1903   Washington, DC   50.00
1909   Washington, DC   50.00
1920   Washington, DC   40.00

REED, David Wilson   Campaigns and Battles of the Twelfth Regiment Iowa Veteran Volunteer Infantry.
1903   Evanston, IL   100.00

REED, Emily   Life of A. P. Dostie.
1868   New York   30.00

REED, I. Richard   100 Years Ago Today: Niagara County in the Civil War as Reported in the Pages of "the Niagara Falls Gazette."   Wraps.
1966   Lockport   30.00

REED, John A. and DICKEY, L. S.   History of the 101st Regiment Pennsylvania Veteran Volunteer Infantry 1861-1865.
1910   Chicago   75.00

REED, John C.   The Brothers' War.
   1905   Boston   30.00
   1906   Boston   25.00
REED, Rowena   Combined Operations in the Civil War.
   1978   Annapolis   32.50
REED, Samuel R.   The Vicksburg Campaign.
   1882   Cincinnati   50.00
REED, William B.   A Northern Plea for Peace, An Address.   Wraps.
   1863   London   15.00
REED, William B.   A Paper Containing a Statement and Vindication
   of Certain Political Opinions.   Wraps.
   1862   Philadelphia   20.00
REED, William Howell   Hospital Life in the Army of the Potomac.
   1866   Boston   50.00
REEDSTROM, Ernest L.   Bugles, Banners and War Bonnets.
   1986   12.98
REESE, Michael, II   Autographs of the Confederacy.
   1981   New York   65.00
REESE, Timothy J.   Sykes' Regular Infantry Division, 1861-1864.
   1990   45.00
**Register of Commissioned Officers of the Vermont Volunteers in the Service
   of the United States.**   Wraps.
   1863   Woodstock   30.00
**Register of Graduates and Former Cadets of U.S. Military Academy 1802-
   1965 Civil War Centennial Edition - II.**
   1965   n.p.   35.00
A Register of Military Events in Virginia   1861-1865, compiled by N. E.
   Warinner.   Wraps.
   1959   n.p.   15.00
**Register of Officers Commissioned in the Volunteer Regiments from the
   State of New York 1861-1865.**
   1868   New York   50.00
Register of the Commandery of the State of Massachusetts, Mollus.
   1912   Cambridge   30.00
Register of the Commandery of the State of Pennsylvania, Mollus.
   1902   Philadelphia   35.00
**Register of the Commissioned and Warrant Officers of the Navy of the Con-
   federate States, to January 2, 1863.**   Wraps.
   (1863)   n.p.   75.00
**Register of the Commissioned Officers and Privates of the New Jersey Vol-
   unteers in the Service of the United States.**
   1863   Jersey City   110.00
**Register of the Commissioned, Warrant, and Volunteer Officers of the Navy
   of the United States.**
   1866   Washington, DC   75.00
**Register of the Confederate Dead . . . Hollywood Cemetery, Richmond, Vir-
   ginia.**   Wraps.
   1869   Richmond   100.00
**Register of the Officers and Cadets of the Virginia Military Institute -
   Lexington, Va.**   Wraps.
   1857   Richmond   50.00

Regulation for the Government of the United States Navy 1865.
    1865   Washington, DC   100.00
Regulations for the Army of the Confederate States, 1863.
    1980   Harrisburg   30.00
Regulations for the Instruction, Formations and Movements of the Cavalry.
    1865   London   100.00
Regulations for the Medical Department of the Army.
    1989   Knoxville   18.75
Regulations for the Recruiting Service of the Army of the United States, Both Regular and Volunteer. Wraps.
    1862   130.00
REICHARDT, Theodore   Diary of Battery A, First Regiment Rhode Island Light Artillery.
    1865   Providence   120.00
REID, Harvey   The View from Headquarters, Civil War Letters of Harvey Reid, edited by Frank L. Byrne.
    1965   Madison   25.00
REID, Jesse W.   History of the 4th Regiment of South Carolina Volunteers.
    1891   Greenville   1000.00
    1892   Greenville   Wraps   225.00
    1975   Dayton   17.50
REID, Whitelaw   After the War: A Southern Tour.
    1866   London   100.00
    1866   Cincinnati   75.00
    1965   New York   Wraps   10.00
REID, Whitelaw   Ohio in the War: Her Statesmen Her General, and Soldiers. 2 Vols.
    1868   Cincinnati   125.00
    1868   New York   125.00
    1893   Columbus   125.00
REIDENBAUGH, Lowell   The 33rd Virginia Infantry.
    1987   Lynchburg   16.45
REINFIELD, Fred   The Story of Civil War Money.
    1959   New York   30.00
The Rejected Stone. See: CONWAY, Moncure D.
REMINGTON, Cyrus Kingsbury   A Record of Battery I, First NY Light Artillery Vols. Otherwise Known as Wiedrich's Battery.
    1891   Buffalo   110.00
REMINGTON, Frederic   Frederic Remington's Own West, edited by Harold McCracken.
    1960   New York   30.00
Reminiscences of an Army Surgeon 1860-1863. Wraps.
    n.d.   n.p.   100.00
Reminiscences of Chicago During the Civil War.
    1914   Chicago   30.00
    1967   New York   15.00
Reminiscences of His Capture and Escape from Prison and Adventures within the Federal Lines by a Member of Mosby's Command, with a Narrative by a C.S. Naval Officer. (Rahm, Frank H. and Archer, Edward). Wraps.
    1895   Richmond   350.00

Reminiscences of the Civil War from Diaries of Members of 103d Illinois
    Volunteer Infantry.
    1904   Chicago   140.00
Reminiscences of the Cleveland Light Artillery.
    1906   Cleveland   110.00
Reminiscences of the Women of Missouri During the Sixties.
    (1913)   Jefferson City   75.00
REMINISCO, Don Pedro Q. (pseud.)   Life in the Union Army . . . A
    History, in Verse, of the 15th Regiment New York Engineers. Wraps.
    1864   New York   50.00
REMLAP, L. T. (pseud.)   See: PALMER, Loomis T.
RENNOLDS, Edwin H.   A History of the Henry County Commands
    Which Served in the Confederate States Army.
    1904   Jacksonville 500.00
    1961   Kennesaw, GA 30.00
    1988   26.00
Reply to the Twenty-seven, by the Editor of the Mobile Daily Advertiser.
    (Langdon, C. C.). Wraps.
    1850   Mobile   100.00
Report in the Senate, Committee on the Conduct of the War. . . . Inquire
    into and Report the Facts Concerning Attack on Petersburg. Report
    114, 38th Congress, 2nd Session, Senate.
    1864   Washington, DC   40.00
Report of Annual Reunions of 64th Regiment N. Y. Vol. Infantry. Wraps.
    1894-97   25.00 each
Report of Board of Visitors, Lee Camp Soldiers Home, Richmond, VA., Dec.
    31, 1908. Wraps.
    1909   Richmond   35.00
Report of Droop Mountain Battlefield Commission.
    1928   60.00
Report of Minnesota Commission, Report of . . . National Military Cemeter-
    ies at Little Rock, Memphis and Andersonville.
    1916   St. Paul   30.00
Report of State Commission for Erection of Monument to Ninth New Jersey
    Volunteers at New Berne, N. C. . . .
    1906   Philadelphia 35.00
Report of the Adjutant & Inspector General of the State of Vermont.
    1862-65   Montpelier Wraps 45.00 each
Report of [the] Adjutant General & Acting Quartermaster General of Iowa.
    To Jan. 1, 1863 2 Vols. 125.00
    To Jan. 1, 1864 65.00
    To Jan. 1, 1865 65.00
    To Jan. 1, 1866 65.00
    To Jan. 1, 1867 40.00
    To Jan. 1, 1868 40.00
Report of the Adjutant General of State of Arkansas for the Period of the
    Late Rebellion and to November 1, 1866.
    1867   Washington, DC 100.00
Report of the Adjutant General of the State of Illinois. Vols. 1-8.
    1900-1902   Springfield   375.00
    Individual volumes 40.00 each

Report of the Adjutant General of the State of Indiana. 8 Vols.
  1865-69   Indianapolis   50.00   each
Report of the Adjutant General of the State of Kansas 1861-1865. 2 Vols.
  1896   Topeka   150.00
Report of the Adjutant General of the State of Kentucky for 1862.
  1863   Frankfort   50.00
Report of the Adjutant General of the State of Kentucky 1861-1866.
  2 Vols.
  1866-67 Frankfort   175.00
Report of the Adjutant General of the State of New Hampshire.
  For Year 1863   35.00
  For Year 1865   2 Vols.   60.00
  For Year 1866   2 Vols.   60.00
  For Year 1868   30.00
Report of the Adjutant General of the State of Oregon.   Wraps.
  For Year 1863   45.00
  For Year 1865   45.00
Report of the Joint Committee on the Conduct of the War. 8 Vols.

  37th Congress, Third Session, Washington, DC   1863
  (Part I)   Army of the Potomac
  (Part II)   Bull Run, Ball's Bluff
  (Part III) Department of the West

  38th Congress, Second Session, Washington, DC   1865
  (Vol. I)   Reports on Army of Potomac and Battle of Petersburg
  (Vol. II)   Reports on Red River Expedition, Fort Fisher Expedition,
         Heavy Ordnance.
  (Vol. III) Reports on Sherman-Johnston, Light Draught Monitors, Massa-
         cre of Cheyenne Indians, Ice Contracts, Rosecrans' Campaigns
         & Misc.

  38th Congress, Second Session, Washington, DC   1866 (Supplemental
         Report.)
  (Part I)   Reports of Sherman, Thomas.
  (Part II) Reports of Pope, Foster, Pleasanton, Hitchcock, Sheridan, Rick-
         etts, Communication & Memorial of Norman Wiard.

  Set of 8 Vols.   400.00
  Individual titles   40.00   each
**Report of the Military Services of Gen. David Hunter During the War of the
  Rebellion.** Wraps.
  1892   New York   35.00
Report of the New York Board of Commissioners, Gettysburg Monuments.
  Wraps.
  1887   Albany   75.00
Report of the Select Committee on the Memphis Riots.
  1866   Washington, DC   40.00
Report of the Select Committee on the New Orleans Riots.
  1867   Washington, DC   45.00
**Report of the Special Committee Appointed to Investigate the Troubles in
  Kansas.** Report 200, 34th Congress, 1st Session, House of Reps.
  1856   Washington, DC   55.00
Report of the Surgeon General of Pa. for . . . 1863. Wraps.
  n.d.   n.p.   70.00

Report on the Subject of the Nature and Treatment of Miasmatic Fevers.
Wraps.
1863   50.00

Report, Annual Reunion & Dinner of the Old Guard Association, Twelfth
Regiment, N.G.S.N.Y. Sat. April 21st, 1894.   Wraps.
1894   New York   40.00

Reports of Experiments with Small Arms for the Military Service, by the
Officers of the Ordnance Dept., U.S. Army.
1984   Arendtsville   15.00

Reports of Extent and Nature of the Materials Available for the Preparation
of a Medical and Surgical History of the Rebellion.
1866   Philadelphia   300.00
See also: Medical and Surgical. . . .

Reports of the Naval Engagements on the Mississippi, Resulting in Capture
of New Orleans.
1862   Washington, DC   75.00

Reports on the Proceedings of the Society at the Annual Meetings.
1877-1913   Cincinnati   600.00

Reports to the Contributors to the Pennsylvania Relief Association for East
Tennessee. Wraps.
1864   Philadelphia   35.00

Representative Men of the South.
1880   Philadelphia   75.00

Republican Imperialism Is Not American Liberty.   Wraps.
(c.1863) n.p.   30.00

RERICK, John H.   The Forty-fourth Indiana Volunteer Infantry.
1880   LaGrange   200.00

Resolutions Adopted by Convention of Republican Party of Mississippi . . . in
Favor of Readmission of That State Into the Union. 40th Cong. 3d Sess.
Senate Doc. 8. Wraps.
1868   Washington, DC   40.00

The Returned Battleflags of the Virginia Regiments in the War Between the
States. Wraps.
1907   Richmond   50.00

The Returned Battle Flags, Presented to the Confederate Veterans at their
Reunion, Louisville, Kentucky June 14, 1905.   Wraps.
1905   St. Louis   100.00

Reunion . . . 12th Wisconsin Infantry.   Wraps.
1904-24   20.00 each

Reunion of Col. Dan McCook's Third Brigade, Second Division, Fourteenth
A.C.
1900   Chicago   100.00

Reunion of the 20th Regiment Indiana Veteran Volunteer Association.
Wraps.
Sept. 1, 1886   40.00
Sept. 1, 1888   40.00
Sept. 4, 5, 1889   40.00

Reunion, First Annual _____ of the Ninth New Jersey Veteran Volunteers.
1887   Elizabeth   35.00

Reunions of Taylor's Battery.
1890   Chicago   175.00

REVERE, Joseph W. **Keel and Saddle.**
    1872   Boston   60.00
    1873   Boston   45.00
Reviews of Jefferson Davis, Constitutionalist; His Letters, Papers and Speeches.
    1924   Jackson, MS   20.00
Revised Regulations for the Army of the United States 1861.
    1861   Philadelphia   65.00
    1861   New York   65.00
    1862   Philadelphia   65.00
    1863   Washington, DC   60.00
    1980   30.00
Revised Report of the Select Committee Relative to the Soldiers' National Cemetery.
    1865   Harrisburg, PA   60.00
REYNOLDS, C. G. **Famous American Admirals.**
    1978   17.00
REYNOLDS, Donald E. **Editors Make War.**
    1970   Nashville   20.00
REYNOLDS, E. W. **The True Story of the Barons of the South.**
    1862   Boston   45.00
    1970   35.00
REYNOLDS, John S. **Reconstruction in South Carolina 1865-1877.**
    1905   Columbia   80.00
    1969   New York   20.00
RHOADES, Jeffrey L. **Scapegoat General: The Story of Major General Benjamin Huger, C.S.A.**
    1985   Hamden   21.50
Rhode Island, Report of the Joint Special Comm. on Erection of Monument at Andersonville, Ga.
    1903   Providence   30.00
RHODES, Charles Dudley **History of the Cavalry of the Army of the Potomac.**
    1900   Kansas City   100.00
RHODES, Charles Dudley **The Lineage of Robert E. Lee: Robert E. Lee, the Westpointer.**
    1932   Richmond   40.00
RHODES, Elisha H. **All for the Union, A History of the 2nd Rhode Island Volunteer Infantry.**
    1985   Lincoln, RI   25.00
RHODES, James A. and **JAUCHIUS**, Dean **Johnny Shiloh: A Novel of the Civil War.**
    1959   Indianapolis   10.00
RHODES, James A. and **JAUCHIUS**, Dean **The Trial of Mary Todd Lincoln.**
    1959   Indianapolis   15.00
RHODES, James Ford **History of the Civil War.**
    1917   New York   35.00
    1919   New York   30.00
    1927   30.00
    1961   30.00

RHODES, James Ford   History of the United States from the Compromise of 1850 to the Final Restoration of Home Rule at the South in 1877. 7 Vols.
     1910   New York   100.00

RHODES, James Ford   Lectures on the American Civil War Delivered Before the Univ. of Oxford . . . 1912.
     1913   London   40.00
     1913   New York   30.00

RHODES, John H.   The History of Battery B, First Regiment Rhode Island Light Artillery.
     1894   Providence   120.00

RHODES, Robert H., edited by   All for the Union.
     1985   25.00

RICE, Allen, edited by   Reminiscences of Abraham Lincoln by Distinguished Men of His Time.
     1886   New York   20.00
     1886   Edinborough   20.00
     1888   New York   15.00
     1909   New York   15.00

RICE, Arnold S.   The Ku Klux Klan in American Politics.
     1962   Washington, DC   30.00

RICE, DeLong   The Story of Shiloh, Jackson.
     1924   TN   30.00

RICE, Harvey Mitchell   The Life of Jonathan M. Bennett.
     1943   Chapel Hill, NC   25.00

RICE, Lawrence D.   The Negro in Texas 1874-1900.
     1988   24.95

RICH, Doris   Fort Morgan and the Battle of Mobile Bay.   Wraps.
     1973   n.p.   20.00

RICH, Edward R.   Comrades!
     1898   Easton   225.00

RICH, Edward R.   Comrades Four.
     1907   New York   325.00

RICH, Jessie Pearl   J. L. M. Curry.
     1949   New York   20.00

RICH, Joseph W.   The Battle of Shiloh.
     1911   Iowa City   55.00

RICHARD, J. Fraise, edited by   The Florence Nightingale of the Southern Army   Experiences of Mrs. Ella K. Newsom Confederate Nurse in the Great War.
     1914   New York and Baltimore   140.00
     1915   New York   125.00

RICHARDS, A. P.   The Saint Helena Rifles.   Wraps.
     1968   Houston   50.00

RICHARDS, Henry   Letters of Captain Henry Richards of the Ninety-third Ohio Infantry.
     1883   Cincinnati   65.00

RICHARDS, Henry M. M.   Pennsylvania's Emergency Men at Gettysburg. A Touch of Bushwhacking.   Wraps.
     1895   Reading   50.00

RICHARDS, John T.   Abraham Lincoln the Lawyer-Statesman.
     1916   Boston and New York   15.00

RICHARDS, Laura E.   Samuel Gridley Howe by His Daughter.
  1935   Boston   10.00
RICHARDS, Laura E. and ELLIOTT, Maude Howe   Julia Ward Howe
  1819-1910. 2 Vols.
  1915   Boston   30.00
RICHARDS, W. J.   God Blessed Our Arms with Victory: The Religious
  Life of Stonewall Jackson.
  1986   New York   8.95
RICHARDSON, Albert D.   A Personal History of Ulysses S. Grant.
  1868   Hartford   15.00
RICHARDSON, Albert D.   The Secret Service, The Field, The Dun-
  geon and the Escape.
  1865   Hartford, CT   30.00
  1866   Hartford, CT   25.00
RICHARDSON, Charles   The Chancellorsville Campaign.
  1907   New York   125.00
RICHARDSON, E. Ramsey   "Little Aleck."
  1932   Indianapolis   35.00
RICHARDSON, Edward H.   Cassius Marcellus Clay, Firebrand of Freedom.
  1976   Kentucky   7.00
RICHARDSON, Elmo R. and FARLEY, Alan W.   John   Palmer   Usher
  Lincoln's Secretary of the Interior.
  1960   Lawrence, KS   15.00
RICHARDSON, James D.   A Compilation of the Messages and Papers
  of the Confederacy. 2 Vols.
  1896-99   Washington, DC   100.00
  1905   Nashville   75.00
  1906   Nashville   75.00
RICHARDSON, Leon Burr   William E. Chandler: Republican.
  1940   15.00
RICHARDSON, Rupert N.   The Frontier of Northwest Texas 1846 to
  1876.
  1963   Glendale   30.00
RICHEY, Homer and LINNEY, C. B.   Memorial   History   of   the   John
  Bowie Strange Camp, United Confederate Veterans.
  1920   Charlottesville   60.00
Richmond Civil War Memorial Ceremony - The One Hundredth Anniversary
  of the Resumption of Academic Duties of the Corps of Cadets/Virginia
  Military Institute at the Almshouse. . . . Wraps.
  1964   Richmond   20.00
Richmond During the War.   See: PUTNAM, Sallie A.
Richmond Magazine, June, 1932. Official Program 42nd Annual Confederate Reunion. Wraps.
  1932   Richmond   25.00
RICKEY and CARROLL   The Trial of Hon. Clement L. Vallandigham.
  1863   Cincinnati   100.00
RICKEY, Don, Jr.   40 Miles a Day on Beans and Hay.   Wraps.
  1985   Norman   11.00
RIDDLE, Albert Gallatin   Recollections of War Times.
  1895   New York   40.00

RIDDLE, Donald W. Congressman Abraham Lincoln.
1957 20.00
RIDDLE, Donald W. Lincoln Runs for Congress.
1948 New Brunswick 10.00
RIDGWAY, John Statistical History of John Ridgway's Vertical Revolving Battery. Wraps.
1865 60.00
RIDLEY, Bromfield L. Battles and Sketches of the Army of Tennessee.
1906 Mexico, MO 200.00
1978 35.00
RIETTI, John C., compiled by Military Annals of Mississippi.
(c.1895) Jackson, MS 650.00
1976 Spartanburg 30.00
1988 22.50
RIETTI, John C. Record of Organization, Service, and the Battles, Skirmishes and Marches of the Mississippi Rifles, 10th Mississippi Regiment,Confederate States Army. . . . Wraps.
1872 n.p. 500.00
RIGGS, David F. East of Gettysburg, Custer vs. Stuart. Wraps.
1970 Bellevue, NE 6.00
1985 Ft. Collins Wraps 6.00
RIGGS, David F. 13th Virginia Infantry.
1988 Lynchburg 19.95
RIGHTON, R. V. Their Flag Never Furled.
1983 Stone Mountain 30.00
RILEY, B. F. Makers and Romance of Alabama History.
n.d. n.p. 75.00
RILEY, Franklin L., edited by General Robert E. Lee After Appomattox.
1922 New York 35.00
1930 n.p. 35.00
RILING, Ray The Powder Flask Book; Treating of the History and Use of the Flask as a Principal Accessory to the Firearm. . . .
1960 60.00
RILING, Ray and Halter, Robert Uniform and Dress of the Army and Navy. . . . For 1861 ed., see: Confederate Imprints P-2417. For 1952 reprint, see: Uniform and Dress of the Army and Navy. . . .
RILING, Ray and HARWELL, Richard Uniform and Dress of the Army and Navy of the Confederate States of America.
1960 Philadelphia 200.00
RINGO, Willis L. Seventh Annual Reunion of the 1st Kentucky (Orphan) Brigade, CSA. Wraps.
1889 Frankfort 50.00
RINGOLD, May Spencer The Role of the State Legislatures in the Confederacy.
1966 Athens, GA 25.00
RIPLEY, C. Peter Slaves and Freedmen in Civil War Louisiana.
1976 Baton Rouge 20.00
RIPLEY, Edward Hastings The Capture and Occupation of Richmond, April 3rd, 1865.
1907 n.p. 75.00

RIPLEY, Edward Hastings   Vermont General, The Unusual War Experiences of _____, edited by Otto Eisenschiml.
   1960   New York   45.00
   1960   New York   Wraps 15.00
RIPLEY, Eliza McHatton   From Flag to Flag: A Woman's Adventures.
   1889   New York   80.00
RIPLEY, Warren   Artillery and Ammunition of the Civil War.
   1970   New York   30.00
RIPLEY, William Y. W.   Vermont Riflemen in the War for the Union 1861-1865 A History of Company F, First United States Sharp Shooters.
   1883   Rutland   165.00
   1981   Rochester   25.00
RISTER, Carl Coke   Fort Griffin on the Texas Frontiers. Wraps.
   1986   Norman   7.95
RISTER, Carl Coke   Robert E. Lee in Texas.
   1946   Norman   30.00
RITCHIE, George Thomas   A List of Lincolniana in the Library of Congress.
   1903   Washington, DC   45.00
RITTENHOUSE, Benjamin F.   Battle of Gettysburg as Seen from Little Round Top. Wraps.
   1887   Washington, DC   50.00
RITTENHOUSE, Jack D.   New Mexico Civil War Bibliography.
   1961   Houston Ltd.   50.00
RITTER, William L.   Biographical Memoir and Sketch of the Third Battery of Maryland Artillery.
   1902   Baltimore   125.00
RIVES, John C.   The Congressional Globe.
   1861   Washington, DC   30.00
RIVES, William Cabell   Correspondence Albemarle County Jan. 12, 1861. . . . Wraps.
   (c.1861)   n.p.   150.00
RIX, Guy S., compiled by   Roster of the Known Living Members of Col. Peter A. Porter's Regiment, 8th N.Y. Heavy Artillery.
   1892   Concord   60.00
ROACH, Alva C.   The Prisoner of War and How Treated.
   1865   Indianapolis   75.00
   1867   60.00
ROARK, James L.   Masters Without Slaves, Southern Planters in the Civil War and Reconstruction.
   1977   New York   12.00
   1977   Wraps 7.00
ROBACK, Henry   The Veteran Volunteers of Herkimer and Otsego Counties in the War of the Rebellion.
   1888   Little Falls   110.00
ROBBINS, E. Y.   The Soldier's Foe.
   1861   Cincinnati   150.00
ROBBINS, Gilbert   The Christian Patriot: A Biography of James E. McClellan.
   1865   Worcester   15.00

ROBBINS, Lois Brown   The South's Finest Hour   Essays on the War Between the States.
    1965   New York   10.00
ROBBINS, Walter R.   War Record and Personal Experiences of . . . , edited by Lilian Rea. Wraps.
    1923   (Chicago)   100.00
Robert E. Lee in Memoriam.
    1870   Louisville   30.00
Robert E. Lee: Soldier, Patriot, Educator, with Special Reference to His Life and Services at Washington and Lee University, Lexington, Va. Wraps.
    (1921) n.p.   25.00
Robert Edward Lee Ceremonies at the Unveiling of the Statue of General Lee. Wraps.
    1932   Richmond   20.00
Robert Love Taylor (Late Senator from Tennessee). Memorial Address, Delivered in the Senate and the House of Representatives of the United States.
    1913   Washington, DC   10.00
Robert Warren, The Texan Refugee.   See: **DIXON**, Samuel H.
ROBERTS, A. L.   As They Remembered: The Story of the 45th Penna. Vet. Vol. Inf. Regt. 1861-65. Wraps.
    1964   New York   25.00
ROBERTS, Allen E.   House Undivided The Story of Freemasonry and The Civil War.
    1964   New York   25.00
    1976   Richmond   25.00
ROBERTS, Captain (pseud.)   See: **HOBART-HAMPDEN**, Augustus Charles
ROBERTS, De Witt C.   Southern Sketches: or Eleven Years Down South; Including / Three Years in Dixie. Wraps.
    1865   Jacksonville, IL   150.00
ROBERTS, Derrell C.   Joseph E. Brown and the Politics of Reconstruction.
    1973   University, AL   15.00
ROBERTS, John N.   Reminiscences of the Civil War. Wraps.
    1925   n.p.   40.00
ROBERTS, Joseph   The Hand Book of Artillery for the Service of the U.S. (Army and Militia) with the Manual of Heavy Artillery.
    1861   New York   50.00
    1863   New York   40.00
    1865   New York   40.00
ROBERTS, Maggie   Home Scenes during the Rebellion.
    1875   New York   30.00
ROBERTS, O. M.   Texas. See: Confederate Military History, Vol. XI (Vol. XV, 1989 reprint ed.).
ROBERTS, Octavia   Lincoln in Illinois.
    1918   Boston   30.00
ROBERTS, W. Adolphe   Brave Mardi Gras.
    1946   Indianapolis   20.00
ROBERTS, W. Adolphe   Semmes of the "Alabama."
    1938   Indianapolis   60.00

ROBERTS, William R.   The Alabama Claims! England's Last Attempt to Destroy the American Republic. Wraps.
1872   Washington, DC   25.00

ROBERTSON, Alexander F.   Alexander Hugh Holmes Stuart 1807-1891.
1925   Richmond   35.00

ROBERTSON, Archibald Thomas   Life and Letters of John Albert Broadus.
1901   Philadelphia   45.00

ROBERTSON, Constance   The Unterrified.
1946   New York   16.00

ROBERTSON, Don   By Antietam Creek.
1960   Englewood Cliffs, NJ   30.00

ROBERTSON, Don   The Three Days.
1959   Englewood Cliffs, NJ   12.00

ROBERTSON, George F.   A Small Boy's Recollection of the Civil War.
1932   Clover, SC   40.00
n.d.   n.p.   30.00

ROBERTSON, James Barr   The Confederate Debt and Private Southern Debts. Wraps.
1884   London   75.00

ROBERTSON, James I., Jr.   The Civil War. Wraps.
1963   Washington, DC   10.00

ROBERTSON, James I., Jr., edited by   The Civil War Letters of General Robert McAllister.
1965   New Brunswick   40.00

ROBERTSON, James I., Jr.   Civil War Sites in Virginia A Tour Guide. Wraps.
1982   Charlottesville   10.00
1987   Charlottesville   Wraps   5.95

ROBERTSON, James I., Jr.   Concise Illustrated History of the Civil War.
1961   Harrisburg   5.00
1971   Harrisburg   5.00

ROBERTSON, James I., Jr.   General A. P. Hill. The Story of a Confederate Warrior.
1987   New York   24.00

ROBERTSON, James I., Jr.   Iowa in the Civil War: A Reference Guide. Wraps.
n.d.   Iowa City   15.00

ROBERTSON, James I., Jr.   Soldiers Blue and Gray.
1988   Columbia   25.00

ROBERTSON, James I., Jr.   The Stonewall Brigade.
1963   Baton Rouge   50.00
1984   Wraps   8.95

ROBERTSON, James I., Jr.   Virginia, 1861-1865, Iron Gate to the Confederacy. Wraps.
1961   Richmond   30.00
1985   Baton Rouge   Wraps   9.00

ROBERTSON, James I., Jr. and McMURRAY, Richard M., edited by   Rank and File, Civil War Essays in Honor of Bell Irwin Wiley.
1976   San Rafael, CA   15.00

ROBERTSON, James Rood   A Kentuckian at the Court of the Tsars The Ministry of Cassius Marcellus Clay to Russia. 1861-1862 and 1863-1869.
1935   Berea College, KY   40.00

ROBERTSON, Jerome B.   Touched with Valor, Civil War Papers and Casualty Reports of Hood's Texas Brigade, edited by Harold B. Simpson.
1964   Hillsboro   35.00

ROBERTSON, John   The Flags of Michigan.
1877   Lansing   45.00

ROBERTSON, John, compiled by   Michigan in the War.
1880   Lansing   90.00
1882   Lansing   75.00

ROBERTSON, Robert S.   Diary of the War by Rob't S. Robertson, 93rd Regt. N.Y. Vols. & A.D.C. to Gen. N. A. Miles, Commanding 1st Brigade, 1st Division, 2nd Army Corps, edited by Charles N. & Rosemary Walker.
1965   n.p.   45.00

ROBERTSON, Robert S.   Personal Recollections of the War. A Record of Service with the Ninety-third New York Vol. Infantry.
1895   Milwaukee   75.00

ROBERTSON, Robert Stoddart   From the Wilderness to Spottsylvania, A Paper Read Before the Ohio Commandery of the Mollus. Wraps.
1884   Cincinnati   40.00

ROBERTSON, William Glenn   Back Door to Richmond,   The Bermuda Hundred Campaign April-June 1864.
1987   Newark   39.00

ROBINS, Edward   William T. Sherman.
1905   Philadelphia   20.00

ROBINSON, Arthur J.   Memorandum and Anecdotes of the Civil War 1862 to 1865. Wraps.
1912   n.p.   40.00

ROBINSON, Benjamin   Delores: A Tale of Disappintment and Distress.
1868   New York   100.00

ROBINSON, Charles   The Kansas Conflict.
1892   New York   25.00
1898   25.00

ROBINSON, Charles S.   A Memorial Discourse Occasioned by the Death of Lieut. Col. James M. Green, Forty-eighth N.Y.S.V. Wraps.
1864   Troy, NY   35.00

ROBINSON, Frank T.   History of the Fifth Regiment, M.V.M.
1879   Boston   80.00

ROBINSON, George F.   After Thirty Years, A Complete Roster by Townships of Greene County, Ohio Soldiers.
1895   Xenia   35.00

ROBINSON, H. L.   Pittsfield, N.H. in the Great Rebellion.
1893   Pittsfield   30.00

ROBINSON, Mrs. J. Enders, edited by   The Restoration of the Name of Jefferson Davis to the Cabin John Bridge, Washington, District of Columbia. Wraps.
1909   New Orleans   15.00

ROBINSON, Leigh   Address Delivered Before R.E. Lee Camp Confederate Veterans . . . Acceptance of Portrait of Gen. William H. Payne. Wraps.
1909   Richmond   30.00

ROBINSON, Leigh   Joseph E. Johnston, An Address. Wraps.
1891   Washington, DC   40.00

ROBINSON, Leigh   The South Before and at the Battle of the Wilderness, Address. Wraps.
1878   Richmond   100.00

ROBINSON, Luther Emerson   Abraham Lincoln as a Man of Letters.
1918   Chicago   10.00

ROBINSON, Oliver S.   The Diary and Letters of Oliver S. Robinson. Wraps.
1968   Kensington, MD   40.00

ROBINSON, Wardwell   History of the 184th Regiment New York State Volunteers. Wraps.
1895   150.00

ROBINSON, William J.   Civil War Diary of Capt. William J. Robinson. Wraps.
1975   n.p.   30.00

ROBINSON, William M., Jr.   The Alabama - Kearsarge Battle. Wraps.
1924   Salem, MA   35.00

ROBINSON, William M., Jr.   The Confederate Privateers.
1928   New Haven, CT   75.00

ROBINSON, William M., Jr.   Justice in Grey A History of the Judicial System of the Confederate States of America.
1941   Cambridge, MA   125.00
1968   New York   35.00

ROBINTON, Madeline R.   An Introduction to the Papers of the New York Prize Court, 1861- 1865.
1945   New York   50.00

ROBLES, Philip K.   U.S. Military Medals and Ribbons.
1971   Rutland, VT   20.00

ROBSON, John S.   How a One-Legged Rebel Lives.
1891   Charlottesville   Wraps   125.00
1898   Durham   Wraps   125.00
1984   Gaithersburg   25.00

ROBUCK, J. E.   My Own Personal Experience and Observation as a Soldier in the Confederate Army.
1911   Birmingham   300.00
1979   Memphis   30.00

ROCKWELL, Alphonso David   Rambling Recollections.
1920   New York   75.00

ROCKWELL, Francis Williams   Address at the Unveiling of the Memorial Tablet of Col. Henry S. Briggs and the Tenth Mass. Infantry.
1907   Pittsfield   20.00

ROCKWELL, W. S.   The Olgethorpe Light Infantry of Savannah in Peace and in War. Wraps.
1894   Savannah   650.00

RODDY, Lee   Robert E. Lee. Wraps.
1981   5.00

RODENBOUGH, Theodore F.   **The Bravest Five Hundred of '61.**
1891   New York   60.00
RODENBOUGH, Theodore F.   **From Everglade to Canon with Second Dragoons.**
1875   New York   750.00
RODENBOUGH, Theodore F.   **Photographic History of the Union and Confederate Cavalry.**
1970   Glendale   30.00
RODENBOUGH, Theodore F., edited by   **Uncle Sam's Medal of Honor 1861-1886.**
1886   New York   50.00
RODENBOUGH, Theodore F. and **HASKIN,** William L.   **The Army of the United States.**
1896   New York   35.00
RODENBOUGH, Theodore F., et al   **History of the 18th Regiment of Cavalry Pennsylvania Volunteers 1862-1865.**
1909   New York   100.00
RODGERS, Robert L.   **"Jeff" Davis and the Pope. Wraps.**
1925   Aurora, MO   50.00
RODGERS, Robert L.   **An Historical Sketch of the Georgia Military Institute, Marietta, Georgia. Wraps.**
1956   Atlanta   20.00
RODICK, Burleigh Cushing   **Appomattox: The Last Campaign.**
1965   New York   20.00
1987   25.00
ROE, Alfred S.   **The Fifth Regiment Massachusetts Volunteer Infantry.**
1911   Boston   80.00
ROE, Alfred S.   **From Monocacy to Danville. Wraps.**
1889   Providence   Ltd.   40.00
ROE, Alfred S.   **In Rebel Prison; or, Experiences in Danville, Va. Wraps.**
1891   Providence   Ltd.   40.00
ROE, Alfred S.   **The Melvin Memorial, Sleepy Hollow Cemetery, Concord A Brother's Tribute, Exercises at Dedication June 16, 1909.**
1910   Cambridge   25.00
ROE, Alfred S.   **The Ninth New York Heavy Artillery.**
1899   Worcester   125.00
ROE, Alfred S.   **Recollections of Monocacy. Wraps.**
1885   Providence   Ltd.   40.00
ROE, Alfred S.   **Richmond, Annapolis, and Home. Wraps.**
1892   Providence   Ltd.   40.00
ROE, Alfred S.   **The Tenth Regiment Massachusetts Volunteer Infantry.**
1909   Springfield   50.00
ROE, Alfred S.   **The Thirty-ninth Regiment Massachusetts Volunteers 1862-1865.**
1914   Worcester   75.00
ROE, Alfred S.   **The Twenty-fourth Regiment, Massachusetts Volunteers, 1861-66.**
1907   Worcester   75.00
ROE, Alfred S. and **NUTT,** Charles   **History of the First Regiment of Heavy Artillery Massachusetts Volunteers.**
1917   Worcester   80.00

ROE, E. P.　　　The Gray and the Blue.
1884　　New York　　15.00
ROE, Louis A.　　　The Battle of the Ironclads.
1942　　New York　　35.00
ROE, Mary　　　E. P. Roe, Reminiscences of His Life.
1899　　New York　　25.00
ROEHRENBECK, William J.　　　The Regiment That Saved the Capital.
1961　　New York　　30.00
ROEMER, Jacob　　　Cavalry: Its History, Management and Uses in War.
1863　　New York　　125.00
ROEMER, Jacob　　　Reminiscences of the War of the Rebellion 1861-1865.
1897　　Flushing　　85.00
ROGAN, Lafayette　　　A Confederate Prisoner at Rock Island. The Diary
of Lafayette Rogan, edited by John H. Hauberg. Wraps.
1941　　Springfield, IL　40.00
ROGERS, A.　　　Abraham Lincoln　A Biography in Pictures with Text.
1939　　Boston　　20.00
ROGERS, Cameron　　　Colonel Bob Ingersoll.
1927　　New York　　35.00
ROGERS, Edward H.　　　Reminiscences of Military Service in the Forty-
third Regiment Massachusetts Infantry.
1883　　Boston　　110.00
ROGERS, F. H.　　　Jeb Stuart's Hat; Included Is How I Lost My Hat, by
Chandler, G. W. Wraps.
1893　　Detroit　　15.00
ROGERS, Fred B.　　　Soldiers of the Overland . . . Services of General
Patrick E. Conner & His Volunteers.
1938　　San Francisco　　110.00
ROGERS, H. C. B.　　　The Confederates and Federals at War.
1974　　n.p. 15.00
1975　　New York　　15.00
ROGERS, Henry Munroe　　　Memories of Ninety Years.
1928　　Boston/New York　　30.00
ROGERS, J. L.　　　The Civil War Battles of Chickamauga and Chatta-
nooga. Wraps.
1942　　Chattanooga　　5.00
ROGERS, J. W.　　　Madame Surratt　A Drama in Five Acts.
n.d.　　Washington, DC　　30.00
1879　　Washington, DC　　40.00
ROGERS, James B.　　　War Pictures Experiences and Observations of a
Chaplain in the U.S. Army in the War of the Southern Rebellion.
1863　　Chicago　100.00
ROGERS, William H.　　　History of the One Hundred and Eighty-ninth
Regiment of New York Volunteers.
1865　　New York　　75.00
1866　　New York　　75.00
ROGERS, William H.　　　William H. Rogers's Personal Experiences.
Wraps.
n.d.　　n.p.　　35.00
ROGERS, William Warren　　　Thomas County (Georgia) During the Civil
War.
1964　　Tallahassee　　20.00

ROHAN, J.   Yankee Arms Maker: The Story of Samuel Colt and His Six-Shot Peacemaker.
1948   New York   Revised edition   35.00
ROLAND, A.   Underwater Warfare in the Age of Sail.
1978   Bloomington   25.00
ROLAND, Charles P.   Albert Sydney Johnston - Soldier of Three Republics.
1964   Austin, TX 75.00
1987   Austin, TX Wraps   12.95
ROLAND, Charles P.   The Confederacy.
1960   Chicago   25.00
ROLAND, Charles P.   Louisiana Sugar Plantation During the American Civil War.
1957   Leiden, Netherlands   35.00
Roll of Honor. Wraps.
1868   Washington, DC   50.00
Roll of Honor: New York at Gettysburg. Wraps.
1898   n.p.   75.00
Roll of Honor, The Soldiers of Champaign County, Ohio Who Died for the Union.
n.d.   n.p.   50.00
Roll of Officers and Members of the Georgia Hussars.
1906   Savannah   185.00
Roll of Survivors of the Mississippi River Ram Fleet and Marine Brigade and Reported Deaths Since Formation of Society in 1887. Wraps.
1899   Belvedere, IL   100.00
Roll of the Officers and Enlisted Men of the 3rd, 4th, 18th, and 19th Kansas Volunteers 1861.
1902   Topeka   110.00
ROLL, Charles   Colonel Dick Thompson, The Persistent Whig.
1948   Indianapolis   25.00
ROLLE, Andrew F.   The Lost Cause, The Confederate Exodus to Mexico.
1965   Norman, OK   30.00
1966   Norman, OK   20.00
ROLLER, John E.   Address: Our Heroes,   The Leaders of a New Reformation. Wraps.
(c.1907) n.p.   25.00
ROLLIN, Frank A.   Life and Public Services of Martin R. Delany, Sub-Asst. Commissioner Bureau Relief of Refugees, Freedmen and of Abandoned Lands and Late Major 104th U.S. Colored Troops.
1883   50.00
1969   New York   30.00
Rolls of the Washington Light Infantry in Confederate Service. Wraps.
1888   Charleston   60.00
ROLPH, G. V. and CLARK, Noel   The Civil War Soldier. Wraps.
1961   Washington, DC   5.00
ROMAN, Alfred   The Military Operations of General Beauregard. 2 Vols.
1884   New York 200.00
ROMBAUER, Robert J.   The Union Cause in St. Louis in 1861.
1909   St. Louis   80.00

ROMINE, W. B.   The Story of Sam Davis.   Wraps.
   1928   Pulaski, TN   35.00
ROMINE, W. B. and ROMINE, Mrs. W. B.   A Story of the Original Ku
   Klux Klan. Wraps.
   1924   Pulaski, TN   45.00
ROOD, Hosea Whitford   Camp Randall Memorial Arch Dedicated in
   June 18-19, 1912. Wraps.
   n.d.   n.p.   25.00
ROOD, Hosea Whitford   The Story of the Service of Company E, and of
   the Twelfth Wisconsin Regiment Veteran Volunteer Infantry.
   1893   Milwaukee   210.00
ROOD, Hosea Whitford, compiled by   Wisconsin at Vicksburg: Report of
   the Wisconsin-Vicksburg Monument Commission.
   1914   Madison   40.00
ROPER, John Herbert   U. B. Phillips, A Southern Mind.
   1984   Macon, GA 17.00
ROPER, Laura Wood   Flo, A Biography of Frederick Law Olmsted.
   1974   Baltimore   15.00
ROPES, Hannah   Civil War Nurse, The Diary and Letters of Hannah
   Ropes, edited by John R. Brumgardt.
   1980   Knoxville   15.00
   1983   15.00
   1986   15.00
ROPES, John C.   The Army Under Pope.   See: Campaigns of the Civil
   War.
ROPES, John C.   The Story of the Civil War.
   1894-1913   New York/London 3 Vols. in 4   75.00
   1933   New York   3 Vols. in 4   75.00
ROSCOE, Theodore   Picture History of U.S. Navy.
   1956   New York   20.00
ROSCOE, Theodore   The Web of Conspiracy.
   1959   Englewood Cliffs   25.00
   1969   Englewood Cliffs   25.00
ROSE, Mrs. S. E. F.   The Ku Klux Klan.
   1914   New Orleans   100.00
ROSE, Thomas Ellwood   Col. Rose's Story of the Famous Tunnel Escape
   from Libby Prison. Wraps.
   n.d.   n.p.   35.00
ROSE, Victor M.   Ross' Texas Brigade.
   1881   Louisville   1400.00
   1960   Kennesaw, GA   30.00
ROSE, Victor M.   The Life and Services of Gen. Ben McCulloch.
   1888   Philadelphia   250.00
   1958   Austin, TX   Ltd.   Boxed 60.00
ROSE, Willie Lee   Rehearsal for Reconstruction, the Port Royal
   Experiment.
   1964   Indianapolis   25.00
ROSECRANS, W. S.   Report on the Battle of Murfreesboro, Tennessee.
   1863   Washington, DC   75.00
ROSENBERG, Morton M.   Iowa on the Eve of the Civil War.
   1972   Norman, OK   20.00
   1972   Norman, OK   Wraps   8.00

ROSENBERG, W. von, edited by   Confederate Land Certificates, Legislative, Executive, and Judicial Action. Wraps.
(1969) Austin, TX   20.00

ROSENBERGER, Francis Coleman   The Cumberland Valley of Pennsylvania in the 1860's. Wraps.
1963 Gettysburg   10.00

ROSENGARTEN, J. G.   The German Soldier in the Wars of the United States.
1886 Philadelphia 80.00

ROSET, J.   A Sermon on the Preservation of the Union; Delivered in the Alms-House on Randall's Island, Friday, January 4, 1861. Wraps.
1861 New York   20.00

ROSKE, Ralph J. and VAN DOREN, Charles   Lincoln's Commando, The Biography of Commander W. B. Cushing, USN.
1957 New York   35.00

ROSS, Fitzgerald   A Visit to the Cities and Camps of the Confederate States.
1865 Edinburgh and London   500.00

ROSS, Fitzgerald   Cities and Camps of the Confederate States, edited by Richard B. Harwell.
1958 Urbana, IL   40.00

ROSS, George   Gathered Leaves A Book of Verse Made from a Physician's Pad Leaflets.
1910 New York   30.00

ROSS, Ishbel   Angel of the Battlefield The Life of Clara Barton.
1956 New York   20.00

ROSS, Ishbel   First Lady of the South.
1954 New York   20.00
1958 New York   20.00

ROSS, Ishbel   The General's Wife: The Life of Mrs. Ulysses S. Grant.
1959 New York   15.00

ROSS, Ishbel   Proud Kate.
1953 New York   15.00

ROSS, Ishbel   Rebel Rose Life of Rose O'Neal Greenhow.
1954 New York   25.00

ROSS, Ishbel   The President's Wife Mary Todd Lincoln.
1973 New York   15.00

ROSS, Sam   The Empty Sleeve, A Biography of Lucius Fairchild, State Historical Society of Wisconsin for the Wisconsin Civil War Centennial Commission.
1964 Madison 55.00

ROSSER, Thomas Lafayette   The Cavalry, A.N.V. Address . . . at the Seventh Annual Reunion of the Association of the Maryland Line . . . February 22, 1889. Wraps.
1889 Baltimore   200.00

Roster and Historical Sketch of A. P. Hill Camp C. W. No. 6, Va. Wraps.
1887   45.00
(c.1915) n.p.   30.00

Roster and Historical Sketch of the 101st Regiment Ohio Volunteer Infantry.
1879 Tiffin   75.00

Roster and Muster Roll, and Chronological Record of the Twenty-sixth Regiment Connecticut Volunteers.
1888   Norwich   100.00

Roster and Record of Iowa Soldiers in the War of the Rebellion, Vols. 1-6.
1908-11   Des Moines   75.00 each

Roster and Sketches of the Several Military Companies Which Were in Regular Service of the Confederate States During the Civil War from Yazoo County, Miss. Collected from the Muster Rolls and Authentic Sources of Reliable Men. . . . Wraps.
1905   Yazoo City, MS   200.00

Roster of Officers and Members of the Society of the Army and Navy of the Confederate States in the State of Maryland. . . .   Wraps.
1883   75.00

Roster of R. E. Lee Camp, No. 2, Confederate Veterans of Alexandria, Va. Wraps.
n.d.   n.p.   35.00

Roster of Regimental Surgeons and Assistant Surgeons in the U.S. Army Medical Department during the Civil War. Wraps.
1989   Gaithersburg   30.00

Roster of Soldiers, Sailors and Marines of the War of 1812, the Mexican War, and the War of the Rebellion Residing in Nebraska June 1, 1891.
1892   Lincoln   50.00

Roster of Soldiers, Sailors, and Marines of the War of 1812, the Mexican War, and the War of the Rebellion, Residing in Nebraska , June 1, 1893.
1893   Lincoln   100.00

Roster of Soldiers, Sailors, and Marines of the War of 1812, the Mexican War and the War of the Rebellion Residing in Nebraska, 1895   (Piper, J. A.)
1895   York   75.00

Roster of Soldiers, Sailors and Marines, Who Served in the War of the Rebellion, World War . . . (and Residing in Nebraska).
1925   Omaha   50.00

Roster of Surviving Members of the 41st Regiment, Ohio Veteran Volunteer Infantry in the War of the Rebellion 1861-1865.   Wraps.
1899   Cleveland   35.00

Roster of the 115th Regiment Illinois Infantry Volunteers Issued by Regimental Reunion Assoc., Decatur, Illinois.   Wraps.
n.d.   n.p.   45.00

Roster of the 147th Regiment Ohio Volunteer Infantry with Age at Enlistment.   Wraps.
1913   West Milton   90.00

Roster of the 134th Regiment O.V.I.   Wraps.
1898   Ohio   75.00

Roster of the 22nd Regiment Infantry Maine Vols. Mustered into U.S. Service at "Camp Pope" Bangor, Maine, October 10, 1862.   Wraps.
1863   Bangor   35.00

Roster of the Living Members of the 102d Regt. Ill. Vols.   Wraps.
1911   (Galesburg)   45.00

Roster of the Officers and Members of the 18th Michigan Volunteer Infantry.
1899   Adrian, MI   75.00

Roster of Wisconsin Volunteers, War of the Rebellion 1861-1865. 2 Vols.
  1886   Madison, WI   130.00
ROTH, Margaret Brobst, edited by   **Well Mary   Civil War Letters of a Wisconsin Volunteer.**
  1960   Madison, WI   30.00
ROTHERY, Agnes   **Houses Virginians Have Loved.**
  1954   New York and Toronto   30.00
ROTHSCHILD, Alonzo   **Lincoln Master of Men.**
  1906   Boston   10.00
ROUNTREE, J. A.   **The Cross of Military Service (C.M.S.) History and Records of men of lineal Confederate descent who served honorably in the Army, Navy or Marine Corps of the United States or its Allies during the period of the World War (April 6, 1917-November 11, 1918.)**
  1927   Birmingham   100.00
ROWAN, Richard Wilmer   **The Story of Secret Service.**
  1937   New York   20.00
ROWE, David W.   **A Sketch of the 126th Regiment Pennsylvania Volunteers. Wraps.**
  1869   Chambersburg   75.00
ROWELL, Adelaide   **On Jordan's Stormy Banks.**
  1948   Indianapolis   20.00
ROWELL, John W.   **Eli Lilly's Battalion.**
  1975   36.00
ROWELL, John W.   **Yankee Artillerymen: Through the Civil War with Eli Lilly's Indiana Battery.**
  1975   Knoxville   25.00
ROWELL, John W.   **Yankee Cavalrymen: Through the Civil War with the Ninth Pennsylvania Cavalry.**
  1971   Knoxville   40.00
  1985   24.00
ROWLAND, Dunbar   **Jefferson Davis, Constitutionalist.** 10 Vols. and index.
  1923   Jackson, MS   500.00
ROWLAND, Dunbar   **Jefferson Davis' Place in History as Revealed in his Letters, Papers and Speeches. Wraps.**
  1923   Jackson, MS   15.00
ROWLAND, Dunbar   **Military History of Mississippi, The Official and Statistical Register of the State of Mississippi.**
  1908   Nashville   175.00
  1988   Columbia   38.00
ROWLAND, Eron   **Varina Howell: Wife of Jefferson Davis.** 2 Vols.
  1927-31 New York   75.00
ROY, Andrew   **Recollections of a Prisoner of War.**
  1905   Columbus   75.00
  1909   Columbus   55.00
ROY, Paul L.   **The Last Reunion of the Blue and Gray. Wraps.**
  1950   Gettysburg   15.00
ROYALL, William L.   **A Reply to "A Fool's Errand, By One of the Fools." Wraps.**
  1880   New York   70.00
ROYALL, William L.   **Some Reminiscences.**
  1909   New York   150.00

ROYSE, Isaac Henry Clay   History of the 115th Regiment Illinois Volunteer Infantry.
 1900   Terre Haute   Ltd.   165.00
ROZWENC, Edwin C., edited by   The Causes of the American Civil War. Wraps.
 1961   Boston   5.00
ROZWENC, Edwin C.   Reconstruction in the South. Wraps.
 1972   Lexington, MA   10.00
RUBY, James S., edited by   Blue and Gray.   Georgetown University and the Civil War.
 1961   Washington, DC   45.00
RUCHAMES, Louis, edited by   A John Brown Reader.
 1960   5.00
RUDISILL, James J.   The Day of Our Abraham, 1811-1899.
 1936   York, PA   Ltd.   100.00
RUDOLPH, E. L.   Confederate Broadside Verse   A Bibliography and Finding List of Confederate Broadside Ballads and Songs.
 1950   New Braunfels, TX   50.00
RUDOLPH, Joseph   Pickups from the "American Way," Early Life and Civil War Reminiscences of Capt. Joseph Rudolph. Wraps.
 1941   Hiram   40.00
RUFFIN, Edmund   The Diary of _____, edited by William K. Scarborough. 2 Vols.
 1972-76   Baton Rouge   60.00
RUFFNER, Kevin C.   The 44th Virginia Infantry.
 1987   Lynchburg   Ltd.   16.95
RUGGLES, A. G.   A National System of Finance. Wraps.
 1862   Fond Du Lac, WI   20.00
RUGGLES, A. G.   Prince of Players, Edwin Booth.
 1953   New York   25.00
RULE, William The Loyalists of Tennessee in the Late War: A Paper . . . 1887. Wraps.
 1887   Cincinnati   40.00
Rules for the Management and Cleaning of the Rifle Musket Model 1863 for the Use of Soldiers.
 1863   Washington, DC   30.00
 1955   Wraps   5.00
 1960   Philadelphia   Wraps   10.00
RUMBAUGH, George P.C.   From Dust to Ashes: A Romance of the Confederacy.
 1895   Little Rock   10.00
RUNYAN, N. P.   A Quaker Scout.
 1900   New York   25.00
RUSH, Benjamin   Letter on the Rebellion, to a Citizen of Washington, from a Citizen of Philadelphia. Wraps.
 1862   Philadelphia   25.00
RUSLING, James Fowler   Men and Things I Saw in the Civil War Days.
 1899   New York   65.00
 1914   New York   50.00
RUSSELL, A. J.   Russell's Civil War Photographs. Wraps.
 1982   8.00

RUSSELL, Don   The Lives and Legends of Buffalo Bill aka William I
Cody, Federal Scout. Wraps.
1982   14.00
RUSSELL, Don   One Hundred and Three Fights and Scrimmages, Th
Story of General Reuben F. Bernard.
1936   Washington, DC   75.00
RUSSELL, L. B.   Granddad's Autobiography. Wraps.
1930   Comanche, TX   Ltd.   75.00
RUSSELL, L. E.   Abraham Lincoln: A Contribution Toward A Bibliogra
phy. Wraps.
1910   Cedar Rapids, IA   20.00
RUSSELL, Phillips   The Woman Who Rang the Bell, The Story c
Cornelia Phillips Spencer.
1949   Chapel Hill, NC   25.00
RUSSELL, William H.   The Battle of Bull Run. Wraps.
1861   New York   45.00
RUSSELL, William H.   The Civil War in America. Wraps.
1861   Boston   90.00
RUSSELL, William H.   My Diary North and South. 2 Vols.
1863   New York   100.00
1863   London   150.00
1863   Boston   100.00
1954   New York   edited by Fletcher Pratt 25.00
1954   Boston   25.00
RUTH, Kent   Great Day in the West. Forts, Posts and Rendezvo
Beyond the Mississippi.
1963   30.00
RUTH, Kent   Landmarks of the West. A Guide to Historical Sites.
1986   University, NE   17.50
RUTHERFORD, Mildred Lewis   Battles and Leaders. The Surrend
and Results. Wraps.
1923   Athens, GA   10.00
RUTHERFORD, Mildred Lewis   Contrasted Lives of Jefferson Dav
and Abraham Lincoln. Wraps.
1927   Athens, GA   10.00
RUTHERFORD, Mildred Lewis   Facts and Figures vs. Myths and Mi
representations. Wraps.
1921   Athens, GA   10.00
RUTHERFORD, Mildred Lewis   Four Addresses. Wraps.
(1916)   Birmingham   10.00
RUTHERFORD, Mildred Lewis   Henry Wirz and Andersonville Priso
Wraps.
1921   Athens, GA   10.00
RUTHERFORD, Mildred Lewis   Henry Wirz, The True History
Andersonville Prison. Wraps.
1924   Athens, GA   10.00
RUTHERFORD, Mildred Lewis   Historical Sins of Omission and Con
mission. Wraps.
1915   Athens   9.00
RUTHERFORD, Mildred Lewis   History of the Ladies Memorial Ass
ciations: Monuments to the Confederate Soldiers. Wraps.
1924   Athens, GA   10.00

RUTHERFORD, Mildred Lewis   Jefferson Davis and Abraham Lincoln
   1861-1865. Wraps.
   1916   Athens, GA   10.00
RUTHERFORD, Mildred Lewis   Secession Was Not Rebellion.   Wraps.
   1923   Athens, GA   10.00
RUTHERFORD, Mildred Lewis   The South Must Have Her Rightful
   Place in History.   Wraps.
   1923   Athens, GA   10.00
RUTHERFORD, Mildred Lewis   The   South's   Greatest   Vindication.
   Stone Mountain Memorial.   Wraps.
   1924   Athens, GA   10.00
RUTHERFORD, Mildred Lewis   Text Books - The South's Responsibil-
   ity. Wraps.
   1924   Athens, GA   10.00
RUTHERFORD, Mildred Lewis   Truths of History.   Wraps.
   n.d.   n.p.   10.00
RYAN, Abram J.   Father Ryan's Poems.
   1879   Mobile, AL   30.00
RYAN, Abram J.   Poems: Patriotic, Religious, Miscellaneous.
   1880   Baltimore   15.00
   1896   New York   10.00
   1903   New York   10.00
RYAN, Andrew   News From Fort Craig.
   1966   Santa Fe   Ltd.   40.00
RYAN, Daniel J.   The Civil War Literature of Ohio.
   1911   Cleveland   125.00
RYDER, John J.   Reminiscences of Three Years' Service in the Civil War.
   By a Cape Cod Boy.
   1928   New Bedford   40.00
RYWELL, Martin   Confederate   Guns   and   Their   Current   Prices.
   Wraps.
   1952   Harriman, TN   30.00
   1958   Harriman, TN   30.00
RYWELL, Martin   The Gun that Shaped American Destiny.
   1957   Harriman, TN   35.00
   1984   Union City entitled: Sharps Rifle: The Gun That Shaped
      American Destiny. Wraps   5.00
RYWELL, Martin   Judah Benjamin, Unsung Rebel Prince.
   1948   Asheville, NC   35.00
RYWELL, Martin   The Trial of Samuel Colt.
   1953   Ltd.   85.00
RYWELL, Martin   United States Military Muskets, Rifles, Carbines
   and Their Current Prices.   Wraps.
   1959   Harriman, TN   20.00
SABRE, Gilbert E.   Nineteen Months a Prisoner of War.
   1865   New York   50.00
SACKETT, Frances Robertson   Dick Dowling.
   1927   Houston   30.00
SAGE, William   The Claybornes: A Romance of the Civil War.
   1902   Boston   15.00
SALA, George Augustus   My Diary in America. 2 Vols.
   1865   London   150.00

SALLEY, Alexander S., Jr., compiled **South Carolina Troops in Confederate Service.** 3 Vols.
 1913-30 Columbia   750.00
 Vol. I   only   60.00
 Vol. II   only   300.00
 Vol. III only   200.00
SALTER, William   **The Life of James W. Grimes, Governor of Iowa.**
 1876   New York   25.00
Samuel Colt Presents   A Loan Exhibition of Presentation Percussion Colt Firearms.
 1961   Hartford   40.00
SAMUEL, Bunford   **Secession and Constitutional Liberty.** 2 Vols.
 1920   New York   125.00
SANBORN, Alvan F.   **Reminiscences of Richard Lathers.**
 1907   New York   Ltd.   50.00
SANBORN, F. B., edited by   **Life and Letters of John Brown, Liberator of Kansas and Martyr of Virginia.**
 1885   Boston 30.00
 1891   Boston 25.00
SANBORN, F. B.   **Recollections of Seventy Years.** 2 Vols.
 1909   Boston 50.00
SANBORN, John B.   **Some Descriptions of the Battles in Which the Commands of General John B. Sanborn . . . Participated in the Departments of Tennessee and Missouri During the Rebellion of 1861-65.** Wraps.
 1900   St. Paul 50.00
SANBORN, Margaret   **Robert E. Lee.** 2 Vols.
 1966-67 Philadelphia 50.00
SANDBURG, Carl   **Abraham Lincoln 1809-1959   The Address Before the United States Congress Washington, D.C., February 12th, 1959.**
 1959   Worcester 75.00
SANDBURG, Carl   **Abraham Lincoln. The Prairie Years.** 2 Vols.
 1926   New York 50.00
 ✓1926   6 Vol. set 100.00
 1945   6 Vol. set 90.00
 1954   New York 30.00
SANDBURG, Carl   **Abraham Lincoln: The War Years.** 4 Vols.
 1939   New York 80.00
SANDBURG, Carl   **Lincoln Collector. The Story of Oliver R. Barrett's Great Private Collection.**
 1949   New York 60.00
 1950   New York 50.00
 1960   20.00
SANDBURG, Carl   **Remembrance Rock.** 2 Vols.
 1948   New York 90.00
SANDBURG, Carl   **Storm Over the Land.**
 1942   New York 20.00
 1957   Autographed 50.00
SANDBURG, Carl and **ANGLE**, Paul   **Mary Lincoln. Wife and Widow.**
 1932   New York 20.00
SANDERSON, James Monroe   **My Record in Rebeldom.** Wraps.
 1865   New York 150.00

SANDS, Benjamin F.   From Reefer to Rear-Admiral.
1899   New York   50.00
SANFORD, George B.   Fighting Rebels and Redskins, Experiences in
Army Life of Colonel _____ 1861-1892, edited by E. R. Hagemann.
1969   Norman, OK   25.00
SANFORD, Paul   Sioux Arrows & Bullets.
1969   20.00
SANFORD, Washington L.   History of Fourteenth Illinois Cavalry and
the Brigades to Which It Belonged.
1898   Chicago   225.00
SANGER, Donald Bridgman and HAY, Thomas Robson   James
Longstreet: I-Soldier II-Politician, Officeholder and Writer. 2 Vols.
1952   Baton Rouge   60.00
1968   Gloucester, MA   45.00
SANGER, George P., edited by   By Authority, the Statutes at Large
and Treaties of the United States of America. Wraps.
1864   Boston   100.00
SANGSTON, Lawrence   The Bastiles of the North. Wraps.
1863   Baltimore   75.00
SANTOVENIA, Emeterio S.   Lincoln in Marti - A Cuban View of
Abraham Lincoln.
1953   Chapel Hill, NC   10.00
SARGENT, F. W.   England, The United States, and The Southern
Confederacy.
1864   London   75.00
SARGENT, F. W.   On Bandaging and Other Operations of Minor
Surgery.
1862   Philadelphia   65.00
SARMIENTO, Ferdinand L.   Life of Pauline Cushman, The Celebrated
Union Spy and Scout.
1865   Philadelphia   35.00
1878   Philadelphia   30.00
(c.1890) New York   30.00
SARTAIN, James Alfred   History of Walker County, Georgia. Vol. 1 (all
pub).
1932   Dalton   80.00
SASS, Herbert Ravenel   Look Back to Glory.
1933   Indianapolis   20.00
SATTERLEE, John L.   The Journal of the 114th 1861-65 (Illinois).
1979   Ltd.   40.00
SAUERS, Richard   A Caspian Sea of Ink; The Meade-Sickles
Controversy.
1989   Ltd.   32.50
SAUERS, R. A., compiled by   The Gettysburg Campaign, June 3 - August
1, 1863. A Comprehensive, Selectively Annotated Bibliography.
1982   Westport   18.00
SAUNIER, Joseph A., edited by   A History of the Forty-seventh Ohio
Veteran Volunteer Infantry.
1903   Hillsboro   195.00
SAVAGE, John   The Life and Public Services of Andrew Johnson.
1866   New York   35.00

SAVAGE, John H.   The Life of John H. Savage, Citizen, Soldier, Lawyer, Congressman . . . Written by Himself.
    1903   Nashville   800.00

A Savoury Dish for Loyal Men.   Wraps.
    1863   Philadelphia   15.00

SAWICKI, James A.   Infantry Regiments of the U.S. Army.
    1982   30.00

SAWYER, E. H.   Gettysburg, The Battle of Gettysburg, July 1st to July 3rd, 1863.   Wraps.
    1936   40.00

SAWYER, Franklin   A Military History of the 8th Regiment Ohio Vol. Infantry, Its Battles, Marches and Army Movements.
    1881   Cleveland   225.00

SAYNER, Donald B.   The Orders of Col. Samuel McPhail 1863 Minnesota Mounted Rangers.   Wraps.
    1973   Tucson, AZ   25.00

SCAIFE, William R.   Confederate Surgeon.
    1985   25.00

SCALES, Alfred M.   The Battle of Fredericksburg   An Address . . . Before the Association of the Virginia Division of the Army of Northern Virginia.   Wraps.
    1884   Washington, DC   100.00

SCALES, Cordella Lewis   "Dear Darling Loulie" Letters of Cordelia Lewis Scales to Loulie W. Irby During the War Between the States, edited by Martha Neville Lumpkin.
    1955   Boulder   55.00

SCHAFF, Morris   The Battle of the Wilderness.
    1910   Boston   45.00
    1986   30.00

SCHAFF, Morris   Jefferson Davis.
    1922   Boston   30.00

SCHAFF, Morris   The Spirit of Old West Point.
    1907   Boston   40.00
    1908   Boston   30.00
    1912   Boston   25.00

SCHAFF, Morris   The Sunset of the Confederacy.
    1912   Boston   50.00
    1985   30.00

SCHALK, Emil   Campaigns of 1862 and 1863.
    1862   Philadelphia   50.00
    1863   Philadelphia   40.00

SCHARF, J. Thomas   History of the Confederate States Navy.
    1887   New York   200.00
    1894   Albany   150.00
    1977   New York   35.00

SCHEE, George W. and MONTZHEIMER, O. H.   Biographical Data and Army Record of Old Soldiers Who Have Lived in O'Brien County, Iowa.
    1909   Primghar, IA   100.00

SCHEIBERT, Justus   Der BurgerKrieg in Den Nordamerikaniscen Staaten Militairisch Beleuchtet fur den Deutschen Offizier.   Wraps.
    1874   Berlin   375.00

SCHEIBERT, Justus   Seven Months in the Rebel States During the North American War, 1863.
  1874   Berlin (In German) 300.00
  1876   Paris (In French)   300.00
  For the 1958 ed. See: Confederate Centennial Studies, No. 9.
SCHELIHA, Viktor E. K. R. Von   A Treatise on Coast-Defence.
  1868   London 300.00
  1971   Westport, CT   35.00
SCHELL, Herbert S.   Dakota Territory During the Eighteen Sixties. Wraps.
  1954   Vermillion, SC   15.00
SCHELL, Mary L.   The Love of Life of Brig.Gen. Henry M. Naglee, Consisting of a Correspondence on Love, War and Politics.
  1867   n.p.   80.00
SCHENCK, Martin   Up Came Hill.
  1958   Harrisburg, PA   40.00
  1985   Gaithersburg   25.00
SCHILDT, John W.   Antietam Hospitals. Wraps.
  1987   Chewsville   6.00
SCHILDT, John W.   Connecticut at Antietam.   Wraps.
  1988   Chewsville   5.00
SCHILDT, John W.   Drums Along the Antietam.
  1972   Parsons, WV   30.00
SCHILDT, John W.   Hunter Holmes McGuire; Doctor in Gray.
  1986   Chewsville   13.95
SCHILDT, John W.   Roads from Gettysburg.
  1979   n.p.   15.00
SCHILDT, John W.   Roads to Antietam.   Wraps.
  1985   Chewsville   7.50
SCHILDT, John W.   Roads to Gettysburg.
  1978   Parsons, WV   25.00
  1982   Parsons, WV   20.00
SCHILDT, John W.   September Echoes - The Maryland Campaign of 1862. Wraps.
  1960   Middletown, MD   35.00
SCHILDT, John W.   Stonewall Jackson Day by Day.   Wraps.
  1980   Chewsville 20.00
SCHILLER, Herbert M.   The Bermuda Hundred Campaign. Operations on the James River, Virginia-May, 1864.
  1988   Dayton   29.95
SCHLEY, Winfield Scott   Forty-five Years Under the Flag.
  1904   New York   35.00
SCHLICKE, C. P.   General George Wright: Guardian of the Pacific Coast.
  1988   Norman   29.95
SCHLUETER, Herman   Lincoln, Labor and Slavery.
  1913   New York   10.00
SCHMITT, Martin F.   General George Crook. His Autobiography. . . .
  1986   9.95
SCHMITT, William A.   The Last Days of the Lost Cause. Wraps.
  1949   Clarksdale   25.00

SCHMUCKER, Samuel M.   The History of the Civil War in the United States.
   1865   Philadelphia   40.00

SCHNECK, B. S.   The Burning of Chambersburg, Pennsylvania.
   1864   Philadelphia   50.00
   1865   Philadelphia   50.00

SCHOFIELD, John M.   Forty-six Years in the Army.
   1897   New York   50.00

SCHOFIELD, Levi T.   Retreat from Pulaski to Nashville, Tenn.
   1909   Cleveland   75.00

SCHOMAEKERS, G.   American Civil War.
   1979   15.00

SCHOTT, T. E.   Alexander Stephens of Georgia: A Biography.
   1988   Baton Rouge   37.50

SCHOULDER, James   Eighty Years of Union.
   1903   New York   25.00

SCHOULER, William   A History of Massachusetts in the Civil War. 2 Vols.
   1868   Boston   75.00

SCHRANTZ, Ward L.   Jasper County, Missouri, in the Civil War.
   1923   Carthage   125.00

SCHREIER, K. F.   Remington Rolling Block Firearms. Wraps.
   1987   Union City   6.95

SCHUCKERS, J. W.   The Life and Public Services of Salmon Portland Chase.
   1874   New York   40.00
   1970   Salem, NH   30.00

SCHULTZ, Harold S.   Nationalism and Sectionalism in South Carolina 1852-1860.
   1950   Durham   20.00

SCHULTZ, John A.   One Year at War: The Diary of Private John A. Schultz, edited by Hobard Lewis Morris, Jr.
   1968   New York   30.00

SCHURZ, Carl   Abraham Lincoln, and the Gettysburg Address and Other Papers by Abraham Lincoln.
   1891   Cleveland   20.00
   1899   Cleveland   15.00

SCHURZ, Carl   The Autobiography of _____.
   1961   New York   20.00

SCHURZ, Carl   Eulogy on Charles Sumner. Wraps.
   1874   New York   20.00

SCHURZ, Carl   The Reminiscences of _____. 3 Vols.
   1907-09 New York   75.00

SCHURZ, Carl   Speech of _____. Wraps.
   1864   Philadelphia   20.00

SCHUSTER, Richard   The Selfish and the Strong.
   1958   New York   15.00

SCHUTZ, Wallace J.   Major-General John Pope and the Army of Virginia.
   1986   18.50

SCHUTZ, Wallace J. and TRENERRY, Walter   Abandoned by Lincoln, A Military Biography of General John Pope.
1990   University, IL   27.50

Schuyler, Hartley and Graham's Illustrated Catalogue of Arms & Military Goods.
1972   New Milford   30.00

SCHWAB, John Christopher   The Confederate States of America.
1901   New York   75.00
1968   New York   35.00

SCHWARTZ, Stephan   Twenty-two Months a Prisoner of War, A Narrative of 22 Months Imprisonment by the Confederates in Texas. . . .
1892   St. Louis   75.00

SCOFIELD, Levi Tucker   The Retreat from Pulaski to Nashville, Tennessee. . . .
1909   Cleveland   150.00

SCOTT, Allan M.   Chronicles of the Great Rebellion.
1864   Cincinnati   30.00
1868   Cincinnati   30.00

SCOTT, Eben Greenough   Reconstruction During the Civil War in the United States of America.
1895   Boston   35.00

SCOTT, Edwin J.   Random Recollections of a Long Life.
1884   Columbia, SC   60.00

SCOTT, Evelyn   The Wave.
1929   New York   10.00

SCOTT, Florence Johnson   Old Rough and Ready on the Rio Grande. Wraps.
1935   San Antonio   40.00

SCOTT, George H.   Vermont at Gettysburg   An Address Delivered before the Society, July 6, 1870, Proceedings of the Vermont Historical Society. New Series Vol I, No. 2.
1930   15.00

SCOTT, H. L.   Military Dictionary.
1862   New York   60.00
1863   New York   30.00
1864   50.00
1956   Harriman, TN   entitled Civil War Military Dictionary, edited by Martin Rywell   Wraps   25.00

SCOTT, J. G. and WYATT, E. A.   Petersburg's Story: A History.
1960   Petersburg   30.00

SCOTT, J. L.   36th Virginia Infantry.
1987   Lynchburg   16.95

SCOTT, J. L.   The 36th and 37th Battalion Virginia Cavalry.
1986   Lynchburg   16.95

SCOTT, James K. P.   The Story of the Battles at Gettysburg.
1927   Harrisburg   40.00

SCOTT, Joe M.   Four Years in the Southern Army.
1897   Mulberry   2000.00
1958   Fayetteville   Wraps   40.00

SCOTT, John   Partisan Life with Col. John S. Mosby.
1867   New York   175.00
1985   Gaithersburg   30.00

SCOTT, John   The Lost Principle; or the Sectional Equilibrium by "Barbarossa."
  1860   Richmond   65.00
SCOTT, John, compiled by   Story of the Thirty-second Iowa Infantry Volunteers.
  1896   Nevada, IA   175.00
SCOTT, Kate M.   History of the 105th Regiment of Pennsylvania Volunteers.
  1877   Philadelphia 140.00
SCOTT, M. W.   Old Richmond Neighborhoods.
  1975   Richmond   35.00
SCOTT, Major R. Taylor   Pickett's Division Association. Address at the Unveiling of the Monument in Hollywood Cemetery, October 5, 1888. Wraps.
  1888   Richmond   40.00
SCOTT, Robert G.   Into the Wilderness with the Army of the Potomac.
  1985   Bloomington   30.00
SCOTT, Samuel W. and ANGEL, Samuel P.   History of the Thirteenth Regiment, Tenn. Volunteer Cavalry, U.S.A.
  1903   Philadelphia 100.00
  1973   Blountville   40.00
  1987   Johnson City   21.95
SCOTT, W. W., edited by   Two Confederate Items, Diary of Capt. H. W. Wingfield and Reminiscences of the Civil War by Judge E. C. Moncure. VSL Bulletin. Wraps.
  1927   Richmond   25.00
SCOTT, William Forse   Philander P. Lane, Colonel of Volunteers in the Civil War 11th Ohio Infantry.
  1920   New York   100.00
SCOTT, William Forse   Roster of the Fourth Iowa Cavalry Veteran Volunteers.
  1902   New York   65.00
SCOTT, William Forse   The Story of a Cavalry Regiment. The Career of the Fourth Iowa Veteran Volunteers.
  1893   New York   145.00
SCOTT, Winfield   The Infantry Tactics. 3 Vols.
  1861   New York   150.00
SCOTT, Winfield   Memoirs, Written by Himself. 2 Vols.
  1864   New York   150.00
  1970   20.00
SCOVILLE, Samuel, Jr.   Brave Deeds of Union Soldiers.
  1915   Philadelphia 20.00
SCRIBNER, Benjamin Franklin   How Soldiers Were Made.
  1887   New Albany, IN   125.00
SCRIBNER, Robert L.   The Stonewall Brigade   Of a Band of Heroes and Their Commanders. Wraps.
  1956   Lexington   15.00
SCRIBNER, Theodore T.   Indiana's Roll of Honor, Vol. II.
  1866   Indianapolis 65.00
Scribner's Monthly. See Appendix: Magazines.

SCRIPPS, John L.   The First Published Life of Abraham Lincoln.
    1900   Detroit   Ltd.   60.00
    1968   New York   30.00
SCRYMSER, James A.   Personal Reminiscences of _____ in Times of
    Peace and War.
    1915   New York   55.00
SCULLY, Everett G.   The Story of Robert E. Lee.
    1905   Portland, ME   25.00
SEABROOK, William L. W.   Maryland's Great Part in Saving the
    Union.
    1913   n.p.   90.00
SEABURY, Samuel D.   The Union Volunteer.   Wraps.
    1878   Portland, ME   20.00
SEAGER, Robert   And Tyler Too, A Biography of John and Julia
    Gardiner Tyler.
    1963   New York   20.00
SEARCHER, Victor   The Farewell to Lincoln.
    1965   New York and Nashville   25.00
SEARING, Laura C. R.   Idyls of Battle and Poems of the Rebellion.
    1864   New York   10.00
SEARS, Louis M.   John Slidell.
    1925   Durham, NC   65.00
SEARS, Stephen W., edited by   The American Heritage Century
    Collection of Civil War Art.
    1974   New York   25.00
SEARS, Stephen W., edited by   The Civil War Papers of George B.
    McClellan.
    1988   New York   34.95
SEARS, Stephen W.   George B. McClellan. The Young Napoleon.
    1988   24.95
SEARS, Stephen W.   Landscape Turned Red. The Battle of Antietam.
    1983   New Haven   20.00
SEATON, Benjamin M.   The Bugle Softly Blows, The Confederate
    Diary of _____, edited by Harold B. Simpson.
    1965   Waco   35.00
SEAWELL, Molly Elliot   The Victory.
    1906   New York   10.00
Secession and East Tennessee: A Poem.
    1864   Philadelphia   30.00
SeCHEVERELL, John Hamilton   Journal History of the Twenty-ninth
    Ohio Veteran Volunteers 1861-1865.
    1883   Cleveland   150.00
Second Reunion of Mahone's Brigade.   Wraps.
    1876   Norfolk   40.00
Secret Correspondence Illustrating the Condition of Affairs in Maryland.
    Wraps.
    1863   Baltimore   200.00
SEDGWICK, John   Correspondence of. 2 Vols.
    1902-03   New York   Ltd.   250.00
SEFTON, James E.   The United States Army and Reconstruction 1865-
    1877.
    1967   Baton Rouge   25.00

SEIBERT, George   Die Berloeung der Stadt Chambersburg-Zeastoung.
     1865   Chambersburg and Philadelphia   125.00
SEIFERT, S.   Farewell My General.
     1954   Philadelphia   15.00
SEITZ, Don C.   Braxton Bragg, General of the Confederacy.
     1924   Columbia, SC   200.00
     1971   Freeport, NY   40.00
SEITZ, Don C.   The Dreadful Decade.
     1926   Indianapolis   20.00
SEITZ, Don C.   Lincoln, The Politician.
     1931   New York   20.00
SELBY, John   The Iron Brigade.   Wraps.
     1973   New York   30.00
SELBY, John   Men at Arms Series: U.S. Cavalry.   Wraps.
     1974   New York   15.00
SELBY, John   The Stonewall Brigade.
     1971   Norwich   20.00
     1973   New York   15.00
SELBY, John   Stonewall Jackson as Military Commander.
     1968   Princeton   35.00
     1968   London   35.00
SELBY, Julian A.   Memorabilia and Anecdotal Reminiscences of
     Columbia, South Carolina.
     1905   Columbia, SC   75.00
     1970   n.p.   25.00
Selected Civil War Maps.
     1961   Washington, DC   50.00
A Selection from the Addresses, Lectures and Papers, with a Biographical
     Sketch of Arthur A. Putnam of Uxbridge, Mass.
     1910   Cambridge   30.00
Selection of War Lyrics.
     1864   New York   30.00
SELFRIDGE, Thomas O., Jr.   Memoirs of _____.
     1924   New York   40.00
     1987   21.95
SELLERS, Alfred J.   Reunions of the Survivors of the 90th Pa. Vol. Inf.
     on the Battlefield of Gettysburg Sept. 2 & 3, 1888 and Sept. 1 & 2, 1889.
     1889   Philadelphia   75.00
SELPH, Fannie Eoline   The South in American Life and History.
     1928   Nashville   60.00
SELPH, Fannie Eoline   Texas (or) The Broken Link in the Chain of
     Family Honors.
     1905   W. Nashville, TN   25.00
SEMMES, Raphael   The Confederate Raider Alabama, edited by Philip
     Van Doren Stern.
     1962   Bloomington   40.00
SEMMES, Raphael   The Cruise of the Alabama and the Sumter.
     2 Vols.
     1864   London   300.00
     1864   London entitled The Log of the Alabama and Sumter.   200.00
     1864   New York   2 Vols. in 1   150.00
     1864   Paris   2 Vols. in 1   100.00

SEMMES, Raphael   My Adventures Afloat . . . Cruises and Services in the "Sumter" and "Alabama."
✓1869   London   2 Vols. in 1   250.00
1869   Baltimore   entitled   Memoirs of Service Afloat During the War Between the States.   125.00
1877   Baltimore   entitled   Services Afloat. . . .   125.00
1887   London   125.00
1887   Baltimore   100.00
1890   100.00
n.d.   New York   100.00
1903   New York   entitled   Service Afloat. . . .   75.00
1987   entitled   Memoirs of Service Afloat. . . .   14.95
SEMMES, Raphael   Rebel Raider: Being an Account of Semmes Cruise in the C.S.S. Sumter, edited by Harper A. Gosnell.
1948   Chapel Hill, NC   30.00
SENOUR, Faunt   Major General William T. Sherman and His Campaigns.
1865   Chicago 50.00
SENOUR, Faunt   Morgan and His Captors.
1864   Cincinnati   60.00
1865   Cincinnati   50.00
1865   Chicago 50.00
SENSENEY, Charles H.   Address Delivered . . . To his Comrades . . . Fiftieth Anniversary . . . of Battery D, First West Virginia Light Artillery. Wraps.
1912   Wheeling   30.00
SENSING, Thurman   Champ Ferguson, Confederate Guerrilla.
1942   Nashville   150.00
1962   Nashville   20.00
Recent reprint   14.95
Sequel to General M'call's Report of the Pennsylvania Reserves in the Peninsula. Wraps.
n.d.   n.p.   20.00
SERGENT, Mary Elizabeth   They Lie Forgotten; The United States Military Academy, 1856- 1861, Together with a Class Album for the Class of May, 1861.   Wraps.
1986   Middletown   20.00
SETTLE, William S.   History of the Third Pennsylvania Heavy Artillery and One Hundred and Eighty-eighth Pa. Vol. Infantry.   Wraps.
1886   Lewistown   125.00
Seventeenth Annual Reunion of the 17th Regiment C.V.I.   Wraps.
1884   Bridgeport   25.00
SEVILLE, William P.   History   of   the   First   Regiment,   Delaware Volunteers.   Wraps.
1884   Wilmington, DE   50.00
1986   16.00
SEWARD, Frederick W.   Reminiscences of War-Time Statesman and Diplomat 1830-1915.
1916   New York   20.00
SEWARD, William H.   The Diplomatic History of the War from the Union, Being the Fifth Volume of the Works of _____, edited by George F. Baker.
1884   Boston   25.00

SEWARD, William H.   Issues of the Conflict.   Terms of Peace,
  Speech.   Wraps.
  1864   Washington, DC   10.00
SEWARD, William H.   Speech for the Immediate Admission of Kansas
  into the Union.   Wraps.
  1856   Washington, DC   10.00
SEYMOUR, Digby G.   The Divided Loyalties   Fort Sanders and the
  Civil War in East Tennessee.
  1963   Knoxville   35.00
  1982   Knoxville   25.00
SHAARA, Michael   The Killer Angels.
  1974   New York   20.00
  1981   New York   25.00
  1987   New York   19.95
SHACKLEFORD, George G.   George   Wythe   Randolph   and   the
  Confederate Elite.
  1988   University, GA   25.00
SHACKLETON, Robert   Strange Stories of the Civil War.
  1907   New York   20.00
Shadows of the Storm.   See: DAVIS, William C.   The   Image   of   War,
  1861-1865.
SHAFFNER, J. F.   Diary of Dr. J. F. Shaffner, Sr. . . .   Wraps.
  1936   Winston Salem, NC   175.00
SHAFFNER, Taliaferro Preston   The War in America.
  1862   London   175.00
SHALHOPE, Robert E.   Sterling Price, Portrait of a Southerner.
  1971   Columbia   20.00
SHANE, John H.   First Regiment Eastern Shore Maryland Infantry at
  Gettysburg July 1863.   Wraps.
  1895   Baltimore   50.00
SHANK, John Daniel   One   Flag,   One   Country   and   Thirteen
  Greenbacks a Month, Letters from a Civil War Private and His Colonel,
  compiled by Edna J. Shank Hunter.
  1980   San Diego   Ltd.   35.00
SHANKS, Henry T.   The Secession Movement in Virginia.
  1934   Richmond   30.00
SHANKS, William F. G.   Person Recollections of Distinguished Generals.
  1866   New York   45.00
SHANNON, Fred Albert   The Organization and Administration of the
  Union Army 1861-65.   2 Vols.
  1928   Cleveland   125.00
  1965   Gloucester   30.00
SHARKEY, Robert P.   Money, Class, and Party   An Economic Study
  of Civil War and Reconstruction.
  1959   Baltimore   25.00
SHATTUCK, Charles H.   The Hamlet of Edwin Booth.
  1969   Champaign, IL   30.00
SHAVER, Lewellyn A.   A History of the 60th Alabama Regiment,
  Gracie's Alabama Brigade.
  1867   Montgomery   500.00
  Recent reprint   20.00

SHAW, Albert   Abraham Lincoln A Cartoon History. 2 Vols.
1929   New York   Boxed   45.00

SHAW, Albert D.   A Full Report of the First Reunion and Banquet of the Thirty-fifth N.Y. Vols.
1888   Watertown   100.00

SHAW, Archer H., edited by   The Lincoln Encyclopedia: The Spoken and Written Words of A. Lincoln Arranged for Easy Reference.
1950   New York   30.00

SHAW, Arthur Marvin   William Preston Johnston.
1943   Baton Rouge   50.00

SHAW, Dale   Titans of the American State - Edwin Forrest, the Booths, the O'Neills.
1971   PA   40.00

SHAW, Edmund   The 110th Regiment, Pa. Vol. at Gettysburg. . . . Wraps.
n.d.   n.p.   100.00

SHAW, Elton Raymond   The Love Affairs of Washington and Lincoln.
1923   Berwyn, IL   10.00

SHAW, Frederick B.   One Hundred and Forty Years of Service in Peace and War, History of the 2nd Infantry United States Army.
1930   Detroit   40.00

SHAW, Horace H.   The First Maine Heavy Artillery.
1903   Portland   125.00

SHAW, James   Our Last Campaign and Subsequent Service in Texas. Wraps.
1905   Providence   Ltd.   40.00

SHAW, James Birney   History of the Tenth Regiment Indiana Volunteer Infantry.
1912   Lafayette   250.00

SHEA, George   Jefferson Davis. Wraps.
1877   London   25.00

SHEA, John C.   The Only True History of Quantrell's Raid Ever Published. Wraps.
1879   Kansas City   300.00

SHEA, John Gilmary, edited by   The Lincoln Memorial: A Record of the Life, Assassination, and Obsequies of the Martyred President.
1865   New York   20.00

SHEERAN, James B.   Confederate Chaplain, A War Journal of Rev. _____, edited by Joseph Durkin.
1960   Milwaukee   25.00

SHELDON, Winthrop D.   The "27th," A Regimental History.
1866   New Haven   75.00

SHELLABARGER, Samuel   Disfranchisement of Rebels, Speech. Wraps.
1866   Washington, DC   15.00

SHELLABARGER, Samuel   Reconstruction, Speech. Wraps.
1866   Washington, DC   10.00

SHELLABARGER, Samuel   Speech, The Relations of the Constitution and of Public Law to Rebellion. Wraps.
1862   Washington, DC   10.00

SHELLENBERGER, John K.   The Battle of Franklin.
1902   n.p.   90.00

SHELLENBERGER, John K.   The Battle of Franklin, Tennessee, November 30, 1864, a Statement of the Erroneous Claims Made by General Schofield. . . . Wraps.
> 1916   Cleveland   Ltd.   125 copies.   100.00

SHELLENBERGER, John K.   The Battle of Spring Hill, Tenn. November 29, 1864. Wraps.
> 1913   Cleveland   80.00

SHELTER, Charles   West Virginia Civil War Literature.   Wraps.
> 1963   Morgantown   30.00

SHELTON, Vaughan   Mask for Treason: The Lincoln Murder Trial.
> 1965   Harrisburg, PA   40.00

The Shenandoah Campaigns of 1862 and 1864, and the Appomattox Campaign.   See: Papers of the Military Historical Society of Massachusetts, No. 6.

SHENFIELD, Lawrence L.   Confederate States of America / The Special Postal Routes.
> 1961   New York   60.00

SHENTON, James P.   Robert John Walker, A Politician from Jackson to Lincoln.
> 1961   New York   15.00

SHEPARD, I. F.   Memorial Day, May 30, 1870, Oration at Jefferson Barracks St. Louis, Missouri.   Wraps.
> 1915   n.p.   10.00

SHEPHERD, Henry E.   Life of Robert Edward Lee.
> 1906   New York and Washington, DC   100.00

SHEPPARD, Eric William   The American Civil War 1864-1865.
> (c.1938) Aldershot   125.00

SHEPPARD, Eric William   Bedford Forrest, The Confederacy's Greatest Cavalry-Man.
> 1930   New York   150.00
> 1930   London   150.00
> 1988   25.00

SHEPPARD, Eric William   The Campaign in Virginia and Maryland June 26th to Sept. 20th, 1862. . . .
> 1911   London   150.00

SHEPPARD, William Arthur   Red Shirts Remembered.
> 1940   Atlanta   75.00

SHEPPARD, William Arthur   Some Reasons Why Red Shirts Remembered.   Wraps.
> 1940   Greer   25.00

Sheridan's Veterans, A Souvenir of Their Two Campaigns in the Shenandoah Valley.   Wraps.
> 1883   Boston   50.00

SHERIDAN, Philip Henry   Citizens of Albany and the State of New York, Unveiling of the Equestrian Statue of General Philip H. Sheridan.
> 1916   New York   30.00

SHERIDAN, Philip Henry   Personal Memoirs.   2 Vols.
> 1888   New York   75.00
> 1891   1 Vol. ed.   50.00
> 1902   New York   2 Vols.   40.00

SHERIDAN, Philip Henry   Report of Operations of the Army of the Shenandoah from Aug. 4, 1864 to Feb. 27, 1865. Wraps.
n.d.   n.p.   30.00

SHERIDAN, Philip Henry   Report of Operations of the Cavalry Corps Army of the Potomac from April 6 to August 4, 1864. Wraps.
n.d.   n.p.   35.00

SHERLOCK, Eli J.   Memorabilia of the Marches and Battles in Which the 100th Regiment of Indiana Infantry Volunteers Took an Active Part.
1896   Kansas City   135.00

SHERMAN, Andrew M.   In the Lowlands of Louisiana in 1863, An Address. Wraps.
1908   Morristown, NJ   60.00

SHERMAN, E. A.   The Engineer Corps of Hell; or Rome's Sappers and Miners Containing the Tactics of the Militia of the Pope. . . .
(c.1890)   100.00

SHERMAN, Henry   The Centennial of the Confederacy, The United States of America, the Situation.
1875   Washington, DC   20.00

SHERMAN, Henry   Slavery in the United States of America.
1860   Hartford   30.00

SHERMAN, John   Recollections of Forty Years in the House, Senate and Cabinet. 2 Vols.
1895   Chicago   60.00
1895   n.p.   50.00
1896   50.00

SHERMAN, John   Speech of Hon. _____ on Emancipation as a Compensation for Military Service Rendered by Slaves. Wraps.
1864   Washington, DC   25.00

SHERMAN, Sylvester M.   History of the 133rd Regiment O.V.I.
1896   Columbus   150.00

SHERMAN, William T.   Address to the Graduating Class of the U.S. Military Academy, West Point, June 15th, 1869. Wraps.
1869   New York   40.00

SHERMAN, William T.   From Atlanta to the Sea.
1961   London   20.00

SHERMAN, William T.   Home Letters of General Sherman, edited by M. A. DeWolfe Howe.
1909   New York   25.00

SHERMAN, William T.   Marching through Georgia, William T. Sherman's Personal Narratives. . . .
1978   New York   20.00

SHERMAN, William T.   Memoirs of General William T. Sherman, by Himself. 2 Vols.
1875   New York   75.00
1886   New York   75.00
1887   New York   75.00
1891   New York   2 Vols. in 1   30.00
1892   New York   75.00
1957   Bloomington, IN   2 Vols. in 1   35.00
1984   Wraps   16.00

SHERMAN, William T.   Official Account of His Great March.   Wraps.
1865   New York   80.00
SHERMAN, William T.   The   Sherman   Letters,   edited   by   Rachel
Sherman Thorndike.
1894   New York   30.00
1969   New York   20.00
SHERMAN, William T.   Story of the Grand March.   Beadle's Dime
Series. Wraps.
n.d.   New York   25.00
SHERMAN, William T.   "War Is Hell!" William T. Sherman's Personal
Narrative of His March Through Georgia, edited by Mills Lane.
1974   Savannah   30.00
SHERMAN, William T.   Who Burnt Columbia? . . .   See: Who Burnt
Columbia?
SHERRILL, Clarence O.   The Grant Memorial in Washington.
1924   Washington, DC   15.00
SHERRILL, Miles O.   A Soldier's Story: Prison Life and Other Incidents
in the War of 1861-'65.   Wraps.
(1904)   (Raleigh)   150.00
SHERRILL, Samuel W.   Heroes in Gray.   Wraps.
1909   Nashville   50.00
SHERWIN, Oscar   Prophet   of   Liberty - The   Life   and   Times   of
Wendell Phillips.
1958   New York   20.00
SHERWOOD, Isaac R.   Memories of the War.
1923   Toledo   70.00
SHIELDS, S. J.   A Chevalier of Dixie.
1907   New York   45.00
SHINGLETON, Royce Gordon   John Taylor Wood   Sea Ghost of the
Confederacy.
1979   Athens   25.00
1982   Athens   25.00
SHINGLETON, Royce Gordon   Richard Peters; Champion of the New
South.
1985   Macon, GA   20.00
SHIPPEN, E.   Thirty Years at Sea: The Story of a Sailor's Life.
1879   Philadelphia 100.00
SHOEMAKER, J. J.   Shoemaker's   Battery,   Stuart   Horse   Artilery,
Pelham's Battalion.
n.d.   Gaithersburg   20.00
SHOFNER, Jerrell H.   Nor Is It Over Yet, Florida in the Era of
Reconstruction 1863-1877.
1974   Gainesville   20.00
SHOMETTE, D. S.   Shipwrecks of the Civil War: The Encyclopedia of
Union and Confederate Naval Losses.   Wraps.
1973   Washington, DC   65.00
SHOREY, Henry A.   The Story of the Maine Fifteenth.
1890   Bridgton   135.00
Short Stories by the Old Battery Boy. (Fislar, John) Wraps.
(c.1920s)   (Venice, CA)   75.00
SHORT, Dewey   Address . . . Battle of Wilson's Creek.   Wraps.
1959   Washington, DC   15.00

SHOTWELL, Randolph Abbott   The Papers of Randolph Abbott Shotwell, edited by J. G. Hamilton. 3 Vols.
1929   Raleigh, NC   100.00
SHOTWELL, Walter Gaston   The Civil War in America. 2 Vols.
1923   London   225.00
SHOTWELL, Walter Gaston   Life of Charles Sumner.
1910   New York   20.00
SHREVE, William P.   The Story of the Third Army Corps Union.
1910   Boston   55.00
SHUMATE, Madge Bocock and MANN, Anne V.   Thomas S. Bocock -
Only Speaker of the Confederate Congress.   Wraps.
1940   Richmond   15.00
SHURTER, Edwin DuBois   Oratory of the South.
1908   New York   70.00
Sickness and Mortality of the Army During the First Year of the War.
Wraps.
1863   Washington, DC   40.00
SIDEMAN, Belle Becker and FRIEDMAN, Lillian, edited by   Europe Looks
at the Civil War, An Anthology.
1960   New York   25.00
SIEBERT, Wilbur Henry The Mysteries of Ohio's Underground Railroads.
1951   Columbus   25.00
SIEPEL, K. H.   Rebel: The Life and Times of John Singleton Mosby.
1983   New York   19.00
SIEVERS, Harry J.   Benjamin Harrison, Hoosier Warrior, 1833-1865.
1952   Chicago   35.00
1960   25.00
SIFAKIS, S.   Who Was Who in the Civil War.
1988   New York   60.00
SIGAUD, Louis A.   Belle Boyd, Confederate Spy.
1944   Richmond   40.00
1945   Richmond   30.00
SIGELSCHIFFER, Saul   The American Conscience, The Drama of the
Lincoln-Douglas Debates.
1973   New York   15.00
SIGILLOGIA   Being Some Account of the Great or Broad Seal of the
Confederate States of America.   Wraps.
1873   Washington, DC   30.00
SILBER, Irwin, compiled by   Soldier Songs and Home-Front Ballads of
the Civil War.   Wraps.
1964   New York   10.00
SILBER, Irwin, compiled and edited by   Songs of the Civil War.
1960   New York   40.00
SILBEY, Joel H.   A Respectable Minority, The Democratic Party in the
Civil War Era, 1860-1868.
1977   New York   10.00
SILLIMAN, Justus M.   A New Canaan Private in the Civil War, edited
by Edward Marcus.   Wraps.
1984   8.00
SILVER, David M.   Lincoln's Supreme Court.
1957   Urbana, IL   30.00

SILVER, James W.   Confederate Morale and Church Propaganda.   See:
   Confederate Centennial Studies, No. 3.
SILVERSTONE, P. H.   Warships of the Civil War Navies.
   1989   38.95
SIMKINS, Francis B.   A History of the South.
   1965   New York   10.00
SIMKINS, Francis B. and PATTON, James Welch   The Women of the
   Confederacy.
   1936   Richmond   50.00
SIMKINS, Francis B. and WOODY, Robert Hilliard   South   Carolina
   During Reconstruction.
   1932   Chapel Hill, NC   75.00
   1966   25.00
SIMMONS, Henry E., edited by   A Concise Encyclopedia of the Civil
   War.
   1965   New York   15.00
   1967   15.00
   1986   4.98
SIMMONS, Louis A.   The History of the 84th Regiment Illinois Vols.
   1866   Macomb   250.00
SIMMONS, William Joseph   The Klan Unmasked.
   1924   Atlanta, GA   50.00
SIMMS, Henry H.   A Decade of Sectional Controversy 1851-1861.
   1942   Chapel Hill, NC   20.00
SIMMS, Henry H.   Life of Robert M. T. Hunter.
   1935   Richmond   35.00
SIMMS, William Gilmore   Sack and Destruction of the City of Columbia,
   SC, edited by A. S. Salley.
   1937   n.p.   35.00
   1971   Freeport, NY   25.00
SIMMS, William Gilmore, edited by   War Poetry of the South.
   1866   New York   30.00
   1867   New York   30.00
SIMON, John Y.   The Personal Memoirs of Julia Dent Grant (Mrs.
   Ulysses S. Grant).
   1975   New York   25.00
SIMON, John Y.   Ulysses S. Grant Chronology.   Wraps.
   1963   n.p.   10.00
SIMONHOFF, Harry   Jewish Participants in the Civil War.
   1963   New York   40.00
SIMONS, Ezra D.   A Regimental History, The One Hundred and
   Twenty-fifth New York State Volunteers.
   1888   New York   125.00
SIMPSON, C. M.   A Good Southerner; The Life of Henry A. Wise of
   Virginia.
   1985   Chapel Hill, NC   28.00
SIMPSON, Edward   A Treatise on Ordnance and Naval Gunnery.
   1862   New York   75.00
SIMPSON, Harold B.   Brawling Brass, North and South.   Wraps.
   1960   Waco   Ltd.   30.00

SIMPSON, Harold B.   Cry Comanche   The 2nd U.S. Cavalry in Texas,
    1855-1861.
    1979   Hillsboro   40.00
    1988   17.50
SIMPSON, Harold B.   Gaines Mill to Appomattox.
    1963   Waco   50.00
    1988   16.95
SIMPSON, Harold B.   Hood's Texas Brigade: A Compendium.
    1977   Hillsboro   100.00
    1977   Hillsboro   Ltd. edition 125.00
SIMPSON, Harold B.   Hood's Texas Brigade in Reunion and Memory.
    1974   Hillsboro   100.00
    1974   Hillsboro   Ltd. ed. of 25 copies 150.00
SIMPSON, Harold B., edited by   Hood's Texas Brigade   In Poetry and
    Song.
    1968   Hillsboro   30.00
SIMPSON, Harold B.   Hood's Texas Brigade: Lee's Grenadier Guard.
    1970   Waco   75.00
    1983   25.00
SIMPSON, Harold B.   The   Marshall   Guards;   Harrison   County's
    Contribution to Hood's Texas Brigade.   Wraps.
    1967   Marshall   15.00
SIMPSON, Harold B.   The Recruiting, Training, and Camp Life of a
    Company of Hood's Brigade in Texas, 1861.   Wraps.
    1962   Waco   Ltd.   40.00
SIMPSON, Harold B.   Red Granite for Gray Heroes.
    1969   Hillsboro   Ltd. Boxed   100.00
SIMPSON, Harold B.   Simpson Speaks on History.
    1986   Hillsboro   15.00
SIMPSON, L. P.   Mind and the American Civil War: A Meditation on
    Lost Causes.
    1989   Baton Rouge   15.95
SINCLAIR, Arthur   Two Years on the Alabama.
    1895   Boston   175.00
    1896   Boston   150.00
    1989   23.95
SINCLAIR, Donald A.   The Civil War and New Jersey: A Bibliography.
    1968   New Brunswick   35.00
    Recent reprint   12.00
SINCLAIR, Harold   American Years   A Novel.
    1938   10.00
SINCLAIR, Harold   The Cavalryman.
    1958   New York   20.00
SINCLAIR, Harold   The Horse Soldiers.
    1956   New York   25.00
    1959   25.00
SINCLAIR, Peter   Freedom of Slavery in the United States.   Wraps.
    n.d.   London   45.00
SINCLAIR, Upton   Manassas.
    1904   New York   15.00
    1923   14.00

SINGLETARY, O. A.   Negro Militia and Reconstruction.
    1957   Austin   20.00
SINGMASTER, Elsie   A Boy at Gettysburg.
    1924   Boston   20.00
SINGMASTER, Elsie   Gettysburg. Stories of the Red Harvest and the Aftermath.
    1913   New York   25.00
SIPES, William B.   The 7th Pennsylvania Veteran Volunteer Cavalry.
    1905   Pottsville   120.00
    1906   Pottsville   85.00
The Sites of War The Civil War Revisited A Guide to What has been Preserved and Restored. Wraps.
    1961   Washington, DC   5.00
SITTERSON, Joseph C.   The Secession Movement in North Carolina. Wraps.
    1939   Chapel Hill, NC   20.00
SIVITER, Anna Pierpont   Recollections of War and Peace 1861-1868, edited by Charles H. Ambler.
    1938   New York   60.00
Sixteenth Regiment Connecticut Volunteers, Excursion and Reunion at Antietam Battlefield, Sept 17, 1889.
    1889   Hartford   30.00
Sixteenth Regiment Connecticut Volunteers, Report of the 23rd Annual Reunion.
    1890   Hartford   25.00
The Sixty-second Pennsylvania Volunteers in the War for the Union. Wraps.
    1889   Pittsburgh   75.00
SKELLY, Daniel A.   A Boys' Experiences During the Battles of Gettysburg. Wraps.
    1932   Gettysburg   30.00
Sketch of the Duplin Rifles. Wraps.
    1895   n.p.   125.00
A Sketch of the Life and Service of General William Ruffin Cox.
    1921   Richmond   75.00
Sketches of War History 1861-1865 Papers Read Before Ohio Commandery, Mollus. 6 Vols.
    1888-1908   Cincinnati   250.00
    Individual volumes   45.00 each
SKINKER, Thomas Keith   Samuel Skinker and His Descendants.
    1923   St. Louis   100.00
SKINNER, H., GUNTER, E., and SANDERS, W.   The New Dietz Confederate States Catalog and Handbook.
    1986   Miami   75.00
SKINNER, Otis   The Last Tragedian Booth Tells His Own Story.
    1939   New York   30.00
SLATTERY, Charles Lewis   Felix Reville Brunot 1820-1898.
    1901   New York   20.00
SLAUGHTER, Frank G.   In a Dark Garden.
    1946   New York   8.00
SLAUGHTER, Philip   A Sketch of the Life of Randolph Fairfax.
    1878   Baltimore   150.00

SLEASE, William Davis   The Fourteenth Pennsylvania Cavalry in the
   Civil War, 1861-1865.
   1915   Pittsburgh   300.00
SLOAN, Benjamin   The Merrimac and the Monitor.   Wraps.
   1926   Columbia   30.00
SLOAN, Edward W.   Benjamin Franklin Isherwood: Naval Engineer, the
   Years as Engineer in Chief 1861-69.
   1965   Annapolis   25.00
   1966   20.00
SLOAN, John A.   North Carolina in the War Between the States.   Wraps.
   1883   Washington, DC   125.00
SLOAN, John A.   Reminiscences of the Guilford Grays, Co. B 27th N.C.
   Regiment.
   1883   Washington, DC   250.00
   1978   Wendell, NC   25.00
Slocum and His Men.
   1904   75.00
SLOCUM, Charles E.   The Life and Services of Major General Henry
   Warner Slocum.
   1913   Toledo, OH   75.00
SLONAKER, John   The U. S. Army and the Negro.   Wraps.
   1971   Carlisle Barracks, PA   15.00
Small Arms 1856.
   1984   Arendtsville, PA   15.00
Small Arms Reports of Experiments with Small Arms for the Military
   Service by Officers of the Ordnance Department, U.S. Army.
   n.d.   Washington, DC   15.00
Small Arms Used by Michigan Troops in the Civil War.   Centennial
   Commission.   Wraps.
   1966   25.00
SMALL, Abner R.   The Road to Richmond, The Civil War Memoirs of
   _____ of the Sixteenth Maine Volunteers, edited by Henry A. Small.
   1939   Berkeley   50.00
   1957   Berkeley   30.00
SMALL, Abner R.   The Sixteenth Maine Regiment in the War of the
   Rebellion.
   1886   Portland   130.00
SMALL, Cassandra Morris   Letters of 1863.
   n.d.   Detroit   35.00
SMALL, William   Camp-Fire Talk on the Life and Military Services of
   Maj. Gen. Judson Kilpatrick.   Wraps.
   1887   Washington, DC   80.00
SMALLEY, George   Anglo-American Memoirs.
   1911   New York   20.00
SMART, James G.   A Radical View.   The Agate Dispatches of
   Whitelaw Reid, 1861-65. 2 Vols.
   1976   Memphis   30.00
SMEDES, Susan Dabney   Memorials of a Southern Planter.
   1887   Baltimore   40.00
   1888   Baltimore   40.00
   1889   London   50.00

1890   New York   entitled **A Southern Planter**   40.00
1956   New York   25.00
1965   New York   25.00

SMEDLEY, R. C.   **History of the Underground Railroad in Chester and the Neighboring Counties of Pennsylvania.**
1969   New York   18.00

SMILEY, David L.   **Lion of Whitehall The Life of Cassius M. Clay.**
1962   Madison, WI   30.00
1969   15.00

SMITH, A. J.   **The Light of Other Days,** edited by J. P. Watson.
1878   Dayton   20.00

SMITH, Abram P.   **History of the Seventy-sixth Regiment, New York Volunteers.**
1867   Syracuse   110.00

SMITH, Adelaide W.   **Reminiscences of an Army Nurse During the Civil War.**
1911   New York   50.00

SMITH, Arthur D. Howden   **Old Fuss and Feathers.**
1937   New York   25.00

SMITH, Benjamin T.   **Private Smith's Journal, Recollections of the Late War,** edited by Clyde C. Walton.
1963   Chicago   25.00

SMITH, C. Carter, Jr., edited by   **Two Naval Journals: 1864, The Journal of Mr. John C. O'Connell, CSN on the C.S.S. Tennessee, and The Journal of Pvt. Charles Brother, SUMC on the U.S.S. Hartford at the Battle of Mobile Bay.** Wraps.
1964   Chicago   20.00
1969   Wraps   8.00

SMITH, Cabell, Mrs.   **Forty Years with the Virginia Division U.D.C.** Wraps.
(c.1935) n.p.   25.00

SMITH, Charles H.   **Bill Arp from the Uncivil War to Date 1861-1903.**
1903   Atlanta   30.00

SMITH, Charles H.   **Bill Arp, So Called A Side Show of the Southern Side of the War.**
1866   New York   25.00

SMITH, Charles M.   **From Andersonville to Freedom.** Wraps.
1894   Providence Ltd.   30.00

SMITH, Charles H.   **The History of Fuller's Ohio Brigade, 1861-1865.**
1909   Cleveland   175.00

SMITH, Charles W.   **Life and Military Services of Brevet Major Gen. Robert S. Foster.** Wraps.
1915   Indianapolis   20.00

SMITH, D. C.   **Lilly in the Valley, Civil War at Mossy Creek.** Wraps.
1986   New Market   7.50

SMITH, Daniel E. Huger, et al, edited by   **Mason Smith Family Letters, 1860-68.**
1950   Columbia, SC   40.00

SMITH, Daniel P.   **Company K, First Alabama Regiment or Three Years in the Confederate Service.**
1984   Gaithersburg   20.00

SMITH, Donald L.   The Twenty-fourth Michigan of the Iron Brigade.
    1962   Harrisburg   60.00
    1987   30.00
    1988   30.00

SMITH, Donnal V.   Chase and Civil War Politics.
    1931   Columbus   30.00

SMITH, E. Delafield   The Peterhoff, Argument of _____ . . . in the
Case of the Prize Steamer Peterhoff, July 10, 1863.   Wraps.
    1863   New York   75.00

SMITH, Edward Conrad   The Borderland in the Civil War.
    1927   New York   30.00

SMITH, Edward Conrad   Thomas Jonathan Jackson 1824-1863.
    1920   Weston, WV   100.00

SMITH, Edward P.   Incidents Among Shot and Shell.
    1868   New York   35.00
    1869   Philadelphia   entitled   Incidents of the United States . . .
    Christian Commission.   35.00
    1871   35.00
    1888   Philadelphia   30.00

SMITH, Elbert B.   The Presidency of James Buchanan.
    1980   20.00

SMITH, Ernest A.   The History of the Confederate Treasury.
    1901   n.p.   40.00

SMITH, F. Hopkinson   The Fortunes of Oliver Horn.
    1902   New York   10.00

SMITH, Francis H.   History of the Virginia Military Institute.
    1989   Bay Shore   39.95

SMITH, Francis H.   Introductory Address to the Corps of Cadets of the
Virginia Military Institute . . . on the Resumption of Academic
Exercises.   Wraps.
    1866   Baltimore   35.00

SMITH, Francis H.   Special Report of the Superintendent of the
Virginia Military Institute.   Wraps.
    1859   Richmond   75.00

SMITH, Francis H.   The Virginia Military Institute.
    1912   Lynchburg, VA   75.00

SMITH, Gene   High Crimes and Misdemeanors The Impeachment and
Trial of Andrew Johnson.
    1977   New York   20.00

SMITH, George B.   Official Army List of the Western States for
August 1862. Wraps.
    1862   Chicago   100.00

SMITH, George G.   The Boy in Gray.
    1894   Macon   50.00
    1903   Nashville   40.00

SMITH, George G.   Leaves from a Soldier's Diary.   Wraps.
    1906   Putnam, CT   50.00

SMITH, George H.   The Positions and Movements of the Troops in the
Battle of New Market Fought May 15th, 1864. . . . Wraps.
    n.d.   n.p.   175.00

SMITH, George Winston   Medicines for the Union Army.   Wraps.
    1962   Madison, WI   15.00

SMITH, George Winston and JUDAH, Charles   Life in the North During the Civil War, A Source History.
    1966   Albuquerque   25.00
SMITH, Goldwin   The Civil War in America.
    1866   London   40.00
SMITH, Goldwin   A Letter to a Whig Member of the Southern Independence Association. Wraps.
    1864   Boston   25.00
SMITH, Gustavus W.   The Battle of Seven Pines.   Wraps.
    1891   New York   125.00
    1974   Dayton, OH 17.50
SMITH, Gustavus W.   Confederate War Papers.
    1884   New York   100.00
SMITH, Gustavus W.   Generals J. E. Johnston and G. T. Beauregard at the Battle of Manassas. Wraps.
    1892   New York   50.00
SMITH, H.   Lincoln and the Lincolns.
    1931   New York   20.00
SMITH, Hampden Harris   J. E. B. Stuart - A Character Sketch.   Wraps.
    (c.1933)   Ashland, VA   60.00
SMITH, Hampden Harris   Jefferson Davis - A Character Sketch.   Wraps.
    (c.1920)   Blackstone, VA   30.00
SMITH, Hampden Harris   Robert E. Lee - A Character Sketch.   Wraps.
    (c.1900)   n.p.   30.00
SMITH, Hampden Harris   Stonewall Jackson - A Character Sketch. Wraps.
    (c.1920)   Blackstone, VA   40.00
SMITH, Harry Allen   The Rebel Yell.
    1954   Garden City, NY   15.00
SMITH, Harry King, Jr.   Some Encounters with General Forrest. Wraps.
    (c.1956) n.p.   30.00
SMITH, Henry B.   Between the Lines. Secret Service Stories Told Fifty Years After.
    1911   New York   90.00
SMITH, Henry I.   History of the Seventh Iowa Veteran Volunteer Infantry During the Civil War.
    1903   Mason City   250.00
SMITH, J. H., compiled by   From Out of the Ashes . . . 1864.
    1964   25.00
SMITH, James E.   A Famous Battery and Its Campaigns . . . The Career of Corporal James Tanner.
    1892   Washington, DC   90.00
SMITH, James Power   General Lee at Gettysburg. A Paper Read Before the Military Historical Society of Massachusetts. . . . Wraps.
    (1905)   Richmond   60.00
SMITH, James Power   The Religious Character of Stonewall Jackson: An Address. Wraps.
    n.d.   Lexington, VA   25.00

SMITH, James Power   Stonewall Jackson and Chancellorsville   A Paper Read Before the Military Historical Society of Massachusetts. . . . Wraps.
1904   Richmond   75.00

SMITH, James Power   With Stonewall Jackson in the Army of Northern Virginia..
1982   Gaithersburg   30.00

SMITH, Jo D.   History of High Bridge.   Wraps.
1987   Richmond   4.75

SMITH, John Day   The History of the Nineteenth Regiment of Maine Volunteer Infantry, 1862-1865.
1909   Minneapolis   100.00
1988   35.00

SMITH, John L.   Antietam to Appomattox with the 118th Pa. Volunteers.
1892   Philadelphia   75.00

SMITH, John L.   History of the 118th Pennsylvania Volunteers - the Corn Exchange Regiment.
1905   Philadelphia   125.00

SMITH, John L., compiled by   History of the Corn Exchange Regiment, 118th Pennsylvania Volunteers.
1888   Philadelphia   125.00

SMITH, John Thomas   A History of the Thirty-first Regiment of Indiana Volunteer Infantry in the War of the Rebellion.
1900   Cincinnati   125.00

SMITH, Joseph A.   An Address Delivered Before the Union League of Philadelphia.   Wraps.
1906   Philadelphia   25.00

SMITH, Joshua   Map and Description of the Main Battlefields, Routes, Camps and Headquarters in the Gettysburg, Wilderness and Appomattox Campaigns.
1900   Chicago   200.00

SMITH, K.   Virginia Military Institute During the War Between the States.   Wraps.
1938   Orange   10.00

SMITH, Myron J., Jr.   American Civil War Navies: A Bibliography.
1972   Metuchen   30.00

SMITH, P. A. L.   Boyhood Memories of Fauquier.
1926   Richmond   25.00

SMITH, Page   Trial by Fire: A People's History of the Civil War and Reconstruction.
1982   New York   30.00

SMITH, Ralph J.   Co. K 2nd Texas Infantry: Reminiscences of the Civil War and Other Sketches.
1962   Waco   Ltd.   40.00

SMITH, Richard H.   Organization of the Protestant Episcopal Church of the Confederate States, A.D. 1861, and Its Reunion with the Protestant Episcopal Church in the United States.   Wraps.
1882   Weldon, NC   50.00

SMITH, Rixey and BEASLEY, Norman   Carter Glass, a Biography.
1939   New York and Toronto   20.00

SMITH, Robert G.   Brief Account of the Services Rendered by the
Second Regiment Delaware Volunteers in the War. Wraps.
1909   Wilmington, DE   45.00

SMITH, S. A. and SMITH, C. C., Jr., edited by   Mobile: 1861-1865   Notes
& Bibliography. Wraps.
1964   Chicago and Mobile   10.00

SMITH, S. E. D.   The Soldier's Friend.
1867   Memphis, TN   80.00

SMITH, Mrs. S. L., compiled by North Carolina's Confederate Monuments
and Memorials.
1941   Raleigh   50.00

SMITH, Stephen   Hand-Book of Surgical Operations.
1863   300.00

SMITH, Sydney K.   Life, Army Record, and Public Services of D.
Howard Smith.
1890   Louisville, KY   250.00

SMITH, Thomas C.   Here's Yer Mule, The Diary of _____.
1958   Waco   Ltd.   60.00

SMITH, Thomas West   The Story of a Cavalry Regiment: "Scott's 900"
Eleventh New York Cavalry.
1897   Chicago   150.00

SMITH, Timothy L.   Revivalism and Social Reform.
1976   12.00

SMITH, Tunstall   James McHenry Howard A Memoir.
1915   Baltimore   175.00

SMITH, W.   A Political History of Slavery. 2 Vols.
1903   New York   60.00

SMITH, W. C.   The Private in Gray: Written by a Private, "Not an
Officer, Only One of the Men."
n.d.   n.p.   300.00

SMITH, Walter George   Life & Letters of Thomas Kilby Smith.
1898   New York   90.00

SMITH, Willard H.   Schuyler Colfax: The Changing Fortunes of a
Political Idol.
1952   Indianapolis   23.00

SMITH, William   The History and Debates of the Convention of the
People of Alabama.
1975   Spartanburg, SC   25.00

SMITH, William A.   Lectures on the Philosophy and Practice of Slavery
. . . in the United States: with the Duties of Masters to Slaves.
1856   Nashville   75.00

SMITH, William Alexander   The Anson Guards, Co. C, 14th Regt N.C.
Vols. 1861-1865.
1914   Charlotte   350.00
1978   Wendell, NC   30.00

SMITH, William B.   On Wheels and How I Came There.
1892   New York   75.00
1893   New York   55.00

SMITH, William Ernest   The Francis Preston Blair Family in Politics.
2 Vols.
1969   New York   60.00

SMITH, William F.   From Chattanooga to Petersburg.
1893   Boston   35.00
SMITH, William R.   The History and Debates of the Convention of the People of Alabama.
1975   Spartanburg, SC   20.00
SMITH, Winston O.   The Sharp's Rifle: Its History, Development and Operation.
1943   New York   50.00
SMITHE, George C.   Glimpses: of Places, and People, and Things, Extracts from Published Correspondence and Other Writings   1861-1886.
1887   Ypsilanti, MI   50.00
SMYTHE, Mrs. A. T., POPPENHEIM, Miss M. B., and TAYLOR, Mrs. Thomas, edited by   South Carolina Women in the Confederacy.
2 Vols.
1903   Columbia, SC   150.00
1907   Columbia, SC   150.00
SMYTHE, Augustine T., Jr.   Torpedo and Submarine Attacks on the Federal Blockading Fleet off Charleston During the War of Secession. Wraps.
1907   VA   40.00
SNEAD, Thomas L.   The Fight for Missouri.
1886   New York   60.00
1888   New York   40.00
SNETSINGER, Robert J., edited by   Kiss Clara for Me: The Story of Joseph Whitney and His Family, Early Days in the Midwest, and Soldiering in the American Civil War.
1969   PA   25.00
SNIDER, Denton   The American Ten Years War 1855-1865.
1906   St. Louis   25.00
SNIDER, Denton   Lincoln and Ann Rutledge.
1912   St. Louis   15.00
SNOW, William P.   Southern Generals.
1865   New York   75.00
1866   New York   60.00
1867   New York   entitled Lee and His Generals. 60.00
1982   15.00
SNOWDEN, Yates   Confederate Books.
1903   Charleston, SC   75.00
SNOWDEN, Yates   Marching with Sherman. Wraps.
1929   Columbia, SC   50.00
SNOWDEN, Yates   War-Time Publications (1861-1865) from the Press of Walker, Evans and Cogswell Co., Charleston, SC. Wraps.
1922   Charleston, SC   75.00
SNYDER, Anne E.   The Civil War from a Southern Stand-Point.
1893   Nashville   45.00
SNYDER, Anne E.   A Narrative of the Civil War.
1899   Nashville   40.00
SOBIESKI, John   Life Story and Personal Reminiscences of Col. John Sobieski.
1900   Shelbyville, IL   60.00
n.d.   Los Angeles   50.00

SOBOL, Donald J.   The Lost Dispatch A Story of Antietam.
   1958   New York   25.00
SOBOL, Donald J.   Two Flags Flying.
   1960   New York   30.00
Society of the Army of the Cumberland, Reunions.
   v.d.   v.p.   15.00 each
Society of the Army of the Potomac, Annual Reunions.
   v.d.   v.p.   10.00 each
Society of the Army of the Tennessee, Reunions.
   v.d.   v.p.   20.00 each
Society of the Army of West Virginia, Proceedings of Meetings.
   v.d.   v.p.   30.00 each
Society of the 74th Volunteer Infantry, Reunion Proceedings and History of
   the Regiment.
   1903   Rockford   150.00
SOKOLOFF, Alice Hunt   Kate Chase for the Defense.
   1971   New York   15.00
The Soldier of Indiana in the War for the Union. (Merrill, Catharine)
   1866   Indianapolis   100.00
   1869   Indianapolis   100.00
Soldier's Aid Society of Northern Ohio, Annual Reports.
   v.d.   v.p.   15.00 each
Soldiers' and Citizens' Album of Biographical Record Containing Personal
   Sketches of Army Men and Citizens Prominent in Loyalty to the Union.
   2 Vols.
   1888-90   Chicago   125.00
The Soldier's Casket. Vol. 1 (all pub) Jan-Dec 1865.
   1865   Philadelphia   150.00
Soldier's Hymns and Psalms.
   (c.1862) New York   50.00
Soldiers' National Cemetery (Gettysburg), Report of.
   1864   Harrisburg   35.00
Soldiers' National Cemetery (Gettysburg), Revised Report.
   1867   Harrisburg   35.00
   1988   12.95
The Soldier's Pocket Manual of Devotions.
   1861   Philadelphia   40.00
Soldiers of Florida. In the Seminole Indian-Civil-Spanish American Wars.
   1983   45.00
SOLEY, James R.   Admiral Porter.
   For additional information, see Appendix: Great Commanders Series.
   1903   New York   30.00
   1903   New York   Ltd.   125.00
SOLEY, James R.   The Blockade and the Cruisers.   See: Campaigns
   of the Civil War.
SOLEY, James R.   The Sailor Boys of '61.
   1888   Boston   50.00
SOLOMON, Eric, edited by   Faded Banners.
   1960   New York   30.00
SOLVICK, Stanley   Let the Drum Beat.
   1988   25.00

SOMERS, Robert The Southern States Since the War 1870-71.
1871 London 125.00
SOMMERS, Richard J. Richmond Redeemed, The Siege at Petersburg.
1981 Garden City, NY 27.50
SORREL, G. Moxley Recollections of a Confederate Staff Officer.
1905 New York 150.00
1917 New York 75.00
1958 Jackson, TN, edited by Bell I. Wiley 40.00
1978 Dayton 30.00
1987 Wilmington, NC 30.00
SOSEY, Frank H. Robert Devoy: A Tale of the Palmyra Massacre.
1903 Palmyra, MO 75.00
SOUDER, Mrs. Edmund A. Leaves from the Battlefield of Gettysburg.
1864 Philadelphia 50.00
The South Besieged. See: DAVIS, William C. The Image of War, 1861-1865.
South Carolina - Confederate Military History. See: Confederate Military History, Vol. V (Vol. VI, 1987 reprint ed.).
"Southern Battlefields," A List of Battlefields on and Near the the Lines of the Nashville, Chattanooga and St. Louis Railway and Western and Atlantic Railroad. Wraps.
(c. 1890) Atlanta 35.00
1906 Nashville 30.00
Southern Bivouac, A Monthly Literary and Historical Magazine.
10.00 per issue.
Vols. 1-2 175.00 each
Vols. 3-9 150.00 each
Southern Famine Relief Fund of Philadelphia.
1867 Philadelphia 25.00
Southern Historical Society Papers. Vols. 1-52. Wraps.
1876-1959 Bound w/wraps bound in 1500.00
1977 reprint bound 1400.00
Individual issues 10.00-20.00 depending on content
1980 Index 150.00
Southern Historical Society, Proceedings of the 2nd Annual Meeting Held in Richmond. Wraps.
1874 Richmond 30.00
Southern Revenge. Civil War History of Chambersburg, PA.
1989 28.95
SOUTHWICK, Thomas P. A Duryee Zouave.
1930 Washington, DC 70.00
SOUTHWOOD, Marion "Beauty and Booty" The Watchword of New Orleans.
1867 New York 40.00
Souvenir Memorial, Col. James C. Carmichael, 157th Regt. N.Y.S.V.
(1891) n.p. 40.00
Souvenir of Excursion to Antietam and Dedication of Monuments of the 8th, 11th, 14th, and 16th Regiments of Connecticut Volunteers. Wraps.
1894 35.00
A Souvenir of the Unveiling of the Richmond Howitzer Monument of Richmond, Va., Dec. 13, 1892.
1893 Richmond 90.00

Souvenir Views of Gettysburg, Pa. Wraps.
  (c.1900) (Gettysburg) 25.00
SPANGLER, Edward W. My Little War Experience with Historical Sketches and Memorabilia.
  1904   York   75.00
SPARKS, A. W. Recollections of the Great War.
  1987   Longview, TX 22.50
SPARKS, A. W. The War Between the States as I Saw It.
  1901   Tyler   400.00
SPAULDING, E. G. History of the Legal Tender Paper Money Issued During the Great Rebellion.
  1869   Buffalo 50.00
SPEAR, William E. The North and South at Antietam and Gettysburg.
  1908   Boston   35.00
SPEARS, Zarel C. and BARTON, Robert S. Berry and Lincoln Frontier Merchants.
  1947   New York   10.00
Special Committee on Volunteering . . . In Filling the Quota of the County of N. Y. 1864 for 500,000 Men.
  1864   New York   50.00
Special Military History of Ohio, Hardesty's Historical and Geographical Encyclopedia.
  1885   New York   160.00
SPEED, James James Speed A Personality.
  1914   Louisville   35.00
  n.d.   n.p.   30.00
SPEED, James Opinion on the Constitutional Power of the Military to Try and Execute the Assassins of the President. Wraps.
  1865   Washington, DC   40.00
SPEED, Thomas The Union Cause in Kentucky 1860-1865.
  1907   New York   75.00
SPEED, Thomas, KELLY, Robert M., and PIRTLE, Alfred The Union Regiments of Kentucky.
  1897   Louisville   250.00
SPEER, Emory Lincoln, Lee, Grant and Other Biographical Addresses.
  1909   New York   60.00
SPEER, John Life of Gen. James H. Lane.
  1896   Garden City 50.00
SPEESE, Andrew J. Story of Companies H, A, and C, 3rd Pa. Cavalry at Gettysburg, July 3, 1863.
  1906   Germantown   75.00
SPENCE, James The American Union.
  1861   London   50.00
  1862   London   40.00
SPENCER, Ambrose A Narrative of Andersonville.
  1866   New York   50.00
SPENCER, Bella Z. Tried and True.
  1868   Springfield 30.00
SPENCER, Carrie Esther, edited by A Civil War Marriage in Virginia: Reminiscences and Letters, compiled by Carrie Esther Spencer, Bernard Samuels and Walter Berry Samuels.
  1956   Boyce   50.00

SPENCER, Cornelia Phillips   The Last Ninety Days of the War in North Carolina.
1866   New York   125.00
SPENCER, Ivor   The Victor and the Spoils: A Life of William L. Marcy.
1959   20.00
SPENCER, John W.   The Confederate Guns of Navarro County.
1984   Corsicana   Ltd.   20.00
SPENCER, John W.   From Corsicana to Appomattox: The Story of the Corsicana Invincibles and the Navarro Rifles.
1984   Corsicana   18.00
SPENCER, John W.   Terrell's Texas Cavalry, The Wild Horsemen of the Plains in the Civil War.
1982   Burnett, TX   13.00
SPENCER, Warren F.   The Confederate Navy in Europe.
1983   University, AL   20.00
SPERRY, Andrew F.   History of the 33d Iowa Infantry Volunteer Regiment.
1866   Des Moines   225.00
1984   30.00
SPICER, William A.   The Flag Replaced on Sumter.   Wraps.
1885   Providence   25.00
SPICER, William A.   History of the 9th and 10th Regiments Rhode Island Volunteers and the 10th Rhode Island Battery.
1892   Providence   60.00
SPRAGUE, Dean   Freedom Under Lincoln.
1965   Boston   7.00
SPRAGUE, Homer B.   History of the 13th Infantry Regiment of Connecticut Volunteers.
1867   Hartford   110.00
SPRAGUE, Homer B.   Lights and Shadows in Confederate Prisons, A Personal Experience 1864-1865.
1915   New York   75.00
SPRAGUE, J. T.   The Treachery in Texas.   The Secession of Texas.   Wraps.
1862   New York   50.00
SPRENGER, George F.   Concise History of the Camp and Field Life of the 122nd Regiment Penna. Volunteers.
1885   Lancaster   150.00
SPRING, Leverett W.   Kansas: The Prelude to the War for the Union.
1885   Boston   30.00
1888   25.00
SPRUANCE, John S.   Delaware Stays in the Union: The Civil War Period: 1860-1865.   Wraps.
1955   Newark   15.00
SPRUILL, F. S.   A Sketch of the Life and Service of General William R. Cox.
1921   Richmond   60.00
SPRUNT, James   Chronicles of the Cape Fear River 1660-1916.
1914   Raleigh, NC   200.00
1916   Raleigh, NC   revised and enlarged   250.00

SPRUNT, James   Derelicts,   An Account of Ships Lost at Sea . . . and a Brief History of Blockade Runners Stranded Along the North Carolina Coast 1861-1865.
    1920   Wilmington, NC   250.00
SPRUNT, James   Tales and Traditions of the Lower Cape Fear   1661-1896.   Wraps.
    1896   Wilmington, NC   100.00
SPRUNT, James   Tales of the Cape Fear.
    1960   Wilmington, NC   Ltd.   45.00
SPURLIN, Charles   West of the Mississippi with Waller's 13th Texas Cavalry Battalion.   Wraps.
    1971   Hillsboro   40.00
SQUIRER, Ephraim   See: LESLIE, Frank
SQUIRES, William Henry Tappey   The Days of Yesteryear: A Sketch Book of Virginia.
    1928   Portsmouth   Ltd.   50.00
SQUIRES, William Henry Tappey   The Land of Decision.
    1931   Portsmouth, VA   60.00
SQUIRES, William Henry Tappey   Unleashed at Long Last, Reconstruction in Virginia April 9, 1865 - Jan 26, 1870.
    1939   Portsmouth   Ltd.   55.00
St. Valentine, Planting the Guns on Kennesaw, A Poem.   Wraps.
    n.d.   n.p.   10.00
STACKPOLE, Edward J.   Chancellorsville.
    1958   Harrisburg   30.00
    Recent reprint   20.00
    1989   Wraps   12.95
STACKPOLE, Edward J.   Drama on the Rappahannock, The Fredericksburg Campaign.
    1957   Harrisburg   25.00
    Recent reprint   20.00
STACKPOLE, Edward J.   From Cedar Mountain to Antietam.
    1959   Harrisburg   35.00
STACKPOLE, Edward J.   Sheridan in the Shenandoah.
    1961   Harrisburg   30.00
    Recent reprint   20.00
STACKPOLE, Edward J.   They Met at Gettysburg.
    1956   Harrisburg   30.00
    1982   Wraps   13.00
STACKPOLE, Edward J. and NYE, Wilbur S.   The Battle of Gettysburg A Guided Tour.   Wraps.
    1960   Harrisburg   30.00
STAFFORD, David W.   In Defense of the Flag, A True War Story.   Wraps.
    1912   Warren   50.00
    1915   Warren   40.00
    1917   Erie   40.00
STAFFORD, Frederick H.   Medals of Honor Awarded for Distinguished Service During the War of the Rebellion.   Wraps.
    1886   Washington, DC   35.00

STAMPP, Kenneth M.   And the War Came The North and the Secession Crisis 1860-1861.
    1950   Baton Rouge   20.00
    1964   Chicago   Wraps   8.00
    1967   Baton Rouge   20.00
    1970   Baton Rouge   Wraps   8.00
STAMPP, Kenneth M., edited by   Causes of the Civil War. Wraps.
    1965   Englewood Cliffs, NJ   8.00
    1974   Englewood Cliffs, NJ   15.00
STAMPP, Kenneth M.   The Era of Reconstruction 1865-1877.
    1965   New York   25.00
STAMPP, Kenneth M.   The Imperiled Union - Essays on Background of Civil War. Wraps.
    1980   New York   9.00
STAMPP, Kenneth M.   The Peculiar Institution Slavery in the Anti-Bellum South.
    1956   New York   25.00
    1963   25.00
    1982   17.50
STAMPP, Kenneth M.   The Southern Road to Appomattox. Wraps.
    1969   El Paso, TX   15.00
STAMPP, Kenneth M. and LITWACK, L. F., edited by   Reconstruction, Anthology. Wraps.
    1976   12.00
STANARD, Beverly   Letters of a New Market Cadet, edited by John G. Barrett and Robert K. Turner, Jr.
    1961   Chapel Hill, NC   25.00
    1988   14.00
STANARD, Mary Newton   John Brockenbrough Newton. Wraps.
    1924   Richmond   50.00
STANARD, Mary Newton   Richmond, Its People and Its Story.
    1923   Philadelphia   40.00
STANDARD, Diffee William   Columbus, Georgia, in the Confederacy.
    1954   New York   25.00
Standing Orders of a Regiment of Volunteers for Its Regulation and Government in the Field and in Camp. Wraps.
    1862   Wilkes-Barre, PA   100.00
STANFORD, Edward   Stanford's New Hand-map of the United States . . . Showing the Boundary of the Seceding States. . . .
    1861   London   100.00
STANLEY, Caroline Abbot   Order No. 11: A Tale of the Border.
    1904   New York   10.00
STANLEY, D. S.   Personal Memoirs of Major-General D. S. Stanley, U.S.A.
    1987   Gaithersburg   25.00
STANLEY, F.   The Civil War in New Mexico.
    1960   New York   45.00
    1960   Denver   35.00
STANLEY, F.   E. V. Sumner Major General U. S. Army.
    1969   n.p.   55.00

STANLEY, R. H. and HALL, George O.   Eastern Maine and the Rebellion.
  1887   Bangor   80.00
STANTON, D., BERQIOST, G., and BOWERS, P., edited by   The Civil War Reminiscences of General M. Jeff Thompson.
  1988   24.95
STANTON, Henry T.   Poems of the Confederacy.
  1900   Louisville, KY   35.00
STANTON, R. L.   The Church and the Rebellion.
  1864   New York   70.00
STANYAN, John Minot   History of the Eighth Regiment, New Hampshire Volunteers.
  1892   Concord   100.00
STAPLES, Thomas S.   Reconstruction in Arkansas 1862-1874.
  1923   New York   75.00
  1964   25.00
STARK, Richard B. and STARK, Janet C.   Surgical Care of the Confederate States Army.   Wraps.
  1958   n.p.   40.00
STARR, Darius   From Spotsylvania Courthouse to Andersonville: A Diary of _____, edited by E. Merton Coulter.   Wraps.
  1957   Savannah, GA   20.00
STARR, Frederick, Jr.   The Loyal Soldier, A Discourse . . . at the Funeral of Major John Barnet Sloan.   Wraps.
  1864   Penn Yan   35.00
STARR, John W., Jr.   Lincoln and the Railroads.
  1927   New York   30.00
STARR, John W., Jr.   Lincoln's Last Day.
  1922   New York   20.00
STARR, Louis M.   Bohemian Brigade, Civil War Newsmen in Action.
  1954   New York   25.00
STARR, Stephen Z.   Colonel Grenfell's Wars - The Life of a Soldier of Fortune.
  1971   Baton Rouge   25.00
STARR, Stephen Z.   Jennison's Jayhawkers.
  1973   Baton Rouge   30.00
STARR, Stephen Z.   The Union Cavalry in the Civil War. 2 Vols.
  1979-81   Baton Rouge   75.00
STARR, Thomas I., edited by   Lincoln's Kalamazoo Address Against Extending Slavery.
  1941   Detroit   Ltd.   20.00
Stars and Stripes in Rebeldom.   See: BATES, William C.
State Historical Markers of Virginia; Listing the Inscriptions on All Such Markers on the Principal Highways of Virginia, with Supplementary Data.   Wraps.
  1948   Richmond   9.00
State of New York, Fiftieth Anniversary of the Battle of Gettysburg 1913.
  1916   Albany   50.00
The State of Sovereignty Record of Massachusetts by a Son of Norfolk.   Wraps.
  1872   Norfolk   20.00

A Statement of the Case of Brigadier Gen. Joseph W. Revere. Wraps.
   1863   New York   40.00

A Statement of the Causes Which Led to the Dismissal of Surgeon General William A. Hammond from the Army. Wraps.
   (c.1870) n.p.   50.00

Statement of the Disposition of Some of the Bodies of Deceased Union Soldiers and Prisoners of War Whose Remains Have Been Removed to National Cemeteries in the Southern and Western States. Wraps.
   1868   Washington, DC   60.00

Statements Made by the Alleged Lincoln Conspirators Under Examination, 1865.
   1980   n.p.   20.00

Statistical Pocket Manual of the Army, Navy and Census of the United States of America.
   1862   Boston   60.00

STATON, Kate E., edited by   Old Southern Songs of the Period of the Confederacy; the Dixie Trophy Collection: Tarboro, N.C.   Wraps.
   1926   New York   80.00

STAUDENRAUS, P. J.   Mr. Lincoln's Washington.
   1967   S. Brunswick   15.00

STAUDENRAUS, P. J., edited by   The Secession Crisis, 1860-1861. Wraps.
   1963   Chicago   10.00

STAUFFER, W. H., et al   Seven Fateful Days of 1865; The Story of Gen. R. E. Lee's Retreat from Petersburg to Appomattox, VA, April 2-9, 1865. Wraps.
   1962   Farmville   25.00

STEARNS, Albert   Reminiscences of the Late War.
   1881   Brooklyn   65.00

STEARNS, Amanda Akin   The Lady Nurse of Ward E.
   1909   New York   50.00

STEARNS, Amos E.   Narrative of _____ A Prisoner at Andersonville. Wraps.
   1887   Worcester   50.00

STEARNS, Austin C.   Three Years with Company K, Sergt. Austin C. Stearns Company K, 13th Mass. Infantry (Deceased), edited by Arthur A. Kent.
   1976   Rutherford   25.00

STEARNS, Charles   The Black Man of the South and the Rebels.
   1872   New York   60.00
   1969   Millwood   15.00

STEARNS, Frank Preston   The Life and Public Services of George Luther Stearns.
   1907   Philadelphia   20.00

STEARNS, William Augustus   A Memorial to Adjutant Stearns.
   1862   Boston   15.00

STEDMAN, Charles Ellery   The Civil War Sketchbook of _____, Surgeon U.S. Navy.
   1976   San Rafael, CA   30.00

STEDMAN, Edmund C.   The Battle of Bull Run.   Wraps.
   1861   New York   75.00

STEED, Hal   Georgia, Unfinished State.
    1976   10.00
STEEL, Edward M., Jr.   T. Butler King of Georgia.
    1964   Athens, GA   15.00
STEEL, S. A.   Explaining of Objection to "Rebel."   Wraps.
    1913   Richmond   25.00
STEEL, S. A.   The Sunny Road: Home Life in Dixie During the War. Wraps.
    n.d.   n.p.   75.00
STEELE, James Columbus   Sketches of the Civil War Especially of Companies A, C, and H, from Iredell County, N.C., and the 4th N.C. Regimental Band.   Wraps.
    1921   Statesville, NC   650.00
STEELE, James W.   The Battle of the Blue of the Second Regiment, K.S.M., Oct. 22 1864.
    1896   Chicago   90.00
STEELE, Matthew Forney   American Campaigns.   2 Vols.
    1909   Washington, DC   75.00
    1922   Washington, DC   75.00
    1935   Washington, DC   75.00
    1951   Washington, DC   80.00
STEELE, Matthew Forney   Atlas to Accompany Steele's American Campaigns, edited by V. J. Esposito.
    1945   n.p.   50.00
    1953   West Point   50.00
STEERE, Edward   The Wilderness Campaign.
    1960   Harrisburg, PA   35.00
    1987   30.00
STEFFEN, Randy   The Horse Soldier.   4 Vols.
    1979-85   Norman, OK
    Vol. I   30.00
    Vol. II   30.00
    Vol. III   30.00
    Vol. IV   30.00
STEFFEN, Randy   United States Military Saddles, 1812-1943.
    1987   Norman   22.95
    Recent reprint   Wraps   14.95.
STEGEMAN, John F.   These Men She Gave: The Civil War Diary of Athens, Georgia.
    1964   Athens   25.00
STEINER, Bernard C.   Life of Henry Winter Davis.
    1916   Baltimore   40.00
STEINER, Bernard C.   Life of Reverdy Johnson.
    1914   Baltimore   55.00
STEINER, Lewis H.   Report of Lewis H. Steiner, M.D. Inspector of the Sanitary Commission, Containing a Diary Kept During the Rebel Occupation of Frederick, MD, and an Account of the Operations of the U.S. Sanitary Commission. . . . Wraps.
    1862   140.00
STEINER, Paul E.   Disease in the Civil War: Natural Biological Warfare.
    1968   Springfield   75.00

STEINER, Paul E.   Medical-Military Portraits of Union and Confederate Generals.
1968   Philadelphia   50.00
STEINER, Paul E.   Physician-Generals in the Civil War.
1966   Springfield   55.00
STEINMETZ, Lee, edited by   The Poetry of the American Civil War.
1960   East Lansing   12.00
STELLE, Abel Clarkson   1861 to 1865 Memoirs of the Civil War, the 31st Regiment Wisconsin Volunteer Infantry.   Wraps.
1904   New Albany   110.00
A Stenographic Report of the Proceedings of the Constitutional Convention Held in Atlanta, Ga., 1877.
1877   Atlanta   45.00
STEPHENS, Alexander H.   A Compendium of the History of the United States from the Earliest Settlements to 1872.
1880   New York and Columbia, SC   150.00
STEPHENS, Alexander H.   A Constitutional View of the Late War Between the States.
1868-70 Philadelphia   2 Vols.   100.00
✓1868   Philadelphia   2 Vols. in 1   60.00
STEPHENS, Alexander H.   A Letter for Posterity: Alex Stephens to His Brother Linton June 3, 1864. Wraps.
1954   Atlanta   7.00
STEPHENS, Alexander H.   Recollections of Alexander H. Stephens, edited by Myrta Lockett Avary.
1910   New York   50.00
STEPHENS, Alexander H.   The Reviewers Reviewed. A Supplement to the War Between the States.
1872   New York   60.00
STEPHENS, Thomas   A New System of Broad and Small Sword Exercise Comprising the Broad Sword Exercise of Cavalry and Artillery. . . .
1861   Milwaukee, WI   150.00
STEPHENSON, Mary Harriet   Dr. B. F. Stephenson - Founder of the Grand Army of the Republic.
1894   Springfield   40.00
STEPHENSON, Nathaniel W.   Abraham Lincoln and the Union.
1918   New Haven   10.00
STEPHENSON, Nathaniel W.   The Day of the Confederacy.
1919   New Haven   15.00
STEPHENSON, Nathaniel W.   Lincoln.
1922   Indianapolis   10.00
1924   Indianapolis   10.00
STEPHENSON, Nathaniel W.   The Question of Arming the Slaves. Wraps.
1913   n.p.   20.00
STEPHENSON, R. Randolph, M.D.   The Southern Side; or, Andersonville Prison.
1876   Baltimore   125.00
STEPHENSON, Richard W., compiled by   Civil War Maps An Annotated List of Maps and Atlases in the Map Collections of the Library of Congress. Wraps.
1961   Washington, DC   20.00

STEPHENSON, Wendell Holmes   The Political Career of General James H. Lane. Contained in Kansas State Hist. Society Pubs. Vol. III, 1930.
1930   Topeka, KS   20.00
STEPHENSON, Wendell Holmes   The South Lives in History.
1955   Baton Rouge   25.00
STEPP, John W. and HILL, I. William, edited by   Mirror of War.
1961   Englewood Cliffs, NJ   20.00
STERKX, H. E.   Partners in Rebellion: Alabama Women in the Civil War.
1970   Rutherford, NJ   30.00
STERKX, H. E.   Some Notable Alabama Women During the Civil War. Wraps.
1962   University, AL   25.00
STERLING, Ada   See: CLAY-CLOPTON, Virginia
STERLING, James T.   Personal Experiences of the Early Days of 1861. Wraps.
1892   Detroit   35.00
STERLING, Pound   See: MAXSON, William P.
STERN, Philip Van Doren, edited by   The Annotated Uncle Tom's Cabin.
1964   New York   20.00
STERN, Philip Van Doren, edited by   The Civil War Christmas Album.
1961   New York   25.00
STERN, Philip Van Doren   The Confederate Navy: A Pictorial History.
1962   New York   30.00
Recent reprint   20.00
STERN, Philip Van Doren   Drums of Morning.
1942   New York   10.00
STERN, Philip Van Doren   An End to Valor, The Last Days of the Civil War.
1958   Boston   40.00
Recent reprint   25.00
STERN, Philip Van Doren   The Man Who Killed Lincoln.
1939   New York   20.00
STERN, Philip Van Doren   Prologue to Sumter.
1961   Bloomington, IN   20.00
STERN, Philip Van Doren   Robert E. Lee, The Man and the Soldier.
1963   New York   15.00
STERN, Philip Van Doren   Secret Missions of the Civil War.
1959   Chicago   40.00
1959   New York   30.00
1960   22.50
STERN, Philip Van Doren   Soldier Life in the Union and Confederate Armies.
1961   Bloomington, IN   25.00
1961   New York   25.00
STERN, Philip Van Doren   They Were There, The Civil War in Action as Seen by Its Combat Artists.
1959   New York   40.00
STERN, Philip Van Doren   When the Guns Roared - World Aspects of the American Civil War.
1965   New York   20.00

STEVENS, C. A.　　The Battle of Gettysburg.　Wraps.
　　1982　　10.00

STEVENS, C. A.　　Berdan's United States Sharpshooters in the Army of the Potomac.
　　1892　　St. Paul, MN　　175.00
　　1972　　Dayton　30.00
　　1984　　30.00

STEVENS, Edwin A.　　The Stevens Battery, Memorial to Congress.
　　(c.1861) n.p.　100.00

STEVENS, George T.　　Three Years in the Sixth Corps.
　　1866　　Albany　100.00
　　1867　　New York　　75.00
　　1984　　25.00

STEVENS, Hazard　　The Battle of Cedar Creek.　Wraps.
　　1987　　10.00

STEVENS, Hazard　　The Life of Isaac Ingalls Stevens.　2 Vols.
　　1900　　Boston　75.00

STEVENS, Henry S.　　Souvenir of Excursion of Battlefields by Society of Fourteenth Connecticut Regiment . . . 1891.
　　1893　　Washington, DC　75.00

STEVENS, John Austin　　Union Defense Committee of the City of New York.
　　1885　　New York　　50.00

STEVENS, John W.　　Reminiscences of the Civil War.
　　1902　　Hillsboro　　750.00
　　1982　　Powhatan　　20.00
　　1984　　20.00

STEVENS, Joseph E.　　America's National Battlefield Parks.
　　1990　　University, OK　　28.95

STEVENS, William B.　　History of the Fiftieth Regiment of Infantry Massachusetts Volunteer Militia.
　　1907　　Boston　　65.00

STEVENSON, Alexander F.　The Battle of Stone's River Near Murfreesboro, Tennessee.
　　1884　　Boston　　65.00
　　1974　　Gettysburg　　30.00
　　1983　　30.00

STEVENSON, B. F.　　Letters from the Army.
　　1884　　Cincinnati　150.00
　　1886　　Cincinnati　125.00

STEVENSON, David　　Indiana's Roll of Honor, Vol. I.
　　1864　　Indianapolis　　90.00

STEVENSON, Joshua Thomas　　Memorial of Thomas Greely Stevenson 1836-1864.
　　1864　　Cambridge　　80.00

STEVENSON, R. Randolph　The Southern Side; or, Andersonville Prison.
　　1876　　Baltimore　100.00

STEVENSON, Thomas M.　　History of the 78th Regiment Ohio Veteran Volunteer Infantry.
　　1865　　Zanesville　　225.00

STEVENSON, William G.   Thirteen Months in the Rebel Army . . . By
An Impressed New Yorker.
    1862   London   75.00
    1862   New York   50.00
    1863   New York   40.00
    1959   New York   15.00
STEWART, Alexander M.   Camp, March and Battlefield.
    1865   Philadelphia   120.00
STEWART, George R.   Pickett's Charge.
    1959   Boston   35.00
    1983   20.00
    1983   Wraps   12.00
STEWART, Lucy Shelton   The Reward of Patriotism.
    1930   New York   60.00
STEWART, Nixon B.   Dan McCook's Regiment, 52nd O.V.I.
    1900   Alliance   145.00
STEWART, Robert L.   History of the 140th Regiment, Pennsylvania
Volunteers.
    1912   Philadelphia   80.00
STEWART, William H.   A Pair of Blankets.
    1911   New York   250.00
    1990   (revised reprint)   Wilmington, NC   30.00
STEWART, William H.   The Spirit of the South.
    1908   New York and Washington, DC   75.00
STIBBS, John Howard   Andersonville and the Trial of Henry Wirz.
Wraps.
    1911   Iowa City   45.00
STICKLES, Arndt M.   Simon Bolivar Buckner Borderland Knight.
    1940   Chapel Hill, NC   50.00
    1987   Wilmington, NC   30.00
STIDGER, Felix G., edited by   Treason History of the Order of Sons
of Liberty.
    1903   Chicago   125.00
STILES, Robert   Address at the Dedication of the Monument to the
Confederate Dead, University of Virginia, June 7, 1893.
    1893   Richmond   75.00
STILES, Robert   Four Years Under Marse Robert.
    1903   New York   75.00
    1977   Dayton   20.00
    1988   Dayton   25.00
STILL, William   Still's Underground Rail Road Records with a Life of
the Author.
    1886   Philadelphia   60.00
    1968   20.00
STILL, William N., Jr.   Confederate Shipbuilding.   Wraps.
    1969   Athens, GA   20.00
    1987   Columbia, SC   19.95
STILL, William N., Jr.   Iron Afloat.
    1971   Nashville   25.00
    1985   Columbia, SC   19.95
    1987   21.95

STILL, William N., Jr.   What Finer Tradition: The Memoirs of
Thomas O. Selfridge, Jr., Rear Admiral, U.S.N.
1987   21.95

STILLE, Charles J.   History of the United States Sanitary Commission.
1868   New York   30.00

STILLE, Charles J.   How a Free People Conduct a Long War.   Wraps.
1862   Philadelphia   30.00

STILLE, Charles J.   Northern Interests and Southern Independence: A
Plea for United Action.   Wraps.
1863   Philadelphia   35.00

STILLWELL, Leander   The Story of a Common Soldier of Army Life
in the Civil War.
1920   Erie, KS   100.00
1983   30.00

STILLWELL, Lucille   Born to be a Statesman,   John Cabell Brecken-
ridge.
1936   Caldwell, ID   45.00

STIMMEL, Smith   Personal Reminiscences of Abraham Lincoln.
1928   Minneapolis   Ltd.   35.00

STINE, J. H.   History of the Army of the Potomac.
1892   Philadelphia   80.00
1893   Washington, DC   75.00

STIPP, Joseph A.   The   History   and   Service   of   the   154th   Ohio
Volunteer Infantry.
1896   Toledo   175.00
n.d.   n.p.   20.00

STOCKARD, Henry Jerome   A Study in Southern Poetry.
1911   New York and Washington, DC   45.00

STOCKTON, Joseph   War Diary (1862-65) of Brevet Brigadier General
Joseph Stockton.   Wraps.
1910   Chicago   95.00
1989   7.95

STOCKWELL, Elisha   Private Elisha Stockwell, Jr.   Sees the Civil
War, edited by Byron Abernethy.
1958   Norman, OK   25.00
1985   8.00

STODDARD, Henry Luther   Horace Greeley: Printer, Editor, Crusader.
1946   New York   12.00

STODDARD, William O.   Abraham Lincoln: The True Story of a Great
Life.
1885   New York   35.00

STODDARD, William O.   Inside the White House in War Times.
1890   New York   25.00

STODDARD, William O., Jr., edited by   Lincoln's Third Secretary . . .
The Memoirs of William O. Stoddard.
1955   New York   15.00

STONE, Edwin M.   Rhode Island in the Rebellion, Battery C, First R.
I. Light Artillery.
1864   Providence   50.00

STONE, Henry Lane   "Morgan's Men."   Wraps.
1919   Louisville   50.00

STONE, Irving   Love Is Eternal   A Novel About Mary Todd and Abraham Lincoln.
    1954   New York   10.00

STONE, James M.   The History of the Twenty-seventh Regiment Maine Volunteer Infantry.
    1895   Portland   50.00

STONE, James M.   Personal Recollections of the Civil War . . . As a Private Soldier in the 21st Vol. Regiment of Infantry.
    1918   Boston   75.00

STONE, Kate   Brokenburn, The Journal of _____, edited by John Q. Anderson.
    1955   Baton Rouge   30.00
    1956   Baton Rouge   30.00
    1972   Baton Rouge   30.00

STONE, William A.   The Tale of a Plain Man.
    n.d.   n.p.   45.00

STONEBRAKER, J. Clarence   The Unwritten South.
    1903   Hagerstown   35.00
    1908   n.p.   30.00

STONEBRAKER, Joseph R.   A Rebel of '61.
    1899   New York   500.00

STOREY, Moorfield   Charles Sumner.
    1900   Boston   10.00

Stories of the Civil War.   Wraps.
    1965   Falls Church   10.00

STORMONT, Gilbert R.   History of the Fifty-eighth Regiment of Indiana Volunteer Infantry.
    1895   Princeton   150.00

STORMONT, John W.   The Economics of Secession and Coercion 1861.
    1957   Victoria, TX   25.00

STORRICK, W. C.   The Battle of Gettysburg.   Wraps.
    1938   Harrisburg, PA   15.00
    1945   15.00
    1959   Harrisburg, PA   10.00

STORRICK, W. C.   Gettysburg.
    1932   Harrisburg, PA   25.00

STORRS, John W.   The "Twentieth Connecticut."
    1886   Naugatuck   85.00

The Story of American Heroism.
    1897   Springfield   80.00

The Story of the "General."   Wraps.
    (c.1900) Nashville, TN   30.00
    n.d.   n.p.   15.00

The Story of the Confederate States' Ship "Virginia" (Once Merrimac) Her Victory Over the Monitor.   Wraps.
    1879   Baltimore   40.00

The Story of the Fifty-fifth Regiment Illinois Volunteer Infantry.
    1887   Clinton, MA   190.00

Story of the 21st Connecticut Volunteer Infantry During the Civil War.
    1900   Middletown   90.00

STORY, Grace Haskell   Haskell, Edward Howard, A Memorial.
    1927   Cambridge   35.00

STOUT, L. H.   Reminiscences of General Braxton Bragg.   Wraps.
    1942   Hattiesburg, MS   Ltd.   60.00

STOUTAMIRE, A.   Music of the Old South: Coloney to Confederacy.
    1932   Rutherford, NJ   20.00
    1972   Rutherford, NJ   23.00

STOVALL, Pleasant A.   Robert Toombs.
    1892   New York   60.00

STOWE, Harriet Beecher   Autographs for Freedom.
    1853   Boston   30.00

STOWE, Harriet Beecher   A Key to Uncle Tom's Cabin; Presenting the Original Facts and Documents Upon Which the Story Is Founded. . . .
    1853   Boston   50.00

STOWE, Harriet Beecher   Men of Our Times.
    1868   Hartford   25.00

STOWE, Harriet Beecher   A Reply to "The Affectionate and Christian Address of Many Thousands of Women of Great Britain and Ireland, To Their Sisters, the Women of the United States of America."
    1863   London   40.00

STOWE, Harriet Beecher   Uncle Tom's Cabin.   2 Vols.
    1852   Boston   700.00   To support this value, condition must be fine.
    1938   Ltd. ed. Club   75.00
    Later printings   40.00-60.00

STOWITS, George H.   History of the One Hundredth Regiment of New York Volunteers.
    1870   Buffalo   110.00

STRAIT, Newton A.   Alphabetical List of Battles, 1754-1900.   Wraps.
    1882   Washington, DC   40.00
    1909   Washington, DC   40.00

STRANG, Edgar B.   General Stoneman's Raid, or The Amusing Side of Army Life.   Wraps.
    1911   Philadelphia   40.00

STRATTON, J. T., compiled by   Portrait Gallery and Library of R. E. Lee Camp, No. 1, Confederate Veterans, Richmond, Virginia.   Wraps.
    1913   Richmond   20.00

STRAUBING, Harold Elk, edited by   Civil War Eyewitness Reports.
    1985   New York   25.00

STREET, James   Tap Roots.
    1946   New York   25.00

STREET, James   By Valour and Arms.
    1944   New York   10.00

STREET, James   The Civil War.
    1953   New York   10.00

STRIBLING, R. M.   Gettysburg Campaign and Campaigns of 1864 and 1865 in Virginia.
    1905   Petersburg, VA   75.00
    1988   25.00

STRIBLING, T. S.   The Forge.
    1931   New York   10.00

STRIBLING, T. S.   The Store.
    1932   New York   10.00

STRICKLER, Theodore D.   When and Where We Met Each Other on Shore and Afloat. Wraps.
1899   Washington, DC   25.00
1899   Philadelphia   25.00
STRIDER, Robert Edward Lee   The Life and Work of George W. Peterkin.
1929   Philadelphia   35.00
STRODE, Hudson   Jefferson Davis.   4 Vols.
Vol. 1   American Patriot.
Vol. 2   Confederate President.
Vol. 3   Tragic Hero.
Vol. 4   Private Letters.
1955-66   New York   Individual volumes   25.00 each
1966   4 Vol. set   150.00
STRONG, Benjamin Thomas   Three Years or During the War.   Wraps.
1913   Olathe, KS   150.00
STRONG, George Templeton   The Diary of _____, edited by Allan Nevins.   4 Vols.
1952   New York   75.00
STRONG, Robert Hale   A Yankee Private's Civil War, edited by Ashley Halsey.
1961   Chicago   20.00
STROTHER, David Hunter   The Old South Illustrated.
1959   Chapel Hill, NC   25.00
STROTHER, David Hunter   A Virginia Yankee in the Civil War: The Diaries of _____, edited by Cecil D. Eby, Jr.
1961   Chapel Hill, NC   30.00
STROUD, D. V.   Inscribed Union Swords, 1861-1865.
1983   Kilgore   Ltd.   35.00
STROYER, Jacob   My Life in the South.
1898   Salem, MA   75.00
STRUNSKY, Rose   Abraham Lincoln.
1914   New York   20.00
STRYKER, Lloyd Paul   Andrew Johnson.
1929   New York   25.00
1930   New York   25.00
STRYKER, William S.   Record of Officers and Men of New Jersey in the Civil War 1861- 1865.   2 Vols.
1876   Trenton   150.00
STUART, A. A.   Iowa Colonels and Regiments.
1865   Des Moines   100.00
STUART, Alex. H. H.   A Narrative of the Leading Incidents of the Organization of the First Popular Movement in Virginia in 1865 . . . to Secure Restoration of Virginia to the Union.
1888   Richmond   50.00
1973   Richmond   20.00
STUART, J. E. B.   Letters of _____ to His Wife 1861, edited by Bingham Duncan.   Wraps.
1943   Atlanta   Ltd.   35.00
STUART, Meriwether   Colonel Ulric Dahlgren and Richmond's Union Underground, April 1864.   Wraps.
1964   VA   15.00

STUART, Meriwether   The Record of the Virginia Forces, A Study in the Compilation of Civil War Records. Wraps.
1960   VA   40.00

STUART, Meriwether   Samuel Ruth and General R. E. Lee Disloyalty and the Line of Supply to Fredericksburg 1862-63. Wraps.
1963   VA   20.00

STURGIS, Thomas   Prisoners of War 1861-1865.
1912   New York   40.00

STURTEVANT, Ralph O.   Pictorial History Thirteenth Regiment Vermont Volunteers War of 1861-1865.
1910   n.p.   150.00

STUTLER, Boyd B.   Captain John Brown and Harper's Ferry. Wraps.
1926   Harpers Ferry   30.00

STUTLER, Boyd B.   Glory, Glory, Hallelujah! The Story of "John Brown's Body" and "Battle Hymn of the Republic."
n.d.   Cincinnati   40.00

STUTLER, Boyd B.   West Virginia in the Civil War.
1963   Charleston   30.00
1966   Charleston   25.00

STYPLE, W. B., edited by   Letters from the Peninsula: The Civil War Letters of General Philip Kearny. Wraps.
1988   Kearny   17.95

STYRON, William   The Confessions of Nat Turner.
1967   New York   15.00

Subdued Southern Nobility by One of the Nobility.
1882   New York   25.00

SUBLETT, Charles W.   57th Virginia Infantry.
1985   Lynchburg   20.00

Suggestions as to Arming the State.
1860   Charleston   100.00

SULLINS, David   Recollections of an Old Man Seventy Years in Dixie 1827-1897.
1910   Bristol   75.00

Sullivan County and the Civil War, Brass Buttons and Leather Boots.
1963   n.p.   Ltd.   40.00

SULLY, Langdon   No Tears for the General, The Life of Alfred Sully, 1821-79.
1974   Palo Alto, CA   20.00

SUMMERS, Festus P.   The Baltimore and the Ohio in the Civil War.
1939   New York   100.00

SUMMERS, Festus P.   A Borderland Confederate.
1962   Pittsburg   30.00

SUMMERS, Festus P.   Johnson Newlon Camden.
1937   New York   20.00

SUMMERSELL, Charles Grayson   The Cruise of CSS Sumter.   See: Confederate Centennial Studies, No. 27.

SUMMERSELL, Charles Grayson   C.S.S. Alabama: Builder, Captain, and Plans.
1985   University, AL   40.00

SUMNER, Charles   Slavery and the Rebellion, One and Inseparable, Speech. Wraps.
1864   Boston   15.00

SUMNER, Charles   Speech . . . , on the Johnson-Clarendon Treaty for the Settlement of Claims.   Wraps.
    1870   Boston   20.00

SUMNER, Charles   Speech of . . . Treatment of Prisoners of War. Wraps.
    1865   New York   25.00

SUMNER, Charles   Speech of Senator Chas. Sumner (on the Bill to Admit Kansas to the Union as a Free State.)   Printed in German. Wraps.
    1860   n.p.   30.00

SUMNER, G. Lynn   Meet Abraham Lincoln   Profiles of the Prairie President.
    1946   New York   10.00

SUMNER, George C.   Battery D, First Rhode Island Light Artillery in the Civil War, 1861-1865.
    1897   Providence   50.00

SUMNER, M. E., edited by   The Diary of Cyrus B. Comstock.
    1987   Dayton   37.50

SUNDERLAND, Glenn W.   Lightning at Hoover's Gap, The Story of Wilder's Brigade.
    1969   New York   35.00

SUNDERLAND, Glenn W.   Wilders Lightning Brigade and Its Spencer Repeaters.   Wraps.
    1984   9.00

Supplement to the Annual Reports of the Adjutant General of the State of Maine for the Years 1861-1866.   Alphabetical Index of Maine Volunteers.
    1867   Augusta   60.00

Supplement to the Congressional Globe Containing the Proceedings of the Senate Sitting for the Trial of Andrew Johnson, President of the U.S. 40th Congress, 2nd Session.
    1868   Washington, DC   100.00

SURBY, Richard W.   Grierson's Raids and Hatch's Sixty-four Days' March.
    1865   Chicago   300.00

Sussex County, A Tale of Three Centuries, compiled by WPA Workers.
    1942   Richmond   30.00

SUTTON, Aaron T.   Prisoner of the Rebels in Texas.
    1978   13.00

SUTTON, J. J.   History of the Second Regiment, West Virginia Cavalry Volunteers.
    1892   Portsmouth   120.00

SWANBERG, W. A.   First Blood, the Story of Fort Sumter.
    1957   New York   20.00
    1957   Special edition signed by author   35.00
    1960   England   18.00
    1984   Wraps   13.00

SWANBERG, W. A.   Sickles, the Incredible.
    1956   New York   40.00
    1956   New York   CWBC edition signed by author   50.00

SWANK, W. D., compiled by   Confederate Letters and Diaries, 1861-
   1865. Wraps.
   1988   Mineral   15.00
SWANN, Leonard A.   John Roach: Maritime Entrepreneur - The Years
   as Naval Contractor   1862-1886.
   1965   Annapolis   25.00
SWASEY, Charles A. G.   American Caricatures Pertaining to the Civil
   War.
   (c.1875) n.p.   75.00
SWEENY, Talbot   A Vindication from a Northern Viewpoint of Gen.
   Robt. E. Lee and His Fellow Officers Who Left the United States Army
   and Navy in 1861. . . . Wraps.
   1890   Richmond   50.00
SWEENY, William M.   A Biographical Memoir of Thomas William
   Sweeny, Brigadier General United States Army.
   n.d.   n.p.   45.00
SWEET, William Warren   The Methodist Episcopal Church and the Civil
   War.
   n.d.   Cincinnati   40.00
SWIERENGA, Robert P., edited by   Beyond the Civil War Synthesis,
   Political Essays of the Civil War Era.
   1975   Westport, CT   20.00
SWIFT, Charles Jewett   The Last Battle of the Civil War. A Paper.
   Wraps.
   1915   Columbus, GA   75.00
SWIFT, Frederick W.   My Experiences as a Prisoner of War. Wraps.
   1888   Detroit   35.00
SWIFT, George W.   Experiences of a Falmouth Boy in Rebel Prisons.
   Wraps.
   1899   Falmouth   50.00
SWIGGETT, Howard   The Rebel Raider.
   1934   Indianapolis   45.00
   1937   Garden City, NY   40.00
SWIGGETT, S. A.   The Bright Side of Prison Life.
   1897   Baltimore   60.00
SWINBURNE, John   A Typical American; or Incidents in the Life of Dr.
   John Swinburne.
   1888   New York   75.00
SWINFEN, David B.   Ruggles' Regiment. The 122nd New York Vols. in
   the American Civil War.
   1982   Hanover   25.00
SWINT, Henry L., edited by   Dear Ones at Home: Letters from Contraband Camps.
   1966   Nashville   20.00
SWINTON, William   Campaigns of the Army of the Potomac.
   1866   New York   75.00
   1867   New York   75.00
   1871   New York   65.00
   1882   New York   65.00
   1988   15.00

SWINTON, William   History of the Seventh Regiment, National Guard, State of New York, During the War of the Rebellion.
   1870   New York   60.00
   1876   New York   50.00
   1886   New York   50.00
SWINTON, William   The Twelve Decisive Battle of the War.
   1867   New York   35.00
   1986   15.00
SWINTON, William   The War for the Union   From Fort Sumter to Atlanta. Wraps.
   (c.1865)   n.p.   25.00
SWISHER, Carl Brent   Stephen J. Field: Craftsman of the Law.
   1963   Washington, DC 10.00
SWISHER, Jacob A., compiled by   The Iowa Department of the Grand Army of the Republic.
   1936   Iowa City   30.00
SWISHER, Jacob A.   Iowa in Times of War.
   1943   Iowa City   40.00
SWISHER, James   How I Know, or Sixteen Years Eventful Experiences.
   1880   Cincinnati   125.00
SWISSHELM, Jane Grey   Crusader and Feminist, Letters of _____, edited by Arthur J. Larsen.
   1934   St. Paul, MN   50.00
SWITLIK, M. C.   The Complete Cannoneer.
   1979   MI 35.00
SWORD, Wiley   Firepower from Abroad. The Confederate Enfield and LeMat Revolver.
   1986   18.00
SWORD, Wiley   Sharpshooter: Hiram Berdan, His Famous Sharpshooters and their Sharps Rifles.
   1988   17.50
SWORD, Wiley   Shiloh: Bloody April.
   1974   New York   40.00
   1983   Dayton   35.00
   1988   Wraps   15.00
SYKES, Edward T.   Walthall's Brigade.
   1905   Columbus, MS   150.00
   1906   n.p.   100.00
   1916   n.p.   75.00
SYLVIA, Stephen W., edited by   North South Trader's Civil War Price Guide. Wraps.
   1988   Fredericksburg   12.00
SYLVIA, Stephen W. and O'DONNELL, Michael J.   Civil War Canteens. Wraps.
   1983   Orange   25.00
SYLVIA, Stephen W. and O'DONNELL, Michael J.   The Illustrated History of American Civil War Relics.
   1978   Orange   35.00
   1985   39.95
   1988   39.95
SYMONDS, Craig L.   A Battlefield Atlas of the Civil War.
   1983   Annapolis   30.00

SYMONDS, H. C.   Report of a Commissary of Subsistence 1861-5.
    1888   Sing Sing   45.00

Synopsis of the Military Career of Gen. Joseph Wheeler, Commander of the Cavalry Corps, Army of the West. Wraps. Incorrectly dated.
    1865 (i.e. 1878) New York   150.00

SYPHER, Josiah R., compiled by   History of the Pennsylvania Reserve Corps.
    1865   Lancaster   100.00

Tabular Statements Showing the Names of Commanders of Army Corps, Divisions and Brigades, United States Army, During the War of 1861 to 1865.
    1887   Philadelphia   100.00

TAFFT, Henry S.   Reminiscences of the Signal Service in the Civil War. Wraps.
    1899   Providence   Ltd.   50.00
    1903   Providence   Ltd.   35.00

TALBOT, Edith Armstrong   Samuel Chapman Armstrong   A Biographical Study.
    1904   New York   30.00

TALCOTT, T. M. R.   Stuart's Cavalry in the Gettysburg Campaign   A Reply to the Letter of Col. John S. Mosby, Published in the "Times Dispatch" of January 30, 1910. Wraps.
    1911   Richmond   100.00

TANCIG, William J.   Confederate Military Land Units.
    1967   Brunswick   30.00

TANKERSLEY, Allen P.   John B. Gordon.
    1955   Atlanta   60.00

TANNER, Robert G.   Stonewall in the Valley.
    1976   Garden City, NY   30.00

TANSILL, Robert   A Free and Impartial Exposition of the Causes Which Led to the Failure of the Confederate States to Establish Their Independence. Wraps.
    1865   Washington, DC   250.00

TARBELL, Ida   He Knew Lincoln.
    1909   New York   10.00

TARBELL, Ida   He Knew Lincoln and Other Billy Brown Stories.
    1922   New York   10.00

TARBELL, Ida   In the Footsteps of Lincoln.
    1924   New York   15.00

TARBELL, Ida   The Life of Abraham Lincoln. 4 Vols.
    1901   New York   30.00
    1909   New York   30.00
    1924   New York   30.00
    1960   2 Vols.   30.00

TARBELL, Ida and DAVIS, J. McCan   The Early Life of Abraham Lincoln.
    1896   New York   12.00
    1974   12.50

TARRANT, Eastham   The Wild Riders of the First Kentucky Cavalry.
    1894   Louisville   250.00
    1969   Lexington   75.00

TATE, Allen   The Fathers.
   1938   New York   10.00
TATE, Allen   Jefferson Davis, His Rise and Fall.
   1929   New York   30.00
TATE, Allen   Stonewall Jackson, the Good Soldier.
   1928   New York   50.00
   1965   Ann Arbor   25.00
TATUM, Edith   When the Bugle Called.
   1908   New York   30.00
TATUM, Georgia L.   Disloyalty in the Confederacy.
   1934   Chapel Hill, NC   50.00
   1970   New York   20.00
TAYLOR, A. Reed   The War History of Two Soldiers: A Two-Sided View of the Civil War. Wraps.
   1970   Alabama   20.00
TAYLOR, Benjamin F.   Mission Ridge and Lookout Mountain, With Pictures of Life in Camp and Field.
   1872   New York   55.00
   1875   Chicago   entitled Pictures of Life in Camp and Field   35.00
TAYLOR, Elizabeth S. W.   Aunt Bet, the Story of a Long Life, a Memoir of Elizabeth S. W. Taylor. . . .
   1927   Winchester   Ltd. 500 copies.   70.00
TAYLOR, Emerson Gifford   Gouverneur Kemble Warren, The Life and Letters of an American Soldier 1830-1882.
   1932   Boston   60.00
   1988   35.00
TAYLOR, Frank H.   Philadelphia in the Civil War 1861-1865.
   1913   Philadelphia   25.00
TAYLOR, George Rogers   The American Railroad Network.
   1956   Cambridge   25.00
TAYLOR, Isaac L.   Campaigning with the First Minnesota A Civil War Diary, edited by Hazel Wolf.
   1944   St. Paul   45.00
TAYLOR, James E.   The James E. Taylor Sketchbook.
   1989   Dayton   85.00
TAYLOR, James E.   With Sheridan Up the Shenandoah Valley in 1864: Leaves from a Special Artist's Sketchbook and Diary.
   1989   Dayton   85.00
TAYLOR, Jeremiah   The Sacrifice Consumed. Life of Edward Hamilton Brewer.
   1863   Boston   30.00
TAYLOR, Joe Gray   Louisiana Reconstructed 1863-1877.
   1974   Baton Rouge   25.00
TAYLOR, Joe Gray   Negro Slavery in Louisiana.
   1963   Baton Rouge   13.00
TAYLOR, John C.   History of the First Connecticut Artillery and of the Siege Trains of the Armies Operating Against Richmond 1862-1865.
   1893   Hartford   180.00
TAYLOR, John C.   Lights and Shadows in the Recollections of a Youthful Volunteer in the Civil War. Wraps.
   n.d.   Ionia   120.00

TAYLOR, John Dykes   History of the 48th Alabama Volunteer Infantry Regiment, C.S.A., edited by William Stanley Hoole.
    1985   University, AL 8.00

TAYLOR, John S.   Sixteenth South Carolina Regiment CSA from Greenville County, S.C.
    1964   n.p.   30.00

TAYLOR, N. G.   Relief for East Tennessee, Address . . . Meeting Cooper Institute. Wraps.
    1864   New York   20.00

TAYLOR, Richard   Destruction and Reconstruction: Personal Experiences of the Late War.
    1879   New York   100.00
    1879   London   200.00
    1890   75.00
    1903   New York   50.00
    1955   New York   edited by Richard Harwell   40.00
    1979   30.00
    1983   30.00

TAYLOR, Rosser Howard   Slaveholding in North Carolina: An Economic View. Wraps.
    1926   Chapel Hill, NC   25.00

TAYLOR, Susie King   Reminiscences of My Life in Camp with the 33rd United States Colored Troops.
    1902   Boston   100.00
    1968   Boston   30.00

TAYLOR, Thomas E.   Running the Blockade.
    1896   New York   125.00
    1896   London   150.00
    1897   London   100.00
    1912   London   75.00
    1971   Freeport, NY   25.00

TAYLOR, Walter H.   Four Years with General Lee.
    1877   New York   150.00
    1878   New York   125.00
    1962   Bloomington   edited by James I. Robertson   35.00
    Recent reprint   22.50

TAYLOR, Walter H.   General Lee: His Campaigns in Virginia.
    1906   Norfolk, VA   150.00
    1975   Dayton   30.00

TAYLOR, William   Cause and Probable Results of the Civil War in America. Wraps.
    1862   London   40.00

TAYLOR, William H.   De Quibus: Discourses and Essays by. . . .
    1908   Richmond   75.00

TAYLOR, William R.   Cavalier and Yankee   The Old South and American National Character.
    1961   New York   30.00

TEAL, Mrs. M. D., et al   The Effect of the Civil War on Music in Michigan.
    1965   Lansing   13.00

TEETOR, Paul R.   A Matter of Hours: Treason at Harper's Ferry.
    1982   Rutherford   25.00

Telegrams Received by the War Department in Relation to the War of the Rebellion.
1876 Washington, DC 100.00

TELFER, William D. **Reminiscences of the First Battle of Manassas: A Camp-Fire Story of the 71st Regiment.**
1864 New York 50.00

TEMPLE, Oliver P. **East Tennessee and the Civil War.**
1899 Cincinnati 125.00
1972 Knoxville Ltd. 50.00

TEMPLE, Oliver P. **Notable Men of Tennessee from 1833 to 1875.**
1912 New York 110.00

TEMPLE, Sarah Blackwell Gober **The First Hundred Years, a Short History of Cobb County in Georgia.**
1935 Atlanta 125.00

TEMPLE, Wayne C. and **RICE**, Glenna A., compiled by **Lincoln Herald Analytical Index 1950-1960.** Wraps.
1962 Harrogate, TN 10.00

Tennesseans in the Civil War, A Military History of Confederate and Union Units with Available Rosters of Personnel. 2 parts.
1964-65 Nashville 100.00
1985 Part 1 40.00
Part 2 40.00
1989 Part 1 40.00
Part 2 50.00

Tennessee - Confederate Military History. See: **Confederate Military History, Vol. VIII** (Vol. X, 1987 reprint ed.).

Tennessee Civil War Veterans Questionnaires, compiled by Gustavus W. Dyer and John Trotwood Moore. 5 Vols.
1985 Easley 200.00

TENNEY, W. J. **The Military and Naval History of the Rebellion in the United States.**
1865 New York 45.00
1866 New York 35.00

Tentative Roster of the Third Regiment, South Carolina Volunteers, Confederate States Provisional Army, edited by A. S. Salley, Jr. Wraps.
1908 Columbia 100.00

TERRELL, W. H. H. **Indiana in the War of the Rebellion.**
1960 Indianapolis 50.00
Recent reprint 32.50

TERRILL, John Newton **Campaign of the Fourteenth Regiment New Jersey Volunteers.**
1884 New Brunswick 125.00

Testimonial to Col. Rush C. Hawkins, 9th Regiment N.Y.V., "Hawkins Zouaves." Wraps.
1863 New York 45.00

Testimony Taken by the Joint Select Committee to Inquire into . . . the Insurrectionary States . . . See: **Ku Klux Conspiracy.**

TEVIS, C. V. **The History of the Fighting Fourteenth.**
1911 New York 120.00

Texas - Confederate Military History. See: **Confederate Military History, Vol. XI** (Vol. XV, 1989 reprint ed.).

Texas, and Its Late Military Occupation and Evacuation. By an Officer of the Army. (Phillips, Edwin D.) Wraps.
1862   New York   350.00

THANE, Elswyth   Yankee Stranger.
1944   New York   15.00
1968   10.00

THARIN, Robert S.   Arbitrary Arrests in the South.
1863   New York   40.00
1969   30.00

THARP, Louise   Three Saints and a Sinner: Julia Ward Howe, Louisa, Annie and Sam Ward.
1956   Boston   10.00

That Dashing Cavalry Commander and Brilliant Orator: Gen'l Judson Kilpatrick. Wraps.
n.d.   n.p.   30.00

THATCHER, Marshall P.   A Hundred Battles in the West, St. Louis to Atlanta 1861-1865.
1884   Detroit   125.00
1987   25.00

THAYER, Eli   History of the Kansas Crusade.
1889   New York   25.00

THAYER, George A.   The Draft Riots of 1863, A Historical Study.
(1916)   n.p.   30.00

THAYER, George A.   "Gettysburg," "As We Men on the Right Saw It." A Paper. Wraps.
1886   Cincinnati   50.00

THAYER, George A.   History of the Second Massachusetts Regiment of Infantry, Chancellorsville. Wraps.
1882   Boston   40.00

THAYER, M. Russell   A Reply to Mr. Charles Ingersoll's "Letter to a Friend in a Slave State." Wraps.
1862   Philadelphia   40.00

THAYER, William M.   A Youth's History of the Rebellion. 4 Vols.
1864-65   40.00
Individual volumes   10.00 each

THAYER, William Roscoe   The Life and Letters of John Hay. 2 Vols.
1915   Boston   25.00
1916   15.00

THEAKER, James G.   Through One Man's Eyes: Letters of _____, Belmont County, Ohio Volunteer, edited by Paul E. Rieger.
1974   Mt. Vernon   25.00

THIAN, R. P.   Notes Illustrating Military Geography of the U.S. 1813-1880.
1979   20.00

This Discursive Biographical Sketch 1841-1902 of Richard Lathers.
1902   Philadelphia   50.00

THOBURN, Thomas C.   My Experiences During the Civil War, compiled by Lyle Thoburn.
1963   Cleveland   35.00

THOMAS, Benjamin P.   Abraham Lincoln.
1952   New York   30.00

THOMAS, Benjamin P.   Lincoln's New Salem.
   1954   New York   10.00
   1988   13.95
   1988   Wraps   7.95
THOMAS, Benjamin P.   Portrait for Posterity.
   1947   New Brunswick   10.00
THOMAS, Benjamin P. and HYMAN, Harold M.   Stanton - The Life and Times of Lincoln's Secretary of War.
   1962   New York   30.00
THOMAS, Clarence   General Turner Ashby The Centaur of the South.
   1907   Winchester, VA   250.00
THOMAS, D. S.   The Gettysburg Cyclorama: A Portrayal of the High Tide of the Confederacy.
   1989   Gettysburg   9.95
THOMAS, David Y.   Arkansas in War and Reconstruction 1861-1874.
   1926   Little Rock   50.00
THOMAS, Edison H.   John Hunt Morgan and His Raiders.
   1975   Lexington   20.00
   1985   Lexington   15.00
THOMAS, Edison H.   The Story of the Jefferson Davis Funeral Train. Wraps.
   n.d.   Louisville   8.00
THOMAS, Edward J.   Memoirs of a Southerner.
   1923   Savannah   100.00
THOMAS, Emory M.   The American War and Peace, 1860-1877.
   1973   Englewood Cliffs, NJ   20.00
THOMAS, Emory M.   Bold Dragoon, the Life of J. E. B. Stuart.
   1986   New York   22.95
THOMAS, Emory M.   The Confederacy as a Revolutionary Experience.
   1971   Englewood Cliffs, NJ   30.00
THOMAS, Emory M.   The Confederate Nation 1861-1865.
   1979   New York   25.00
THOMAS, Emory M.   The Confederate State of Richmond.
   1971   Austin   30.00
THOMAS, Emory M.   Travels to Hallowed Ground: A Historian's Journey to the American Civil War.
   1987   Columbia   19.95
THOMAS, George H.   The Military Correspondence of Maj.Gen. _____. Wraps.
   1925   n.p.   30.00
THOMAS, H. H.   The Story of Allen and Wheelock Firearms.
   1965   Cincinnati   50.00
THOMAS, Hampton S.   Some Personal Reminiscences of Service in the Cavalry of the Army of the Potomac. Wraps.
   1889   Philadelphia   80.00
THOMAS, Henry W.   History of the Doles-Cook Brigade, Army of Northern Virginia, C.S.A.
   1903   Atlanta   175.00
   1988   45.00
THOMAS, Howard   Boys in Blue from the Adirondack Foothills.
   1960   Prospect   40.00

THOMAS, J. A. W.　　A History of Marlboro County.
　1897　Atlanta　140.00
THOMAS, John L.　　The Liberator William Lloyd Garrison: A Biography.
　1963　Boston　14.00
THOMAS, John P.　　Career & Character of General Micah Jenkins. Wraps.
　1903　Columbia, SC　Ltd.　150.00
THOMAS, John P.　　The History of the South Carolina Military Academy.
　1893　Charleston, SC　150.00
THOMAS, Theresa　　Tall Grey Gates.
　(1942)　New York　75.00
THOMAS, Wilbur　　General George H. Thomas, The Indomitable Warrier.
　1964　New York　50.00
THOMASON, John W., Jr.　　Jeb Stuart.
　1930　New York　40.00
　1934　New York　30.00
　1941　New York　30.00
　1946　New York　30.00
　1948　New York　30.00
　1958　New York　30.00
THOMASON, John W., Jr.　　Lone Star Preacher.
　1941　New York　40.00
　1955　30.00
THOMES, W. H.　　Running the Blockade.
　1875　Boston　100.00
　1888　Chicago　50.00
THOMPSON, Bradford F.　　History of the 112th Regiment of Illinois Volunteer Infantry.
　1885　Toulon　150.00
THOMPSON, C. Mildred　　Reconstruction in Georgia.
　1915　New York　Wraps　65.00
　1964　Gloucester　22.50
THOMPSON, Charles Willis　　The Fiery Epoch 1830-77.
　1931　Indianapolis　20.00
THOMPSON, Edwin Porter　　History of the First Kentucky Brigade.
　1868　Cincinnati　300.00
THOMPSON, Edwin Porter　　History of the Orphan Brigade.
　1898　Louisville　325.00
　1973　Dayton 30.00
THOMPSON, Gilbert　　The Engineer Battalion in the Civil War. Wraps.
　1910　Washington, DC　150.00
　1919　125.00
THOMPSON, Heber S.　　Diary of _____, 7th Penna. Cavalry.　Wraps.
　(191-)　Pottsville　50.00
THOMPSON, Heber S.　　The First Defenders.
　1910　n.p.　80.00
THOMPSON, Henry T.　　Ousting the Carpetbagger from South Carolina.
　1926　Columbia　100.00

THOMPSON, Henry Yates   An Englishman in the American Civil War, The Diary of _____, edited by Christopher Chancellor.
1971   New York   25.00

THOMPSON, James Monroe   Reminiscences of the Autauga Rifles, edited by William Stanley Hoole. Wraps.
1984   University, AL 8.00

THOMPSON, Jerry D.   Colonel John Robert Baylor: Texas Indian Fighter and Confederate Soldier. Wraps.
1971   Waco, TX   30.00

THOMPSON, Jerry D.   Henry Hopkins Sibley: Confederate General of the West.
1987   Natchitoches, LA   25.00

THOMPSON, Jerry D.   Mexican Texans in the Union Army.
1986   El Paso, TX 7.50

THOMPSON, John C.   History of the Eleventh Regiment Rhode Island Volunteers by R. W. Rock (pseud.).
1881   Providence   60.00

THOMPSON, Joseph Parrish   Bryant Gray: The Student, The Christian, The Soldier.
1864   New York   50.00

THOMPSON, Joseph Parrish   Revolution Against Free Government. Wraps.
1864   Philadelphia   30.00

THOMPSON, Joseph Parrish   The Sergeant's Memorial by His Father.
1863   New York   30.00

THOMPSON, M. Jeff   Memoirs, edited by Donal J. Stanton, Goodwin F. Berquist and Paul C. Borners.
1988   Dayton   24.95

THOMPSON, Magnus S.   From the Ranks to Brigadier-General   The Service Record of Col. Elijah V. White 1861-1865. Wraps.
1923   n.p.   140.00

THOMPSON, Mildred   Reconstruction in Georgia.
1971   Marietta, GA   18.00

THOMPSON, S. Millett   Thirteenth Regiment of New Hampshire Volunteer Infantry in the War of the Rebellion 1861-1865.
1888   Boston   100.00

THOMPSON, Samuel Bernard   Confederate Purchasing Operations Abroad.
1935   Chapel Hill, NC   75.00
1973   Gloucester 25.00

THOMPSON, Seymour Dwight   Recollections with the Third Iowa Regiment.
1864   Cincinnati   145.00

THOMPSON, W. Fletcher, Jr.   The Image of War.
1960   New York   25.00

THOMPSON, Wesley S.   The Free State of Winston, a History of Winston County, Alabama.
1968   Winfield   28.00

THOMPSON, Wesley S.   Tories of the Hills.
1953   Boston   20.00

THOMPSON, William Y.   Robert Toombs of Georgia.
1966   Baton Rouge   25.00

THOMSON, O. R. and RAUCH, W. H.   History of the "Bucktails" Kane Rifle Regiment of the Pennsylvania Reserve Corps.
1906   Philadelphia   100.00
1988   40.00

THOMSON, Orville   From Philippi to Appomattox, Narrative of the Service of the 7th Indiana Infantry.
(190-)   n.p.   175.00

THORNBROUGH, Emma Lou   Black Reconstructionists. Wraps.
1972   3.00

THORNBROUGH, Emma Lou   Indiana in the Civil War Era, 1850-1880. Wraps.
1965   Indianapolis   25.00

THORNWELL, J. H.   Hear the South The State of the Country.
1861   New York   30.00

THORP, Willard   A Southern Reader.
1955   New York   30.00

THORPE, John H.   Roster of Nash County Confederate Soldiers.
1925   Raleigh   150.00

THORPE, Sheldon B.   History of the Fifteenth Connecticut Volunteers.
1893   New Haven   100.00

Three Rebels Write Home: Edgar Allan Jackson, James Fenton Bryant, Irvin Cross Wills and Miscellaneous Items. Wraps.
1955   Franklin   Ltd.   35.00

Three Weeks at Gettysburg. Wraps.
1863   New York   60.00

Thrilling Stories of the Great Rebellion by a Disabled Officer.
1865   Philadelphia   25.00

THURSTON, W. S.   History of the 111th Regiment O.V.I.
1894   Toledo   200.00

THWAITES, Reuben Gold, edited by   Civil War Messages and Proclamations of Wisconsin War Governors.
1912   Madison   35.00

TIBBETTS, E. D.   From Maine to Gettysburg, 1863-1913.
1913   60.00

TIBBETTS, George W.   A Brief Sketch of the Cleveland Grays.
n.d.   n.p.   65.00

TICKNOR, Francis Orray   The Poems of Francis Orray Ticknor, edited by Michelle Cutliff Ticknor.
1911   New York   25.00

TIDWELL, William A.   Come Retribution.   The Confederate Secret Service and the Assassination of Lincoln.
1988   38.50

TIDWELL, William A.   Confederate Spy Country, 1861-1865.
1979   Fairfax   15.00

TIEBOUT, Samuel   The Civil War Diary of Samuel Tiebout, 5th N. Y. Vol. Infantry, edited by Bruce T. McCully. Wraps.
1943   Cooperstown   20.00

TIEMANN, William F., compiled by   The 159th Regiment Infantry, New York State Volunteers.
1891   Brooklyn   80.00

TILGHMAN, T. F.   The Confederate Baggage and Treasure Train End Its Flight in Florida: A Diary of Tench Francis Tilghman.
n.d.   n.p.   20.00

TILLEY, John S.   Facts the Historians Leave Out A Youth's Confederate Primer. Wraps.
1951   Montgomery, AL   15.00

TILLEY, John S.   Lincoln Takes Command.
1941   Chapel Hill, NC   30.00

TILLINGHAST, Pardon Elisha   History of the Twelfth Regiment Rhode Island Volunteers in the Civil War 1862-1865.
1904   Providence   75.00

TILNEY, Robert   My Life in the Army   Three Years and a Half with the Fifth Army Corps.
1912   Philadelphia   100.00

TILY, James   The Uniforms of the United States Navy.
1968   New York   30.00

TINKCOM, Harry Marlin   John White Geary, Soldier-Statesman 1819-1873.
1940   Philadelphia   25.00

TINSLEY, Henry C.   Observations of a Retired Veteran.
1904   Staunton   100.00

TIPTON and BLOCKER   Gettysburg, The Pictures and the Story. Wraps.
1913   Gettysburg   30.00

TIVY, Joseph A.   Souvenir of the Seventh Containing a Brief History of It.
(190-)   Detroit   160.00

To the Memory of William M. Stanley Whose Soldier's Grave Is Unmarked by Shaft or Stone.
1965   Tyler, TX   Ltd.   30.00

To the People of the South, Senator Hammond and the Tribune by Troup. Wraps.
1860   Charleston   40.00

TOBIE, Edward P.   First Maine Cavalry. Historical Sketch & Recollections. Wraps.
n.d.   n.p.   50.00

TOBIE, Edward P.   History of the First Maine Cavalry.
1887   Boston   160.00
1987   45.00

TOBIE, Edward P.   Personal Recollections of General Sherman. Wraps.
1889   Providence   Ltd.   35.00

TOBIE, Edward P.   Service of the Cavalry in the Army of the Potomac. Wraps.
1882   Providence   Ltd.   35.00

TOBIE, Edward P.   A Trip to Richmond as Prisoner of War. Wraps.
1879   Providence   Ltd.   25.00

TOBITT, John H.   What I Heard in Europe During the "American Excitement."
1865   New York   25.00

TODD, Albert   The Campaigns of the Rebellion.
1884   Manhattan, KS   40.00

TODD, Frederick P.   **American Military Equipage, 1851-1872   Vol. I.**
    1980   New York   85.00
TODD, Frederick P.   **American Military Equipage, 1851-1872   Vol. II -**
State Forces.
    1982   New York   55.00
TODD, Frederick P.   **Cadet Gray; A Pictorial History of Life at West**
Point as Seen Through Its Uniforms.
    n.d   New York   30.00
TODD, Frederick P.   **Soldiers of the American Army 1775-1954.**
    1954   Chicago   35.00
TODD, George T.   **First Texas Regiment.**
    1909   Jefferson, TX   2000.00
    1963   Waco   Ltd.   50.00
TODD, Helen   **A Man Named Grant.**
    1940   Boston   15.00
TODD, Richard C.   **Confederate Finance.**
    1954   Athens   30.00
TODD, William   **The Seventy-ninth Highlanders, New York Volunteers**
in the War of the Rebellion.
    1886   Albany   90.00
TOEPFER, Ray Grant   **The Scarlet Guidon.**
    1958   New York   10.00
TOEPPERWEIN, Herman   **Rebel in Blue, A Novel of the Southwest**
Frontier 1861-1865.
    1963   New York and Toronto   15.00
    1972   Fredericksburg, TX   10.00
TOLBERT, Frank X.   **Dick Dowling at Sabine Pass.**
    1962   New York   30.00
TOLBERT, Noble J., edited by   **The Papers of John Willis Ellis.**
2 Vols.
    1964   Raleigh, NC   30.00
TOLMAN, N. F.   **The Search for General Miles.**
    1968   New York   25.00
TOMES, Robert   **The War With the South.** 3 Vols.
    1862-66   New York   125.00
    1865   New York   entitled **The Great Civil War**   125.00
TOMLINSON, Everett T.   **For the Stars and Stripes.**
    1909   Boston   15.00
TONEY, Marcus B.   **The Privations of a Private.**
    1905   Nashville   100.00
    1907   Nashville   75.00
TOOMBS, Robert   **The Correspondence of Robert Toombs, Alexander**
H. Stephens and Howell Cobb.
    1913   Washington, DC   25.00
TOOMBS, Samuel   **New Jersey Troops in the Gettysburg Campaign**
from June 5 to July 31, 1863.
    1888   Orange   60.00
    1988   30.00
TOOMBS, Samuel   **Reminisicences of the War, Comprising a Detailed**
Account of the Experiences of the Thirteenth New Jersey Volunteers.
    1878   Orange   100.00

TOOMEY, D. C.   The Civil War In Maryland.
    1983   Baltimore   18.00
TOPPAN, George L.   Notes Upon United States and Confederate States
    Stamps and their Varieties. Wraps.
    1906   New York   10.00
TOPPER, C. C.   Civil War Relics from South Carolina.
    1988   Fairfax   Ltd. 1000   35.00
TOTTEN, B. J.   Naval Text-Book and Dictionary for the Use of the
    Midshipmen of the U.S. Navy.
    1862   125.00
TOURGEE, Albion W.   An Appeal to Caesar.
    1884   New York   30.00
TOURGEE, Albion W.   An Appeal to Pharaoh, The Negro Problem and
    Its Radical Solution.
    1889   New York   30.00
TOURGEE, Albion W.   Bricks Without Straw.
    1880   n.p.   30.00
    1969   Baton Rouge   edited by Otto H. Olsen 10.00
TOURGEE, Albion W.   A Fool's Errand, and the Invisible Empire.
    1880   New York   30.00
TOURGEE, Albion W.   A Royal Gentleman and Zouri's Christmas.
    1881   New York   15.00
TOURGEE, Albion W.   The Story of a Thousand.
    1896   Buffalo   150.00
TOURGEE, Albion W.   The Veteran and His Pipe.
    1888   Chicago   15.00
TOUSARD, Louis De   American Artillerist's Companion. 3 Vols.
    1969   New York   90.00
TOUSEY, Thomas G.   Military History of Carlisle and Carlisle
    Barracks.
    1939   Richmond   23.00
TOWER, Henry M.   Historical Sketches Relating to Spencer, Mass.
    1903   Spencer, MA   50.00
TOWNSEND, Cyrus Brady   Three Daughters of the Confederacy.
    1905   New York   15.00
TOWNSEND, E. D.   Anecdotes of the Civil War in the United States.
    1884   New York   20.00
TOWNSEND, George Alfred   Campaigns of a Non-Combatant.
    1866   New York   30.00
    1950   Chapel Hill, NC   entitled **Rustics in Rebellion**   20.00
    1982   22.50
TOWNSEND, George Alfred   Katy of Catoctin Or the Chain-Breakers.
    1959   Cambridge, MD   10.00
TOWNSEND, Harry C.   Townsend's Diary, Last Months of the War.
    1907   Richmond   110.00
TOWNSEND, John   The South Alone Should Govern the South.
    Wraps.
    1860   Charleston, SC   100.00
TOWNSEND, Luther T.   History of the Sixteenth Regiment, New
    Hampshire Volunteers.
    1897   Washington, DC   75.00
    1902   With supplement   130.00

TOWNSEND, Richard W. The Passing of the Confederate Suggested by the Account Given of the Decrepit Appearance of the Confederate Veterans, During their March Through the Streets of Lumberton, N.C. . . .
1911   New York   75.00

TOWNSEND, Thomas S.   The Honors of the Empire State in the War of the Rebellion.
1889   New York   75.00

TOWNSEND, William H.   Lincoln and His Wife's Home Town.
1929   Indianapolis   30.00

TOWNSEND, William H.   Lincoln and Liquor.
1934   New York   15.00

TOWNSEND, William H.   Lincoln and the Bluegrass.
1955   Lexington   40.00

TOWNSEND, William H.   Lincoln, the Litigant.
1925   Boston   25.00

TOWNSEND, William H.   The Lion of Whitehall.
1967   Dunwoody, GA   15.00

TRACIE, Theodore C.   Annals of the Nineteenth Ohio Battery Volunteer Artillery.
1878   Cleveland   135.00

TRACY, J. Perkins   The Blockade Runner.   Wraps.
1896   New York   60.00

TRAIN, George Francis   Great Speech on the Withdrawal of McClellan and the Impeachment of Lincoln.   Wraps.
1865   New York   40.00

Transactions of the McLean County Historical Society, Bloomington, Illinois.
1890   Bloomington   75.00

TRASK, B. H.   61st Virginia Infantry.
1988   Lynchburg   19.95
1989   16.95

TRAVIS, Benjamin F.   The Story of the Twenty-fifth Michigan.
1897   Kalamazoo   175.00

TREDWELL, Daniel M.   A Catalogue of Books and Pamphlets Belonging to Daniel M. Tredwell, Relating to the Great Civil War. . . .
1874   New York   200.00

TREDWELL, Daniel M.   On the Construction of Improved Ordnance. . . . Wraps.
1862   50.00

TREFOUSSE, Hans Louis   Ben Butler. The South Called Him Beast!
1957   New York   25.00
1974   New York   26.00

TREFOUSSE, Hans Louis   The Cause of the Civil War - Institutional Failure, or Human Blunder?
1977   New York   10.00

TRELEASE, Allen W.   Reconstruction, The Great Experiment.
1971   New York   20.00

TRELEASE, Allen W.   White Terror, The Ku Klux Klan Conspiracy and Southern Reconstruction.
1971   New York   25.00

TREMAIN, Henry Edwin   The Closing Days About Richmond.   Wraps.
1884   Edinburgh   200.00

TREMAIN, Henry Edwin   Last Hours of Sheridan's Cavalry.
    1904   New York   45.00
TREMAIN, Henry Edwin   Sailors' Creek to Appomattox Court House,
    edited by John Watts DePeyster.   Wraps.
    1885   New York   75.00
TREMAIN, Henry Edwin   Two Days of War: A Gettysburg Narrative and
    Other Excursions.
    1905   New York   70.00
TRENT, William P.   Robert E. Lee.
    1899   Boston   30.00
TRESCOT, William Henry   Memorial of the Life of J. Johnston Petti-
    grew.
    1870   Charleston, SC   150.00
TREXLER, Harrison Anthony   The Confederate Ironclad "Virginia"
    ("Merrimac").
    1938   Chicago   40.00
TREXLER, Harrison Anthony   Slavery in Missouri 1804-1865.   Wraps.
    1914   Baltimore   30.00
TREZEVANT, D. H.   The Burning of Columbia, SC.   Wraps.
    1866   Columbia   90.00
    n.d.   Columbia   5.00
The Trial and Death of Henry Wirz.   Wraps.
    1908   Raleigh   40.00
Trial of Andrew Johnson, President of the United States.   3 Vols.
    1868   Washington, DC   75.00
    1970   Jersey City   145.00
The Trial of Hon. Clement L. Vallandigham.
    1863   Cincinnati   100.00
Trial of John Y. Beall, As a Spy and Guerrillero.   Wraps.
    1865   New York   200.00
The Trial of the Assassins and Conspirators at Washington City, D.C., May
    and June 1865, For the Murder of President Abraham Lincoln.
    1865   Philadelphia   125.00
Trial of the Officers and Crew of the Privateer Savannah, on the Charge of
    Piracy.
    1862   New York   125.00
Tribune Almanac and Political Register 1860-65.   Wraps.
    10.00 each
TRIMBLE, Harvey Marion   History of the Ninety-third Regiment Illi-
    nois Volunteer Infantry.
    1898   Chicago   150.00
TRIMBLE, Issac   Our Infantry.   Wraps.
    n.d.   n.p.   125.00
The Trip of the Steamer Oceanus to Fort Sumter and Charleston . . . . By a
    Committee.
    1865   Brooklyn, NY   50.00
TROBRIAND, Philippe Regis de   Four Years with the Army of the
    Potomac.
    1889   Boston   80.00
    1988   Gaithersburg   45.00

TROBRIAND, Philippe Regis de   Quatre Ans de Campagnes a L'Armee
du Potomac. 2 Vols.
1867-8   Paris   90.00
TROLLOPE, Anthony   North America.
1862   Philadelphia   2 Vols.   60.00
1951   New York   2 Vols. in 1   20.00
Troop Movements at the Battle of Cold Harbor.
1964   Richmond   60.00
TROTTER, William   Bushwhackers! The Civil War in North Carolina,
Volume II - The Mountains.
1988   Greensboro   19.95
TROTTER, William   Ironclads and Columbiads: The Civil War in North
Carolina, Volume III - The Coast.
1989   Greensboro   19.95
TROTTER, William   Silk Flags and Cold Steel. The Civil War in North
Carolina. Vol. I The Piedmont.
1988   Greensboro   19.95
TROWBRIDGE, John T.   Cudjo's Cave.
1864   Boston   40.00
TROWBRIDGE, John T.   The Drummer Boy.
n.d.   20.00
TROWBRIDGE, John T.   My Own Story, With Recollections of Noted
Persons.
1903   Boston   30.00
TROWBRIDGE, John T.   A Picture of the Desolated States and the
Work of Reconstruction.
1868   Hartford   100.00
1956   New York   entitled   The Desolate South 1865-66, edited by
Gordon Carroll   30.00
1970   20.00
TROWBRIDGE, John T.   The South: A Tour of its Battle Fields and
Ruined Cities.
1866   Hartford   75.00
1867   Hartford   50.00
TROWBRIDGE, John T.   The Three Scouts.
1865   Boston   25.00
TROWBRIDGE, Luther S.   A Brief History of the Tenth Michigan
Cavalry.
1905   Detroit   110.00
TROWBRIDGE, Luther S.   Michigan at Gettysburg.
1889   Detroit   85.00
TROWBRIDGE, Luther S.   The Operations of the Cavalry in the Get-
tysburg Campaign.
1888   Detroit   40.00
TROWBRIDGE, Luther S.   The Stoneman Raid of 1865, a Paper.
Wraps.
1888   Detroit   35.00
TRUDEAU, Noah Andres   Bloody Roads South: The Wilderness to
Cold Harbor, May-June, 1864.
1989   Boston   19.95

TRUESDALE, John   The Blue Coats, And How They Lived, Fought and
    Died for the Union.
    1867   Philadelphia   30.00
TRUMBULL, Henry Clay   The Captured Scout of the Army of the
    James. A Sketch of the Life of Sgt. Henry H. Manning.
    1869   Boston   75.00
TRUMBULL, Henry Clay   The Knightly Soldier, A Biography of
    Major Henry Ward Camp, Tenth Conn. Volunteers.
    1865   Boston   40.00
    1871   35.00
    1892   Philadelphia   35.00
TRUMBULL, Henry Clay   War Memories of an Army Chaplain.
    1898   New York   40.00
    1906   New York   30.00
Trumpet of Freedom. Wraps.
    1864   Boston   35.00
TUBBS, Charles   Osceola in the War of the Rebellion.
    1885   Wellsboro   75.00
TUCKER, Beverley   Address of _____ To the People of the United
    States 1865, edited by James Harvey Young. Wraps.
    1948   Atlanta   15.00
TUCKER, Beverley   The Partisan Leader.
    1861   New York   100.00
TUCKER, George Wellford   Lee and the Gettysburg Campaign.
    1933   n.p.   60.00
TUCKER, Glenn   Chickamauga.
    1961   Indianapolis   35.00
    1972   Dayton   20.00
    1984   Dayton   17.50
    1985   Dayton   20.00
    1986   Dayton   Wraps   11.95
TUCKER, Glenn   Front Rank.
    1962   Raleigh   50.00
TUCKER, Glenn   High Tide at Gettysburg.
    1958   Indianapolis   30.00
    1973   Dayton   19.95
    1988   Dayton   19.95
    1988   Dayton   Wraps   11.95
TUCKER, Glenn   Lee and Longstreet at Gettysburg.
    1968   Indianapolis   30.00
    1987   Dayton   Wraps   8.95
TUCKER, Glenn   Zeb Vance - Champion of Personal Freedom.
    1965   Indianapolis   25.00
TUCKER, Nathaniel Beverley   A Key to the Disunion Conspiracy.
    The Partisan Leader. Secretly Printed in Washington (in the year 1836)
    . . . for circulation in the Southern states. But afterwards Suppressed.
    2 Vols in 1.
    1861   New York   150.00
    1933   New York   50.00
TUCKER, S.   Arming the Fleet: U.S. Navy in the Muzzle-loading Era.
    1989   Annapolis   38.95

TUCKER, St. George   A Dissertation on Slavery: With a Proposal for the Gradual Abolition of It in the State of Virginia. Wraps.
1861   New York   50.00

TUCKERMAN, Henry T.   The Rebellion: Its Latent Causes and True Significance. Wraps.
1861   New York   10.00

TUMBLETY, Francis   A Few Passages in the Life of Dr. _____, The Indian Herb Doctor Including His Experience in the Old Capitol Prison, to Which He Was Consigned. . . . Wraps.
1866   Cincinnati   150.00

TUNNARD, W. H.   A Southern Record: The History of the Third Regiment Louisiana Infantry.
1866   Baton Rouge   800.00
1970   Dayton   edited by Edwin C. Bearss   35.00
1988   Dayton   35.00

TUNNELL, Ted   Crucible of Reconstruction. War, Radicalism, and Race in Louisiana, 1862-1877.
1984   Baton Rouge   25.00

TUNSTALL, Nannie Whitmell   "No. 40" A Romance of Fortress Monroe and the Hygeia. Wraps.
1890   Richmond   35.00

TURCHIN, John B.   Noted Battles for the Union During the Civil War in the United States of America 1861-5 - Chickamauga.
1888   Chicago   125.00

TURNER, Ann   Guide to Indiana Civil War Manuscripts. Wraps.
1965   Indianapolis   25.00

TURNER, Edward Raymond   The New Market Campaign May 1864.
1912   Richmond   60.00
1988   14.95

TURNER, George Edgar   Victory Rode the Rails.
1953   Indianapolis   65.00

TURNER, Joseph Addison   Autobiography of "The Countryman," edited by Thomas H. English. Wraps.
1943   Atlanta   15.00

TURNER, Justin G. and LEVITT, Linda   Mary Todd Lincoln - Her Life and Letters.
1972   New York   15.00

TURNER, Maxine   Navy Gray.
1988   University, AL   24.95

TURNER, W. A.   Even More Confederate Faces.
1983   Orange   35.00

TUTHILL, Richard S.   With Sherman's Artillery at the Battle of Atlanta. Wraps.
n.d.   Chicago   30.00

Twelfth U.S. Infantry 1798-1919, Its Story - By Its Men.
n.d.   New York   45.00

The 25th Regiment Connecticut Volunteers in the War of the Rebellion.
1913   Rockville, CT   100.00

TWITCHELL, Albert Sobieski   History of the Seventh Maine Light Battery.
1892   Boston   175.00

TWITCHELL, Albert Sobieski   Reunion Poems.
    1883   Gorham   15.00

Two Diaries from Middle St. Johns Berkeley, S.C. Feb-May 1865 Journals Kept by Susan R. Jervey and Charlotte S. J. Ravenel and Reminiscences of Mrs. Waring Henagan. Wraps.
    1921   n.p.   Ltd.   50.00

TWYMAN, R. W. and ROLLER, D. C.   The Encyclopedia of Southern History.
    1979   Baton Rouge   75.00

TYLER, C. W.   The Scout: A Tale of the Civil War.
    1911   Nashville   75.00
    1912   Nashville   50.00

TYLER, Lyon G.   A Confederate Catechism.   Wraps.
    1935   n.p.   5.00

TYLER, Lyon G.   Confederate Leaders and Other Citizens Request the House of Delegates to Repeal the Resolution of Respect to Abraham Lincoln the Barbarian. Wraps.
    1928   Richmond   20.00

TYLER, Lyon G.   General Lee's Birthday.   Wraps.
    1929   n.p.   5.00

TYLER, Lyon G.   John Tyler and Abraham Lincoln   Who Was the Dwarf?
    1929   Richmond   20.00

TYLER, Lyon G.   Virginia Principles Address.   Wraps.
    1928   Richmond   20.00

TYLER, Mason Whiting   Recollections of the Civil War.
    1912   New York   55.00

TYLER, Ronnie C.   Santiago Vidaurri and the Southern Confederacy.
    1973   Austin   20.00

TYLER, Samuel   Memoir of Roger Brooke Taney.
    1872   Baltimore   15.00

TYLER, William N.   The Dispatch Carrier and Memoirs of Andersonville. Wraps.
    1892   Port Byron, IL   65.00

TYRNER-TYRNAUER, A. R.   Lincoln and the Emperors.
    1962   New York   15.00

ULMER, George T.   Adventures and Reminiscences of a Volunteer. Wraps.
    1892   Chicago   30.00

The Un-Civil War, Some Maps and Views of the South During 1861-1865. Wraps.
    1974   Tiger Cave, PA   Ltd.   15.00

Uncle Daniel's Story of Tom Anderson and Twenty Great Battles   By an Officer of the Union Army.
    1886   New York   30.00

Under the Maltese Cross, Antietam to Appomattox, The Loyal Uprising in Western Pennsylvania.
    1910   Pittsburgh   150.00

UNDERWOOD, Adin B.   The Three Years' Service of the Thirty-third Mass. Infantry Regiment.
    1881   Boston   70.00

UNDERWOOD, George C.   History of the 26th Regiment of North
   Carolina Troops.
   1901   Goldsboro, NC   250.00
   1978   Wendell, NC   20.00
UNDERWOOD, John C.   Monument to the Confederate Dead at Chicago.
   1896   Chicago   40.00
   1897   Chicago   25.00
UNDERWOOD, John Levi   The Women of the Confederacy.
   1906   New York and Washington, DC   150.00
UNDERWOOD, Larry   The Butternut Guerillas: A Story of Grierson's
   Raid.
   1981   KY   13.00
Uniform and Dress of the Army and Navy of the Confederate States . . . .
   For 1861 ed., see: Confederate Imprints P-2417.
   1952   New Hope   Ltd.   50.00
Uniform Regulations for the Army of the United States. Wraps.
   1961   Washington, DC   10.00
The Uniformed Battalion of the Veterans of the 7th Regiment, N.G., N.Y.
   1861-1892.
   1893   New York   30.00
The Union Army A History of Military Affairs in the Loyal States 1861-65,
   Records of the Regiments. . . . 8 Vols.
   1908   Madison   500.00
The Union League of Philadelphia.
   1902   Philadelphia   10.00
United Confederate Veterans, Reunion.   Wraps.
   15.00 each
United Daughters of the Confederacy, Programs at Conventions.   Wraps.
   1915-56   10.00 each
United Daughters of the Confederacy - Treasured Reminiscences.   (John K.
   McIver Chapter, SC.) Wraps.
   1982   SC   10.00
The United Service,   A Quarterly Review of Military and Naval Affairs,
   Philadelphia. Vol. I-XVI, 1879-96.
   25.00 each
The United States Army and Navy Journal, and Gazette of the Regular and
   Volunteer Forces.   52 issues per volume. Wraps.
   Vol. I   Bound   150.00
   Vol. II   Bound   150.00
The United States Biographical Dictionary and Portrait Gallery of Eniment
   and Self-made Men.
   1876   Chicago   110.00
United States Christian Commission for the Army and Navy, Annual
   Reports, 1863-65. Wraps.
   20.00 each
U.S. Christian Commission, Record of the Federal Dead. Wraps.
   1865   Philadelphia   75.00 per volume
U.S. 46th Cong., 1st Sess., Senate, Es. Doc. 37 Proceedings and report of the
   board of Army officers convened . . . in the case of Fitz-John Porter. . .
   4 Vols.
   1879   Washington, DC   200.00

U.S. Infantry Tactics . . . for the Use of Colored Troops.
　　1863　　Washington, DC　　250.00
U.S. Infantry Tactics.
　　1861　　Philadelphia　100.00
　　1862　　Philadelphia　100.00
　　1863　　Philadelphia　100.00
The U. S. Sanitary Commission of the United States Army . . . Its Works and Purposes.
　　1864　　New York　　75.00
U.S. Sanitary Commission　A Sketch of Its Purposes and Its Work.
　　1863　　Boston　　75.00
U.S. Sanitary Commission Publication, Our Daily Fare.　Nos. 1-12 June 8, 1864-June 21, 1864.
　　Complete as issued　　175.00
U.S. Sanitary Commission Camp Inspection Return.
　　1861　　50.00
U.S. Sanitary Commission, Bulletins of.
　　1863-65 12 issues per year　　7.00 per issue
U.S. Sanitary Commission, Statement of the Object and Methods.
　　1863　　New York　　30.00
United States Service Magazine.
　　40.00 per volume
Univ. of PA Medical Alumni in the Civil War.　Wraps.
　　1961　　40.00
Unveiling of Monument to the First Maine Cavalry at Gettysburg, Oct. 3, 1889.
　　1889　　Boston　　30.00
Unveiling of the Equestrian Statue of Philip H. Sheridan.
　　(1961)　　Albany　　25.00
UPSHUR, Abel P.　　A Brief Enquiry into the True Nature and Character of our Federal Government.　Wraps.
　　1863　　Philadelphia　30.00
UPSHUR, John N.　　The Battle of New Market, an Address.　Wraps.
　　1903　　n.p.　125.00
UPSON, Theodore F.　　With Sherman to the Sea, The Civil War Letters, Diaries, and Reminiscences of _____, edited by Oscar Osburn Winther.
　　1943　　Baton Rouge　　35.00
　　1958　　Bloomington　　30.00
　　1977　　25.00
UPTON, E.　A New System of Infantry Tactics.
　　1867　　New York　50.00
　　1868　　New York　50.00
UPTON, Emory　　The Military Policy of the United States.
　　1904　　Washington, DC　　35.00
　　1907　　30.00
　　1912　　30.00
　　1917　　Washington, DC　　30.00
UPTON, L. M.　　Battle of Wilson's Creek.　Wraps.
　　1951　　Springfield, MO　　13.00
URBAN, John W.　　Battle Field and Prison Pen.
　　1882　　Philadelphia　　50.00

URBAN, John W.   In Defense of the Union: or Through Shot and Shell and Prison Pen.
1887   n.p.   30.00

URBAN, John W.   My Experiences Mid Shot and Shell and in Rebel Den.
1882   Lancaster, PA   60.00

URQUHART, David   The Right of Search - Two Speeches.
1862   London   50.00

URWIN, Gregory J. W.   Custer Victorious: The Civil War Battles of George Armstrong Custer.
1983   Rutherford 35.00
1990   Wraps   9.95

URWIN, Gregory J. W.   The United States Infantry: An Illustrated History, 1775-1918.
1988   London and New York   24.95

UTLEY, Robert M.   Cavalier in Buckskin,   George Armstrong Custer and the Western Military Frontier.
1988   University, OK   19.95

UTLEY, Robert M.   Custer and the Great Controversy.   Origin and Development of a Legend.
1980   17.50

UTLEY, Robert M.   Frontier Regulars.   The United States Army and the Indian. 1866-1891.
1973   New York   25.00

UTLEY, Robert M.   Frontiersmen in Blue - The U.S. Army and the Indian.
1967   New York   20.00

UTLEY, Robert M.   The Indian Frontier of the American West, 1846-1890.   Wraps.
1984   Albuquerque   15.00

UTLEY, Robert M., edited by   Life in Custer's Cavalry; Diaries and Letters of Albert and Jennie Barnitz, 1867-1868.
1977   New Haven   18.00

VAIL, Enos B.   Reminiscences of a Boy in the Civil War.
1915   Brooklyn   75.00

VAIL, I. E.   Three Years on the Blockade.
1902   New York   65.00

VAILL, Dudley Landon   The County Regiment   A Sketch of the 2nd Regiment of Connecticut Volunteer Heavy Artillery.
1908   Litchfield   75.00

VAILL, Theodore F.   History of the Second Connecticut Volunteer Heavy Artillery Originally the Nineteenth Connecticut Vols.
1868   Winsted, CT   85.00

VALE, Joseph G.   Minty and the Cavalry.
1886   Harrisburg   140.00

VALENTINE, E. G.   Dawn to Twilight: Work of Edward V. Valentine.
1929   Richmond   30.00

VALENTINE, Herbert E., edited by   Dedication of the Boulder Commemorating the Service of the Twenty-third Regiment Mass. Vol. Infantry.   Wraps.
1905   Salem   25.00

VALENTINE, Herbert E.   Story of Company F, 23d Massachusetts Volunteers.
1896   Boston   70.00
VALLANDIGHAM, James L.   Life of Clement L. Vallandigham.
1972   Baltimore   30.00
1872   New York   30.00
Valley News Echo Monthly Civil War Newspaper. 50 issues.
1965   Hagerstown, MD 100.00
Valuable American Historical Library of the Late Major Edward Willis of Charleston, SC. Wraps.
1914   40.00
The Valuable Papers of the Late Hon. Gideon Welles, Auction Catalog Jan. 4th, 1924. Wraps.
1924   n.p.   40.00
VAN ALSTYNE, Lawrence   Diary of an Enlisted Man.
1910   New Haven   75.00
VANCE, Wilson J.   Stone's River, The Turning-Point of the Civil War.
1914   New York   125.00
VANCE, Zebulon B.   The Last Days of the War in North Carolina, An Address. Wraps.
1885   Baltimore   100.00
VANCE, Zebulon B.   The Papers of Zebulon Baird Vance, Vol. 1 1843-1862, edited by Frontis W. Johnston.
1963   Raleigh, NC   15.00
VAN CLEAF, Aaron R., compiled by   History of Pickaway County, Ohio and Representative Citizens.
1906   Chicago 110.00
VANDERHUESSEL, Jerry   Crowns of Thorns and Glory.
1988   19.95
VANDERSLICE, Catherine H.   The Civil War Letters of George Washington Beidelman.
1978   New York   25.00
VANDERSLICE, John M.   Gettysburg, Where and How the Regiments Fought and Troops They Encountered.
1897   Philadelphia   40.00
1899   New York   40.00
1899   Chicago   35.00
1983   35.00
VANDER VELDE, Lewis G.   The Presbyterian Churches and the Federal Union 1861-1868.
1932   Cambridge   30.00
1932   London   40.00
VAN DEUSEN, Glyndon G.   Horace Greeley Nineteenth-Century Crusader.
1953   Philadelphia   20.00
VAN DEUSEN, Glyndon G.   The Life of Henry Clay.
1937   25.00
1979   Westport   35.00
VAN DEUSEN, Glyndon G.   Thurlow Weed: Wizard of the Lobby.
1947   Boston   25.00
VAN DEUSEN, Glyndon G.   William Henry Seward.
1967   New York   25.00

VAN DE WATER, Frederic F.   Glory-Hunter, A Life of Gen. Custer.
   1934   Indianapolis   45.00
   1964   New York   15.00
VANDIVER, Frank E., edited by   Confederate   Blockade   Running
Through Bermuda 1861-1865.
   1946   Austin, TX   75.00
   1947   50.00
   1970   40.00
VANDIVER, Frank E.   Jefferson Davis and the Confederate States.
Wraps.
   1964   Oxford   15.00
VANDIVER, Frank E.   Jubal's Raid, General Early's Famous Attack on
Washington in 1864.
   1960   New York   35.00
   1974   Westport   20.00
   1988   25.00
   1988   Wraps   15.00
VANDIVER, Frank E.   The Making of a President: Jefferson Davis,
1861. Wraps.
   1962   Richmond   20.00
VANDIVER, Frank E.   Mighty Stonewall.
   1957   New York   40.00
   1957   Ltd. signed edition   60.00
   1974   Westport   50.00
   1988   30.00
VANDIVER, Frank E.   Ploughshares into Swords.
   1952   Austin   75.00
   1977   35.00
VANDIVER, Frank E.   Rebel Brass The Confederate Command System.
   1956   Baton Rouge, LA   45.00
   1971   Westport   30.00
VANDIVER, Frank E.   Their Tattered Flags.
   1970   New York   30.00
VANDIVER, Frank E., et al   Essays on the American Civil War.
   1968   Austin, TX   20.00
VAN DOREN, Mark   The Last Days of Lincoln A Play in Six Scenes.
   1959   New York   25.00
VAN HORNE, John Douglass   Jefferson Davis and Repudiation in Mississippi. Wraps.
   1915   n.p.   20.00
VAN HORNE, Thomas B.   History of the Army of the Cumberland. 3
Vols. (2 Vols. - Text, 1 Vol. - Atlas).
   1875   Cincinnati 400.00
   1988   Wilmington, NC   2 Vols.   60.00
VAN HORNE, Thomas B.   The Life of Maj. Gen. George H. Thomas.
   1882   New York   50.00
VAN NESS, W. W.   The National School for the Soldier.
   1862   New York   30.00
VAN NOPPEN, Ina Woestemeyer   Stoneman's Last Raid.
   1961   Raleigh, NC   25.00

VAN SANTVOORD, Cornelius   The One Hundred and Twentieth Regiment New York State Volunteers.
1894   Rondout   85.00
1983   New York   18.00
VANSCOTEN, M. H.   The Conception, Organization and Campaigns of Company "H" 4th Penn. Reserves, compiled by Mrs. M. H. France.
1883   Tunkhannock   110.00
1885   Tunkhannock   100.00
VAN ZANDT, K. M.   Force With Fanfare: The Autobiography of _____.
1968   Fort Worth   20.00
VASVARY, Edmund   Lincoln's Hungarian Heroes, The Participation of Hungarians in the Civil War 1861-1865.   Wraps.
1939   Washington, DC   40.00
VAUGHAN, Alfred J.   Personal Record of the Thirteenth Regiment, Tenn. Infantry C.S.A. by Its Old Commander.
1897   Memphis   150.00
1975   Brentwood Ltd.   20.00
VAUGHT, Elsa, edited by   The Diary of an Unknown Soldier Sept. 5, 1862 to December 7, 1862.
1959   Van Buren, AR   30.00
VAUGHTER, John Bacon   Prison Life in Dixie Giving a Short History of Inhuman and Barbarous Treatment of Our Soldiers by Rebel Authorities, edited by Serg. Oats.
1880   Chicago   60.00
VAUTIER, John D.   History of the 88th Pennsylvania Volunteers.
1894   Philadelphia   140.00
1986   30.00
VELAZQUEZ, Loreta Janeta   The Woman in Battle.
1876   Richmond   50.00
1876   Hartford   40.00
1890   New York   entitled The Famous Female Spy   30.00
VENABLE, C. S.   The Campaign from the Wilderness to Petersburg. Address.   Wraps.
1879   Richmond   150.00
VENABLE, Matthew Walton   Eighty Years after or Grandpa's Story.
1929   Charleston, WV   70.00
VERNE, Ilian   Phil, The Scout.   The War Library Vol. 7, No. 233. Wraps.
1887   New York   30.00
VERNE, Jules   North Against South, a Tale of the American Civil War.   2 Parts in 1.
1888   London   60.00
VICKERS, George Edward   Last Charge at Gettysburg.   Wraps.
1899   Philadelphia   30.00
VICKERS, George Morley   Under Both Flags.
1896   Boston   45.00
1896   Chicago   40.00
1896   Philadelphia   40.00
VICTOR, Orville J.   The History, Civil, Political and Military of the Southern Rebellion.   4 Vols.
1861-68   New York   80.00

VICTOR, Orville J.   Incidents and Anecdotes of the War.
    1862   New York   20.00
    1866   New York   20.00
VIELE, Egbert   Hand-Book for Active Service.
    1861   New York   60.00
    1968   New York   20.00
VILAS, William F.   A View of the Vicksburg Campaign.
    1908   Madison   40.00
VILLARD, Henry   Lincoln on the Eve of '61.
    1941   New York   15.00
VILLARD, Henry   Memoirs of Henry Villard, Journalist and Financier
1835-1900. 2 Vols.
    1904   Boston   40.00
VILLARD, Oswald Garrison   John Brown. . . . A Biography Fifty Years
After.
    1910   New York   50.00
    1910   Boston   50.00
    1911   Boston   50.00
    1965   20.00
VILLIERS, Brougham   Anglo-American Relations 1861-1865.
    1920   New York   30.00
VINCENT, Thomas M.   Abraham Lincoln and Edwin M. Stanton.
Wraps.
    1890   Washington, DC   25.00
    1892   Washington, DC   20.00
VINTER, Thomas H.   Memoirs of _____.
    1926   Philadelphia   60.00
Virginia at Gettysburg 1917 Ceremonies Attending Dedication of the Virginia Memorial on the Battlefield of Gettysburg. . . .
    (1917)   Richmond   100.00
The Virginia Campaign of 1862 Under General Pope.   See: Papers of the Military Historical Society of Massachusetts, No. 2.
Virginia - Confederate Military History.   See: Confederate Military History, Vol. III (Vol. IV, 1987 reprint ed.).
Virginia Guidebook. Wraps.
    1961   Williamsburg, VA   15.00
Virginia Historical Society, Collections of.
    Vols. I-VI   35.00 each
VLOCK, Laurel F. and **LEVITCH**, Joel A.   Contraband of War, William Henry Singleton.
    1970   New York   20.00
VOEGELI, V. Jacque   Free But Not Equal, the Midwest and the Negro During the Civil War.
    1969   Chicago   15.00
A Voice from Rebel Prisons Giving an Account of Some of the Horrors of the Stockades at Andersonville, Milan, and Other Prisons by a Returned Prisoner of War. Wraps.
    1865   Boston   60.00
VOLCK, Adelbert J.   Confederate War Etchings.   29 plates loose in folder.
    (1880-90)   (Philadelphi)   Ltd. to 100 sets   1600.00

The Volunteers' Roll of Honor.   Wraps.
    1864   Philadelphia   30.00
VON ABELE, Rudolph   Alexander H. Stephens, A Biography.
    1946   New York   30.00
VON HOLST, H. E.   John C. Calhoun.   Wraps.
    1980   Edgemont, PA   6.00
VON HOLST, Hermann   John Brown, edited by Frank P. Stearns and
John C. Calhoun.
    1888   Boston   35.00
VOORHIS, Jerry, Sr.   The Life and Times of Aurelius Lyman Voorhis.
    1976   New York   30.00
W. D. B.   See: BICKHAM, W. D.
WADDELL, Alfred Moore   Some Memories of My Life.
    1908   Raleigh, NC   50.00
WADDELL, James D., edited by   Biographical Sketch of Linton Stephens.
    1877   Atlanta   75.00
WADDELL, James I.   C.S.S. Shenandoah: The Memoirs of Lieutenant
Commander James I. Waddell, edited by James D. Horan.
    1960   New York   35.00
WADDELL, Joseph A.   Annals of Augusta County, Virginia . . . with a
Diary of the War 1861-5 and A Chapter on Reconstruction.
    1886   Richmond   90.00
    1888   Richmond   75.00
WAGENKNECHT, Edward   Abraham Lincoln   His Life, Work and
Character.
    1947   New York   10.00
WAGNER, William F.   Letters of William F. Wagner, Confederate Sol-
dier, edited by J. M. Hatley and L. B. Huffman.
    1983   Wendell, NC   15.00
WAGSTAFF, Henry McGilbert   State Rights and Political Parties in
North Carolina, 1776-1861.
    1906   Baltimore   25.00
WAHL, P. and TOPPEL, D.   The Gatling Gun.
    1965   New York   60.00
WAINWRIGHT, Charles S.   A Diary of Battle, The Personal Journals
of _____, edited by Allan Nevins.
    1962   New York   60.00
WAITE, Otis F. R.   Claremont War History: April 1861 to April 1865
New Hampshire Regiments.
    1868   Concord 55.00
WAITE, Otis F. R.   New Hampshire in the Great Rebellion . . .
    1870   Claremont   60.00
WAITE, Otis F. R.   Vermont in the Great Rebellion.
    1869   Claremont   20.00
WAITT, Ernest Linden, compiled by   History of the Nineteenth Regi-
ment Massachusetts Volunteer Infantry.
    1906   Salem 65.00
    1988   25.00
WAITT, R. W.   Confederate Military Hospitals in Richmond.   Wraps.
    1964   Richmond   25.00

WAITZ, Julia Ellen (Le Grand)   The Journal of Julia Le Grand: New Orleans 1862-1863.
   1911   Richmond   75.00
WALCOTT, Charles F.   History of the Twenty-first Regiment Massachusetts Volunteers.
   1882   Boston   75.00
WALKER, Aldace F.   The Vermont Brigade in the Shenandoah Valley 1864.
   1869   Burlington   50.00
WALKER, C. Irvine   The Life of Lieut. Gen. Richard Heron Anderson.
   1917   Charleston, SC   150.00
WALKER, C. Irvine   Rolls and Historical Sketch of the Tenth Regiment, So. Ca. Volunteers.
   1881   Charleston, SC   300.00
   1985   Lexington, VA   25.00
WALKER, Charles D.   Memorial V.M.I. Biographical Sketches of the Graduates . . . Who Fell During the War.
   1875   Philadelphia   125.00
WALKER, Charles M.   Sketch of the Life . . . of Oliver P. Morton.
   1878   Indianapolis   30.00
WALKER, Edward A.   Our First Year of Army Life, An Anniversary Address Delivered to First Regiment of Connecticut Volunteer Heavy Artillery. Wraps.
   1862   New Haven   50.00
WALKER, Francis A.   General Hancock.
   For additional information, see Appendix: Great Commanders Series.
   1894   New York   30.00
   1894   New York   Ltd. 125.00
   1895   30.00
   1897   New York   30.00
   1987   30.00
WALKER, Francis A.   Hancock in the War of the Rebellion. Wraps.
   1891   n.p.   50.00
WALKER, Francis A.   A History of the Second Army Corps in the Army of the Potomac.
   1886   New York   75.00
   1891   New York   60.00
   1985   40.00
   1988   40.00
WALKER, G. C.   Yankee Soldiers in Virginia Valleys: Hunter's Raid.
   1989   Roanoke Ltd.   30.00
WALKER, Georgiana Gholson   The Private Journal of Georgiana Gholson Walker 1862-1865.   See: Confederate Centennial Studies, No. 25.
WALKER, Jeanie Mort   Life of Capt. Joseph Fry, the Cuban Martyr.
   1875   Hartford   65.00
WALKER, Margaret Walker   Jubilee.
   1966   Boston   15.00
WALKER, Peter F.   Building a Tennessee Army: Autumn 1861. Wraps.
   1957   TN   15.00

WALKER, Peter F.   Vicksburg: A People at War, 1860-1865.
> 1960   Chapel Hill, NC   30.00
> 1987   Wilmington, NC   25.00
> 1987   Wilmington, NC   Wraps   8.95

WALKER, Richard L.   Camp Life of a Confederate Boy of Bratton's Brigade, Longstreet's Corps.
> 1984   25.00

WALKER, William C.   History of the Eighteenth Regiment Conn. Volunteers.
> 1885   Norwich   75.00

WALKLEY, Stephen   History of the 7th Connecticut Volunteer Infantry.
> 1905   Southington, CT   90.00

WALL, Alexander J.   A Sketch of the Life of Horatio Seymour 1810-1886.
> 1929   New York   Ltd.   50.00

WALL, Bernhardt   Following Abraham Lincoln 1809-1865.
> 1943   Lime Rock, CT   25.00

WALL, H. C.   Historical Sketch of the Pee Dee Guards.
> 1983   30.00

WALL, Joseph Frazier   Henry Watterson Reconstructed Rebel.
> 1956   New York   15.00

WALLACE, Elizabeth C.   Glencoe Diary: The War-Time Journal of . . . , edited by Eleanor and Charles Cross.   Wraps.
> 1968   VA   20.00
> 1983   Wendell, NC   20.00

WALLACE, Francis B.   Memorial of the Patriotism of Schuylkill County.
> 1865   Pottsville   50.00

WALLACE, Isabel   Life and Letters of Gen. W. H. L. Wallace.
> 1909   Chicago   75.00

WALLACE, John   Carpet-bag Rule in Florida.   Wraps.
> 1888   Jacksonville   300.00
> 1986   20.00

WALLACE, Lee A., Jr.   5th Virginia Infantry.
> 1988   Lynchburg   16.95

WALLACE, Lee A., Jr.   Guide to Virginia Military Organizations 1861-1865.
> 1964   Richmond   40.00
> 1986   Lynchburg   40.00

WALLACE, Lee A., Jr.   Under the Stars and Bars: A History of the Surry Light Artillery.
> 1975   OH 25.00

WALLACE, Lewis   Ben Hur: A Tale of the Christ.
> 1880   40.00

WALLACE, Lewis   Lew Wallace: An Autobiography. 2 Vols.
> 1906   New York   120.00

WALLACE, Robert C.   A Few Memories of a Long Life, edited by John Carroll.
> (1916)   (Helena)   25.00

WALLACE, Willard M.   Soul of the Lion, A Biography of General Joshua L. Chamberlain.
1960   New York   40.00
1960   Edinburgh   40.00

WALLIS, S. Teakle   Address . . . Delivered at the Academy of Music, in Baltimore, April 20th, 1874, on Behalf of the Lee Memorial Assoc. Wraps.
1875   Baltimore   10.00

WALSH, William S., edited by   Abraham Lincoln and the London Punch.
1909   New York   15.00

WALTER, R. S.   A Ride for Life at Gettysburg.
1896   Front Royal, VA   40.00

WALTERS, John B.   Merchant of Terror General Sherman and Total War.
1973   Indianapolis   15.00

WALTERS, Judith Allison   Brief Biographies of 12 Illinois Men Who Fought in the Civil War. Wraps.
1975   Washington, DC   6.00

WALTHALL, Ernest Taylor   Hidden Things Brought to Light.
1933   Richmond   Ltd.   40.00

WALTON, Clyde C.   Illinois and the Civil War. Wraps.
1961   Springfield   10.00

WALTON, William   Army and Navy of the United States: From the Period of the Revolution to the Present day. Green wrappers in cloth portfolios.
1889-95   Philadelphia   1200.00
Same on Japanese vellum   2500.00
1900   Philadelphia   (usually bound in 2 Vols.) 1500.00

WALTON, William Martin   An Epitome of My Life: Civil War Reminiscences.
1965   Austin   40.00

The War 1861-1865 As Depicted in Prints by Currier and Ives. Wraps.
1960   n.p.   10.00

War Between the States . . . . Wraps.
1938   Hattiesburg, MS   100.00

War Days in Fayetteville, North Carolina, Reminiscences of 1861 to 1865.
1910   (Fayetteville, NC)   75.00

The War for the Union, 1861-1865: A Record of Its Defenders, Living and Dead, from Steuben County, Indiana; and History of Veteran Organizations and Kindred Associations.
1888-89   n.p.   150.00

War History of the National Rifles, Company A, Third Battalion District of Columbia Volunteers of 1861.
1887   Wilmington, DE   175.00

War Letters of a Disbanded Volunteer.   See: BARBER, Joseph

War Lyrics and Songs of the South.
1866   London   75.00

War Papers and Personal Reminiscences, 1861-1865 Read Before the Commandery of the State of Missouri, Mollus. Vol. I (all pub).
1892   St. Louis   75.00

War Papers of the Confederacy. Wraps.
 1961 Charlottesville, VA 20.00
War Papers Ohio Commandery. 4 Vols.
 1888 165.00
War Papers Read Before the Commandery of the State of Maine, Mollus.
Vols. 1-4.
 1898-1908 Portland 35.00 each
War Papers Read before the Commandery of the State of Wisconsin, Mollus.
4 Vols.
 1891-1914 Milwaukee 50.00 each
War Papers Read Before the Indiana Commandery, Mollus, Vol. I (all
issued).
 1898 Indianapolis Ltd. 85.00
War Papers Read Before the Michigan Commandery, Mollus. 2 Vols.
 1893-98 Detroit 150.00
War Record, General I. F. Shepard 1861-1864. Wraps.
 (1889) n.p. 30.00
War Records. Wraps.
 1907 Columbia 30.00
 1908 Columbia 30.00
War Records, South Carolina College Cadets in the War. Wraps.
 1908 Columbia 36.00
War Sketches and Incidents. Iowa Commandery, Mollus. 2 Vols.
 1893-98 Des Moines 130.00
War Talks in Kansas, A Series of Papers Read Before the Kansas Comman-
dery, Mollus.
 1906 Kansas City 200.00
WARD, Dallas T. **The Last Railroad Flag of Truce During the Civil**
War. Wraps.
 n.d. Raleigh, NC 15.00
WARD, Dallas T. **War Songs of the Blue and Gray As Sung By the**
Brave Soldiers of the Union and Confederate Armies.
 n.d. New York 30.00
WARD, Fanny B. **History of Battery "I," First Ohio O.L.A.**
 n.d. n.p. 250.00
WARD, George W. **History of the Excursion of the Fifteenth Mas-**
sachusetts Regiment.
 1901 Worcester 30.00
WARD, George W. **History of the 2nd Pennsylvania Veteran Heavy**
Artillery.
 1904 Philadelphia 75.00
WARD, James A. **That Man Haupt, A Biography.**
 1973 Baton Rouge 25.00
WARD, Joseph R. C. **History of the 106th Regiment Pennsylvania Volun-**
teers, 2nd Brigade, 2nd Division, 2nd Corps.
 1883 Philadelphia 125.00
 1906 Philadelphia 100.00
WARD, Lester F. **Young Ward's Diary,** edited by B. J. Stern.
 1935 New York 55.00

WARD, Margaret Ketcham   Testimony Before U.S. Senate Committee on Relations Between Labor and Capital. Wraps.
- 1936   Birmingham   100.00
- 1965   Birmingham   50.00
- 1977   Birmingham   20.00

WARD, Susan Hayes   George H. Hepworth, Preacher, Journalist, Friend of the People - The Story of His Life.
- 1903   New York   30.00

WARD, W. H.   Records of Members of the Grand Army of the Republic, with a Complete Account of the 20th National Encampment. . . .
- 1886   75.00

WARDEN, Robert   An Account of the Private Life and Public Services of Salmon P. Chase.
- 1874   Cincinnati   30.00

WARE, Edith Ellen   Political Opinion in Massachusetts During Civil War and Reconstruction.
- 1916   New York   20.00
- 1969   20.00

WARE, Eugene F.   The Indian War of 1864.
- 1911   Topeka   125.00
- 1960   New York   35.00
- 1960   NE Wraps   15.00

WARE, Eugene F.   The Lyon Campaign in Missouri: Being a History of the First Iowa Infantry.
- 1907   Topeka   125.00

WARFIELD, Edgar   A Confederate Soldier's Memoirs.
- 1936   Richmond Ltd.   200.00

WARING, George E., Jr.   Whip and Spur.
- 1875   Boston   75.00
- 1886   Boston Ltd.   110.00
- 1897   New York   50.00

WARING, Malvina Sarah   One Old Reb.
- 1929   Columbia, SC   50.00

WARING, Mary   Miss Waring's Journal 1863 and 1865, edited by Thad Holt, Jr. Wraps.
- 1964   Chicago   40.00

WARINNER, N. E.   A Register of Military Events in Virginia, 1861-1865. Wraps.
- 1959   Richmond   10.00

WARMOTH, Henry Clay   War, Politics and Reconstruction.
- 1930   New York   50.00

WARNEFORD, R. N.   Running the Blockade.
- 1863   London   200.00

WARNER, Abraham J.   The Private Journal of Abraham Joseph Warner.
- 1973   San Diego Ltd.   50.00

WARNER, Ezra J.   Generals in Blue.
- 1964   Baton Rouge   30.00
- 1977   Baton Rouge   30.00
- 1984   Baton Rouge   30.00
- 1986   Baton Rouge   30.00

WARNER, Ezra J.   Generals in Gray.
    1959   Baton Rouge   30.00
    1965   Baton Rouge   25.00
    1983   Baton Rouge   25.00
    1986   Baton Rouge   25.00
WARNER, Ezra J. and YEARNS, W. Buck   Biographical Register of the
    Confederate Congress.
    1975   Baton Rouge   30.00
Warren and Danner's Pocket Guide Book of Gettysburg and the Battlefield
    with Map.
    n.d.   n.p.   20.00
Warren County Civil War Centennial Commemoration, The Battle of Front
    Royal, May 19-20, 1862. Wraps.
    n.d.   n.p.   15.00
WARREN, Edward   A Doctor's Experiences in Three Continents.
    1885   Baltimore   150.00
WARREN, G. H.   Fountain of Discontent: The Trent Affair and Freedom
    of the Seas.
    1981   Boston   27.50
WARREN, G. K.   An Account of the Operations of the 5th Army Corps
    Commanded by Maj.-Gen. G. K. Warren, at the Battle of Five Forks,
    April 1, 1865. Wraps.
    1866   New York   40.00
WARREN, H. N.   Declaration of Independence and War History, Bull Run
    to Appomattox.
    1894   Buffalo, NY   75.00
WARREN, Horatio N.   Two Reunions of the 142nd Regiment Penna.
    Vols.
    1890   Buffalo   75.00
WARREN, Kittrell J.   Life and Public Services of an Army Straggler,
    edited by Floyd C. Watkins. Wraps.
    1961   Athens   25.00
WARREN, Louis A.   Lincoln's Gettysburg Declaration.
    1964   Fort Wayne   Ltd.   25.00
    1974   15.00
WARREN, Louis A.   Lincoln's Youth Indiana Years Seven to Twenty-
    One 1816-1830.
    1958   New York   20.00
    1959   New York   15.00
WARREN, M. A.   Historic Buildings of Edenton, North Carolina. Wraps.
    n.d.   Edenton   10.00
WARREN, R.   The Prairie President: Living Through the Years with
    Lincoln.
    n.d.   Chicago   15.00
WARREN, Robert Penn   Band of Angels.
    1955   New York   10.00
WARREN, Robert Penn   Jefferson Davis Gets His Citizenship Back.
    1980   Lexington, KY   25.00
WARREN, Robert Penn   John Brown - The Making of a Martyr.
    1929   New York   125.00
WARREN, Robert Penn   The Legacy of the Civil War.
    1961   New York   40.00

WARREN, Robert Penn   Wilderness, A Tale of the Civil War.
1961   New York   15.00
WARREN, Rose Harlow   A Southern Home in War Times.
1914   Broadway, NY   40.00
WARRINER, N. E., compiled by   A Register of Military Events in Virginia, 1861-1865. Wraps.
1959   Richmond   15.00
WASH, W. A.   Camp, Field and Prison Life; containing sketches of service in the South, and the experience, incidents and observations. . . .
1870   St. Louis   200.00
WASHBURN, Emory   Can a State Secede? Wraps.
1865   Cambridge   25.00
WASHBURN, George H.   A Complete History of the 108th Regiment N. Y. Vols. Together with Roster, Letters, Rebel Oaths of Allegiance, Rebel Passes, Reminiscences. Wraps.
1887   New York   60.00
1894   Rochester   140.00
WASHBURN, William D., Jr.   Gettysburg. Wraps.
1908   Minneapolis   25.00
Washington and Lee University, Lexington, Virginia. Historical Papers, No. 6 - 1904.
1904   Lynchburg   125.00
WASHINGTON, John   They Knew Lincoln.
1942   New York   20.00
WASHINGTON, Mrs. James Madison   How Beauty Was Saved and Other Memories of the Sixties.
1907   New York   40.00
WASON, Robert Alexander   Babe Randolph's Turning Point, An Episode of the Civil War.
1904   Chicago   Ltd.   150.00
WASSON, R. Gordon   The Hall Carbine Affair.
1948   New York   55.00
WATERBURY, J. B.   Something for the Knapsack. Wraps.
1862   New York   75.00
WATERMEIER, Daniel J., edited by   Between Actor and Critic. Selected Letters of Edwin Booth and William Winter.
1971   Princeton   30.00
WATERS, Williard O.   Confederate Imprints in the Henry E. Huntington Library Unrecorded in Previously Published Biographies of Such Material. Wraps.
1929   n.p.   25.00
1930   n.p.   25.00
WATHEN, R. N.   The First Manassas: Correspondence Between General R. S. Ewell and G. T. Beauregard. Wraps.
1885   TN   10.00
WATKINS, Lizzie Stringfellow   The Life of Horace Stringfellow.
1931   Montgomery, AL   45.00
WATKINS, Raymond   The Greenville County Historical Society, The Hicksford Raid. Wraps.
1978   VA   20.00

WATKINS, Sam R.   "Co. Aytch" Maury Grays First Tennessee Regiment.
  1882   Nashville   600.00
  1900   Chattanooga   300.00
  1952   Jackson   edited by Bell I. Wiley   35.00
  1982   Dayton   20.00
  1987   Wilmington   25.00
  1987   Wilmington   Wraps   9.00
WATSON, Benjamin Franklin   Addresses, Reviews and Episodes, Chiefly Concerning the "Old Sixth" Massachusetts Regiment.
  1901   New York   75.00
WATSON, Benjamin Franklin   An Oration Delivered at Huntington Hall, Lowell, Massachusetts April 19, 1886.
  1886   New York   35.00
WATSON, Lady Elizabeth   Fight and Survive: A History of Jackson County, Arkansas in the Civil War.
  1973   Newport   25.00
WATSON, Thomas E.   Bethany A Story of the Old South.
  1929   Washington, DC   30.00
WATSON, Thomas Shelby   The Silent Riders. Wraps.
  1971   Louisville   7.00
WATSON, Virginia   The Featherlys.
  1936   New York   15.00
WATSON, William   Letters of a Civil War Surgeon, edited by Paul Fatout. Wraps.
  1961   W. Lafayette, IN   20.00
WATSON, William   Life in the Confederate Army Being the Observations and Experiences of an Alien in the South During the American Civil War.
  1888   New York   160.00
  1888   New York   150.00
  1983   New York   30.00
WATSON, William   The Adventures of a Blockade Runner.
  1892   London   75.00
  1893   London   75.00
  1898   London   75.00
WATSON, Winslow C.   Eulogium Commemorative of Gorton T. Thomas. Wraps.
  1862   Burlington   30.00
WATTERSON, Henry   "Marse Henry," an Autobiography. 2 Vols.
  1919   New York   40.00
WATTERSON, Henry   Abraham Lincoln, An Oration. Wraps.
  1899   Louisville   10.00
WATTS, D. W., compiled by   Civil War Battles in Winchester and Frederick County, VA, 1861-1865.
  1960   Boyce   20.00
WAUCHOPE, George Armstrong   Henry Timrod: Man and Poet. Wraps.
  1915   Columbia   25.00
WAY, Virgil G.   History of the Thirty-third Regiment Illinois Veteran Volunteer Infantry.
  1902   Gibson City, IL   140.00

WAYDE, Bernard   Along the Potomac. The War Library Vol. 2, No. 256. Wraps.
   1887   New York   30.00

WAYLAND, John W.   Battle of New Market Memorial Address. Wraps.
   1926   New Market, VA   40.00

WAYLAND, John W.   John Kagi and John Brown.
   1961   Strasburg, VA   25.00

WAYLAND, John W.   The Pathfinder of the Seas.
   1930   Richmond   50.00

WAYLAND, John W.   Robert E. Lee and His Family.
   1951   Staunton, VA   45.00

WAYLAND, John W.   Stonewall Jackson's Way.
   1940   Staunton, VA   200.00
   1956   Staunton, VA   75.00
   1969   Verona, VA   50.00
   1984   Dayton   45.00

WAYLAND, John W.   Twenty-five Chapters on the Shenandoah Valley.
   1957   Strasburg   50.00

WAYNE, Henry C.   The Sword Exercise, Arranged for Military Instruction.
   1860   Washington, DC   35.00

WEAVER, Ethan Allen   Owen Rice, Christian, Scholar and Patriot, A Genealogical and Historical Memoir. Wraps.
   1911   Germantown   40.00

WEAVER, R. M.   The Southern Tradition at Bay; a History of Postbellum Thought.
   1968   New York   15.00

WEAVER, Ward   Hang My Wreath.
   1941   New York   10.00

Webb and His Brigade at the Angle, Gettysburg.
   1916   Albany   60.00

WEBB, Alexander S.   An Address Delivered at Gettysburg . . . at the Dedication of the Monument, 72nd Pa. Vols. Wraps.
   1883   Philadelphia 40.00

WEBB, Alexander S.   The Peninsula   McClellan's Campaign of 1862. See: Campaigns of the Civil War.

WEBB, Richard D., edited by   The Life and Letters of Captain John Brown.
   1861   London   35.00

WEBB, W. L.   Battles and Biographies of Missourians, or The Civil War Period of Our State.
   1900   Kansas City   125.00
   1903   125.00

WEBB, Willard   Crucial Moments of the Civil War.
   1961   New York   25.00

WEBBER, Richard H.   Monitors of the US Navy 1861-1937. Wraps.
   n.d.   Washington, DC   15.00

WEBER, John B.   Autobiography of John B. Weber.
   1924   Buffalo   30.00

WEBER, Thomas   The Northern Railroads in the Civil War.
   1952   New York   50.00
   1953   New York   35.00
   1970   35.00
WEBSTER, Dan and CAMERON, Don C.   History of the First Wisconsin Battery Light Artillery.
   1907   Washington, DC   140.00
WEBSTER, William G.   Army & Navy Pocket Dictionary.
   1863   New York   75.00
WECTER, D.   When Johnny Comes Marching Home.
   1970   Westport   25.00
WEDDELL, Alexander Wilborne   Richmond, Virginia in Old Prints, 1737-1887.
   1932   Richmond Ltd.   250.00
WEDDLE, Robert S.   Plow Horse Cavalry, The Caney Creek Boys of the 34th Texas.
   1974   Austin   20.00
WEED, Cora Chaplin, compiled by   Handbook for Iowa Soldiers' and Sailors' Monument.
   1898   n.p.   30.00
WEEDEN, William B.   War Government, Federal and State in Massachusetts, New York, Pennsylvania and Indiana 1861-1865.
   1906   Boston   30.00
The Weekly Southern Spy: an Account of the Events, Progress and Spirit of the American War.   Vol. 1, No. 1   June 29, 1861.   Periodical.
   1861   Baltimore   300.00
WEEKS, Della Jerman   Legends of the War.
   1868   Boston   25.00
WEEKS, Stephen B.   The University of North Carolina in the Civil War, An Address . . . June 5, 1895.   Wraps.
   1896   Richmond   85.00
WEICHMAN, Louis   A True History of the Assassination of Abraham Lincoln and the Conspiracy of 1865.
   1975   New York   20.00
WEIGLEY, Russell F.   Quartermaster General of the Union Army - A Biography of M. C. Meigs.
   1959   New York   40.00
WEIK, James W.   The Real Lincoln A Portrait.
   1922   Boston   15.00
WEINER, Jonathan M.   Social Origins of the New South: Alabama 1860-1865.
   1978   Baton Rouge   30.00
WEINERT, R. P. and ARTHUR, R.   Defender of the Chesapeake: The Story of Fort Monroe.
   1989   Shippensburg   19.95
WEISBERGER, Bernard A.   Reporters for the Union.
   1953   Boston   20.00
WEISER, George   Nine Months in Rebel Prisons.
   1890   Philadelphia   50.00
WEISS, Francis   Reminiscences of Chevalier Karl De Unter-Schill, Later Known as Colonel Francis Weiss.
   1903   Troy, NY   30.00

WEITZEL, Godfrey   Richmond Occupied, edited by Louis H. Manarin. Wraps.
   1965   Richmond   30.00
WELCH, G. M.   Border Warfare in Southeastern Kansas, 1856-59.
   1977   12.00
WELCH, Spencer Glasgow   A Confederate Surgeon's Letters to His Wife.
   1911   New York   500.00
   1954   Marietta   30.00
WELCH, William L.   23rd Massachusetts Infantry. Personal Narratives of Events in the War of the Rebellion.
   1890   RI   50.00
WELCHER, F. J.   The Union Army, 1861-1865; Organization and Operations. Vol. I- The Eastern Theater.
   1987   Bloomington   75.00
   1989   75.00
WELD, Stephen Minot   War Diary and Letters of Stephen Minot Weld 1861-1865.
   1912   Cambridge   Ltd.   300.00
   1979   Boston   Ltd   50.00
WELLER, Edwin   A Civil War Courtship, the Letters of Edwin Weller from Anitetam to Atlanta.
   1980   Garden City   15.00
WELLER, Edwin   Civil War Courtship, the Letters of Edwin Weller from Antietam to Atlanta, edited by William Watson.
   (1980)   15.00
WELLES, Gideon   Civil War and Reconstruction, edited by Albert Mordell.
   1959   New York   7.00
WELLES, Gideon   Diary of _____, Lincoln's Secretary of the Navy. 3 Vols.
   1911   Boston   75.00
   1960   New York   edited by Howard K. Beale   Boxed   75.00
WELLES, Gideon   Lincoln and Seward.
   1874   New York   30.00
   1969   New York   15.00
WELLMAN, Manly Wade   Giant in Gray. Wade Hampton.
   1949   New York   60.00
   1980   Dayton   35.00
   1988   Dayton   35.00
WELLMAN, Manly Wade   Harpers Ferry Prize of War.
   1960   Charlotte, NC   15.00
WELLMAN, Manly Wade   The Kingdom of Madison; A Southern Mountain Fastness and Its People.
   1973   Chapel Hill, NC   18.00
WELLMAN, Manly Wade   Rebel Boast: First at Bethel - Last at Appomattox.
   1956   New York   30.00
WELLMAN, Manly Wade   They Took Their Stand.
   1959   New York   30.00

WELLMAN, Paul I.   The House Divides, the Age of Jackson and Lincoln from the War of 1812 to the Civil War.
 1966   Garden City, NY   25.00
WELLS, Damon   Stephen Douglas The Last Years, 1857-1861.
 1971   Austin, TX   10.00
WELLS, David A.   Our Burden and Our Strength.   Wraps.
 1864   Boston   10.00
WELLS, Edward L.   Hampton and His Cavalry in '64.
 1899   Richmond   150.00
WELLS, Edward L.   Hampton and Reconstruction.
 1907   Columbia, SC   125.00
WELLS, Edward L.   A Sketch of the Charleston Light Dragoons.   Wraps.
 1888   Charleston   100.00
WELLS, J. W. and STRAIT, N. A.   An Alphabetical List of the Battles of the War of the Rebellion.   Wraps.
 1883   Washington, DC   30.00
WELLS, James M.   The Chisolm Massacre: A Picture of "Home Rule" in Mississippi.
 1878   Washington, DC   60.00
 1969   New York   30.00
WELLS, James M.   "With Touch of Elbow" or Death Before Dishonor.
 1909   Philadelphia   110.00
 1909   Chicago   80.00
WELLS, Robert W.   Wisconsin in the Civil War.   Wraps.
 1962   Milwaukee   20.00
 1964   Milwaukee   15.00
WELLS, Rosa Lee   General Lee, A Great Friend of Youth.
 1950   New York   20.00
WELLS, Seth J.   The Siege of Vicksburg.
 1915   Detroit   75.00
WELLS, Tom H.   The Confederate Navy.
 1971   University, AL   30.00
WELLS, William, edited by   The Original United States Warship "Monitor."
 1899   New Haven, CT   50.00
WELSH, P.   Irish Green & Union Blue; The Civil War Letters of _____.
 1987   Bronx   22.95
WENTZ, Henry   The Autobiography of a Soldier Boy and Business Man.   Wraps.
 1924   Shelby, OH   150.00
WERLICH, Robert   "Beast" Butler   The Incredible Career of Major General Benjamin Franklin Butler.
 1962   Washington, DC   30.00
WERNER, Edgar A., edited by   Historical Sketch of the War of the Rebellion from 1861 to 1865.
 1890   Albany, NY   35.00
WERNER, Herman   On the Western Frontier with the United States Cavalry. . . .   Wraps.
 1934   n.p.   60.00

WERSTEIN, Irving   Abraham Lincoln vs. Jefferson Davis.
    1959   New York   10.00
WERSTEIN, Irving   1861-1865: The Adventure of the Civil War Told with Pictures.   Wraps.
    1960   Paterson, NJ   55.00
    1969   New York   10.00
WERSTEIN, Irving   July 1863 - The Incredible Story of the Bloody New York City Draft Riots.
    1957   New York   10.00
    1971   New York   entitled The Draft Riots, July 1863   20.00
WERSTEIN, Irving   Kearny the Magnificent.
    1962   New York   30.00
WERSTEIN, Irving   The Many Faces of the Civil War.
    1961   New York   15.00
WERT, J. D.   From Winchester to Cedar Creek: The Shenandoah Campaign of 1864.
    1987   Carlisle   22.50
WESCOTT, M. Ebenezer   Civil War Letters 1861 to 1865 Written to My Mother.   Wraps.
    1909   Mora, MN   40.00
WESLEY, Charles H.   The Collapse of the Confederacy.
    1937   Washington, DC   50.00
WESSELS, William L.   Born to Be a Soldier . . . William Wing Loring.   Wraps.
    1971   Fort Worth   20.00
West Point and the War.   Wraps.
    1863   St. Louis   25.00
West Virginia - Confederate Military History.   See: Confederate Military History, Vol. II (Vol. III, 1987 reprint ed.).
WEST, Emmet C.   History and Reminiscences of the Second Wisconsin Cavalry Regiment.   Wraps.
    1982 (reprint)   MI   10.00
WEST, G. M.   St. Andrews, Florida,   plus appendix containing the official record of the vessels employed on the Blockading Fleet of St. Andrews Bay.
    1922   St. Andrews   75.00
WEST, George B.   When the Yankees Came: Civil War and Reconstruction on the Virginia Peninsula, edited by Parke Rouse, Jr.   Wraps.
    1977   Richmond   8.00
WEST, John C.   A Texan in Search of a Fight.
    1901   Waco   350.00
    1969   Waco   25.00
WEST, Nathaniel   Ancestry, Life and Times of Henry Hastings Sibley.
    1889   St. Paul   60.00
WEST, Richard S., Jr.   Gideon Welles, Lincoln's Navy Department.
    1943   New York   40.00
    1974   Westport   20.00
WEST, Richard S., Jr.   Lincoln's Scapegoat General - A Life of Benjamin F. Butler 1818-1893.
    1965   Boston   30.00
WEST, Richard S., Jr.   Mr. Lincoln's Navy.
    1957   New York   30.00

WEST, Richard S., Jr.   The Second Admiral: Life of David Dixon Porter, 1813-1891.
  1937   New York   40.00
WEST, W. Reed   Contemporary French Opinion of the American Civil War. Wraps.
  1924   Baltimore   20.00
WESTBROOK, Robert S.   History of the 49th Pennsylvania Volunteers.
  1898   Altoona   175.00
WESTCOTT, Allan   Mahan on Naval Warfare.
  1918   Boston   50.00
WESTERVELT, William B.   Lights and Shadows of Army Life as Seen by a Private Soldier.
  1886   Marlboro   60.00
WESTON, David   Among the Wounded. Wraps.
  1864   Philadelphia   50.00
WESTON, Edward P.   The Christian Soldier Boy . . . An Address. Wraps.
  1862   Portland   15.00
WESTON, George M.   The Progress of Slavery in the United States.
  1857   Washington, DC   45.00
WESTON, J. B.   Picket Pins and Sabers: The Civil War Letters of . . . .
  1971   Ashland   9.00
WESTON, James A.   Services Held in the Chapel of Rest, Yadkin Valley, NC at the Funeral of the Late Capt. Walter Waightstill Lenoir. Wraps.
  1890   New York   125.00
WESTRATE, E. V.   Those Fatal Generals.
  1936   New York   30.00
WEYGANT, Charles H.   History of the One Hundred and Twenty-fourth Regiment N.Y.S.V.
  1877   Newburgh   130.00
  1986   30.00
WHALEY, Elizabeth J.   Forgotten Hero: General James B. McPherson.
  1955   New York   35.00
WHAN, Vorin E., Jr.   Fiasco at Fredericksburg.
  1961   State College, PA   35.00
  1986   25.00
WHARTON, H. M.   War Songs and Poems of the Southern Confederacy 1861-1865.
  1904   Philadelphia   75.00
WHEARE, K. C.   Abraham Lincoln and the United States.
  1949   New York   10.00
  1964   London   10.00
WHEELER, A. O.   Eyewitness; or, Life Scenes in the Old North State, Depicting the Trials and Sufferings of the Unionists.
  1865   Boston   200.00
WHEELER, Francis B.   Monograph on the Monitor. Wraps.
  1884   Poughkeepsie, NY   40.00
WHEELER, Joseph   Alabama.   See: Confederate Military History, Vol. VII (Vol. VIII, 1987 reprint ed.).
WHEELER, Joseph   Fitz-John Porter. Speech. Wraps.
  1886   Washington, DC   40.00

WHEELER, Kenneth W., edited by For the Union, Ohio Leaders in the Civil War.
1968   Columbus   20.00
WHEELER, Richard   Sherman's March.
1978   New York   25.00
WHEELER, Richard   The Siege of Vicksburg.
1978   New York   20.00
WHEELER, Richard   Sword Over Richmond An Eyewitness History of McClellan's Peninsula Campaign.
1986   New York   21.95
WHEELER, Richard   Voices of the Civil War.
1976   New York   20.00
WHEELER, Richard   We Knew Stonewall: An Eyewitness Biography.
1977   New York   15.00
WHEELER, Richard   We Knew William Tecumseh Sherman.
1977   New York   20.00
WHEELER, Richard   Witness to Appomattox.
1989   New York   19.95
WHEELER, William   In Memoriam . . . Letters of _____ of the Class of 1855 Y. C.
1875   Cambridge   75.00
WHEELOCK, Julia S.   The Boys in White.
1870   New York   60.00
WHEELWRIGHT, Jere   The Gray Captain.
1954   New York   25.00
WHELAN, Charles E.   Bascom Clarke. The Story of a Southern Refugee.
1913   Madison, WI   30.00
WHERRY, William M.   The Campaign in Missouri and the Battle of Wilson's Creek, 1861. A Paper Read Before the Missouri Historical Society of St. Louis. Wraps.
1880   St. Louis, MO   65.00
WHIDDEN, John D.   Ocean Life in the Old Sailing-Ship Days.
1912   Boston   75.00
WHIPPLE, George M.   History of the Salem Light Infantry from 1805 to 1890.
1890   Salem, MA   35.00
WHIPPLE, J. Raynor and STORER, Malcom   Shinplasters of the Civil War. Wraps.
1942   n.p.   20.00
WHIPPLE, Wayne   Tad Lincoln: A True Story.
1926   New York   10.00
WHIPPLE, Wayne   The Heart of Lee.
1918   Philadelphia   20.00
WHIPPLE, Wayne   The Story Life of Lincoln.
1908   n.p.   10.00
WHISNER, Will. C.   Mark Ellis, or Unsolved Problems.
1899   Morgantown, WV   35.00
WHISTLER, French and Kirk   130th Regiment, Penna. Vol. Inf. at Antietam Dedication of the Monument to the Regiment on the Antietam Battlefield on Sept. 17, 1904. Wraps.
n.d.   n.p.   30.00

WHITAKER, Walter C.   Richard Hooker Wilmer, Second Bishop of Alabama. 2 Vols.
    1907   Philadelphia   85.00
WHITCOMB, Caroline E.   History of the Second Massachusetts Battery (Nim's Battery) of Light Artillery.
    1912   Concord, NH   65.00
WHITE, A. R.   The Blue and the Gray.
    1898   n.p.   35.00
WHITE, Andrew Dickson   A Letter to William Howard Russell. Wraps.
    1863   London   25.00
WHITE, E. V.   The First Ironclad Naval Engagement of the World. Wraps.
    1906   New York   40.00
WHITE, E. V.   History of the Battle of Ball's Bluff. Wraps.
    (c.1900) Leesburg, VA   175.00
    1902   Leesburg, VA   150.00
WHITE, H. M., edited by   William S. White, D.D. and His Times.
    1983   12.00
WHITE, Henry Alexander   Robert E. Lee and the Southern Confederacy.
    1897   New York   100.00
    1910   New York   75.00
    1969   New York   20.00
WHITE, Henry Alexander   Stonewall Jackson.
    1909   Philadelphia   60.00
WHITE, Horace   The Life of Lyman Trumbull.
    1913   Boston   25.00
WHITE, Horace   The Lincoln and Douglas Debates,   An Address. Wraps.
    1914   Chicago   15.00
WHITE, John E.   My Old Confederate, An Address.   Wraps.
    1908   Atlanta   20.00
WHITE, Laura   Robert Barnwell Rhett: Father of Secession.
    1931   New York   35.00
    1965   Gloucester, MA   25.00
WHITE, Leslie Turner   Look Away.
    1943   Philadelphia   20.00
WHITE, Mary Virginia Saunders   Robert E. Lee.   Wraps.
    1935   Cleveland, OH   20.00
WHITE, Melvin Johnson   The Secession Movement in the United States 1847-1852. Wraps.
    1910   n.p.   30.00
WHITE, Richard Grant, edited by   Poetry of the Civil War.
    1866   New York   25.00
WHITE, Robert   West Virginia.   See: Confederate Military History, Vol. II (Vol. III, 1987 reprint ed.).
WHITE, Ruth   Yankee from Sweden.
    1960   New York   15.00
WHITE, William W.   The Confederate Veteran.   See: Confederate Centennial Studies, No. 22.

WHITE, William and Ruth   Tin Can on a Shingle: The Full Story of
the Monitor and the Merrimac.
1957   New York   20.00
WHITEHEAD, A. C.   Two Great Southerners, Jefferson Davis and
Robert E. Lee.
1912   New York   30.00
WHITEHORNE, J. W. A.   The Battle of Cedar Creek: Self-Guided Tour.
Wraps.
1987   Strasburg   6.95
WHITEMAN, Maxwell   While Lincoln Lay Dying.
1968   Philadelphia Ltd.   30.00
WHITFORD, William Clarke   Colorado Volunteers in the Civil War; The
New Mexico Campaign in 1862. Wraps.
1906   Denver   150.00
1962   Chicago   30.00
1971   15.00
WHITING, William   Military Arrests in Time of War. Wraps.
1863   Washington, DC   25.00
WHITING, William   The War Powers of the President, and the Legislative Powers of Congress in Relation to Rebellion, Treason and Slavery.
Wraps.
1863   Boston   30.00
WHITLEY, Edythe Johns Rucker   Sam Davis, Confederate Hero.
1947   n.p.   35.00
1971   Nashville   15.00
WHITMAN, George Washington   Civil War Letters of _____, edited by
Jerome M. Loving.
1975   Durham, NC   20.00
WHITMAN, Walt   Death of Abraham Lincoln.
1962   Chicago   40.00
WHITMAN, Walt   Specimen Days and Collect.
1882-83 Philadelphia   40.00
WHITMAN, Walt   The Wound Dresser: Letters Written to his Mother.
1949   20.00
WHITMAN, Walt   Walt Whitman's Civil War, edited by Walter
Lowenfels.
1960   New York   7.00
1961   15.00
WHITMAN, William E. S. and TRUE, Charles H.   Maine in the War for
the Union: A History.
1865   Lewiston   55.00
WHITNEY, A. H.   War Ballads, The Brave Days of Old.
1884   Chicago   20.00
WHITNEY, Henry Clay   Life on the Circuit with Lincoln.
1892   Boston   35.00
1940   Caldwell, ID   15.00
1950   Caldwell, ID   15.00
WHITNEY, John H.   The Hawkins Zouaves: (Ninth N.Y.V.) Their Battles and Marches.
1866   New York   150.00

WHITNEY, Louisa M.   Goldie's Inheritance, A Story of the Siege of Atlanta.
1903   Burlington, VT   25.00

WHITRIDGE, Arnold   No Compromise: The Story of the Fanatics Who Paved the Way to the Civil War.
1960   New York   15.00
1974   CT   25.00

WHITSITT, William H.   Genealogy of Jefferson Davis, Address Delivered October 9, 1908, before Lee Camp, No. 1, C.V. Wraps.
1910   Richmond   35.00

WHITSITT, William H.   Genealogy of Jefferson Davis and of Samuel Davis.
1910   New York   75.00

WHITSON, Mrs. L. D.   Gilbert St. Maurice.
1874   Nashville   60.00

WHITTAKER, Frederick A.   A Complete Life of General George A. Custer.
1876   New York   120.00

WHITTIER, John Greenleaf   In War Time and Other Poems.
1864   Boston   15.00

WHITTLESEY, Charles   War Memoranda, Cheat River to the Tennessee 1861-1862.
1884   Cleveland   75.00

Who Burnt Columbia? Official Depositions of William Tecumseh Sherman and Gen. O. O. Howard. Wraps. Part 1, all published.
1873   Charleston, SC   125.00

WIARD, Norman   Marine Artillery as Adapted for Service on the Coast and Inland Waters. Wraps.
1863   New York   75.00

WIARD, Norman   Wiard's System of Field Artillery.   Wraps.
1863   New York   100.00

WICKER, T.   Unto This Hour.
1984   New York   15.00

WIECZERZAK, Joseph W.   A Polish Chapter in Civil War America.
1967   New York   20.00

WIGGINS, Gary   Dance & Brothers. Texas Gunmakers of the Confederacy, edited by Stephen Sylvia.
1986   Orange, VA   29.95

WIGHT, Willard E.   Some Wartime Letters of Bishop Lynch.   Wraps.
1957   n.p.   10.00

WILBUR, C. K.   Antique Medical Instruments. Wraps.
1987   W. Chester   12.95

WILD, Frederick W.   Memoirs and History of Capt. F. W. Alexander's Baltimore Battery of Light Artillery, USV.
1912   Baltimore   165.00

WILDER, Theodore   The History of Company C, Seventh Regiment, O.V.I.
1866   Oberlin   150.00

The Wilderness Campaign, May-June, 1864.   See: Papers of the Military Historical Society of Massachusetts, No. 4.

The Wilderness Campaign Organization of the Army of the Potomac. Wraps.
> 1864   n.p.   25.00

WILDES, Thomas Francis   Record of the One Hundred and Sixteenth Regiment, Ohio Infantry Volunteers in the War of the Rebellion.
> 1884   Sandusky   200.00

WILEY, Bell I.   The Common Soldier of the Civil War, The Life of Billy Yank, The Life of Johnny Reb.
> 1942 and 1952   2 Vols. Boxed   75.00
> 1958   New York   2 Vols. in 1   30.00

WILEY, Bell I.   Confederate Women.
> 1975   Westport   30.00
> 1976   30.00

WILEY, Bell I.   Embattled Confederates.
> 1964   New York   30.00
> 1969   New York   15.00
> Recent reprint   20.00

WILEY, Bell I.   Kingdom Coming, The Emancipation Proclamation of Sept. 22 1862, An Address Delivered at the Chicago Historical Society Sept 21, 1962. Wraps.
> 1963   Chicago   25.00

WILEY, Bell I.   The Life of Billy Yank the Common Soldier of the Union.
> 1952   Indianapolis   40.00
> 1971   New York   10.00
> 1983   Baton Rouge   Wraps   10.00
> 1986   Baton Rouge   Wraps   10.00

WILEY, Bell I.   The Life of Johnny Reb.
> 1943   Indianapolis   40.00
> 1971   New York   30.00
> 1986   Baton Rouge   Wraps   9.95

WILEY, Bell I.   The Plain People of the Confederacy.
> 1943   Baton Rouge   60.00
> 1944   Baton Rouge   50.00
> 1971   Gloucester, MA 15.00

WILEY, Bell I.   The Road to Appomattox.
> 1956   Memphis   40.00

WILEY, Bell I.   The Role of the Archivist in the Civil War Centennial. Wraps.
> 1960   Georgia   10.00

WILEY, Bell I.   Southern Negroes 1861-1865.
> 1953   New York   50.00

WILEY, Bell I.   They Fought for the Union.
> 1949   New York   30.00

WILEY, Bell I. and MILHOLLEN, Hirst D.   They Who Fought Here.
> 1959   New York   30.00

WILEY, Eral Wellington   Four Speeches by Abraham Lincoln. . . .
> 1972   New York   30.00

WILKES, Charles   Autobiography of _____, U.S. Navy 1798-1877, edited by William J. Morgan, et al.
> 1978   Washington, DC   30.00

WILKES, George   McClellan: From Ball's Bluff to Antietam. Wraps.
1863   New York   30.00
WILKES, George   McClellan: Who He Is and What He Has Done.
1863   New York   30.00
WILKESON, Frank   Recollections of a Private Soldier in the Army of the Potomac.
1887   New York   75.00
1972   Freeport   30.00
WILKIE, Franc B.   Pen and Powder.
1888   Boston   125.00
WILKINSON, Herbert A.   The American Doctrine of State Secession. Wraps.
1934   Baltimore   25.00
WILKINSON, John   The Narrative of a Blockade-Runner.
1877   New York   250.00
1983   Lexington, MA   30.00
WILKINSON, Norman B.   The Brandywine Home Front During the Civil War.
1966   Wilmington, DE   25.00
WILLARD, Benjamin J.   A Record of the Things Which Happened to Capt. Benjamin J. Willard, Pilot and Stevedore.
1895   Portland, ME   50.00
WILLETT, Elbert D.   History of Company B (originally Pickens Planters) 40th Alabama Regiment C.S.A. 1862-1865.
1902   Anniston   400.00
1963   n.p.   75.00
Recent reprint   35.00
WILLETT, James R.   Rambling Recollections of a Military Engineer. Wraps.
1888   Chicago   80.00
WILLEY, Robert   The Iron 44th.
(c.1982) n.p.   30.00
WILLEY, William P.   An Inside View of the Formation of the State of West Virginia.
1901   Wheeling   40.00
WILLIAMS, Alfred B.   Hampton and His Red Shirts: South Carolina's Deliverance in 1876.
1876   Charleston, SC   75.00
1935   Charleston, SC   50.00   Variant copies abound, made up of sheets from the 1935 edition and later printed pages. The variant copies have inferior stamping on the covers.
WILLIAMS, Alpheus S.   From the Cannon's Mouth The Civil War Letters of . . . , edited by Milo M. Quaife.
1959   Detroit   35.00
WILLIAMS, Ben Ames   House Divided.
1947   Boston   20.00
1947   Boston   2 Vols.   30.00
WILLIAMS, Ben Ames   The Unconquered.
1953   Cambridge   25.00

WILLIAMS, C. R., compiled by　　　Southern Sympathizers, Wood County Confederate Soldiers and a Sketch of the Night Hawk Rangers of Wood, Jackson, Wirt, and Roane Counties in West Virginia.
(c.1960)　Parkersburg　65.00

WILLIAMS, Charlean　　　The Old Town Speaks.
1951　Houston　75.00

WILLIAMS, Charles　　　The Life of Rutherford Birchard Hayes. 2 Vols. Diary and Letters. 5 Vols.
1928　Columbus　7 Vols.　125.00

WILLIAMS, E. B.　　　Knapsack and Rifle, or Life in the Grand Army.
1886　50.00

WILLIAMS, E. F. and HUMPHREYS, H. D., edited by　Gunboats and Cavalry as Told to J. P. Pryor and Thomas Jordan by Nathan Bedford Forrest. Wraps.
1965　Memphis　25.00

WILLIAMS, Edward F., III　　　Fustest with the Mostest - The Military Career of Tennessee's Greatest Confederate Lt. Gen. Nathan Bedford Forrest. Wraps.
1969　TN　25.00

WILLIAMS, Edward P.　　　Extracts from Letters to A.B.T. from _____ During His Service in the Civil War 1862-64.
1903　New York　100.00

WILLIAMS, Ellen　　　Three Years and a Half in the Army, or History of the Second Colorados.
1885　New York　275.00

WILLIAMS, Emma Inman　　　Historic Madison, The Story of Jackson County, Tenn.
1946　Jackson　60.00

WILLIAMS, Flora McDonald　　　Who's the Patriot?　A Story of the Southern Confederacy.
1886　Louisville, KY　30.00

WILLIAMS, Frances L.　　　Matthew Fontaine Maury.
1963　New Brunswick, NJ　50.00

WILLIAMS, Francis Howard　　　The Burden Bearer-An Epic of Lincoln.
1908　Philadelphia Ltd.　30.00

WILLIAMS, George F.　　　Bullet and Shell.
1882　New York　35.00
1883　New York　25.00

WILLIAMS, George W.　　　A History of the Negro Troops in the War of the Rebellion.
1888　New York　80.00
1969　New York　20.00

WILLIAMS, Hermann Warner, Jr.　　　The Civil War:　The Artists' Record. Wraps.
1961　Boston　25.00

WILLIAMS, Hermann Warner, Jr.　　　Civil War Drawings. Wraps.
1974　New York　6.00

WILLIAMS, J. R.　　　The Confederate Fiddle.
1962　Englewood Cliffs, NJ　15.00

WILLIAMS, James　　　The Rise and Fall of the Model Republic.
1863　London　150.00

WILLIAMS, James   The South Vindicated. Being a Series of Letters. . . .
1862   London   150.00
WILLIAMS, James M.   From That Terrible Field, Civil War Letters of
_____, edited by John K. Folmar.
1981   University, AL   18.00
WILLIAMS, John A. B.   Leaves from a Trooper's Diary.
1869   Philadelphia   50.00
WILLIAMS, John C.   Life in Camp, A History of the Nine Months' Service of the 14th Vermont Regiment.
1864   Claremont   65.00
WILLIAMS, John M.   The Eagle Regiment, 8th Wis. Inf'try Vols.
1890   Belleville   130.00
WILLIAMS, John Sharp   Address to Company "A" Confederate Veterans.
Wraps.
1904   Memphis   50.00
WILLIAMS, John Skelton   Our Advance from Appomattox, An Address. Wraps.
(1907)   n.p.   35.00
WILLIAMS, K. J.   Ghost Ships of the Mersey: A Brief History of Confederate Cruisers with Mersey Connections. Wraps.
1987   Birkenhead   5.00
WILLIAMS, Kenneth Powers   Lincoln Finds a General. 5 Vols.
1949-59 125.00
Individual volumes 25.00 each
1985   Wraps   10.95
WILLIAMS, Noble C.   Echoes from the Battlefield.
1902   Atlanta   35.00
WILLIAMS, R. H.   With the Border Ruffians: Memories of the Far West, 1852-1868, edited by E. W. Williams.
1982   Lincoln   31.00
1982   Lincoln   Wraps   9.95
WILLIAMS, Rebecca Yancey   The Vanishing Virginian.
1940   New York   25.00
WILLIAMS, Samuel   The Lincolns and Tennessee.
1942   Harrogate   15.00
WILLIAMS, Samuel C.   General John T. Wilder, Commander of the Lightning Brigade.
1936   Bloomington   80.00
WILLIAMS, Sidney S.   From Spottsylvania to Wilmington, N.C. By Way of Andersonville and Florence. Wraps.
1899   Providence Ltd.   40.00
WILLIAMS, T. Harry   General Ewell to the High Private in the Rear.
Wraps.
n.d.   n.p.   30.00
WILLIAMS, T. Harry   Hayes of the Twenty Third.
1965   New York   50.00
WILLIAMS, T. Harry   The History of American Wars. From Colonial Times to WWI.
1981   New York   25.00
WILLIAMS, T. Harry   Lincoln and His Generals.
1952   New York   25.00
1958   25.00

WILLIAMS, T. Harry   Lincoln and the Radicals.
1941   Madison, WI   20.00
1972   Wraps   14.00
WILLIAMS, T. Harry   McClellan, Sherman and Grant.
1962   New Brunswick   25.00
WILLIAMS, T. Harry   P. G. T. Beauregard, Napoleon in Gray.
1954   Baton Rouge   50.00
1955   Baton Rouge   40.00
1960   Baton Rouge   40.00
1981   25.00
WILLIAMS, T. Harry   The Selected Essays of T. Harry Williams.
1983   Baton Rouge   20.00
WILLIAMS, T. Harry   With Beauregard to Mexico.
1956   Baton Rouge   Ltd.   45.00
WILLIAMS, William G.   Days of Darkness: The Gettysburg Civilians, An Historical Novel.
1987   Shippensburg   19.00
Williamson County, Franklin, Tennessee, 1864-1964, Civil War Centennial, Battle of Franklin. . . .   Wraps.
1964   n.p.   15.00
WILLIAMSON, James J.   Mosby's Rangers, A Record of the Operations of the Forty-third Battalion of Virginia Cavalry.
1896   New York   250.00
1909   New York   200.00
1982   n.p.   25.00
WILLIAMSON, James J.   Prison Life in the Old Capitol and Reminiscences of the Civil War.
1911   West Orange   125.00
WILLIAMSON, Joel   After Slavery, The Negro in South Carolina During Reconstruction 1861-1877.
1967   Chapel Hill, NC   30.00
WILLIAMSON, Mary L.   A Confederate Trilogy for Young Readers: The Life of Gen. Robert Edward Lee; Lt. Gen. T. J. 'Stonewall' Jackson; and Maj.Gen. J. E. B. Stuart.
1989   Harrisonburg   23.00
WILLIAMSON, Mary L.   The Life of Gen. Robert E. Lee for Children in Easy Words.
1893   Richmond   25.00
1895   Richmond   25.00
WILLIAMSON, Mary L.   The Life of Gen. Thomas J. Jackson.
1899   Richmond   30.00
1914   Richmond   20.00
WILLIAMSON, Mary L.   The Life of J. E. B. Stuart.
1914   Richmond   30.00
WILLINGHAM, Robert M., Jr.   No Jubilee, The Story of Confederate Wilkes.
1976   Washington, GA   15.00
WILLIS, Edward   Memorials of Gen. _____ Commandant of the 12th Georgia Infantry.   Wraps.
1890   Richmond   40.00

WILLIS, Henry A. The Fifty-third Regiment Massachusetts Volunteers.
1889 Fitchburg 65.00
WILLIS, Henry A. Fitchburg in the War of the Rebellion.
1866 Fitchburg 60.00
WILLISON, Charles H. Reminiscences of a Boy's Service with the 76th Ohio in the 15th Army Corps Under General Sherman. . . .
1908 Menasha, WI 200.00
WILLS, Charles W. Army Life of an Illinois Soldier.
1906 Washington, DC 110.00
WILLS, Mary Alice The Confederate Blockade of Washington, D. C. 1861-62.
1975 Parsons, WV 15.00
WILLSON, Arabella M. Disaster, Struggle, Triumph; Adventures of 1,000 "Boys in Blue."
1870 Albany 60.00
WILLSON, Beckles John Slidell and the Confederates in Paris.
1932 New York 40.00
1970 New York 22.50
WILMER, L. Allison, JARRETT, J. H. and VERNON, G. W. F. History and Roster of Maryland Volunteers War of 1861-1865. 2 Vols.
1898-99 Baltimore 150.00
1987 Silver Spring, MD 75.00
WILMER, Richard H. The Recent Past From a Southern Standpoint.
1887 New York 30.00
WILSON, Augusta Jane Evans Macaria.
1896 New York 75.00
(c.1910) New York 40.00
WILSON, C. R. Baptized in Blood: The Religion of the Lost Cause, 1865-1920.
1980 Athens 25.00
1983 22.00
Wraps 10.00
WILSON, D. and SIMON, J., edited by Ulysses S. Grant: Essays and Documents.
1981 Carbondale, IL 14.00
WILSON, Edmund Patriotic Gore - Studies in the Literature of the American Civil War.
1962 New York 40.00
1984 Wraps 14.00
WILSON, Ephraim A. Memoirs of the War.
1893 Cleveland 150.00
WILSON, Forrest Crusader in Crinoline: The Life of Harriet Beecher Stowe.
1941 Philadelphia and London 20.00
WILSON, Francis John Wilkes Booth.
1929 Boston/New York 35.00
1929 Boston/New York Ltd. 55.00
WILSON, H. W. Ironclads in Action. 2 Vols.
1896 Boston 80.00

WILSON, Henry   History of the Anti-Slavery Measures of the Thirty-seventh and Thirty-eighth United States Congresses.
1864   Boston   30.00
WILSON, Henry   History of the Reconstruction Measures.
1868   Hartford   30.00
WILSON, Henry   History of the Rise and Fall of the Slave Power in America. 3 Vols.
1872   Boston   100.00
1879   Boston   75.00
1969   40.00
WILSON, Hill   John Brown, Soldier of Fortune.
1913   Lawrence, KS   15.00
WILSON, J. L.   The Code of Honor; or Rules for the Government of Principals and Seconds in Duelling. Wraps.
1959   Kennesaw   10.00
WILSON, James Grant   Biographical Sketches of Illinois Officers engaged in the War Against the Rebellion of 1861. Wraps.
1862   Chicago 275.00
WILSON, James Grant   General Grant.
For additional information, see Appendix: Great Commanders Series.
1897   New York   20.00
1897   New York   Ltd. 125.00
WILSON, James Grant   The Life and Public Services of Ulysses Simpson Grant. Wraps.
1885   New York   20.00
WILSON, James Harrison   General Edward Francis Winslow, A Leader of Cavalry in the Great Rebellion. Wraps.
1915   New York   40.00
WILSON, James Harrison   The Life and Services of Brevet Brigadier-General Andrew Jonathan Alexander.
1887   New York   50.00
WILSON, James Harrison   Life and Services of William Farrar Smith.
1904   Wilmington, DE   30.00
WILSON, James Harrison   The Life of Charles A. Dana.
1907   New York   25.00
WILSON, James Harrison   The Life of John A. Rawlins.
1916   New York   75.00
WILSON, James Harrison   The Life of Ulysses S. Grant.
1868   Springfield, MA   15.00
WILSON, James Harrison   Under the Old Flag. 2 Vols.
1912   New York   100.00
1971   Westport   45.00
WILSON, John A.   Adventures of Alf Wilson.
1880   Toledo   125.00
1897   Washington, DC   50.00
1972   Marietta   Wraps 10.00
WILSON, John Laird   Battles of the Civil War in the United States. 2 Vols.
1878   New York   80.00
WILSON, John Laird   Story of the War: Pictorial History of the Great Civil War.
1881   Chicago   65.00

WILSON, Joseph   Naval Hygiene.
  1870   Washington, DC   75.00
WILSON, Joseph T.   The Black Phalanx.
  1888   Hartford   100.00
  1890   Hartford   100.00
  1891   Hartford   100.00
WILSON, Lawrence   Itinerary of the Seventh Ohio Volunteer Infantry
  1861-1865.
  1907   New York   250.00
  2 Vol. edition   250.00
WILSON, LeGrand J.   The Confederate Soldier, edited by James W.
  Silver.
  1902   Fayetteville, AR   1000.00
  1973   Memphis   30.00
  Recent reprint   15.00
WILSON, Rufus Rockwell   Uncollected Works of Abraham Lincoln.
  2 Vols.
  1947   Elmira, NY   30.00
WILSON, Rufus Rockwell, edited by   Lincoln Among His Friends.
  1942   Caldwell, ID   10.00
WILSON, Rufus Rockwell, edited by   Lincoln in Caricature.
  1945   Elmira, NY   40.00
  1953   New York   20.00
WILSON, Sarah   Life of _____, Experiences During the War of the
  Rebellion.   Wraps.
  n.d.   n.p.   100.00
WILSON, Suzanne Colton, compiled by   Column South with the 15th
  Pennsylvania Cavalry.
  1960   Flagstaff   55.00
WILSON, Thomas B.   Reminiscences of Thomas B. Wilson.   Wraps.
  (1939)   Nashville   250.00
WILSON, William B.   A Few Acts and Actors in the Tragedy of the Civil
  War.
  1892   Philadelphia   35.00
WILSON, William L.   A Borderland Confederate, Civil War Letters and
  Diaries of _____, edited by Festus P. Summers.
  1962   Pittsburgh   30.00
WILSON, Woodrow   Robert E. Lee, An Interpretation.
  1924   Chapel Hill, NC   15.00
WILTON, Mark   Fremont, The Pathfinder, The War Library Vol. 7 No.
  252.   Wraps.
  1887   New York   30.00
WILTSE, Charles M.   John C. Calhoun, Nullifier 1829-1839.
  1949   IN   15.00
WILTSE, Charles M.   John C. Calhoun, Sectionalist 1840-1850.
  1951   IN   20.00
WIMSATT, Josephine Cleary   Recollections.
  1926   Tientsin, China   75.00
WINANT, Lewis   Pepperbox Firearms.
  1952   New York   50.00
WINDER, William H.   Secrets of the American Bastile.   Wraps.
  1863   Philadelphia   55.00

WINDLER, Penny Nichols   Placid.   A Collection of Authentic Tales
   Centering Around Placid Plantation, Person and Granville Counties,
   North Carolina, During the Period 1861 through 1865.
   1961   Warwick, VA   50.00
WINDOLPH, Charles   I Fought with Custer.   Wraps.
   1987   University, NE   6.95
WINDROW, John E.   John Berrien Lindsley.
   1938   Chapel Hill, NC   35.00
WING, Samuel B.   The Soldier's Story A Personal Narrative.
   1898   Phillips   55.00
WINGATE, George W.   History of the Twenty-second Regiment of
   N.G.S.N.Y.
   1896   New York   90.00
WINGATE, George W.   Last Campaign of the Twenty-second Regiment
   N.G.S.N.Y.   Wraps.
   1864   New York   40.00
WINGFIELD, Marshall   A History of Caroline County, Virginia.
   1924   Richmond   60.00
WINGFIELD, Marshall   General A. P. Stewart, His Life and Letters.
   1954   Memphis   75.00
WINKLER, Angelina V.   The Confederate Capital and Hood's Texas
   Brigade.
   1894   Austin   375.00
WINKLER, Frederick C.   Letters of Frederick C. Winkler - 1862 to 1865.
   1963   Milwaukee Ltd.   50.00
WINKLEY, J. W.   John Brown, The Hero.
   1905   Boston   25.00
WINKS, Robin W.   Canada and the United States: The Civil War
   Years.
   1960   Baltimore   25.00
WINSLOW, Arthur   Francis Winslow: His Forebears and Life.
   1935   Norwood, MA   Ltd.   50.00
WINSLOW, Hattie Lou and MOORE, Joseph R. H.   Camp   Morton   1861-
   1865.   Wraps.
   1940   Indianapolis   20.00
WINSLOW, Richard Elliott   General John Sedgwick, the Story of a
   Union Corps Commander.
   1982   Novato, CA   20.00
WINSLOW, William Henry   Southern Buds and Sons of War.
   1907   Boston   20.00
WINSOR, Bill   Texas in the Confederacy.
   1978   Hillsboro   40.00
WINSTON, Robert W.   Andrew Johnson, Plebian and Patriot.
   1928   New York   30.00
WINSTON, Robert W.   High Stakes and Hair Trigger.
   1930   New York   30.00
WINSTON, Robert W.   Robert E. Lee.
   1934   New York   20.00
WINTER, William   Life and Art of Edwin Booth.
   1893   New York   30.00
WINTERS, Erastus   Serving Uncle Sam in the 50th Ohio.   Wraps.
   1905   East Walnut Hills   160.00

WINTERS, John D.   The Civil War in Louisiana.
   1963   Baton Rouge   35.00
   1979   Baton Rouge   30.00
   1985   Baton Rouge   30.00
WIRTH, C. L.   Restoration of Ford's Theatre.   Wraps.
   1963   Washington, DC   20.00
Wisconsin at Andersonville, Report of the Wisconsin Monument Commission
   Appointed to Erect a Monument at Andersonville, Georgia.
   1911   Madison   25.00
Wisconsin at Vicksburg, Report of the Wisconsin-Vicksburg Monument Commission Including the Story of the Campaign and Siege of Vicksburg in
   1863.
   1914   Madison   40.00
Wisconsin Volunteers, War of the Rebellion 1861-1865.
   1914   Madison   80.00
WISE, Barton H.   The Life of Henry A. Wise of Virginia.
   1899   New York   60.00
WISE, George   Campaigns and Battles of the Army of Northern Virginia.
   1916   New York   175.00
WISE, George   History of the Seventeenth Virginia Infantry, C.S.A.
   1870   Baltimore   200.00
   1969   Arlington   30.00
WISE, George M.   Marching Through South Carolina: Another Civil
   War Letter of _____, edited by Wilfred W. Black.
   1957   n.p.   25.00
   1957   Wraps 20.00
WISE, H. A.   Drawing Out the Man: The V.M.I. Story.
   1980   Charlottesville   18.00
WISE, Henry A.   Seven Decades of the Union.
   1872   Philadelphia 30.00
WISE, Jennings Cropper   The Long Arm of Lee. 2 Vols.
   1915   Lynchburg, VA 125.00
   1959   New York   2 Vols. in 1 40.00
   1988   Richmond   2 Vols. 59.00
WISE, Jennings Cropper   The Military History of the Virginia Military
   Institute 1839-1865.
   1915   Lynchburg   100.00
WISE, Jennings Cropper   Personal Memoir of the Life and Services of
   Scott Shipp.
   1915   Lexington   75.00
WISE, Jennings Cropper   Sunrise of the Virginia Military Institute as a
   School of Arms, Spawn of the Cincinnati.   Wraps.
   1958   Lexington   50.00
WISE, John S.   Memorial Address, Delivered . . . May 15, 1864.   Wraps.
   n.d.   n.p.   30.00
WISE, John S.   The End of an Era.
   1899   Boston 40.00
   1901   Boston 30.00
   1902   Boston 30.00
   1964   20.00
   1965   New York   17.50

WISE, Stephen R.   Lifeline of the Confederacy: Blockade Running During the Civil War.
1988   Columbia   24.95

WISTAR, Isaac J.   Autobiography of Isaac Jones Wistar 1827-1905. 2 Vols.
1937   Philadelphia   50.00

WISTER, F. K., edited by   Sarah Butler Wister's Civil War Diary. Wraps.
1978   13.00

WISTER, Francis   Recollections of the 12th U.S. Infantry and Regular Division 1861-1865. Wraps.
1887   Philadelphia   30.00

WISTER, Owen   Ulysses S. Grant and the Seven Ages of Washington.
1928   New York   15.00

WITHERS, Robert Enoch   Autobiography of an Octogenarian.
1907   Roanoke   125.00

Within Fort Sumter; or, a View of Major Anderson's Garrison Family for One Hundred and Ten Days. By One of the Company. Wraps.
1861   New York   100.00

WITHINGTON, William Herbert   Michigan in the Opening of the War. Wraps.
1889   Detroit   25.00

WITKOWSKI, W.   Civil War Trivia. Wraps.
1987   Boston   7.95

WITTENMYER, Annie   Under the Guns.
1895   Boston   50.00

WOLCOTT, Walter   The Military History of Yates County, N. Y.
1895   Penn Yan   100.00

WOLDMAN, Albert A.   Lincoln and the Russians.
1952   Cleveland   15.00

WOLF, Hazel Catherine   On Freedom's Altar, The Martyr Complex in the Abolition Movement.
1952   Madison   15.00

WOLF, Simon   The American Jew as Patriot, Soldier and Citizen.
1895   Philadelphia   75.00

WOLFE, Samuel M.   Helper's Impending Crisis Dissected. Wraps.
1860   Philadelphia   60.00

WOLSELEY, Garnet Joseph (Viscount)   The American Civil War: An English View, edited by James A. Rawley.
1964   Charlottesville   35.00

WOLSELEY, Garnet Joseph (Viscount)   The Story of a Soldier's Life. 2 Vols.
1903   Westminster   125.00

WOMACK, James J.   Civil War Diary of Capt. _____, Co. E 16th Tenn. C.S.A. Wraps.
1961   McMinnville   35.00

WOMACK, Robert J.   Call Forth the Mighty Men.
1987   29.95

WOOD, C. J., MD   Reminscences of the War . . . Narrative of the Morgan Raid in Indiana and Ohio . . . Fall of Richmond . . . Flight of Jeff Davis . . . and Hanging of Col. Orton and Major Dunsbar, Two Rebel Spies at Franklin, Tenn., in 1863.
(1880)   (Washington, DC)   100.00

WOOD, David W., compiled by   History of the 20th Ohio Veteran Volunteer Infantry Regiment.   Wraps.
1876   Columbus   140.00

WOOD, Edward A., II   Dr. Eugene V. H. Hall, Veteran of the Civil War.   Wraps.
1956   Chicago   20.00

WOOD, Forrest G.   Black Scare.
1970   Berkeley, CA   15.00

WOOD, George L.   The Seventh Regiment: A Record.
1865   New York   120.00
1865   New York   entitled Famous Deeds by American Heroes: A Record of Events from Sumter to Lookout Mountain.   65.00

WOOD, Helen Everett, edited by   Delevan Arnold, A Kalamazoo Volunteer in the Civil War.   Wraps.
1962   Kalamazoo   15.00

WOOD, James H.   The War: Stonewall Jackson, His Campaigns and Battles The Regiment as I Saw Them.
1910   Cumberland 250.00

WOOD, John Sumner   The Virginia Bishop: A Yankee Hero of the Confederacy.
1961   Richmond   25.00

WOOD, L. C.   The Haydock's Testimony: A Tale of the American Civil War.
1907   25.00

WOOD, Leonora A.   Abraham Lincoln.
1942   Piedmont, WV   10.00

WOOD, Oliver E.   The West Point Scrap Book.
1871   New York   75.00
1874   New York   35.00

WOOD, Robert C.   Confederate Hand-Book, A Compilation of Important Data . . . Relating to the War Between the States.
1900   New Orleans   60.00

WOOD, W. B. and **EDMONDS**, J. E.   A History of the Civil War in the United States 1861-1865.
1905   New York   60.00
1905   London   75.00
1910   New York   40.00
1959   New York   entitled Military History of the Civil War 25.00

WOOD, W. D.   A Partial Roster of the Officers and Men Raised in Leon County, Texas, for the Service of the Confederate States.
1963   Waco Ltd.   35.00

WOOD, W. Kirk   A Northern Daughter and a Southern Wife   The Civil War Reminiscences and Letters of Katherine H. Cummings 1860-1865.   Wraps.
1976   Richmond   18.00

WOOD, Wales W.   A History of the Ninety-fifth Regiment Illinois Infantry Volunteers.
1865   Chicago   175.00
WOOD, William   Captains of the Civil War, Vol. 31 of Chronicle of America.
1921   New Haven   15.00
WOOD, William Nathaniel   Reminiscences of Big I.
1909   Charlottesville   800.00
1956   Jackson edited by Bell I. Wiley   50.00
1987   Wilmington, NC   25.00
WOODBURN, James Albert   The Life of Thaddeus Stevens.
1913   Indianapolis   20.00
WOODBURY, Augustus   Ambrose Everett Burnside.
1867   Providence   35.00
WOODBURY, Augustus   A Narrative of the Campaign of the 1st Rhode Island Regiment in the Spring and Summer of 1861.
1862   Providence   50.00
WOODBURY, Augustus   The Preservation of the Republic. Wraps.
1862   18.00
WOODBURY, Augustus   The Second Rhode Island Regiment. A Narrative of Military Operations.
1875   Providence   75.00
WOODFORD, Frank B.   Father Abraham's Children, Michigan Episodes in the Civil War.
1961   Detroit   15.00
WOODHALL, D. M.   Manual of Arms Compiled Pursuant to Regimental Orders for the 10th Regiment N.G.S.N.Y.
1865   75.00
WOODLEY, T.   Thaddeus Stevens.
1934   Harrisburg   60.00
WOODMAN, Harold D., edited by   The Legacy of the American Civil War.
1973   New York   10.00
WOODRUFF, George H.   Fifteen Years Ago: or, The Patriotism of Will County.
1876   Joliet   80.00
WOODRUFF, Matthew   A Union Soldier in the Land of the Vanquished, Diary of Sgt. Matthew Woodruff in Louisiana Jun. - Dec. 1865, edited by F. N. Boney.
1969   University, AL   30.00
WOODRUFF, William E.   With the Light Guns in '61-'65. Reminiscences of Eleven Arkansas, Missouri, and Texas Light Batteries, in the Civil War.
1903   Little Rock   350.00
Recent reprint   25.00
WOODS, Joseph Thatcher   Services of the 96th Ohio Volunteers.
1874   Toledo   200.00
WOODS, Joseph Thatcher   Steedman and His Men at Chickamauga.
1876   Toledo   150.00
WOODWARD, Ashbel   Life of General Nathaniel Lyon.
1862   Hartford   40.00

WOODWARD, Ashbel   Memoir of General Nathaniel Lyon of the 1st Brigade Missouri Vols.
1866   Boston   30.00

WOODWARD, C. Vann   Mary Chesnut's Civil War.
1981   New Haven and London 30.00
Recent reprint Wraps 16.95

WOODWARD, C. Vann   Reunion and Reaction, The Compromise of 1877 and the End of Reconstruction.
1951   Boston 15.00
1966   15.00

WOODWARD, C. Vann   The Burden of Southern History.
1960   Baton Rouge   20.00
1970   10.00

WOODWARD, C. Vann   The Private Mary Chesnut. Wraps.
1984   12.00

WOODWARD, Evan M.   History of the 198th Pennsylvania Volunteers.
1884   Trenton   75.00

WOODWARD, Evan M.   History of the 3rd Pennsylvania Reserve.
1883   Trenton   120.00

WOODWARD, Evan M.   Our Campaigns.
1865   Philadelphia   75.00
1899   75.00

WOODWARD, Helen   William E. Woodward, Years of Madness.
1951   New York   25.00

WOODWARD, Joseph J.   Outlines of Chief Camp Diseases of U. S. Armies.
1863   Philadelphia   80.00

WOODWARD, Joseph J.   The Hospital Steward's Manual.
1862   Philadelphia   75.00

WOODWARD, Joseph T.   Historic Record and Complete Biographic Roster 21st Maine Volunteers.
1907   Augusta 120.00

WOODWARD, W. E.   Meet General Grant.
1928   New York   20.00
1939   New York   15.00
1940   New York   15.00

WOODWARD, W. E.   Years of Madness.
1951   New York   15.00

WOODWORTH, Steven E.   Jefferson Davis and His Generals, The Failure of Confederate Command in the West.
1990   University, KS   25.00

WOOLFOLK, George Ruble   The Cotton Regency.
1958   New York   20.00

WOOLLEY, Edwin C.   The Reconstruction of Georgia. Wraps.
1901   New York   30.00

WOOLSEY, Jane Stuart   Hospital Days. Wraps.
1870   New York   200.00

WOOLSEY, Theodore D.   Remarks on the Alabama Claims from the New Englander for July, 1869. Wraps.
1869   New Haven   40.00

WOOLSON, Alvin M.   First O.V.H.A., Company M.
1914   Toledo   110.00

WOOLWORTH, Solomon   Experiences in the Civil War.   Wraps.
    1903   Newark   80.00
    1904   Newark   80.00
    1905   n.p.   60.00
WORDEN, J. L., GREENE, S. D., and RAMSEY, H. A.   The Monitor and the Merrimac.
    1912   New York   40.00
WORK, Henry C.   Marching Through Georgia.
    1889   Boston   30.00
WORLEY, Ted R., edited by   At Home in Confederate Arkansas, Letters to and from Pulaski Countians 1861-1865.   Wraps.
    1955   Pulaski, AR   30.00
WORLOCK, Wilbur W.   Poetic War Record of Drake's Veteran Zouaves of Elizabeth, N. J.   Wraps.
    1885   Elizabeth   30.00
WORMELEY, Katharine Prescott   The Other Side of War; with the Army of the Potomac.
    1889   Boston   75.00
WORMELEY, Katharine Prescott   The United States Sanitary Commission A Sketch of the Purpose and Its Work.
    1863   Boston   25.00
WORMSER, Richard   The Yellowlegs. Story of the U. S. Cavalry.
    1966   New York   20.00
WORSHAM, John H.   One of Jackson's Foot Cavalry.
    1912   New York   200.00
    1964   Jackson   edited by James I. Robertson   40.00
    1987   Wilmington, NC   Wraps 9.95
WORSHAM, William J.   The Old Nineteenth Tennessee Regiment.
    1902   Knoxville   250.00
    1973   Blountville   35.00
WORTH, Jonathan   Correspondence, edited by J. G. De R. Hamilton. 2 Vols.
    1909   Raleigh, NC   40.00
WORTHINGTON, Glenn H.   Fighting for Time . . . Or, the Battle That Saved Washington.
    1932   Baltimore   100.00
    1985   19.95
    1988   19.95
WORTHINGTON, Thomas   Brief History of the 46th Ohio Volunteers.
    1877-80 Washington, DC   100.00
WORTHINGTON, Thomas   A Correct History . . . Gen. Grant at Shiloh.   Wraps.
    1880   Washington, DC   50.00
WORTHINGTON, Thomas   Shiloh, or The Tennessee Campaign of 1862.   Wraps.
    1872   Washington, DC   50.00
WRAY, William J.   History of the 23rd Pennsylvania Volunteer Infantry, Birney's Zouaves.
    1904   Philadelphia 110.00
WRIGHT, Arthur A.   The Civil War in the Southwest.
    1964   Denver   30.00

WRIGHT, Charles   A Corporal's Story, Experiences in the Ranks of Company C, 81st Ohio Vol. Infantry.
   1887   Philadelphia Ltd.   135.00
WRIGHT, E. N.   Conscientious Objectors in the Civil War.
   1931   Philadelphia   50.00
   1961   New York   15.00
WRIGHT, Henry H.   A History of the Sixth Iowa Infantry.
   1923   Iowa City   65.00
WRIGHT, Howard C.   Port Hudson, Its History from an Interior Point of View. Wraps.
   1961   Baton Rouge   15.00
WRIGHT, John H., compiled by   Compendium of the Confederacy: An Annotated Bibliography, Booklets, Pamphlets, Serials. 2 Vols.
   1989   Wilmington, NC   150.00
WRIGHT, John S.   Citizenship Sovereignty. Wraps.
   1863   Chicago   45.00
WRIGHT, John S.   Reply to Hon. Charles G. Loring Upon "Reconstruction." Wraps.
   1867   Chicago   15.00
WRIGHT, Louise   A Southern Girl In '61; The Wartime Memories of a Confederate Senator's Daughter.
   1905   New York   50.00
WRIGHT, Marcus J.   Arkansas in the War 1861-1865.
   1963   Batesville   50.00
WRIGHT, Marcus J., edited by   General Officers of the Confederate Army.
   1911   New York   150.00
WRIGHT, Marcus J., General Scott.
   For additional information, see Appendix: Great Commanders Series.
   1893   New York   40.00
   1893   New York   Ltd.   125.00
   1894   New York   40.00
WRIGHT, Marcus J., edited by   List of Field Officers in the Confederate States Service plus List of Regiments and Battalions in the Confederate States Army 1861-1865.
   1897   Washington, DC   300.00
WRIGHT, Marcus J.   Tennessee in the War.
   1908   New York   125.00
WRIGHT, Marcus J.   Texas in the Civil War 1861-1865, edited by Harold B. Simpson.
   1965   Hillsboro   40.00
   1984   Hillsboro   15.00
WRIGHT, Stuart Thurman   Historical Sketch of Person County [NC].
   1974   Danville   20.00
WRIGHT, Thomas J.   History of the Eighth Regiment Kentucky Volunteer Infantry.
   1880   St. Joseph, MO   275.00
WRIGHT, William C.   The Secession Movement in the Middle Atlantic States.
   1973   Rutherford   20.00
WUBBEN, Hubert H.   Civil War Iowa and the Copperhead Movement.
   1980   Ames, IA   25.00

WULSIN, Lucien   Roster of Surviving Members of the 4th Regiment Ohio Volunteer Cavalry with a Brief Historical Sketch of the Regiment.
   1891   Cincinnati   100.00
WULSIN, Lucien   The Story of the 4th Regiment Ohio Vet. Vol. Cavalry.
   1912   Cincinnati   150.00
WYETH, John Allan   Life of General Nathan Bedford Forrest.
   1899   New York   150.00
   1900   New York   125.00
   1904   New York   110.00
   1959   New York   entitled That Devil Forrest: Life of General Nathan Bedford Forrest   40.00
   1989   16.95
WYETH, John Allan   With Sabre and Scalpel.
   1914   New York   100.00
WYETH, John J.   Leaves from a Diary Written While Serving in Co. E, 44th Massachusetts, Dept of N.C. Sept 1862 - June 1863.
   1878   Boston   75.00
WYMAN, Lillie B. C.   A Grand Army Man (Augustine A. Mann) of Rhode Island.
   1925   Newton Ltd.   30.00
WYNES, Charles E., edited by   The Negro in the South Since 1865.
   1965   University, AL   15.00
Yankee Notions (Jan. - Dec., 1862.)
   1862   New York   150.00
YATES, Bowling C.   Historical Guide for Kennesaw Mountain National Battlefield Park and Marietta, Georgia.   Wraps.
   1976   Marietta   10.00
YATES, Bowling C.   History of the Georgia Military Institute, Marietta, Georgia.   Wraps.
   1968   Marietta   20.00
YATES, Richard E.   The Confederacy and Zeb Vance.   See: Confederate Centennial Studies, No. 8.
Ye Book of Copperheads.   Wraps.
   1863   Philadelphia   45.00
YEARNS, Wilfred Buck   The Confederate Congress.
   1960   Athens   25.00
YEARNS, Wilfred Buck, edited by   The Confederate Governors.
   1985   Athens   29.50
YEARNS, Wilfred Buck and BARRETT, John G., edited by   North Carolina Civil War Documentary.
   1980   Chapel Hill, NC   20.00
   1986   19.95
YEARY, Mamie, compiled by   Reminiscences of the Boys in Gray 1861-1865.
   1912   Dallas   325.00
   1986   75.00
YEATMAN, James   Report to the Western Sanitary Commission, St. Louis, Dec. 17, 1863.   Wraps.
   (1863)   (St. Louis)   30.00
YORK, Brantley   The Autobiography of _____.
   1910   Durham, NC   50.00

YOUNG, Agatha   The Women and the Crisis.
   1959   New York   25.00
YOUNG, Bennett H.   Confederate Wizards of the Saddle.
   1914   Boston 250.00
   1958   Kennesaw, GA   60.00
   1988   35.00
YOUNG, Bennett H.   Dr. Gander of Youngland.
   (1921) Louisville   65.00
YOUNG, Bennett H.   The South in History.   Wraps.
   (1910) Nashville, TN   40.00
YOUNG, Charles P.   History of Crenshaw Battery, Pegram's Battalion.
   Wraps.
   1904   Richmond   200.00
YOUNG, Ford E.   The Third Day at Gettysburg.
   1981   20.00
YOUNG, James C.   Marse Robert, Knight of the Confederacy.
   1929   New York   25.00
   1931   New York   20.00
YOUNG, James Harvey   Anna Elizabeth Dickinson and the Civil War.
   Wraps.
   1944   MI   20.00
YOUNG, Jesse Bowman   The Battle of Gettysburg.
   1913   New York   75.00
   1976   Dayton   17.50
YOUNG, Jesse Bowman   What a Boy Saw in the Army.
   1894   New York   50.00
YOUNG, John Preston   The Seventh Tennessee Cavalry (Confederate)
   A History.
   1890   Nashville 275.00
   1976   Dayton   17.50
YOUNG, John Russell   Around the World with General Grant. 2 Vols.
   1879   New York   50.00
YOUNG, John Russell   Men and Memories, edited by May D. Russell
   Young.
   1901   New York   40.00
YOUNG, Lot D.   Reminiscences of a Soldier of the Orphan Brigade.
   Wraps.
   (1918) Paris, KY   30.00
YOUNG, Stark   So Red the Rose.
   1934   New York   40.00
   1935   30.00
   1951   20.00
ZABRISKIE, George A.   John Brown: Saint or Sinner?
   1949   Ormond Beach, FL   20.00
ZARA, Louis   Rebel Run.
   1951   New York   30.00
ZETTLER, Berrien McPherson   War Stories and School-Day Incidents
   for the Children.
   1912   New York   350.00
ZINCKE, F. Barham   Last Winter in the United States.
   1868   London   70.00

ZINN, Jack   The Battle of Rich Mountain.   Wraps.
   1971   Parsons, WV   10.00
   1972   Parsons, WV   10.00
ZINN, Jack   R. E. Lee's Cheat Mountain Campaign.
   1974   Parsons, WV   30.00
ZORN, W. A.   Hold at All Hazards: The Story of the 29th Alabama
   Infantry.
   1987   Jesup   27.50
ZORNOW, William Frank   Lincoln and the Party Divided.
   1954   Norman   15.00
ZUBER, Richard L.   Jonathan Worth, A Biography of a Southern
   Unionist.
   1965   Chapel Hill, NC   25.00
ZUBER, Richard L.   North Carolina During Reconstruction. Wraps.
   1975   Raleigh, NC   4.00
ZUBER, William P.   My Eighty Years in Texas, edited by Janis B. May-
   field.
   1971   Austin   25.00

CONFEDERATE IMPRINTS

Material printed in the Confederate States during the Civil War is considered to be of Confederate Imprint. This designation also applies to material printed in other countries for the Confederacy and brought through the blockade. However, material printed during the War in federally occupied areas of the South, New Bern, New Orleans, etc., during the period of occupation is not of Confederate Imprint. Official publications of the Confederate States Government in Richmond date from February 1861 through March 1865. Since Confederate Imprints are identified by place and date of publication, the dates of secession constitute a necessary guideline.

1. South Carolina — Dec. 20, 1860	Thus, a work published in South Carolina on or before December 20, 1860, 'till the end of the War is a Confederate Imprint, etc.

1. South Carolina — Dec. 20, 1860
2. Mississippi — Jan. 9, 1861
3. Florida — Jan. 10, 1861
4. Alabama — Jan. 11, 1861
5. Georgia — Jan. 19, 1861
6. Louisiana — Jan. 26, 1861
7. Texas — Feb. 1, 1861
8. Virginia — Apr. 17, 1861
9. Arkansas — May 6, 1861
10. North Carolina — May 20, 1861
11. Tennessee — June 8, 1861
*12. Missouri — Aug. 19, 1861
*13. Kentucky — Dec. 9, 1861

*Rump sessions of the Missouri and Kentucky legislatures passed ordinances of secession and these states were admitted into the Confederacy on August 19 and December 9, 1861. For this reason, the Confederate flag contained thirteen stars. In reality, both Kentucky and Missouri were divided states and neither contributed much in the way of Confederate Imprints. Thus far, only two Confederate Imprints have been assigned to Kentucky and four to Missouri.

Confederate Imprints are a world unto themselves. In this volume, they are listed by subject in numerical sequence in accordance with the standard guide to the field, CONFEDERATE IMPRINTS: A BIBLIOGRAPHY by Parrish and Willingham. This thousand-page plus tome lists all known Confederate Imprints with locations noted and a cross-reference section for converting entries in earlier Confederate checklists.

Since Confederate Imprints are grouped by subjects, it is necessary to look under the proper heading to find a particular volume. If you have a Confederate Imprint which is an official publication of the Confederacy, or a Confederate state, look under that heading, i.e., Tennessee official publications will be listed under Tennessee. Non-official publications are divided into categories. Select the category that best suits your title and give it a try. Failing this, try another category. Our apologies if this seems confusing, but almost all of those who collect and sell Confederate Imprints are used to this system. We thought on the matter, but couldn't come up with an easy way to convert to a single alphabetical listing. However, if it's any consolation, rare Confederate Imprints are few and far between these days.

UNIFORM AND DRESS

OF THE

ARMY

OF THE

CONFEDERATE STATES

ADJUTANT AND INSPECTOR GENERAL'S OFFICE,
RICHMOND, SEPTEMBER 12, 1861.

The work styled the "Uniform and Dress of the Army of the Confederate States," for which a copyright has been secured by Blanton Duncan, is published by authority.

S. COOPER,
Adjutant and Inspector General.

RICHMOND:
CHAS. H. WYNNE, PRINTER, 94 MAIN STREET
LITHOGRAPHS BY E. CREHEN.
1861.

CONFEDERATE IMPRINTS

CONFEDERATE GOVERNMENT

OFFICIAL PUBLICATIONS

CONSTITUTION

P-7   **Constitution of the Confederate States of America,** In Congress - March 9, 1861 - Amended Constitution. . . .
(1861)   (Montgomery, AL)   15,000.00

P-9
C-6   **Constitution of the Confederate States of America.** Adopted unanimously by the Congress of the Confederate States of America, March 11, 1861.
1861   Milledgeville   600.00

P-16
C-10   **Constitution of the Confederate States of America.**
1861   Richmond   400.00

P-18
C-12   **Provisional and Permanent Constitutions,** together with the acts and resolutions of the first session of the Provisional Congress States.
1861   Montgomery, AL   350.00

CONGRESS

P-23
C-15   **Acts and Resolutions of the first session** of the Provisional Congress of the Confederate States.
1861   Montgomery, AL   200.00

P-27
C-17   **Acts and Resolutions of the third session** of the Provisional Congress of the Confederate States, held at Richmond, Va.
1861   Richmond   125.00

P-28
C-18   **Acts and Resolutions of the fourth session** of the Provisional Congress of the Confederate States, held at Richmond, Va.
1862   Richmond   150.00

P-29
C-19   **The statutes at large of the Provisional Government of the Confederate States** . . . from . . . February 8, 1861, to . . . February 18, 1862. . . . Edited by James M. Matthews.
1864   Richmond   325.00

P-30
C-20   **The statutes at large of the Confederate States of America** . . . first session . . . first Congress; 1862. . . . Edited by James M. Matthews.
1862   Richmond   100.00

P-31
C-21   **The statutes at large of the Confederate States of America** . . . second session . . . first Congress; 1862. . . .
1862   Richmond   100.00

P-32
C-22   **The statutes at large of the Confederate States of America** . . . third session . . . first Congress; 1863. . . .
1863   Richmond   100.00

P-33 C-23	**The statutes at large of the Confederate States of America** . . . fourth session . . . first Congress; 1863-64. . . . 1864 Richmond 100.00
P-34 C-24	**The statutes at large of the Confederate States of America** . . . first session . . . second Congress; 1864. . . . 1864 Richmond 100.00
P-42 C-29	**Compilation of the Tariff Act of the Confederate States of America,** approved May 21st, 1861. . . . 1861 New Orleans 300.00
P-43 C-30	**A Digest of the Military and Naval Laws of the Confederate States,** arranged by Capt. W. W. Lester and William J. Bromwell. 1864 Columbia, SC 200.00
P-44 C-31	**Digest of Military and Naval Laws of the Confederate States,** from the commencement of the Provisional Congress to the end of the first Congress under the permanent constitution. Analytically arranged by Capt. W. W. Lester, of the Quartermaster-General's Office, and Wm. J. Bromwell, of the Department of State, attorneys-at-law. 1864 Columbia, SC 500.00
P-46 C-33	**Laws for the Army and Navy of the Confederate States.** 1861 Richmond 350.00
P-50 C-36	**Laws of the Provisional Congress of the Confederate States** in relation to the War Department. 1861 Richmond 325.00
P-55 C-41	**Tariff of the Confederate States of America approved by Congress, May 21, 1861** . . . "Treasury Circular, no. 10." 1861 Charleston, SC 75.00
P-58 C-42	**An act recognizing the existence of war** between the United States and the Confederate States. . . . 1861 Montgomery, AL 250.00
P-59 C-43	**An act relative to prisoners of war** . . . Approved May 21, 1861. 1861 Montgomery, AL 75.00
P-60 C-44	**An act to amend an act entitled "An act recognizing the existence of war** . . . , and concerning letters of marque, prizes and prize goods. . . . 1861 Montgomery, AL 150.00
P-65 C-50	**An act to perpetuate testimony in cases of slaves** abducted or harbored by the enemy, and of other property seized, wasted, or destroyed by them. No. 270. . . . 1861 Richmond 150.00
P-80 C-62	**An act to reduce the currency, and to authorize a new issue of** treasury notes. — An act to levy additional taxes for the common defence and support of the government. — An act to organize forces to serve during the war. 1864 Richmond 60.00
P-85 C-66	**An act to amend the tax laws.** 1864 Richmond 25.00
P-228 C-73	**Address of Congress to the people of the Confederate States.** 1864 Richmond 100.00

P-246
C-77
Proceedings of the Congress on the announcement of the death of Col. Francis S. Bartow. . . .
1861   Richmond   225.00

P-247
C-78
Proceedings on the announcement of the death of Hon. John Tyler. . . .
1862   Richmond   125.00

P-257
C-87
Report of the Joint select committee appointed to investigate the condition and treatment of prisoners of war.
1865   Richmond   150.00

P-258
C-88
Report of the Joint select committee appointed to investigate the condition and treatment of prisoners of war.
1865   Richmond   125.00

SENATE

P-308
C-110
(Senate bill, no. 13). A bill to be entitled An act in relation to the public printing.
1863   Richmond   40.00

P-331
C-130
Letter from Gen. Wise . . . to Hon. Jas. Lyons . . . endorsing and enclosing the memorial of Generals Hardee, Stevenson and other officers. . . .
1863   Richmond   50.00

P-346
C-536
Resolutions Adopted by Company "H," "I" and "K" Thirteenth Virginia Infantry. January 28, 1865.   Broadsheet.
(1865)   (Richmond)   100.00

P-385
C-171
(Senate bill, no. 121). A bill declaring the mode of ascertaining the value of the tithe deliverable to the government under existing laws.
1864   Richmond   30.00

P-394
C-180
Amendment to Senate bill (S. 129) to provide for the employment of free negroes and slaves to work upon fortifications, and to perform other labor connected with the defenses of the country.
1864   Richmond   60.00

P-404
C-191
(Senate engrossed bill, no. 121). A bill declaring the mode of ascertaining the value of the tithe deliverable to the government under the true construction of existing laws.
(1865)   Richmond   30.00

P-417
C-203
Amendment proposed by the Committee on Finance, to the bill (H.R. 229) to provide more effectually for the reduction and redemption of the currency.
1865   Richmond   30.00

P-419
C-204
Resolution of the Legislature of the State of North Carolina in relation to the pay of disabled soldiers.
1865   Richmond   35.00

P-422
C-206
Resolutions Passed at a Meeting of the 14th Regiment of Virginia Infantry, in Relation to the Condition of the Country and the Conduct of the War.
(1865)   (Richmond)   150.00

P-448 C-227	**Directory of the Confederate States Senate,** for the second session of the second Congress, commencing November 7, 1864. 1864 Richmond 70.00
P-453 C-230	**Rules for conducting business in the Senate** of the Confederate States of America. 1864 Richmond 350.00

HOUSE OF REPRESENTATIVES

	House Bills. There are copious numbers of miscellaneous House bills and resolutions; most are valued: 25.00–30.00 each
P-800 C-530	**Resolutions Passed at a Meeting of the Ninth Virginia Infantry,** January 25, 1865. 1865 Richmond 150.00
P-807 C-537	**Resolutions Adopted by Humphrey's Mississippi Brigade,** Army of Northern Virginia. Broadside. (1865) (Richmond) 125.00
P-879	**Evidence taken before the committee of the House of Representatives** appointed to enquire into the treatment of prisoners at Castle Thunder. 1863 Richmond 225.00

PRESIDENT

	President's Messages. Numerous copies of Presidential Messages exist; in general, these are valued: 25.00–40.00 each
P-897 C-608	**Message of the President.** 1861 Montgomery, AL 150.00

ARMY

P-991	**Circular. The disgraceful and cowardly conduct** of many officers and men, who seek to avoid actions with the enemy and other dangers and hardship. . . . Broadside, on full color pages. 1863 Franklin, TN 750.00
P-993	**Head Quarters Wheeler's Cavalry Division 1863,** General Order No. 4. Broadside. 1863 n.p. 150.00
P-994	**Wheeler's Cavalry Corps,** General Order No. 2, Feb. 10, 1864. Broadside. 1864 n.p. 150.00
P-999	**Gen. Forrest to his troops.** Broadside. 1865 Gainesville, AL 1500.00
P-1000	**FORREST,** Nathan Bedford **Maj. Gen. N. B. Forrest's Address to His Command.** Broadside. 1864 Tupelo, MS 2000.00
P-1006	**LONGSTREET,** James, Lt.Gen. **General Orders, No. 7.** (Morristown, TN) Broadsheet. 1864 Morristown, TN 150.00

P-1124   **JOHNSTON**, Albert Sidney   **Soldiers of the Army of the Mississippi.** Broadside.
1862   Corinth, MS   1200.00

P-1159
C-700   **BRAGG**, Braxton   **Pursuant to the orders** of the President, I assume the permanent command of the Forces in this Department. . . . Broadside.
1862   Tupelo, MS   750.00

P-1164   **BRAGG**, Gen. Braxton   **General Orders No. 94,** Tupelo, Mississippi, July 8, 1862.
1862   Tupelo, MS   150.00

P-1164   **BRAGG**, Gen. Braxton   **General Orders No. 96,** Tupelo, Mississippi, July 10, 1862.
1862   Tupelo, MS   350.00

P-1234
C-669   **Resolutions of the Texas Brigade.** Army.
1865   n.p.   150.00

P-1260   **Address of Generals Johnston & Beauregard** after the Battle of Manassas, to the Soldiers. . . . Broadside.
1861   n.p.   925.00

P-1265   **General Orders No. 75.** A new banner is entrusted to-day, as a battle-flag to the safe keeping of the Army of the Potomac. . . . Broadside.
1861   Centreville, VA   500.00

P-1347
C-786   **Soldiers of Hood's Division: Your country calls you!** Will you not give a willing response in her hour of peril? . . . Broadside.
1864   n.p.   400.00

P-1413
C-773   **Head Quarters, District of Texas, New Mexico and Arizona.** General Orders, No.- . Broadside.
1863   Caricites, TX   75.00

P-1431
C-774R   **General orders. Houston, 1865.** Nos. 1-31; January 1-May 20, 1865. No. 19 issued at Galveston. Army.
1865   Houston   75.00 each

P-1447   **Head Quarters, District of Texas, New Mexico and Arizona.** Special Orders, No. 27. Broadside.
1864   Houston   75.00

P-1449   **Head Quarters, District of Texas, New Mexico and Arizona.** Special Orders, No. 118. Broadside.
1865   Houston   75.00

P-1517
C-748   **General Order.** The money issued by the Confederate government is secure, and is receivable in payment of public dues, and convertible into 8 per cent. bonds. Broadside.
(1862)   Charleston, (WV)   400.00

P-1529
C-749   **To the People of Western Virginia.** The Army of the Confederate States has come among you to expel the enemy. . . . Broadside.
1862   Charleston, (WV)   600.00

P-1542
C-797-2   **General orders. Head Quarters Trans.-Miss. Dept.** Shreveport, 1863. Nos. 1-61; March 7-December 10, 1863.
1863   Shreveport   60.00 each

P-1544   **Head Quarters Trans-Mississippi Department,** Shreveport, La., April 1, 1865. General Orders, No. 31.
1865   Shreveport   500.00

P-1544   **Head Quarters Trans Mississippi Department,** Shreveport, La.
H-798-2   General Orders, No. 29.   Broadside.
1865   Shreveport   150.00

P-1598   **Resolutions of Forsberg's Brigade,** Wharton's Division.   Army.
C-697   1865 n.p.   150.00

P-1599   **A Message from the Army of the Valley of Virginia.**   Broadside.
C-698   1865   Richmond   200.00

DISTRICT COURTS

P-1639   **Decisions of Hon. James D. Halyburton,** judge of the Confederate
C-848   States District Court for the Eastern District of Virginia, in the cases of John B. Lane and John H. Leftwich, in relation to their exemption, as mail contractors, from the performance of military service. District Courts.
1864   Richmond   100.00

DEPARTMENT OF JUSTICE

Communications and Reports of Attorney General. There are many copies of these items, generally valued: 20.00–40.00 each

NAVY DEPARTMENT

P-1681   **Communication from Secretary of Navy . . .** Transmitted with
C-861   Message of the President . . . March 10, 1863.
1863 Richmond   30.00

P-1682   **Communication from the Secretary of the Navy . . .** [relative to
C-862   "a flour and grist mill and baker," established by the Department, at Albany, Georgia].
1865   Richmond   30.00

P-1683   **Communication of Secretary of the Navy . . .** [conveying the
C-863   information that "no coals were taken from the steamer 'Advance,' in October last, or at any other time, for the naval service"].
1865   Richmond   60.00

P-1706   **Register of the commissioned and warrant officers** of the Navy
C-881   of the Confederate States. . . .
1863   Richmond   325.00

P-1711   **Regulations for the Navy of the Confederate States.** 1862. . . .
C-885   1862   Richmond   900.00

P-1714   **Report of the Secretary of the Navy . . .** November 5, 1864.
C-888   1864   Richmond   150.00

PATENT OFFICE

Reports of the Commissioner of Patents. Copies of patent reports are valued: 40.00 each

P-1737
C-902
Rules and directions for proceedings in the Confederate States Patent Office.
1861   Richmond   300.00

POST-OFFICE DEPARTMENT

Reports of the Postmaster General. These numerous reports are generally valued: 40.00 each

P-1750
C-911
Instructions for postmasters east of the Mississippi River. Broadside.
(1864)   (Richmond)   150.00

P-1756
C-917
Report of the Postmaster-General to the President, April 29, 1861.
(1865)   Richmond   125.00

BUREAU OF PUBLIC PRINTING

Reports of the Superintendent of Public Printing. These reports, printed in Richmond, 1864, are valued: 30.00 each

DEPARTMENT OF STATE

P-1783
C-839
Correspondence of the Department of State, in relation to the British consuls resident in the Confederate States.
1863   Richmond   100.00

SURGEON-GENERAL'S OFFICE

P-1969
C-1042
Guide for inspection of hospitals and inspector's report.
(186-)   Richmond   150.00

P-1971
C-1044
Hospital Regulations. Gen'l Hospital, No. 3, Lynchburg, July 1, 1863. Broadside.
(1863)   (Lynchburg, VA)   400.00

P-1984
C-1057
A Manual of military surgery. Prepared for the use of the Confederate States Army . . . By order of the Surgeon-General.
1863   Richmond   1000.00

TREASURY DEPARTMENT

Abstracts, Estimates and Communications from Secretary of Treasury. These items are generally valued: 20.00–25.00 each

P-2193
Produce Loan - Instructions. (Debow, James D. B.)
(1862)   (Jackson, MS)   100.00

WAR DEPARTMENT

| P-2210 C-1208 | **Army regulations,** adopted for the use of the Army of the Confederate States. . . . |
| | 1861   New Orleans   250.00 |

| P-2213 | **Army regulations,** adopted for the use of the Army of the Confederate States. . . . |
| | 1861   Raleigh   250.00 |

| P-2215 C-1211 | **Army regulations,** adopted for the use of the Army of the Confederate States. . . . |
| | 1861   Richmond   200.00 |

| P-2216 C-1212 | **Articles of War.** An Act for Establishing Rules and Articles for the Government of the Armies of the Confederate States. |
| | (1861)   (Raleigh)   300.00 |

| P-2217 C-1214 | **Articles of War,** for the government of the armies of hte [*sic*] Confederate States. |
| | 1861   Charleston   300.00 |

| P-2218 C-1215 | **Articles of War,** for the government of the Army of the Confederate States. |
| | 1861   Montgomery   300.00 |

Secretary of War - Communications and Correspondence. Most of these items are valued: 20.00–30.00 each

| P-2324 C-1341 | **Gen. Beauregard's Official Report of the "Battle of Manassas."** |
| | (1861)   (Richmond)   850.00 |

| P-2327 C-2482 | **STARK,** Alexander W.   **Instruction for field artillery. . . .** |
| | 1864   Richmond   600.00 |

| P-2330 C-1358 | **Letter from the Secretary of War** . . . March 31, 1862, communicating copies of the official reports, on file in this department, of the battle of Bethel, on the 10th of June, 1861. |
| | 1862   Richmond   75.00 |

| P-2343 C-1372 | **Official Report of the Battle of Chickamauga.** |
| | 1864   Richmond   400.00 |

| P-2347 C-1376 | **Official Reports of Battles.** Published by Order of Congress. |
| | 1864   Richmond   500.00 |

| P-2348 C-1377 | **Official Reports of Battles.** |
| | 1864   Richmond   300.00 |

| P-2349 C-1378 | **Official Reports of Battles** . . . Published by Order of Congress. |
| | 1864   Richmond   500.00 |

| P-2355 C-1385 | **Proceedings to the Court of Inquiry** relative to the fall of New Orleans. Published by order of Congress. |
| | 1864   Richmond   300.00 |

| P-2361 C-1390 | **Regulations for the Army of the Confederate States, 1862.** |
| | 1862   Richmond   150.00 |

| P-2362 C-1391 | **Regulations for the Army of the Confederate States, 1862.** |
| | 1862   Richmond   200.00 |

| P-2364 C-1392 | **Regulations for the Army of the Confederate States, 1863.** Corrected and enlarged with a revised Index. . . . |
| | 1863   Richmond   350.00 |

P-2365
C-1393
Regulations for the Army of the Confederate States, 1863.
1863 Richmond   250.00

P-2369
C-1397
Regulations for the Army of the Confederate States, 1864.
Revised and enlarged with a new and copious index. Third and only reliable edition. . . .
1864   Richmond   200.00

P-2372
C-1399
Regulations for the Army of the Confederate States, 1861.
1861   New Orleans   300.00

P-2374
C-1401
Regluations for the Army of the Confederate States, and for the Quartermaster's Department and Pay Department.
1861   Richmond   200.00

P-2375
C-1402
Regulations for the Army of the Confederate States. . . Also Containing the Articles of War, and the Acts of Congress for the Organization of the Army of the Confederate States.
1861   New Orleans and Jackson   600.00

P-2379
C-1410
MECHLING, W. T.   Regulations of the Army of the Confederate States, 1862: Containing a Complete Set of Forms for the Quartermasters, Subsistence, Ordnance, and Medical Departments of the Army. . . .
1862   Austin   500.00

P-2384
C-1415
Report of Brig. Gen. John S. Williams of operations in East Tennessee, from 27th September to 15th October, 1863.
1864   Richmond   200.00

P-2385
C-1416
Report of Brigadier General R. S. Ripley, of Operations from August 21, to September 10, 1863. With Sub-Reports. Published by Order of Congress.
1864   Richmond   750.00

P-2391
C-1422
Report of Major General Hindman, of his operations in the Trans-Mississippi District. . . .
1864   Richmond   350.00

P-2393
C-1423
Report of Major General Loring of Battle of Baker's Creek, and Subsequent Movements of His Command.
1864   Richmond   150.00

P-2402
C-1431
Report of the Secretary of War . . . April 28, 1864.
Department.
1864   Richmond   60.00

P-2403
C-1432
Report of the Secretary of War . . . November 3, 1864.
1864   Richmond   60.00

P-2406
C-1435
Reports of the operations of the Army of Northern Virginia, from June 1862, to and including the battle of Fredericksburg, Dec. 13, 1862. . . . 2 Volumes.
1864   Richmond   300.00

P-2407
C-1436
Response of Secretary of War, to the resolutions of the Senate, adopted December 5th, 1864. . . .
1864   Richmond   40.00

P-2416
C-1448-3
Uniform and dress of the Army.
1861   Richmond   2000.00

P-2417 C-1449	**Uniform and dress of the Army of the Confederate States.** . . . 1861 Richmond 3500.00
P-2423 C-1342	**General Orders** from the Adjutant and Inspector-General's Office, Confederate States Army, in 1862. . . . 1863 Charleston, SC 375.00
P-2424 C-1343	**General Orders** from Adjutant and Inspector-General's Office . . . from January, 1862, to December, 1863. . . . 1864 Columbia 375.00
P-2425 C-1344	**General orders** from the Adjutant and Inspector-General's Office, Confederate States Army, for the year 1863, with a full index. 1864 Richmond 400.00
P-2426 C-1345	**General Orders** from the Adjutant and Inspector-General's Of- fice, Confederate States Army, from January 1, 1864, to July 1, 1864, inclusive. . . . 1864 Columbia 250.00 Variant copy, front wrap and title page information differ. 250.00
P-2429 C-1348	**General Orders.** Adjutant and Inspector-General's Office. Nos. 1- 112; January 1-December 30, 1862. 1862 Richmond 20.00 each
P-2430 C-1349	**General orders.** Adjutant and Inspector-General's Office. Nos. 1- 164, January 3-December 30, 1863. 1863 Richmond 20.00 each
P-2446 C-1759	**Ordinances passed by the [North Carolina] State Convention** at its Second Adjourned Session. (1862) (Raleigh, NC) 300.00
P-2493 C-1406	**Regulations for the Government of the Ordnance Department** of the Confederate States of America. 1862 Richmond 400.00
P-2502	**Authority to Impress.** Sir: Under the authority of an act of Congress passed March 26th, 1863 . . . you are . . . empowered to impress army supplies. . . . Broadside. 1863 Richmond 200.00
	Quartermaster General's Circulars. Many copies exist of these various circulars; most are valued: 20.00-30.00 each

ALABAMA

P-2609 C-1454	**Ordinances adopted by the people of the State of Alabama,** in Convention, at Montgomery . . . Andrew B. Moore, Governor. William M. Brooks, President of the Convention. 1861 Montgomery 300.00
P-2612 C-1455-2	**Report and Resolutions, from the Committee of Thirteen,** upon the formation of a provisional and permanent government between the seceding states. 1861 Montgomery 300.00

P-2623
C-1459
Acts of the Called Session, 1862, and of the Second Regular Annual Session of the General Assembly of Alabama . . . commencing on the 27th day of October and second Monday in November, 1862.
1862   Montgomery   400.00

ARKANSAS

P-2710
C-1485
Ordinances of the State Convention, which convened in Little Rock, May 6, 1861.
1861   Little Rock   250.00

FLORIDA

P-2724
C-1496
Constitution or Form of Government for the People of Florida, as Revised and Amended at a Convention of the People . . . at . . . Tallahassee on . . . [January 3, 1861], together with the Ordinances Adopted by the Convention.
1861   Tallahassee   750.00

P-2727
C-1499
Journal of the Proceedings of the Convention of the People of Florida . . . at the Capitol in . . . Tallassee [sic], on . . . January 3, 1861].
1861   Tallahassee   500.00

P-2728
C-1500
Ordinances & Resolutions Passed by the State Convention of the People of Florida . . . in . . . Tallahassee January 3, 1861.
1861   Tallahassee   750.00

P-2730
C-1502
Proceedings of the Convention of the People of Florida, Called Sessions . . . at the Capitol in Tallahassee, on . . . [February 26 and April 18, 1861].
1861   (Tallahassee)   500.00

P-2734
C-1504
Acts and Resolutions, 12th General Assembly of Florida, Tallahassee: Office of the *Floridian & Journal.*
1862   Tallahassee   100.00

P-2745
C-1510
Journal of the Proceedings of the House of Representatives - State of Florida - Tallahassee: Office of the *Floridian & Journal.*
1861   Tallahassee   500.00

GEORGIA

P-2768
C-1518
Journal of the public and secret proceedings of the Convention of the poeple of Georgia, held in Milledgeville, and in Savannah in 1861 . . . with the ordinances adopted.
1861   Milledgeville   225.00

P-2778
C-1521
Acts of the General Assembly of the State of Georgia, passed . . . at an annual session in November and December, 1861.
1861   Milledgeville   75.00

P-2779
C-1522
Acts of the General Assembly . . . passed . . . at an annual session in November and December, 1862; also extra session of 1863.
1863   Milledgeville   125.00

P-2780   **Acts of the General Assembly** . . . passed . . . at an annual session
C-1523   in November and December, 1863; also, extra session of 1864.
          1864   Milledgeville   100.00

P-2787   **A code of the State of Georgia.** . . .
C-1531   1861   Atlanta   100.00

P-2791   **Papers relative to the mission of Hon. T. Butler King,** to Europe.
C-1538   1863   Milledgeville   100.00

P-2885   **Georgia.** Militia. General orders . . .   No. 24, Dec. 27, 1862.
          Small broadside.
          1862   Milledgeville   200.00

LOUISIANA

P-2991   **Acts Passed by the Twenty-seventh Legislature of the State of**
C-1620   **Louisiana,** in Extra Session at Opelousas, December, 1862, &
          January, 1863.
          1864   Natchitoches   500.00

P-2993   **Acts Passed by the Sixth Legislature of the State of Louisiana.**
C-1621   at its Extra Session, Held in . . . Shreveport, on the 4th of May,
          1863.
          1863   Shreveport   500.00

P-3001   **Important Acts of the Louisiana General Assembly** Passed at the
C-1624   Session of 1864. Published by Direction of . . . Henry W. Allen,
          Governor of Louisiana.
          (1864)   Shreveport   500.00

P-3012   **By Authority. No. 41.** An Act to provide for the support of the
C-1625   families of officers, soldiers and marines. . . No. 21. An Act to
          raise an army for the defence of . . . Louisiana . . . No. 42. An
          Act to organize the militia for the defences of the State.
          Broadsheet.
          (1863)   (Shreveport)   400.00

P-3033   **The Confederate government stands greatly in need of old iron.**
          1862   New Orleans   250.00

P-3047   **ALLEN,** Henry W.   **Inaugural Address of Governor** . . . to the
H-1637-1   Legislature of . . . Louisiana. Delivered at Shreveport Jan. 25,
          1864.
          (1864)   (Shreveport)   500.00

P-3275   **To the People of New Orleans.** Mayoralty of New Orleans, City
          Hall, April 25, 1862. . . . (Appeal to citizens to resist Federal
          invasion.) Broadside.
          1862   New Orleans   1000.00

MISSISSIPPI

P-3282   **Journal of the State Convention,** and ordinances and resolutions
C-1655   adopted in March, 1861.
          1861   Jackson   150.00

P-3292   **Laws** . . . passed at a called session . . . July 1861.
C-1659   1861   Jackson   75.00

P-3293
C-1660
Laws ... passed at the regular session ... November & December 1861, and January, 1862.
1862   Jackson   75.00

P-3294
C-1661
Laws ... passed at a called and regular session ... Dec. 1862 and Nov. 1863.
1864   Selma   75.00

P-3297
C-1664
Laws ... passed at a called session ... February and March, 1865.
1865   Meridian   75.00

NORTH CAROINA

P-3443
C-1756
Ordinances and resolutions passed by the State Convention of North Carolina, at its several sessions in 1861-'62.
1862   Raleigh   300.00

P-3444
C-1757
Ordinances of the State Convention, published in pursuance of a resolution of the General Assembly, (ratified 11th Feb., 1863). Bound with P-3494, P-3495, P-3497, P-3502, P-3503, and P-3504.
1863   Raleigh   250.00

P-3484
C-1789
Executive and legislative documents. Session 1862-'63. Documents 1-24.
1863   Raleigh   50.00

P-3486
C-1791
Executive and legislative documents. Extra sessions 1863-'64.
1864   Raleigh   125.00

P-3487
C-1792
Executive and legislative documents. Session of 1864-'65.
1865   Raleigh   40.00

P-3493
C-1795
Private laws of the State of North Carolina, passed by the General Assembly at its session of 1860-'61. Private laws of the State of North Carolina, passed by the General Assembly, at its first extra session, 1861. Bound with P-3500.
1861   Raleigh   100.00

P-3498
C-1800
Private laws of the State of North Carolina, passed by the General Assembly at its adjourned session of 1863. Bound with P-3499, P-3505 and P-3506.
1863   Raleigh   75.00

P-3499
C-1801
Private laws of the State of North Carolina, passed by the General Assembly at its adjourned session of 1864. See P-3498.

P-3500
C-1802
Public laws of the State of North Carolina, passed by the General Assembly, at its session of 1860-'61; together with the Comptroller's statement of public revenue and expenditure. Public laws of the State of North Carolina, passed by the General Assembly, at its first extra session of 1861. See P-3493.

P-3501
C-1803
Public laws of the State of North Carolina, passed by the General Assembly, at its second extra session, 1861.
1861   Raleigh   75.00

P-3502
C-1804
Public laws of the State of North Carolina, passed by the General Assembly, at its session of 1862-'63. See P-3444.

P-3503 C-1805	**Public laws of the State of North Carolina,** passed by the General Assembly, at its adjourned session of 1862-'63. See P-3444. 1863 Raleigh
P-3504 C-1806	**Public laws of the State of North Carolina,** passed by the General Assembly at its called session of 1863. See P-3444. 1863 Raleigh
P-3505 C-1807	**Public laws of the State of North Carolina,** passed by the General Assembly at its adjourned session of 1863. See P-3498. 1863 Raleigh
P-3506 C-1808	**Public laws of the State of North Carolina,** passed by the General Assembly at its adjourned session of 1864. See P-3498. 1864 Raleigh
P-3514 C-1816	**Journal of the Senate of the General Assembly of the State of North Carolina,** at its extra session, 1861. Bound with P-3605. 1861 Raleigh 50.00
P-3515 C-1817	**Journal of the Senate of the General Assembly of the State of North Carolina,** at its first session, 1862. Bound with P-3516 and P-3606. 1862 Raleigh 160.00
P-3516 C-1818	**Journal of the Senate of the General Assembly of the State of North Carolina,** at its second session, 1863. See P-3515. 1863 Raleigh
P-3605 C-1844	**Journal of the House of Commons of the General Assembly of the State of North Carolina,** at its second extra session, 1861. See P-3514. 1862 Raleigh
P-3606 C-1845	**Journal of the House of Commons of North Carolina,** at its session 1862-'63. Journal of the House of Commons of North Carolina at its adjourned session 1862-'63. See P-3515. 1862 Raleigh
P-3656 C-1861-2	**Statements of the Comptroller of Public Accounts** for the two fiscal years ending Sept. 30, 1861 and 1862. 1862 Raleigh 125.00
P-3723 C-1861-9	**Cases at law,** argued and determined in the Supreme Court of North Carolina, at Raleigh, June term, 1863. 1863 (Raleigh) 175.00
P-3732 C-1863-1	**Reports of Cases at Law,** Argued and Determined in the Supreme Court of North Carolina, June term. 2 Vols. 1863-64 n.p. 250.00
P-3739 C-1863-4	**List of wounded from the State of North Carolina.** In the battle of Richmond, from June 26th to July 1st, 1862. . . . 1862 n.p. 125.00

SOUTH CAROLINA

P-3758
C-1871

Convention Documents. Report of the Special Committee of Twenty-one, on the communication of His Excellency Governor Pickens, together with the reports of heads of departments, and other papers.
1862   Columbia   125.00

P-3761
C-1873

Declaration of the immediate causes which induce and justify the sesession of South Carolina from the federal union; and the ordinance of secession.
1860   Charleston   500.00

P-3795

An ordinance to dissolve the Union. . . .   Charleston Mercury Extra. Broadside.
(1860)   (Charleston)   3000.00

P-3831
C-1900

Acts of the General Assembly . . . passed in December, 1862, and February and April, 1863. . . .
1863   Columbia   50.00

P-4048
C-2104

Message no. 1 of His Excellency, F. W. Pickens, to the Legislature, at the regular session of November, 1862.
1862   Columbia   75.00

P-4084
C-2122

Correspondence between the commissioners of the State of So. Ca. to the government at Washington and the President of the United States. . . .
1861   Charleston   100.00

P-4119
C-2135

Census of the city of Charleston, South Carolina, for the year 1861 . . . by Frederick A. Ford.
1861   Charleston   100.00

TENNESSEE

P-4128
C-2139

Public acts . . . passed at the extra session of the thirty-third General Assembly, April, 1861.
1861   Nashville   75.00

P-4132
C-2141

Senate [and House] Journal of the Second Extra Session of the . . . General Assembly of . . . Tennessee, which convened at Nashville . . . [April 25, 1861]. 2 vols in 1.
1861   Nashville   500.00

P-4141
C-2146

Regulations adopted for the Provisional Force of the Tennessee Volunteers. . . .
1861   Nashville   500.00

P-4147
C-2150

The Constitution of the State of Texas, as amended in 1861. The constitution of the Confederate States of America. The ordinances of the Texas Convention: and an address to the people of Texas. . . .
1861   Austin   400.00

P-4150
C-2152

A declaration of the causes which impel the State of Texas to secede from the federal union.
1861   Austin   1000.00

P-4181 C-2171	General Laws of the Ninth Legislature of the State of Texas. 1862 Houston 275.00
P-4183 C-2173	General Laws of the Tenth Legislature of . . . Texas. 1864 Houston 350.00

VIRGINIA

P-4353 C-2255	New Constitution of Virginia, Proposed for Adoption, by the Convention. 1861 (Richmond) 175.00
P-4354 C-2256	The New Constitution of Virginia, with the amended bill of rights, as adopted by the Reform Convention of 1850-51, and amended by the Convention of 1860-61. Bound with P-4387 and P-4388. (1861) (Richmond) 60.00
(N/P) C-2257	Addresses delivered before the Virginia State Convention by Hon. Fulton Anderson, commissioner from Mississippi, Hon. Henry L. Benning, commissioner from Georgia, and Hon. John S. Preston, commissioner from South Carolina, February 1861. 1861 Richmond 150.00
P-4355 C-2258	Documents. Richmond, 1861. Nos. 1-54 (lacking no. 39 which apparently was not printed). 1861 Richmond 300.00
P-4381 C-2267	An Act for the Relief of Families of Soldiers and Sailors from Virginia, within the Lines of the Enemy. . . . 1864 (Richmond) 100.00
P-4385 C-2271	Acts of the General Assembly . . . passed in 1861. . . . 1861 Richmond 60.00
P-4386 C-2272	Acts of the General Assembly . . . passed in 1861-62. . . . 1862 Richmond 60.00
P-4387 C-2273	Acts of the General Assembly . . . passed at called session, 1862 . . . . See P-4354. 1862 Richmond
P-4388 C-2274	Acts of the General Assembly . . . passed at adjourned session, 1863. . . . See P-4354. 1863 Richmond
P-4390 C-2275	Acts of the General Assembly . . . passed at called session, 1863 . . . . Bound with P-4391. 1863 Richmond 60.00
P-4391 C-2276	Acts of the General Assembly . . . passed at session of 1863-64 . . . . See P-4390. 1864 Richmond
P-4395 C-2278	Virginia-General Assembly-Documents. 2 Vols. 1862 Richmond 300.00
P-4396 C-2279	Documents. 1861-62. Richmond, 1862. Nos. 1-68. 1862 Richmond 15.00
P-4492	(Senate) Bill No. 66. To amend . . . act Passed March 29, 1862. . . . (1863) (Richmond) 60.00

P-4499
C-2295
Journal of the Senate of the Commonwealth of Virginia: begun and held at the Capitol in the city of Richmond, on Monday, the second day of December, in the year one thousand eight hundred and sixty-one — being the eighty-fifth year of the Commonwealth.
1861   Richmond   300.00

P-4616
C-2357
Journal of the House of Delegates of the State of Virginia, for the session of 1861-62. Bound with P-4617.
1861   Richmond   75.00

P-4617
C-2358
Journal of the House of Delegates of the State of Virginia, for the extra session, 1862. See P-4616.
1862   Richmond

P-4618
C-2359
Journal of the House of Delegates of the State of Virginia, for the called session of 1862. Bound with P-4619.
1862   Richmond   150.00

P-4619
C-2360
Journal of the House of Delegates of the State of Virginia, for the adjourned session, 1863. See P-4618.
1863   Richmond

P-4620
C-2361
Journal of the House of Delegates of the State of Virginia, for the called session of 1863. Bound with P-4621.
1863   Richmond   75.00

P-4621
C-2362
Journal of the House of Delegates of the State of Virginia, for the session of 1863-64. See P-4620.
1863   Richmond

P-4665
To Arms! To Arms!! Brave Men of the West. Headquarters, Va. Forces Staunton, June 7, 1861. Broadside.
1861   Staunton, VA   750.00

P-4672
C-2377
Resolutions of Wise's Brigade.
1865 n.p.   75.00

UNOFFICIAL PUBLICATIONS

MILITARY
(Military Texts, Manuals, etc.)

P-4723
C-2393
ARENTSSCHILDT, Friedrich von   **Instructions for Officers and Non-Commissioned Officers of Cavalry,** on Outpost Duty . . . With an abridgment of them by . . . F. Ponsonby . . . [with illustrations in text].
1861   Richmond   750.00

P-4731
C-2614
BARDE, Alexandre   **Histoire Des Comites De Vigilance Aux Attakapas.**
1861   Saint-Jean-Baptiste   2000.00

P-4734
C-2615
The battle of Fort Sumter . . .
1861 Charleston, SC   400.00

P-4744   BROUN, W. Leroy   Notes on Artillery: from . . . Mordecai,
C-2397   Dahlgreen [sic] . . . Gibbon and Benton. By . . . Lieutenant
Artillery Virginia Volunteers.
1862   Richmond   300.00

P-4747   BUCKHOLTZ, Louis von   Tactics for officers of infantry,
C-2400   cavalry and artillery. . . .
1861   Richmond   250.00

P-4748   BUGEAUD DE LA PICONNERIE, Thomas Robert, *duc d'Isly*
C-2401   The practice of war. By C. F. Pardigon.
1863   Richmond   300.00

P-4750   BYRNE, Edward P.   Partisan Rangers! By authority of the War
Department, I am now engaged in organizing a regiment of
cavalry and a battery of horse artillery, for partisan service. . . .
Broadside.
(1861)   (Bowling Green, KY)   1250.00

P-4755   CARY, R. Milton   Skirmishers' Drill and Bayonet Exercise (as
C-2402   Now used in the French Army). . . .
1861   Richmond   375.00

P-4767   CLAGHORN, Joseph S.   Abstract of Heavy Artillery Drill. . . .
1861 Savannah, GA   850.00

P-4776   [Confederate Roll of Honor.]
(1864)   (Charleston, SC)   600.00

P-4779   COOKE, John Esten   The life of Stonewall Jackson. By a
C-2563   Virginian. . . .
1863   Richmond   900.00

P-4791   CURRY, John P.   Volunteers' camp and field book. Contain-
C-2408   ing useful and general information on the art and science of
war, for the leisure moments of the soldier. By John P. Curry.
1862   Richmond   200.00

P-4796   DAVIS, James Lucius   The trooper's manual: or, Tactics for light
C-2409   dragoons and mounted riflemen. . . .
1861   Richmond   250.00

P-4797   DAVIS, James Lucius   The trooper's manual: or, Tactics for light
C-2410   dragoons and mounted riflemen. . . .
1861   Richmond   325.00

P-4801   DAVIS, Nicholas A.   The campaign from Texas to Maryland.
C-2621   1863   Richmond   3500.00

P-4804   Marginalia; or, Gleanings from an army notebook. By "Personne."
C-2623   1864   Columbia, SC   300.00

P-4836   GILHAM, William   Manual of instruction for the volunteers
C-2418   and militia of the Confederate States. . . .
1861   Richmond   250.00

P-4837   GILHAM, William   Manual of instruction for the volunteers
C-2419   and militia of the Confederate States.
1862   Richmond   275.00

P-4848
C-2578
A Complete Biographical Sketch of "Stonewall" Jackson; giving a full and accurate account of the leading events of his military career, his dying moments. . . . [Hallock, Charles.]
1863   Augusta, GA   600.00

P-4850
C-2421
HARDEE, William Joseph   **Rifle and infantry tactics.** . . . (First edition). 2 Vols.
1861   Mobile   300.00

P-4854
C-2425
HARDEE, William Joseph   **Rifle and infantry tactics.** . . . (Third edition). 2 Vols.
1861   Mobile   300.00

P-4858
C-2429
HARDEE, William Joseph   **Rifle and infantry tactics.** . . . (Ninth edition). 2 Vols.
1863   Mobile   500.00

P-4859
C-2430
HARDEE, William Joseph   **Rifle and infantry tactics.** . . .
1862   Raleigh, NC   400.00

P-4862
HARDEE, William Joseph   **Rifle and light infantry tactics.** . . . School of the Soldier, School of the Company and Instructions for Skirmishers.
1861   Jackson, MS   150.00

P-4864
C-2433
HARDEE, William Joseph   **Rifle and light infantry tactics.** . . . 2 Vols. in 1.
1861   Memphis   350.00

P-4865
C-2434
HARDEE, William Joseph   **Rifle and light infantry tactics.** . . . 2 Vols.
1861   Nashville   300.00

P-4867
C-2435
HARDEE, William J. **Rifle and light infantry tactics.** . . .
1861   New Orleans   400.00

P-4870
C-2436
HARDEE, William Joseph   **Rifle and light infantry tactics.** . . . 2 Vols. in 1. With plates.
1861   Richmond   600.00
Without plates   400.00

P-4877
C-2628
HARRIS, W. A. **The record of Fort Sumter,** from its occupation by Major Anderson. . . .
1862   Columbia, SC   400.00

P-4891
C-2633
JACKSON, Henry W. R.   **Historical Register,** and Confederates Assistant to National Independence. Containing a discovery for the preservation of butter, together with other valuable recipes, and important information for the soldier. . . .
1862   Augusta, GA   500.00

P-4892
C-2634
JACKSON, Henry W. R.   **The Southern Women of the Second American Revolution,** Their Trials, &c. Yankee Barbarity Illustrated. Our Naval Victories and Exploits of Confederate War Steamers. Capture of Yankee Gunboats, &c.
1863   Atlanta   850.00

P-4898
C-2513
KANE, George Proctor   **To All Marylanders in the Confederate States.**
(c.1864)   (Richmond)   200.00

P-4899
C-2637
Prisoner of War, or Five Months Among the Yankees, Being a narrative of the crosses, calamities, and consolations of a Petersburg Militiaman during an enforced summer residence north, by A. Rifleman. (Keiley, Anthony M.)
(1865)   Richmond   500.00

P-4904
C-2441
LEE, Charles Henry **The judge advocates vade mecum:** Embracing a general view of military law and the practice before courts martial. . . .
1863   Richmond   200.00

P-4906
C-2443
LEE, James Kendall **The Volunteer's Hand Book:** containing an abridgment of Hardee's Infantry Tactics, adapted to the use of the percussion musket in squad and company . . . by James K. Lee, of the First Regiment of Virginia Volunteers.
1861   Raleigh, NC   350.00

P-4909
C-2446
LEE, James Kendall **The Volunteer's Hand Book:** containing an abridgment of Hardee's Infantry Tactics, adapted to the use of the percussion musket in squad and company. . . . Twentieth Thousand.
1861   Richmond   450.00

P-4910
C-2447
LEE, James Kendall **The Volunteer's Hand Book.**
1861   Richmond   300.00

P-4911
C-2448
LEE, James Kendall **The Volunteer's Hand Book** . . . (Third edition).
1861   Richmond   250.00

P-4912
C-2449
The school for guides, for the use of the Army of the Confederate States. . . . (LeGal, Eugene)
1861   Savannah   325.00

P-4913
C-2450
School of the guides, or The Practical Soldier; designed for the use of the Militia of the Confederate States. (Le Gal, Eugene).
1861   New Orleans   650.00

P-4914
C-2451
The school of the guides, for use of the Army of the Confederate States, with questions. . . .
1862   Richmond   400.00

P-4924
C-2590
JACKSON, James W.   **Life of James W. Jackson,** the Alexandria Hero, the Slayer of Ellsworth, the First Martyr in the Cause of Southern Independence. . . . Published for the benefit of his family.
1862   Richmond   450.00

P-4938
C-2593
McCABE, James Dabney   **The life of Thomas J. Jackson.** By an ex-cadet. Second edition.
1864   Richmond   500.00

P-4942
C-2454
MAHAN, Dennis Hart   **An elementary treatise on advanced-guard,** out-post, and detachment service of troops, and the manner of posting and handling them in presence of an enemy.
1861   New Orleans   400.00

P-4947
C-2459
MAHAN, Dennis Hart   **A treatise on field fortifications.** . . .
1862   Richmond   300.00

P-4953	MARMONT, Auguste F. L. Viesse De The spirit of military
C-2462	institutions. . . .
	1864 Columbia 400.00

P-4958	MAURY, Capt. D. H. Skirmish Drill for Mounted Troops.
H-2462-2	1861 Richmond 400.00

P-4963	Memoranda of Facts Bearing on the Kentucky Campaign.
C-2528	(Richardson, Dr.)
	(1862) n.p. 500.00

P-4966	To the Men of Albemarle. Broadside.
C-2529	1863 Charlottesville 575.00

P-4972	The Officer's Manual, Napoleon's Maxims of War.
C-2463	1862 Richmond 300.00

P-4973	A Narrative of the battles of Bull Run and Manassas Junction,
C-2641	July 18th and 21st, 1861. . . .
	1861 Charleston, SC 450.00

P-4979	NOLAN, Lewis Edward Cavalry; its history and tactics. . . .
C-2464	1864 Columbia, SC 600.00

P-4980	Obituary. The Late Captain George Pettigrew Bryan.
	1864 Raleigh, NC 750.00

P-4987	PATTEN, George Washington Cavalry drill and sabre exercise;
C-2468	compiled agreeably to the latest regulations of the War Depart-
	ment. . . .
	1862 Richmond 700.00

P-4990	POLLARD, Edward Alfred The first year of the war.
C-2643	1862 Richmond 150.00

P-4992	POLLARD, Edward Alfred The first year of the war. . . .
C-2645	1862 Richmond 250.00

P-4994	POLLARD, Edward Alfred Observations in the North:
C-2647	eight months in prison and on parole.
	1865 Richmond 350.00

P-4996	POLLARD, Edward Alfred The second year of the war.
C-2650	By Edward A. Pollard, author of "Black diamonds," etc. . . .
	1863 Richmond 300.00

P-4998	The Seven Days Battles in Front of Richmond. An Outline
C-2652	Narrative of the Series of Engagements Which Opened at
	Mechanicsville. . . . Compiled from the Detailed Accounts of the
	Newspaper Press. (Pollard, Edward A.)
	1862 Charleston 350.00

P-5001	POLLARD, Edward Alfred The seven days' battles in front
C-2654	of Richmond.
	1862 Richmond 400.00

P-5015	REA, D. B. Sketches from Hampton's cavalry. . . .
C-2658	1864 Columbia, SC 600.00

P-5020	RICHARDSON, John H. Infantry tactics, or, rules for the
C-2469	exercise and manoeuvres of the Confederate States infantry. . . .
	1862 Richmond 500.00

P-5021 C-2470	**RICHARDSON, John H. Infantry tactics, or, rules for the** exercise and manoeuvres of the Confederate States infantry. . . . 1864 Shreveport 300.00
P-5022 C-2471	**RICHARDSON, William H. A manual of infantry and rifle tactics.** . . . 1861 Richmond 250.00
P-5023 C-2472	**ROBERTS, Joseph The Hand-book of artillery.** 1861 Richmond 650.00
P-5024 C-2473	**ROBERTS, Joseph The Hand-book of artillery.** By Capt. Joseph Roberts, Fourth Regiment Artillery United States Army. 1861 Richmond 400.00
P-5026 C-2475	**ROBERTS, Joseph The Hand-book of Artillery.** Second edition revised and enlarged. 1862 Richmond 600.00
P-5033	**Sacred to the memory of Joseph S. Jones,** son of W. H. & S. E. Jones. Born April 21, 1834. Was killed at the Battle of Sharpsburg, September 17th, 1862. . . . Broadside. 1862 n.p. 750.00
P-5043 C-2479	**SCOTT,** Winfield **Infantry-tactics;** or rules of the exercise and manoeuvres of infantry. . . . 1862 Raleigh, NC 250.00
P-5047 C-2661	**Sack and Destruction of the City of Columbia, S.C.** to which is added a list of the property destroyed. (Simms, William Gilmore) 1865 Columbia, SC 1400.00
P-5048 C-2544	**SIMONS, James Address to the officers of the Fourth Brigade,** giving the grounds for his resignation . . . 1861 Charleston, SC 150.00
P-5049 C-2605	**SLAUGHTER, Philip A Sketch of the Life of Randolph Fairfax, a Private in the Ranks of the Rockbridge Artillery,** Attached to the "Stonewall Brigade." . . . Including a Brief Account of Jackson's Celebrated Valley Campaign. By . . . Editor of the "Army and Navy Messenger." 1864 Richmond 750.00
P-5053	**SLOSS, Thomas M. Ralley! Freeman, ralley! . . .** Broadside. 1862 (Florence, AL) 750.00
P-5084 C-2485	**Instruction for heavy artillery;** prepared by a board of officers for use of the Army of the United States. 1861 Charleston, SC 350.00
P-5085 C-2486	**Instruction for heavy artillery;** prepared by a board of officers, for the use of the Army of the United States. 1862 Richmond 350.00
P-5087 C-2487	**The ordnance manual for the use of the officers** of the United States Army. Second edition. 1861 Charleston, SC 250.00
P-5088 C-2488	**The ordnance manual for the use of the officers** of the United States Army. Second edition. 1861 Richmond 250.00

P-5092
C-2490

VIELE, Egbert Ludovickus   **Hand-book of field fortifica-tions and artillery;** also manual for light and heavy artillery. With illustrations.   By Egbert L. Viele, late U.S.A. Captain Engineers, Seventh Regiment, N.G.
1861   Richmond   250.00

P-5100
C-2662

WARDER, T. B. and **CATLETT**, James M.   **Battle of Young's Branch;** or, Manassas Plain, fought July 21, 1861. . . .
1862   Richmond   750.00

P-5114
C-2664

WEST, Beckwith   **Experience   of   a   Confederate   States prisoner.** . . .
1862   Richmond   500.00

P-5116
C-2491

WHEELER, Joseph   **A revised system of cavalry tactics,** for the use of the cavalry and mounted infantry, C.S.A.
1863   Mobile   400.00

P-5121
C-2665

WILSON, Frank I.   **The Battle of Great Bethel,** (Fought June 10, 1861).
1864   Raleigh, NC   850.00

POLITICS, ECONOMICS AND SOCIAL ISSUES

P-5151

ARRINGTON, A. H. **To the voters of the 5th Congressional District of North Carolina,** composed of the counties of Orange, Granville, Wake, Franklin, Warren and Nash. Broadside.
1863   Hilliardston, NC 200.00

P-5160

A Good Work on Foot. Mr. H. W. R. Jackson, the author of several volumes that have appeared during the war, recently set apart a certain percentage of his sales . . . for . . . a Free School for the Orphans of Deceased Soldiers. . . . (*Atlanta Intel-ligencer*). Broadside.
(1864)   (Atlanta)   75.00

P-5179
C-2882

BERRY, Harrison   **Slavery and abolitionism,** as viewed by a Georgia slave.
1861   Atlanta   600.00

P-5182
C-2692

BILBO, William N.   **The Past, Present, and Future of the Southern Confederacy:** An Oration delivered . . . in . . . Nashville, Oct. 12, 1861.
1861   Nashville   400.00

P-5184

Blum's Farmers' and Planters' Almanac, for the year 1862: being the second after bissextile or leap year. . . .
1861   Salem, NC   150.00

P-5187
C-4980

Blum's Farmers' and Planters' Almanac, for . . . 1865.
(1864)   Salem, NC   450.00

P-5207
C-2701

BUCHANAN, W. Jefferson   **Maryland's hope; her trials and interests in connexion with the war,** by W. Jefferson Buchanan.
1864   Richmond   450.00

P-5230
C-2954

Central Southern Railroad Company. Sixth Annual Report of the Board of Directors . . . to the Stockholders, 1861.
1861   Nashville   175.00

P-5236 CHAMPOMIER, P. A.   Statement of the sugar crop of Louisiana,
C-2903 of 1861-62.
        1862   New Orleans   200.00

P-5260 Clarke's Confederate Household Almanac, 1863, being the third
C-4983 year of the independence of the Confederate States of America.
        1863   Vicksburg, MS   225.00

P-5261 Clarke's Confederate Household Almanac.
C-4984 1863   Vicksburg, MS   150.00

P-5287 The Confederate States Almanac, and repository of useful
C-4987 knowledge, for 1862.
        1861   Vicksburg, MS   250.00

P-5288 The Confederate States Almanac . . . second edition.
C-4988 1861   Vicksburg, MS   275.00

P-5289 The Confederate States Almanac, and repository of useful
C-4989 knowledge, for . . . 1863.
        (1863)   Vicksburg, MS   450.00

P-5290 The Confederate States Almanac, and repository of useful
C-4990 knowledge. For the year 1864. . . .
        1863   Mobile, AL   275.00

P-5291 The Confederate States Almanac, and repository of useful
C-4991 knowledge, for . . . 1865.
        (1864)   Mobile, AL   450.00

P-5293 The Confederate States Almanac for . . . 1862.
C-4992 1862   Nashville   250.00

P-5297 Confederate States Almanac for the year of our Lord 1864. . . .
C-4995 1863   Mobile   275.00

P-5299 Confederate States Almanac for the year of our Lord 1864. . . .
C-4996 1863   Macon   275.00

P-5311 Official Report of the Proceedings of the Convention of Rail
        Road Presidents . . . at Montgomery, Alabama, April 26, 1861.
        1861   Montgomery   300.00

P-5322 Cumberland Almanac, for . . . 1862 . . . calculated for . . .
C-5000 Nashville . . . and with slight variation . . . for Kentucky, Missis-
        sippi, and Alabama.
        (1861)   Nashville   600.00

P-5330 DE BOW, James Dunwoody Brownson   The interest in slavery of
C-2886 the Southern non-slaveholder.
        1860   Charleston, SC   300.00

P-5334 DE JARNETTE, Daniel C.   The Monroe Doctrine . . .
C-2728 1865   (Richmond)   100.00

P-5364 EDWARDS, Weldon Nathaniel   Memoir of Nathaniel Macon, of
C-2573 North Carolina.
        1862   Raleigh   250.00

P-5367 For President, Jefferson Davis, of Mississippi.   For Vice Presi-
C-2744 dent, A. H. Stephens, of Georgia. . . .   Broadside. Four variant
        printings and sizes.
        1861   n.p.   300.00

P-5380 FANNING, David The Narrative of Colonel David Fanning
C-2624 (A Tory in the Revolutionary War With Great Britain). . . .
1861 Richmond 3500.00

P-5392 FREMANTLE, Sir Arthur James Lyon Three months in the
C-2670 Southern States: April, June, 1863.
1864 Mobile 650.00

P-5415 GHOLSON, Thomas S. Speech of Hon. Thos. S. Gholson, of
C-2887 Virginia, on the policy of employing negro troops, and the duty
of all classes to aid in the prosecution of the war. . . .
1865 Richmond 125.00

P-5417 GILMER, John H. Confederate States vs. John H. Gilmer. . . .
C-2750 1862 Richmond 75.00

P-5478 HALL, William A. The Historic Significance of the Southern
C-2764 Revolution. A lecture delivered . . . in Petersburg, Va. . . . by
Rev. William A. Hall, of New Orleans Battalion Washington
Artillery.
1864 Petersburg 400.00

P-5481 HARDEE, William Joseph, and GOETZEL, S. H. Memorial to
C-3279 the Congress of the Confederate States.
1863 Mobile 75.00

P-5486 HAYNE, Paul H. M.M.S. of Volume First of the work entitled:
Politics of South Carolina, F. W. Pickens' Speeches, Reports, &c.
1864 (Columbia) 300.00

P-5519 JAMISON, David Flavel The life and times of Bertrand Du
C-2587 Guesclin: a history of the fourteenth century. 2 Vols.
1864 Charleston, SC 300.00

P-5528 JONES, Charles C., Jr. Monumental remains of Georgia.
C-2636 Part first.
1861 Savannah 250.00

P-5529 JONES, Joseph Agricultural resources of Georgia. Address
C-2918 before the Cotton Planters Convention of Georgia at Macon,
December 13, 1860.
1861 Augusta, GA 250.00

P-5583 MACMAHON, T. W. Cause and contrast: an essay on the
C-2784 American crisis.
1862 Richmond 175.00

P-5609 The Merryman habeas corpus case, Baltimore. The proceedings
C-2787 in full and opinion of Chief Justice Taney. . . .
1861 Jackson, MS 150.00

P-5613 Miller's Planters' and Merchants' State Rights Almanac, for the
year . . . 1861: Being the . . . First of Southern Independence.
Second edition (at head of title).
(1860) Charleston, SC 150.00

P-5614 Miller's Planters' and Merchants' State Rights Almanac, for the
year . . . 1862: Being the . . . 2nd of Southern Independence.
(1861) Charleston, SC 150.00

P-5615 Miller's Planters' & Merchants' State Rights Almanac, for the
C-5026 year of our Lord 1862. . . .
1861 Charleston, SC 175.00

P-5702 C-2804	**The Oath of Allegiance to the United States** (Palmer, B. M.) (1863) n.p. 400.00
P-5703 C-2805	**A Vindication of Secession and the South** from the Strictures of Rev. R. J. Breckinridge . . . in the Danville Quarterly Review. (Palmer, B. M.) 1861 Columbia, SC 400.00
P-5713 C-2675	**PETTIGREW,** James Johnston **Notes on Spain and the Spaniards,** in the summer of 1859, with a glance at Sardinia. 1861 Charleston, SC 500.00
P-5732	**State of the Planters' Bank of Tennessee, and Branches, June 29, 1861.** (1861) n.p. 60.00
P-5735 C-2648	**POLLARD,** Edward Alfred **The Rival Administrations:** Richmond and Washington in December, 1863. 1864 Richmond 500.00
P-5736 C-2824	**POLLARD,** Edward Alfred **The Southern Spy.** Letters on the policy and inauguration of the Lincoln war. . . . Second edition. 1861 Richmond 200.00
P-5763 C-2992	**Proceedings of the fourteenth annual meeting** of the stockholders of the Raleigh and Gaston Rail Road Company. . . . 1864 Raleigh, NC 80.00
P-5778 C-2831	**RICHARDSON,** George W. **Speech . . . in Committee of the Whole,** on the report of the Committee on Federal Relations, in the Convention of Virginia, April 4, 1861. 1862 Richmond 150.00
P-5779 C-5033	**Richardson's Almanac, 1862.** (1861) Richmond 275.00
P-5780 C-5034	**Richardson's Virginia and North Carolina Almanac,** for the year of our Lord 1862. 1861 Richmond 200.00
P-5781 C-5035	**Richardson's Virginia and North Carolina Almanac,** for the year of our Lord 1862. . . The first of the Southern Confederacy. (1861) Richmond 350.00
P-5802 C-5047	**Richardson's Virginia and North Carolina Almanac,** for the year of our Lord 1865, being the first after bissextile or leap year. 1865 Richmond 250.00
P-5832 C-2835	**ST. PAUL,** Henry **Our Home and Foreign Policy.** 1863 (Mobile) 400.00
P-5852 C-2840	**SEGAR,** Joseph Eggleston **Speech of Joseph Segar,** Esq., of the York District in the House . . . of Delegates of Virginia, . . . Directing the Governor of Virginia to Seize, by Military Force, the U.S. Guns at Bellona Arsenal, and on the Secession of Virginia. (1861) (Richmond) 500.00
P-5858 C-2843	**SMEDES,** William C. **Letter of William C. Smedes . . .** of Vicksburg, Miss., in Vindication of the Southern Confederacy. 1861 Jackson, MS 400.00

P-5864 SMITH, William Russell   The history and debates of the
C-2845 Convention of the people of Alabama . . . in which is preserved
the speeches of the secret sessions and many valuable state
papers.
1861   Montgomery   500.00

P-5870 S. S. (Sons of the South) (sideways on front wrapper surrounded
by decorative printer's ornaments).
(1862)   n.p.   2000.00

P-5876 The Confederate. By a South Carolinian.
C-2716 1863   Mobile   500.00

P-5878 The Southern Almanac, for 1863.
C-5050 (1862)   Lynchburg, VA   450.00

P-5907 SPENCE, James   The American union; its effect on national
C-2846 character and policy, with an inquiry into secession as a
constitutional right, and the causes of the disruption. . . .
1863   Richmond   200.00

P-5921 The Stranger's guide and official directory for the city of
C-2676 Richmond. . . .
1863   Richmond   350.00

P-5973 THORNWELL, James Henley   The state of the country. . . .
C-2861 1861   Columbia, SC   150.00

P-6009 Turner's North Carolina almanac, for the year of our Lord 1864:
C-5060 being bissextile, or leap year, the eighty-eighth of American
independence. . . .
1864   Raleigh, NC   200.00

P-6025 Review of certain remarks made by the President when requested
C-2873 to restore General Beauregard to the command of Department no.
2. (Villere, Charles J.)
1863   Charleston, SC   225.00

P-6030 Address of the President of the Va. Central Railroad Co., to the
C-3011 Stockholders, on the Subject of Withdrawal of the Mails by the
Postmaster General. (Fontaine, E.)
1864   Richmond   250.00

P-6038 Election, Wednesday, November 6th, 1861. For President,
C-2735 Jefferson Davis. . . . Broadside.
1861   (Richmond)   250.00

P-6061 Warrock's Virginia and North Carolina Almanac for the year of
C-5064 our Lord 1865, being the first after bissextile or leap year. . . .
(c.1864)   Richmond   200.00

P-6064 Circular. Letter from Gen. West . . . Meridian, Miss., Aug. 12,
1863, to my Fellow-Citizens of . . . Mississippi. . . . Broadsheet.
(1863)   (Meridian, MS)   400.00

P-6073 WIGGS, A. R.   Hal's travels in Europe, Egypt, and the Holy
C-2679 Land. . . .
1861   Nashville, TN   200.00

P-6090 An appeal for peace sent to Lieut. Gen. Scott, July 4, 1861.
Signed by the Women of Maryland.   Broadside.
1861   n.p.   400.00

P-6094 C-2879	YANCEY, William Lowndes Speeches . . . made in the Senate of the Confederate States during the session commencing on the eighteenth day of August, A.D., 1862. 1862 Montgomery 275.00
P-6096 C-2611	YOUNG, Robert A. Personages: A Book of Living Characters. 1861 Nashville 100.00
P-6109 C-3026	CHISOLM, John Julian A manual of military surgery, for the use of surgeons in the Confederate Army. . . . 1861 Charleston, SC 1500.00
P-6112 C-3028	CHISOLM, John Julian A manual of military surgery, for the use of surgeons in the Confederate Army. . . . 1862 Richmond 1000.00
P-6132 C-3041	PORCHER, Francis Peyre Resources of the Southern fields and forests, medical, economical and agricultural. Being a medical botany of the Confederate States. . . . 1863 Charleston, SC 1700.00 (1864) Charleston, SC 1000.00
P-6133 C-3042	PORCHER, Francis Peyre Resources of the Southern fields and forests, medical, economical and agricultural. Being also a medical botany of the Confederate States. . . . 1863 Richmond. 1500.00
P-6144 C-4971	South Carolina Hospital Aid Association. 1862 Richmond 400.00
P-6145 C-3044	WARREN, Edward An epitome of practical surgery, for field and hospital. 1863 Richmond, VA 1800.00

MAPS AND PRINTS

P-6180 C-3053	Plan of the Western Seat of War. 1861 New Orleans 335.00
P-6183 C-3056	MCRAE, A. T. Map of the battle ground of Greenbrier River. (1861) Richmond 750.00
P-6185 C-3057	MANOUVRIER, J., & Co. Map of the present seat of war in Missouri. (1861) New Orleans 750.00
P-6191 C-3060	MITCHELL, Samuel P. Sketch of the country occupied by the Federal & Confederate armies on the 18th & 21st July 1861. (1861) Richmond 750.00
P-6203 C-3065	Topographical sketch of the battle of Bethel, June 10th, 1861. (1861) n.p. 750.00
P-6204 C-3066	Map of the State of Virginia containing the counties, principal towns, railroads, rivers, canals & all other internal improvements. 1862 Richmond 650.00
P-6206 C-3067	Map of the State of Virginia containing the counties, principal towns, rail-roads, rivers, canals & all other internal improvements. (Cover title: New map of Virginia) 1862 Richmond 1000.00

BELLES-LETTRES

P-6208
C-3069
ABRAMS, Alexander St. Clair   The Trials of the Soldier's Wife: A Tale of the Second American Revolution.
1864   Atlanta   1000.00

P-6232
Battle Hymn of the Virginia Soldier! Broadside.
(1861)   n.p.   75.00

P-6242
C-3170-1
God and Liberty! Broadside verse.
(186-)   n.p.   100.00

P-6245
C-3126
The boys and girls stories of the war. Contents: General Stonewall Jackson, Commodore Foot [sic] and Colonel Small, etc.
(1863)   Richmond   750.00

P-6246
C-3072
BRADDON, Mary Elizabeth   **Aurora Floyd.**
1863   Richmond   400.00

P-6278
C-3165
The Confederate Soldier's wife parting from her husband! Broadside verse.
(1861)   n.p.   100.00

(N/P)
C-3157-5
Battle Hymn of a Virginia Soldier. Broadside verse.
(186-)   n.p.   100.00

P-6284
C-3166
Country, home and liberty. Broadside verse.
(1861)   n.p.   50.00

P-6293
C-3082
DAVIS, Mrs. Mary Elizabeth (Moragne)   **The British partizan:** a tale of the olden time. By a lady of South Carolina.
1864   Macon, GA   300.00

P-6301
C-3085
DICKENS, Charles   **Great Expectations.**
1863   Mobile   750.00

P-6307
C-3088
EDGEVILLE, Edward   **Castine. . . .**
1865   Raleigh, NC   350.00

P-6309
C-3089
Silas Marner, the Weaver of Raveloe. By the author of "Adam Bede," "The Mill on the Floss," and "Scenes of Clerical Life." (Eliot, George, pseud. of Marian Evans.)
1863   Mobile   750.00

P-6311
The Exodus.
(1861)   n.p.   150.00

P-6313
C-3138
FANE, Julian Henry C. and **BULWER-LYTTON**, Edward Robert **Tannhauser; or, The battle of the bards . . .** by Neville Temple and Edward Trevor.
1863   Mobile   200.00

P-6329
C-3170
The Georgia Volunteer. Broadside verse.
(1861)   Savannah   100.00

P-6342
C-3171-1
Hark! O'er the Southern hills. . . . Broadside verse.
(186-)   n.p.   150.00

P-6353
C-3095
DERRINGTON, W. D.   **The deserter's daughter.**
1865   Raleigh, NC   450.00

P-6357
C-3141
HILL, Theophilus Hunter   **Hesper, and other poems . . .**
1861   Raleigh, NC   200.00

P-6367
C-3096
HUGO, Victor Marie **Les miserables. . . .** Issued in five parts.
1863-64   Richmond   800.00

P-6368 **Hurrah for Jeff. Davis.** By a Lady Rebel—written after the
C-3177 battle of Bull Run. Broadside.
 1861 n.p. 60.00

P-6393 **L. R.** (pseud.) **Dear liberty, or Maryland will be free.**
C-3180-1 Broadside verse.
 (186-) Richmond 100.00

P-6396 **LAMB,** Robert **Rally around the stars and bars!** Broadside
C-3181 verse.
 (1861) n.p. 125.00

P-6400 **The Last Race of the Rail-Splitter.** Broadside.
C-3182 (1861) n.p. 150.00

P-6409 **Lines on the death of the Confederate Gen. Albert Sidney**
C-3185 **Johnston, of Ky. . . .** Broadside verse.
 (1862) n.p. 150.00

P-6415 **LYTTON,** Sir E. Bulwer **A Strange Story.**
C-3102 1863 Mobile 750.00

P-6420 **MCCABE,** James Dabney **The aid-de-camp; a romance of the**
C-3104 **war.**
 1863 Richmond 250.00

P-6427 **MARTIN,** William Maxwell **Lyrics and Sketches.** By William
C-3146 Maxwell Martin.
 1861 Nashville, TN 250.00

P-6428 **The dying Confederate's last words.** Broadside verse.
C-3167-1 (186-) n.p. 100.00

P-6436 **MUNDT,** *Frau* Clara **Henry VIII, and his court, or Catherine**
C-3105 **Parr.** A historical novel, By L. Muhlbach. 2 Vols.
 1865 Mobile 350.00

P-6437 **MUNDT,** *Frau* Clara **Joseph II. and his court . . .** by L.
C-3106 Meuhlbach. . . . 4 Vols.
 1864 Mobile 750.00

P-6443 **North Carolina. A call to arms! ! !** Broadside verse.
C-3192 1861 Raleigh, NC 100.00

P-6457 **Hurrah for Dixie! Broadside verse.**
C-3176 (1861) n.p. 175.00

P-6459 **Southrons, hear your country call you!** By Albert G. Pike, of
 Arkansas. To the tune of Dixie. Broadside.
 1861 (Memphis, TN) 400.00

P-6467 **PRESTON,** Mrs. Margaret (Junkin) **Beechenbrook; a rhyme of**
C-3149 the war.
 1865 Richmond 200.00

P-6474 **Prison Bill of fare,** by a prisoner of war, composed, written and
C-3199 spoken at the exhibition of the "Prisoners of War Dramatic
 Association". . . . Broadside verse.
 1861 (Richmond) 250.00

P-6484 **RANDALL,** James Ryder **Maryland. Air - "My Normandy!"**
 Broadside. 2 columns.
 n.d. n.p. 150.00

P-6512 C-3216	**Texan Rangers.** Broadside verse. 1861 Galveston, TX 750.00
P-6520 C-3154	**SHEPPERSON,** William G., edited by **War Songs of the South,** **edited by "Bohemian".** . . . 1862 Richmond 250.00
P-6543 C-3210	**South Carolina.** Broadside verse. 1861 Charleston, SC 150.00
P-6550	**Southern Song of Liberty.** Broadside. (1861) (Richmond) 60.00
P-6562 C-3213	**STANTON,** Henry Thompson **Awake in Dixie** . . . [by] H.T.S. Broadside verse. Feb. 24, 1862. 1862 Winchester, VA 150.00
P-6571 C-3215	**Tennessee! Fire away!** Broadside verse. (1861) n.p. 150.00
P-6573 C-3111	**THACKERAY,** William Makepeace **The adventures of Philip** **on his way through the world.** . . . 1864 Columbia, SC 1000.00
P-6577 C-3217	**TIMROD,** Henry **Ode on the meeting of the Southern Con-** **gress.** Broadside verse. (1861) n.p. 225.00
P-6585 C-3219-1	**TUCKER,** Henry St. George **The Southern Cross.** . . . Broadside verse. 1861 Selma, AL 150.00
P-6586 C-3112	**TUCKER,** Nathaniel Beverley **The partisan leader.** . . . 1862 Richmond 500.00
P-6603 C-3113	**WARREN,** Ebenezer W. **Nellie Norton:** or, Southern Slavery and the Bible. A scriptural refutation of the principal arguments upon which the abolitionist rely. A vindication of Southern slavery from the Old and New Testaments. 1864 Macon, GA 650.00
P-6606 C-3224	**WHITAKER,** D. K. **Maryland in chains** . . . *Richmond Exam-* *iner*, May 14, 1861. Broadside verse. 1861 Richmond 150.00
P-6607 C-3132	**Grandpapa and One of His Stories.** (Williams, Mary Temple) 1863 Richmond 1000.00
P-6608 C-3114	**WILSON,** Mrs. Augusta Jane (Evans) **Macaria; or, Altars of** **Sacrifice.** 1864 Richmond 500.00
P-6609 C-3115	**WILSON,** Mrs. Augusta Jane (Evans) **Macaria; or, Altars of** **Sacrifice.** Second edition. 1864 Richmond 500.00

MUSIC AND ENTERTAINMENT

P-6633 C-3254	**The bold soldier boy's song book.** n.d. Richmond 150.00
P-6637 C-3256	**BRANSON,** Thomas A. **The Jack Morgan songster.** 1864 Raleigh, NC 325.00

P-6638 BURROWES, John F. Burrowes' Piano-Forte Primer, containing
C-3257 the rudiments of music, calculated either for private tuition, or,
teaching in classes. Revised and enlarged, with additions and
alterations, by W. C. Peters.
1864   Richmond   750.00

P-6639 Social Hop. You are respectfully solicited to attend a "soiree," to
be given at the court-house, in Camden, on Monday evening,
December the 26th, commencing at 9 o'clock. The proceeds to be
devoted to the establishment of a "soldier's home." Broadside.
1864   Camden, AR   900.00

P-6641 Grand Military ball. The pleasure of your company is respect-
C-3239 fully solicited at a ball to be given at Camp Carondelet, near
Manassas, Tuesday evening, February 25th, 1862. Broadside.
1862   Richmond   500.00

P-6642 The Cavalier Songster. Containing a Splendid Collection of
C-3258 Original and Selected Songs. Compiled and arranged expressly
for the Southern Public.
1865   Staunton, VA   450.00

P-6651 The Dixie Land Songster. Published by Blackmar and Bro.,
C-3259 Augusta, Ga.
1863   Macon, GA   750.00

P-6679 Benefit of Mr. W. H. Crisp! and positively the last night of the
season! By desire of many patrons, Mr. & Mrs. W. H. Crisp will
take their farewell of their Mobile patrons and friends in
Sheridan Knowles' celebrated play of the Wife! . . . Broadside.
1863   Mobile, AL   400.00

P-6685 MOORE, William D. The new Confederate flag song book.
1864   Mobile, AL   275.00

P-6720 The Punch songster.
C-3265 1864   Richmond   150.00

P-6728 The Libby Prison Minstrels! . . . Thursday evening, Dec. 24, 1863.
C-3243 Programme. . . . Broadside.
1863   Richmond   600.00

P-6763 Songs of the South.
C-3271 1864   Richmond   175.00

P-6764 Songs of the South.
1864   Richmond   650.00

P-6772 The Stonewall Song Book: being a collection of patriotic,
H-3273 sentimental, and comic songs.
1863   Richmond   400.00

P-6773 The Stonewall Song Book: being a collection of patriotic,
sentimental and comic Songs. Fourth edition (at head of title.)
1863   Richmond   850.00

SHEET MUSIC

There are over 800 titles of sheet music, and numerous copies of
many of these titles still abound. Some exceptions follow, but, in
general, sheet music is valued: 50.00–75.00 each

P-6787– P-7655	**Collection of 322 pieces of sheet music printed in the Confederacy.** Many with colored or pictorial covers. 1861-65 20,000.00
P-6917 C-3385	**Confederate Flag;** written by Mrs. C. D. Elder; music by Sig. G. George. (c.1861) Augusta, GA and New Orleans 100.00
P-7469 C-3821	**The Song of the South.** . . . (Huber, James H.) 1861 Louisville 150.00
P-7560 C-3899	**SCHRENK, J. Tiger Rifles Shottisch.** 1861 New Orleans 100.00

EDUCATION

P-7658 C-3985	**Regulations for the University of Alabama, Tuscaloosa.** With . . . Army Regulation. . . . 1861 Nashville 600.00
P-7671 C-4030	**BRANSON, Levi First Book in Composition** . . . especially designed for . . . Southern Schools. 1863 Raleigh, NC 450.00
P-7674 C-4031	**BROWNE, George Y. Browne's Arithmetical Tables** . . . for beginners. 1865 Atlanta 350.00
P-7680 C-4034	**Caesar's Commentaries on the Gallic War,** with a vocabulary and notes by William Bingham . . . of the Bingham School. 1864 Greensboro, NC 300.00
P-7682 C-4036	**CAMPBELL, William A. The child's first book.** 1864 Richmond 250.00
P-7685 C-4039	**CHAUDRON, Adelaide De Vendel Chaudron's spelling book** . . . . Fourth edition - thirtieth thousand. 1865 Mobile 300.00
P-7686 C-4040	**CHAUDRON, Adelaide De Vendel Chaudron's spelling book** . . . Fifth edition - fortieth thousand. 1865 Mobile 200.00
P-7690 C-4043	**CHAUDRON, Adelaide De Vendel The Second Reader.** . . . Second edition. Adopted . . . in . . . schools of Mobile. 1864 Mobile 500.00
P-7694 C-4046	**COLBURN, Warren Intellectual Arithmetic** . . . Revised and adapted to the use of schools in the Confederate States by Thos. O. Summers. 1862 Nashville 500.00
P-7705 C-4074-1	**CUSHING, E. H., edited by The New Texas Reader.** Designed for the use of schools in Texas. 1864 Houston 1500.00
P-7706 C-4048	**DAGG, John L. The Grammar of the English Language.** Book First (all published). 1864 Macon, GA 300.00
P-7722 C-4052	**The First Confederate Speller.** . . . By an association of Southern Teachers. 1861 Nashville 600.00

544

| P-7755 C-4058 | **Illustrated Alphabet.** (Lithographed in red and blue.) (1863) Columbia, SC 1500.00 |

P-7755
C-4058
Illustrated Alphabet. (Lithographed in red and blue.)
(1863)   Columbia, SC   1500.00

P-7756
C-4059
JOHNSON, L. ✻ **An elementary arithmetic, designed for beginners. . . .**
1864   Raleigh, NC   325.00

P-7757
C-3996
JOYNES, Edward S.   **Education After the War.** A Letter Addressed to a Member of the Southern Educational Convention, Columbia, S.C., 28th April, 1863.
1863   Richmond   250.00

P-7761
C-4061
LANDER, S.   Our own school arithmetic.
1863   Richmond   300.00

P-7801
C-4067
MOORE, Mrs. Marinda Branson   **The Dixie Speller.** To follow the First Dixie Reader.
1864   Raleigh, NC   450.00

P-7803
C-4068
MOORE, Mrs. Marinda Branson   **The first Dixie reader; designed to follow the Dixie primer.**
1863   Raleigh, NC   375.00

P-7806
C-4070
MOORE, Mrs. Marinda Branson   **The Geographical reader,** for the Dixie children. Issued with 6 double page maps. Occurs with maps colored and uncolored.
1863   Raleigh, NC   1500.00

P-7828
C-4006
North Carolina University, Chapel Hill Catalogue of the trustees, faculty and students of the University of North Carolina, 1861-'62.
1862   Raleigh, NC   75.00

P-7837
C-4967
By-laws of the Orphan House of Charleston. . . .
1861   Charleston, SC   50.00

P-7873
C-4083
The Confederate First Reader . . . for the younger children in the schools and families of the Confederate States. (Smith, Richard M.)
1864   Richmond   500.00

P-7879
C-4086
SMITH, Richard McAllister   **The Confederate spelling book.**
1865   Richmond   125.00

P-7880
C-4087
Louisiana English Grammar. Published by order of . . . Henry W. Allen, Governor of Louisiana. (Smith, Roswell C.)
1865   Shreveport, LA   650.00

P-7881
C-4088
SMITH, Richard McAllister   **Smith's English grammar, on the productive system. . . .**
1863   Richmond   375.00

P-7883
C-4090
SMYTHE, Charles W.   **Our Own Elementary Grammar,** intermediate between the primary and high school grammars.
1863   Greensboro, NC   500.00

P-7886
C-4093
SMYTHE, Charles W.   **Our Own Primary Grammar, for** . . . **beginners.** Third edition.
1863   Greensboro, NC   500.00

P-7889
C-4013
South Carolina College Catalogue of the trustees, faculty and students, of the South Carolina College, January, MDCCCLXI.
1861   Columbia, SC   100.00

P-7891   **South Carolina College.** Broadside.
          1861   Columbia, SC   200.00

P-7895   **South Carolina Institution for the Education of the Deaf and**
C-4015   **Dumb, and the Blind.** Fourteenth annual report.
          1862   Columbia, SC   75.00

P-7908   **STERLING,** Richard and **CAMPBELL, J.D.**   **Our own first**
C-4096   **Reader;** for . . . schools and families.
          1862   Greensboro, NC 600.00

P-7909   **STERLING,** Richard **Our own first reader . . .**
C-4097   1862   Greensboro, NC 150.00

P-7915   **STERLING,** Richard and **CAMPBELL, J. D. Our Own Second**
C-4101   **Reader:** for schools and families (With wood-cuts).
          (1862)   Greensboro, NC & Richmond   500.00

P-7921   **STERLING,** Richard **Our Own Third Reader:** for the use of
C-4105   schools and families.
          (1863)   Greensboro, NC & Richmond   350.00

P-7923   **STEWART,** Kensey Johns **A geography for beginners.**
C-4107   1864   Richmond 150.00

P-7938   **Virginia Military Institute. Register of the officers and cadets** of
C-4019   the Virginia Military Institute, Lexington, Virginia, July 1863.
          1863   Richmond 350.00

P-7940   **The Virginia Primer. . . .**
C-4110   1864   Richmond 400.00

P-7942   **The Virginia Speller and Reader.** (With wood-cuts)
C-4111   1865 Richmond 600.00

P-7945   **Virginia University, Charlottesville University of Virginia.** List
C-4022   of the distinguished, proficients & graduates, session 1860-61. . . .
          Broadside.
          1861   Charlottesville 350.00

P-7963   **WHATLEY,** Richard **Elements of Logic.**
C-4116   1861   Nashville 275.00

P-7965   **WILEY,** Calvin Henderson, et al **Address to the people of North**
C-3984   **Carolina.**
          (1861)   (Raleigh, NC)   125.00

P-7968   **WILEY,** Calvin Henderson   **Circular, to the authorities and**
C-4025   **People of North Carolina.**
          1863   Greensboro, NC 175.00

P-7976   **An Analytical, Illustrative and Constructive Grammar.**
C-4120   1862   Raleigh, NC   250.00

P-7978   **YORK,** Brantley **York's English grammar revised and adapted to**
C-4121   **Southern schools.**
          1864   Raleigh, NC   250.00

P-7993   **JACKSON,** Thomas J., et al   **Anecdotes for Our Soldiers. No. 3.**
C-4565   (186-)   (Charleston, SC) 200.00

P-8005   **ARMSTRONG,** George D. **"The good hand of our God upon us."**
C-4122   A Thanksgiving Sermon, preached on occasion of the Victory of
          Manassas, July 21st, 1861. . . .
          1861   Norfolk, VA   300.00

| P-8007 | **The Army Hymn-Book.** |
| C-4239 | 1863   Richmond   600.00 |

P-8107	**Minutes of the Lowe Canoochee Association,** in session with the
C-4337	**Mill Creek Church, Bulloch County, Georgia,** from the 11th to
	the 13th October, 1862. . . .
	1862 n.p. 100.00

P-8247	**Minutes of the forty-second anniversary of the State Convention**
C-4385	**of the Baptist Denomination in S.C.,** held at Greenville, July
	25th-28th, 1862.
	1862 Columbia, SC 100.00

P-8267	**Minutes of the Tennessee Association, of Baptists, Held with the**
C-4402	**Dandridge Church.** . . .
	1861 Morristown, TN 300.00

P-8348	**Bible** . . . **The soldier's pocket Bible.** Issued for the use of the
C-4579	army of Oliver Cromwell. (Original title page.) The soldier's
	pocket Bible. . . .
	(186-) Charleston, SC 200.00

| P-8357 | **The New Testament.** |
| C-4213 | 1861   Nashville   750.00 |

| P-8360 | **The New Testament of our Lord and Saviour Jesus Christ.** . . . |
| C-4215 | 1862   Atlanta   350.00 |

| P-8361 | **The New Testament of our Lord and Saviour Jesus Christ.** . . . |
| C-4216 | 1862   Atlanta   350.00 |

P-8393	**BROADDUS,** Rev. Andrew **It Is a Fearful Thing to Live,**
C-4590	**Dedicated to Our Faithful Soldiers.**
	(186-) (Raleigh, NC) 100.00

| P-8410 | **Bethel.** |
| C-4578-1 | (186-)   n.p.   150.00 |

P-8411	**BURROWS,** John L. **The Christian Scholar and Soldier.**
C-4600	**Memoirs of Lewis Minor Coleman,** Professor in the University of
	Virginia - Lt. Col. of First Reg't. Va. Artillery.
	1864 (Raleigh) 350.00

| P-8416 | **Shiloh. A Sermon.** |
| C-4849 | (1862)   n.p.   250.00 |

| P-8436 | **The Christian officer.** |
| C-4608 | (186-)   (Charleston, SC)   175.00 |

| P-8445 | **A Collection of Sabbath School hymns** . . . |
| C-4241 | 1863   Raleigh, NC   300.00 |

| P-8453 | **The Confederate hero and his heroic father.** |
| C-4615 | (c.1862)   Charleston, SC   175.00 |

P-8464	**Curious and Useful Questions on the Bible** . . . for Sunday
	Schools and Families.
	1864 Goldsborough, NC 150.00

| P-8500 | **DOGGETT,** David Seth   **A nation's Ebenezer** . . . |
| C-4136 | 1862   Richmond   50.00 |

P-8526	**ELLIOTT,** Stephen **Address of** . . . to the Thirty-ninth Annual
C-4140	Convention of the Protestant Episcopal Church . . . of Georgia.
	1861 Savannah 75.00

P-8531 C-4144	ELLIOTT, Stephen God's presence with our army at Manassas! 1861 Savannah 275.00
P-8543 C-4153	ELLIOTT, Stephen "Vain is the help of man." A Sermon preached in . . . Savannah on . . . September 15 . . . the day of fasting, humiliation, and prayer. . . . 1864 Macon, GA 300.00
P-8571 C-5066	Proceedings of the Grand Chapter of Alabama (Freemasons), at the Annual Convocation, held in . . . Montgomery . . . December 4, 1860. 1861 Montgomery 150.00
P-8572 C-5067	Proceedings of the Grand Chapter of Alabama (Freemasons), at Two Annual Convocations held in . . . Montgomery . . . December 1861 and 1862. 1863 Montgomery 250.00
P-8573 C-5068	Proceedings of the Grand Chapter of Alabama (Freemasons), at the Annual Convocation held in . . . Montgomery . . . December 8, 1863. 1864 Montgomery 200.00
P-8578 C-5072	Proceedings of the annual communication of the Grand Lodge of Alabama. . . . 1861 Montgomery 100.00
P-8579 C-5073	Proceedings of the annual communication of the Grand Lodge of Alabama. . . . 1862 Montgomery 100.00
P-8628 C-5093	Proceedings of the Grand Lodge of Free and Accepted Masons of North Carolina. . . . 1865 Raleigh, NC 125.00
P-8648 C-5102	Free masonry and the war. Report of the committee under the resolutions of 1862, Grand Lodge of Virginia. . . . 1865 Richmond 150.00
P-8661 C-5112	By-laws and list of members of Richmond Lodge, No. 10. . . . 1864 Richmond 100.00
P-8662 C-5113	By-Laws and List of Members of Richmond Randolph Lodge No. XIX, Ancient York Masons. 1864 Richmond 125.00
P-8699 C-2576	FURMAN, James Clement Sermon on the death of Rev. James M. Chiles, preached at Horeb Church, Abbeville District, S.C., on Sunday, 29th of March, 1863. 1863 Greenville, SC 150.00
P-8715 C-4669	GRANBERY, John An Address to the Soldiers of the Southern Armies. (186-) (Raleigh, NC) 60.00
P-8720 C-4674	GRASTY, John Sharshall A Noble Testimony. (186-) Raleigh, NC 50.00
P-8756 C-4689	HEBER, Reginald Noah's carpenters. (186-) Raleigh, NC 50.00

P-8771	HARRISON, Dabney Carr Minister of the Gospel and Captain
C-2582	in the Army of the Confederate States of America.
	1863 Richmond 250.00

| P-8775 | HORNADY, Henry Carr   How to be saved. |
| | (186-)   Macon, GA   100.00 |

P-8785	HOWE, George Discourse in commemoration of the life and
C-2583	labors of Rev. George Cooper Gregg. . . .
	1862 Columbia, SC 100.00

| P-8792 | Hymns for the camp. . . . |
| C-4246 | 1864   Raleigh, NC   350.00 |

| P-8794 | Hymns for the camp. Second edition. . . . |
| C-4247 | 1862   Raleigh, NC   400.00 |

| P-8795 | Hymns for the camp. |
| | (1862)   Raleigh, NC   600.00 |

| P-8797 | Hymns for the camp. Third edition. . . . |
| C-4248 | (186-)   Raleigh, NC   400.00 |

| P-8813 | It is I! Broadside. |
| C-4716-1 | (1861)   (Richmond)   50.00 |

P-8826	JONES, Charles Colcock, Sr. Religious instruction of the
C-2888	negroes. . . .
	(1862) Richmond 350.00

| P-8828 | JONES, John   The Southern soldier's duty. . . . |
| C-4161 | 1861   Rome   350.00 |

| P-8854 | A Letter to a Son in Camp. |
| C-4735 | (1863)   (Petersburg)   100.00 |

| P-8904 | MCGILL, John   Faith, the victory. . . . |
| C-4275 | 1865   Richmond   200.00 |

| P-8910 | MACLEOD, Norman   Wee Davie. |
| C-3130 | 1864   Richmond   600.00 |

P-8957	Minutes of the seventy-fourth annual session of the South
C-4468	Carolina Conference of the Methodist Episcopal Church, South,
	held in Chester, S.C., commencing Thursday, December 12th,
	1861.
	1862 Charleston, SC 75.00

P-8965	MILES, James W. God in History. A Discourse delivered
C-4170	before the Graduating Class of the College of Charleston.
	1863 Charleston, SC 300.00

| P-8988 | The Muster. |
| C-4769 | (186-)   (Charleston, SC)   60.00 |

P-9030	PALMER, Benjamin Morgan A discourse before the General
C-4175	Assembly of South Carolina, on December 10, 1863. . . .
	1864 Columbia, SC 100.00

P-9033	PALMER, Benjamin Morgan The Oath of Allegiance to the
C-4790	United States, discussed in its moral and political bearings.
	1863 Richmond 500.00

| P-9040 | Patriotic Prayer for the Southern cause. |
| C-4221-1 | (186-)   n.p.   225.00 |

P-9043 C-4254	**The Southern Zion's Songster;** hymns designed for Sabbath Schools, prayer and social meetings, and the camps. 1864 Raleigh, NC 500.00
P-9067 C-4222	**Prayers and other devotions for the use of the soldiers of the Army of the Confederate States.** (186-) Charleston, SC 100.00
P-9068 C-4223	**Prayers suitable for the Times in Which We Live.** 1861 Charleston, SC 275.00
P-9084 C-4478	**Minutes of the General Assembly of the Presbyterian Church in the Confederate States. . . .** 1861 Augusta, GA 75.00
P-9094	**Minutes of the Presbytery of Cherokee,** at their fall and spring sessions 1861 and 1862. 1862 Marietta, GA 225.00
P-9114	**Minutes of the Presbytery of South Carolina,** spring session, Held at Retreat Church, Pickens. . . . 1861 Columbia, SC 50.00
P-9131	**Minutes of the Primitive Ebenezer Association,** Held with the Mount Gilead Church, Washington County, [Georgia] . . . 21st September, 1861. (1861) n.p. 200.00
P-9132	**Minutes of the Primitive Ebenezer Association,** Held with the Friendship Church, Wilkinson County [Georgia] . . . September . . . 30th, 1862. (1862) n.p. 200.00
P-9133	**Minutes of the Primitive Ebenezer Association,** Held with the Mountain Spring Church, Jones County [Georgia] September. . . . . . . 29th, 1863. (1863) n.p. 200.00
P-9134	**Minutes of the Primitive Ebenezer Association,** Held with the Pleasant Plains Church, Wilkinson County [Georgia], September . . . 26th 1864. (1864) n.p. 200.00
P-9164 C-4518	**Journal of Proceedings of an Adjourned Convention** . . . of the Protestant Episcopal Church in the Confederate States of America, held in . . . Columbia . . . from Oct. 16th to Oct. 24th . . . 1861. 1861 Montgomery 250.00
P-9170 C-4522	**Proposed Constitution and Digest of Revised Canons for** . . . the Protestant Episcopal Church in the Confederate States of America. 1861 Columbia, SC 250.00
P-9217 C-4232	**The army and navy prayer book.** 1865 Richmond 400.00
P-9218 C-4233	**Prayer book for the camp.** 1863 Richmond 400.00
P-9223 C-4234	**QUINTARD,** Charles T. **Balm for the weary and the wounded.** By Rev. C. T. Quintard, chaplain 1st Tenn. Reg't, C.S.A. 1864 Columbia, SC 400.00

P-9232 C-2600	**RAMSEY**, James Beverlin **True eminence founded on holiness.** A discourse occasioned by the death of Lieut. Gen. T. J. Jackson . . . May 24th, 1863. 1863 Lynchburg, VA 200.00
P-9259 C-4261	**ROOT**, Sidney **Primary Bible questions for young children.** Third edition. 1864 Atlanta 100.00
P-9293	**SHERWOOD**, Adiel **Conversation in a Tent.** (1862) Macon, GA 125.00
P-9323 C-4864	**The soldier's almanac. 1863.** 1863 Richmond 125.00
P-9334 C-4250	**The Soldier's hymn book. . . .** 1863 Charleston, SC 400.00
P-9349 C-4972	**Proceedings of the State Bible Convention of South Carolina. . . .** 1862 Columbia, SC 50.00
P-9351 C-4194	**STILES**, Joseph Clay **National rectitude the only true basis of national prosperity.** 1863 Petersburg 100.00
P-9382 C-4890	**THORNWELL**, James H. **Our danger and our duty.** By Rev. J. H. Thornwell, D.D. (186-) Charleston, SC 200.00
P-9383 C-2859	**THORNWELL**, James H. **Our danger and our duty.** 1862 Columbia, SC 300.00
P-9402 C-4286	**TUCKER**, John Randolph **The Bible or Atheism.** (186-) (Richmond) 225.00
P-9420 C-4902	**The Victory Won: a Memorial of the Rev. William J. Hoge, D.D.,** late pastor of the Tabb Street Presbyterian Church, Petersburg, Va. (Moore, T. V.; Hoge, Moses D.; et al). 1864 Richmond 200.00
P-9445	**The Westminster shorter catechism. . . .** 1862 Richmond 75.00
P-9459 C-4925	**Whither Bound?** By the Chaplain 10th Virginia Cavalry. (186-) (Raleigh, NC) 100.00

NEWSPAPERS

Newspapers, Confederate.   30.00−75.00 each (per issue).

Parrish and Willingham's *Confederate Imprints* does not list newspapers. We understand a new catalogue is being prepared.

C-5123	**The Richmond Age,** a Southern Eclectic Magazine. Vol. I, No. II February, 1864. 1864 Richmond 75.00
C-5146	**The Commission; or Southern Baptist Missionary Magazine.** Vol. 5, No. 10, and Vol. 6, Nos. 1 and 2. April, July and August, 1861. 1861 Richmond 125.00
C-5152	**The Countryman,** Turnwold, Georgia, Oct. 6, 1862 Vol. III, No. 2. 1862 Turnwold, GA 100.00

C-5211   **The Memphis Appeal,** Sept. 1, 1864. Extra (printed in Atlanta, GA)
1864   Atlanta   500.00

C-5232   **The North Carolina Journal of Education.**   Vol. V, No. 1. January, 1862.
1862   Greensborough, NC   35.00

UNLISTED

A Song of the Trinity. Air - 'Rock of Ages.' Broadside. Dec. 30, 1864.
1864   Augusta   250.00

Allen's Lone Star Ballads - Telegraph Print, Houston, Lone Star Banner of the Free!   As sung in concert for the benefit of soldiers' families, Dec. 26, 1862.
1862   Houston   300.00

Antanga Citizen, Prattville, AL. Nov. 12, 1863. (Newspaper)
1863   Prattville, AL   125.00

APEL, H. **Prose Specimens for Translation into German,** with copious vocabularies and explanation.
1862   London   60.00

BEAUREGARD, Gen. G. T.   **General Orders No. 43,** Corinth, Mississippi, May 18, 1862.
1862   Corinth   500.00

BRAGG, Gen. Braxton   **General Orders No. 210,** Courts Martial Lt. W. H. Mearse, 1st Arkansas Regiment, for drunkeness and Pvt. J. W. Alcorn, Co. H, 9th Texas Regiment for stealing fifty pounds of ammunition, ordering the left side of his head to be shaved and that he be marched in front of the troops.
1863   250.00

By Telegraph, Direct! Natchez Courier. Natchez, Mississippi. Wednesday, June 4, - 10 1/2 a.m. Later News Further from Richmond. Killed and Wounded, Natchez Fencibles (caption-title). Broadside.
(1862)   Natchez, MS   400.00

Confederate Association, Marshall, TX. Broadside.
1863   Marshall, TX   350.00

Constitutionalis(t) Extra. Sunday Evening, April 30, 1865.   Terms of Agreement Between Gens. Johnston and Sherman. Broadside.
(1865)   (Augusta, GA)   750.00

The Courier - Extra. Charleston, S.C. February 18, 1861 - 5 P.M. By Telegraph. Southern Congress. Inaugural Speech of President Davis. Broadside.
1861   Charleston, SC   1500.00

The Courier Extra. Broadside.
1861   Charleston, SC   400.00

Daily Rebel Extra, Chic[k]amauga, Tennessee, Nov. 25, 1863.   Broadside.
1863   Chickamauga, TN   350.00

Head Quarters Army of Tennessee, General Bragg. Broadside.
1863   Tullahoma   150.00

Headquarters Port Hudson, July 8, 1863 . . . Nobly have the troops performed their duty in the defence of this position. . . .
1863   Port Hudson, LA   800.00

In Equity - Charleston District.
1861   Charleston, SC   75.00

JOHNSTON, Gen.   **General Orders No. 22,** The System of Cavalry Tactics prepared by Maj.Gen. Joseph Wheeler is adopted for the use of the Cavalry of the Army of Tennessee.
(186-)   (Dalton, GA)   250.00

Mississippian Extra (caption-title above Confederate flag and firing cannon). Monday, April 7, 1862 - 12 M . . . Victory! Victory!! Broadside.
1862   (Jackson, MS)   650.00

New Orleans Almanac, 1861.
1861 New Orleans   200.00

Official Returns, J. S. Rollins, Conservative (Confederate Democrat) . . . A. Krekel, Radical (Union-Republican).   Broadside.
1862   Columbia, MO   200.00

The ordinance of secession: a poll to take the sense of the qualified voters of this commonwealth upon the ratification or rejection of 'An Ordinance to repeal the ratification of the Constitution of the United States of America, by the State of Virginia . . . adopted in convention . . . on the 17th day of April, 1861. . . . '
1861   n.p.   500.00

Proceedings of the M. W. Grand Lodge of Texas (Freemasons), at Its Twenty-eighth Annual Communication, Held at . . . Houston . . . June . . . 1864.
1864   Houston   300.00

Receipt for Tanning, Washington, Arkansas, 1863.   Broadside.
1863   Washington, AR   500.00

Rules of the House and joint rules of both houses of the legislature of Texas.
1863   Austin   250.00

SCRUGGS, Phineas T.   **Committee of Thirteen.**   Broadside.
1861   (Marshall, TX)   200.00

South Carolina Female Collegiate - Columbia, S.C.
1861   Columbia, SC   200.00

Southern Cultivator, Augusta, GA, June 1861.
1861   Augusta, GA   75.00

State Journal Extra   Broadside.
1864   n.p.   200.00

Tax in kind: Instructions on various procedures for taxing in kind.
1863   Richmond   30.00

Texas Republican, Marshall, Texas, 1862.
1862   Marshall, TX   200.00

To Churchmen: Memorial to the General Council of the Protestant Episcopal Church in the Confederate States. . . .
1862   Montgomery   60.00

Traitors and Rebels of Wheeling, Va., who voted May 23, 1861 for the infamous Ordinance of Secession, adopted by the usurpers in the Richmond, Va. convention.

1861   (Richmond)   350.00

WADE, Col. W. B., et al   **H.Q. District of Mississippi and East Louisiana,** Special Orders No. 62.

n.d.   n.p.   200.00

Western Department, Murfreesboro, Tenn., Feb. 23, 1862. Orders No. 3. Under great necessity temporary possession may be taken wagons, teams, and othe property of our citizens for the use of the army. . . . Broadside.

1862   Murfreesboro, TN   600.00

WHEELER, Maj. Gen. Joseph   **General Order No. 7** - June 3, 1863. Broadside.

1863   Tullahoma, TN   400.00

The *Atlas* To Accompany
THE OFFICIAL RECORDS

Between 1891 and 1895 the War Department issued 175 double page plates of maps and views to accompany the Official Army Records. These plates measure 29 1/2 inches wide by 18 1/2 inches high. The image, or printed area, is 27 inches by 16 1/4 inches, thus there are generous margins on all sides. The plates were issued five at a time, folded through the center, and laid loose in a coarse gray paper wrapper. The entire compilation was appropriately entitled *Atlas to Accompany the Official Records.*

Most of the loose plates were later bound into volumes — by various binders at various times, there is no standard binding for an *Official Records Atlas.* Unfortunately, most of the binders took the easy way out and sewed the plates through the center — thus greatly diminishing the plates utility and value — who wants a map sewn through the middle with parts missing, since it can't be read in the crease?

Most of the atlas plates are printed in four colors and a fifth color, brown, was used for some views. Most of the maps have more than one map or scene — some small, some large. The design and quality of the engravings is the best available at that time — in many aspects better than what is available today. The engravers and printer-craftsmen who did these plates are long gone and haven't been replaced.

The atlas plates contain detailed and accurate maps, scenes and troop movement for the Civil War. They show trees, creeks, bridges and structures. In many cases homes are shown with the owners' names. Anything that was known was put down. As historians and relic hunters can attest, the *Official Records Atlas* plates are by far the most detailed and accurate source for the period. These original plates show details not visible in any subsequent reprints as all reprints of the *Official Records Atlas* were reduced in size with loss of fine detail and wording. Plus, in later reprints, many of the subtle colors and shading in the originals were lost in reproduction.

We suggest binding the *Official Records Atlas* plates as follows:

•Discard the gray paper wrappers; they are quite acidic, on poor paper and will continue to deteriorate.

•Have your bookbinder "tab" each map individually and bind the tabbed plates into two volumes. By "tab", I mean he should glue a strip of acid-free paper to the crease of each map and sew through the strips for binding. Thus, the maps are not sewn through the crease and will lie completely flat after being bound. The maps should be bound in order. This should be no problem as the 178 map pages are clearly numbered.

•The volumes should be stamped on the spine as follows:

OR Atlas	OR Atlas
Volume I	Volume II
No. 1-90	No. 91-178

Hopefully, these suggestions, gained from binding probably fifty volumes of atlas plates over twenty years, will be helpful.

CONFEDERATE MILITARY HISTORY
Extended Edition

At the time Evans published the regular volumes of Confederate Military History, he also printed what he called "extended" editions. These volumes were identical to the regular edition in binding, yet contained many more biographical sketches than the regular editions —a multiple of twenty times in some cases.

The difference between the "regular" and "extended" editions is apparent from a comparison of page counts. Indeed, this is how one differentiates the two editions. The "extended" editions were evidently inserted in sets sent to particular states in place of that states regular edition, i.e., sets sold in Virginia would have the Virginia volume in extended format. Thus, there is no such thing as a set with all" extended" volumes; the only one I know was the one put together to reprint *Confederate Military History* in all "extended" format.

Fine, so far. However, for some of the extended titles, i.e., *Confederates Living in the North, Missouri,* there are only one or two copies known. Why did Evans go to the expense and trouble of producing an extended edition, yet print probably less than twenty copies for some titles? If anyone can convincingly explain this bibliographic riddle, I will be glad to trade a set of the "extended" edition for the answer to the question.

How To Tell The Difference Between
The *REGULAR* and *EXTENDED* EDITION Of
CONFEDERATE MILITARY HISTORY.

STATE	PAGES REGULAR EDITION	PAGES EXTENDED EDITION
Maryland	190	453
West Virginia	142	302
Virginia	697	1300
North Carolina	359	818
South Carolina	429	936
Georgia	469	1076
Alabama	456	869
Mississippi	282	519
Tennessee	352	810
Kentucky	267	598
Missouri	231	456
Louisiana	327	636
Arkansas	424	609
Texas	273	718
Florida	216	371

GREAT COMMANDERS SERIES

This series of eighteen biographies of outstanding American military commanders of the 18th and 19th centuries included: five early-American commanders, three Confederate commanders and ten Union commanders. The biographies were commissioned by D. Appleton & Company of New York, and published by that house at intervals between 1892 and 1913.

Each biography was published simultaneously in a Standard Edition (green colored cloth binding with gold lettering on spine) and a DeLuxe Edition (beige colored cloth binding with title label on spine). Internally, both editions are identical, except the pages of the Standard Edition have been trimmed to about 19 1/2 cm (7.7 in.) and bound in green cloth, while the pages of the DeLuxe Edition are about 22 cm (8.7 in.) and bound in beige cloth. The DeLuxe Edition is limited to 1,000 numbered copies.

Below is a listing of the eighteen biographies giving author, title, and date of publication.

Early-America Commanders (5)

Brady, C. T.	"Commodore Jones"	1900
Greene, F. V.	"General Greene"	1893
Parton, J.	"General Jackson"	1892
Howard, O. O.	"General Taylor"	1892
Johnson, B. T.	"General Washington"	1894

Confederate Commanders (3)

Mathes, J. H.	"General Forrest"	1902
Hughes, R. M.	"General Johnston"	1893
Lee, F.	"General Lee"	1894

Union Commanders (10)

Mahan, A. T.	"Admiral Farragut"	1892
Soley, J. R.	"Admiral Porter"	1913
Wilson, J. G.	"General Grant"	1897
Walker, F. A.	"General Hancock"	1894
Pennypacker, I. R.	"General Meade"	1901
Michie, P. S.	"General McClellan"	1901
Wright, M. J.	"General Scott"	1893
Davies, H. E.	"General Sheridan"	1895
Force, M. F.	"General Sherman"	1899
Coppee, H.	"General Thomas"	1893

OFFICIAL RECORDS OF
THE UNION AND CONFEDERATE ARMY
— Checklist —

One of the more onerous tasks in Civil War books is trying to put a set of *Official Records* in proper order and then determine if the set is complete. Later reprints have serial numbers on the spine which make the job easier. However, the original edition didn't feature serial numbers for the first volumes and often the original set is found in such poor condition that it is impossible to read the spine lettering.

By utilizing the following checklist one can assemble a set of *Official Records* and be sure the job is done right. Woefully, the world will now know that volumes 54 and 55 were never published, and the supply of supposedly incomplete sets (those lacking these two volumes) at a good prices will probably end.

VOLUME	PART NO.	SERIAL NO.	VOLUME	PART NO.	SERIAL NO.
SERIES I			SERIES I		
1		1	22	1	32
2		2	22	2	33
3		3	23	1	34
4		4	23	2	35
5		5	24	1	36
6		6	24	2	37
7		7	24	3	38
8		8	25	1	39
9		9	25	2	40
10	1	10	26	1	41
10	2	11	26	2	42
11	1	12	27	1	43
11	2	13	27	2	44
11	3	14	27	3	45
12	1	15	28	1	46
12	2	16	28	2	47
12	2 (supp.)	17	29	1	48
12	3	18	29	2	49
13		19	30	1	50
14		20	30	2	51
15		21	30	3	52
16	1	22	30	4	53
16	2	23	31	1	54
17	1	24	31	2	55
17	2	25	31	3	56
18		26	32	1	57
19	1	27	32	2	58
19	2	28	32	3	59
20	1	29	33		60
20	2	30	34	1	61
21		31	34	2	62

VOLUME	PART NO.	SERIAL NO.
34	3	63
34	4	64
35	1	65
35	2	66
36	1	67
36	2	68
36	3	69
37	1	70
37	2	71
38	1	72
38	2	73
38	3	74
38	4	75
38	5	76
39	1	77
39	2	78
39	3	79
40	1	80
40	2	81
40	3	82
41	1	83
41	2	84
41	3	85
41	4	86
42	1	87
42	2	88
42	3	89
43	1	90
43	2	91
44		92
45	1	93
45	2	94
46	1	95
46	2	96
46	3	97
47	1	98
47	2	99
47	3	100
48	1	101
48	2	102
49	1	103
49	2	104
50	1	105
50	2	106
51	1	107
51	2	108
52	1	109
52	2	110

VOLUME	PART NO.	SERIAL NO.
53		111
*54		112
*55		113

*These volumes were reserved for additional material but were never published, thus, do not exist.

VOLUME	PART NO.	SERIAL NO.
SERIES II		
1		114
2		115
3		116
4		117
5		118
6		119
7		120
8		121
SERIES III		
1		122
2		123
3		124
4		125
5		126
SERIES IV		
1		127
2		128
3		129
General Index		130

PERIODICALS

From the beginning of the War, through the end of the Century, various monthly magazines, both here and abroad, featured articles on the Civil War, ranging from worthless prose to valuable first-hand accounts. In sum, the issues with good Civil War material are valued at about $25 each. However, an indigence of motivation and energy on the editor's part precludes a listing and sorting of this material in this publication. Periodicals in this category containing Civil War articles are:

CENTURY MAGAZINE
HARPER'S MAGAZINE
SCRIBNER'S MONTHLY
ATLANTIC MONTHLY
BLACKWOOD'S MAGAZINE